# REASONS
# FOR
# REALISM

*Selected Essays of James J. Gibson*

James J. Gibson (Davis, California, 1978).

# REASONS
# FOR
# REALISM

*Selected Essays of James J. Gibson*

*Edited by*
**Edward Reed** and **Rebecca Jones**
*University of Minnesota*

**LEA** LAWRENCE ERLBAUM ASSOCIATES, PUBLISHERS
1982   Hillsdale, New Jersey                    London

Lawrence Erlbaum Associates, Inc., Publishers
365 Broadway
Hillsdale, New Jersey 07642

**Library of Congress Cataloging in Publication Data**

Gibson, James Jerome, 1904–
    Reasons for realism.

    (Resources for ecological psychology)
    Bibliography: p.
    Includes indexes.
    1. Visual perception—Addresses, essays, lectures.
2. Space perception—Addresses, essays, lectures.
3. Motion perception (Vision)—Addresses, essays,
lectures.  4. Environmental psychology—Addresses,
essays, lectures.  I. Reed, Edward (Edward S.)
II. Jones, Rebecca.  III. Title.  IV. Series.
BF241.G49   1982        153.7        82-8867
ISBN 0-89859-207-0                   AACR2

Printed in the United States of America
10   9   8   7   6   5   4   3   2   1

# Contents

# RESOURCES FOR ECOLOGICAL PSYCHOLOGY

A series of volumes edited by:
**Robert E. Shaw, William M. Mace, and Michael T. Turvey**

REED AND JONES ● *Reasons for Realism: Selected Essays of James J. Gibson*

# Foreword

The publication of this collection of the papers of my husband, James J. Gibson, is an event that I welcome and that I consider timely. I welcome it because many of the papers are not available, either because they were never published but existed only as memoranda written for his students (known to them as "purple perils"), or because they were published in places that are not easily accessible, like the selections from *Motion Picture Testing and Research*. That book is little known and is owned by few libraries, but it is full of ideas and research that still seem fresh and innovative. I wish it could have been reprinted in full. I consider this collection of papers timely too, because James Gibson's last book, *The Ecological Approach to Visual Perception*, presented in full and readable form what might be considered the culmination of wisdom attained over a long career of independent and persistent thinking about the problem of how we obtain knowledge of the world, its layout, its furnishings, and what happens in it. The ideas are radical, never bent to tradition nor made to please an antagonist or even a friend. For this reason, the short time succeeding the book's publication has witnessed a flow of publications in which the book has been praised, attacked, or supplemented with suggestions by would-be helpers. The critics are many, both friendly and unfriendly, but always seriously concerned. For this reason, the elucidation provided by a collection of papers foreshadowing and underlying the evolution of the thinking that went into *The Ecological Approach to Visual Perception* is very important.

That is how I think of this collection of papers; they provide a kind of intellectual history of how a devoted scientist and epistemologist pursued a problem that has concerned earlier scientists and philosophers for many centuries. His way of looking at the problem and the concepts he generated to handle it were changed many times over the nearly 50 years that James Gibson worried about it. I would like to sketch a kind of outline of how the changes evolved. His autobiography provides many details (although it was written 13 years before his death, and many more could now be added); I seek only to indicate periods that may organize the papers usefully and historically.

His earlier work, beginning with a thesis on "Reproduction of Visually Perceived Forms," is quite in the tradition of the times and shows a young man exercising his experimental skills in a number of directions. These early papers, frequently originating in experiments conducted with students in a class in advanced experimental psychology, are not included here. They ranged widely over perception, verbal learning, memory, and even conditioning. (They included two papers with me as co-author, one on conditioning and one on retroactive inhibition, and two with Gertrude Raffel Schmeidler, one of his best undergraduate students, one on "primary" memory and one on conditioning.) The only early paper included in this collection is the one on automobile driving (1938), with Lawrence Crooks, an automotive engineer, as co-author. It is purely descriptive and theoretical and at the time it seemed far off the track of James Gibson's own work and the psychophysical style then characteristic of perceptual research. But the reviewer (E. G. Boring) wrote him, "I love your paper about how Lewin drives a car." You could not describe the perceptual process that controls driving in psychophysical terms, and even Boring recognized it. It is remarkable now to see how persuasively it engages one in the concept of "affordance," only thought of as a concept and given a name 35 years later.

The first period of research and theorizing that was uniquely his own and that made him a reputation as a perception psychologist was the work on adaptation to curvature and tilt. The research and the ideas were innovative and important, because they flatly contradicted the assumption that perception is compounded of simple sensations that correspond with points of light or color. All the work has stood the test of time, and the results are basic facts for textbooks now. Alas, they are sometimes interpreted as evidence for a new kind of element, to be paired with a "feature detector" in the nervous system. That was not how they were interpreted by my husband at the time, but they were still in the tradition of psychophysics. He thought of them as interpretable in terms of "dimensions" of experience with positive and negative poles, a little like an "opponent process" theory. Gestalt psychologists thought of them as grist for their mills, Köhler seeing in the negative aftereffects evidence for processes of "dynamic redistribution" in the brain. None of these papers are republished in this book, because the mainstream of James Gibson's thinking soon turned in another direction, away even from what he later called "global psychophysics," a term suggested by R. B. MacLeod at a conference on perception held at Cornell in 1953, following an International Congress of Psychology in Montreal.

World War II took him off to the Army Air Force, where he was faced at once with problems of how we perceive and control locomotion perceptually in a real world. How different it was from everything that he had worked on in the laboratory! The only earlier work that related to the air force research and theorizing is the paper on automobile driving, which did consider control of locomotion in a moving vehicle. The selections from the book entitled *Motion Picture Testing and Research* (a title that fails to indicate what much of the book was about) speak for themselves. The reality of the practical problem of flying and landing a plane took over, and the old "cues for depth" had to go, for they all assumed a static environment and a static perceiver. Motion must contain its own information; but something must persist, too. The idea that took hold in the course of this revolution of thinking was that of the ground as persistent and stable, and of flow patterns in relation to the ground and the observer during locomotion as information for where one is going. Gradients over the ground furnish information for depth and distance in a static situation too, and this possibility was explored in considerable detail in his 1950 book, *The Perception of the Visual World*.

Following the war, he continued to work for several years on gradients as information for depth, but after our move to Cornell he became ever more interested in movement and locomotion and their role in perceiving. He had many students at this time who helped push the research and thinking and helped formalize the description of the new kind of information. They included Frank Rosenblatt, Walter Carel, Bill Purdy, John Hay, Howard Flock, and others. Some of them went to work for General Electric and used their new found knowledge to design simulated landing systems. This was the practical side; but the theoretical side grew too, as the concepts of invariants and transformations became better defined.

The third period in the progress of James Gibson's thinking I like to call the "systems" approach. It was not "systems theory" in any formal sense, but it was his own way of thinking about systems involved in perceiving. He gave up the notion of the "retinal image" as being the basis of visual perception and began to think of visual perception as an active process of "looking" (searching for change and invariants), which involved a much enlarged receptive system that is not just receptive. Adjustments of eyes, head and trunk are all involved and the perceiver is not static. He moves around and as he does so the scene is continuously changing, and the flow of stimulation as well. This view is explored in detail in his book, *The Senses Considered as Perceptual Systems* (1966), but it is also foreshadowed in a number of the papers in this collection, the earliest (and my favorite) being, "Visually controlled locomotion and visual orientation in animals," published in the *British Journal of Psychology* in 1958. The editor, Ian Hunter, perceived it as novel, but he welcomed it and wrote: "May I take this opportunity to say how much I enjoyed reading your paper. It isn't often that editorial chores can be joined with enjoyment, but they were in this case. My impression is that the paper is a first-rate piece of work for which many people will be grateful and I am glad to think that it is to appear in our journal.''

A fourth period in his thinking began as *The Senses Considered as Perceptual Systems* was being written. The concept of information took over from "stimulus" and "stimulation" and was elaborated over a period of years. Stimulation as it had been previously conceived was inadequate to explain not only the perceptual control of locomotion as a continuously ongoing organized process, but especially numerous instances of pick-up of structure, such as edges, when there are literally no lines or edges present in a static stimulus array. The concept of "layout" is essential, but a changing array over time must also be conceived, and the possibility of amodal information granted. Transformations and changes are abstract, not represented modally, and yet they bear information for persisting structure in the layout. Deletion and accretion at an edge, for instance, provide information for occlusion, for something "going behind," persisting but not momentarily "represented." Furthermore, the same information for the shape of an object can be obtained by exploring it manually, or by looking at it as it moves around or as the observer moves around it.

The concept of information that specifies objects and events in the world and is available to an active perceiver became the focus of my husband's work and thinking for a decade at least. How is the information itself to be described? Can it be described successfully in the physicists' terms, as classic psychophysics described the stimulus? It soon became clear that such a description was totally inadequate for describing an array that exists over a spatial layout and over time, where things move and change, and yet in which persistence of invariant aspects like ground, sky, horizon, and many properties of things, like substance, is specified. The solution seemed to be a new kind of physical description appropriate for the properties of the world, its surfaces and substances, that living creatures must know about to function successfully. Beginning with the world as perceived visually, he called this new physics "ecological optics."

In the summer of 1970, his Navy sponsors supported a conference at Cornell on ecological optics. As I look at the many photographs taken during this week-long meeting, it seems to me that it was an historic occasion, giving birth to a new theory of perception. Most of the old students came, and friends from other universities—David Lee from Edinburgh, Bob Shaw from Minnesota, Gunnar Jansson, and Sverker Runeson from Uppsala. Concepts like the "ambient optic array" (the basis of the new optics) and disturbances of structure in the array that specify events were heatedly discussed and argued over.

"Ecological optics" was developed in constantly greater detail as the book about it, *The Ecological Approach to Visual Perception*, was being written. But this was no hurried production. The book was 10 years in the writing, thinking, and rethinking. Many seminars and many memoranda written for them (and rewritten next week or next year) went into it. Folders of notes for all my husband's seminars exist, and I am sorry one or two could not be included more completely as examples of the progress of a theory. Before the book was finished, a new concept was introduced—the concept of "affordances." A careful description of the information for perception, even as it approaches elegance in the form of a mathematical statement, does not convey sufficiently the reciprocity of a creature and the environment, especially its own niche or habitat. This mutuality of creature and environment is the basis of the need for an ecological optics, one that is meaningful for a living creature. The surfaces and substances of this environment provide opportunities of diverse kinds for the creature's activities, offering it support for living successfully in the world. These opportunities are its "affordance" (a made-up word).

The concept of affordances brought the new theory back to the functionalist outlook characteristic of the book on the perceptual systems, greatly enriching it. The pieces now all fitted together, with the information spelled out and its functional significance stressed. A phenomenological description of perception made sense again too. What is perceived, by an ordinary person, by a child in any culture, or by a chimpanzee? It is the affordances of things—what to do with them, what they mean. This last idea has left us, as did the earlier ones, with decades of research to perform, but it points a way to go.

I have said nothing about another aspect of my husband's work that is represented in the papers selected for this book. That is the work on the perception of pictures. It does not represent any one historical period, and it seems at first glance out of the mainstream, not in the direct line of a theory's evolution. He was always interested in drawings (as witness his thesis on reproduction of forms and an early paper on "What is a form?"). But it became very clear to him, especially during his World War II experience, that a psychology of perception based on drawings (as so much of it had been) simply would not do. In a real world, things are solid and extended; we move around in it, and often things move around us. It turned out that what seemed at first to be complications produced by all this change are really advantages, and that static perception, on the other hand, is drastically impoverished. Yet we do get information from pictures, to some extent the same information that we get by way of real ambient arrays. How does this come about? It is possible because pictures are not representations of a real ambient array; they are presentations of information for a static perceiver, intended to specify the affordance of an event, a place, a person, and so on, in a pictorial medium—a flat surface that one can paint or mark on. They may convey excellent information about something, as caricature can do for a person. But they are a special case. The way they do it is not by copying the ambient array, and they always contain dual information—for the picture's surface, as well as for the affordances that the artist intended to represent. James Gibson's interest in this problem, though perhaps secondary, was unflagging and very much influenced by two friendships extending over the last 15 or 20 years of his life, one with Sir Ernst Gombrich, the other with Frank Malina, editor of *Leonardo*. Sometimes we went to see them, and sometimes they came to Ithaca, especially Professor Gombrich, who was for 7 years a Professor-at-Large at Cornell. When they were together, the conversation waxed furiously, the time flew, and theories were tossed about. Malina's journal, *Leonardo*, appealed especially to my husband because it attempted to bring together the wisdom of artists, psychologists, philosophers of art, and even technical experts.

I have often mentioned people in this preface, because they played such an enormous role in my husband's thinking. He was an exceedingly sociable person, and he loved to argue with a worthy opponent. When he met his friend, Julian Hochberg, after an interval of a few months, they would continue the argument exactly where they had left off. All the people I have mentioned and many others, particularly his students, played such a vital role in the progress of his thinking that I doubt it would have matured as it did without their stimulation. My husband is not here to dedicate this book, but I think if he could, he would dedicate it to these friends and students.

**Eleanor J. Gibson**

# Acknowledgments

We are deeply indebted to the many people who have given us help and advice throughout the preparation of this volume and we offer each of them our sincere thanks. Without the initial encouragement of the late James J. Gibson, and the continuing support of Eleanor J. Gibson, this book could not have been produced. Anne and Herbert Pick also provided a great deal of useful advice and helpful criticism, for which we are grateful. We owe thanks to Bill Mace for orchestrating much of the production of the original manuscript, and we are grateful to Patti Mace and the University of Connecticut students who helped with the typing. We also thank Eleanor Gibson for providing the marvelous photographs and Steve Ristvedt for skillfully reproducing many of the figures.

We owe a special debt to the people whose work we have included. We are very grateful to Eleanor Gibson for her splendid foreword and for allowing us to reprint the essays on perceptual learning she co-authored with her husband. We are also indebted to Gunnar Johansson for allowing us to reprint his "Letter to J. J. Gibson" (1970). We owe thanks to Anthony Barrand and Mike Riegle for allowing us to publish James Gibson's address, "A history of the ideas behind ecological optics" which they transcribed and edited; and we are grateful to Lawrence Crooks, N. M. Glaser, George Kaplan, Horace Reynolds, and Kirk Wheeler, whose work appears in this volume.

The support staff at the Center for Research in Human Learning, University of Minnesota, especially Kathleen Casey Olson and Sue Salm, have aided us in innumerable ways. We gratefully acknowledge their help and the support we received through grants to the Center from the National Institute of Child Health and Human Development (HD-01136) and the National Science Foundation (NSF/BNS-77-22075).

The American Psychological Association kindly waived their reprint fees, making production of this book financially feasible, and we appreciate their generosity. Finally, we extend our thanks to the following organizations for their permission to reproduce copyrighted materials: Academic Press, Inc.; The American Psychological Association; The Association for Educational Communications and Technology; The British Psychological Society; Daedalus; Irvington Publishers, Inc.; The Journal Press; North-Holland Publishing Co.; Pergamon Press; The Psychonomic Society; D. Reidel Publishing Co., The State University of New York Press, Inc.; and Paul Theobald and Co.

**Edward Reed**
**Rebecca Jones**

# REASONS
# FOR
# REALISM

*Selected Essays of James J. Gibson*

# General Introduction

Edward Reed
and Rebecca Jones

James J. Gibson's numerous theoretical and empirical contributions to the understanding of how people perceive are innovative, controversial, often radical, and always profound. Many of his ideas have revolutionized the science of perception, and his influence continues to grow throughout the world. This book is a collection of the most important of Gibson's essays on the psychology of perception. Drawing from the entire corpus of Gibson's papers, we have selected over three dozen works dealing with such diverse topics as ecological optics, event perception, pictorial representation, and the conceptual foundations of psychology. Our goals in preparing this volume were twofold: first, to provide easy access to Gibson's most outstanding papers and talks, including some that were previously unpublished; and second, to provide an intellectual biography of Gibson by including essays from the different periods of his career.

The theme of this book is Gibson's realism, his conviction that we can directly perceive the world as it is, if we only try, and his view that psychologists must seek to understand the world if they are to explain how we become aware of it and act upon it. Throughout his career, Gibson's research and theorizing exemplified this realism. Although his early work (Gibson, 1929, 1937b, 1941a; Gibson & Mowrer, 1938) was firmly rooted in empiricism and behaviorism, Gibson's realistic approach nevertheless is apparent in the painstaking care he took in describing the context and function of the behavioral or perceptual abilities under study. After his first book (Gibson, 1947), Gibson strove to articulate and clarify his reasons for realism (Costall, 1981; Lombardo, 1973; Mace, 1977; Ch. 4.5), and they are well developed in his last book, *The Ecological Approach to Visual Perception* (1979a).

For Gibson, realism was more than a philosophy; it was a demanding way of pursuing science. He was committed to the view that (Gibson, 1950a): "The construction of a theory is most useful when the theory is 'vulnerable,' that is to say, when future experiments can but do not disprove it [p. vii]." As is evident in all his research, he labored hard to render his theories falsifiable, and, in so doing, he treated as hypotheses what most experimenters are content to leave as assumptions. For example, whereas most experimenters assume they know what the relevant stimuli in their experiments are, Gibson devoted much of his career to discovering what can count as a stimulus for a perceiver. He frequently found that traditional assumptions about the nature of stimuli were incorrect. Gibson's commitment to realism motivated him to seek clarity and consistency in his ideas, and to establish as precise a correspondence as possible between his ideas and the available facts. He never tired of testing hypotheses, modifying his theories, and facing up to facts.

The essays included herein exemplify Gibson's realistic approach to science. He was merciless in his critiques, especially of his own work, and was never content merely to patch up old ideas. Behind Gibson's critical approach to psychology was his purpose of furthering our understanding of how people apprehend and act upon the real world in which they live. He strove to formulate an *ecological* approach to perception and psychology.

From Gibson's broad range of interests, we have chosen four topics of central importance to his thinking and have organized the book around them with the goal of capturing both the breadth of Gibson's thought and his penetrating depth of analysis. The first section is devoted to the creation and development of *ecological optics,* a discipline invented by Gibson to provide a psychologically appropriate and empirically based description of the information available in light. The papers chosen for Section 2 deal with the analysis of environmental events and emphasize the information for perceiving object motions and animal movements. The papers in the third section are concerned with picture perception and document Gibson's attempt to answer the question of how pictures perform their representational function. Finally, Section 4 contains papers in which Gibson discussed the general implications of his ecological approach to perception for the science of psychology. Gibson's approach motivated the revision of many important concepts such as perceiving, acting, knowing, and development, all of which are discussed in the fourth section.

Each of the four topics is represented by approximately a half dozen published and several unpublished essays illustrating the development and refinement of Gibson's ideas on that topic. Each section is introduced by a short essay that places the papers in an historical context and relates the contents to relevant work by Gibson and others. We have also added editorial footnotes to many of the papers[1] referring readers to more recent literature on the topic, and cross-referencing the many connections within Gibson's work. Because this book is in part an intellectual biography, a personal and historical introduction is appropriate. Thus, we are honored and delighted that Professor Eleanor J. Gibson, the one contemporary perceptionist of stature equal to J. J. Gibson, has agreed to introduce this collection of her husband's work. We have also reprinted J. J. Gibson's (1967) autobiography to provide his own view of his life and work.

A collection of essays cannot provide as thorough an analysis of any one issue as do Gibson's (1947, 1950a, 1966b, 1979a) books, nor have we tried to do so herein. The essays in this volume were chosen to complement Gibson's major books, and to make available material that otherwise would have been difficult to obtain (such as the material from Gibson's first book, reprinted in Chs. 1.1, 2.2, and 3.1). Our criteria for selection included whether the essay made a significant contribution to one of the section topics, whether it represented a major theoretical statement, or whether it included a critical review of earlier work, or suggestions for future research. The papers within each section are presented in chronological order to show the development of Gibson's thinking on that section's topic. However, where important later comments on a paper were brief, we placed them out of chronological order, together with the original essay.

Some of the essays printed herein were previously unpublished, and a special word about them is in order. Because of his commitment to precision of thought and statement, Gibson often wrote and rewrote short papers dealing with a single topic or presenting a single argument. Many of these notes became what are known as "purple perils" (also called "purple pearls"). These were usually short, spirited papers that were distributed to colleagues or to members of Gibson's perennial weekly seminar on perception. They were intended to provoke comments on the way Gibson had formulated an argument, problem, or issue. When Gibson used these manuscripts in writing his books or papers (as he frequently did), invariably he would expand, modify, and further clarify them. Although Gibson consented to our publishing some of these hitherto unpublished papers, none of them was written with publication in mind. We have included some of these purple perils for two reasons: First, they offer great insight into Gibson's creative processes, revealing how he developed and transformed his ideas. Second, many of the unpublished essays we have included deal with important topics not discussed elsewhere by Gibson, and thus they show some of the new vistas that he was exploring.

Our final editorial contribution is a complete bibliography of Gibson's published papers, reviews, and films. This appears at the end of the book, along with a compilation of all the references cited in the essays and introductions. We hope that these bibliographies are convenient and useful for readers.

---

[1]Editorial footnotes are identified by the phrase "(Eds.)" at the end, to distinguish them from Gibson's notes.

The present volume illustrates as thoroughly as possible a few of Gibson's many interests. However, space limitations have prevented us from drawing as complete a portrait as could be drawn. In organizing the volume, we decided to concentrate on Gibson's theoretical contributions rather than on his experimental work. To do justice to either side of Gibson's career would require a volume in its own right, and we have selected papers to fit into a single book. Nevertheless, several experiments are included in otherwise theoretical essays (e.g., in Chs. 2.7, 4.1, 4.2, and 4.4), and they provide a flavor of Gibson's commitment to experimentation. For the reader interested in pursuing Gibson's more empirical work, we have referred to many of his experiments in our section introductions, and we have referenced reviews of experimental research by Gibson and others in footnotes.

Space limitations have also prevented us from including three theoretical essays of great importance to the understanding of Gibson's intellectual development. These are his essay on adaptation with negative aftereffect (Gibson, 1937b), his review of the concept of set (Gibson, 1941a), and the outline of his perceptual psychophysics (Gibson, 1959a). Each of these papers contains a major statement of Gibson's thinking on a central topic in perception, and it is impossible to understand his career fully without considering them. However, because each one approaches monograph length, we have chosen to review briefly their significance instead of reprinting them.

Gibson's research and theorizing on adaption to curvature and slant (Gibson, 1933, 1937a, b; Gibson & Radner, 1937; Radner & Gibson, 1935) illustrates his early use of a realistic research strategy and led to his development of the concept of dimensional properties in perception. Gibson's experiments on adaptation originally were performed to test the empiricist hypothesis that visual adaptation to curvature imposed by prismatic spectacles is due to the discrepancy between visual (falsely curved) and tactile (veridically rectilinear) space. Initially, Gibson (1933) eliminated the corrective tactile and kinesthetic input by having prism-wearing observers sit motionless while fixating a single point. The amount of adaptation with negative aftereffect decreased but was still evident. Then Gibson attempted a stronger test: Observers without prisms were asked to inspect actually curved lines. In this situation, where there was no visual-tactile discrepancy whatsoever, almost all observers nevertheless exhibited slight, but consistent, adaptation with negative aftereffect.[2] These were startling results for a committed empiricist!

Gibson's theory of these and other adaptation phenomena (Gibson, 1937b) reflects his concern with giving a realistic account of the perceptual situation, that is, with discovering what stimuli are psychologically real for perceivers. From the adaptation results, he argued that neither punctate sensory elements nor Gestalt forms are basic to perception, but rather that entire dimensions of stimuli

---

[2]This effect has come to be called the "Gibson effect."

are perceptually important. This early emphasis on relational aspects of stimulation provided an important basis for much of his later thinking about stimuli in terms of dimensional gradients (Chs. 1.1, 2.2, 3.1), the contrastive features of those dimensions (Chs. 1.8, 4.2), and, finally, the invariants across variations in stimulation (Ch. 1.2). In recent years, Gibson's adaptation with negative-aftereffect paradigm has come to be used by neuropsychologists as a tool for discovering the selective sensitivities of neural mechanisms of vision (Braddick, Campbell, & Atkinson, 1978; Mollon, 1977a, b) and audition (Eimas & Miller, 1978).

Gibson's work on the concept of set (Gibson, 1941a) elucidates the variety and nature of the cognitive factors that affect behavior and perception. This was a topic of long-standing interest for Gibson, whose dissertation (Gibson, 1929) was an investigation of the role of experience (as opposed to Gestalt organization principles) in schematizing reproduction memory for forms (Bartlett, 1932). Experience, organization, expectation, motivation, and hypothesis testing had all been considered forms of set, and these sets were supposed to modify existing patterns of behavior. The idea that behaviors vary along a continuum from stimulus-bound (involuntary) to cognitively based (voluntary) is at the heart of the concept of set. However, Gibson argued that upon inspection the alleged dimension of stimulus-bound to cognitively based behavior simply disappears, leaving behind a number of factors, none of which is well defined. Although many of these factors obviously play a role in behavior and perception, Gibson urged that the concept of set be either abandoned or refined, so that the nature and scope of the effects of cognition and motivation on perception could be identified with more clarity, and without the limitations imposed by the artificial and relatively meaningless distinction between voluntary and involuntary action. Gibson's later discussions of Gestalt theory (Ch. 4.1), perceptual development and learning (Ch. 4.2), cognition (Ch. 3.2), memory (Ch. 2.5), and behavior (Chs. 4.6, 4.9) all owe much to his early paper on set.

Gibson's essay, "Perception as a function of stimulation," which appeared in Volume 1 of Koch's series, *Psychology: A Study of a Science* (1959a), is a clear and powerful statement of the generalized hypothesis of psychophysical correspondence. In this essay, Gibson argued for a psychophysics of perception in which every aspect of the phenomenal world has a corresponding variable in the energy flux of stimulation. The clarity and precision with which Gibson articulated this radical proposal facilitated his later theorizing and led to his ultimate rejection of this theory. There was and is a great deal of evidence supporting the correspondence hypothesis, but Gibson later showed that perceptual psychophysics is not sufficiently ecological to provide an adequate theory of vision (Chs. 1.6, 4.4; Gibson, 1979a, p. 149). Ecological information is so rich that the implied one-to-one mapping between stimulation and perception in this psychophysical theory is untenable (Ch. 4.8), and the idea of a real *versus* a phenomenal environment is unworkable (Gibson, 1971b; Ch. 4.9). Finally, perception involves more than just awareness; it involves the ability to control one's activity within one's surroundings. In his later theorizing, Gibson (1966b, 1979a; Chs. 2.4, 4.4, 4.8) abandoned the conjecture that stimulation determines perception, developing the alternative hypothesis that stimulus information constrains perception and behavior.

In addition to the previous three papers, we have left out many other important and interesting essays on social psychology (Gibson, 1950b, 1951a, 1953a) on perceptual systems other than the visual system (Gibson, 1962a), and a large number of papers on visual perception (Gibson, 1948, 1950c, 1952b, 1958a, c). Despite these omissions, this collection does include the most important contributions to the study of vision by the 20th century's most important perceptionist. Gibson's genius lay mainly in his ability to seize on the best problems, to never let them go, to address all the facts relevant to a problem, and never to be satisfied with halfway solutions. This volume is a record of Gibson's intellectual odyssey through the classical problems of the psychology of perception to his creation of the new problems of perception that we must now try to face. We may succeed in dealing with these novel issues and problems if we follow J. J. Gibson and think—passionately and deeply—for ourselves.

# James J. Gibson
# Autobiography*

I was born in 1904 in a little river town in southeastern Ohio. The Muskingum Valley had been settled very early by New Englanders. The Indians had long since disappeared, but arrowheads still turned up in the spring ploughing, and my father had a large collection. A river town, with a dam and a water-powered mill smelling of grain, is a memorable place for a small boy.

My mother taught all the grades in a country school until she married my father. He had learned to be a surveyor for railroads after a couple of years in college. Soon after I began school, his job took him into raw new country in the West. His family went along; only after some years in the Dakotas and Wisconsin did we settle down in a suburb of Chicago. By that time, at the age of eight, I knew what the world looked like from a railroad train and how it seemed to flow inward when seen from the rear platform and expand outward when seen from the locomotive. The son of a railroad man had a better opportunity than others in those days to see things: sawmills, mines, ore-boats, mountains, canyons, deserts, rivers, viaducts, tunnels, and the geometrical wonder of steel rails tracing an even path over a wrinkled earth.

By the time I was fully settled in school I had two younger brothers. We lived within walking distance of Lake Michigan. But I never learned to be a swimmer; I had rather climb trees, and I conquered a whole grove in the backyard with my brothers. But they were four and eight years younger; I was something of a solitary youth and I had few outside friends until nearly through high school. There, at the age of sixteen, my entry into social life was provided by a teacher who cast me in a play. I was a wicked courtier.

*History of Psychology in Autobiography (Vol. 5), E. G. Boring & G. Lindzey (Eds.) Copyright 1967 by Irvington Publishers, Inc. Reprinted by permission.

I delighted in acting. For the next twenty years I sought every opportunity to try out for parts in the "little" theater. Amateur players are a special fraternity, I think, with peculiar ego-needs, and my proudest moments have been obtained on the stage. The achieving of a dramatic role, the expressing of a character, has given me deeper satisfaction than the playing of any of the other roles that an academic career affords—or the military, scientific, professional, or administrative roles. Wherever I have lived, the North Shore, Northwestern University, Princeton, Smith College, and Cornell, the amateur theater has made a bridge between college and community and across disciplines, and those who are addicted to it, as I was before I became deaf, are persons to my taste.

The only thing I remember learning in high school was Euclidean geometry. The beauty of geometrical insight and geometrical proof made a lasting imprint on my thinking; I recall asking the teacher whether every theorem that *was* true could be *proved* true. After secondary school I went to Northwestern for lack of any other planning of where I might go to college. It was just down the lake shore, and I could commute from home.

In 1922 I transferred from Northwestern to Princeton (which strangely would accept a Midwestern sophomore without much Latin, but not a freshman) and found myself out of place again except among the little theater enthusiasts. My friends in college were the eccentrics instead of the club members. I had no ideas what I wanted to do or be, choosing to major in philosophy and spending the summers as an inadequate bank clerk, a bewildered oilfield laborer, and a miserable salesman. It was the Princeton celebrated by F. Scott Fitzgerald. I was an emancipated youth but, alas, not a gilded one. I was deeply impressed by that environment, like the unhappy novelist himself, but I dimly realized that I did not like it. However, in my last year we put on a production of a blood-and-thunder play of the twelfth century from the manuscript of which Shakespeare had stolen the plot of Hamlet. The characters were the same even if their speeches were bombast. It was a great success, especially the duelling, which I had coached, and we took it to New York for two nights. I fell in love with our Ophelia who had been borrowed from the cast of the Garrick Gaieties. This last was the first "intimate revue" produced in New York, and I became a familiar backstage visitor. Philosophy was neglected. I scraped through the comprehensive exams in May, however, and she came to my commencement in 1925. To be sure, she jilted me during the following year, when I was a graduate student, but I had become a sophisticate. I could stroll casually through a stage door.

At the beginning of my senior year I had taken a course in experimental psychology run in permissive fashion by H. S. Langfeld, newly arrived from Harvard. The eight students were a mixed group but an *esprit de corps* developed. Some catalyst was present that precipitated four psychologists from them: Bray, Gahagan, Gibson, and Schlosberg. Langfeld was delighted with us; he had a touch of the German professor, but he winked at the horseplay with which we enriched the laboratory exercises. Toward the end of the year he was able to offer three of us assistantships. This stroke of luck gave me an identity; I was an academic; not a philosopher, but even better, a psychologist.

My lack of aptitude for business had been clearly demonstrated, and my father was willing to take the burden of two sons in college at the same time. Graduate study in psychology suited me. I brought to it a taste for pragmatism in philosophy and I soon became excited by the behaviorist revolution. Howard Crosby Warren, the founder of Princeton psychology after James Mark Baldwin, was a friend and a champion of Watson, who spoke to the colloquium. I thought him brash. The next year Langfeld brought E. B. Holt to the department from Harvard, and we took to his ideas with enthusiasm. Holt was a slow writer but a great teacher. He had a contempt for humbug and a clarity of thought that has never been matched. He had shown how cognition might itself be a form of response, and he was engaged in extending conditioned-reflex theory to social behavior, amending the gaps in the published textbook that his student Floyd Allport had recently written. He shocked his students by violent p edictions in the mildest possible manner of speaking.

Holt's motor theory of consciousness provided a way of encompassing the facts of Titchener without either trying to refute them or simply to forget about them. It was a more elegant theory than that of any other behaviorist. For thirty years I was reluctant to abandon it, and it is still very much alive today, but the experimental evidence is now clearly against it. Awareness seems to me now an activity but not a motor activity, a form of adjustment that enhances the pickup of information but not a kind of behavior that alters the world. Instead of the contrast between consciousness and behavior that used to preoccupy us, I think we should look for the difference between observational activity and performatory activity. But this is getting ahead of the story.

Graduate instruction at Princeton was not split up into different fields. It was centered around a weekly colloquium at which we made frequent reports in the form of papers written out and read. The faculty then criticized. There was a group of young instructors, including Leonard Carmichael who lectured on the evolution of the nervous system. We also learned from each other and from graduate students in other disciplines. The Graduate College, where we lived, had a life of its own apart from the University. It stood on a hill a mile from the campus. Its dean had won the only academic battle ever lost by Woodrow Wilson in placing it there. We had dinner in gowns in a great hall. The trappings were a mere imitation of Oxford, no doubt, but this did not bother us, for the intellectual air was bracing and the conversations were wide-ranging. The wine cellar included in the plans for the building was empty, but New Jersey applejack was to be had, and a stomach for it could be learned, if not a taste.

I did my thesis on the drawing of visual forms from memory to refute the just-published results of Wulf at Berlin, a student of Koffka's, purporting to show that memories changed spontaneously toward better Gestalten. The drawings of *my* subjects differed from the originals only in accordance with laws of perceptual habit, not laws of dynamic self-distribution, I concluded with great confidence. Form perception was learned. Otherwise one fell into the arms of Immanuel Kant. I was a radical empiricist, like Holt, who suspected that the very structure of the nervous system itself was learned by neurobiotaxis in accordance with the laws of conditioning. Little did I know that within six months I would be facing Koffka himself weekly across a seminar table.

I reported my research one spring under the wing of Langfeld at a meeting of Titchener's invited group of experimentalists. The great man sat at the head of a table, like Jehovah in black broadcloth, with an enormous cigar emerging from a great white beard. I received a few words of advice, very penetrating, as I recall. He inspired genuine awe, for he quite simply knew more psychology than anyone else. But my generation had no need for his theory or his method. His influence was on the wane and he died soon after. I was later deeply influenced by Boring's modification of the Titchenerian theory, a modification that permitted psychophysics to go about its business, but not by analytical introspection. The assumption that all consciousness, or even all cognitive consciousness, can be reduced to sensory elements is surely untenable.

So it was that in 1928 I was considered qualified to teach psychology. I went to Smith College (at $1800 a year). Harold Schlosberg went to Brown; Chuck Bray stayed at Princeton. At Smith I was to remain for many years. And within my first week I met that extraordinary man Kurt Koffka, a kind of person entirely new to my experience.

Koffka had been brought to Northampton by William Allen Neilson, who installed him in an old house off the campus, permitted him to import assistants from Russia, Poland, Germany, and elsewhere, and let him experiment to his heart's content. Neilson had not consulted his department of psychology in making this research appointment, and the teaching staff did not quite know whether to be honored or offended. But Koffka promptly set up a weekly seminar to which we were cordially invited.

Koffka did most of the talking, and I listened regularly from 1928 to 1941. I sometimes reported my own work and I occasionally ventured to argue with him, for my bent was skeptical and pragmatic. Koffka hated positivism. The emerging doctrines of Gestalt theory seemed to me tenderminded, but I learned a great deal, for the seminar was centered on evidence and the analysis of evidence. In 1933, after the original research funds had been exhausted, Koffka became a member of the department, teaching one course. He then began to put together the *Principles of Gestalt Psychology* (1935), requiring his undergraduates to summarize sections of his manuscript in class as he went along. This strange method of teaching, you might suppose, would soon bring his course enrollment to zero (the worst of all fates at a college), but, on the contrary, the girls were dazzled. He chose the brightest. It was a serious book, dedicated to difficult problems, and there was no compromise with difficulty.

Of course it is also true that Koffka loved Smith College and that women melted in his presence. It was once explained to me that such worship of an odd-looking man with a high-pitched voice came from the fact that he gave absolute attention to any girl he met. But I do not pretend to understand why they worshipped him. He wrote one of the great books of this century, as I came to realize later. It took a long time for the *Principles* to sink in, and I had to reject the notion of organization and reinterpret the notion of structure before I could assimilate it, but Koffka, along with Holt, was a main influence on my psychological thinking.

I had my own teaching, of course, during all this time. There were never less than nine class hours a week. I had a regular course in social psychology that ran throughout the year. After fifteen years of it I knew the field pretty well, but I never tried to publish in it. I also did my stint of teaching the introductory course and the beginning experimental course. But my specialty was advanced experimental psychology, which met six hours a week for thirty-two weeks a year. There were always eight to a dozen seniors in it, and we ran experiments on every possible problem. They were generally new experiments, with little or no published evidence as to what the results might be. Bright students, especially girls, will work like demons when the outcome will be a contribution to knowledge. At the high point of this course the students would choose a problem from my offerings, run the subjects, analyze the data, and write up a report at the rate of one a month. I still have copies of the best of these papers, and every so often I find a published experiment that was first performed essentially by one of my students in the thirties. A good many *were* publishable. The apparatus was makeshift (but it was used only once), the statistics were elementary (but one gets a feeling for reliability), and a satisfying number of the questions we put to test gave clear answers. There must have been 500 or more such projects in my years at Smith, and I am sure that they constitute my main backlog of psychological knowledge. And there is still another backlog in the files of unanswered questions that I had to dream up in order to keep ahead of those lovely creatures who had a zeal for discovering how the mind works.

One year, 1930 to 1931, there were eight or nine girls in the course who were all smart (and all pretty). The mysterious catalyzer of an intellectual group developed. We made astonishing discoveries—that a conditioned withdrawal-reflex would transfer to the unconditioned hand, for example (with E. G. Jack & G. Raffel, 1932). We had a lovely time and ended the year with a splendid picnic. Five of the group went on to become psychologists. Two of them, Eleanor Jack and Sylvia MacColl, with another from a previous year, Hulda Rees, became graduate assistants at Smith. That year, 1931 to 1932, was an illustrious one for me. As a prosperous bachelor with a salary of $2500 in the deep depression, I could take around all three girls at once, and they were charming as well as being my professional colleagues. We had weekends in New York and mountain climbing expeditions to New Hampshire. By summer I was in love with the prettiest of all and pursued her to Illinois where she was persuaded to marry me in September.

This is the place, perhaps, to jump ahead and speak of my wife's part in the psychological history here being attempted. I will say nothing about our personal live save that we have had a fine time, have raised two handsome offspring who seem to be intellectuals like ourselves, and have had our share of adventures. We have never been a "research team," as many married scientists have, for we collaborate only indifferently. She went to Yale for a year and got a degree with Clark Hull in a burst of mutual admiration. She was and is a very tough-minded investigator, for all of being a nice girl. Down deep she is a Hullian, as I am a Holtian; a rat-behaviorist, as I am a philosophical behaviorist. The influence of Koffka was weaker on her than on me. She is bored by the epistemological problem, whereas I am fascinated by it. Nevertheless, we converge in the developing belief that the weakness of the stimulus-response formula in American psychology lies on the side of the stimulus, not on that of the response. The experiments on learning that convince her of this are not the same as the experiments on perception that convince me of it, but we agree on where to look for the trouble, and we both think that modern psychology is in deep trouble.

We have no patience with the attempts to patch up the S-R formula with hypotheses of mediation. In behavior theory as well as psychophysics you either find causal relations or you do not. After much travail we managed to write a paper together ten years ago on perceptual learning (with E. J. Gibson, 1955). Perception, as we said, is a matter of differentiating what is outside in the available stimulation, not a matter of enriching the bare sensations of classical stimulation. We barely touched upon the many questions that arise, however, and agreed upon scarcely more than a few slogans. Leo Postman saw this paper as a threat to the whole theory of association (Postman, 1955), and it was, but he rightly argued that an alternative theory of perceptual learning had not been spelled out. References to "the Gibsons' theory of perception," therefore, have given us a bit of a turn, for we were neither wholly in agreement at the time nor was that paper a theory.

In the last few years, however, we have been working semi-independently on different levels of the input side of the S-R formula. We now have a theory. At this moment I have finished a book entitled *The Senses Considered as Perceptual Systems* (1966b) and my wife has nearly finished one on perceptual learning and development. The one is consistent with the other. I have formulated a theory of stimulus information and redescribed the sense organs as mechanisms for picking it up. She has examined the ways in which growth and experience enhance the pickup of the invariants that carry information. As a whole it is new, and the theory has radical implications for all parts of psychology. But once more I have gotten ahead of the story.

Returning to 1932, I did an experiment that summer before getting married. I had previously been using a pair of spectacle frames with optometrist's trial-prisms in them to verify the old result that one soon learned to reach for things in the right direction despite their apparent displacement. I had also observed the curvature adaptation that resulted from wearing the prisms and assumed that this too was a correcting of visual experience by tactual, in accordance with Bishop Berkeley's theory of visual perception. But there was disturbing evidence against this presumably self-evident explanation (even in Stratton's original experiment of this type), and I thought of a control experiment that would surely put the doctrine of sensory empiricism back on its feet. I would look at a field of *actually* curved lines equivalent to the prismatic distortion for as long as I could stand to do so and show that no change in apparent curvature would then occur. But to my astonishment it did occur. Apparent curvature still decreased and straight lines thereafter looked curved in the opposite direction.

This result was shocking to an empiricist. How could sensory experience be validated except against other sensory experience? It might, of course, be validated against behavior, which came to the same thing, but there had *been* no behavior in my experiment. I could only conclude that the perception of a line must be like the sensation of a color or temperature in being susceptible to the negative afterimage caused by some process of physiological normalization. This was equally puzzling, however, for it called in question the very notion that perceptions were based on physiological sensations. This crucial experiment (see 1933), subsequently elaborated in many ways, has motivated my thinking for thirty years.

I never pursued the more strenuous experiment of wearing distorting spectacles for weeks or months, as Ivo Kohler did in Innsbruck in the mid-thirties, and I failed to discover the full range of phenomenal adaptation to visual distortion that he did (Kohler, 1951). His results are even more destructive of classical theories than mine. Distortion of the visual feedback from movements of the observer, it now appears, is even more important than a distortion of visual *form* with a stationary observer. If I had followed up this lead I might have come sooner to my present conviction that optical transformations in time are the main carriers of information, not optical forms frozen in time.

I continued to work on various problems in the decade before the war. A great deal of encouragement for research came from the annual opportunity to report it at the meetings of the Psychological Round Table, a somewhat raffish group of young psychologists in the East, founded on the inflexible principle that members became emeritus at the age of forty. Promotion of assistant professors was not rapid in those days and elevation to membership in the Society of Experimental Psychologists, which was full up with venerable holdovers from Titchener's day, was not to be expected. At its first meeting the group voted tolerantly *not* to call itself the Society of Experimenting Psychologists. It was concerned *not* to issue invitations on the basis of weighty deliberation. On Saturday night a scientific address was delivered on sexual or scatological questions. Despite the lightheartedness of these meetings, discussions and new ideas were fruitful, and criticism was sharp.

In 1937 one of my friends, an engineer, was a bug on automobiles, and it was the time of the first driver clinics. The tests being given, I felt, were nonsense, for the skill of driving a car (on which I prided myself) had never been analysed. So we analysed it (with L. E. Crooks, 1938). Lewin had begun to formulate his theory of behavior as locomotion, with fields, valences, and vectors, but it was static and did not apply very well to visually-guided real locomotion, so other concepts had to be worked out—the clearance-lines of obstacles, the margin of safety considered as a ratio, and the temporal flow of the necessary information for accelerating, decelerating, and steering. Our paper was not spectacular, but the problems encountered came up again in my wartime work on aircraft landing (see 1947; with Olum & Rosenblatt, 1955) and my later attempt at a general theory of locomotion (1958b). No fact of behavior, it seems to me, betrays the weakness of the old concept of visual stimuli so much as the achieving of contact without collision—for example, the fact that a bee can land on a flower without blundering into it. The reason can only be that centrifugal flow of the structure of the bee's optic array specifies locomotion and controls the flow of locomotor responses.

As the reader may gather, I prefer radical solutions to scientific problems whenever possible. General explanations are always preferable to piecemeal explanations (''models'' as they are nowadays called), and this is all that is meant by a radical theory. As the depression deepened in the thirties, I became convinced that a radical solution of politico-socio-economic problems was possible. Social psychology looked a great deal easier then than it does now. Marxian socialism provided the only general theory for social action, and it was internally consistent as compared to the intellectual muddles of liberalism, and rational as compared to the stupidities of fascism. I was converted from skepticism and pragmatism to radicalism almost overnight in a strange way: by reading *The Education of Henry Adams*. In this effete and indecisive American I seemed to recognize myself. The old American radicals, men like Thorstein Veblen (with whose nephew I had taken a course in non-Euclidean geometry at Princeton), were men who had rightly been soured by the rationalizations of satisfied citizens, but they could accomplish nothing because they had no political backing. The mass support for social reform could only come, of course, from Labor. So I became a left-winger and joined the Labor movement.

A group of us on the Smith faculty took out a charter as Local 230 of the American Federation of Teachers. It was, I think, the first such college union. We bored from within the American Association of University Professors. We sent a delegate to the Northampton trade union council. The lack of any feeling for socialism among the local unionists puzzled me, and I must have puzzled them. President Neilson, who often was invited to AAUP dinners, was hurt by our minority, for he considered himself a radical. So he was, of course, but with a difference. We never did persuade any public or secondary school teachers to join our local. My wife and I once went up to organize the Dartmouth faculty, who in truth were exploited worse than we were, but we got so distracted by a round of parties on the Carnival weekend that the necessary papers went unsigned.

The truth is, I suppose, that the intellectual radicals of the depression years, and even the Communist Party, never got to the really hungry people. Marx could not foresee this. Social behavior was less predictable than we thought it was. I have reluctantly given up theorizing about politico-economic problems. The Society for the Psychological Study of Social Issues, which I helped to found and the motivation of which I understood, has become a group that I no longer understand. No one has a theory any more, only a conscience. And this is too bad, for, as Lewin said, there is nothing as practical as a good theory.

The failures of international politics in that era were heartbreaking to one of my generation. Things might have been different and Hitler might have been prevented if statesmen and parties had been wiser, that is, if they had understood what was going on. But to understand, to be able to explain and predict, entails the knowing of laws. It is our own fault if we do not know the laws. Because no radical solution to the problems of politics has been found does not mean that it does not exist. Psychologists are simply, on an absolute scale, dullards.

When the war came in 1941, I felt little idealism about it. Nevertheless, it was as good a war as could be expected if there had to be one, and there were opportunities for a psychologist to make a practical contribution. I left in the middle of the year and spent some months in Washington where the program of psychological research units in the Army Air Force was being organized. I then spent eighteen months in Fort Worth, Texas, at the headquarters of the Flying Training Command and another two and one-half years at Santa Ana Army Air Base in California.

Psychological research units were mainly needed for personnel selection. At one time, something like the equivalent to the entire college population of the country was being trained for flying duty of one sort or another, and selection for aptitude was essential. There was some research on training, of which I will speak, but testing was our main responsibility. Most of the psychologists recruited for this job were experimentalists like myself, not test psychologists. There was to be an entirely new approach to aptitude testing.

One of the new ideas was to use motion picture screening for the presentation of test items. And another, more obvious, was the development of tests for the visual perception of space. The Army Air Corps had to be at home in the "wild blue yonder." The motion picture unit became my responsibility and the ancient problem of space perception was my burden. It was worrisome, for, as I gradually came to realize, nothing of any practical value was known by psychologists about the perception of motion, or of locomotion in space, or of space itself. The classical cues for depth referred to paintings or parlor stereoscopes, whereas the practical problems of military aviation had to do with takeoff and landing, with navigation and the recognition of landmarks, with pursuit or evasion, and with the aiming of bullets or bombs at targets. What was thought to be known about the retinal image and the physiology of retinal sensations simply had no application to these performances. Birds and bees could do them, and a high proportion of young males could learn to do them, but nobody understood *how* they could.

The Aviation Psychology Program included four or five research units besides the motion picture unit. We made tests for aircrew aptitudes, hundreds upon hundreds of them; and we tested the tests in the Anglo-American tradition of statistical prediction. We validated against the criteria of pass-fail in the flying schools, and the navigator, bombardier, and gunnery schools, and thus lifted ourselves by our own bootstraps. We analysed the factors in the correlations between tests and struggled to interpret them. But I, at least, have never achieved a promising hypothesis by means of factor-analysis. The so-called "spatial" abilities extracted from existing tests still seem to me unintelligible. The fact is, I now think, that the spatial performances of men and animals are based on stimulus-information of a mathematical order that we did not even dream of in the 1940's. There are invariants of structure or pattern under transformation. Moreover, the information is so redundant in natural situations, with so many covariant equivalent variables and so many ways of getting information that substitute for one another, that the isolation of cues for testing these perceptual skills is a problem we will not soon solve. Perceiving is flexible, opportunistic, and full of multiple guarantees for detecting facts. It is no wonder that the hope of fairly sampling perception with paper-and-pencil tests, pictorial tests, or even motion picture tests has not been realized. And the building of apparatus to simulate the stimulus-information in life situations is difficult when one does not know what the information is.

 The test-construction work of my own unit has been described elsewhere (1944, 1947) and need not be repeated. Adapting the motion picture for group testing was a fascinating problem. Our test films were partly shot and were always processed and printed in a militarized motion picture studio staffed with industry personnel who had simply put on uniforms. Air Force training films were also produced in this studio where the Hal Roach comedies had been made. We also had the facilities of Hollywood available. I became as sophisticated about film studios as I had been about the stage. I learned a great deal about the technology of film-making and something about the psychology of the sort of perception that the film can mediate. A true understanding of this sort of vicarious experience would be a triumph for both psychology and the cinema if it could be achieved. But there is a vast gulf between what the film expert knows and what the perception psychologist knows. The cinematographer knows how to convey astonishing versions of reality on a sheaf of light-rays but cares nothing for the eye. The psychologist thinks he knows about the eye but has never paid any attention to the subtleties in the sheaf of rays. The two do not communicate.

Toward the end of the war my research unit was finally asked to work on a problem that had long interested us, the question of how a training film taught, or conveyed information, and what kinds of subject matter the cinema was uniquely adapted to teach. The previous experimental literature on educational films in schools and colleges and the controversies over "visual education" were almost useless. The Air Force had been using training films on an unprecedented scale for all sorts of purposes and literally hundreds of them were available: for orientation, for morale, for propaganda against picking up girls not approved by the USO, and for instruction in all the classes of all kinds of training schools down to technical films on how to rivet aluminum. The AAF Production Unit in Culver City would make a training film on any subject whatever. But nobody had any clear idea as to whether or not they did any good. We had been analysing some of the shooting scripts of instructional films in advance of production to see if we could develop a theory of what a motion picture shot could do that nothing else could. And this led to an experiment.

R. M. Gagné, who had once been my student in peacetime and who was the only other pure experimental psychologist ever assigned to us as an officer, worked on it with me. Essentially what we did was to take an instructional film that we considered excellent and compare it with the best possible illustrated manual and the best possible illustrated lecture on the same material. The auditory instruction with the motion sequences ran only fifteen minutes; the written and oral instruction with the static pictures was fuller and ran thirty minutes. Despite the time difference, aviation cadets learned significantly more from the teaching with the graphic displays. The reasons were fairly clear. What had to be learned was a system of how to aim at a moving target (fighter plane) from a moving platform (bomber). As the situation changed, the action changed. The film *showed* how one thing varied with another; the book and the talk could graph it, represent stages of it, and describe it in several ways, but could not display the continuous covariation in time. Moreover, and this impressed me, the film could make use of the "subjective camera," taking the point of view of the learner and displaying how the situation would look to *him,* not merely what things looked *like.* The experiment is more fully described in my book (1947, Ch. 10).

Gagné and I also worked on aircraft recognition, the discrimination and identification of small dark silhouettes against the sky with only slight differences in form. It was a life-and-death matter in certain theaters of the war. Weeks of training were spent on it in all branches of the service. Perhaps no other such peculiar perceptual skill has ever been so widely learned and taught. A large number of instructors was required, and it once seemed to me that half the English professors of America must be serving their country by teaching the subject. But how to do it? The psychologist Renshaw, at Ohio State, had early convinced the military that the secret of recognition was promptness and the way to get quick perceptual reactions was to give quick stimuli, that is, to show photographic slides of airplanes with a tachistoscope. The English professors were endlessly flashing pictures on a screen so as to speed up their students' perceptions. The only thing that could be said for such training was it was less boring than most military courses. The trouble was that when the boys got overseas they could not recognize aircraft.

By the end of 1943 there began to be disillusion with the Renshaw flash system, and a few aviation psychologists were allowed to take a crack at the problem. An airplane has to be recognized in any of its possible orientations. We advocated the use of solid models, the changing shadows of solid models on a translucent screen, motion picture shots, and instead of pictures, caricatures or cartoon drawings of the different airplanes that exaggerated their distinctive features. Gagné and I did a lot of nice research on the kind of learning involved in this perceptual skill (Gibson, 1947, Ch. 7). We learned more about the perception of objects, I think, than we would ever have done by running standard laboratory experiments on form-perception. For one thing, I got a nagging suspicion that nobody ever really sees a flat form in life, that is, a picture of a thing. One sees a continuous family of perspective transformations, an infinity of forms, that somehow specifies the solid shape of the object. This puzzle remained with me for twelve years until I was able, in collaboration with my wife, to conclude that the invariants in a family of transformations are effective stimuli for perception (with E. J. Gibson, 1957).

The suggestion that it is the distinctive features in the transformations of objects, not the forms as such, that enable us to recognize them is a very fruitful if radical hypothesis. What a caricaturist does is to freeze the differences between one human face and all others in a drawing, emphasizing the differences and omitting the similarities. A caricature therefore is not usefully understood as a distortion of a face or a misrepresentation, for it specifies the person and conveys information about him. This is information in the recently discovered meaning of the term which implies that a stimulus is definable as what it is *not* instead of as what it *is*.

I was lucky in the war, for unlike most I got to work finally at what I could best do. I did not care much for military life (the few psychologists who revelled in it were not ones I respected), but I made a lot of friends, and putting my education to a practical test was a new education. I discovered that what I had known before did not work. I learned that when a science does not usefully apply to practical problems there is something wrong with the theory of the science. So, after writing up my contribution to the shelf of volumes on aviation psychology, I got out, returned to my teaching at Smith, and began at once to write a book on visual perception that took off from new assumptions. This was *The Perception of the Visual World* (1950a).

Koffka had died, and my wife and I felt that the spark had gone out in the old Smith College department, so we were glad to go to Cornell in 1949. Unhappily, she could no longer teach as she had done since 1932 (with time out) under Neilson's canny policy of hiring husbands and wives in the same department and getting two for the price of one-and-a-half. Smith has experienced no difficulty with the supposed evils of nepotism, and it is a pity that universities will not try the experiment of tolerating spouses. I doubt that they put their heads together any more than other academic pairs.

The book came out during the first year at Cornell. The crux of it came in the third chapter where the experience of the *visual world* was contrasted with the experience of the *visual field*. The former was the awareness of one's surroundings; the latter was an awareness of one's visual sensations when the eyes were fixated. I was out to give an explanation of the former, not of the latter. Depth and distance and objects of constant size and shape were *seen*, I suggested, not judged or inferred, and the question was how this could be explained. The perceptual impression was primary and the sensory impressions were secondary, being obtained only with an introspective attitude. The "cues for depth" were what depth and distance looked like when they were not simply seen as depth and distance. The real stimuli for perception (I should have said stimulus-*information* for perception) were gradients of the retinal image (I should have said *invariants* of the *optic array*).

The main new idea I introduced was that of optical texture, which enabled me to define and illustrate gradients of the *density* of optical texture. Such a gradient was asserted to be in psychophysical correspondence with the recession or slant of a phenomenal surface. This assertion has been checked by a good many experimenters in the last fifteen years and it seems to hold up. At least it does if optical "texture" is treated generally as the overall structure of the optic array. It subdivides into many other hypotheses that cannot be detailed here.

The idea that such a gradient might be a stimulus opened up a quite new possibility of explaining how perception might be veridical, for the gradient of density was a consequence of the perspective projection of light from the real surfaces of the environment. The correspondence of phenomenal surfaces to physical ones might be thus accounted for without any appeal to innate intuition, or the correction of sensations by past experience, or a spontaneous organization of the sensory data in the brain—in short, with no appeal to any theory of perception whatever. Here was a new basis for a realist solution to the epistemological problem.

My sixteen years at Cornell have been largely devoted to the developing, testing, and sometimes the altering of the ideas set forth in the *Visual World*. They keep generating fresh ideas and opening up new explanations. A great number of exploratory experiments and some twenty or more published ones have come out pretty much as expected. Most of these involve surface-perception in one way or another: extending to the edges of surfaces; the layout of surfaces; the motions of surfaces, both rigid and non-rigid; the perception of human faces as elastic surfaces; the tactual perception of surface-layout; and recently the perception of impending collision with a surface (Schiff, 1965).

These experiments are not concerned any more with the perception of space but with the perception of the features of the world, the furniture of the environment, and what they afford. The old puzzle of depth-perception, I think, can be dismissed. Space, so-called, is not separable from meaning. An example is provided by the experiments done by my wife and Richard Walk on detection of a "visual cliff" (Gibson & Walk, 1960). Animals and babies are very sensitive to the optical information that specifies depth downward at an edge. This specifies (or "means," if I may use the term) a falling-off place. For a terrestrial animal it affords falling and hence injury. It might be expected therefore that this unique discontinuity in a transforming optic array would be readily picked up by terrestrial animals. Their behavior shows that it is. But this result does not in the least imply that animals and babies possess innate depth perception in the sense intended by Immanuel Kant. It implies that their visual systems first detect those gross features of the layout of the world that are important for animals and babies. That information for a cliff is in the ambient light. The notion that they are born with depthless visual sensations to which the third dimension is added by *any* operation, learned or unlearned, now seems to me quite ridiculous.

There was a period in the 1950's when we explored the possibilities and the limitations of the kind of visual perception that is mediated by still pictures, drawings, photographs, and the like. I learned from it a great respect for painters and the art of painting. I was bewildered by the continuing controversy of art considered as representation versus art in the styles loosely called nonrepresenta-tive. I have come to think that the futile debates about nonrepresentative art stem from our ignorance about the information in light. Psychologists and artists have misled one another; we have borrowed the so-called cues for depth from the painters, and they in turn have accepted the theory of perception we deduced from their techniques.

Eventually I came to realize how unlike the pictorial mode of perception is from the natural one. The former is perception at second hand; the latter is perception at first hand. The framed optic array coming from a picture to an eye is quite unlike the natural optic array coming from the world to an eye. The latter is only a sector, a sample, of the total ambient array. Eyes evolved so as to see the world, not a picture. Since this became clear to me I have tried to give up any use whatever of the term "retinal image." The assumption that there is a picture on the retina has led to all sorts of unnecessary and insoluble problems, problems for psychology, art, and optics. I have ventured to assume that classical instru-mental optics comprises a set of convenient fictions for a rather dull branch of applied physics and that a new ecological optics can be worked out (1961a).

I now assume that perception does not depend on sensory impressions at all, but instead only on the pickup of stimulus information. Sense data are incidental symptoms of experience, not its foundation, and the effort of Titchener and his predecessors to make an inventory of them was almost wholly wasted.

The theory of perception as the registering of information and of perceptual learning as the education of attention to information in the available stimulation applies as well to touching, listening, smelling, and tasting as it does to looking. It illuminates the evolution of perceptual skills of man. The theory will be open to examination with the publication of my new book (1966b) and the forthcoming one written by my wife on perceptual learning. I have had to contradict the most venerable doctrines of sensory physiology, and she has had to throw away the laws of association, seemingly the only foundation for empiricism since Locke. It is too soon to say whether the alternative ideas will catch on in physiology, psychology, and education. We shall see.

In conclusion, a kind of self-examination may be revealing. What I have most wanted to do all my life is to make a contribution to knowledge. If you feel you are doing this it is much more fun than running things, or being a military commander, a departmental chairman, a participant in the brotherhood of workers, a mountain climber, or even an actor. And it seems to me that one can contribute to knowledge without being very bright (which I am not) but merely by being stubborn about it. Such a contribution, of course, has to be expounded and clarified, and this is where teaching comes in. It is a two-way process, and no one does it for himself. One must listen as well as talk; read as well as write. Knowledge is not knowledge until it is preserved in dusty libraries for the future. But despite all that, the big satisfaction comes from the thinking that first went into it, the satisfaction of seeing old facts and new data fall into place.

I have been a lucky member of a rich society that has made it materially easy for someone who wants to contribute to knowledge to do so. At least it has been easy since the Great Depression. I have been given all the breaks. I have had time for thinking and writing at most of the havens provided for the leisure of the theory class, as someone put it. I have been to Oxford University (1955-56), the Institute for Advanced Study at Princeton (1958-59), and the Center for Advanced Study in the Behavioral Sciences (1963-64). They are wonderful places. My career has been made possible by the fact of endowments, and my research has been generously supported by the federal taxpayer. I am a creature of a prosperous age.

I seem to be, to my surprise, a member of a large profession. There are some 20,000 psychologists in this country alone, nearly all of whom have become so in my adult lifetime. They are all prosperous. Most of them seem to be busily applying psychology to problems of life and personality. They seem to feel, many of them, that all we need to do is consolidate our scientific gains. Their self-confidence astonishes me. For these gains seem to me puny, and scientific psychology seems to me ill-founded. At any time the whole psychological applecart might be upset. Let them beware!

I have, in my time, experienced the gratification of having people unburden themselves about their emotional problems and the fascination of getting inside the complex personality of another. I have felt the urge to help others. I even think I might have been a successful clinician. But nothing that I know as a scientist would have helped me to be one.

As to my personal peculiarities, the principal one is my deafness. I have had to wear a hearing aid for the last twenty years, and the loss seems to be progressive. The earliest of the surgical remedies for otosclerosis failed in my case and the later ones would probably not do me much good. The standard wisecrack that it must be a great advantage to be able to turn off the noises of the world at will gives me a hollow laugh. Deafness is isolating. For some reason I could never learn to pick up the visual information for lip-reading, although I have occasionally tried. On the other hand, I think I am fairly acute at understanding facial and gestural expressions. This is a contradiction I cannot resolve. I have tended to compensate for deafness by advertising it instead of trying to hide the necessary apparatus. Most people, in face-to-face conversation, react appropriately to this signal, and to them one is grateful. A few are disconcerted and, worst of all, a few shout. Conversation is nevertheless fairly satisfactory. The main frustration is in group discussion and in the failure of auditory localization. It is very hard for someone to realize that when he calls to me I do not know which way to look for him.

It is interesting that my vision has held up well even past the age when presbyopia limits the unaided acuity of most persons. I use my eyes for all sorts of purposes; I have educated them, and I sometimes wonder if that has anything to do with it.

I think I have a new solution to the ancient puzzle of how animals and men perceive. It is pieced together, of course, from selected bits of all the old solutions, but it has one new piece that makes everything fit—the concept of available stimulus-information and the relegation of stimulus-energy to its own level. There are other psychologists who have thought about perception almost as I do, but not quite. The one with whom in recent years I have been in strikingly near agreement is Albert Michotte, of Louvain—in everything but the notion of external information and external meaning. (His death, since this was first written, is a great loss to psychology.) It is a notable lesson in the convergence of experimental science that such a man as he and such a one as I, from totally different backgrounds, should have found ourselves agreeing so thoroughly and so delightedly—he, a student of Cardinal Mercier and I of the materialist Holt; he, a believer and phenomenologist and I a skeptic and behaviorist; he, a member of the conservative Belgian nobility, a prince of the Catholic Church, and I a Midwestern Sunday-school radical with an underlying suspicion of popery. We got the same results. This is what counts. It makes one believe in the possibility of getting at the truth.

# 1

# FOUNDATIONS OF ECOLOGICAL OPTICS

Edward Reed
and Rebecca Jones

## INTRODUCTION

The papers in this section document the origin and development of ecological optics, the discipline created by Gibson for the analysis of the information for vision. The study of ecological optics is a crucial component of the ecological approach to vision, together with the description of what is in the environment to be perceived, and the account of how organisms detect and use information. Although this section focuses on ecological optics, the analysis of optical information depends both on the nature of the environment to be seen and on the activities of animals in detecting that information. Thus, all three components of the ecological approach are touched upon herein.

The founding of ecological optics is one of Gibson's greatest contributions to perception. It provides a framework for analyzing information at a level appropriate to the facts of the environment, and, as Gibson argued, it provides us with "new reasons for realism" (Ch. 4.5). The papers in this section reveal the research and theorizing that led to the development of ecological optics and illustrate Gibson's search for the proper analysis of information in stimulation, from the concept of retinal gradients (Ch. 1.1), to the notion of optical motions and transformations (Ch. 1.2), to the idea of disturbances in the nested structure of the optic array (Ch. 1.7).

The section begins with a selection from Gibson's report on his wartime research for the Air Force, *Motion Picture Testing and Research* (1947). The demands of practical problems, such as pilot selection and training, motivated Gibson to question the assumptions underlying the classical formulation of space perception. It had always been assumed that we see depth along the line receding from us by means of depthless sensory cues that are reorganized or interpreted to yield perceived depth. Gibson rejected these assumptions when the classical theory failed drastically to provide a useful framework for working on practical problems of vision.

Gibson's attempt to provide a more useful and realistic theory of space perception involved the formulation of a new account of what is perceived and a new description of the variables in stimulation. According to his new "ground theory," we do not perceive "space" but rather the continuous ground surface extending underneath all other surfaces and edges in the environment. This novel account of "space" perception led to the formulation of Gibson's well-known concept of *texture gradients* as stimuli for vision. Gibson argued that the dimension of stimulation corresponding to geographical distance is the perspective compression of ground texture projected onto the retina. The claim was that perceived depth correlates with these retinal gradients of texture.

Many psychophysical experiments were performed to determine how texture gradients correlate with perceived size (Gibson, 1947, pp. 196–217; Gibson & Purdy, 1954), perceived slant (Flock, 1964a, b; Gibson & Cornsweet, 1952), and the perception of surfaces as such (Gibson, 1950c; Gibson & Carel, 1952; Gibson & Dibble, 1952; Gibson, Purdy, & Lawrence, 1955). Gibson's gradient theory explained a considerable number of facts and had many practical applications. However, the theory that geographical and retinal topography are correlated did not account for the effects of object motion on the retinal image. This presented a critical problem for Gibson, because he was interested in the visual control of locomotion and the perception of motion (Gibson, 1954b).

In "Optical motions and transformations as stimuli for visual perception" (Ch. 1.2), Gibson extended his gradient theory to include transformations caused by motion, thereby amending the gap in his earlier theory. Building on the work of Musatti (1924), Metzger (1934), and Wallach and O'Connell (1953), Gibson and his colleagues demonstrated that certain transformations of shadow forms are seen as projections of rigid and elastic objects in motion (Gibson, 1958c; Gibson & Gibson, 1957; von Fieandt & Gibson, 1959). On the basis of these results, Gibson formulated the then radical theory that the retina is sensitive to optical transformations per se. In other words, he argued that *higher-order variables* constitute stimuli for vision.

As recounted in "A history of the ideas behind ecological optics" (Ch. 1.6), there were several difficulties with the theory of perceptual psychophysics based on higher-order stimulus variables that led Gibson eventually to reject it. One problem was that the correspondence between gradients of compression of retinal texture and the perceived slant of surfaces was inexact (Flock, 1964a, b; Purdy,

1958). Such approximation was not adequate for Gibson, who believed that precise causal relations were the foundations of theorizing (Autobiography, p. 12). A more pernicious problem with the higher-order variable theory was that it lacked a clear differentiation between proximal and distal stimuli. As Gibson would have said, the distinction between the two was "muddled"; what was in the environment to be seen was apt to be confused with the information available for seeing it. This problem became especially clear in Gibson's work on visual perception during observer movement, because observer movement produces transformations of retinal stimulation that are not correlated with environmental texture.

Gibson's introduction of the notion of *optical structure* (Gibson, Purdy, & Lawrence, 1955) was the first step in revising the proximal–distal distinction toward an ecological concept. Optical structure differs from both retinal (proximal) gradients and the (distal) gradients of ground surface texture. Unlike proximal stimulation, optical structure is not altered by an observer's movements, and, unlike distal objects, it can affect an observer's perceptual systems.

In "The information contained in light" (Ch. 1.3) and "Ecological optics" (Ch. 1.4), Gibson expanded the notion of optical structure into the theory of information and began to specify what his new discipline of ecological optics entailed. A fundamental concept introduced in these papers is the *optic array*. In an illuminated environment, light reverberates off every substantial surface and is structured by the layout and pigmentation of those surfaces. Thus, at every point of observation, there is a visual solid angle of 360°, whose nested arrangement of optical borders and transitions corresponds to the layout of that environment. The structured light available at a point of observation constitutes the ambient optic array. Ecological optics is devoted to the study of the optic array and, in particular, to the analysis of the optical information it contains.

The analysis of the optical basis of vision was a life-long challenge for Gibson. In his early work (Chs. 1.1, 1.2; Gibson, 1950a; Gibson, Olum, & Rosenblatt, 1955), he relied heavily on projective geometry in analyzing optical stimulation of the retina. With the development of ecological optics, Gibson began to deemphasize the use of projective geometry, because it was not adequate for describing the complex nesting of optical transitions and the transformations found in the optic array. In Chapter 1.5 we have included an exchange of letters between Gibson and Professor Gunnar Johansson of Uppsala University in Sweden, which deals with the question of how to analyze visual information.

Johansson (1950, 1964) has developed an impressive extension of the Gestalt analysis of proximal stimuli to the study of visual motion and space perception, based in large part on projective geometry. In the 1950s and 1960s, Gibson and Johansson often discussed their mutual concern with the analysis of the information for perceiving found in changing patterns of stimulation. In his letter, Johansson articulated some of his disagreements with ecological optics, and with Gibson's (1966b; cf. Ch. 4.4) theory of perceptual systems. In his reply, Gibson attempted to meet Johansson's questions and criticisms, thereby clarifying his own views.

Johansson had several questions for Gibson, concerning the nonprojective analysis of optical structure given in Gibson's (1966b; Ch. 1.4) ecological optics, and concerning the importance of locomotion for perceiving. Johansson agreed with Gibson on the need for analyzing patterns of change in stimulation but argued that projective geometry is perfectly suited to this task. Also, although Johansson agreed that the emphasis placed on ambiguity in static displays by other perceptionists is misleading, he noted that even patterns of change in proximal stimuli are not uniquely specific to their environmental source. Therefore, Johansson argued that organisms must contribute certain stimulus decoding principles to the process of perceiving, if they are to see veridically. Johansson further suggested that Gibson's emphasis on locomotion obscured the important question as to whether space perception is possible on the basis of sight alone.

In his reply to Johansson, Gibson emphasized that, whereas projective geometry may be adequate for the description of visual proximal stimuli, it is inadequate for analyzing the nested structure of the optic array. Gibson argued that his emphasis on locomotion is proper, because seeing space involves seeing one's position with respect to the rest of the environment, and this visual proprioceptive ability is intimately bound up with locomotion (Chs. 2.3 and 2.4; Gibson, 1979a, Ch. 13). Although Gibson and Johansson never completely agreed on the theory of visual perception, their mutual understanding and respect enriched both of their theories.

A decade after the new discipline of ecological optics was introduced, many of Gibson's students and colleagues gathered at Cornell for an ecological optics workshop. In his opening address to the workshop, entitled "A history of the ideas behind ecological optics" (Ch. 1.6), Gibson reviewed many of the puzzles he had discovered in trying to apply physical and physiological optics to the study of vision. He argued that these theories, which have been used to describe the optical basis of vision for milennia, have only misled us, because they offer inadequate insight into how light carries *information*. Gibson's address gives a fascinating account of certain problems in traditional optics and perceptual theory that led him to formulate the concept of optical structure and to propose the study of ecological optics.

"On the analysis of change in the optic array" (Ch. 1.7) was written for a special issue of *The Scandinavian Journal of Psychology,* dedicated to Gunnar Johansson in honor of his retirement. Here, Gibson further contrasted his and Johansson's approaches to describing optical structure. In extending traditional optical analyses, Johansson has emphasized the investigation of optical elements and their motions, conceived of as projections of environmental elements to the eye. Alternatively, Gibson proposed to investigate the structure nested at all levels of the solid visual angle constituting an optic array. The primary failing of the projective analysis of optical structure, Gibson argued, is its inability to offer a concrete description of occlusion, the accretion and deletion of optical texture resulting from the covering and uncovering of one surface by another, from some point of view (cf. Ch. 2.7). The obscuring and revealing of surfaces by one another is a primary fact of environmental layout that must be included in any analysis of optical information.

The ecological approach to perception involves much more than ecological optics, although that discipline serves as the approach's foundation. Another important area of research for ecological psychology is *ecological physics* (cf. Ch. 2.9). This is the study of what there is in the environment to be perceived. Whereas ecological information for perception is available in the media of the environment (chemical, acoustical, and optical structure over time in air or water, mechanical information over time at the boundaries of two or more surfaces), what that information specifies, and what organisms therefore perceive, are the *surfaces* and *substances* of the environment in various combinations (Gibson, 1948; 1950b; 1979a, Part One).

In "What is involved in surface perception?" (Ch. 1.8), Gibson extended and refined the ecological physics of surfaces presented in his last book, *The Ecological Approach to Visual Perception*. Ecological physics is concerned with the properties of surfaces that are relevant to perceiving and acting creatures. In his analysis of surface properties, Gibson relied in part on Gestalt phenomenology (Gibson, 1950b; Katz, 1935); however, he showed that the properties under discussion are not merely phenomenal but also are real.

Gibson devoted most of his lifetime to answering the question of what is the information for perceiving. In so doing, he attempted to avoid the sterile reductionism of physicalist analyses and the restrictive subjectivism of phenomenalism, while adopting and improving the best aspects of both approaches. It is fitting therefore that this section on ecological optics ends with a critique and refinement of the theory of surface perception from his last book, which was written only a few months after that book appeared. Gibson believed that good questions are difficult to answer, and that a stubbornly critical outlook offers the only hope of success at answering them.

# 1.1

# Perception and Judgment of Aerial Space and Distance As Potential Factors in Pilot Selection and Training*

## EVIDENCE THAT SPACE PERCEPTION IS IMPORTANT IN THE SELECTION AND TRAINING OF PILOTS

Aerial space may be defined as the visual surroundings extending away from the observer and bounded in any direction by the horizon, the surface of the earth and the sky. It may be distinguished from local space primarily by its voluminousness and long range of distances. Local space is the kind to which we are accustomed; it is inclosed by walls and restricted in range by them. Even out of doors in a civilized environment the spatial scene is cut up and confined to localized areas by buildings and other objects which obliterate the horizon. It is aerial space which constitutes the environment of the flier.

Persons who are adapted to going out and making the ordinary judgments of distance in the city are usually misled by the extent of distances in the desert, mountains, on water, or from a plane. Generally, aerial distances are poorly estimated by such persons because they are unfamiliar with the visual cues present in the situation for space perception. The spatial adjustments which are adequate in local or room-sized space are not adequate for flying a plane. It may be assumed that the pilot must possess or acquire the ability to perceive aerial space accurately.* * *

The maneuver of landing a plane is considered an outstanding example in which accurate perceptual judgment is needed by the pilot. One analysis of the problem of landing (Miller, 1947) concluded that the principle difficulties en-

---

*A selection from Chapter 9 of Gibson, 1947, pp. 179–195, written in collaboration with N. M. Glaser. Omitted material is marked by * * *.

countered by primary student pilots were stalling-out correctly, placing the glid-ing turn correctly, maintaining a straight approach leg, and breaking the glide at the correct height. More specifically, learning to land a plane depended on the ability to learn and use visual cues for height, distance, direction, and velocity of motion in space.

The results of factor analyses provide quantitative evidence that spatial skills are present in operating an airplane. An analysis (in Miller 1947) of the intercor-relations between daily grades on various maneuvers yielded three rotated factors named: (1) Perceptual Judgment; (2) Headwork; (3) Motor Technique. Percep-tual judgment had the highest loadings for spins, landings, traffic, and forced landings. It is defined as "the ability to make rapid and accurate judgments of distance, speed, and altitude."* * *

If the perception of aerial space and distance are of such importance for the selection and training of fliers, it is obvious that psychological tests and training methods need to be devised with which to select and train them. This cannot be done effectively until the nature of space and distance perception is understood. It is the purpose of this chapter to provide a theory for a clearer understanding of space perception and to describe the experiments and tests involved in the theory. A systematic analysis of aerial space and distance should, if correct, have many practical applications to the problems of pilot selection and training.

## THE TRADITIONAL PSYCHOLOGICAL PROBLEM OF DEPTH PERCEPTION AND THE EMPHASIS ON OCULAR CUES

### The Assumption of the Binocular Basis of Depth Perception

If it can be taken as proved that the pilot has to be able to judge tridimensional space in order to fly successfully, what is the sensory basis for the perception of such space? This question is, of course, the ancient problem of how we see a world which appears to extend away from us rather than a flat world, analogous to a picture, corresponding to the image formed on the retina of the eye. The accepted answer to this question—the answer given in the literature of aviation medicine and also by most of the textbooks in psychology and physiological optics—is that depth perception has its basis primarily in the existence of two eyes. The fact of binocular parallax, or stereoscopic vision, is commonly referred to as the main explanation of depth perception. It is usually stated that the binocular cue is supplemented by "monocular" cues for the perception of dis-tance, but these are usually thought of as secondary.[1] It is supposed that these

---

[1] For more on this distinction, see Gibson (1950a, pp. 71f & pp. 131f). (Eds.)

latter signs or indicators of depth are not innate but are learned in the course of experience and therefore have little to do with the pilot's intrinsic or essential ability to see depth. These monocular cues are usually listed as including such factors as linear perspective, transposition of objects, shadows and shading, aerial perspective, and occasionally a few others. They will be discussed in the next section. The question which arises here is whether the accepted emphasis on binocular vision is correct insofar as it concerns flying.

A good deal of evidence can be adduced to show that visual cues which are *not* dependent on the spatial separation of the two eyes are of much greater significance for the kind of distance perception which fliers need than has been realized in the past. The evidence will be listed in the following paragraphs.

*The Perception of Distance by Persons with Only One Eye.*  There has been a sufficient number of monocular pilots who flew successfully to suggest that binocular vision is at least not absolutely essential for adequate flying performance. The most famous of these was Wiley Post, who was admittedly an excellent flier. If space can be judged successfully with the use of only one eye, then the monocular cues of the normal pilot with two eyes must also be capable of producing space perception. Probably the normal pilot has even better capacity for such perception because of the fact that each eye supplements the monocular vision of the other eye, quite apart from the binocular dispartiy of the two images, and because two eyes yield a wider field of vision than one eye alone.[2] Training or experience may or may not be necessary for monocular space perception; the point is simply that the capacity is present.

*The Perception of Depth in Photographs and Pictures.*  It is a familiar fact that depth perception can be produced artificially in the stereoscope, i.e., by presenting separately to each eye the picture which it alone would see in the corresponding real three-dimensional scene and superposing the two different pictures by prismatic lenses. The vivid perception of depth which results is taken to be a proof of the effectiveness of binocular or stereoscopic vision. What is less familiar is the fact that a striking depth effect can be seen if two *identical* photographs are substituted in the stereoscope for the two pictures taken from slightly different points of view. The depth effect in this case is frequently comparable to that obtained with genuine stereoscopic viewing. Similarly, if a single photograph of a three-dimensional scene is viewed in such a way as not to emphasize the flatness and the frame of the picture, the observer frequently gets as much effect as if he were looking through a stereoscope. As Schlosberg (1941) and others have shown, the explanation is apparently that one sees depth in these single pictures because they are viewed through a lens which minimizes the surface quality of the picture and which hides its frame. This is the method by

---

[2]Cf. Jones & Lee (1981). (Eds.)

which stereoscopic photographs are viewed. The conclusion must be that a considerable part of the depth effect obtained with the stereoscope itself is not a genuine binocular effect at all but instead is dependent on the monocular stimuli for depth present in the single photographs but ordinarily inhibited by the circumstances under which they are viewed.[3] These cues lose much of their effectiveness under the customary conditions for looking at photographs because they are contradicted by the cues which make the picture a flat rectangular surface. If the conclusion is valid for stereoscopic photographs it must also be valid for ordinary binocular seeing, i.e., it is implied that a considerable part of the depth effect in ordinary vision is not binocular but monocular in origin.

*The Diminishing of the Binocular Cues with Distance.* It is a possibility that aerial distance perception at long range is mediated somewhat differently from distance perception at short range and that while binocular cues are important in the latter situation, they are less important in the former. It is likely that the depth effect produced by binocular parallax becomes ineffective beyond a certain distance from the observer. The eyes are about two and one half inches apart. For objects in near space, this is enough to produce parallax; or otherwise stated, there will be a disparity between the images in the right and the left eye, which serves as one kind of stimulus for the perception of depth. But for objects in far space, the retinal disparity in the two eyes presumably becomes so minute as no longer to be an adequate stimulus for seeing depth and, for all practical purposes, the two eyes have identical images. At just what distance from the observer this occurs does not seem to be agreed upon; the range of stereoscopic vision is sometimes given as under a hundred feet and by others is estimated at a distance of as much as a thousand yards. All such estimates seem to be based on calculations rather than on empirical measurement of the effect of disparate retinal vision in real space. They assume that the just-noticeable retinal angle of disparity as determined with a stereoscopic apparatus is the determining factor for the maximum distance at which one can still see binocular depth in the open air. The actual range of stereoscopic vision, therefore, is not known. It is fairly certain, however, that the other binocular cue of the degree of convergence (with correlative accomodation) of the eyes has a fairly short range. At longer ranges, both convergence and accommodation disappear. They are, of course, essential for normal vision but as criteria of distance they are limited to what has been called room-sized space and are ineffective for the perception of aerial space. The only conclusion that can safely be drawn is that since the effectiveness of the binocular cues decreases with distance, the monocular cues are probably increasingly significant at large distances, and may even be the only cues available at such distances. Presumably it is this long range distance perception which is important to fliers.

The evidence above all points to the conclusion that the visual stimuli for depth

---

[3]Julesz's (1971) method of studying binocular stereopsis avoids this problem. (Eds.)

*not* dependent on the spatial separation of the two eyes—the so-called monocular cues—need to be taken into account in selecting and training fliers for effective space perception.

## The Monocular Cues for Depth Perception

The list of accepted cues for the perception of depth has very largely remained unchanged since the discovery of the stereoscope. The non-binocular cues are sometimes called signs or indicators or criteria of depth to imply that they have not the same status of elementary sensations as has the fact of binocular retinal disparity. They are conventionally thought of as having to be interpreted rather than being sensed and they are assumed to be learned rather than innate. The list usually includes some or all of the following factors: *linear perspective* (such as converging railroad tracks), the *apparent size of objects of known size* (which decreases with distance from the observer), the *changes due to atmospheric conditions such as haze* (aerial perspective and blurring of outlines), *monocular parallax* (change of appearance with change of the observer's position), *interposition* (the superimposing of near objects on far objects), *shadow patterns* (the light-and-shade relations yielding relief) and sometimes the *angular location of the object on the ground* (position of the object on the retinal dimension beginning with the observer and ending with the skyline). *Accommodation* is also sometimes given as a monocular cue for near depth. It is evident that all of these cues are not on the same explanatory level. Some of them will explain not how the distance of an object is visible but only how one object can be seen at a greater distance than another. For example, interposition and shadow patterns give the *relative* location of objects but do not produce the impression of a space which is continuous in the third dimension. Although all these cues have been described by many observers, they have in general not been experimentally isolated or systematically varied in relation to the perception of distance. They are described somewhat differently by different writers and have not been brought together into a consistent theory explaining how they can function. Nevertheless, if they are as significant for the perception of distance by fliers as seems likely, it is important that such a theory be formulated. If they are to be used as a basis for tests of the ability to judge distance or if they are to be described with sufficient exactness so that they can be used in training, they must be redefined. An attempt to define them and to formulate a theory will be made. Before doing so, however, it would be well to look into the question of the kind of space which they are required to explain.

## The Kind of Distance Perception Required for Flying

When one describes the cues for the perception of distance in the terms above, the perception referred to is the distance of a particular object rather than the impression of continuous distance. Conceiving the problem in a traditional way, distance perception in general consists of the ability to judge the distances of a number of specific objects. This, however, is not the space in which the pilot flies. What he perceives is continuous space. It is almost never a single distance which he needs to judge, but a dimension of distance. There is invariably beneath him a continuous terrain, and what he discriminates is the location of all points on this terrain rather than specific distances to given points. Objects on or above this terrain may be momentarily of great importance, it is true, but they are judged in terms of a continuum of distance or, in other words, a background of three-dimensional space.

Traditionally conceived tests for the perception of distance have concentrated on the problem of how well an observer can judge the relative distance of two objects, or how accurately he can equate the distance of two objects. But the judgments a flier makes are in terms of appropriate changes of speed and direction of flight in relation to the distance of the ground. Such distance judgments always involve the "here" position of the observer at one end of the distance to be judged. It might be suggested that the practical value of depth or distance perception is that it makes possible locomotion through a continuous space which includes obstacles, and that both the obstacles and the locomotion itself involve the absolute distance from here to there.

Tests for depth perception, therefore, should aim to set up a kind of judgment similar to this. And the theory behind it should be a theory of a continuous space with an underlying terrain in which the observer is himself located and in which he can move.

## THE STIMULUS VARIABLES FOR THE PERCEPTION OF DISTANCE AND CONTINUOUS SPACE IN THE OPEN AIR

The problem of three-dimensional vision, or distance perception, is basically a problem of the perception of a *continuous surface* which is seen to extend away from the observer. All spaces in which we live include at least one surface, the ground or terrain. If there were no surface, there would be no visual world, strictly speaking. Whether we stand on it or fly over it, the ground is the basis of visual space perception both literally and figuratively. It is obvious enough that we could not stand or walk without the ground, but it is equally true that a pilot cannot fly purposefully without the ground and its horizon to guide and orient him. If by reason of fog or darkness the ground is invisible, an instrument must be provided to give him a substitute for it, an artificial horizon. The terrain, of course, is not all there is to the visual world. Objects stand out against the ground and they are usually what demand our attention. But an array of objects by themselves does not make up visual space; it is constituted instead by the ground or surface against which these shapes and figures appear. The visual world consists of object-surfaces on a background of an extended ground surface. This is what is implied by the "figure-ground" distinction in perceptual psychology. If we ask how the distances of these objects are seen and discriminated, it would be a mistake to disregard the surface of the background which connects and lies behind them. This mistake has regularly been made in most theories of depth perception. We need to explain not the "cues" or "indicators" to the distance of specific objects but instead the dimension or sensory continuum of distance, as such, which once visible, determines how distant all the objects within it are.[4]

This view of the problem is in contrast to the classical formulation which asks how the retina of the eye can see a third dimension in the sense of a theoretical line extending outward from the eye. Points on this line at different distances must all be identical so far as the retina is concerned. Nevertheless we do see depth. How can this be? The solution to this dilemma is to recognize that visible distance does not consist of a line extending outward from the eye. The question to ask is not how do we see such a line but how do we see the substratum—the surface which extends away from us in the third dimension. The image of this surface is obviously *spread out* across the retina.

Figure 1 illustrates the two formulations of the problem. The points A, B, C, and D cannot be discriminated by the retina. Distance along this line is a fact of geometry but not one of optics or of visual perception. But the points W, X, Y, and Z at corresponding distances can be discriminated by the retina. They represent the retinal image which corresponds to an extended substratum. It may be noted that the retinal points become progressively closer together as the distance increases.

If this view is correct, it is necessary to see a continuous surface in order to have an accurate sense of continuous distance. The sky may be a background but is not a surface. Distance appears to end at the skyline and the sky itself does not have a determinate distance. Single aircraft or clouds in the sky are of course objects having a surface, but since there is no background surface behind them, their distances ought in theory to be difficult to estimate, and in actual fact they are. The stimulus variables which make possible the perception of such a continuous surface must necessarily consist of continuous differential stimulation on the retina. The retinal image of the surface must differ significantly at different points corresponding to those which are farther or nearer. There must, in other words, be retinal *gradients* of stimulation. The present use of the term "gradient" may be explained by the following illustration. It is sometimes stated that one of the monocular indicators for the perception of distance of a point in space is its retinal location on the up-and-down dimension which begins with the lower margin of the visual field and ends with the horizon. Usually the lower margin of the visual field includes an image of the observer's feet and body—it always includes at least a faint marginal image of his cheeks and nose. The observer

---

[4]Boring (1933) and Gibson (1937b) discuss the concept of sensory and perceptual dimensions in more detail. (Eds.)

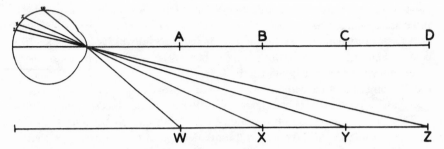

FIG. 1. Two formulations of the problem of distance perception.

himself and the skyline are two points of reference on the retina and the distance of the object from the observer may thus be estimated on the basis of its visible up-and-down relationship to these two points of reference. Let us consider this statement. It is very doubtful if this retinal dimension should be thought of as a sensory variable *as such* for the perception of distance. It would be a stimulus only if there were differential stimulation yielding an extended *surface* in perception. The up-and-down location of a retinal point has a distance value only when it is located in relation to a gradient of retinal stimulation. The retinal limits of the skyline on the one extreme and the "bottom" of the field (the body) at the other are limits within which gradients of stimulation may lie, and, as we have already implied, a gradient of stimulation must exist if a continuous distance is to be perceived extending into the third dimension.

The sensory variables which underlie the perception of distance as defined above can now be described. The list will be found to differ considerably from the familiar list of cues for depth perception. The variables proposed are intended to be genuine dimensions of the stimuli affecting the retina, like the stimuli for color and brightness, and to differ from them chiefly in that the dimension is spread across the retina in the form of a gradient and that it is of a more complex order. To what extent they are learned or innate need not be discussed at this stage. They are all systematically related to the perception of a continuum of distance embodied in a substratum extending out to the horizon.

## The Retinal Gradient of Texture

The difference between the perception of a surface, such as a flat wall, and the perception of an area without surface, such as the sky, has been investigated in the psychological laboratory. According to Metzger (1930) and also Koffka (1935) the difference lies in the fact that the surface corresponds to a retinal image having minute irregularities, spots, or differences in stimulation from point to point, whereas the area without surface corresponds to a retinal image which is in effect completely homogeneous. The area is differentiated in the former situation and undifferentiated in the latter. The term which Metzger and Koffka use for this sensory quality is *microstructure*. When an area of the visual field has microstructure, a surface is visible at a determinate distance; when the area has no microstructure, nothing is seen but "film color" and no determinate distance is visible.[5]

It is possible to go a step farther and to point out that the retinal image may vary between extremely coarse and extremely fine differentiation. In order to include the extremes of this stimulus variable, it will here be called not microstructure but "texture." As a first approximation to a definition, it may be suggested that retinal texture is the size of the "spots" and of the gaps between them in a differentiated visual image.

Any surface, such as the ground, obviously possesses texture. If it extends away from the observer, the retinal texture becomes greater. Figure 1 already discussed, indicated the way in which the retinal image becomes more "dense" as one passes from point W to point Z. There will exist a continuous gradient of texture from coarse to fine with increasing distance of the surface. A retinal gradient of this sort is in fact an adequate stimulus for the perception of continuous distance whether or not it is produced by an actual surface extending into the third dimension. The effectiveness of this stimulus variable may be illustrated by three examples. In Figure 2, there is a gradient of texture from coarse to fine running from the bottom to the top of the picture and, correspondingly, a continuous increase in the visible distance of the surface. In Figure 3, the same effect may be seen but with a texture of different character, i.e., a texture having elements of different shape and different mean size. The *gradients* in both pictures are, however, similar. It is an incidental fact that these texture gradients were produced by photographing a ploughed field in the first illustration and a stubble field in the second; it is nevertheless true that the only effective stimulus for distance perception in the pictures is the variable of texture. Figure 4 may appear to be an even more convincing demonstration of the stimulus variable, since the gradient of texture was here constructed artificially. The line-segments in this illustration were drawn increasingly smaller from the bottom to the top of the picture and so likewise were the vertical and horizontal spaces between them. The impression of a level terrain extending away from the observer is compelling.

It may be noted that the stimulus-correlate of distance in these illustrations is not the gross retinal size of the texture-elements but their *relative* size within the gradient. For example, the size of the line-segments in Figure 4, i.e., the elements of the texture, could have been twice as large at the bottom of the picture and would then have been twice as large all the way up the picture to the horizon; the resulting impression of distance, would, however, have remained the same.

---

[5] This and related claims were tested by Gibson & Dibble (1952), Gibson & Waddell (1952) and Gibson, Purdy & Lawrence (1955). Cf. Ch. 1.6. (Eds.)

FIG. 2. Distance as produced by a natural gradient of texture.
(Figure variant of original. Eds.)

FIG. 3. Distance as produced by a different natural gradient of texture.
(Figure variant of original. Eds.)

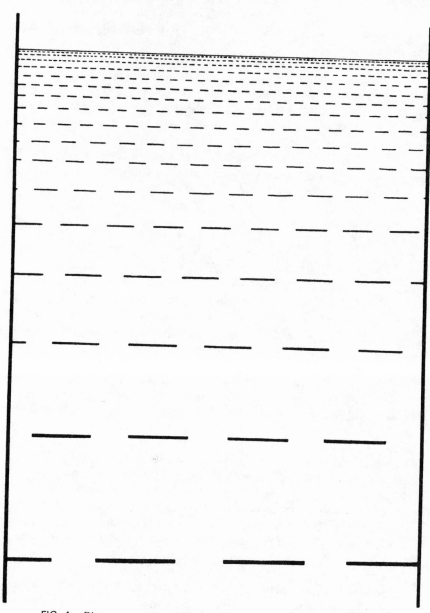

FIG. 4.   Distance as produced by an artificially constructed gradient of texture.

This implies that in perceiving distance over real terrain, it is a matter of indifference to the observer whether the overall texture of the terrain is made up of large or small elements—whether for example it is produced by sand, grass, brush, or trees.

It should also be noted that the line elements of Figure 4 were so drawn as not to fall one behind the other in straight lines converging to the horizon. This would have introduced the factor of linear perspective, which ought to be considered separately. The stimulus variable in that illustration was intended to be one of "pure" texture. The texture gradient is, however, a kind of perspective in the broad sense of that term and it is related to linear perspective inasmuch as in the case of both variables retinal size decreases with distance and vanishes at the horizon. All the retinal gradients to be described as stimulus variables for distance perception are analogous to perspective at least in respect to being extended on the surface of the retina. The variable just described, therefore, might well be given the name of *texture-perspective*.

## The Retinal Gradient of Size-of-Similar-Objects

In almost every kind of terrain which the flier is likely to meet, and in most of the spaces of everyday life, objects are present in addition to the substratum itself. Commonly there are classes or types of similar objects scattered about or lined up in the environment. Houses, fence posts, telegraph poles, fields, and even hills tend to be of similar physical size and shape, as do chairs, tables, and people. If there are more than a few of these similar objects in the visual field, there can exist a gradient of decreasing retinal size corresponding to their distance from the observer. The principle involved is the familiar one of size perspective. If more than one *homogeneous type* of object is present, there will be more than one gradient, and it may be assumed that different gradients may exist at the same time such as, for example, one for trees and another for houses. Gradients of size and gradients of texture are obviously analogous and the one merges into the other when the objects in the visual field become sufficiently numerous.

If the objects on the terrain are lined up in rows, or if extended objects like roads and fields having linear contours are present, the size perspective becomes linear perspective. This stimulus for distance is more familiar than the others, but it is merely a special case of the principle that retinal size decreases with distance until it vanishes, or becomes infinitesimal, on the horizon.

It should be pointed out that size perspective and linear perspective, when considered as retinal gradients, are stimulus correlates of continuous physical distance. They are to be distinguished from the traditional "cue" for distance perception of the apparent size of familiar objects, i.e., of objects whose real size is remembered from past experience. The comparison of an absolute retinal size and a remembered size and the inferring of the distance, assuming it to occur, is not an adequate explanation for the perception of a continuum of distance. The explanation proposed here does not assume the perceiving of absolute sizes as such but only the ability to react to a continuous gradient of retinal sizes.

The facts of texture perspective and size perspective as described refer to the *retinal image* of the terrain in two dimensions. The resulting *perception* of an extended terrain in three dimensions is characterized by objects and terrain features which do *not* shrink in size toward the horizon. Instead, they appear to maintain a substantially constant size and are perceived at a distance. The relation between this constancy of perceived size and the perception of distance will be discussed later.

### The Retinal Gradient of Velocity During Movement of the Observer

A third stimulus variable for the perception of distance is one which is particularly applicable to the flying situation since it occurs during movement of the observer. It bears some relation to the cue of monocular motion parallax. When an observer moves, and particularly when he is flying or driving, the visual world is represented by images which also move across the retina of the eye. The simplest form of this retinal motion may be described by the statement that the image of the world expands radially outward on the retina as one moves straight forward. The expanding optical picture ahead as one drives a car is the most familiar example, and it has probably been noticed by nearly everyone. If, instead, one looks backward, the world (considered as a flat image) contracts inward on the retina as one moves away from it. The center of this expansion, the point from which it radiates, is the point toward which the observer is moving. There is a center of contraction at the opposite pole, i.e., the point he is moving away from. During ordinary locomotion, the center of expansion is on the horizon.[6]

Now under such circumstances the retinal motion of the image corresponding to the terrain is subject to the principle of perspective. There exists, in other words, still another type which will be called retinal motion perspective. The *rate* of expansion of the image of any point or object is inversely proportional to the distance of that point or object from the observer.[7] There is, in other words, a continuous gradient of the velocity of the ground as it "goes by;" the gradient begins with a maximum at the points of the terrain nearest the observer and ends with zero movement at the horizon. This rule holds no matter in what direction

---

[6]This idea was formalized in Gibson, Olum & Rosenblatt (1955). Lee (1974, 1980a) has developed the formalism and reviews empirical and theoretical research related to optical information during locomotion. (Eds.)

[7]From this one can derive the optical information specifying the observer's time to contact with a surface when either the observer or surface is moving. Such information is useful for avoiding a "looming" object (Schiff, Caviness & Gibson, 1962; Schiff, 1965) and it is also useful for controlling one's movement through the environment so as to avoid obstacles (Lee, 1976, 1980b). (Eds.)

one looks. Such a gradient of velocities is capable of determining a continuum of distance and, within this dimension, the distance of any point or object is determinate from its retinal velocity.

When a retinal gradient of velocity exists in the way described, the perception which results is not that of a visual environment which moves but of a stationary world in which the observer himself moves. If the observer is not moving but is, let us say, sitting at a desk, it is nevertheless true that his head will move from time to time and that the image of his visual world moves on the retina. Optically speaking, the world is "alive" with retinal motion produced by only the ordinary slight displacements of the head and body, and the gradients of motion which result are ever present stimuli for the visible continuum of distance.

The description above leaves out of account a number of the characteristics of motion perspective, and makes no mention of several complicating factors. When the motion of the observer is not parallel to the terrain, as when a pilot lands an airplane, the formulation given must be modified. The effect of eye movements on motion perspective also needs to be considered. These matters will be discussed in a later section. For the present purpose of listing the sensory bases for distance perception, the description above will suffice.

## The Retinal Gradients Arising from Atmospheric Transmission of Light

The cue of aerial perspective as ordinarily described provides another kind of retinal gradient which is a continuous correlate of distance. The retinal image of a terrain stretching away to the horizon is constituted by light which at one extreme has passed through only a few feet of air and at the other extreme has passed through many miles of air. The character of the light stimulus varies with the amount of atmosphere through which it has been transmitted. The resulting color quality becomes less saturated and bluer with increasing atmospheric distance. The color is also described as being increasingly blurred or filmlike in appearance with increasing lengths of aerial transmission, and the outlines within the image become less sharp. It is possible that these latter variations should be considered in relation to the texture variable. The exact stimulus-variations involved have not been worked out in detail. They are effectively employed by painters but they have not been fully described in terms of physiological optics.

## The Retinal Gradient of Binocular Disparity

A number of visual stimulus dimensions have just been defined which are concomitants of distance and which are presumably stimuli for the perception of space as the flier sees it. They are all based on gradients of stimulation in a single retina; that is to say, they do not depend on differences in stimulation between the two eyes. There is, in addition, however, the fact of binocular retinal disparity, or stereopsis, which has received most of the attention devoted to the problem of distance perception in the past. This variable can be defined, like the others, in terms of a gradient of stimulation, with only the addition of the fact that the stimulation referred to is a binocular rather than a monocular effect.

Assuming for the moment that the observer's eyes are fixated on the horizon, the retinal image of the terrain in the right eye will differ from that in the left eye. This difference at any given point is called retinal disparity, and is due to the different positions of the two eyes in relation to the terrain. Near points and objects on the terrain are displaced horizontally in the image of one eye relative to the other. This relative displacement decreases with increasing distance and becomes zero at the horizon itself. There is, in short, a gradient of disparity in the combined retinal field. It is, like the others already described, a vertical gradient, running up the field from the observer's body at one extreme to the horizon at the other. Any point on the terrain corresponds to a disparity which is inversely proportional to the distance of that point from the observer. It must be supposed that this variable is a stimulus-correlate of perceived distance.

This description holds true when the eyes are fixated on the horizon. If instead, the eyes are fixated on a near point, the disparity is zero at that point and reaches a maximum at the horizon. But this disparity is opposite in kind to that existing in the former situation; it is "uncrossed" rather than "crossed," or positive where the former was negative. The *gradient* of disparity with respect to its sign is therefore the same when the eyes are fixated on a near point as when they are fixated on a far point, or for that matter when they are fixated at any point. An increase in positive disparity being equivalent to a decrease in negative disparity, the gradient may run from minus to zero or from zero to plus and still be the same gradient. The stimulus which is concomitant with distance, therefore, is not simply disparity as such but disparity relative to a gradient which may lie anywhere on a scale of negative to positive.

## The Relation of Other So-Called Cues for Depth to the Variables Above

All of the traditional cues for depth perception have been incorporated or reinterpreted in the variables listed, except for interception or superposition of contours and the distribution of shadows and shading. Interception is capable of determining the relative distance of two or more objects but, by its very nature, it is not a variable which can establish a continuum of distance. It has to do with the establishing of the figure-ground relationship and the relation of "behind" or "in front of" rather than with distance perception as such. The distribution of shadows produced by objects and the gradients of shading appearing on three-dimensional shapes are determiners of what is properly called relief or relative depth, but this is not the same thing as the sensory continuum of distance. They will not be discussed further, nor will any analysis be given of the retinal gradient associated with accommodation—a kind of "blur" gradient.

# 1.2 Optical Motions and Transformations as Stimuli for Visual Perception*

How do we see the motions of objects around us? The way to go about answering this question is to note the kinds of physical motion that occur in the human environment and then to examine the kinds and variables of optical stimulation that correspondingly occur. The isolation and control of these variables with suitable optical apparatus will make possible an experimental psychophysics of kinetic impressions. The desirability of such a psychophysical approach has been pointed out in an earlier paper (Gibson, 1954b) and the following proposals modify or make explicit a number of suggestions there made.

## DISTINCTION BETWEEN PHYSICAL MOTIONS AND OPTICAL MOTIONS

Ever since Isaac Newton supposed that the motions of things revealed the forces behind them and thereby the causes of all events, physics has been concerned with the observation of motions. The beauty of the idea for physics is that it applies to *all* things: stars and planets; stones, machines, and animals; particles and atoms. Of these motions, however, only a certain class is the concern of perceptual psychology. The things whose motion is visible are substances which, in the first place, differentially reflect or emit light and, in the second place, are

*Psychological Review*, 1957, *64*, 288–295. Part of an American Psychological Association Presidential address, 1955. A motion picture, Gibson (1955b) illustrating the text is available. Copyright 1957 by the American Psychological Association. Reprinted by permission.

not either too far away or too small. The motion of the wind is invisible because gaseous substances transmit light instead of reflecting it. The motion of the heavenly bodies is invisible because their angular change of position is too small per unit of time. And the motion of microscopic bodies is invisible because their boundaries reflect an optical texture too small for the eye to resolve. But the environment of man contains an enormous variety of surfaces which do project focusable light to his eye, and these are the bodies the psychologist must be interested in. For when they fall, rise, turn, roll, bend, flow, twist, writhe, stretch, or break, an eye can register this event and the animal possessing the eye can respond to it.

We may observe that physical motions can be classified as *rigid* or *nonrigid*, the former being characteristic of crystalline substances and the latter of elastic or fluid substances. Rigid physical motions are exemplified in mechanics; they are analyzable into components of translation and rotation on or around any of three axes, and they have been studied since the time of Newton. Nonrigid physical motions are exemplified in biology since the growth and also the reactive movements of living animals are generally of this sort (LeGros Clark & Medawar, 1945).

The motions of the physical environment might also be classified as *connected* or *nonconnected*. In the former the parts of the moving substance remain adjacent, even if not rigid, whereas in the latter they do not and are not even considered parts of the "same" substance. Instead they are treated as separate motions of different objects. The separations and fusions, attractions and repulsions, or collisions of things, animals, and people are all of this sort.

Physical motions are given to an eye only in the form of optical motions. An optical motion is an event in the *optic array,* that is, in the light reflected from an illuminated environment to an eye or, rather, to any position in the air where an eye might be placed (Gibson, Purdy & Lawrence, 1955). An eye is an organ for exploring an optic array. The solid sector of this array which an eye takes in is the basis of patterned vision; neither objects nor their motions could affect the eye except by means of it. External motion can be seen only if some differentiated part of the array is displaced relative to the rest of it, or to some other part, or if parts move relative to one another. There has to be some change of its pattern, considered as a projection to a point.

An optical motion, then, is a projection in two dimensions of a physical motion in three dimensions.[1] The projection may be taken either as on the surface of a sphere centered at the eye or as on a plane in front of the eye. When locomotor movements of the observer are to be considered, the former is preferable (Gibson, Olum & Rosenblatt, 1955), but when, as here, they are not involved, the plane projection is better. The one can be converted into the other if

---

[1]See Ch. 2.6 for a critique of this claim. (Eds.)

necessary. Our question is, What kinds of optical motion occur which might serve as stimuli for perception?

## KINDS AND VARIABLES OF OPTICAL MOTION

How can optical motions be described or specified? The question has to do with the motions of a texture or pattern in a two-dimensional array. Tentatively, there seem to be two general possibilities. First, one could divide the pattern into convenient elements, describe the positions of all the elements by pairs of coordinate values, and finally describe the motions of all the elements by the successive pairs of values. Or one could describe the motions of the elements by direction and speed at successive moments of time. This procedure is analytical. Second, a non-analytical method of specifying optical motion is possible. One could simply take the pattern as given, and then use the operation defining a *perspective transformation* in geometry to describe a family of changes of pattern.[2] This method does not exhaust all the varieties of optical motion, as will be evident, but it has advantages for an experimenter who needs to produce an artificial optical array.

*Continuous perspective transformations.* In geometry, any form or pattern on one plane which is a projection of a form or pattern lying on some other plane is called a *perspective transformation.* These forms are static. When the point of projection (the focus of the sheaf of lines which connect the pair of forms, point for point) is near the two planes, we speak of a *central* or *polar* projection; when this point of projection is at a very great distance from the planes, we speak of a *parallel* projection. (It may be useful to recall that the "plans" and "elevations" of an architect are cases of parallel projection, but that his drawing for the client's eyes is a case of polar projection. This latter is the case we are chiefly concerned with.) When the two planes are parallel, the difference between the projected form and the given form is one of size only; it is called a *similarity* transformation. When the two planes are not parallel, the difference between the forms is that to which common meaning applies the term "perspective," or sometimes the term "foreshortening." In geometry, both the difference of size and that of shape are classed as perspective transformations.

We can now speak of motion. When the angle or the distance of the first plane relative to the second plane is altered, the projected form is correspondingly altered. The fact is that the relation between any earlier and any later projected form is *also* a perspective transformation. The relation holds between any two of its stages in times. Hence, the motion in question may be described as a continuous series of perspective transformations. It is a relation between a temporal series or family of static forms, not merely between two forms. Any such moving

---

[2]See Ch. 1.7 for a more sophisticated development of these two possibilities. (Eds.)

transformation can be analyzed by six parameters corresponding to the six components of the possible movements of the first plane—that is, three of translation and three of rotation.

*Families of continuous perspective transformations.* It can now be observed that all optical motions resulting from the rigid physical motions of the flat face of an external object are continuous families of perspective transformations, as defined above. These are optical motions as taken on a plane in front of the eye. The six parameters of optical motion can be visualized as (a) vertical translation of the pattern in the plane, (b) horizontal translation of the pattern, (c) enlargement or reduction of the pattern, (d) horizontal foreshortening of the pattern, (e) vertical foreshortening of the pattern and (f) rotation of the pattern in the plane.

These parameters of transformation are for the case of a *polar* projection. As the focus of projection is taken at an increasing distance from the two planes, one approaches the case of a *parallel* projection. For the latter case, three of the six parameters have been altered in character, namely (c), (d), and (e) above, while (a), (b), and (f) remain unaltered. Enlargement or reduction of the pattern has vanished; horizontal foreshortening becomes a mere horizontal flattening; and vertical foreshortening becomes vertical flattening.

These "pure types" of optical motion can be observed on a motion picture screen (Gibson, 1955b). An irregular or regular contour shape or an irregular or regular group of spots can be made to undergo continuous perspective transformations, and the observer can note the various types of motion in the plane of the screen. One can note, for example, that in types (d) and (e) a square is transformed into a trapezium with polar projection, but is transformed into a flattened rectangle with parallel projection. The interesting fact, however, is that for types (c), (d), and (e) with polar projection it is *very difficult to notice* the motion in the plane. Instead, one sees a sort of "virtual" object or surface which (c) moves toward or away from the screen, (d) rotates on its vertical axis, or (e) rotates on its horizontal axis. One sees, in other words, rigid motion in depth. The suggestion is that the parameters of transformation are stimuli for the phenomenal parameters of the motion in space of one face of an object.

The rotations in depth are similar in some respects to the kinetic depth effect obtained by Wallach and O'Connell (1953). Such effects have been observed for Lissajous figures (Fisichelli, 1946), and long ago for the silhouette of a rotating windmill against the horizon (Boring, 1942, p. 270). All these apparent rotations are said to be characterized by ambiguity as to the direction of rotation, and by spontaneous reversals in the direction of rotation. The apparent rotations shown in the film, however, are *not* characterized by ambiguity or reversals of direction when the transformations are those obtained with polar projection, but only when the transformations are those obtained with parallel projection.

A psychophysical experiment has been performed on the degree of perceived semirotation in depth as a function of the transformation sequence (Gibson & Gibson, 1957).

## APPARATUS FOR PRODUCING CONTINUOUS PERSPECTIVE TRANSFORMATIONS IN THE OPTIC ARRAY

The method used to display the geometrical transformations on a motion picture screen was not by "animation" of film; the procedure, rather, was to photograph the window of a device which might be called a shadow transformer. Details of its construction are given in the report of the experiment (Gibson & Gibson, 1957). It will here be described only as it suggests possibilities for a psychophysics of motion perception. It consists of a translucent screen with a point source of light on one side and an observer symmetrically on the other side. In the square luminous window, dark shapes, patterns, or textures can be made to appear. They are shadows, not objects, so that only two grades of intensity exist, surface texture and binocular disparity are eliminated, and accommodation and convergence are controlled for this sector of the optic array to the eye. The variables of form and transformation are thus isolated for study.

In the diverging ray sheaf from the point source to the translucent window a mount can be placed, a pane of transparent material large enough so that it can be moved without its edges being projected on the screen. Forms, patterns, or textures cut from gummed paper or masking tape can be attached to this mount, or it can be traced with ink or even sprinkled with talcum powder, so that shadows of many varieties are projected on the screen. The mount can be rotated on any of three axes, or translated in any of three dimensions. Hence, considering the mount and the screen as two geometrical planes, changes in the position of the mount will yield all possible perspective transformations of the shadow relative to the shadow caster, and likewise all parameters of continuous perspective transformation of the shadow itself. Previous shadowcasting devices, most recently Wallach and O'Connell's (1953), have not been constructed for this systematic purpose. They have also not utilized polar projection. For purposes of comparison, the present aparatus can also be illuminated by a projector beam at 80 ft. instead of a point source at 5 ft.; the former yields an approximately parallel projection. The use of a transparent mount obviates the necessity of any visible support for the shadow caster, or of having the shadow it casts extend below the bottom of the window.

The optical geometry of the apparatus is given in Fig. 5 for a size transformation. It may be noted that the converging ray sheaf to the eye is the geometrical opposite of the diverging ray sheaf. The relation of the shadow to its "virtual object" (by analogy with the "virtual image" in a mirror) is simply the reverse of the relation of the shadow to the shadow caster. This reversal does not affect the transformations in any other way. It is true that the motions perceived are opposite to those of the shadow caster, but this does not present a paradox if one remembers that vision depends on the optic array, not on the way an optic array can be artificially produced.

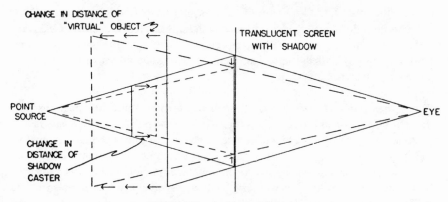

FIG. 5. The shadow transformer.

## INTERNAL DEPTH OF TRANSPARENT OBJECTS
## AND COLLECTIONS OF OBJECTS

So far, consideration has been limited to continuous transformations of textures corresponding to the opaque face of an object. What about the optical motions corresponding to the physical motions of transparent objects, or things with different parts in depth, or rigid collections of things like a forest of trees or a tangle of wire? The phenomenon termed "stereokinesis" (Metzger, 1953, Ch. 13 and references) and the kinetic depth effect of Wallach and O'Connell (1953) involve an impression of *internal depth*. The "virtual object" of these experiments is often a collection of posts or a figure of bent wire.

The complex optical motions of these experiments can be analyzed by considering different parameter values of the same perspective transformation corresponding to the different planes of depth of the object. This suggestion becomes clearer with a concrete example. If, with the shadow transformer, one casts a shadow on the screen through several parallel sheets of glass, each of which has been sprinkled with talcum powder, the composite shadow looks something like the Milky Way in the night sky. When the sandwich of mounts is *moved,* however, the perception separates into clear planes of depth, each layer of nebulous material standing in front of its neighbor. The effect is shown in the film (Gibson, 1955b).

The internal depth of the virtual object produced by the moving shadow of a bent wire, or by an arrangement of vertical sticks on a horizontal turntable, has been frequently studied. The writer suspects that it will yield to the kind of analysis proposed. The depth is similar to binocular stereoscopic depth; a unifying hypothesis would be that the simultaneous disparity of binocular images is only a special geometrical case of the successive disparities of a continuous image. Both rest on the geometry of parallax, that is, the projection of a collection of objects in space to a point in space, and this has led Tschermak (1939) to include both under the term "parallactoscopy." Both are transformations in the most general sense of the term, and perhaps both sorts of disparity should be treated as transformations.[3]

*The impression of surfaces meeting at a corner.* With the apparatus described, one can also produce the impression of *more* than one flat face of an object moving in depth. If two transparent mounts are joined to make an angle, and if both are given some opaque texture of any kind, the combined shadow looks like a plane surface so long as the combined mounts are kept stationary. When they are moved, however, the shadow becomes two faces or surfaces making a corner. The relative slant of one surface to the other can be judged with some accuracy.

## WHAT IS THE STIMULATING EFFECT OF NONPERSPECTIVE TRANSFORMATIONS IN THE OPTIC ARRAY?

If the rigid mechanical motions of the physical environment are represented by one kind of geometrical transformations in the pattern of light, are the nonrigid biological motions of the environment represented by a *different* kind of geometrical transformations in the pattern of light? The difference is suggested when the geometer describes topology as "rubber sheet geometry." This is concerned with changes of bidimensional form *other* than the changes heretofore described. Considering an organism in silhouette, its reactive movements cannot be compounded of the six pure types of optical motion considered above. Neither can its growth be described as magnification. Medawar, a biologist following D'Arcy Thompson, seems to have demonstrated that the change of shape of the human figure from infancy to adulthood, disregarding the change of size, is a specific continuous transformation which can only be suggested in words.[4] A "tapered stretch" describes it approximately (LeGros Clark & Medawar, 1945, pp. 177 ff.). The change is monotonic, i.e., it keeps the same trend. Geometrically, there are different *forms* of change of bidimensional form. Conceivably, the visual mechanism is sensitive to these forms of change.

The shadow transformer can be adapted to display nonperspective transformations if an elastic or flexible sheet is used for the transparent mount which carries the shadow-casting form or texture, and if this is stretched or bent in some way. Preliminary observations suggest that the resulting perception of motion is corre-

---

[3]Cf. Lee (1969, 1971). (Eds.)
[4]Todd, Mark, Shaw & Pittenger (1980) develop this idea further. (Eds.)

spondingly elastic instead of rigid. There are technical difficulties in controlling such optical motions. But if apparatus can be built for systematically producing them, it will be open to the perceptual psychologist to study such phenomena as animate, expressive, and physiognomic movements in the manner of psychophysics.

## DISJUNCTIVE OR SEPARATE OPTICAL MOTIONS

The converting of a single form on a plane into *two* forms is something which goes beyond the continuous transformations heretofore considered. There is, instead, a discontinuity in both the temporal and the spatial series. The geometer is tempted to describe it by saying that there is a breaking or tearing of the surface, thus falling back on a physical analogy.

If certain parts of a connected optical pattern undergo one kind of transformation while other parts undergo another kind, it might be predicted that the perceived surface will become two perceived surfaces, each composed of the parts carrying the same transformation. This is obvious when one set of parts moves in one direction and the other in a different direction, and the fact was recognized in Wertheimer's law of "common fate" as a determiner of sensory organization (Metzger, 1953, Ch. 13).[5] It should equally be true, however, when one set of parts carries a slant transformation or a size transformation different from that of the other; the texture will break into two textures each moving in its own tridimensional way. Some of these possibilities have been investigated by using a "sandwich" of mounts in the apparatus, and the film illustrates a few of these possible dual disjunctive motions. Perceptual separation does result. Evidently when the parts of an optical texture undergo *joint motion* this does not have to be understood as a set of motions with the same velocity in the same direction.

It is also possible to note what happens when *all* the parts of a connected optical pattern move, each in a different direction: the pattern becomes many smaller objects, like a swarm of ants. This result also suggests that what connected the elements of the pattern in the first place was their nonmotion relative to one another; in the optic array, after all, stability is only a special case of transformation. Research on the problem of how elementary motions might be *organized* into a single unitary motion has been performed by Johansson (1950), Duncker (1929), and Metzger (1953).

The varieties and dimensions of optical motion in which the parts are *not* connected in adjacent order are of formidable complexity. It is not even clear how to go about classifying them. Disjunctive optical motions are, however, the

---

[5]See Johansson (1950), Mace (1974) and Restle (1979) for reviews of theory and experiments on applying a "common fate" analysis to retinal displacements. (Eds.)

stimuli by virtue of which we see occurrences, happenings, and actions in the world around us. There is certainly order and lawfulness in them, for Michotte (1954/1963) has studied the impressions of causality induced by higher order variables of nothing more objective than the motions of separate spots. These abstract variables are clearly discriminable by observers, for the impressions can be made to come or go as the experimenter varies certain spatiotemporal conditions.

## CONCLUSIONS

If the optical geometry here expounded is correct, there is a possible basis in optical stimulation for the ability to distinguish between and among rigid, elastic, and multiple moving things. The basis lies in different mathematical modes of transformation and motion. The implication is that we see both the constant and the changing properties of things in this way. We see them not because we have formed associations between the optical elements, not even because the brain has organized the optical elements, but because the retinal mosaic is sensitive to transformations as such. These are stimuli for perception.

Is it really plausible, one might ask, to call anything as apparently abstruse as a continuous series of transformations a *stimulus*? A bit of evidence may here be convincing. A puff of air to the cornea of the eye is a stimulus for the blink reflex in the pure and original sense of the term. The fact is that when an observer with the apparatus described is near the screen, a rapid expansion of the shadow until it fills the screen will also produce a blink reflex.[6] The latter event ought to be considered as much a stimulus as the former.

---

[6]This experiment is reported in Schiff, Caviness & Gibson (1962). (Eds.)

# 1.3 The Information Contained in Light*

Let us consider the results of a recently published experiment (Walk, Gibson, & Tighe, 1957). A rat was placed on an elevated wooden runway, four inches wide and thirty inches long. It is well known that rats very seldom fall off such a runway. Three inches below it a sheet of clear plate glass extended outward on both sides, so arranged as to reflect as little light as possible upward. The rat could in fact descend to this solid surface and walk on it; the question was whether he would do so. The three inch drop was just such that the glass could not be touched by the rat's nose, or the vibrissae, unless his front feet were on it. Conceivably the existence of the glass surface could be given to the rat's ears by auditory echolocation, or to his eyes by highlights on the surface, or dust, but these possibilities were the same on both sides of the runway. The question was whether a difference in the light transmitted *through* the glass to the rat's eyes would determine his behavior.

A coarsely patterned paper was fixed immediately under the glass on one side of the runway but sixty inches under the glass on the other side, the two being equally illuminated.

The optical texture of the light reflected from the physical texture of the paper and projected to the station point of the rat was, therefore, about 15 times smaller and denser on one side than on the other. As the rat moved, the optical shearing of texture at the edge of the platform, the relative motion parallax, was about 15 times greater on one side than on the other. Assuming that a rat, having little

*Acta Psychologica*, 1960, *17*, 23–30. Copyright 1960 North Holland Publishing Co. Reprinted by permission. This paper is a revision of a paper presented at the Symposium on Space Perception at the International Congress of Psychology, Brussels, 1957.

overlap in the fields of binocular vision, cannot register the disparity of two simultaneous projections to slightly different points, these were the *only* differences between the stimuli from the two sides of the runway to which the rat might respond.

A large number of hooded rats were placed in this situation. They explored the runway and peered over both edges. Eventually most of them descended. About 90 per cent descended to the optically near surface instead of the optically far surface, even though a physically identical surface was present. Insofar as the glass was represented in the optical texture because of imperfect transparency, it was equivalent on the two sides and could only have attenuated the results. The cause of the difference could only have been the different distances of the light reflecting papers, since the results of a control experiment, in which they were placed just under the glass on *both* sides, were that the rats descended with equal frequency to both sides.

I have a particular interest in this experiment because in the first place it seems to me very ingenious, and in the second place one of the collaborators was my wife. The authors call their device an "optical cliff." They have proved that a rat will not attempt to descend a vertical drop disproportionate to its body size, but will descend one proportionate to its body size, depending on visual stimulation. It ventures over a step but not a cliff. One might interpret this fact in all sorts of ways. Terrestrial animals may have a direct "fear of falling," or one based on a distaste for colliding with the ground *after* falling. Perhaps they dislike "loss of support," or like to maintain contact with a solid substratum.[1] They might be said to perceive distances in terms of visual cues and then interpret the vertical distances in terms of falling, jumping, or stepping down. They might be supposed to have an innate perception of falling-off-places and an instinctive avoidance of them, or to have a learned perception and a habit based on past experience with falling. Walk, Gibson, and Tighe, the experimenters, actually investigated the latter alternatives; they found that rats reared in complete darkness discriminate the depth of a drop-off just as well as do rats reared in a lighted environment. But I do not want to discuss nativism and empiricism, or instinct, or even space perception in the usual sense of the term. Instead, I would like to call attention to the external stimulus in this experiment, the light, and then to make the strange assertion that this light contains information or carries meaning. I wish to argue that the geometrical relations of the reflecting solids were *given* in the light, or *specified* by the light.

We have long assumed, certainly since Bishop Berkeley made such a point of it, that light carried very little information to the eye about the object from which it comes. The light as such cannot possibly specify the distance of the object, we suppose, and consequently not its size. At best we can obtain only cues or "clues" to its shape and slant, to its velocity, and to its pigmentation or color.

---

[1] Gibson (1977b; 1979a, Ch. 9) later argued that terrestrial animals on a visual cliff perceive that the edge of the cliff affords stoppage of locomotion (cf. Ch. 4.9). (Eds.)

Nevertheless, we would admit that light carried information about its source in some sense of that term, inasmuch as we can detect, with a spectroscope, the temperature of the source, e.g., that of the sun, or of an incandescent body. By analysis of the spectral lines one can even determine the chemical elements of which the luminous object is composed. If light yields information to a spectro-scope why not to an eye?

If this manner of speaking be allowed, we can proceed to analyse the informa-tion in light which an eye might be expected to register. It will be terrestrial information, not astronomical, and it will be that carried by reflected light, not radiant light. Physical optics is only partially helpful here; we are concerned with what might be called *ecological* optics, or *environmental* optics. Of the many functions of light, we need to examine that of illumination. When it is multiply reflected in a clear medium, by opaque surfaces of imperfect smoothness, rays are projected inward to every possible station point in the medium. That is, at any point, the ambient light will have different intensities (and compositions) in different directions. Such a conjunction of rays, taken in small angular units of minutes or seconds of arc is what I call an *optic array*. Its transitions yield an optical *texture*. To this, many of the principles of projective or perspective geometry can be applied. *An optic array may plausibly be supposed to carry information about the objects from which it is projected*, that is the layout of textured surfaces from which it is reflected. Such a layout always fills at least a hemisphere of the optic array, as does the terrain under an open sky, and may fill the whole spherical array, as do the surfaces of a room. By a "layout" I mean such geometrical properties of surfaces as *edges, corners, slants, convexities* or *concavities*.

The optic array for the rat in the experiment consisted of a finely textured upper hemisphere (not represented in Figure 6) coming from a ceiling and walls with a light source above. In the lower hemisphere there was a large sector of light from the unpainted wooden surface of the runway, coarsely textured by the grain of the wood, and two sectors of the same texture-pattern but different texture-density. Note that the downward sector is partly occluded by the rat's own body (also not represented in Figure 6). The principle meridians of this array, produced by the corners and edges of surfaces, were coincident with the direction of the force of gravity. The latter, of course, is specified by other senses than vision, and hence the downward direction was given to the rat by multiple information.

Please note that nothing whatever has been said about retinal images. These depend on the ocular equipment of the animal, that is, on the placing of the eyes in the head, on accommodation, on the kind of eye-movements that are possible, and so on. Different species of animals have different retinal images and some, with compound eyes like those of the invertebrates, do not even have retinal images, but all can register the structure of an optic array, and do so continuously over time. This structure, after all, is what makes retinal images possible.

The information in ambient light is always potential information. Whether or

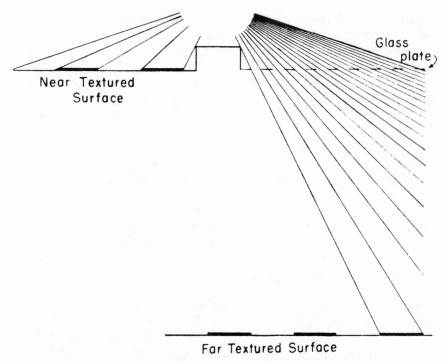

Near Textured
Surface

Glass
plate

For Textured Surface

FIG. 6. A cross-section of the light at the station-point of a rat. The diagram is schematic. The lines represent transitions of intensity, showing that the optical texture is more compact at one edge of the runway than at the other. The optical texture of the runway surface is not shown, nor the relative motion of textures at the edges of the runway, nor the textures of the upper semicircle of the cross-section.

not an animal or a man can register it depends on the anatomy and physiology of the sensory channel, on the stage of growth or maturation of the system, and even perhaps on the level of practice or attention in picking up the information. The edges of the substratum and the amount of depth at the edges, in the experimental situation described, were specified in the light to the rat's station-point whether or not he perceived them. They were conveyed by variables of texture-density and texture-motion.

## THE INFORMATION IN OPTICAL GEOMETRY

What are the general properties of optical structure that might specify corresponding properties of the environment? Wavelength as such tells the eye nothing about a surface, although a spectral distribution of wavelengths might do so. Intensity as such does not correspond to anything about a surface (only to the amount of illumination) although a set of relative intensities might be expected to correspond to a set of relative reflectances or surfaces. So the variables to be analysed are those of structure, pattern, or texture. The actual analysis of these variables, however, is not easy. A natural optic array is a hierarchy of structure, having patterns within patterns, or forms within forms down to an almost infinitesimal detail. The mathematical methods for environmental optics are not immediately obvious. However a number of principles can be safely stated.

### 1. Presence or absence of texture

A homogeneous region of the optic array corresponds to an unobstructed medium of air; a textured region of the array corresponds to a relatively solid surface. The former is perceived by us as a filmy or unsubstantial color; the latter as a surface-color. These patches of the visual field have very different meanings for locomotion. The one means free progress; the other an obstacle. The one implies empty space, or "nothing;" the other implies filled space, or "something." What information could be more important than this? In the downward direction of the array, texture specifies not an obstacle but a substratum. This means *support,* that is to say the upward push of the ground on the feet. Absence of texture in the downward direction would correspond to *loss* of support, and would normally be accompanied by falling.

### 2. Pattern or form of a texture

Optical texture may take various forms depending on the kind, spacing, and regularity of the transitional elements. It may be grainy, pebbled, mottled, aligned, irregular, or sinuous. It is highly various because the structure of the reflecting surfaces in the environment is highly various. Water, grass, wood, or rock are thus specified fairly well in light. Let us note an important fact about the form of an optical texture: it is invariant, as the geometer says, under a transformation. For example, if two textures, one composed of triangles and the other of rectangles, both underwent magnification or perspective foreshortening they would still be composed of triangles and rectangles respectively. Another important fact about the form of a texture is that it stays constant when the intensity of the light is altered. The structure of an optic array, that is, is independent of the energy level of the array.

### 3. Texture with a closed contour

A cone of the optic array with internal texture and a sharp boundary corresponds to a solid detached object in the environment. Such a bounded region of the visual field, without reference to texture, has been said to induce the figure-ground phenomenon in perception. But note the following. A cone of the optic array with a sharp boundary but *without* internal texture corresponds to a hole in the environment, such as the mouth of a cave or a window on the sky. To this stimulus, the phenomenal properties of the figure-ground phenomenon do not apply; they are in fact reversed. One might conclude from this that contour and texture are not separate and independent stimuli in the world (we have only made them so artificially in outline drawings) and that these two properties of light are informative only in combination.

These considerations lead me to suspect that object-perception and its complement "hole perception" are not based on figure-ground perception as we have supposed but are, on the contrary, simpler and more direct. How will the Gestalt Theorists reply to this suggestion?

### 4. Shape and size of contour as such: Abstract form

The shape of a closed contour without motion or texture does not specify the shape of an object in the environment. It is only ambiguous information, since there is a whole family of solids at various inclinations which might project it to the station point. Likewise the size of a contour does not specify the size of an object, since a small-near object would be equivalent to a large-far object. By the same reasoning, the so-called cue of linear perspective, the convergence of a pair of straight contours, does not specify the recession in depth of the face of an object, the edges of the object may or may not be physically parallel. This, together with the other cues, is in truth only a probabilistic indicator of the environmental surfaces. But all these cues are obtained by considering only the abstract forms in the light, the contours in isolation. Our habit of doing so probably comes from making and looking at outline drawings. If we had considered the structure of a natural optical array, which consists of forms *within* forms, we should not have been driven to the theory of the cues or clues for space perception, nor led to the theory of the figure-ground phenomenon as an improvement on it.

### 5. Density of texture as such

The compactness of an optical texture in itself is ambiguous, since it may correspond to a near surface of fine structure or a far surface of coarse structure. But a difference in density of the *same* texture-pattern corresponds to a difference in distance of the same substance, with a higher probability. A *gradient* of density of the same texture corresponds to the direction of increasing distance of a surface composed of the same substance, with an even greater probability.

A stepwise increase of density at a contour combined with an increase of parallactic motion at the contour, specifies an edge of a surface in the environment, or one surface *behind* another. The amount of difference gives the amount of depth. This information was presumably that to which the rats were reacting in the experiment described. If the parallax at the edge is covariant with kinaesthetic stimuli from movement of the head and body the information about a solid environment becomes as statistically reliable as anyone could hope for.

### 6. Transformation

A transformation of the pattern of an optic array, both the whole and all its parts, corresponds to a change of the station-point, that is, to a change in the animal's point of view. Considering the whole set of surfaces composing the environment, one of them is magnified, one of them is minified, and everything between is altered in perspective. Both the contours and the textures undergo a perspective (or projective) transformation with a movement of the observer. The information provided an animal for the guidance and control of its locomotion by this fact need not be described here since it has been discussed elsewhere (Gibson, 1958b). The point I wish to urge here is that changes of form and texture of this sort, far from destroying the information that "form" is supposed to convey about objects, are in fact the best information obtainable about objects. A family of transformations over time, I suggest, should be considered a stimulus for an eye. A change of pattern is optically just as much a fact as a nonchange of pattern, and there is no good reason to assume that eyes register unchanging pattern as a primary process, and change as a secondary process. The eyes of insects, for example, may well be much more sensitive to a pattern which undergoes change than to one which does not. Is it not likely that our concern with "form perception" is a theoretical prejudice reflecting our concern with pictures? An eye is *not* like a camera and, most fundamentally, it is unlike in that it registers *continually*, without film-replacement; moreover, moving an eye forward, or up or down, or sideways enhances the perception instead of spoiling the picture.

### 7. Invariant Properties

A great many properties of a tridimensional environment are unaltered in a bidimensional projection to a point. They are, as the geometer says, invariant under projection. A straight contour in the optic array is a guarantee of a straight edge in the world. An angle in the array guarantees an angle in the environment. A triangle means a triangular shape, and a conic section specifies at least another conic section. What I have called the pattern or form of a texture is the same in all its perspectives. Each perspective is a transformation of what it would be if the station-point were different. The gradient of the spacing or density of the texture will differ, for example. But it is the same texture. Most generally, the adjacent order of texture-elements is preserved in any projection; only the distances and angles between elements are altered. As long as a reflecting solid body in the environment keeps its physical continuity there will be optical continuity in the projection, and *only* so long as it does. Here, I suggest, in the stimulus, is to be found the ultimate solution for the puzzle of the phenomenal constancy of objects, and the apparent rigidity of the phenomenal environment during locomotion.

## CONCLUSION

I have tried to justify with examples the hypothesis that light conveys information about things. Nothing has been said about binocular disparity, or color constancy, or relief, or shadows, or distance-estimation, although these could have been fitted in. The suggestion is that light, in its projective function, contains more information than any pair of eyes is ever likely to pick up in a life-time of exploration. Under optimal conditions of illumination there is generally more than enough information for perception—it is redundant. But, unlike a wordy or repetitious speaker, light uses a language rich with meanings of endless subtlety. If the air is clear the information in light is perfectly clear and the fault is ours if we fail to take it in.

# 1.4 Ecological Optics

## PART I: ECOLOGICAL OPTICS*

The overall problem of vision is that of understanding those activities of men and animals which depend on the stimulation of their eyes. This includes not only problems like the discrimination of wavelength, intensity, and flicker, but also the study of surface, form, space and motion. For vision in this general sense of the term, classical optics, taken straight, is not an adequate basis. It creates troublesome puzzles and contradictions of theory. Perhaps students of vision should reconsider some of the fundamental assumptions about light which they have borrowed from physics.

A large part of physical optics is admittedly not appropriate for the study of vision, nor relevant to it. The theory of design of optical instruments is of great importance, but it cannot be taken over and applied to the eye. For an eye is *not* an optical instrument, despite all the textbook comparisons. An eye is logically prior to any optical instrument, and incommensurable with it. An instrument is something which is intended, in the last analysis, to be used by an eye.

We are accustomed to say that the stimulus for an eye is light, and in truth it has long been known that the stimulus for the kind of photoreceptor found in a lower animal is the light falling on it. The effective limits of wavelength and intensity have been measured. Accordingly it is easy to assume that the stimulus for the eye of a higher animal is the light falling on a mosaic of photoreceptors. But this analogy is misleading, for the characteristic activity of an eye is not that

---

*Vision Research, 1961, *1*, 253–262. Copyright 1961 by Pergamon Publishers, Inc. Reprinted by permission.

of a simple photoreceptor. An eye proper, including both the chambered organ of the vertebrates or the higher mollusks and the compound organ of the higher insects, enables its possessor to respond not only to light but also to the things from which light is reflected. Just what does stimulate such an eye? What is it naturally adapted to register? To what is it sensitive, considered as an organ instead of a mosaic of cells? "Light" is much too simple an answer. A better answer is needed, and one might begin by suggesting that an eye registers *ambient* light. The remainder of this paper will be an effort to elaborate this answer.

The use of the term "ambient" suggests the light that surrounds an individual on all sides. This is part of what is intended. But I wish to refer more particularly to the light which arrives from all directions at a position in space and which does so whether or not an individual is stationed at that position. If this light has different intensities in different directions, instead of the same intensity in all directions, I propose to call it an *optic array*. It is an array because the variation of intensities makes an *arrangement*.

In our world, which is primarily composed of air and surfaces, the air transmits light and the surfaces reflect it. They reflect light diffusely, not regularly, since mirrors are rare in nature. Moreover, they reflect in multiple fashion, from one surface to another and to yet another. The outcome of diffuse reflection and multiple reflection is a reverberating flux of light in the transmitting medium. When analyzed in terms of rays, such a reverberating flux consists of a dense intersecting network made up of pencils of rays. A pencil can be defined as a cluster of lines meeting at a common point, and there will be two types of pencil, divergent and convergent. The divergent pencils are cases of light radiating from a point source on a surface; the convergent pencils are cases of light coming to a point of observation in the medium. The former might be called "radiant" and the latter "ambient." Each of the convergent pencils of light in an ordinary illuminated environment is an optic array.

The radiant pencils issuing from point-sources can be properly treated as physical energy and measured as such. But I suspect that the convergent pencils to a point of observation should be treated as *potentially stimulating* energy, not energy as such, and that they cannot be measured in the same way. The ray of ambient light, I will suggest, should be conceived as different from the ray of radiant light.[1]

I cannot discover that the facts about ambient light have ever been fully recognized in optics, or in any allied discipline. They are more or less recognized in books on perspective, or perspective geometry. But this discipline came to a halt many years ago, having achieved a satisfactory set of rules for the making of pictures by artists and architects. The special rules applied to a *picture plane* and a *station point*. We should not allow these special rules of pictorial perspective to

---

[1]For more details, see Gibson (1979a, p. 48ff.) (Eds.)

take the place of a general study of environmental perspective. The viewing of pictures is by no means the same problem as the viewing of the environment, but many writers have tended to confuse them.

The above set of facts is also more or less implicit in the technology of making images on viewing screens. The concept of *projection* uses the idea of a pencil of rays intersecting in a point, thereby analyzing the correspondence between an object and its image. Taken abstractly, the concept is the basis of projective geometry. But neither of these disciplines is directly relevant to the problem of vision. The term ''projection'' is unfortunate when applied to the light stimulating an eye since this event is more like introjection than projection. The practice of illuminating engineering likewise depends on the same set of fundamental facts, but it does not seem to have been formulated or exploited.[2]

These considerations have convinced me that psychologists, physiologists and others concerned with vision should try to define a special branch of optics appropriate for their problems. I suggest that it be called *ecological optics*. It would be concerned strictly with light in its capacity to stimulate eyes. It would be physics, in a sense, because it deals with a form of physical energy. It would be ecological because it deals with the relation of this energy to a concrete environment which reflects light. I venture to propose a set of assumptions for ecological optics. They are useful in putting a foundation under the kind of visual experiments I have been doing. They may also prove useful to other experimenters but, even if not, they should at least provoke a re-examination of optical theory.

## 1. THE CONCEPT OF AN OPTIC ARRAY

The primary assumption is that the natural stimulus for the ocular equipment of the higher animals is what I have called an *optic array*. An optic array is the light converging to any position in the transparent medium of an illuminated environment insofar as it has different intensities in different directions. Differences in spectral composition may accompany the differences of intensity. Geometrically speaking, it is a pencil of *rays* converging to a point, the rays taking their origin from textured surfaces, and the point being the nodal point of an eye.[3] We have already noted that rays may diverge from a reflecting point (or a luminous point) as well as converge to a point of observation but that a divergent pencil of rays is *not* an optic array. The essence of an optic array is that it has pattern or structure. The radiant pencil has no pattern.

---

[2]Benedikt (1979) has begun to develop these ideas with reference to architectural structures. (Eds.)

[3]This claim is the main point of discussion in the following paper, ''A Note on Ecological Optics.'' (Eds.)

It should be noted that if the medium of the illuminated environment is not transparent, if it wholly scatters the reverberating flux of light by reason of fog or dust, then no optic array can exist in that medium. Likewise no optic array can occur in complete darkness.

## The Optic Array as a Stimulus

The above assumption may astonish some readers. An optic array is extended and enduring whereas the word "stimulus" suggests something punctate and momentary, like a pinprick. An optic array is external to the eye. It cannot act all at once. Above all, it violates the accepted belief that the retinal image is the stimulus. I am suggesting, however, that we re-examine the meaning of that term.[4]

It is just as reasonable to suppose that a sense organ can be stimulated as to suppose that a single receptor-cell can be stimulated. So can a whole sensory system. Each has its own level or order of stimulation. An optic array is the proper stimulus for an ocular system. A retinal image is the proper stimulus for a retina, considered by itself. But we should not be preoccupied with it to the exclusion of other facts. A single eye admits only a *sector* of a complete optic array at any one time. But the ocular equipment of an active animal, as we shall note, can respond by one method or another to a complete spherical array. As we know, the first responses of a man to an optic array, if he is awake, are to focus, fixate, modulate its intensity, and above all *explore* it. The optic array is a *potential* stimulus. It is also a *global* stimulus rather than a *punctate* stimulus.

Retinal stimulation and ocular stimulation have to be distinguished. One is inside the eye and the other outside. The steady application of an image to the human retina (by artificially "stabilizing" it) results in a wholly ineffective stimulus after a short time. But the steady application of an optic array to an eye, which is the natural condition, does not so result. The movements of the eye prevent it. Another proof of the distinction is the fact that both the compound eye of an insect and the camera-eye of a vertebrate can respond to an optic array, but that only the latter kind of an eye has a retinal image. The optic array is an essential feature of all vision; the retinal image only of vision in some animals.

In speaking of the optical stimulus one must distinguish between simultaneous action and successive action. For the kind of animal with a panoramic ocular system, with eyes on each side of the head, the whole optic array is a simultaneous stimulus, or nearly the whole of it. For animals like ourselves with forward-pointing eyes the optic array is physically present at the station-point but it has to be sampled in successive overlapping sectors. In short, a single eye in a given

---

[4]In this discussion, the two issues of what is the stimulus for vision and of what is the retinal image are not separated. A separate discussion of the stimulus concept can be found in Ch. 4.3, and the retinal image concept is discussed in Chs. 1.6 and 2.6 (Eds.)

posture registers no more than half of an array but an ocular system is constructed either to register a whole array or to explore it. By either mechanism animals react to their surroundings. How the nervous system integrates the successive patterns of retinal input and makes them equivalent to a simultaneous pattern of input is, of course, a question.

The eyes are different in different species of animals but the natural stimulus for all animals is the optic array, that is, the *differences* in ambient light. The latter is the "adequate" stimulus for vision. It is the circumstance under which eyes developed during the millions of years of evolution. Artificial or "in-adequate" stimuli of all sorts can be applied to eyes, of course, and this is how we study vision experimentally. Some of these are quite unlike the natural stimulus; some are like it. At one extreme, electrical current can be used to excite the retina. If the subject will fixate on verbal command, a measured beam of light can be thrown into the eye and presumptively on the retina. Or a picture can be put in front of an eye, and this can reproduce part of a natural optic array—a sort of window opening on an environment other than the present one. This is a favorite method of psychologists. The possibilities of controlling light rays to one or both eyes are endless. Psychophysical experiments on vision have unlimited pos-sibilities. But in constructing optical devices we should remember, I think, the kind of stimuli that eyes are equipped to register.

## The Set of Optic Arrays at Differing Station Points

Animals with eyes move about in the environment. The optic array at one position will, in general, be different from that in any other position. That is, its pattern will be different. It will be so by virtue of the laws of parallax and perspective. No two "perspectives" of the world are ever exactly the same. The change from one stationary optic array to another is itself assumed to be a kind of stimulus for an ocular system. All eyes, including the compound type, are known to be sensitive to "motion" and this assumption is, therefore, reasonable. One might even suppose that the optic array at a moving viewpoint is just as much an effective stimulus as the array at a stationary viewpoint (Gibson, 1958b).

The set of changes from one to another optic array in a given environment and the set of moving optic arrays come to the same thing. They are equivalent to the *complete* set of all stationary arrays in that environment. This is an abstract notion, more familiar to geometers than to students of vision. Nevertheless it is a useful concept. It defines the permanent possibilities of optical stimulation for the environment in question. It is potential stimulation, of course, and the actual or effective stimuli for a particular animal or man will always fall short of it no matter how thoroughly he inspects his part of the world. The notion of an unlimited reservoir of potential stimuli for the eyes to explore is a very fruitful one for visual theory.

The change of pattern from one stationary optic display to another can be termed a transformation of pattern. For animals with a panoramic ocular system, the whole global transformation arising from a change of location is a simultaneously present potential stimulus. It probably serves as a controlling input for their locomotion. For animals like ourselves, with forward-pointing eyes, matters are more complicated. The whole transformation of the array during locomotion can be registered only by successive sampling, but the simultaneous mismatch of the two slightly different arrays at the two eyes can be picked up in front, and this sensitivity to binocular parallax is undoubtedly a compensating advantage.[5]

## 2. THE CONTENT OF AN OPTIC ARRAY

An optic array was said to consist of "rays." But in ecological optics, I believe, a ray should not be conceived as a beam of light, not even as one which vanishes to a geometrical line, but as the transition between one beam, and the next. It is the locus of a change in light energy over the array. Considered in two dimensions, the array would consist not of spots or patches but of the boundaries between them. This means that if an optic array had no transitions along either meridian, if it were homogeneous with respect to energy and spectral composition, it would not be a stimulus for an eye and would not be an array at all. The energy of the ambient light could be measured by instruments but it would not stimulate an eye to its characteristic activity. There are many facts to support this inference.

The concept of a beam of light which becomes vanishingly thin but still retains a given intensity and spectral character is troublesome. Such a fiction may be useful for geometrical optics, and convenient for the tracing of rays through refracting media, but it cannot stimulate an eye. A transition, however, *can* stimulate an eye. The rays of ecological optics, being the loci of transitions, are not infinitely dense as they are supposed to be in pure geometry. Ecological optics does not have to be concerned with the problem of waves or particles nor with the laws of refraction, reflection, and diffraction. It is primarily concerned with margins, borders, contrasts, ratios, differences, and textures in the array.

The stimulating properties of an array thus depend on what is loosely called its structure. It will have both microstructure and macrostructure. An ordinary daylight array will have a fine structure at the level of seconds of arc, a coarse structure at the level of minutes, and a gross structure at the level of degrees. Outdoors, the upper half of the array will come from the sky and the lower from the earth. The fine structure corresponds to the rays coming from very small or very distant things; the gross structure corresponds to those coming from very large or very near things. The levels of structure exist whether or not an attentive

---

[5]The issue of frontal *versus* panoramic vision is more complicated than this; cf. Hughes (1977). (Eds.)

eye is in a position to pick them up. Within what limits they are registered is another question. It depends on what kind of eyes the animal has, not on ecological optics.

We must not confuse optical structure with material structure. The texture of focusable light is not the same as the texture of the surface which reflected it, although the one tends to *correspond* to the other in important respects. The precise geometrical relation between the layout of opaque substances in space and the layout of luminous transitions in an optic array has to be determined by ecological optics.

There is a great advantage in defining the optical stimulus in terms of the transitions between patches or spots of light, not the spots or patches themselves. It encourages the use of relational magnitudes in visual experiments instead of the absolute magnitudes borrowed from physics. Physiologists used to assume that the elementary stimulus for vision was a narrow beam of light, measured for wavelength and intensity, that could be applied to a single receptor, and then to suppose that the whole of vision could be derived from knowledge of these elementary stimuli and their effects. It seems to me that this program has failed. It would be better to start from the fact that an optic array as a stimulus is independent of the intensity of light over a wide range of intensities, that is, degrees of illumination. From noon to sunset the *contrasts* are the same. Only as light energy, and only when taken piecemeal, is the optic array different from noon to sunset. This hypothesis seems to show disrespect for the labors of photometry and radiometry. I do not mean to be glib about the measurement of light. I only wish to suggest that there are profound difficulties in all present efforts to do so in a way that is relevant to an eye. We do see the difference between noon and sunset, to be sure, and our eyes still have some function as photoreceptors, but this is not their *characteristic* function.

## 3. THE STIMULUS VARIABLES IN AN OPTIC ARRAY

The essential stimulus variables in "light" have, since Newton, been taken to be wavelength and intensity, or amount of energy. These can be measured in fundamental physical units. Hue is in psychophysical correspondence to wavelength, and brightness to energy. When saturation is included, corresponding to wavelength "purity" or some such measure, one gets the three supposedly basic dimensions of sensory experience. A beam of light can vary in these three physical ways and, correspondingly, a patch of color in experience can vary in three ways. Vision is then supposed to be based on color-sensations. The formula is simple and is tied to simple physical measurement. The trouble with it is that, however amended and supplemented, it does not fit all the facts, not even all the facts of color vision. Ecological optics would assume that the essential stimulus variables for vision are *not* to be found in a beam of light and are *not* wavelength and amount of energy. Instead, the stimulus variables depend on the optic array, and must be discovered by analyzing its structure. Variables of structure or pattern, to be sure, cannot so easily be tied to the fundamental measures of physics. They seem inexact. Nevertheless if the old theory is inadequate, a beginning must be made on a new one. If "color" does not account for vision, let us see if "pattern" will do so, and perhaps then discover that color phenomena will fall into line. Or, putting it in another way, perhaps we cannot understand how the retina works unless we understand how the eye works.

The transitions in a natural optic array are primarily transitions of intensity. These depend on the layout, the chemical and structural composition, and the illumination of the solids, liquids, and gases of the environment. That is, they depend on the edges, corners, and other irregularities of reflecting surfaces. The intensity transitions are usually accompanied by spectral transitions (changes in the wavelength distribution relative to the spectrum of the illumination), but these are secondary. The fundamental variables of an optic array would then be ones like the following:

(a) Abruptness of transition, or what is loosely called "sharpness" of the boundary. A penumbra is at one extreme and an edge is at the other. How to measure this variable is still a question.

(b) Amount of transition. It seems likely that this variable should be measured as a ratio or fraction of the adjacent intensities, not as the absolute difference between them.

(c) Shape of the boundary, e.g., rectilinear, curved, or pointed.

(d) Closure of the boundary or non-closure.

(e) Density of transitions, or number per unit angle of the array.

(f) Change in the density of transitions; also the rate of change of density. The latter is the "gradient" of density of texture.

(g) Motion of one boundary relative to others; or motion of each boundary relative to all the others. The latter might be called a "transformation." There can also be gradients of motion.

(h) Presence or absence of transitions within a closed boundary of the array.

This list might be extended indefinitely. It consists of "significant" variables (of which more later). They have all been isolated experimentally and shown to be effective stimuli. But they are only the ones I happen to have studied, and there are many other potential stimuli in an optic array.

## 4. THE INFORMATION CARRIED BY STIMULUS VARIABLES IN AN OPTIC ARRAY

When defined as above, the variables of an optic array may *carry information* about the environment from which the light comes. This is a central hypothesis for ecological optics. By "carry information," I mean only that certain variables in an array, especially a moving array, will correspond to certain properties of edges, surfaces, things, places, events, animals, and the like—in short to environmental facts. They will not, of course, replicate but only specify such facts.

This hypothesis is perfectly capable of being investigated, and the extent to which it is true or false can be determined. The difficulty has been that no discipline acknowledges the responsibility of doing so—of finding the connections between optical stimuli and their natural sources. The problem falls between ecology, optics, physiology and psychology. There has been plenty of speculative theorizing about the so-called cues for perception but no empirical study of whether a cue is in fact a clue to its object. The late Egon Brunswik called for a study of the "ecological validity" of cues (1956) but few have heeded him. However, he believed that the only relations that could be found between "proximal" stimuli and "distal" objects were statistical probabilities, and this made the problem seem overwhelmingly difficult. I cannot believe that it is so. The notion of an optic array puts the problem on a geometrical basis, not a statistical one, although an element of probability no doubt remains.

There are almost certainly laws by which some variables in the optic array specify some environmental facts. They need to be investigated. Here are some tentative ones to start with:

(a) A sharply bounded sector of the optic array specifies an object in the world; a penumbra specifies a shadow in the world.
(b) A textured patch of the array specifies an obstructing surface in the world; a homogeneous patch specifies air. This is "surface quality" vs. "film quality."
(c) The kind of texture in a patch of the array specifies the kind of substance composing the surface—water, sand, grass, fire.
(d) A rectilinear boundary in the array specifies a straight edge in the world. Angles specify angles, and curves specify curves although, of course, the shape of an object is not specified by its form in the array.
(e) A gradient of density of the *same kind* of texture in the array specifies the direction of recession of a continuous surface.
(f) A transformation of the pattern and texture of the whole array specifies a change of station point.
(g) A transformation of a textured and bounded patch of the array, in isolation, specifies a displacement of an object in the world.

There are surely also complements and corollaries of such laws which will tell us what optical variables do *not* specify environmental facts. For example, optical size does not specify the physical size of an object. But magnification specifies the coming closer of an object and minification the opposite with considerable reliability. The intensity of a patch in the array does not specify the reflectance of a surface in the world. But relative intensities over the whole array might specify the relative reflectances of the whole layout of surfaces. If the stimuli, once naively thought to provide information about the environment, turn out not to do so others may be discovered which do. There is no reason to conclude that knowledge of the world is impossible because "light" is empty of information.

## Invariant Properties under Transformation of an Array

It was noted earlier that the optic array at one position is different from that in another, and that waking animals continually move about. As slight a change of viewpoint as 2½ inches horizontally yields a change in the structure of the array—one that we are used to calling a "disparity" where retinal images are concerned. Consider the change of form and texture for any change of station point. Only some properties of the array change, not all of them. There are *variant* properties of such an array and *invariant* properties. Some "variables" are altered, others are constant. The invariant variables, as they might be called, have not been specified and listed, but they can be, and this is another task for ecological optics.

From projective geometry we know that when a form undergoes a perspective transformation some features are altered and others are not. The same rule holds for the overall structure of an optic array.

The reason why invariants need to be isolated and studied is that they are potentially stimuli. Variants and invariants need to be distinguished. In the past we have assumed that an altered pattern at the eye is simply a different stimulus for the eye. This is not true for an unaltered property. It remains constant and is therefore the *same* stimulus. The unaltered property provides a possible basis for the impression of a constant object or a rigid surface (Gibson & Gibson, 1957). On this theory, the variants in an optic array specify motions of objects or of the individual; the invariants specify the permanent characteristics of the layout of the environment. Here is a radical departure from previous theorizing.

The classical explanation of the constancy of phenomenal objects with respect to shape and size has been to ascribe it to some higher mental process. None has been verified. Actually the problem is one of the constancy of the whole phenomenal environment, not merely of objects. As such it is part and parcel of the study of vision. The theory suggested explains the constancy of phenomenal space as well as that of objects in space. I omit color constancy, but I suspect it can be explained in a similar way by reference to invariants under change of illumination.

The problem of the control of locomotion by vision and the perception of moving objects has scarcely been touched on by psychologists. When the variant properties of a moving optic array have been separated from the invariant ones the necessary stimulus information will, I think, become evident (Gibson, 1958b).

## 5. SOME IMPLICATIONS

These assumptions about light clarify some old puzzles and suggest many new experiments. The advantages that occur to me are as follows:

1. The concept of an optic array enables us to investigate vision without having to choose between sensation and perception. The known facts cannot be separated into these two categories, and the theoretical separation is becoming meaningless. For example, color-perception and surface-perception need to be studied in relation to one another.

2. The defining of higher orders of optical stimuli enables us to perform simple psychophysical experiments on qualities of experience previously called "perceptual." For example, gradients of optical texture can be used as stimuli for impressions of slant-depth.

3. The optic array permits the defining of *relational* magnitudes in the light entering an eye as well as *absolute* magnitudes of stimulus energy, and suggests new experiments in which pattern and sequence are systematically varied instead of frequency and intensity. For example, parameters of optical transformation can be used as stimuli.

4. The notion of an optic array which emanates from surfaces resolves the ancient theoretical puzzle of the "third dimension."

5. By providing a theory of the relation between the proximal stimulus and its distal source it promises to put the problems of size, shape, and color constancy on a new footing, to be treated as problems of vision instead of some little-understood kind of mental activity.

6. The optic array puts the retinal image in its proper place as one stage in the process of seeing in animals having chambered eyes.

7. It destroys the misleading analogy between the retinal image and a picture, while clarifying the relation between them. A picture is a human means of reproducing a part of a natural optic array.

8. It also enables us to bypass some of the long-standing paradoxes concerning the retinal image considered as a picture. For example, instead of worrying about double and single impressions from the two eyes we are led to consider information pickup in a conjugated binocular system.

9. The optic array requires us to consider the responses of the eye and the responses of the retina as each affects the other instead of treating them separately. The orienting and exploratory movements of the eyes developed in parallel with the structure of the retina.

10. Finally, if potentially stimulating light carries information about the environment, as ecological optics may demonstrate, the ancient problem of veridical perception is solved.

## 6. SUMMARY

I have made some tentative suggestions about how to further the study of vision by modifying our assumptions about light. They have been dignified by the term "ecological optics." An optic array was defined, and three main assumptions were made. They seem to be as follows:

1. There is a set of optic arrays in every habitable environment when it is illuminated.
2. Some correspondence exists between the structure of a local optic array and the structure of the local environment, also between the set of arrays and the whole environment.
3. The variables of structure in an array and a set of arrays are potential stimuli for an ocular system.

These hypotheses provide a novel basis for the study of the eyes. They suggest an assumption which common sense would like to accept but which students of vision have thought they had to reject, namely:

An ocular system is essentially a mechanism for registering the information about the environment in a set of optic arrays. It thereby makes possible the control of behavior with respect to the environment.

## PART II: A NOTE ON ECOLOGICAL OPTICS*

The foregoing chapter on ecological optics, by R. M. Boynton, is both a description and a critique of what I believe to be an emerging discipline. The critique is welcome, but the description is so incomplete that I take this opportunity to say so, even at the risk of sounding ungracious.

A chapter on the subject could have been written by me, and the reader may wonder why I did not grasp the opportunity. The reason is that ecological optics cannot be treated in one chapter. It claims to be more than a special branch of optical science; it is more radical and more far-reaching than that. It is the basis for a new theory of vision and is itself based on a new conception of the environment to be perceived. It implies a new answer to the old question of how knowledge is possible. I have doubts that "visual science will be advanced" by it—more likely visual science will be upset although, of course, an upset is sometimes an advance. For these reasons, ecological optics needs to be treated in the context of a whole book on visual perception, and such a book is forthcoming.[6]

---

*The Handbook of Perception, Volume 1. E. C. Carterrette & M. P. Friedman (Eds.) Copyright 1974 by Academic Press, Inc. Reprinted by permission. This paper was written as a response to Boynton (1974).

[6]Gibson (1979a). (Eds.)

I argue that the established branches of optics are appropriate for the study of visual sensations but not for the study of visual perception. I maintain that visual perception is not based on having sensations but on attention to the information in light. The essence of ecological optics is the demonstration that there *is* information in ambient light. The common assumption of physical, geometric, and physiological optics, however, is that there is *no* information in light, that is, no information about the ordinary things from which the light is reflected. A good deal of hedging goes on in perceptual theory today in the attempt to avoid facing this issue, but I am convinced that it is unavoidable. And this is the reason why ecological optics is theoretically crucial. The kind of optics one accepts determines one's theory of perception.[7]

Students of traditional optics, like students of sensory physiology, tend to be impatient with what they consider philosophical issues. They like to believe that science progresses by the accumulation of facts, not by polemics. Yet when Boynton asserts (pp. 300–301) that "we are not in visual contact with objects, or edges, facets, faces, or textures. We are in contact only with photons," this assertion is loaded with epistemology. It is a strictly philosophical conclusion. I disagree with it. There is a misunderstanding of the metaphor of "visual contact," one that goes back to Johannes Müller, and it is one that I discussed repeatedly in *The Senses Considered as Perceptual Systems* (Gibson, 1966b). It leads to the doctrine that all we can ever *see* (or at least all we can ever see *directly*) is *light*.

The heart of ecological optics is the concept of the ambient optic array at a point of observation. The ambient *array* is to be distinguished from the ambient *light*. The former constitutes stimulus information the latter constitutes stimulus energy. Boynton thoroughly approves of the concept of ambient light energy coming to a point (I call it a "Boynton point") but he is doubtful of the concept of a purely relational array or structure. He catches me up for having once defined it in terms of rays, and he is quite right to do so. The formula of a "dense intersecting network of rays" was a mistake; all I meant to imply by it was that the steady state of illumination in a living-space is *projective*. I now define an ambient optic array as a nested set of adjacent *solid angles,* not *rays,* each solid angle corresponding to one of the large faces or small facets of the environment. The solid angles are separated by contours or contrasts. These contours I take to be mathematically definite, and to be independent of an observer. So defined, the array as such is invariant from noon to sunset.

In this theory contours or contrasts are optical facts, and are more important for useful vision than intensities. It becomes reasonable to assume that some mechanism of the visual system registers contours directly, without first having to register the different intensities in the form of brightness sensations on either

---

[7]This claim is further discussed in Jones & Pick (1980), Mace (1974, 1977), and Neisser (1977). (Eds.)

side of each contour and only thus to detect the differences. This is what I meant by suggesting that visual sensations were irrelevant for visual perception; I meant sensations, not sensitivity. Boynton, like most of us until recently, identifies the problem of information pickup with that of having sensations, but this is a confusion. The mechanism of information pickup entails sensitivity but is not one of getting and then interpreting the so-called data of sense.

Boynton says that, for me, "there is no need to be particularly concerned about the mechanisms in whatever pickup device is used to analyze the array; one needs to know only about the array itself." But of course I *do* need to be concerned with the mechanisms of information pickup; the difference between us is that I am led to postulate a device that samples the structure of the ambient array whereas he is led to postulate a device that operates on a set of neural signals from the retinal mosaic.

We are both suspicious of the eye-camera analogy, although I go further than he does in rejecting the usefulness of the concept of the retinal image. He still believes that "the discovery of the retinal image was of monumental importance for the proper understanding of vision" (p. 290). I maintain that it was only important for the understanding of *vertebrate* vision, the kind of vision based on the chambered eye, and that the optic array is more important for vision in general, which can be based on either the chambered eye or the compound eye. In short I maintain that the chambered eye with an image-forming lens is only one way of sampling the information in ambient light; the eye consisting of tubes each pointing in a different direction achieves the same end without a focusing lens and with no focused image. The seeing of the environment does not, then, depend on the formation of an image. This conclusion has quite radical implications for perception. I am not quite sure whether Boynton accepts it or not.

In this connection he again points out my error in 1959 of conceiving an ambient array as a dense set of rays. I did say that the array consisted of "focusable light," thinking only of the eye with a lens and forgetting that "focusable light never converges but always diverges, it is the job of a lens to produce the convergence that causes the focus" (p. 298). Boynton is right. Rays radiate. What converges are visual solid angles. But he is not right, I think, in saying that the error is carried over into my 1966 book.

Incidentally, I now call the apex of all the visual angles in an array a *point of observation,* not a *station point.* The reason is that a point of observation is almost never stationary, and the structure of an optic array is almost never frozen but changing. The station point of a picture projected on a transparent plane, in perspective geometry, is not to be confused with the point of observation for an ambient array, in ecological optics. The two are not so similar as I once thought. The "laws of perspective" are not the same as the invariants in an optic array.[8]

Boynton has become convinced that ambient light as well as radiant light

---

[8]Cf Chs. 3.3 and 3.4 (Eds.)

should be accorded some treatment in optics. He proposes that intensity vectors toward a point (a *point sink*) should be recognized as well as intensity vectors from a point (a *point source*). How is this conception of ambient *light,* drawn from physical optics, related to my conception of an ambient *array,* drawn from a new sort of abstract geometrical optics? This is an important question. I want to say that the former is stimulus energy while the latter is stimulus information. But he does not agree, and wishes to "breathe some physical life into the geometric concepts" that I have introduced. The reader is invited to reconcile these different formulas, if he can.

The purpose of ecological optics is not to explain the visibility of stars, or lighthouses, or spectral colors. It is not to improve the design of optical instruments or the prescribing of spectacles. It is not concerned with dazzle, or afterimages. Its purpose is to explain how animals see their environment, chiefly illuminated surfaces, and this explanation has been sadly neglected. Ecological optics is less concerned with seeing light than with the seeing of things by *means* of light. Consequently, I believe that it can *bracket* the disciplines of radiomety, photometry, and psychophysics and base itself on the *invariant* properties of an optic array. These geometric concepts may well prove to be more lifelike than the physics of photons.

The invariants in a changing optic array over time permit the student of vision to investigate problems that otherwise he could not touch. Traditional optics, physical, geometric, and physiological, simply cannot handle the fact that we live in a cluttered environment of opaque surfaces and hence that some things are hidden at some points of observation. But ecological optics invites the study of occluding edges, angular and curved, and the changing occlusion that results from a moving point of observation. Any surface is revealed by an appropriate movement, both the back side of an object and the background of it. Disocclusion at one edge is usually accompanied by occlusion at another. The optical transitions that specify the changing occlusion have been worked out (Gibson, Kaplan, Reynolds, & Wheeler, 1969). The perception is of *one surface behind another*. The observer does not see a patchwork with depth added; he does not see space; he does not see a figure on a ground. He perceives an occluded surface without having any sensations to correspond with that surface. Presumably the perception is based on an invariant over time.

A frozen optic array therefore is never in one-to-one projective correspondence with the cluttered environment that we actually perceive. Still less is a retinal image or a picture of some selected sector of the cluttered environment. What we see is not a projection, an image, or a picture, but a layout of surfaces. And the information for perceiving this layout is got by noticing what is invariant under changes of the array produced by the exploratory movements of the observer himself.

# 1.5 On Theories for Visual Space Perception

## PART I: A LETTER TO GIBSON* FROM GUNNAR JOHANSSON, UNIVERSITY OF UPPSALA, SWEDEN

Dear Friend,

For many years we have both been engaged in experimental research and theoretical work aiming at a better understanding of visual space and object perception. A main theme has been the important role played by changing stimulus patterns, thus, event perception, as contrasted to static perception. During these years we have exchanged many personal communications which, for me, have been highly stimulating.

The purpose of the present paper is to continue the discussion about some parts of your recent book: *The Senses Considered as Perceptual Systems*, in which we were involved during your visit to Uppsala some months ago. Both I, personally, and other members of the Uppsala group had some important objections to the applications of "ecological optics" in your book. I promised to analyze this conception a little further and to communicate the result in a discussion paper. Here you have our point of view. I hope that a discussion of some essential divergences may be fruitful for both of us.

I will analyze your construct "ecological optics" in two ways: first, from a systematic point of view, and then I intend to scrutinize the validity of your application of its basic rules in your theory of space perception.

---

*Scandinavian Journal of Psychology*, 1970, *11*, 67–74, Copyright 1970 by Almqvist & Wiksell. Reprinted by permission of the publisher and author.

## WHAT IS "ECOLOGICAL OPTICS"?

From several declarations in your book it seems clear that you regard ecological optics as a special but very little studied field of general optics. I hope that I have understood your book aright when I say that the main function of ecological optics is to *develop a model for how reflected light carries visually decodable information about an organism's environment* (see e.g. 1966b, p.186).

In terms of distal-proximal stimuli this means that you start with the distal environment and ask what information about it is available proximally at the eye. Such detailed knowledge is, to be sure, a highly important condition for a theory of visual space perception, and I regard your consequent endeavor in this respect as a highly important contribution.

In your discussion the central question is an analysis of the information available in the optical convergence points in space, given by the network of rays from reflected light. (The reader is reminded that the optical convergence point (the station point) is a point where rays reflected from the environment cross. Light rays cross in every point in a room reflecting light and such a crossing is a necessary condition for the functioning of an eye or a camera. Fig. 7 gives a diagrammatic illustration taken from Gibson's book.)

Formulated in this way the problem is primarily a geometrical one. It has direct relevance for the study of the eye as an optical instrument, but also for other optical instruments, for instance the camera. However, it has the same relevance for the perspective drawer. In this way ecological optics in accordance with your treatment has a close relationship to the most classical part of optics, namely geometrical optics on the one hand and the geometry of perspective on the other. I will in the following briefly touch upon both these fields.

In your treatment you stress the very special character of ecological optics. You speak about the "quite unfamiliar laws of ecological optics" and that known laws of physical optics need to be supplemented with these laws (p.188). You also say that "this protodiscipline cannot be expected to have the mathematical elegance of classical optics but it is closer to life" (p.187). I want to stress another position. I agree wholeheartedly in your endeavor to develop an optics specially adapted to our common theoretical problems, but I think that in the two above-mentioned branches of geometry and optics we have rather adequate basic principles and rules ready for borrowing.

### Ecological Optics as a Part of Geometrical Optics

Currently, optics is divided into three parts: geometrical optics (where the "ray" conception has fundamental relevance), physical optics (primarily wave theory), and quantum optics (= interaction between light and matter).

Geometrical optics introduces the concept of "ray" and studies, among other things, how light is reflected from more or less opaque surfaces, how it is

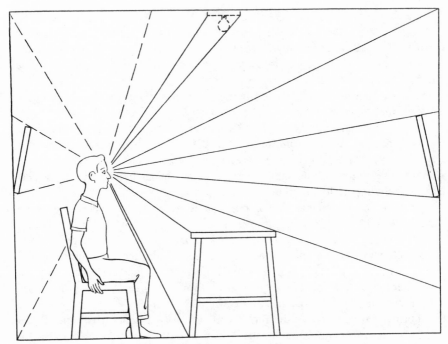

FIG. 7.   The effective array at a stationary convergence point (Stage 5). The solid
lines represent the sample of the total optic array that is admitted to a human eye
in a given posture. The dashed lines represent the remainder of the array, which
is available for stimulation but not effective at this moment.

refracted, etc. In this way it gives the well known principles for image generation
from reflected rays crossing in a point in space. In fact, the insight that rays from
a surrounding hemisphere are crossing in every point in space is the basis for
optical image generation—even if this fact is not often explicitly pointed out.
From this point of view, ecological optics may be regarded as a special application of geometrical optics. Optical image generation is macroscopic in character
in the same way as you have stressed for ecological optics and it is submitted to
the well developed mathematics of geometrical optics. The "image" may be
regarded as a convenient way of describing some of the information available in
the convergence point. Used in this way it is a geometrical concept rather than a
visual one.

## Ecological Optics and Perspective Geometry

In your book *Perception of the Visual World* (1950a) you made much use of the
laws of perspectivity. The perspectivity gradients played a central role in your
theory structure.

   In the present book you seem to be rather disappointed with the results of experimental work along these lines. The concept of gradients has vanished. (Parenthetically I wish to say that this is a reaction which perhaps will prove to be a little premature.) However, I know that you are aware of the close relationship between perspective geometry and your ecological optics. But even here you have a well developed science: perspective geometry was the origin of projective geometry. Thus, you have here again the powerful mathematical tools of a highly developed and sophisticated science.

Information contained in the optical convergence point, or the station point, may be described in many different but theoretically equivalent ways. Now, you want to leave the traditional picture plane method and use a construct with hemispheres. This, I think, depends on your ambition to discuss vision in terms of wide-angle perspective. From a geometrical point of view this is adequate. The question is not, however, a very important one, it is just a question of choice between spherical and linear representation of the same information contained in the convergence point. What is of key importance is the knowledge that all the visually useful information in reflected light is available in the optical crossing point loosely represented by the pupil of the eye.

## About Multiple Reflection and Information About Illumination

What I have so far touched upon concerns primarily the stimulus counterpart for contour vision and perception of forms. In traditional terms this is the stimulus background for *shape constancy*. There is, however, a third part of the system you have named ecological optics, and in my opinion the most "ecological" part of it. This concerns the consequences of multiple light reflection between surfaces in terms of reduction of energy and change of spectral characteristics. Both the number of reflections and type of reflecting surfaces have specific effects and give the ray a "history." These ecological characteristics of light are highly important for perception of illumination. They are the stimulus counterpart for *brightness constancies and color constancies*.

I am a little astonished to find that you have not explicitly treated this section of the ecology of light. (You have mentioned it at p.12.). These aspects of the information contained in the convergence point (and surely used by the visual apparatus) seem to give special problems for proximal stimulus analysis. Here, perhaps, your declaration about the lack of adequate methods for stimulus analysis is more justified than ever.

## INFORMATION ABOUT THE THIRD DIMENSION IN THE CONVERGENCE POINT

After these comments on your treatment of the optical-geometrical relation between environment and convergence point (distal stimulus $->$ proximal stimulus) we can take the next step. This concerns the essential question of the information about space available at the station point. If we regard the light reflection to a convergence point as a geometrical projection (in accordance with projective geometry) we can speak about the visual "reconstruction" of physical space from proximal light distribution as a reversal of this process, thus a *reverse projection*.

The general problem is well known from Bishop Berkeley. We can express it in the following questions: How is specific 3-D perception possible from the information available in the convergence point? How is the third dimension given in vision? We know that the classical cue theory for static perception is unsatisfactory. It does not cover the ordinary type of visual perception: perception of changes and of motion. However, there is an important difference between your theoretical positions in this field and my own, and my main purpose with the present paper is to sort out this controversy.

I will start with an effort to summarize from your text (Gibson, 1966b), your present position in the following two statements. I hope that you will find my digest of your text correct.

1. It is not possible for the eye to get specific and veridical information about space from a single static convergence point (pp.198–199). (You argue with data from the Ames distorted room.)

2. A set of convergence points in space can, taken as a unit, bring about specific and veridical information about this space (pp. 191–192, stage 3). Locomotion (motion) of the eye through a series of convergence points yields a successive combination of information in the same way and therefore gives specific 3-D information (p.199) about a rigid environment.

I borrow Figure 8 from your book as a very clear but static illustration of the effect of locomotion.

These statements seem to me to form the basis of your main theorem: the visual system receives optically no specific information about the environment when it is in a static state but a moving organism obtains such information due to its motion. You assume that it is gained from combining information available in a set of static points along the motion track. There we have our main point of controversy.

Let me comment on your position.

1. You state that there is no specific 3-D information available in one single static convergence point. Here I agree and will add that we have at our disposal also decisive geometrical arguments for this position; arguments of ecological optics-type taken from projective geometry (equivalent configurations). These arguments are given in, e.g., Johansson (1964) and Johansson & Jansson (1968), but also in the theoretical discussions behind Ames's demonstrations.

2. The second statement concerns motion and changing patterns of proximal stimulus information. Your position would have been correct there also if you had included a highly important restriction. But it is lacking. Without *a priori* assuming the existence of 3-D rigidity there is no specific information about space available in the visual stimulus, even in connection with locomotion. The

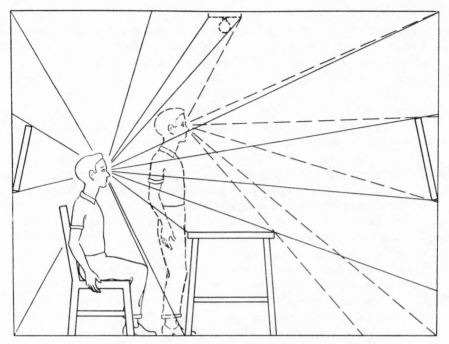

FIG. 8.    The transformation of the optic array obtained by a locomotor movement (Stage 6). The solid lines represent the optic array before the observer stands up, the dashed lines after he has moved. The path of locomotion of the head is forward and upward. The whole array is transformed, including the invisible portion behind the head, but the latter is not represented in the drawing.

visual apparatus has to introduce a set of decoding principles for data treatment with the assumption that the expanding and changing proximal patterns represent motion in a rigid 3-D world. Taken *per se* the changing information pattern due to locomotion does not contain specific information about a 3-D space.

I know that you dislike any attempt to introduce what may be regarded as subjective components in visual perception (like "assumptions," "schemata" etc.) Your main thesis has been that there is available in the proximal stimulus all the information needed and that the problem is to find an adequate stimulus description in terms of higher order variables. Now, you have changed your position when it is a question of static perception, but seem to believe in the possibility of keeping the position when it is a question of the case of changing stimulation where the changes are due to locomotion.

As you know, I am of the same opinion as you regarding the need for reformulating the traditional description of the stimulus. We also have the same position regarding the decisive importance of motion and changing visual stimulation for an understanding of visual perception. For that same reason I feel that it is necessary to make it clear what is valid in your approach and what is an erroneous consequence of an incomplete analysis.

When you restrict your discussion about information in visual change to changes caused by locomotion it seems to me that you stop half way. You stop at locomotion instead of analyzing the more pure case concerning a stationary eye and its changing stimulation due to motions and form changes of objects. Locomotion in 3-D space surely introduces non-optical components of sensory information as well. So far as I understand however, there is no place for such added information in your ecological optics.

You may answer that a main theme of your book is to demonstrate how the different sense channels interact and form unitary perceptual systems and that perhaps we have here the most important example of such interaction. I agree wholeheartedly. I am convinced that space perception in a freely moving animal or man is the result of a highly complex interaction between vision and a number of different receptor systems for mechanical forces.

Our discussion here, however, concerns the isolated visual component. Our problem is to find out how much pure optical information in a convergence point can contribute to the organism's orientation in its environment. Therefore, in the interest of theoretical clarity I want to stress the distinction between possible optical information and possible mechanical information.

From this follows the question: Is space perception from visual perception necessarily due to interaction with non-visual sense channels (outside the eye)? This is, I think, a crucial question for theoretical development.

In order to get an answer to this question, the appropriate step is, of course, to study the visual effects of changing optical structures in an approximately static convergence point. Suppose that we are able to demonstrate experimentally that this condition can also give specific (and perhaps veridical) space perception. The consequence would be that we had shown that bodily motion is not a necessary condition for specific 3-D perception from optical motion. And we would also know that isolated optical stimulation of this type is enough for obtaining space perception.

We have, as you well know, many such affirmative results. You have given excellent affirmative answers yourself. Your "looming" experiments with various species have convincingly demonstrated how expanding patterns on resting retinas yield perception of motions in depth. I could also mention the kinetic depth effects (Wallach & O'Connell, 1953) or my own studies about motion perception already referred to.

Strangely enough, in your arguments for what I will call the locomotor theory (p.199) you have pointed to the looming effects as experimental support. I hope that you will agree when I stress that these effects are, on the contrary, an argument for the proposition that an eye resting in space is able to get specific 3-D perception from changing stimulation. If so, let us make it clear that it is continuous optical change in the convergence point that is the decisive condition. Whether such changes are due to locomotion or to moving objects is rather equivalent from the point of view of 3-D information.

We have to accept that (1) there is geometrically no specific information about space available in the pattern of change in the station point, and (2) that the visual system obtains specific information from such stimulus patterns. This poses a problem which you have not solved.

There is also another important reason for me to say that your theory for motion perception is not sufficiently developed. You have not taken into consideration a highly important characteristic of the perceptual pick-up of optical information.

I am aiming at the property of the visual decoding for which I once used the term *motion analysis* (Johansson, 1950; see also 1958,1964). The term refers to the automatic and unavoidable splitting up into unitary components of the complex pattern of change in the optical convergence point. This analysis follows simple laws of mechanics. Its consequence is that a complex pattern of optical change in the station point is perceptually split up and grouped into mutually equal and divergent components. This function of the visual system seems to be a necessary condition for the visual ability to perceive a rigid world and rigid objects from the complex optical information flow at the eye.

I have discussed (Johansson, 1958) how this characteristic of the visual treatment of stimulus data not only makes it possible to get adequate information about locomotion *or* about object motion, but also to perceive both types of event *at the same time*. Locomotion gives one component of change in the whole pattern and the object motion another and these components are perceptually perfectly separated. A hunting animal, for instance, seems to perceive in a perfect way its motion over a field and simultaneously the motion of the prey. The same analysing principle is at work when we are able to walk along a crowded sidewalk or to drive our car in ordinary city traffic. We visually perceive our own motion and the motion of several distinct objects at the same time. It seems appropriate to point to the fact that the ear demonstrates an analogous analysing capacity. From the complex wave pattern of the eardrum we are able to distinguish a chosen voice in party chatter or one of the instruments in an orchestra.

But, let us now return to our main point of controversy: the role of the organism. Above I have characterized your position in this respect as the result of an incomplete analysis. Thus, I mean that a more thorough analysis brings about a deviating position. Therefore, in order to give you an object for your criticism, let me sketch out the structure of my own theory. It has been developed on the basis of experiments, which I have tried to make as critical as possible for the problem.

I will stress that the visual system itself, in a decisive way, contributes to the perceptual outcome from the proximal stimulus flow also to an eye approximately at rest. The efficiency of the system is given by a set of rules for stimulus data treatment (the programming of the visual computer, if you accept this metaphor), rules which work in an automatic way, but which result in veridicality when the proximal stimuli are projections from moving rigid objects and/or a rigid environment in motion relative to the eye. The principle of motion analysis mentioned above may be regarded as a general summarizing formulation of these decoding principles.

Such rules have been shown experimentally to work in a blind, mechanical way and leave basically nothing for subjective choice. Therefore, I prefer to regard them as indicating a primary neurological "wiring." Their basic effect seems to be to filter out rigidity in space.

Together with my co-workers, I have tried to give some special and preliminary formulations of these stimulus decoding principles (Johansson, 1964; Johansson & Jansson, 1968). Further analyses are found in Marmolin & Ulfberg (1967), Jansson & Runeson (1969), and Jansson & Borjesson (1969). Much more. experimental and theoretical work remains, but I think that we begin to discern the main lines. This means that I (and I think all members of the Uppsala group) hope to be able to arrive at generally valid and specific formulations of perceptual rules for visual stimulus data treatment.

It is our opinion that our research program will help us to avoid a not uncommon appeal to subjectivity in the basic functions of the visual apparatus, but at the same time to avoid following the pendulum swing to the other extreme: an unstructured belief in stimulus information.

It is, of course, appropriate to characterize the theory outlined above as purely nativistic. Your own theory, then, would be described as belonging to the empiricist type. I regard, however, these two old polar categories as rather unsatisfactory for the purpose of characterizing both our theories. The structure I have outlined here concerns the primary biological programming of the visual system and has thus concentrated on the nativistic component. But for a more complete theory we must include also the ability to adapt to induced distortions of various kinds. We are dealing with both basic and rather rigid decoding principles (apparently common for all types of visual systems of retinal type) as one category and, as another, as a more or less advanced ability to adapt the outcome from this primary decoding scheme when needed. This may perhaps be regarded as some kind of analog to a basic programming together with a possibility of changing some instructions and constants within the program of a computer. What is your own opinion in this respect?

## PART II: A REPLY TO JOHANSSON* FROM JAMES J. GIBSON

Dear Friend,

It is 19 years since you published *Configurations in Event Perception* and I published *The Perception of the Visual World*. During all these years we have

---

*Scandinavian Journal of Psychology,* 1970, *11,* 75–79. Copyright 1970 by Almqvist & Wiksell. Reprinted by permission.

been in fundamental agreement about the perception of events and the perception of space. That is why our disagreements are worth discussing. Each of us always knows what the other is talking about, at the very least, and this is a very satisfying situation. I understand your criticisms and I will try to meet them, or at least some of them.

## ECOLOGICAL OPTICS

First, about ecological optics. You say that I seem to regard it as a special branch of the existing science of optics, but a neglected branch. You imply that ecological optics could be derived from physical and geometrical optics without introducing any radically new postulates. Well, when I think about it, I disagree. It seems to me that ecological optics is a discipline of *higher order* than physical optics, and that the new definitions and postulates give us a truly different level at which to study light. The *seeing of light* is a problem in sensory physiology. But *the seeing of things by means of light* is so different a problem that the very meaning of the term ''light'' is altered. The light that radiates from a source and the light that illuminates the surfaces of a room are different because new laws emerge for the latter. What I am saying, in a sense, is that there are Gestalt laws not only for physical objects and not only for the brain, but also for light.

You say that the aim of ecological optics is to explain ''how reflected light carries visually decodable information about an organism's environment.'' That is approximately right but I have two reservations about it. First, the light which reverberates in the air instead of being propagated through empty space reaches a steady state. It is not just reflected light, but *multiply* reflected light. It ''fills'' the air. It does not therefore so much *carry* information as *contain* information. The information exists in the set of all the ambient arrays at each of the station points. The air, in other words, is filled with geometrical projections, not just with waves or particles. Second, the information in an ambient array, consisting of geometrical projections, is not the kind that can be coded and decoded as messages and signals can. It is information in a quite different meaning of the term.

I do not believe that the existing disciplines of physical and geometrical optics can explain how light carries or contains information about the environment so long as light is conceived merely as radiant energy or rays. Rays can carry information about the *atoms* of a surface that radiates light, or is excited to emit it, but not about the gross layout, structure, and composition of the surface.

If, as you seem to suggest, we simply borrow the rules of physical and geometrical optics we must assume that an observer has to *construct* a perception of his environment out of light rays; that is, he must build up a picture of the world from elementary point sensations. You and I both know the theoretical difficulties to which this leads. My solution of this theoretical problem is to assume that there are genuine units in the array of ambient light, units that are not reducible to a distribution of points of light, or to a matrix of independent stimuli.

I think you are assuming that the information in the array of light coming to a convergence point *has* to be analyzed in terms of the direction, the amplitude, and the wavelength of each ray at that point. I agree that this analysis is possible but I do not think it is appropriate for the study of perception. The information can be analyzed in terms of relations, contrasts, discontinuities, and invariants. Your kind of information could be transmitted along a fiber of the optic nerve as a signal; my kind of information could not be transmitted in this way—in fact it could not be transmitted at all. But then I do not believe that the visual system is a channel for transmitting signals from the retina to the brain. I believe it is a system for *sampling* the ambient array.

I do not deny, of course, that visual sensations from the retina can be noticed—afterimages for example—but I assert that they are irrelevant for perception. Optical information as I conceive it is not conveyed over a channel; it is picked up by an active observer. And that means that the observer's brain cannot be compared to a computer, or to a processor of information delivered to it. It means that the environment does not send messages to a little perceiver in the head of an animal. And it means that the concept of information used by the mathematical theory of communication, however suggestive, is not applicable to vision considered as a perceptual system.

## INFORMATION FOR THE PERCEPTION OF A RIGID SPATIAL ENVIRONMENT

Next we come to a deeply puzzling problem that has concerned us both for many years. We agree that optical *change* in some sense of that term contains information for the perception of space. You speak of "changing form" where I speak of "transformation." You still like to talk about the third dimension of "space" where I like to talk about the "layout" of surfaces. But despite our use of different terms we both understand the importance of a changing array as distinguished from a frozen array in time. There is less ambiguity in a changing array than there is in a frozen array, and we seem to agree about this. The difficulty between us arises, I think, from the assumptions I have made about the ecological *causes* of optical change. Let me try to make them explicit.[1]

I assume there are four different kinds of material events that give rise to four distinct kinds of optical change. They are, first, rigid motions of objects relative to a stationary earth with a stationary observer, second, elastic motions of certain substances when the remaining environment and the observer are stationary, third, locomotions of the observer in a stationary environment, and fourth, elastic movements of the observer's extremities, such as his hands. I assume that the fundamental layout of the environment is rigid, since it is mostly matter in the

---

[1]For further discussion see Chs. 1.7, 2.6–2.8, & 4.7 (Eds.)

solid state, not viscous or liquid. Hence a motionless observer is surrounded by an optic array which is for the most part frozen in time. He thus detects his immobility relative to the environment and this information is much more trustworthy than what might be provided by the joints, muscles, and vestibular organs, since he may have to work in order to stay in the same place, like a bird in a wind. When he moves (actively or passively) this ambient array undergoes "motion perspective" (as I call it) and he thus detects his locomotion relative to the environment (Gibson, Olum & Rosenblatt, 1955).

I then assume that the optical change resulting from either the motion of a rigid object or the locomotion of an observer is of a special mathematical kind, whereas the optical change resulting from the *elastic* motion of an external surface or that of one's own skin is of a *different* mathematical kind. Being different, they are capable of being distinguished. The rigidity and non-rigidity of things can thus be detected. The difference has to be noticed of course; it has to be picked up by the visual apparatus, but that does not mean that the brain has to know *a priori* that space is rigid. I don't think that there are any built-in assumptions in the brain, but it is a great distinguisher of differences! (Gibson, 1969a).

I think it is a fact, a geological fact, that the surface of the earth tends to be rigid and tends to be composed of evenly distributed units. This is the basis of the assumption that the laws of perspective projection hold for terrestrial space.

You say that I overstate the importance of the locomotion of the observer in space perception and neglect the importance of the motion of objects. But surely the locomotion of the observer is necessary for large-scale space perception, for the awareness of the whole environment. Do you not agree that the *ground*, the *earth*, is the fundamental frame of reference for both locomotions and the motions of objects? Motion perspective for the surface of the earth is therefore the first case to analyze. The same laws no doubt will apply to both kinds of motion but the detecting of locomotion by vision is required for the *control* of locomotion (Gibson, 1958b). However I have never doubted or denied that depth perception can arise from the motion of objects relative to the earth with no motion of the observer relative to the earth.

My guess is that the optical change over time in the optic array is what specifies both the locomotion of the observer and the motion of an object whereas the *non-change* over time in the changing array is what specifies the spatial arrangement of the environment and of the object in the environment. If I am right about this, then we shall have to understand the mathematical *invariants* under optical transformation instead of the old-fashioned "cues for depth" if we hope ever to understand space perception.

This last point may well be a crucial one for understanding the difference between our positions. The truly *specifying* information for the layout of the faces of an object or of the surfaces of the environment may be something that only emerges over time. It takes time since an invariant can only be detected if something does not vary along with something else that does. Such an invariant, you must agree, could not be transmitted over a nerve in the way a signal can be transmitted. It would have to be detected, registered, or "picked up" by an active perceptual system that works in a radically different way than the channels of sensory input work.[2]

My notion of invariant properties during the course of change in the optic array is an alternative to your notion of applying vector analysis to the change in the optic array. You try to reduce the highly complex changes of the array to the simplest component motions (is that right?) whereas I try to separate the parameters of change in the array from the properties that do *not* change. Your motion analysis follows the laws of mechanics, as you say, and appeals to analytic geometry whereas my theory says that optical changes occur at a different level of abstraction than do mechanical motions and appeals to what has sometimes been called synthetic geometry.

Perhaps your analytic approach and my synthetic approach can be reconciled in the end, but for the present I cannot do so. Your idea that the information for ego-motion and that for object-motion are different *components* of change in the optic array is a good one. As I would put it, the first is "propriospecific" information and the second is "exterospecific." But I do not understand how you can say that this idea of component changes is derived from mechanics and vector analysis. The components are properties of the optic array, not the velocities of bodies in space.

I suggested a year ago (Gibson, 1968a) that the changes in an optic array should not be called "motions" at all. They are changes that can *specify* environmental motions or locomotions without having to be *like* the motions that are specified. Hence what gives rise to the *perception* of motion is not itself motion. This is a radical conclusion, I must admit, and it is disconcerting. But I predict you will be forced to it, as I was, by the evidence. The hypothesis that a displacement of the retinal image over the retina is necessary for any kind of perception of motion is simply incorrect as I tried to show. And yet you seem to accept that hypothesis when you advocate the analysis of complex motions into simple components.

My reasons for believing that the rigidity of the terrestrial world in general and the elasticity of certain parts of it are distinguishable have been set forth recently in another publication (Gibson, 1969a) and need not be repeated here. It is a deeply puzzling problem, as I said at the beginning, but it goes to the heart of many other problems and we must try to solve it.

## THE CONTRIBUTION OF THE PERCEIVER TO HIS PERCEPTION

You argue that the visual system itself *contributes to* the perceptual outcome resulting from stimulation. You have a theory of how this contribution is made in

---

[2]Cf. Gibson (1966b, Ch. 2; 1979a, Ch. 14; Chs. 2.5 & 4.8). (Eds.)

terms of rules for treating the stimulus data. You say that my theory of stimulus information goes to an extreme and does not recognize the contribution of the organism to perception. This is your final and most general criticism.

My answer is that it is false to put into opposition the contribution of the perceiver and the contribution of the external stimulation. It is impossible to weigh the subjectivity of perception against the objectivity of perception. They are not commensurable. If perception is essentially an act of attention, as I maintain, and is not to be confused with imagination, hallucination, or dreaming then the perceiver does not *contribute* anything to the act of perception, he simply *performs* the act.

When you postulate rules for treating the stimulus data or principles for decoding the data you are taking, it for granted that the data themselves are insufficient for perception. You imply that they are meaningless. Both nativist and empiricist theories of perception begin with this assumption. The nativist assumes innate ideas (or the basic "programming" of the nervous system in computer terms) whereas the empiricist assumes acquired memories (or new connections in the nervous system). But both theories are alike in supposing that perception is a process of contributing to the data of sense. My theory of available stimulus information outside the eyes of an observer and explored by him avoids *both* nativism and empiricism.

For me, perception is an awareness of the world.[3] An awareness of the self *accompanies* it but does not *contribute* to it. Proprioception, as I put it, goes along with perception but is not the same thing. There is a subjective aspect and an objective aspect to every phenomenal experience but this does not mean that there is some degree of subjective *determination* of objective perception. The old idea that a perception is determined partly from the outside and partly from the inside is nothing but a muddle of thought. So when you argue that we should avoid the two extremes of perceptual theorizing, the "appeal to subjectivity" on the one hand and the "belief in stimulus information" on the other, I do not agree for I think the issue is false. It is just as false as the issue between nativism and empiricism.

My theory of perception is not going to be clear unless you understand that it goes hand in hand with a theory of *proprioception*. One cannot be aware of the world without also being more or less aware of existing in the world, sometimes staying in the same place and sometimes moving about or being moved. If this had been clear to you you would not have said that I had a "locomotor theory" of space perception. Locomotion is one biological function and space perception is another; the former does not explain the latter. I think you still believe that the third dimension must be added to depthless sensations by motion. But I do not any longer believe in the "cues for depth." I think a perceiver picks up information about the layout of the environment directly, and does so the more readily when the object moves or when he himself moves.

---

[3]This definition is expanded in Gibson (1979a, p. 239). (Eds.)

# 16 A History of the Ideas Behind Ecological Optics: Introductory Remarks at the Workshop on Ecological Optics*

## INTRODUCTION

This discipline of "ecological optics" is now 10 years old (Gibson, 1958b, 1961a, 1966b; also Purdy, 1958) and it's time to see where it's got to. What I am going to discuss today is first a series of difficulties or problems that I personally could not resolve and that pushed me in the direction of ecological optics. Then, second, I will describe a set of discoveries made by us or by others which also led up to ecological optics. Third, I will say what I think the differences are between physical optics, geometrical optics, and ecological optics. Everybody including me has been confused about these different kinds of optics. Physical optics is a branch of physics. Geometrical optics, a sort of discipline used mostly by instrument designers, is semi-mathematical. Then, of course, there is physiological optics. I think the first book entitled *Physiological Optics* (Helmholtz, 1866) was published about a hundred years ago. In my opinion physiological optics, over 100 years, has failed to explain the phenomena of perception, although it's had an enormous success in providing a basis for ophthalmology and optometry and for the study of visual sensations. At the end I will give out a glossary of terms or definitions that are more or less in use in ecological optics[1] and that set of definitions will unquestionably provide grounds for argument for the rest of the week.

---

*This paper was the opening address at the Workshop on Ecological Optics, held at Cornell University, Ithaca, New York, in June 1970. The address was transcribed and edited by Anthony G. Barrand and Mike Riegle. It has not been published previously.

[1]This refers to an earlier version of the glossary appearing as Appendix One in Gibson (1979a). This glossary was distributed at the workshop. (Eds.)

# I

What are the difficulties that led me in the direction of these hypotheses? I can think of five.

1. The difficulty of interpreting the results of Metzger's experiments on the *Ganzfeld*.
2. The insufficiency of Koffka's distinction between the proximal and distal stimulus.
3. The anomalies in my old idea of retinal gradients of texture.
4. The defects of the formula: perception is a function of stimulation.
5. The difficulties with the assumption that gradients of velocity were retinal.

These are the difficulties I'm going to talk about. They are familiar to many of you.

First is the difficulty of interpreting the results of the famous experiment on homogeneous visual stimulation, the so-called *Ganzfeld* experiment or "total-field" experiment (only I think it's misnamed) in terms of retinal image optics. Metzger (1930) set up a very large, semi-panoramic, finely-grained plaster wall in front of subjects' eyes and asked, "What do you see?". When he made the illumination dim enough, the subjects said, "I see nothing." ("I see fog or film or sky or something of that sort.") Koffka used this as a basic result in *The Principles of Gestalt Psychology* (Koffka, 1935, pp. 111–124), and there has been a long series of repetitions of the experiment, all somewhat different, with a great deal of discussion (e.g., Avant, 1965; Cohen, 1957; Gibson & Waddell, 1952; Hochberg, Triebel & Seaman, 1951). What I interpret the experiment to mean is given in the memo called "Homogeneous optical stimulation and its implications for visual perception."[2]

As I say, Metzger faced his observer with a large, smooth, plaster wall, similar in principle to the theatrical cyclorama. In contrast, my observations, or the best ones, were made with hemispheres of diffusing plastic in front of the eyes (or a hemisphere of diffusing glass in front of the face in my original study; either eyecaps or a sort of face mask). The important fact to know about my apparatus, as opposed to Metzger's, is that it makes accommodation impossible, not just difficult. You can't accommodate your eyes for a diffusing surface either ¼ inch in front of your eyes or 1½ inches in front of your nose. It makes accommodation impossible, whereas in Metzger's experiment and in many of the repetitions, accommodation has been theoretically possible because the panoramic screen was anywhere from two to four feet from the subject. To make accommodation fail you have to have your screen extremely carefully painted and the plaster must be very fine. If there is even a speck of dirt on it, it will spoil the experiment.

---

[2]Unpublished manuscript, 1969, Cornell University archives. A package of "purple perils" was distributed to all attendees of the 1970 workshop. (Eds.)

I am saying that if the light coming to the nodal point of the eye has no discontinuities of intensity in different directions, then it is impossible to accommodate. That simple fact you will not find stated in any textbook of optics or physics. I finally realized that fact, and it is one of the reasons for developing ecological optics—that there is such a thing as unfocussable light. Ray theory can't account for this fact. Rays imply radiant light and the focussing of rays by a lens, whereas this fact implies *ambient* light. So, what this experiment demonstrated is that when the light available to the eye is wholly undifferentiated, then a retinal image cannot exist. It suggests that the ambient light at a point of observation is more fundamental for the theory of vision than the retinal image is, although we have taken the latter to be fundamental. If the light entering the eye is unfocussable, the light stimulating the retina will still constitute *stimulation* for the retina but it will not constitute stimulus *information*.

A vertebrate eye can extract information from ambient light only when the ocular system can form an image, and for this the ambient light must be structured. It must constitute an optic array having an arrangement. That is the central hypothesis of ecological optics. An "optic array" is best defined as a set of adjacent solid angles, at a point of observation, *not* as a set of light rays intersecting at a point, a "sheaf," so-called (an infinitely dense set of light rays all intersecting at a point). So, my definition implies *differences* of intensity in different directions, and that, I suggest, is distinguished from *different* intensities in different directions. Is that too subtle or is there not implied an important theoretical difference that we can discuss? My definition implies margins or contrasts in the array, not a distribution of intensities over the optic array.[3] The advantage of this definition is that margins or contrasts are included in the definitions of optics and do not have to be "explained" by physiology. That is, margins or contrasts of light outside the eye are invariant with changes of illumination from dawn to sunset. In a sense we have solved a large number of optical and perceptual problems by this new assumption. So in this case we must begin to think of the retina in a quite different way—not only as a receptor mosaic, but also as an organ. Conceived as a set of photo-receptors, the retina, when stimulated by homogeneous light will still send impulses up the optic nerve. The "classical" theory of perception (and also the theory of information processing for that matter) says that the impulses in the optic nerve are the basis of visual perception, and they have to be processed.

Well now, what possible theory would account for the fact that there are impulses in the optic nerve when you look into a clear blue sky and still you see "nothing?" There's still stimulation by light and there's still a train of impulses in the nerve but there's no perception. You may have a sensation of light. Hochberg and I used to work on this ten years ago. I'm still puzzled by this business and it has led to the present notions. But if you conceive of the retina as

---

[3]This idea is further developed in Gibson (1979a, pp.50–52) and in Ch. 1.7. (Eds.)

simply a part of a system for extracting information from an external array of light, then when stimulated by homogeneous light this organ is non-functional. That is, the retina considered as an organ for picking up structure isn't working because there isn't any structure. Your eye cannot function when you've got a half ping-pong ball in front of it or when you look into the clear blue sky. You cannot explore the array, and all the functions or activities of an ocular system are rendered non-functional by this condition, even though there is input for the system. In short the system cannot perceive although it is sensitive to light as such. That's the first difficulty that led up to the new concepts.

The second difficulty was the insufficiency of the old distinction between the distal stimulus and the proximal stimulus. I looked up the history of this distinction a few years ago. It was first formulated by Heider, I think, before it ever came to this country,[4] and was also adopted by Egon Brunswik (1940, 1944, 1956). Koffka (1935, pp. 79-80) used the distinction as a fundamental part of his *Principles of Gestalt Psychology*. You remember that the proximal stimulus was the retinal image and the distal, or distant, stimulus was the object in the world—so Koffka said and so Heider had assumed. Heider wrote a paper called "Thing and medium" (Heider, 1926/1959) in which he asked the question whether in the air (or in the medium between the object and the image) the object or thing in some sense existed, and he concluded that it did not, as physical optics also concludes. But that's one of the doctrines challenged by ecological optics.

What was this insufficiency? One part of it is that the objects in the world outside are not just objects, strictly speaking. Some of them are places and some of them are persons, who are not quite objects, and some are events. And I don't think we can describe an event as being an object. There may be still other types of stimulus sources. So it is more clear, I believe, to distinguish between the sources of light stimulation and the light stimulation proper. That, in turn, leads to a distinction between sources of light, such as the sun and these tubes (pointing to the fluorescent lamps on the ceiling.—Eds.) which send out photons and the sources of *reflected* light. The latter, I think, are different. If you read your textbook of physics, you will not find that there is any difference at all, between a surface reflecting light and a surface radiating light. The theory of reflection in physical optics is that when light falls on a surface, it's not just that a ray comes in and goes off again at an angle, it is that the atoms of the surface are stimulated to emit light. This is shocking! Reflection is reduced in physics to stimulated emission. At one level, of course, they're right, but that's not the level at which *we* need to discuss light.

The next objection to Heider's and Brunswik's and Koffka's distinction between the proximal and distal stimulus is that the distal stimulus, the source, is not a stimulus at all. That, of course, was really Koffka's point, that the object

---

[4]Much of Heider's work pertaining to perceptual theory and to the proximal-distal distinction is collected in Heider (1959). (Eds.)

does not stimulate the eye. Ninety-some percent of American psychologists and most ordinary people forget this when they write about objects and stimuli. I, as you know, wrote a paper (Gibson, 1960c) objecting to this confusion and I try never, never, to speak of an object as being a stimulus; or of an event as being a stimulus. They are sources of stimulus information. *Light* is a stimulus, and people and objects and events are *sources* of stimulus information, in a way to be discovered. So that's another objection; the sources are not the stimuli at all.

The word "stimulus" is a "weasel" word. For example, Koffka's failure to distinguish the proximal and distal stimuli sharply led to ambiguities. An important ambiguity was the term "microstructure" as used by Koffka (1935, pp. 114–115) and Metzger (1930). "Microstructure" was not assigned either to the world on the one hand or to the retinal image on the other, but had a sort of dual assignment to both worlds. In Metzger's experiment with the plaster wall which was looked at by an observer, if you turned the illumination up high he could see the surface at a fixed distance and in a specific color and at a specific slant, and *only* then could he see the surface. Metzger meant by "microstructure" the actual sand grains in the fine-textured plaster of his wall. But at the same time he meant the fine grain of the retinal image at the back of the eye when you *looked* at this plaster wall. Now that's an objectionable position to hold.

For those of you who are interested, we have a book by Brodatz (1966) consisting of photographs of what he calls "textures." It will illustrate the fact that not all the structures of substances can be called textures. Some of them are forms within forms. There are hierarchies of size-level in a sandy, pebbled beach, for example, which makes it inappropriate for us to use the single word "texture" to describe what a material surface is composed of. Moreover, Metzger and Koffka applied the word "texture" or "microstructure" to both the light and the substance. But Brodatz' photographs show that the texture of the light is entirely incommensurate with the texture of the material surface. If you study the photos you will observe the difference between the structure of the world and the structure of the light coming to an eye from the world. They've *got* to be distinguished, which is what Koffka didn't do. It's only the latter that contains *information* about the former.

When in the old book on the *Visual World* (Gibson, 1950a) I first introduced the term "texture," I wasn't any clearer about it. I meant by "texture" both texture in the world and texture in the light, and I thought the latter was in one-to-one projective correspondence with the former. I did, however, introduce the term "optical structure" and that concept leads to the notion of the "ambient array" and the "*structure* of the ambient array" at different levels of size. This is much better.

The third difficulty was the anomalies in my 1950 concept of "retinal gradients of texture." (I always meant to imply by this the *density* of retinal texture.) Gradients of density in the retinal image, I argued (Gibson, 1950a pp. 77–100), were *stimuli* for perception of slant. Did I mean a stimulus in the same sense that a needle sticking in you is a stimulus for a reflex? So I implied at the time. But this is incorrect. There are other anomalies that arose from these concepts. I had to assume that a picture in front of the eye was equivalent to a retinal image. And I did so assert in Chapter 4 of the *Visual World*. You could compare the retinal image to a picture, I argued, and the comparison had been valid ever since the first discoveries of optics. If one image happens to be right side up and the other upside down, that's no problem. We know that the *mind* turns the retinal image right side up again, or we *learn* to turn it right side up, according to Stratton (1896, 1897).

But this is not so. I now realize that a picture and a retinal image are entirely incommensurate. There's no comparison at all between the two, if for no other reason than simply this: a picture is something to be looked at by an observing eye and a retinal image is not to be looked at by an observing eye. You're up to your neck in the morass of the theory of "the-little-man-in-the-brain" the minute you make that assumption.

I began to doubt the assertion that the retinal image is equivalent to a picture, and when you begin to doubt that, you've got to go off in some quite new direction. I also began to doubt the concept of retinal gradients of density as stimuli for the perception of slant. That was my bright idea in 1950. Space perception of the world is made up of different slants. Slant was a variable, like the color or intensity of light. It was a sensation, I thought. And psychophysics (sacred psychophysics!) was going to be able to discover the correspondence between the gradient of density of texture and the slant of a surface.

For example, Howard Flock spent four years investigating this hypothesis (Flock, 1964a, 1964b, 1965). I suspect that he is still charmed by it, but it's just no good. It will not work.[5] You can't verify it. The original experiment on slant perception was done with a translucent screen and on the screen, from behind, we cast images of different gradients of density of texture, increasing density upward in different degrees or increasing density downward in different degrees. Subjects were asked to judge the slant of the surface that they saw as a result of this picture, but there was no simple psychophysical correspondence. What the subject saw was a *picture* of a slanted surface; or, even when you put the slanted surface behind a hole, there was a strong tendency for the slant of the surface to be *less* than that predicted by the gradient. The surface tended to come up and fill the hole, in the way that a film color does. At any rate we couldn't verify the tendency for slant to be in psychophysical correspondence with the gradient of density of texture.

I now suggest that the so-called variable of the slant of a surface away from the perpendicular to the line of sight is *not* a variable of which the world is made. Instead, the world is made of dihedral angles and curves, which are of a higher order than a simple metric variable like slant. The important variables are not

---

[5]See Gibson (1979a, pp. 149–150) for more discussion. (Eds.)

neat, metric ones that go from zero to a maximum. The concepts of corner, edge, convex and concave curves, protuberance or indentation are the components, I now think, of which the visual world is made.

Next difficulty, the fourth. In 1959, I published a chapter in the first volume of the Koch series entitled "Perception as a function of stimulation" (Gibson, 1959a). This was the high water mark of the psychophysical hypothesis that perception is to be accounted for by psychophysical correspondences, in the same way that sensation had been accounted for by psychophysical correspondences. But the notion of psychophysical functions for perception is not as good as it once sounded. To make perception dependent on stimulation, I had to postulate "higher order variables of stimulation." I meant by that variables of energy of higher order than frequency and intensity. But when anyone asked me what I meant by a "higher order variable," I couldn't explain. It was not simply the number of variables in a formula, nor was it the higher derivatives in calculus. It was a vague term. I should have talked about "invariance," or "invariant variables," but I hadn't thought enough about it at that time. So the notion of psychophysical functions in perception is something to be discussed at this workshop, perhaps, but I am prepared, at the moment, to say that I don't think the "variable" concept is going to work very well. We'll see. I have that puzzle for the moment unresolved. But certainly there were defects in the formula that perception is a mathematical *function* of a variable of stimulation.

There was a fifth difficulty having to do with the notions of "retinal motion" and "optical motion." Twenty years ago the idea was that there were gradients of velocity in a visual field, and that these gradients of velocity were analogous to the gradients of density of texture (Gibson, 1950a, pp. 117–137). Instead of the cue of motion parallax we now had a mathematical gradient of velocity along a meridian of the retinal image. No doubt this was an advance. But I had assumed that the velocity was taken relative to the retina. How in the world can you perceive a motion, I thought, unless a pencil of light scratches the retina in the way I scratch my skin? One perceives cutaneous motion by scratching the skin with a point; one perceives visual motion by scratching the retina with the point of a pencil of rays. Nobody ever doubted that and I didn't either. But this is very troublesome. The retina is undergoing tremor all the time and, furthermore, at some rate (roughly of the order of 5–10 per second) it makes saccadic jumps from one position to another, and the fact is that these movements of the eye, although they produce a motion of the retinal image relative to the retina, are not perceived at all. So it simply cannot be that the motion of the retinal image over the retina is the stimulus for the perception of motion.[6]

---

[6]This point is further substantiated by recent experiments on the amount of eye movements caused by normal head rotation (with seated posture). Traditionally, the vestibulo-ocular-reflex was supposed to eliminate any significant motion of the eyes due to bodily movements; however, recent experimental tests have falsified that assumption. Even with the small amount of head rotation

Is it possible, then, that we perceive motion not because there is optical motion relative to the retina but because there is optical motion relative to other motions? That is, you never perceive motion except as a "Gestalt," except in relation to other motions. So the gradient of velocities over an array is not many motions but only *one* motion which the ocular system picks up. That formula is what I would now substitute for the old notion of gradients of single stimulus velocities which have to be integrated by the brain. And that leads to the hypothesis that the gradient, the "Gestalt," is in the ambient optic array, not on the retina (Gibson, 1968a). There are insoluble paradoxes connected with the old assumption that what gives rise to the perception of motion is motion of the retinal image relative to the retina.

## II

So much for the difficulties of the old optics that suggested a new optics. Let me go on to some positive evidence. There was a series of discoveries, some made here at Cornell, which led in the new direction.

Many years ago I did experiments on what I called "adaptation to curvature" with a "negative aftereffect" (Gibson, 1933, 1937b). The original discovery of this curvature adaptation (and there are many other kinds), had been made with the procedure of wearing spectacles that bias the structure of the light entering the eyes instead of merely helping the eye to focus the rays, as ordinary spectacles are supposed to do. In about 1952 I read a book by Ivo Kohler of Innsbruck on the spectacle-wearing experiments (Kohler, 1951/1964). I was forced to realize that phenomenal adaptation to these optical distortions need not be retinal adaptations at all. You realize that when you are wearing spectacles on your head you move your head around, and you also move your eyes behind the spectacles. If you get adaptation of the phenomenal world under these conditions it cannot possibly be accounted for by local adaptation on the retina, because the retina is continually moving. Kohler originally called this discovery a "conditional after-effect" on the retina. He posed the fantastic idea that every time you moved your eye you changed the local state of adaptation of the retina. This is almost as astonishing as the original Helmholtzian theory that every time you move your eye, you shift the retinal local sign of each single receptor of the retina to just that extent you have moved your eye. What Ivo Kohler really proved, I think, is that the adaptation need not be retinal at all.

His discovery led me to suspect that the adaptation can occur for the whole visual system, not just for the retina. By the visual system I mean the eye-head exploratory system, not just the receptor mosaic on the retina. At least this much

produced by a casually seated person, there is a significant amount of eye movement not compensated for by reflex action (Skavenski, Hansen, Steinman & Winterson, 1979; Steinman & Winterson, 1980). (Eds.)

is clear, that the formula of the transposability of form over the retina, going back to Mach and the theorists of "Gestalt-quality," does not even approximately touch on the dimensions of the problem we must face. It isn't enough that a triangle is the same triangle whether it falls on one or another place on the retina. That much the physiologists have faced up to. It's not enough that forms are transposable over the retina; it's that the motion of the retina seems to be almost irrelevant in picking up the structure of what I now call the ambient optic array. So that this process of adaptation is adaptation to the structure of the light entering the eye, not of the retinal image.

A second discovery that led up to ecological optics came from an experiment done in Morrill Hall[7] with a device called the optical pseudotunnel (Gibson, Purdy, & Lawrence, 1955). This was a forty-foot layout which could produce the information for the perception of a cylindrical solid surface into which subjects looked, with the light inside the cylinder coming from a mysterious (non-visible) source. What could give this impression of a solid cylindrical tunnel was a non-solid set of large sheets of plastic with holes cut in them. Subjects looked through the holes into the distance. There were up to 30 sheets of plastic. If we worked very hard to make the cut edges of these sheets sharp then, when we used either all black or all white sheets, subjects would see nothing except a black or a white fog. That was because there were no contrasts in the optic array to the eye and therefore the eye could not detect the edges. The edges were there, but white-to-white or black-to-black doesn't give a contrast, and so there was no structure in the array. But then by alternating black and white sheets, the illumination being the same, the array was made to consist of a series of concentric rings. In *that* case you saw a solid cylindrical surface, painted black and white, going off for about 40 feet. Every subject reported that if the experimenter should put a ball at the other end of the tunnel it would roll all the way down to where he was seated. Subjects only began to report that it wasn't solid when the number of alternating sheets of black and white was reduced to eight or less. The information for surface perception was no longer compelling.

It was this experiment that led to the hypothesis of an optic array as contrasted with the retinal image. Above all, it led to the hypothesis of stimulus information as contrasted with stimulus energy. That is, I thought of this experiment as one in which *information,* not just stimulation, was controlled. Whether I had 4, 14, or 40 black-and-white rings in the array, the *amount* of light energy was identical, but the density of the array made for the perception of a solid surface in one case and of a non-solid non-surfacy thing in the other case. So we had controlled stimulus information, not just variables of stimulation, so I believed.

The optical tunnel was one experiment and similarly, at about the same time, my wife was working on the so-called "optical cliff" experiment with Dick

[7]Morril Hall was the building in which the Psychology Department at Cornell University was housed prior to its move to Uris Hall (where it is now). (Eds.)

Walk (Walk & Gibson, 1961). It was a pseudo-cliff, like the pseudo-tunnel. The optical cliff was an apparatus in which there was a perfectly solid glass surface on which a baby or a rat or chick could locomote, except that at a certain point the source of the optical texture which had been just under the glass dropped to being 6 feet below it. A virtual though not a substantial cliff was so produced, if the glass was perfectly clear, and hence, invisible. And as you remember, animals and babies refused to locomote over the edge, the optical but not substantial edge, because presumably they were afraid to. This experiment showed the importance of an animal's requirement for support, not only mechanical support (a substance under his feet to keep him from falling) but also *optical* support. Terrestrial animals need to *see* their feet in optical contact with a textured surface. They need optical information for support as well as vestibular, kinesthetic and tactual information. These two experiments encouraged me to believe that we could control the stimulus information in light for the perception not of space, but of the layout of the environment, including the ground under one's feet.

Third in our list of discoveries was the use of motion pictures for the study of motion. This work led to the realization that there is a special kind of motion in the world. I had been brought up on the idea that Isaac Newton's laws of motion are basic and so they are in a limited way. They are the basis of mechanics and of machine civilization. Newtonian motions are important, but as one investigates the laws of visual perception, one begins to realize that optical motion is altogether different from material motion. For example, the optical motions in a field of view when I am moving have no inertia. Maybe the photons of radiant energy, the stimuli for the photoreceptors, have inertia in some sense, but displacements or transformations in the field of view are non-inertial. At any rate that's worth discussing.

We also discovered, in the movie that my wife and I made on optical transformations as information for the perception of changing slant (Gibson, 1955b, 1957a; Gibson & Gibson, 1957), that there was great power in these *optical* motions to yield perception of events, of the *sources* of these motions in the world. This research and that of Johansson at Uppsala on event perception (Johansson, 1950) made us realize the potency of these optical changes. Note that these experiments do much more than yield simply the classical results on the perception of depth. It had long been known that motions could produce "depth effects";[8] they were "cues" for depth. What we were discovering were the parameters of optical transformations.

This set of experiments also led to the hypothesis that the perception of the rigidity of surfaces in motion underlies the facts of so-called "constancy" of shape and size. Size and shape constancy have been for a century an unsolved

---

[8]Braunstein (1976) reviews this literature. (Eds.)

puzzle in psychology. Despite all the experiments still being published on the phenomena, it looks as if we are no closer to a solution than we were at the start. If this rigidity hypothesis is right, then a deeper and more general problem takes the place of the old constancy problem. The puzzle of the invariance of phenomenal shape despite variation of retinal image-shape becomes irrelevant. This leads to what we will discuss later in the workshop, namely the hypothesis of "formless invariants" as constituting the information for objects and for the rigidity of the world during either motions of objects or locomotion of the observer.

Then, fourth, there is a whole series of experiments on the perception of the "terrain" or ground. For example, there were several experiments on the estimation of distance, along the ground on the grassy quadrangle in front of Morrill Hall (e.g., Purdy & Gibson, 1955). This was almost the first time, as far as I know, that a serious attempt was made at psychophysical judgments in a natural environment, rather than an artificial, simplified, laboratory set-up.[9] These experiments on the perception of the ground led to the hypothesis of the two hemispheres of the ambient optic array, the upper hemisphere corresponding to the sky and the lower hemisphere corresponding to the earth below the horizon. These experiments on terrain perception involved a bicycle with a target on it which could go off for 200 yards. The subject could see correctly how the target on the bicycle fractionated the distance to various marks along the ground, out to the end of the quadrangle. This accuracy was in radical contrast to what we know about distance judgments for objects in the sky, namely that they are very poor. In general you can't tell whether an object in the sky is large or small, far or near.

So there is a contrast between the definiteness of earth perception and the indefiniteness of sky perception. The hypothesis is that the information for the layout of surfaces in the lower hemisphere is rich, whereas the information for layout of objects in the sky is much impoverished.

### III

I have given you a sampling of the difficulties and the discoveries that led up to ecological optics. I said that I would also talk about the difference between physical optics, geometrical optics, and ecological optics. But what I am going to do is simply ask this question: According to each of these kinds of optics, how does one see an illuminated surface? That is, how is it *possible* to see an illuminated surface?

According to physical optics, the surface is only visible because the atoms of that surface are stimulated to emit photons by other photons falling on the surface. In short one sees the surface by virtue of the fact that it radiates light. It

---

[9]Some of the experiments reported in Gibson (1947) and discussed in Chs. 1.1, 2.2, and 3.1 herein were among the first naturalistic experiments on the psychophysics of perception. (Eds.)

is assumed that one must see light in order to see surfaces. And that is one of the hypotheses that I think can be challenged. I suggest that the seeing of surfaces by means of light is not *dependent* on the seeing of light.

If you assume that one has to see light, to have sensations of light, before one can see differences by means of light, you are in danger of falling into the pit of believing that there are no real surfaces in the world. This is a philosophical trap. Of course, there are surfaces! The ground does not consist of atoms colliding with the soles of the feet! The physicists who fall into this trap are confused about their levels of analysis. If light, in short, is taken to be mere radiation, instead of taking it to be a structured array (as I propose) you are in danger of falling into the error of Eddington (1929).

So much for physical optics. What does geometrical optics have to say about the possibility of seeing illuminated surfaces? According to geometrical optics, abstract rays of light are lawfully reflected from a surface. But the only kind of surface you ever read about in this business is the perfectly planar surface, the mirror or the perfectly *smooth* surface of a lens. This optics is able to deal with mirror images, and it permits the design of optical instruments. But it doesn't explain how we see the surfaces of the environment. There is talk of something called "scatter reflection" in classical optics but the attempts to mathematize it have not been very successful. And physicists don't seem to talk about it much because it's messy. In short the existing information about geometrical reflection of rays doesn't explain why most surfaces are visible.

What does ecological optics have to say about the seeing of surfaces? We take for granted the illumination of surfaces by radiant light. We assume that the reverberation of multiple-reflected light in a terrestrial medium reaches a steady state almost instantly. Having assumed that, we give up all further reference to photons, photon paths, and rays, and we talk about ambient light, consisting of a point in a medium at which there is the common apex of a whole array of solid angles. We no longer have points and bundles of rays, but rather solid angles coming to a point from the faces of objects. So we no longer define ambient light as different intensities in different directions, but as differences of intensity in different directions, and thereby say that a set of visual solid angles constitutes an optic array (see Gibson, 1966b, pp. 186–223).

We're led to the conception of an ambient optic array whose structure is invariant. We then have an explanation of how a surface is visible; it is visible by means of the structure of this array.

# 1.7

## On the Analysis of Change in the Optic Array*

Seven years ago Gunnar Johansson and I wrote papers that were published together.[1] We first acknowledged how much we agreed about event perception and then went on to say wherein we disagreed. It is the same now. We have common problems but our approaches differ. I would like to present him with another attempt to spell out the difference. My ecological optics is somewhat clearer now than it was and the terms in which I want to describe the optic array are more explicit.

Ecological optics asks two questions. First, how does the optic array at a point of observation carry information about the environment? This means information about both the persisting layout of the environment and the events that occur in the environment, the chief of which are changes in layout. I include under changes of layout rigid displacements of detached objects (mechanical motions) and non-rigid deformations of surfaces (water, mud, rubber, and living skin).

The second question is an extension of the first. How does the optic array at a *moving* point of observation carry information about the environment? This means information about persisting layout and change of layout, as in the first question, but it also of necessity means information about the movement of the point of observation itself, that is, locomotion. In this case a reconsideration of the relation between perception and proprioception is unavoidable, which is theoretically upsetting. Johansson formerly argued that this problem could be deferred. But I now think it is part of the problem of perception.

---

*Scandinavian Journal of Psychology, 1977, 18, 161–163. This issue of the journal was dedicated to Professor Gunnar Johansson of Uppsala University. Copyright 1977 by Almqvist and Wiksell, publishers. Reprinted by permission.
[1]Reprinted as Ch. 1.5 herein. (Eds.)

The principal hypotheses in answer to these two questions are as follows. An event is specified by a local change in the ambient array while locomotion is specified by a global change of the ambient array. The surface layout of the environment is specified by invariants of structure. In some respects the layout is specified by the structure of an unchanging array (as we have long realized from the classical studies of "space" perception) but it is specified in *more* respects by the invariants that underlie a changing array. The reason is that, for a set of opaque surfaces, more of them are specified when the perspectives are changing than when they are arrested, as when the observer is motionless.

We might agree that the above questions are good ones and that the hypotheses are at least promising. But the terms *array, structure,* and *change* have not been defined. What exactly *is* the ambient optic array? How can change of the array be analyzed and distinguished from non-change? Just here is where basic disagreement can enter in, and where approaches may differ. Consider first the notion of an array, and second the notion of a *changing* array.

An optic array can be thought of in two quite different ways, as a set of elements or as a manifold of parts. It might consist of spots or points in an otherwise empty extent or it might consist of adjacent forms in a wholly filled structure. The spots or points would correspond to bodies or atoms in space. The adjacent forms would correspond to the faces and facets of opaque surfaces in the terrestrial environment. In the first case space is empty, a vacuum. In the second case space is filled, a plenum. It is interesting to note that Democritus' theory of atoms in a void was appealing to early physicists because the atoms had vacancies to move in, whereas the parts of Aristotle's plenum could not move.[2] The atoms of a surface in modern optics correspond one-to-one with the focus-points of an image, whereas the faces and facets of surfaces in ecological optics correspond to the nested forms of a structure. The former correspondence is produced by a bundle of rays intersecting in a common point, a "pencil" of rays in projective geometry, whereas the latter correspondence is produced by a manifold of visual solid angles all having a common apex at the point of observation. The latter conception is unfamiliar, especially inasmuch as the solid angles are nested and each is unique. An optic array consisting of solid angles is very different from an optic array consisting of lines.

Similarly, *change* of an optic array can be thought of in quite different ways, as a set of motions of the elements of the array, or as a change in some or all of its parts. In the first case the elements can be either points or forms. If the elements are points some of them can be displaced relative to other fixed points, or relative to the empty field. But a point cannot be transformed in the way a form can be enlarged or foreshortened; instead a tranformation can be reduced to a set of

---

[2]This same distinction is also used in modern physics, where the "absolute" (empty) space of classical mechanics has come to be replaced by fields of force and a relativistic space-time-matter plenum (see Berkson, 1974). (Eds.)

displacements of points. A form can be displaced, it is true, but only when there is an empty field around it. If, on the other hand, the optic array is conceived as a manifold of adjacent parts, simple displacement of a part is not possible; the form will destroy another form when it is moved. It seems to follow that change of an optic array can only be analyzed as a set of motions when the physical theory of atoms-in-a-void is borrowed for the two-dimensional array. If the array is conceived as a manifold of parts, a filled structure, then motion analysis will not apply and a different kind of analysis must be invented that allows parts to appear and disappear in special ways. But there is no branch of mathematics that does this, so far as I know. Seemingly, we have not even *thought* about the geometry of appearance and disappearance, or creation and destruction. We only think about stimuli that go *on* and then *off* like lamps controlled by a switch.

The motions of optical elements in an array can be compared to the motions of material bodies in space, and then the powerful mathematics developed for mechanics and kinetics is available for the analysis of an array. This is what Johansson has developed with such success, together with his students, beginning with his monograph on "Configurations in Event Perception" (1950). It has only to be assumed that motions in two dimensions are related to motions in three dimensions by *projection*. One perceives depth through motion. Just as points are grouped into an object by proximity so moving points are grouped into a moving object by their common motion. One of the great achievements of Johansson was to take Wertheimer's vague law of "common fate" and give it precision and elegance by vector analysis.

In contrast to this precise analysis, the alternative that I have been struggling to formulate can only suggest that an optic array undergoes *disturbances of structure* including parts that come and go in various ways, some of them reversible and some not. Neither the motions of points nor the transformations of forms will describe these disturbances. They are brought about by the coming into sight and the going out of sight of surfaces (at occluding edges or at the horizon of the earth) during the locomotions of an observer and the motions of objects. These are reversible. And optical disturbances are also brought about by the going out of *existence* and the coming into *existence* of surfaces during the death and destruction or growth and creation of objects. These environmental events are not reversible. Difficult as it may be to formulate the parameters of all these optical disturbances it seems to me that we should try to do so.

The history of experiments on the perception of space and motion has been characterized by the assumption that objects and events in three dimensions are "projected" into forms and motions in two dimensions. A one-to-one correspondence is implied by that term and we then infer that the only problem is that of the third dimension of how the forms and motions are perceived in "depth." But this is not the right problem for perception. A one-to-one correspondence between a three-space and a two-space is impossible with opaque surfaces. The true problem is how surfaces are perceived when they are temporarily occluded, or hidden, or covered, that is, when they are not projected in the array at a fixed point of observation. The true problem is superposition, how two things are seen *in front* and *behind,* and how one thing is seen with both a *near side* and a *far side*. We should ask not how one can see the *depth* of the environment but how one can see a *cluttered* environment. The forms in the array corresponding to surfaces in the layout do not just move, they undergo what I call deletion and accretion (Gibson, Kaplan, Reynolds, & Wheeler, 1969). Progressive one-sided deletion or accretion specifies an occluding edge. This is an entity that, although not recognized in geometry, is an essential feature of an environment.

My way of analyzing a changing optic array takes into account this neglected fact. It is not so exact as Johansson's way. His way leads to more straightforward experiments than mine does. His experiments fit into the psychophysical tradition and mine do not. But he seems to suppose that since a physical event can be analyzed into the motions of physical elements, its optical counterpart can be analyzed into the motions of optical elements. If he does suppose this, I do not agree. Johansson's analysis will work for what might be called a *flat* event seen from the front, or a *transparent* event, with the essential parts of the machine or the man always projected in the array.[3] It will work for the motions and collisions in a frontal plane of objects like billiard balls. But it will not work for an ordinary event where one part goes out of sight behind another part and then comes back into sight again. I want to study the perception of ordinary events. This will be hard to do. But it will lead the psychology of perception in new directions, I think, and it will free our thinking from the last vestiges of the hopeless muddle of space perception, the lost third dimension, and the cues for depth.

---

[3]See Gibson (1976a) for a more detailed discussion of transparency. (Eds.)

# 1.8
## What is Involved in Surface Perception?*

The theory put forward in *The Ecological Approach to Visual Perception* (1979a) begins with the properties of surfaces instead of the traditional qualities of objects: color, form, location, and motion. What properties of a *surface* are perceivable? The following proposals extend what was said in Chapter 2 of that book. I can think of at least nine such surface properties. Most of them have been noticed by phenomenologists, but I assume that they are also *real*.[1]

Several facts about surfaces as distinguished from objects should be noted. First, a surface is not *discrete* like a detached object and thus surfaces are not denumerable. Instead, a surface is nested within superordinate surfaces. Second, a surface does not have a *location* as an object does, a locus in space. Instead, it is part of what I call the environmental *layout* it is situated relative to the other surfaces of the habitat underlaid by the ground, the surface of support. A Newtonian body has location relative to the three coordinate axes of mathematical space but these axes are not perceived; they are *thought of*. Hence the problem of how we *perceive* space is a false problem, and the unsolved puzzle of how we might perceive *locations* in space (on the basis of cutaneous or retinal "local signs") is a false puzzle. Third, a surface does not have a *color* in the sense of that term employed in physical optics, and does not have a *form* in the sense of that term used in plane geometry.

---

*Unpublished manuscript, May, 1979. (Cf. Gibson (1950c)).

[1]Husserl, the founder of phenomenology, considered objective properties to be outside of the stream of consciousness, but within consciousness as a whole (see Aquila, 1977, Ch.1). Later phenomenologists have argued that, while objective properties are real, they are nevertheless constituted by a subject (Thinès, 1977, Ch. 1). (Eds.)

An object, in this theory, is only a surface that stands out from the rest of the surface layout, the ground, because it is bounded by an occluding edge. This is an ecological fact, to which the figure-ground phenomenon is incidental.

What perceivable properties *does* a surface have? Here is a partial list: hard to soft, luminous or reflecting, illuminated to shaded, high to low reflectance, uniform to speckled reflectance, smooth to rough texture, opacity to transparency, dull to shiny, and hot to cold.[2] Note that some of these are accessible to both the visual and the haptic system in corroboration, some are accessible only to vision, and the last is accessible only to the skin system.

*1. The Property of Being Rigid, Viscous, or Fluid.* This is observable by palpating, prodding, or pounding the surface without seeing it, by seeing the "impact-character" of a collision without feeling it (as has recently been shown by Runeson at Uppsala)[3], or by both together. This distinguishing of rigidity-viscosity and firmness-softness, is a good beginning basis for later differentiating the variety of substances in the environment, and babies seem to do so at an early age (E. J. Gibson, Owsley & Johnston, 1978; E. J. Gibson, Owsley, Walker & Megaw-Nyce, 1979) long before they learn to apply names to them.

*2. The Property of Being Radiant or Reflecting.* A luminous surface emits light; an ordinary surface only reflects illumination. How are they distinguished visually? (e.g., Wallach on the quality of being luminous).[4] If heat accompanies the light, the source can also be detected by turning one's skin from side to side.

*3. The Property of Being Weakly or Strongly Illuminated.* If any surface in a layout is illuminated all of them are illuminated, and there are ambient optic arrays at all points in the air. But some faces of the layout are relatively "lighted" while some are relatively "shaded," and this fact is independent of the amount of light in the air. It depends on the inclination of the surface to the direction of the source, for one thing. How do we see whether a surface is in weak light or in strong light? A surface in weak light during the morning will be in strong light during the afternoon, and *vice versa*. *Ratios* of luminance among the visual solid angles of the ambient array must have something to do with it. You cannot tell by touching a surface, of course, whether and how much it is illuminated.

*4. The Property of High to Low Reflectance of the Incident Light.* The reflectance of a reflecting surface is intrinsic to the substance, i.e., the kind of sub-

---

[2]These are dimensional properties, and this analysis is descended from Gibson's (1933, 1937b, 1948) early theorizing on dimensional properties in perception. (Eds.)

[3]Runeson (1977) developed Michotte's (1963) work on the perception of causality with reference to classical mechanics and to ecological physics. (Eds.)

[4]See Wallach (1976, Ch.1). (Eds.)

stance it is. Reflectance is a diagnostic ratio, a fraction. The relative reflectances of all the surfaces in the layout are also invariant. How do we see them despite all the *fluctuations* of terrestrial and artificial illumination? I suggested in my new book (Gibson, 1979a, p. 86 ff.) that a *persistent* structure in an ambient optic array underlies the *changing* structure caused by the movement of the sun across the sky and the resulting interchange between surfaces that are lighted and shaded. Perhaps in this way one can see *both* the relative slants of surfaces in the layout and their relative reflectances. They are what persist; shadows fluctuate. The fact is that we can see the convexities and the colors of the surface layout *underneath* the shadows.

*5. The Property of Having Uniform or Non-uniform Reflectance.* The reflectance of a surface may be uniform or the surface may be speckled, spotted, patterned, pigmented, variegated, or the like. It is not enough merely to say that a surface has an intrinsic "color." A substance is often a conglomerate. The *natural* spotting of a surface characterizes the substance that underlies it, as does its texture (see below). But that fact is complicated by the presence in the human habitat of *artificially* spotted flat surfaces like drawing-pads and canvases, walls, screens, and writing paper. The original unspotted surface can often be recognized. The spots, traces, or deposits are man-made. Apart from what we call *stains* or *dirt* they are said to be *graphic*. And apart from those we call *purely decorative* they *stand for something other than the surface itself.* Hence they may induce a mediated awareness of this "other" along with the direct perception of the surface. These complex facts tend to confuse everybody, and the study of this kind of mediated perception is full of perplexities. But most of the experiments that illustrate Gestalt theory were carried out with man-made tracings on a surface.

*6. The Property of Being Smooth or Rough and, if the Latter, Whether the Texture is Coarse or Fine and, in either Case, What Form it Takes.* This property, especially the form of texture (rippled, pebbled, granular, ridged) is very characteristic of the underlying substance. It can be seen with exactness whenever the illumination has a prevailing direction, or is "glancing," but not so well when it is equal from all directions; then the illumination is said to be "flat." The smoothness, fineness, and roughness of a texture can be detected by rubbing it, as Katz (1925) showed (cf. Gibson, 1966b, p. 126 ff.).

*7. The Property of Being Dull or Shiny (Lustrous).* This property is related to its being unpolished or polished (specular). Luster seems to depend on the presence in the optic array of "highlights" on the surface. The property of being polished can be observed by rubbing the surface with the tips of the fingers. Is this the same as the property of being lustrous?

*8. The Property of Being Opaque or Transparent.*    The ordinary substances of the habitat transmit none of the incident light (they reflect some portion and absorb the rest). Their surfaces are opaque. A few natural substances transmit some or much of the light. Their surfaces, *if the interface is a flat plane*, are said to be transparent, more exactly semi-transparent. There is refraction at the surface, i.e., the rays of radiation are *bent*, but if a surface of pure water is unrippled, or if a sheet of clear glass is polished, the visual solid angles of an optic array have *essentially* the same structure and are not "distorted" by the surface (cf. the research on the wearing of distorting spectacles). I think this is what is meant by saying that the still surface of a pool or the parallel plane surfaces of the glass plate are *transparent:* one can perceive the essential properties of another surface behind it or, as we say, one can "see through it." Note that a *translucent* sheet (ground, pebbled, or diffusing) allows the passage of light but disrupts the structure of an array. An *opaque* sheet or screen blocks both the light and its structure. The edge of a transparent sheet does not *hide* or *conceal* but the edge of a translucent sheet does, as much as the edge of an opaque sheet. There can also be semi-transparent sheets that are only *partially* concealing or blurring, as some of Metelli's demonstrations seem to suggest.[5]

*9. The Property of Being at a Higher or Lower Temperature than the Skin.*    What we call hot, warm, neutral, cool, or cold "to the touch" is *relative* temperature. Psychologists have emphasized the sensation, but the useful perception of the state of the substance is what matters (Gibson, 1966b, Ch. 7). It is based on the direction and amount of heat flow into or out of the tissue. You cannot see this; you can only feel it.

## Persisting and Non-Persisting Surface Properties[6]

We can now observe that the most persistent properties of a surface are those numbered 4, 5, 6, 7 and 8, reflectance, natural spotting, texture, shininess, and transparency. The most changeable property of a surface is number 3, that of being lighted or shaded. This is because the general illumination in the medium fluctuates with day and night, with white light at noon and red light at sunset, with the sun going behind and coming out of a cloud, with the flickering of firelight or torchlight. Also the incident illumination on a surface fluctuates with the change from morning to afternoon, with the dappling of light under the trees in a wind, with the shifts of lighting as one carries a torch at night; and of course with the arbitrary "ons" and "offs" of artificial illumination. So transient is the illumination on a surface that one might even question whether or not it should be considered a "property" of the surface.

---

[5]Gibson (1976a) discusses transparency at greater length. Metelli (1974) and Kanizsa (1979, Ch.9) review this area of research. (Eds.)

[6]Cf. Ch. 4.7. (Eds.)

A somewhat more persisting property is number 9, the temperature of the surface and its substance. Number one, solidity, is quite stable at the ordinary temperatures of terrestrial substances, except for ice which melts at a not unusual level. Number two, being luminous, depends on a very hot substance (apart for the exceptional case of luminescence).

The perception of the properties of the persisting substances of the habitat is necessary if we are to know what they afford, what they are good for. But substances change with aging, fermenting, ripening, cooking, and melting. We can see the change in the surface. Persistence is not permanence. The widely accepted assumption that the child learns to apprehend the "permanence" of objects when he acquires the "object concept" is misleading and unnecessary. The question is this: how do we perceive which properties of a surface are persisting, which are fluctuating, and which are changing irreversibly?

## Fluctuation in the Ambient Optic Array

Substances change and surfaces undergo periodic changes of illumination but neither can be seen without a specifying change of some sort in the ambient optic array at a point of observation. Fluctuations of the shadow-structure of an array have not been studied experimentally under controlled conditions; only an unchanging shadow-structure.[7]

For example, you can see the surface of a lamp or a lighting fixture as luminous when it is radiating and non-luminous when it is not, in relation to the other surfaces of the room, with a steady-state optic array. If, however, the luminosity fluctuated like the surface of a flame, would not this discrimination be more exact and the perception more vivid?

You can see a shadow cast on a flat surface as a shadow if it has a penumbra, but as a stain on the surface if you eliminate the penumbra with a drawn line (the "ringed" shadow of Hering). Moreover, an artificial penumbra will convert a real stain into a shadow (MacLeod, 1932). But the apparent stain with a ring around it will be converted back into a shadow if the latter comes and goes, i.e., fluctuates, according to my observation. Similarly a patch of light that looks like a spot of white will be seen for what it is if it fluctuates.

You can see the convexities and concavities of a non-flat surface (the relief), by means of the stationary pattern of light and shade in the array, but only with some ambiguity. The convexities and concavities reverse if you are able to make the illumination seem to come from the opposite direction. If, however, the light source is actually moved back and forth over the layout so that the lighted and shaded surfaces interchange, and the shadow-structure of the array fluctuates, the relief is no longer ambiguous and does not reverse. So I conclude on the basis of informal motion picture studies.

---

[7]See Katz (1935), Hurvich & Jameson (1966), and Kanizsa (1979, Chs. 7,8, & 10) for reviews of work on color, brightness, shading and organization. (Eds.)

You can see the dullness or luster of a surface in a fixed array according as highlights are absent or present (cf. Beck, 1972). But it seems to me that the luster becomes more evident when you move the vase (or your head) and thus cause the highlights to shift relative to the texture.

You can see the transparency of a surface with an unchanging optic array, and this can be simulated experimentally, as noted above. But it can *also* be simulated when some of the interspersed spots of an array have one coherent motion and the remaining spots have another.[8] This change involves permutation of adjacent order. Two separated surfaces are vividly seen, the superposed surface being transparent.

The experiments reported in Chapter 9 of my new book (Gibson, 1979a) suggest that the optical information for seeing *surfaciness* is density in the array, a variable of *fixed* pattern. But the above experiment on interspersed random textures (Chapter 10), and Kaplan's experiment on the gain or loss of texture on one side of a contour (Chapter 11)[9], suggest that the information for seeing the *unity* or *coherence* of a surface has to do with *changing* pattern in time, not with fixed pattern. I mean the persisting aspects of the changing pattern. I suggested (p. 179 ff.) that what counts for surface perception is the *preservation* of adjacent order, that is, the *continued non-permutation* of order. Consider that the Brownian movement of spots in a microscope is what specifies a non-surface, a group of particles. Then the continuous unbroken connectedness of a true surface at the ecological level of reality is specified by what I can only call the absence of Brownian movement![10]

Note that a persistently unchanging pattern of a natural optic array specifies a great deal about the surfaces surrounding an observer: that they do not change during the period of observation. A changing pattern of the natural array specifies still more about the surfaces: how they change during the period of observation and how the observer moves. Possible ambiguities are eliminated. The *artificially arrested* pattern of the peculiar optic array coming from a picture is a different matter; you cannot always tell whether the state of a pictured surface is a persisting one or is only the instantaneous cross-section of a changing state.

## The Ecological Level of Reality[11]

A surface is the interface between a substance and the medium. The notion of a substance and of degrees of substantiality should not be confused with the physical concept of matter; it is connected with the complicated "states" of matter the gaseous state being wholly insubstantial and the liquid to solid states being increasingly substantial (for terrestrial animals). Continuous substantial surfaces

---

[8]See Gibson (1979a, pp.179–180) and also Mace & Shaw (1974). (Eds.)

[9]See Ch. 2.7. (Eds.)

[10]This hypothesis was strikingly confirmed by Lappin, Doner & Kottas (1980). (Eds.)

[11]Cf. Ch. 4.9. (Eds.)

are not real for physics, but they are primary realities for ecology and for the kind of psychology founded on it.

Animals perceive surfaces and their properties, since animal behavior must be controlled by what the surfaces and their substances afford. (They also perceive the *layout* of surfaces and what the invariants of layout afford, but that is not the main concern of this essay.) There is a need to study the perception of surfaces with a realistic attitude as well as with a phenomenological attitude. The approach advocated is much closer to Gestalt theory than it is to input processing theory ("information" processing, so-called). It is a sort of *ecological* Gestalt theory.

# 2 MOVEMENT AND MOTION: THE PERCEPTION OF ACTION AND EVENTS

Edward Reed
and Rebecca Jones

## INTRODUCTION

The papers in this section represent Gibson's work in the area that traditionally has been called motion perception. His contribution to this field of research is unique, because he alone approached the problem of perceiving motion with a concern for the visual planning and control of bodily movements. All other investigators of visual motion perception, from Mach (1875) to Braunstein (1976), have assumed that the fundamental problem of motion perception is to explain how we see the motion of discrete elements in the field of view, and as a result, their theories are severely limited. Gibson's theory of the perception of both action and events stands alone as a comprehensive account of how active, moving observers perceive the motion of objects and their own bodily movements within the structured environment.[1]

The motivation for Gibson's expansion of the traditional domain of motion perception came from his concern with practical aspects of vision, such as steering a car (Ch. 2.1),

---

[1]Following Gibson (1954b) we use "movement" to refer to displacements of the self, and "motion" to refer to displacements of objects. This terminology calls attention to Gibson's important distinction between the perception of environmental events and the perception of the self acting within the environment. (Eds.)

flying a plane (Ch. 2.2), and general orientation (Ch.2.3). Based on his consideration of these basic functions of vision, Gibson (1954b, 1958c; Ch. 2.6) argued that
the problem of motion perception, traditionally conceived as a single problem,
actually involves three related problems: the perception of objects in motion, the
perception of changes within a more or less stable environment, and the perception of the self moving through the environment. Distinguishing among these
kinds of motion perception led to Gibson's discovery that useful perception
requires movement through environmental space and time and that movement, in
turn, requires perceptual guidance. In emphasizing bodily movement in perceiving, Gibson was able to integrate his novel theory of space perception (Ch. 1.1;
1950a) with his radical account of motion perception (Ch. 2.2). After the development of ecological optics and the theory of information pickup (Chs. 1.3,
1.4, 4.4), Gibson's account of space and motion perception formed the basis for
his general theory of orientation, locomotion, proprioception, and event perception (Chs. 2.3-2.9).

"A theoretical field analysis of automobile driving" (Ch. 2.1), Gibson's
earliest study of movement perception, arose out of his interest in understanding
the perceptual aspects of automobile steering, a skill on which he prided himself.
Dissatisfied with the usefulness of learning theories then current for explaining
the planning and guiding involved in this practical activity, Gibson and his
colleague, Crooks, ingeniously adapted Lewin's (1936) field theory of social
behavior to explain the visual control of driving. As if following Lewin's advice
that "there is nothing so practical as a good theory," Gibson and Crooks elaborated a theoretical account of how drivers can maneuver within the field of safe
travel by using varieties of perceptual information. This is the oldest essay of
Gibson's included in this volume, and, in its anticipation of his later ideas about
visually controlled movement (Gibson, 1979a; Lee, 1976) and the theory of
affordances (Gibson, 1977b; Ch. 4.9), this paper reveals some of the lasting
influence of Gestalt field theory on Gibson's thinking.

The research reported in "The ability to judge distance and space in terms of
the retinal motion cue" (Ch. 2.2) represents Gibson's first attempt to relate his
ground theory of space perception (Ch. 1.1) to the problem of layout perception
during movement. Here again a practical problem, the perception of distance by
airplane pilots, motivated the extension and refinement of Gibson's theory so that
it could apply to perception outside the laboratory. As a result of considering the
perceptual requirements of airplane landing, Gibson formulated an account of
what he then called the "retinal motion cue" for perceiving both the layout of the
stable, three-dimensional environment and one's movements with respect to that
environment. The crucial role of changing stimulation in perception, established
in this paper, was fundamental to all of Gibson's later thinking.

In "Visually controlled locomotion and visual orientation in animals" (Ch.
2.3), Gibson integrated the results of his studies on layout perception (Gibson,
1952b; Gibson & Mowrer, 1938), motion perception (Gibson & Gibson, 1957;

Ch. 1.2), and movement perception (Chs. 2.1, 2.2; Gibson, Olum, & Rosenblatt, 1955) into a comprehensive theory explaining the perception of the environment and of the self moving through the environment. Rejecting S-R models as inappropriate for explaining purposive actions, and rejecting the theory of cognitive maps because of its failure to consider the perceptual information required for the control of locomotion, Gibson formulated his own theory of the planning and execution of movements. This theory included, first, an account of the information available in changing stimulation for the spatial layout of the environment and for the locomotion of observers through that environment, and, second, the articulation of formulae describing how animals might use such information. This theory of visually guided movement represents an early version of the ecological approach to ambulatory vision, which later was refined and elaborated (Gibson, 1979a, Ch. 13; Lee, 1976, 1980b).

Gibson's work on self perception during movement led him to reconsider the traditional accounts of proprioception and the relation between acting and perceiving. In "The uses of proprioception and the detection of propriospecific information" (Ch. 2.4), he outlined an ecological theory of proprioception. Beginning with the idea that all perception is based on information in stimulation (Chs. 1.3, 4.3, 4.4), Gibson developed a theory of propriospecific information and its functions. This theory included a description of the information available to specify the self and its movements and suggestions of ways in which animals might detect and use that information. Thus, he rejected both the traditional theory that holds proprioception to be based on the stimulation of proprioceptors, and the modern theory that holds proprioception to be an outcome of a comparison between stimulus inputs and efferent outputs. Instead, Gibson argued that proprioception is based on the detection of propriospecific information by all the perceptual systems. In this paper, and especially in his book, *The Senses Considered as Perceptual Systems* (1966b), Gibson extended this radical theory of proprioception to explain how perceiving and acting are related. Rejecting the theory that the sensory–motor dichotomy applies to perceiving and acting, he proposed that each involves both sensory and motor processes. He argued that perceiving and acting constitute two general types of purposive behavior with different (yet mutually supportive) functions. The function of perceiving is to investigate the environment, to formulate goals, and to guide action, whereas the function of acting is to execute movements, to accomplish goals, and to provide new information for perception. This distinction between perceiving and acting is the basis for Gibson's characterization of the process of perceiving as the adjustment of perceptual systems to environmental structures by means of the detection of information.

Gibson's persistent emphasis on the perceptual guidance of behavior led him to formulate a new theory of the functions and mechanisms of the external as well as the propriospecific senses. "The problem of temporal order in stimulation and perception" (Ch. 2.5) brings together several different strands of Gibson's thinking concerning the exteroceptive function of the perceptual systems. Because the normal biological use of the senses is to enable mobile creatures to plan and control their actions, Gibson argued that perception takes place over time and that all perception—even the perception of stable aspects of the environment—is based on changing stimulation. To explain the mechanisms of perception in organisms that purposefully move their sense organs in order to perceive, Gibson revised and extended Lashley's theory of temporal organization in the nervous system. For Gibson, the mechanisms of perception are not central responses to peripheral receptor activity but are processes of coordination between an observer and relevant aspects of the environment. Perception is accomplished by the purposive attunement of this coordination process (involving the movements of the body, both effector and receptor organs as well as neural loops between effectors and receptors) to information contained in changing patterns of energy in the media of the environment.

In "What gives rise to the perception of motion?" (Ch. 2.6), Gibson presented a detailed account of the information available in the changing optic array for motion and of the processes involved in scanning the array with the visual system. He argued that the information for motion cannot be motion on the retina, because such motions occur several times a second when our eyes move without there being any motion in the world. Instead, he argued that there are unique changing structures in the ambient optic array that serve as the information for both object motion and observer movements. A local deformation of the optic array specifies the motion of a detached object against a persisting background, a progressive deformation along the equatorial region of the optic array specifies head rotation, and motion perspective (a global expansion or contraction of the array, originating and receding at its polar regions) specifies locomotion in a stable environment. An animal apprehends these and other kinds of events by running its eyes over structured ambient light, coordinating a complex of afferent–efferent loops to the information specifying the event to be detected. Cognition, memory, motivation, and other factors affect which aspects of an event are attended to, and the organization of the processes of attending, but they do not affect the information itself.

The visual perception of motion and movement thus depends on structured ambient light that results from changes and persistences in the environment. In "The change from visible to invisible: A study of optical transitions" (Ch. 2.7), Gibson and his colleagues examined the optical information specifying the different types of events that involve a change from invisible to visible, such as going out of and coming into sight as well as going out of and coming into existence. They showed that each type of motion in the world gives rise to unique optical deformations or transitions in the ambient optic array. A particularly important case for Gibson was the occlusion or concealing of one surface by another, which always occurs during locomotion. When observers move, they change their point of view, so that objects that were hidden by nearer surfaces come into view. A reverse of the movement puts them out of sight. The information for the occlusion or disocclusion of one surface by another consists of the progressive accretion and deletion of optical texture in the ambient array.

The fact that a surface that has gone out of sight because of a change in point of view will come back into sight when a reverse movement is made is the "principle of reversible occlusion" (Gibson, 1970b, 1979a, pp. 191-195). Reversible occlusion is fundamental to the theory of event perception because it explains the perceived continuity and coherence of the world: The world behind our heads does not go out of existence, and there is optical information that specifies its persistence. Furthermore, the puzzle of the relation between perceived space and motion, raised in Gibson's early work on visual guidance of vehicles (Chs. 2.1 & 2.2), begins to be solved by the theory of occlusion. What cannot be seen from here now may be seen from here in a while (visual prediction of occluded motion: Gottsdanker, 1956; Reynolds, 1968; Rosenbaum, 1975), or it may be seen from there now (visual perception of another person's perspective on a scene: Gibson & Pick, 1963), or it may be seen from there in a while (cognitive mapping: Heft, 1981; McIntyre, Hardwick, & Pick, 1976; Menzel, 1978). The theory of occlusion explains why visual space and motion perception are inextricably connected, and why the visual perception of motion is intimately related to the visual perception of self-movement. To see one's position and movement within the environment involves seeing what is out of sight from here, and also seeing how to move to make it come into sight.

Gibson's concern with motion and movement perception led him to believe that an understanding of how we perceive spatially and temporally extended events is crucial to any theory of perception. In "The problem of event perception" (Ch. 2.8), Gibson tackled this challenging problem from an ecological point of view. Included is a definition of an event, a classification of ecological events, and an analysis of the information for events. The ecological approach to events requires transcending both the physical and phenomenal viewpoints of events. Ecological events are not just motions of objects in physical space, because the directions, orientations, occlusions, and qualitative changes of environmental objects are what matters to observing organisms; nor are events merely sequences of states of awareness; they are distinctly real environmental happenings. Gibson's work on events demonstrates that a scientific description of the environment at the ecological level of reality (Ch. 4.9) is both possible and fruitful.

Magical events are events that appear to break the ecological laws of physics, or the laws we tacitly know about events. In "Ecological physics, magic, and reality" (Ch. 2.9), Gibson postulated several laws of ecological physics and, in the context of these laws, examined how magicians can suppress the information for actually occurring events, while at the same time providing information for impossible events. The explanation of questions about the conditions under which existing surfaces can be seen or can exist unseen leads to important issues in event perception and clarification of the laws of ecological physics.

The central issues of perceptual theories in the past have always been the recognition and detection of patterns, objects, and space. Within this conceptual framework, motion and bodily movement become secondary, conceptualized as merely the detection of displacements of elements, objects or the body. The immense variety of biologically important events, including the events involved in bodily actions, have by and large been ignored. Until Gibson's work, questions concerning these biologically basic functions of event perception and visual self-movement perception had barely been raised. Gibson's decades-long insistence that the fundamental problem of visual perception is to explain how moving animals simultaneously perceive both the eventful environment and their actions within it has enriched the psychology of perception enormously.

# 2.1 A Theoretical Field-Analysis of Automobile-Driving*

Of all the skills demanded by contemporary civilization, the one of driving an automobile is certainly the most important to the individual, in the sense at least that a defect in it is the greatest threat to his life (Stoeckel, May & Kirby, 1936). But despite the consequent importance of knowledge about the nature and acquisition of this skill, no more than a beginning in this direction has been made by psychologists, and that chiefly in the field of devising tests to measure some of its inferred components (DeSilva, 1935). A systematic set of concepts is needed in terms of which we can describe precisely what goes on when a man drives an automobile, and such a theory, if it is to be useful, must have practical as well as psychological validity. The following paper has been written in the effort to make a systematic description of this sort.

When this undertaking was first proposed, the effort was made to base the analysis upon the more familiar concepts of present-day psychology—habits, attitudes, and response-sequences. In this effort, however, the writers had but small success. Very little in the way of a useful theory emerged. They finally concluded that the task of the automobile driver is so predominantly a perceptual task, and that the *overt* reactions are so relatively simple and easily learned, that the analysis has to be carried out on a perceptual level and with concepts more appropriate to this requirement. Their alternative was, therefore, to utilize concepts like the "field" of the driver, "valences," and the general cross-sectional method employed by Lewin (1936).

*American Journal of Psychology, 1938, 51, 453–471, written in collaboration with L. E. Crooks. Copyright 1982 by E. J. Gibson. Reprinted by permission. The original note to this article reads, "This article is the outcome of discussions between a psychologist and a practical student of driving."

From this starting point it was possible to formulate a theory better suited to the facts at hand. We may assume that driving is a type of locomotion through a "terrain" or field of space. It is psychologically analogous to walking or running, except that driving is locomotion by means of a tool; that is to say, the automobile can be thought of as a tool for more effective locomotion in the same way that a club is a tool for more effective striking. The primitive function of locomotion is to move the individual from one point of space to another, the "destination." In the course of simple locomotion "obstacles" are met with, i.e. are seen, and the locomotion itself must be appropriately modified in order to avoid them. "Collision" with an obstacle stops locomotion and may produce bodily injury. Locomotion is therefore guided chiefly by vision, and this guidance is given in terms of a "path" within the visual field of the individual such that obstacles are avoided and the destination ultimately reached. These concepts of *terrain, destination, obstacle, collision* and *path* should be applicable to any type of locomotion, whether that of the infant learning to walk, the open field runner in football, or the operator of an automobile. It might seem more logical to apply them first to the simpler types, but nevertheless we shall attempt to work them into a theory of automobile driving, with the idea that a general hypothesis which would cover the more difficult problem would assuredly include valid principles for the solution of the simpler ones.

## THE FIELD OF SAFE TRAVEL AND THE NATURE OF STEERING

The visual field of the driver is a rather special sort of field in several respects. It is selective in that the elements of the field which are pertinent to locomotion stand out, are attended to, while non-pertinent elements, such as "scenery," normally recede into the background. The most important part of the terrain included in this pertinent field is the road. Within the boundaries of the road lies, according to our hypothesis, an indefinitely bounded field which we will name the *field of safe travel*. It consists, at any given moment, of the *field of possible paths which the car may take unimpeded.*[1] Phenomenally it is a sort of tongue protruding forward along the road. Its boundaries are chiefly determined by objects or features of the terrain with a negative "valence" in perception—in other words obstacles. The field of safe travel itself has a positive "valence," more especially along its mid-line. By *valences,* positive or negative, we refer to the meanings of objects by virtue of which we move toward some of them and away from others. The valences of objects with respect to locomotion may be

---

[1]The field of safe travel can be expressed formally as a field within which the time to contact of the driver's vehicle and any object is sufficiently long to afford maneuvering around that object. Lee (1976, 1980b) has derived a dimensionless invariant of optical flow that characterizes the optical information for optimally safe travel. (Eds.)

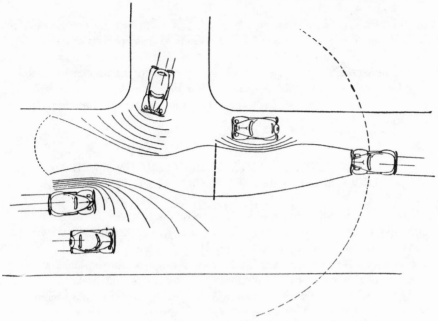

**FIG. 9.**  The field of safe travel and the minimum stopping zone of a driver in traffic.

(If, in this and the following figures, the page is turned around and the figure is viewed from what is now the right, the reader may the better be able to empathize the situation, since he will then have the point of view of the driver of the car whose field of safe travel is under discussion.)

quite different ones from their valences with respect to eating or esthetic enjoyment when the individual is not simply propelling himself between them.[2] For instance, a hot-dog wagon has a negative valence with respect to locomotion, but a positive one with respect to appetite.

Fig. 9 is a representation of this field at a specific instant. The field of safe travel, it should be noted, is a spatial field but it is not fixed in physical space. The car is moving and the field moves with the car *through* space. Its point of reference is not the stationary objects of the environment, but the driver himself. It is not, however, merely a subjective experience of the driver. It exists objectively as the actual field within which the car can safely operate, whether or not the driver is aware of it.[3] It shifts and changes continually, bending and twisting with the road, and also elongating or contracting, widening or narrowing, according as obstacles encroach upon it and limit its boundaries. As will later be evident, other factors may also serve to constrict these boundaries, but for the present we may point out that its depth is limited by frontal obstacles such as

---

[2]Because of this property, valences are not affordances (cf. Ch. 4.9). (Eds.)

[3]This contradicts the Gestalt notion of two environments, one phenomenal, one physical (cf. Ch. 4.9 and Gibson, 1971b). (Eds.)

other vehicles, policemen and stop lights, and its width by "marginal" obstacles like curbs, ditches, soft shoulders, walls, parked cars, pedestrians or "white lines."

It is now possible to define precisely the operation of steering an automobile. *Steering, according to this hypothesis, is a perceptually governed series of reactions by the driver of such a sort as to keep the car headed into the middle of the field of safe travel.*[4]

## THE DETERMINANTS OF ACCELERATING AND DECELERATING, AND THE MINIMUM STOPPING ZONE

Collisions are avoided during all kinds of locomotion by one of two methods—changing the direction of the motion or stopping it. For the driver of the car this means steering away, or decelerating. Having offered a hypothesis for the former, we have next to consider the problem of what factors determine the response of taking the foot off the throttle or stepping on the brake.

First, however, the question arises: What initiates and maintains locomotion itself? In the simplest case we may suppose that speed of locomotion is a function of the urge within the individual toward his destination. This directed motive—"vector" if one prefers the word—may be consciously represented by the experience of "hurry." It is, of course, perfectly true that people frequently drive an automobile without any specific destination. Driving "for pleasure" may be considered, however, in common with most play, the using of a tool or a skill for its own sake. If driving is locomotion with a tool—a very ingenious, elaborate, and versatile tool—it is not surprising that like most tools its manipulation, once acquired, may be an end in itself. Speed of locomotion in this situation becomes a very complex matter; but, limiting ourselves to the simpler case, it appears that locomotion is maintained and augmented by a motive of the simplest kind to be found in all behavior—that of "going somewhere."

Accelerating is then a function of this motive. To what may we ascribe decelerating? Once more, to take the simplest case and disregarding such limits on speed as legal taboos, we may suppose that it occurs when the field of safe travel visibly contracts, and that stopping, like steering, is primarily an avoidance reaction to obstacles. In the diagram of Fig. 9, for example, if the car ahead, which is apparently passing the other, is instead turning into the side street, then the field of safe travel will be cut off and our driver will, it is to be hoped, stop.

We do not, however, have as yet a sufficiently precise description. How much

---

[4]In later discussions of locomotion Gibson (1979a, Ch.13) abandoned the notion of a series of reactions in favor of the concept of action systems which seek optima that are specified by perceptual information. (Eds.)

contraction of the field of safe travel can occur, and what is the relation between contraction and deceleration? The answer is given by another field concept. There is within the field of safe travel another zone, phenomenally less precise but behaviorally and objectively just as real, which is set by the minimum braking distance required to stop the car. It is the zone within which our driver could stop if he had to, and it can be supposed to be present implicitly in every driver's field. How accurately it accords with reality is another question. Unlike the field of safe travel, the size of this *minimum stopping zone* is dependent on the speed of the car—and also, it may be noted, on the condition of the road-surface and of the brakes (Stoeckel, May & Kirby, 1936, p.176). The driver's awareness of how fast he is going does not consist of any estimate in miles per hour; instead, he is aware, among other things, of this distance within which he could stop.

Normally, the forward margin of the minimum stopping zone is well behind the forward boundary of the field of safe travel. Speed may be increased up to the point where the zone nears the size of the field, and when this happens driving begins to feel "dangerous." For the experienced driver, the car is in a sense projected to its potential location at the front of this zone. Hence, when the field of safe travel contracts by reason of an obstacle which encroaches upon it, deceleration occurs *in proportion as the forward margin of the field recedes toward the minimum stopping zone.*

A sudden frontal contraction or a shearing off of the field of safe travel, which cuts it down to or below the minimum stopping zone, produces in the driver a feeling of imminent collision, sometimes approaching panic, and an immediate and maximum braking reaction. There is an "emergency." Much more frequently, however, there occurs a gradual contraction of the field, and, as it approaches the front boundary of the zone, there follows a gradual slowing reaction of such strength as to keep the zone continually smaller than the field.

The ratio of depth-of-field to depth-of-zone which tends to be maintained in given traffic conditions by a given driver is probably to a large extent habitual. It might be designated as the *field-zone ratio* and thought of as an index of cautiousness. The ratio may be expected to decrease when the driver is in a hurry.[5]

Expressions of the foregoing principle may be found in such common-sense rules as never driving so fast that one cannot stop within the "assured clear course," and never "overdriving" one's brakes or one's headlights. Inattentiveness in the driver usually means that objects in the terrain or inside the car which are not pertinent to locomotion stand out in his visual field and that consequently his field of safe travel, if it exists at all, may become incorrectly bounded. The

---

[5]Except for emergencies, more efficient brakes on an automobile will not in themselves make driving the automobile any safer. Better brakes will reduce the absolute size of the minimum stopping zone, it is true, but the driver soon learns this new zone and, since it is his field-zone ratio which remains constant, he allows only the same relative margin between field and zone as before.

*objective* field of safe travel contracts until it threatens to get below the stopping-zone, or does so, without a corresponding contraction of the *behavioral* field.[6] Frequently, it may be suggested, the remedy is not merely increased vigilance or tension in the driver, but the development by learning of semi-automatic perceptual habits and motor habits such that a safe margin is maintained between stopping zone and field of safe travel.[7]

When an obstacle suddenly cuts off the field of safe travel well inside of the stopping zone—an "emergency"—an entirely new field may open up which did not exist an instant before (Fig. 10). Obstacles such as the shoulder of the road, or the curb, or even a shallow ditch which just previously had a minus valence may take on a positive valence and become no longer obstacles but a field of travel. The possibilities for the opening up of a new field depend on the driver's sensitivity to the pertinent field as a whole, and upon the degree to which this field is imbued with meaning for locomotion. The negative valences of obstacles vary in strength, some being more-to-be-avoided than others. The experienced and skillful driver is able to shift his field of travel with considerable flexibility in case of an "emergency" and thereby avoid a collision. In such a case the field of safe travel is highly relative. It might be called the field of safest travel.

The bearing of our hypothesis on the problem of high speed driving is not hard to make out. A good road which is free from traffic offers a very much expanded field of safe travel. The driver's urge toward his destination, especially if he is one who tends to maintain a fairly constant field-zone ratio, will result in high speed. He tends to feel that a higher ratio between field and zone than is demanded by safety is wasteful of time. With increasing speed, however, the minimum stopping zone extends farther and farther down the road. Accordingly the field of safe travel must at all times extend even farther down the road in proportion. Even with a perfectly clear highway a limit to this extension is eventually reached, since obstacles become harder to see as their distance increases, the acuteness of human vision being what it is. Since, at very high speeds, the driver's attention must be fixed at greater and greater distances—for he has to operate farther and farther ahead in his visual field and scan the road for increasingly minimal cues—the purely sensory task of seeing the zone and the

---

[6]This statement is consistent with the Gestalt distinction between the phenomenal and the physical environment (see above, note 3). (Eds.)

[7]The relative importance of effortful attention and of habit in safe driving needs to be worked out. It seems to be assumed, on the basis of what motorists say to police officers after accidents, that most accidents are "caused" by inattention. Hence, it is concluded, drivers need to be warned sternly of their responsibility to be attentive. Such an inference is characteristic of the theological psychology of legal thinking. It is more likely that drivers need to be taught safe habits, among which is the habit of attending to the field-zone ratio. Contemporary safety campaigns tend to emphasize the factor of vigilance and to play upon the fear-motive to such an extent that the development of correct habits may be hampered in some drivers. These campaigns (e.g. *And Sudden Death*) may be more successful in producing attitudes of timidity than in improving the average driver's performance. If drivers *knew how* to drive safely most of them would do so.

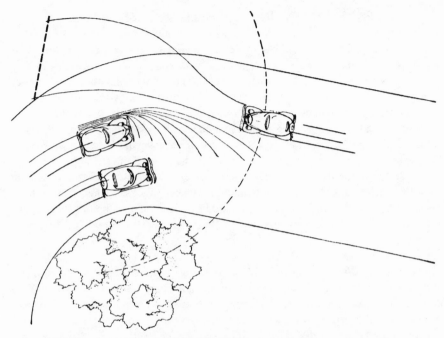

FIG. 10.   Sudden reorganization of the field of safe travel to meet an emergency. An unforeseen contraction of the old field below the minimum stopping zone.

field correctly is more difficult, the strain is greater, and chances for error multiply.

These two fields which have been proposed cannot of course be conceived of as visible, strictly speaking, in the sense that an object with a contour is visible. Nor are their boundaries sharply defined as are lines and contours, although for convenience we may diagram them as if they were. They are *fields within which certain behavior is possible*. When they are perceived as such by the driver, the seeing and the doing are merged in the same experience. Since their boundaries are set by behavioral possibilities, these boundaries are more or less correct and appear as transitions more or less sharp depending on the skill and experience of the driver. Driving skill largely consists, we suggest, in the organization, within the pertinent visual field of the driver, of a correctly bounded stopping zone for the entire repertory of speeds, roads, and surface conditions, and a field of safe travel which is precisely moulded to the actual and potential obstacles in the total field at any given instant. In other words, the field must be shaped in accordance with the objective possibilities for locomotion. If we add that there are concurrent motor reactions which maintain a safe and constant ratio between these two, and which keep the car running in the middle of the field of travel, we shall have described the basic operations of driving an automobile.

## FACTORS LIMITING THE FIELD OF SAFE TRAVEL

*1. Natural Boundaries.*    So far we have said that the driver's field of travel is limited and shaped by obstacles which encroach upon it, but this statement is by no means complete. Limits to this field of the possible seen paths which the car may take may be set, not only by obstacles, but also by physical and physiological factors. Such limitations are, first, the distance at which daylight vision becomes inadequate, because of purely optical factors; secondly, the margins of the field lighted by headlights; thirdly, constriction of the field by fog, snow, *etc.;* fourthly, the diminishing or even the destruction of the field by glare from oncoming headlights; and, finally, such physical limits as the horizon at the top of a hill which the driver is approaching. All these factors, when they cause a diminishing of the field-zone ratio, should bring about a reaction of deceleration. Outside of these natural boundaries of the field there lurk what we shall call *potential* obstacles.

*2. Inflexibility at Higher Speeds.*    Another fact which limits the field of potential paths of the car is that it may not include sharp turns at high speed. The field, of course, conforms to the turns of the road and to obstacles on its edges, but it cannot conform by curving more than a certain amount for a certain speed without the occurrence of skidding. One may conceive that the centrifugal force which produces a skid operates as a kind of potential obstacle which encroaches on the concave side of a field of safe travel (Fig. 11). The field becomes less flexible, more rigid or straighter, with higher speed, for the reason that, if one turns too sharply, one is literally likely to "run into" a skid. This description of skidding may at first sound implausible because we tend to identify skidding with the obstacle *into which* we may skid; but an examination of Fig. 11 will show that, while the field of possible paths is bounded on the right by actual obstacles, it is bounded on the left by the potential skid which would occur if the car were swung into it. At a given speed, the feeling of losing *traction* with the road is projected into the terrain ahead in such a way as to make certain paths impossible.

*3. Obstacles and their "Clearance Lines."*    It has already been stated that obstacles limit the field of safe travel by virtue of their minus valence for locomotion. The open terrain between the obstacles, if it leads off toward the destination, has a plus valence. This negative valence of an obstacle, we could suppose, is an indicator of the consequences of collision with the object in question. The child learning to walk about probably learns these valences rather readily. An object or place which is attractive to the child induces locomotion toward it. In the course of such locomotions, the child bumps against fixed objects in his field, such as furniture, and, as a result of these collisions, acquires a repertory of avoidance responses to them. These avoidances are superimposed

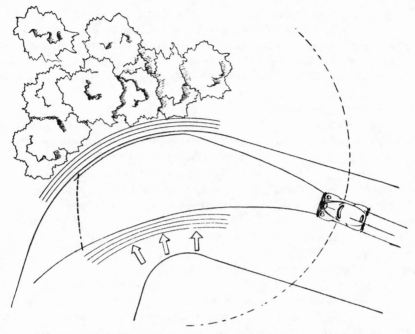

FIG. 11.   Inflexibility of the field of safe travel at high speed. The field is bounded on the right by fixed obstacles and on the left, at this speed, by a projected feeling of the potential skid.

on the general activity of locomotion, and, taking place as they do only in the immediate neighborhood of the obstacle, they can be represented in the child's field by a negative valence of the obstacle and of the space immediately surrounding it. We can thus suppose that every obstacle comes to have a sort of halo of avoidance, and that this halo can be represented by "lines of clearance" surrounding it. In analogy with contour lines on a map, we could draw lines of equal negative valence around an obstacle, each line as it gets closer to the obstacle representing a greater intensity. Locomotion in a field containing obstacles would then be a matter of moving *toward* the destination and at the same time *away* from obstacles. The resultant of these two tendencies, summating the motives (vectors) at each point, yields the *path* of locomotion.[8]

For the automobile driver these concepts can be taken over in their entirety. The driver has learned at least the essentials of locomotion when he learned to walk, and learning to drive is mostly learning the use of the tool. His field of safe travel is at every moment bounded and shaped by the halos of obstacles in the

---

[8]The possibility that this analysis carried further is capable of explaining "round-about" behavior is worth considering. Lewin suggests that the detour performance requires a "restructuring" of the field and "insight"—an extra hypothesis which may not be necessary. (Eds.: cf. the discussion at the end of Ch. 2.3 and Gibson, 1979a, pp. 195-200.)

terrain. It is a reasonable hypothesis, moreover, that the more injurious a collision with an obstacle would be, the more it is avoided and the greater is the extent of its clearance-lines. Some obstacles would then affect the field of safe travel more than others. For example, a heavy bus approaching at great speed would have more clearance-lines than a model-T Ford; and a precipice would have more clearance-lines than a shallow ditch.

4. *Moving Obstacles.* We are now in a position to deal with obstacles more fully. Two cases must be distinguished: that for stationary and that for moving obstacles. In the former case (curbs, trees, parked cars) the clearance lines radiate from the physical location of the obstacle and affect the field of safe travel as it impinges on this location. Figs. 9–11 have represented this state of affairs. For a moving obstacle (vehicle, person, animal) the clearance lines radiate from *the point where the obstacle will be when the driver's car comes closest to it,* or in other words from the point of potential collision.[9] Consequently one may for example steer *toward* the present position of a moving pedestrian (Fig. 12), since, in effect, one is steering away from where he will be when the car reaches him. Likewise a car ahead going in the same direction may, at high speeds, actually be inside the field of safe travel without affecting it, since its clearance-lines are projected far ahead in the field where it would be if it stopped (Fig. 13). In general, the greater the speed of a moving obstacle, the farther ahead of it are its clearance-lines projected. Likewise, for all obstacles moving toward the driver, whether from the front or from one side, the greater their speed, the more do their clearance lines encroach upon the field of safe travel. Finally, the more unpredictable the movement of an obstacle, the more extensive are its clearance-lines. Examples would be cars behaving "strangely," blind men, children (especially on bicycles), and old people. A street-car should have few and narrow clearance-lines to the side, since its lateral movement is usually predictable and negligible. A parked car with a driver visibly sitting in it should have a wider halo than one without a driver, since the former may suddenly pull away from the curb.

It should be remarked here that the correct location of the clearance-lines of a moving vehicle ahead demands, not only a sort of projection of this vehicle to the proper point in its own path, but also the correct projection of one's own car to the point of intersection of the two paths. Both one's own and the other person's field of safe travel are jointly involved. An example is given in Fig. 14. In other words an "estimate" of the speed of the obstacle plus an "estimate" of the speed of one's own car are combined—although the term *estimate* is misleading since there seems to be no conscious process of calculation involved. Here is a case of a highly complex situation, involving relationships between two speeds of movement, which would not be an easy problem to solve with pencil, paper, and

---

[9]This is related to the focus of expansion (see Chs. 1.2 and 2.2) in locomotion. (Eds.)

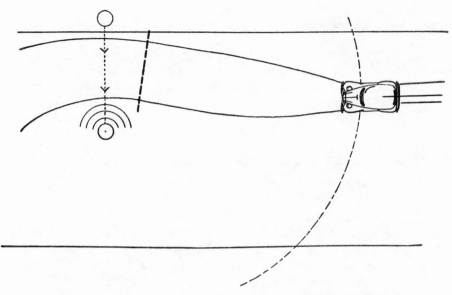

FIG. 12. The field of safe travel as determined by the *future* clearance-lines of a moving pedestrian.

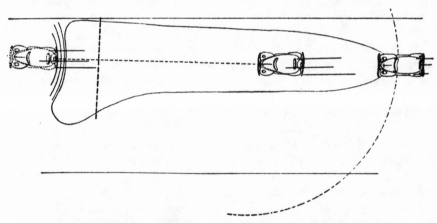

FIG. 13. The field of safe travel at relatively high speed, where a moving obstacle is physically within the field but where its projected clearance-lines determine the forward margin of the field.

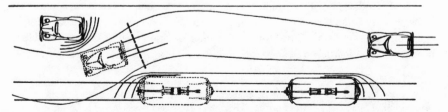

FIG. 14. A driver attempting to pass a street-car before reaching a parked car. At this instant the field of safe travel looks open, since the clearance-lines of the trolley are projected as indicated for the moment when he will be passing it.

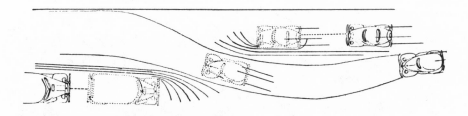

FIG. 15.    A driver passing with intent to cut in. An integration of three perceived speeds of movement is involved in the seeing of this open field of safe travel.

formulae; but for the skillful driver the perceptual field-situation may be immediate, clear, and (let us hope) accurate. Complex "estimates" of speed and location are represented in the experience of the driver only by the simple seeing of an open or a closed field of safe travel. In Fig. 15, which represents a driver passing the car ahead in the face of an oncoming driver, there is involved a projection of *three* cars, with *three* speeds of movement, to their correct positions at a future instant. Here indeed is a very extraordinary type of perceptual "constancy-phenomenon."[10]

5. *Potential Obstacles.*    In addition to the actual obstacles which at any moment are encroaching upon the field of travel to some degree, there may be in the pertinent field *barriers to sight* which also throw out lines of clearance. For the trained driver, any intervening object from behind which a moving obstacle might suddenly cut into the field of travel—a building, a blind corner, or even a parked car—radiates clearance lines (Fig. 16), because it has a secondary or indirect negative valence. The limits to the field of safe travel imposed by darkness beyond the headlight-zone, by fog and by curves or by the brow of a hill ahead, likewise constitute such barriers. Behind them there are *potential* obstacles. There may or may not be *actual* obstacles behind them; the objective field of safe travel may or may not be clear; but, since the driver can react only to his subjective field, the latter is properly shaped and limited by these barriers.

It must be admitted that for the average driver potential obstacles do not have the potency of visible obstacles. Very frequently one of these barriers to sight is not recognized, its negative valence is not perceived, and the field of safe travel is incorrectly related to the objective possibilities for locomotion. Psychologically this fact is not surprising, for the existence of a potential obstacle behind the barrier must be learned by experience and its negative valence transferred to the

[10]The movement-perceptions of the three objects in question are subject in a very striking way to the principle of "constancy." When one considers the actual stimulus-cues for the perceived speed of the approaching car, the to-be-passed car, and finally the driver's own car, and realizes that these speeds are perceived in relation to a phenomenally stationary road, the degree of "phenomenal regression" away from the stimuli and toward "reality" is astounding.

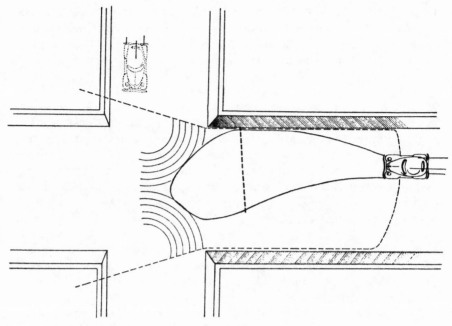

FIG. 16.    A blind corner constituting a barrier to vision and its effect on the field
of safe travel.
At this moment the clearance-lines of potential obstacles cut off the field.

barrier. Probably each new type of sight-barrier which is met necessitates a new
process of learning. More frequently, a barrier representing potential obstacles of
low valence is disregarded. Even the most cautious driver undoubtedly drives on
faith under certain circumstances. For example, a blind stop-street which enters
the highway ahead does not usually affect the field of safe travel, although
occasionally it conceals an automobile which will not stop at the intersection. A
green traffic-signal is interpreted as a *guarantee* that the field will remain open
and that unseen cars on the crossroad will not enter it. It is invariably assumed
that the road does not end abruptly in a stone wall just out of sight over the brow
of the hill ahead—a very probable assumption, to be sure, but still an assumption. It is also generally assumed that the absence of warning signs by the
highway means the absence of obstacles for which one should be warned.

The driver's field of safe travel, as he reacts to it, is delimited, we now see, by
*probable* as well as by seen obstacles. Equally, it is not delimited by *improbable*
obstacles. The more probable types of obstacles are usually indicated by highway signs, crossing signals, and the like, to which the driver supposedly learns
to react as he would to the obstacles themselves. But the highway signs vary
considerably in different parts of the country, and they are usually put up without
any regard for the actual probabilities of the obstacles in question. The average
driver becomes dimly aware that he must calculate the probabilities of the road

for himself without much dependence on highway signs and consequently comes to perceive them as merely legal obstacles to which he must conform, when he does, for reasons distinct from the necessities of location. Their negative valence is based on potential legal consequences rather than potential collision.

6. *Legal Obstacles and Legal Taboos.*   The field of safe travel is modified, not only by the various types of obstacles already described, but also by perceived symbols—more specifically by signals, gestures, signs and markings. The traffic signal showing red and the traffic policeman with arms outstretched are the most obvious examples. Arm signals and the stoplights of the car ahead are cues which enlarge its clearance lines or shift them to one side. Highway markings indicating lanes and the areas around fireplugs are symbolic obstacles, as are "private" signs on driveways and roads. Finally, "stop" signs at intersections, blinkers, and a variety of highway signs, "slow," "curve," "school," "speed limit 20 m.p.h." and the like, affect the field of safe travel with varying degrees of effectiveness. Too frequently they are not reliable indicators of the objective possibilities for locomotion and, as we have suggested, become purely legal taboos. A sign which is not occasionally "reinforced" will in the end no longer stand for anything, as students of the conditioned response are well aware.

There are, accordingly, in the pertinent field of the driver, obstacles whose negative valence is partially or wholly legal. This fact is illustrated by their greatly increased negative valence when a traffic policeman is present in the field as compared with the same field without the policeman. Likewise, maneuvers, which are warranted by the visible field-conditions but are legally tabooed, are seldom made in the visible presence of the law, as for example passing on curves where the field of view is unrestricted, or at a clear intersection where another road enters only from the right. Traffic laws being absolute can agree only roughly with the actual facts of dangerous driving. From the point of view of the driver who undertakes to drive safely but also skillfully and efficiently, the unrealistic legal restrictions present a problem of compromise.

## THE FIELD OF THE OTHER DRIVER

It has been said that driving an automobile is a highly individualistic activity. There is no way of communicating with another driver except by way of the horn, or by arm signals—neither of which is a particularly sociable mode of interaction. As a consequence perhaps of this anonymity on the road, the situation is one conducive to competitive rather than cooperative attitudes. Each driver tends to think of his own task and to regard the other drivers merely as obstacles.

On the other hand, the driver does take into account the field of the other person. It is always assumed, for example, that *the other driver sees you.* The clearance lines of an approaching car are projected, not as if it were simply an inanimate moving obstacle or an incalculable agent, but on the assumption that it is avoiding you as much as you are avoiding it. More specifically, it is assumed that the other driver's field of safe travel does not overlap yours. To speak of an "assumption" is, of course, inadequate, but the behavioral fact remains. For example, when a driver sees two cars approaching on a two-lane road and the rear car swings out to pass with the intention of cutting in before the various paths meet, the driver is usually very much aware of his own menacing aspect in the field of the passing driver. Frequently he uses his advantage to the utmost, maintaining speed despite his dubiously open field of safe travel, in the bold manner of a dog facing a canine trespasser on home ground (Fig. 17).

Another example is the use of the horn, by which one announces one's presence as an obstacle encroaching on the other person's field. If the other person behaves as if he did *not* see you—if his field of safe travel is apparently incorrect—then his clearance lines encroach unduly on one's own field. In this situation blowing the horn simply expands one's *own* clearance lines in the other person's field, advertising that "I am a dangerous obstacle," and one goes on the

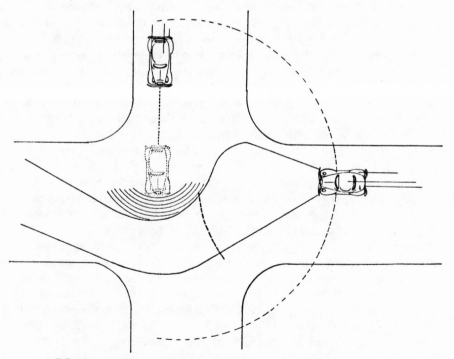

FIG. 17.  Bluffing at an intersection.
A driver projecting his field of safe travel on the assumption that he is a formidable obstacle in the other driver's field.

faith that this expansion of clearance lines in the other's field will indirectly clear up one's own at present constricted field. The obstacle, one trusts, will stop.

Occasionally, however, the obstacle itself may decide to advertise its dangerousness and behave in a powerful and unyielding fashion. We then have the situation of mutual bluffing. Each driver expands his own clearance lines to the utmost, maintaining speed or using the horn, and they may persist even up to the point where their respective minimum stopping zones touch. At this point we may leave them to their fate.

## THE CAR ITSELF AS A FIELD

The perceptions of the driver are organized into a number of spatial fields, each being a sort of projection of the behavioral opportunities, each being a space within which certain behavior is possible and outside of which it is impossible. Within the field pertinent to locomotion are the field of safe travel, the minimum stopping zone, and on some occasions the field of the approaching driver or pedestrian. When the driver prepares to stop, overtake, or make a turn, his pertinent field *includes the road behind* for the reason that he must not encroach too suddenly on the field of safe travel of a potential driver who is coming up fast from the rear. The rear-vision mirror is the usual mediator of this rearward field. Finally, there is still another field which needs to be taken into account—that of the car in which the driver is sitting. We suggested that the car was a tool whose use was locomotion. It is also a sort of field which yields a variety of perceptual cues and which invites and supports specific actions. The impressions constituting it are kinesthetic, tactual, and auditory, as well as visual, and they interact with the impressions from the terrain to produce the totality of cues on which the driving-process is based. The "feel" of the car or the "behavior" of the car are terms which indicate what is meant by this particular field of experience.

In the first place, locomotion involves a feeling of contact with the terrain together with a feeling of exerting force against it. In the case of the driver these feelings are referred to the car; the actual impressions are secondary and indirect. The feeling of driving on an icy surface is similar to the feeling of walking on ice despite the different cues and different muscular movement involved. The perception of *traction* is therefore an important feature of the driving process.[11] Under extreme conditions, as when rain freezes on the road, locomotion takes place predominantly by means of kinesthetic and tactual cues from the car-field. The driver "feels his way" along the road. It is evident that he projects his actual impressions into the car-field and may be said to feel the road with the car in the same sense that one feels the ground with a walkingstick.

---

[11]This is a foreshadowing of Gibson's later hypothesis that information is available to perceptual systems, not to sense channels (cf. Gibson, 1966b, p. 54ff., p. 230). (Eds.)

In the second place locomotion involves a constant orientation with respect to the path. The car, as we have already suggested, is kept pointed into the middle of the field of safe travel; the two are kept in alignment. The car is, therefore, something which can be oriented, pointed or aligned, and this characteristic depends on those sensory cues which go to make up the car-field. During a skid the car becomes disoriented with respect to its path. If the driver, however, maintains *his own* orientation to it and if the skid is only a moderate one, he can correct the car's orientation by simply steering into the middle of the field of safe travel.[12] But if the skid turns the car completely around or if the driver is unskilled, his own personal orientation to the path may be lost. The car is then "out of control," primarily because the *driver* is disoriented.

In the third place, locomotion involves the maintenance of an upright position. The tilt of the car on a high-crowned road and the corresponding pull of the wheel, the centrifugal force and the sway on a sharp curve, all contribute to the driver's sense of his car and the feeling of its stability or lack of it.[13]

Enough has been said to indicate the nature of the car field. This field which the driver inhabits is one in which the impression and the action are especially intimately merged. The impression and the action imply one another. In common with other tools, it has a set of potentialities—a certain repertory of performances which the skillful driver knows and utilizes fully and of which even the tyro is forced to take some account. A high degree of driving skill demands a complete sensitivity to and control over this field. If this demand is fulfilled, the car tends to become, like any properly used tool, simply a sort of physical extension of the driver's body.


## APPLICATION

The situation which faces highway-safety officials in dealing with a public who insist on killing themselves at an ever-increasing rate is similar to that of a bewildered parent dealing with a bad child. Despite past failure, the only thing the parent knows to do is to admonish him oftener and spank him harder. A wise procedure would be first to try to understand what is going on in the child's head. Frequently the child does not *want* to misbehave, and most assuredly the driver does not *want* to kill himself.

Intelligent measures toward educating the public to drive safely can only be taken when the performance of driving an automobile is thoroughly understood. Programs of testing and experimenting are necessary, but useful only if they have some theory to go on. Discussion of the problem should be disinterested rather than merely admonitory, should adopt the driver's point of view rather than the

---

[12]Note that our definition of steering obviates the necessity of any "rule" for getting out of a skid.
[13]Cf. Gibson (1952b) and Gibson & Mowrer (1938). (Eds.)

safety engineer's, should start from normal rather than abnormal driving, and should emphasize what the driver ought to do rather than what he ought not to do.

If driving is to be taught successfully—and there are already courses in a number of adult education and public school systems—it must be taught in terms which the driver will recognize. The concepts employed must refer to operations which the driver understands. If teaching is to be more than merely the memorizing of the local legal restrictions, the "causes" of accidents as listed in statistical tables, a list of "bad driving" practices, and a series of assorted "don'ts," then a systematic theory of driving is needed which can be verified by observation and experimentation. The theory which has been described is an effort in this direction.

Safe and efficient driving is a matter of living up to the psychological laws of locomotion in a spatial field. The driver's field of safe travel and his minimum stopping zone must accord with the objective possibilities, and a ratio greater than unity must be maintained between them. This is the basic principle. High speed, slippery roads, night driving, sharp curves, heavy traffic, and the like are "dangerous," when they are, because they tend to put the driver's field of safe travel out of correspondence with reality. The various "bad driving practices" are bad, when they are, for a reason and not simply because the traffic cop says so. The reason lies in the psychological principles; the "rules of the road" follow from these principles and it is the principles, not the rules, which need to be taught.

The skillful driver recognizes the valences of obstacles quickly and automatically and projects their clearance-lines correctly. He knows the boundary lines of a potential skid on the curve ahead in precise relation to his speed, the road surface, and the characteristics of his car. A sudden shift of the events in his field will lead to an immediate reorganization of the field-relations and not to a disintegration of them in panic. He calculates the other driver's field of travel with sagacity and never allows it to overlap his own. Finally, he does all these things because he has learned to do them, not because he is frightened into a continual state of strained attention.

# 2.2

The Ability to Judge
Distance and Space
in Terms of the Retinal
Motion Cue*

The distance perception heretofore discussed (in Ch. 1.1) has been that of a stationary observer. The flier, however, is in motion. It is primarily because he is in motion that distance perception is so important to him. The stimulus of retinal motion perspective as a basis for distance has been described only in part. Its nature and application to the perception of aerial space during flight may next be considered.

## TYPES OF RETINAL STIMULATION IN RELATION TO VISUAL MOTION PERCEPTION

The retina may be stimulated by motion, or more exactly, the retinal image may undergo motion, in two general ways. The first and simplest is relative displacement. In this case the image corresponding to an object is displaced in relation to the image corresponding to the rest of the world, i.e., the image of the background against which the object-image is located. This is the stimulus that exists when an object in the visual scene moves. The relative displacement is the same whether the eyes follow the moving object or not. The second may be called deformation. In this less familiar type of stimulation, the image is distorted as a whole; it stretches or expands or contracts rather than merely being transposed. This sort of change obviously does not physically occur in real objects, or at least

*This selection contains pp.219-230 of Gibson (1947) and was written in collaboration with N. M. Glaser. Chapter 1.1 contains portions of earlier sections of this chapter of Gibson (1947), and chapter 3.1 contains a portion of a later chapter of the same volume.

solid objects, but it happens all the time to our retinal images—especially to the image of the terrain or background. The fact to be especially noted is that the retinal image over the whole retina, the image representing the entire visual field, may undergo this kind of motion, i.e., may flow at different rates in different parts.[1]

Having distinguished between retinal displacement and retinal deformation, the kinds of visually perceived motion which correspond to them can be stated. The general rule may be formulated that whenever the *observer himself* moves, the retinal image corresponding to the whole visual field undergoes deformation. The converse is also true. When the observer's body is motionless, there is *no* deformation of the retinal image as a whole.

When *objects* move, the corresponding object-images within the retinal image of the field undergo relative displacement (and may also undergo deformation if the objects move toward or away from us) but the retinal background-image of the whole field does not undergo deformation. This rule holds even though the eyes may move from one fixation to another or may fixate a moving object, *so long as the head does not move*, i.e., so long as the *position* of the eyes in space does not change.

When *both* the observer and objects move in a three-dimensional space, there occurs both deformation of the retinal background-image, and displacement (possibly with deformation) of the retinal object-images. Both the observer's own movement and the movement of objects are perceived simultaneously, under normal circumstances, without any interference between the two kinds of perception.[2]

The importance of these distinctions lies in the fact that deformation of the retinal background-image yields not only the perception of subjective motion but provides a powerful stimulus for space perception. Different aspects of this deformation are specific not only to the direction of one's motion and to the velocity of one's motion, but also to its angle of inclination of the surface at which one is looking, to the distance of all points of the surface, and in fact to the distance of all stationary objects in one's field of vision. Considered as a stimulus-correlate for distance, the flowing deformation of the retinal image is identical with what we have called retinal motion perspective.

In order to avoid complicating the discussion unnecessarily one assumption should be made at this point. For the sake of simplicity and for the time being, it will be assumed that the eyes of the moving observer are always fixated at an infinitely distant point such as the horizon, and therefore motionless in his head.

---

[1]This distinction between retinal motions due to object *motion* as versus those due to an organism's *movement* through the environment is further analyzed in Gibson (1954b). Cf. 1950a, p. 132, p. 224. (Eds.)

[2]This duality of perceiving later became a central theme of Gibson's (1979a, Ch.10) ecological theory of vision. Visual perception of self-movement—which Gibson (1950a, p.124) later termed "visual kinesthesis" or "visual proprioception"—is a necessary accompaniment of the visual perception of external objects and events by an observer. (Eds.)

In other words we will disregard movements of the eyes, particularly pursuit movements. The retinal displacement produced when the eyes of a moving observer themselves rotate can be considered independently and therefore the problem can be deferred.[3]

*Retinal Motion Perspective.*   When the observer moves, the retinal image flows at different rates on his retina in an exactly inverse relation to the distances of the corresponding points or objects in the world. The more distant the point, the less its velocity. The line of the horizon, for example, does not move on the retina. Objects at distances which are for practical purposes infinite will not move either. Consider the appearance of the visual world on a clear night, when the observer is flying or driving a car through it. The stars, the moon, and the horizon do not undergo any deformation whatever; their distance is so great that the observer does not change position in relation to them or, in other words, the parallax is zero. But the terrain and the objects on it flow across the visual field, slowly at distant points and more and more rapidly at points nearer the observer. The differences in the rate of flow are dependent on differences in distance, since the nearer points change their direction from the observer, and are therefore retinally displaced, faster than the further points. There exists a certain degree of parallax which is inversely proportional to the distance. Considering this fact as a matter of different velocities stimulating the retina at the same moment, the phenomenon is what we have termed motion perspective.[4]

In addition to the fact that the velocity of this retinal flow approaches zero for very distant objects and vanishes, therefore, at the horizon, it also approaches zero and vanishes at two specific points in the visual world—the point toward which the observer is moving and its opposite, the point he is moving away from. For example, it is a familiar fact that an object in the direct line of an observer's progress yields retinal motion only to the extent that it expands; the exact point on the object at which locomotion is aimed does not move at all. Optically speaking, therefore, the world expands radially outward as the observer moves into it, and, assuming he looks backward, contracts radially inward as he moves away from it. The expansion may be noticed when one drives a car on a straight road, particularly at night, and looks at a distant point ahead. The corresponding contraction is most easily observed from the rear end of a train.

Figure 18 shows diagramatically the general character of retinal motion

---

[3]Hay (1966) gives a mathematical account of the effects of eye and head movement on these optical displacements and deformations; cf. Lee and Lishman (1977a,b) for further discussion. (Eds.)

[4]Implicit in this account is the idea that motion parallax is a special case of motion perspective (see Gibson, *et al.*, 1955; Gibson *et al.*, 1959). Motion perspective is the general case of optical flow produced by a moving observer, and motion parallax is the special case of motion perspective where there is no gradient of retinal deformation. Under these special circumstances the distinction between retinal displacement and retinal deformation breaks down. Hence, motion parallax can be produced by object motion or by bodily movement, but the perceptual effects of these two modes of production are not identical (cf. Rogers & Graham, 1979). (Eds.)

FIG. 18.   Retinal motion perspective looking ahead.

perspective as it exists when the observer is moving and looking straight ahead over a level terrain. The arrows are vectors and the length of each arrow represents the retinal velocity in the field of view at that particular point in the field.[5] These velocities exist, of course, as *continuous gradients* rather than as separate *displacements* on the retina. The retinal image is deformed as a whole. A gradient of velocity is a rate of change of velocity, not a velocity as such. The distinction is important, since the hypothesis will be advanced that the *gradients* in the retinal field and the direction of these gradients rather than the velocities themselves are the effective stimuli for the perception of distance, space, and locomotion.

In Figure 18 it should be noted that there is a gradient of velocities varying from zero at the horizon to a maximum at the near region of the ground. From the observer to the horizon in any direction, this gradient of *velocity* is repeated. The *direction* of all retinal velocities is radially outward from the point toward which one is moving, i.e., from the "center of expansion." In Figure 18 the center of expansion is on the horizon because the observer is assumed to be moving parallel to the terrain.

Figure 19 shows the motion perspective when the eyes are looking not ahead but to the right, as for example in looking out the side window of a plane or train. All velocities vanish at the horizon. They reach their maximum at the point directly under the observer, which point of course cannot be represented in the diagram. The vanishing of all velocities at the horizon is analogous in this

---

[5]Eye and head movements deform these *retinal* vectors, but cannot deform the externally existing optic array vectors (cf. Ch.2.6). (Eds.)

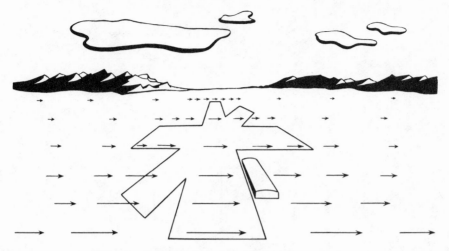

FIG. 19.    Retinal motion perspective looking to the right.

diagram to the vanishing of all sizes on the horizon, and in fact the gradient of decreasing velocity upward on the flat visual field is similar to the corresponding gradient of retinal size. In this diagram, at least, retinal motion perspective is similar to size perspective and to linear perspective. Unlike size, however, motion has the characteristic of direction.

If one were to *reverse the direction* of the arrows in Figure 19 or in other words make the field move in the opposite way, the diagram would represent the view of an observer who is looking straight to the *left* of his line of motion instead of to the right. Similarly, reversing the direction of the arrows in Figure 18, which would have the effect of making the retinal field contract instead of expand, would represent the view of an observer looking in the opposite direction to his line of motion, that is, looking backward. There are, therefore, two opposite poles in optical space at which retinal motion is zero, the center of expansion forward and the center of contraction backward on the line of the observer's locomotion. These poles exist independently of retinal motion perspective. They are cues for the perception not of distance but of the direction of locomotion.

The third diagram, Figure 20, represents the motion perspective when the observer moves forward but looks vertically downward, as for example in looking through the bomb bay doors of an airplane. The velocity of the terrain going by is greatest at its nearest point—the one vertically below the observer. The velocities decrease radially and symmetrically from this maximum point and, merging with the family of gradients already described, finally diminish to zero at the encircling rim of the horizon. By visualizing all of these views as if they were continuous and connected, a fairly complete picture may be gained of the retinal gradients of motion perspective and their interrelations.

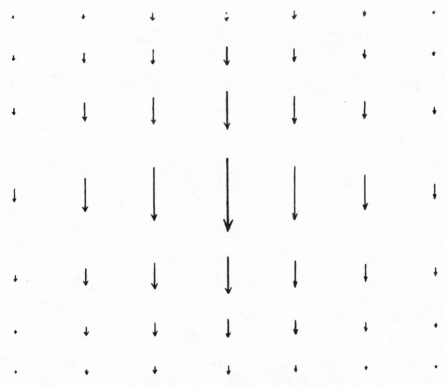

FIG. 20.    Retinal motion perspective looking down.

The answer to the question of how the retina is stimulated if the observer looks vertically upward into a clear sky during locomotion is probably obvious—there is no motion stimulus at all. If nothing is seen but sky there is no visual sense of one's own movement. Likewise there is no visual experience of a world of objects in three dimensions. Motion perception presupposes the stimulus of texture—the existence of objects or surfaces producing a differentiated retinal image. Only when there is such an image can retinal displacement or deformation occur. If the retinal stimulus is perfectly homogeneous or uniform at all points, as it is when we see nothing but clear sky, no motion can be perceived. If there are clouds in the sky, the surfaces formed by them will show retinal motion perspective and if the clouds are near enough to the observer, as occasionally happens in flying, the motion perspective will be noticeable. Figure 21 gives the appearance of the world ahead when flying under a solid overcast or "ceiling." If the cloud is sufficiently solid to be a visible surface, the motion perspective will be precisely analogous to that of a physical ceiling.

FIG. 21.    Motion perspective with a ceiling.

*The Effect of Eye Movements on Gradients of Velocity.*    It is now possible to consider the relation of eye movements to retinal motion perspective. When the eyes follow a moving object or rotate from one fixation point to another the retinal background image obviously shifts across the retina itself. This shift is a displacement of the image of the visual field, not a deformation of it. Suppose that the eyes are fixated not on the motionless horizon as we have heretofore assumed but on a nearby point on the ground. During such a fixation, the retinal velocities in the field are quite different from those represented in the diagrams and one might suppose that retinal motion perspective is thereby destroyed. The retinal velocity at the point fixated is now zero; the velocity of that point has been just canceled by an opposite velocity induced by the rotation of the eye. The velocity at all other retinal points is affected by this compensatory velocity—it is in fact added to each of them. The horizon, for example, moves on the retina at the rate which the now fixated point formerly possessed. The fact is, nevertheless, that the observer sees essentially the same thing as if he looked at the horizon—a three-dimensional world in which he himself moves.

The explanation of this fact is that when a constant opposite velocity is added to a continuous series of different velocities, the relation between them remains unchanged. The adding of velocities is algebraic in the sense that a positive velocity in one direction may be canceled by a negative velocity in the other. The *gradient* of retinal velocities with respect to their direction is therefore unaffected by pursuit movement of the eyes.[6] Since we know that the observer has the same experience of visual locomotion whether he fixates the horizon or watches the ground going by, we must suppose that the effective stimulus for such perception is the gradient of velocities in the retinal field—the direction and rate of change of velocities along a retinal axis—rather than the velocities themselves. The perceptual mechanism involved is similar to that already discussed for the gradient of retinal disparity.

*The Perception Resulting from Retinal Motion Gradients.* The visual movement which has been described in the previous pages is the movement which occurs on the surface of the observer's retina—it is not of course the same thing as the movement which he sees or experiences. The aim has been to define the physiological and optical stimuli for his perceptions of space and locomotion. It is on the basis of these stimuli that he flies an airplane or otherwise gets around in an extended world. The observer does not "see" his retinal images, although his retinal images are of course the conditions of his seeing. Images are two-dimensional, whereas his perceptions are three-dimensional. The visual field which undergoes deformation, for example the expansion shown in Figure 21, is the retinal field; the visual world resulting does not expand correspondingly but is seen as perfectly stable. Why does the world not expand when the stimulus image expands?

The answer must lie in the fact that the world possesses a third dimension and that the observer sees himself moving in this dimension. In all probability the expansion of the retinal image is an effective stimulus for perceived locomotion and for distance perception and by virtue of this fact it is *not* a stimulus for a perceived expansion of the visual world. This explanation suggests that if we could see the terrain of Figure 21 as a flat image, we would also see it as one which instead of extending into the third dimension expands in two dimensions. If it can be assumed that retinal motion perspective during locomotion is normally a stimulus for distance, then it is only reasonable that it should not be a stimulus for deformation.

The customary terms to describe the fact that objects do not undergo expansion or contraction when their position is changed relative to the observer are "shape constancy" and "size constancy." These phenomena are, however, probably only special cases of the general constancy of a continuous three-dimensional terrain.

---

[6]Gibson, Smith, Steinschneider & Johnson (1957) showed that visual discrimination of velocity was equally accurate for observers tracking or fixating a display (i.e., discriminations were equivalent where there were equivalent retinal motion gradients, although there were different absolute retinal speeds). (Eds.)

*Motion Perspective when the Observer's Movement is not Parallel to the Terrain; Application to the Problem of Landing an Airplane.* Up until the present we have been dealing with the situation where the observer moves on the ground or parallel to the ground. This is the case during most of the ordinary small movements of human activity, and during walking, driving, and straight and level flying. However, the ability to judge distance and space is most critical not in these situations but in the situation where the observer is moving *toward* the ground as he is when landing an airplane. We are now in a position to describe the retinal motion stimuli of the pilot during a landing and the way in which they are indicative of the direction, velocity, and angle of his glide, and of his distance or altitude from points on the ground.

The fundamental difference between the retinal gradients of motion during level flight and during a glide is that the optical center of expansion, the point toward which the observer is moving, is no longer on the horizon, but is on the ground.[7] Retinal motion therefore vanishes both on the rim of the horizon and at another point in the field—the center from which the motion radiates. Consider the case which is theoretically simplest—that of vertical descent with the observer looking straight down along the line of locomotion. The retinal velocity will be zero at the center of expansion, will increase to a maximum at points halfway between the center and the horizon, at 45° from the line of locomotion, and will then decrease and finally vanish at the horizon itself, at 90° from the line of locomotion. This pattern of the gradients of expansion will be symmetrical and will be quite different in character from the gradients existing during level flight.

The gradients during a glide aimed at a point *between* the one vertically below and the horizon are a combination of the two situations described. They are diagrammed in Figure 22. The center of expansion is the point at which the glide is now aimed; if the glide is made steeper, it moves downward and if the glide is made shallower it moves upward toward the horizon. The center is, in other words, an indicator of the direction of one's flight—of where one is going at the present moment. If the glide should be continued unchanged this zero point of the retinal gradients is the point where the wheels will touch ground. It therefore enables the pilot to see whether he is overshooting or undershooting the field. A plane, it should be noted, cannot be "aimed" by lining it up with a distant point like a rifle or even like an automobile; its nose never points exactly in the direction in which it is going but somewhat upward from this direction; in a cross-wind furthermore, the nose points to one side of the true direction of flight. The cue therefore by which flight can be guided or aimed has to be external to the plane itself and must be looked for in the visual scene ahead. Langewiesche

---

[7]G. C. Grindley has described this and some other aspects of the phenomenon in a brief report to the British Flying Personnel Research Committee. Whether a discussion of the phenomenon has been published could not be determined at the time of writing this report.

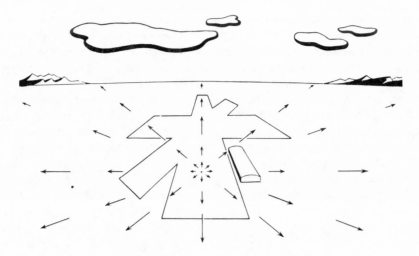

FIG. 22.   Retinal motion gradients during a landing glide.

(1944, Ch.16) has described what is in effect the center of expansion cue in the terminology of the flier. He explains a method for estimating the landing point on the runway even before one turns into the approach by observing the center of expansion during the base leg, noting its angular distance below the horizon, and then projecting it in imagination on the runway, allowing for wind. He makes special note of the fact that, in a normal glide, what we have here called the center of expansion is always a specific angular distance below the horizon. This angle is, in fact, the characteristic gliding angle of the plane being flown. In the absence of power, that is in the event of forced landing, the point-of-present-aim cannot be made to rise above this angular distance; in other words the glide cannot be "stretched." The ability to judge this visual angle enables the flier to see at all times how far on the terrain he could glide with a dead engine.

The optical center of expansion is therefore an exact indicator of the direction of a glide and a means of seeing whether the present line of flight will or will not take the plane to the point the pilot wants to get to—a point, let us say, just above the near end of the runway. It is also an indicator of the angle of glide or the rate of descent. The angle of glide is in fact the visible angular distance between the horizon and the center of expansion. With an unfamiliar plane, or with unfamiliar wind conditions which may steepen or lengthen the glide, it becomes very important for a pilot to be able to see this angle of descent in the three-dimensional space in front of him rather than having to guess it or remember it from past experience.

In the landing situation of Figure 22, the distance of the pilot from the center of expansion and his altitude from the ground directly below him need to be judged with a considerable degree of accuracy. What are the criteria or indicators of this distance and altitude? The coarseness of texture and the size of objects on the ground directly ahead are obvious correlates of these distances, as is increasing binocular depth or relief. A high tower or building on the airfield will provide a cue to the pilot's altitude; when the top of the tower just cuts the horizon, its height will be the same as his altitude. But the expansion gradients themselves vary concomitantly with distance from the ground and provide a basis for judging it. During a descent at uniform speed, the rate of the retinal expansion at its maximal points increases as the distance from the ground decreases. Under a given set of conditions this overall rate of expansion at any moment indicates the altitude. The fact that the ground directly below the plane goes by faster as the altitude decreases has been frequently described and discussed as a cue for landing. But this fact is only one aspect of the more general phenomenon of an increase in the rate of expansion over the entire field. The debated question as to how student pilots should use their eyes during landings ought to be considered in the light of the general phenomenon of expansion at *all* visible points.

The pilot's ability to estimate his ground speed both during landings and during straight and level flight, for what it is worth, is dependent wholly on the perception of retinal motion. We are referring now to ground speed rather than air speed, which latter is given by the air-speed meter, auditory cues, and others. At any given altitude, the over-all rate of the retinal pattern of gradients is directly proportional to his ground speed. Since the visual cue for speed and one of the cues for altitude are, if this analysis is correct, the same stimulus, it follows that visual judgments of speed and altitude are interrelated. The conclusion seems to be supported by the observation that speed appears to decrease as a plane gains altitude and increase as it loses altitude.

In summary, the retinal pattern of motion stimulation has aspects which are specific to a number of corresponding aspects of aerial space—ones which are of great significance to the job of flying. In addition to the dimension of distance on a continuous terrain they include the direction of flight and its angle to the ground, the altitude or distance above the ground and the velocity of flight.

The analysis of the retinal motion pattern that has been presented is admittedly theoretical. Some empirical verification is furnished by the motion-picture test derived from it which is next to be described, but that is insufficient.[8] The theory needs to be formulated more exactly by the use of methods similar to those of projective geometry. Only a beginning has been made in such a task. Such functions as have been derived are omitted here in view of their incompleteness. The generalizations that have been made have been checked, however, by geometrical methods or by empirical study of motion-picture images on a screen. A motion-picture image is, of course, analogous to a human retina insofar as two dimensional gradients are concerned. The generalizations, therefore, are believed to be sound.[9]

---

[8]The experiments mentioned are not reprinted here. (Eds.)

[9]Warren (1976) used a similar motion picture method to test visual perception of self movement. (Eds.)

# 2.3 Visually Controlled Locomotion and Visual Orientation in Animals*

## I. INTRODUCTION

The locomotion of animals seems to be controlled by optical as well as by other kinds of stimulation for, in many species, locomotor behavior ceases when optical stimulation fails, as in total darkness. In bats, to be sure, we now know that locomotion occurs in darkness under the guidance of auditory stimulation, or echolocation (Woodworth & Schlosberg, 1954, p. 359 ff.), but this interesting discovery only serves to emphasize the importance of vision for the majority of animals in the business of getting about the environment, of avoiding obstacles, and of seeking food. Students of animal behavior have long been concerned with locomotion at the level of reflexes and forced movements, but not at the level of averting collisions or of approaching goals: there is a considerable literature on phototropisms, taxes, and kineses (e.g. Fraenkel & Gunn, 1940), but almost nothing on such acts as the pursuit of prey or the flight from a predator.[1] The reason for this failure is probably connected with the generally accepted assumption that the ability of an animal to respond to *light* and the ability of an animal to respond to *objects* are quite different problems. The first is supposed to be

*British Journal of Psychology, 1958, 49, 182-194. Copyright 1958 by the British Psychological Society. Reprinted by permission. The original note to this paper reads: "The first draft of this paper was written in 1955-6 at Oxford University under a Fulbright award. The author wishes to thank Prof. George Humphrey, members of the Institute of Experimental Psychology, and others at the University for kindnesses beyond the demands of academic courtesy. He also thanks these and many other investigators visited during the year for cordial and stimulating discussion."

[1]For more on this distinction, see Ch. 4.6. (Eds.)

physiological and the second psychological. A tropism implies only a sensory process, but a response to an object at a distance implies a perceptual process and this is much more complex. The physiologist is willing to study the former but he is glad to turn over the latter to the psychologist. The problem of how we respond to objects at a distance has been, in truth, a puzzle for psychologists ever since Bishop Berkeley. Depth or space perception has been taken to be an internal process involving the interpreting or organizing of sensations. Theories of this process have never achieved either simplicity or plausibility and, if it is a process of association, the difficulty arises of why animals do not make more errors than they do in the acquisition of locomotor behavior. The writer has argued (1950a) that the only way out of this theoretical muddle is to discard the original assumption about sensory response to light on the one hand and perceptual response to objects on the other. Perhaps the distinction was based on a mistaken conception of vision in the first place. If the theories of space perception do not provide an adequate explanation for the visual control of locomotion in animals, let us forget about the former and pay heed to the latter. Locomotion is a biologically basic function, and if that can be accounted for then the problem of human space perception may appear in a new light. The question, then, is how an animal gets about by vision. How does it react to the solid surfaces of the environment without collision whenever there is enough light to see them by? What indicates to the animal that it is moving or not moving with reference to them? What kind of optical stimulation indicates approach to an object? And how does the animal achieve contact without collision? What governs the aiming and steering of locomotion? (The problem of ''roundabout behavior'' in the presence of a ''barrier,'' as it appears in the writings of Lewin (1933, 1935) and later Hull (1938, 1952) is a different question. It is as close as psychologists have come, however, to a psychology of locomotion.)

## II.  POSTULATES FOR A GENERAL THEORY OF THE VISUAL CONTROL OF LOCOMOTION

The starting point for a theory of locomotion in the higher animals would be the fact that they have evolved eyes (Walls, 1942) which can register not merely light but the objects of an illuminated environment. The optical basis for this assertion has been accumulating for years but the conclusion has not generally been drawn despite its having radical implications for a theory of behavior. The function of a highly developed mosaic of visual receptors is to respond to what might be called the *projective* capacity of light. When light is many-times reflected in all directions from an array of surfaces—when it ''fills'' the environment as we say—it has the unique property that reflected rays will converge to any point in the medium. The objective environment is projected to this point. If an eye is placed at this point, it can register a sector of the projection by the familiar process of the formation of an image. The central hypothesis of the theory to be presented is that the *patterns* and the *changes of pattern* of this projection are stimuli for the control of locomotion relative to the objects of the environment. For the sake of explicitness, it might be well to list the assumptions singly. The first six assumptions deal with the projection of light to the position of a motionless animal, that is, with the optic array to a stationary point. The remaining postulates assume an animal in motion and deal with the optic array to a moving point.

1. *The locomotor environment of animals consists of the surfaces or interfaces between matter in the solid state and matter in a liquid or gaseous state. This generalization holds for aquatic, terrestrial, or aerial environments, and for animals at various phylogenetic levels.*

2. *Solid surfaces generally reflect rather than transmit light. They also generally prevent rather than permit locomotion. Consequently, the remaining liquid or gaseous regions of the environment constitute a* medium *both for the transmission of light and for the movements of organisms.*

3. *If the environment is illuminated there will occur a many-times reflected flux of light in the medium. If the solid surfaces and their parts vary in reflectance a projection of these differential reflectances is obtainable at any point in the medium.[2] That is, the rays converging to this point will have different intensities (and frequency compositions) in different directions. They constitute what may be termed an* optic array.

4. *An eye is a device which registers some portion of the "pattern" or "texture" of an optic array to a station point. Conversely, the pattern of an array is a stimulus for an eye.*

This postulate needs explanation. Eyes, to be sure, are of different types in different animals (Walls, 1942). At one extreme, a pair of eyes can include nearly the whole pattern of a 360° optic array, each eye registering an approximate hemisphere with little overlap. This is the case with fish. At the other extreme, a pair of eyes can register overlapping sectors or cones of the frontal optic array, each picking up the same pattern from a slightly different station point. This is the case with primates in whose case the eyes are mobile and coordinated, being capable of exploratory (saccadic) fixations and convergences. The total array can then be registered only by rotating the eyes and head. The registration process is successive, not simultaneous, since different angular sectors of the array are picked up at successive moments of time. Nevertheless, by a mechanism as yet not well understood, successive registration seems to be equivalent to simultaneous registration.

---

[2]This is a simplified statement, holding for an ideally diffuse illumination. In other conditions of illumination, what we loosely call "shadows" as well as reflectances must enter into consideration. The extent to which animals can discriminate in their behavior between shadows and solid surfaces is a complex problem which can here be omitted.

The pattern of an optic array was said to be a "stimulus" for an eye. For animals with fixed eyes on either side of the head this assertion is plausible. Each eye registers its own hemisphere. For animals with mobile eyes at the front of the head, however, the assertion is not so obvious. The total pattern of the spherical array is then, strictly speaking, a *potential* stimulus as distinguished from the *momentarily effective* stimulus which exists for a single eye-posture. The pattern of a single entering sheaf of rays is only a sample of the whole pattern projected to a point in space. But the whole pattern may and will be picked up if the animal looks around. In an even more abstract sense the whole flux of focusable light pervading the medium is a potential stimulus which can be sampled at various station-points in the medium, although it must be explored by locomotor rather than by oculomotor action. It is, of course, unorthodox to assume that the focusable light converging to an eye is something to which the word "stimulus" should be applied. We have generally believed that only the focused light constituting the retinal image excites receptors. But this physiological conception of the stimulus has been a source of paradox and confusion in psychology. In fact, it does not apply. The image is a stimulus for the retinal mosaic, to be sure, but not for an eye. Focusable light is the stimulus for an eye, which responds first by focusing it. The image is no more than a *response-produced* stimulus.[3] A retinal image is not a thing with definite boundaries in any case. The retina continually moves behind it, with both large and small excursions, so as to bring the fovea to different bits of detail. A continually new sample of the pattern of the world gets projected on the retina. Images are the necessary means by which an animal exploits the capacity of light to project reflecting surfaces to any given point in a transmitting medium. The light converging to such a point is the external, stable, and relatively permanent stimulus for an eye.

5. *The presence or absence of a solid environmental surface in any part of the optic array is specified by the textured or textureless character, respectively, of that part. In other words, textured light indicates the differentially reflecting structure of a solid surface, which stops locomotion. Untextured or homogeneous light indicates an unobstructed medium of water or air, into which locomotion can proceed indefinitely* (Gibson & Dibble 1952). *The presence of a solid* object *in the environment is specified by a textured cone in the optic array with a distinct boundary, and the absence of an object is guaranteed by the absence of such a stimulus* (Gibson, 1951a).

This assumption, it may be noted, contradicts the classical distinction between

---

[3]After Gibson developed his theory of stimulus information to replace the older conception of stimuli (Chs. 1.3, 1.4, 1.6, 4.3, 4.4) it became clear that this formula was inadequate, because it treated the act of scanning for information as a mere response. Gibson (1966b, Ch. 12) later developed a theory of active information pick-up. Attempts to use an S-R theory for explaining the perception of self movement are still being made, although the term "reafference" has replaced "response-produced stimulus" (see Ch. 2.4, and the discussions of reafference in Gallistel, 1980). (Eds.)

sensory and perceptual processes. The present tacit agreement as to where the responsibility of the visual physiologist ends and the responsibility of the visual psychologist begins is thereby destroyed.

6. *In so far as the physical solids of the environment are rigid and permanent (as contrasted with fluid and movable) the pattern of the optic array at any point in the medium is unique and permanent. That is to say, there is, and will be, one and only one pattern for each station point. It is also assumed that no considerable section of a natural environment is a duplicate of another—that models or copies of environing spaces are created only by man. An important consequence of this assumption is that the* difference *between the patterns of the optic arrays at any two station points is a unique difference which depends only on the difference between the points* (Nicod, 1930). *We may call it a unique transformation.*

7. *An animal which moves passes through a continuous series of station points. Each eye is therefore presented with a continuous family of transformations, and this family is unique to the particular path of locomotion. With an animal which does* not *change its position, the eyes are presented with what may be called a continuous non-transformation of the optic array, that is, a static pattern.*

The classical geometry of perspective will describe the static pattern of the optic array, that is, the projection of an environment to a stationary point. The geometry of "motion perspective" (Gibson, Olum & Rosenblatt, 1955) will describe the "flow pattern" of the optic array, that is, the projection of an environment to a moving point. The geometry of motion perspective has been exemplified by an analysis of aerial flight with reference to a plane surface. It is interesting to note that the flow pattern is independent of the static pattern that carries it; the same flow pattern may be embodied in any number of static patterns.

8. *An eye is a device which registers the flow pattern of an optic array as well as the static pattern of an array. Conversely, such a family of continuous transformations is a stimulus for an eye. There are quite specific forms of continuous transformation, and the visual system can probably discriminate among them* (Gibson & Gibson, 1957). *This mode of optical stimulation is an invariable accompaniment of locomotor behavior and it therefore provides "feedback" stimulation for the control and guidance of locomotor behavior. It might be called* visual kinesthesis.

The last assumption asserts something like an unrecognized sense modality. Visual kinesthesis is, of course, supplementary to the recognized mode of proprioceptive kinesthesis. It differs, however, in several ways. First, it seems to provide information about movements of the animal relative to the environment, not about movements of parts of the body relative to other parts, as the muscle-sense does. Secondly, it seems to provide information about displacements rather than information about accelerations and gravitational forces, as the vestibular sense does. Thirdly, the displacements registered have reference to the stable solid surfaces of the environment; displacements with reference to the medium of air or water, in the case of flying or swimming animals, are given only by proprioceptive kinesthesis. Kinesthesis has long been defined as the sense of bodily motion. It was described by Sherrington fifty years ago (1906). It depends on the sensitivity of receptors in the muscles and joints to compression, on the sensitivity of a statocyst to force, and also on the sensitivity of the skin to deformation. Visual kinesthesis depends on the sensitivity of a retinal mosaic to an overall change of pattern. To suggest that the eye can serve as a kinesthetic organ is somewhat upsetting; for one thing it violates our notion of the eye as an exteroceptor in Sherrington's classification of exteroceptors, proprioceptors, and interoceptors. There is some inadequacy, however, in all attempts at anatomical classification of fixed senses. Kinesthesis, as usually understood, is actually several different forms of sensitivity to several different kinds of motion: of the muscles, the joints, the endolymph, and the skin. Why not admit optical motion? The fact is that animals seem to pick up stimulus information from the sea of energy around them through multiple channels and in various ways. Seemingly redundant information is not neglected; on the contrary, many supplements and concomitants and combinations of energy seem to be received at the same time. And the transformations in the field of view are very useful information.[4]

Consider the case of a fish maintaining its position over the bottom of a flowing brook, or the case of a bird hovering over the same bit of land in a wind. It must move relative to the medium in order to be motionless relative to the solid substratum. For this, obviously, it must rely on vision. It has to maintain an unchanging pattern of the optic array. Transformation of the array is an index of motion relative to the substratum, and a completely reliable one. By visual kinesthesis the animal can coordinate its behavior to the environment while at the same time by muscular kinesthesis it can coordinate its locomotion to the medium.

Is there evidence to show that the ocular mechanism in animals can actually register the flow pattern of an optic array, as assumed? Animals, including insects, are said to be very sensitive to "motion," and there is observational evidence from zoology and ethology (Tinbergen, 1951) suggesting that animals make specific responses to specific kinds of moving objects in the environment. If they are sensitive to objective motion in the environment it is likely that they are also sensitive to subjective movement in the environment (Gibson, 1954b), but the question has not been specifically studied. There is, of course, plenty of evidence to show that animals have pattern vision in varying degrees, and experiments on form discrimination make a large literature in comparative psychology. Whether they have *change-of-pattern* vision is another question, and this has scarcely been investigated. But it is very likely that they do. The compound

---

[4]Lishman and Lee's (1973, 1975; Lee & Lishman, 1977b) experiments with a "swinging room" have shown that such visual information for controlling self movement does exist and is used. (Eds.)

eyes of insects, particularly those with a relatively coarse mosaic, may prove to have greater acuity for differences between transformations than they do for differences between forms. There is evidence to prove that human observers are very sensitive to optical motions. They can detect motion parallax in the field of view with very great precision (Graham, 1951), and they can utilize the shadow transformations on a translucent screen for accurate judgments of changing depth (Gibson & Gibson, 1957).

## III. FORMULAE FOR A THEORY OF VISUAL CONTROL OF LOCOMOTION[5]

We are now prepared to apply the postulates to the problem of how an animal gets about in a stable environment, approaching goals, avoiding obstacles, and even responding to moving objects such as a prey or a predator. By these assumptions, transformations of the total optic array to a moving point serve for the control of locomotion relative to the total environment. Transformations of a smaller bounded cone of the optic array (a closed contour with internal texture in the visual field of the animal) serve for the control of locomotion relative to an object in the environment. A formula will be given for each of the following aspects of locomotor behavior: beginning forward locomotion, ceasing locomotion, reversing locomotion; steering toward a specific place or object; approaching without collision; avoiding obstacles; pursuit of a moving object; and avoiding a moving object. The formulae will be in verbal rather than mathematical form, but they are capable of the latter kind of statement.

### (i) Starting, Stopping, and Backing-up

The flow pattern of the optic array during forward displacement vanishes during nondisplacement and is reversed during backward displacement (seventh assumption). A human observer who attends to his visual sensations can note a sort of "expansion" or "contraction" of the patchwork of colors in his frontal visual field as he moves forward or backward. Actually there is a centrifugal flow of the structure of the optic array from a pole in the direction of displacement, the flow being graded in proportion to the nearness of the corresponding surface (Gibson *et al.* 1955). (This graded centrifugal flow of an optic array from an environment of solids has the interesting property of being capable of continuing indefinitely without the consequence that the pattern as a whole becomes larger. Elements or forms of the pattern are magnified as the corresponding objects get nearer, but new elements emerge to take their place in the array. The structure of such an array consists of forms within forms to an unlimited density. The reason for this fact is that the environment of animals is itself structured at any level of

---

[5]See Gibson (1979a, pp 232–234) for modified versions of these formulae. (Eds.)

magnitude; it is composed not only of mountains and trees but also of crystals and cells.) There is a corresponding centripetal flow toward a pole in the direction opposite the displacement. These flow patterns depend on the configuration of the reflecting surfaces in the environment but they are independent of any *particular* configuration. To begin locomotion, therefore, is so to contract the muscles as to make the forward optic array flow outward. To stop locomotion is to make the flow cease. To reverse locomotion is to make it flow inward. To speed up locomotion is to make the rate of flow increase and to slow down is to make it decrease. An animal who is behaving in these ways is optically stimulated in the corresponding ways, or, equally, an animal who so acts as to obtain these kinds of optical stimulation is behaving in the corresponding ways.

### (ii) Steering and Aiming

The center of the flow pattern during forward movement of the animal is the direction of movement. More exactly, the part of the structure of the array from which the flow radiates corresponds to that part of the solid environment toward which he is moving. If the direction of his movement changes, the center of flow shifts across the array, that is, the flow becomes centered on another element of the array corresponding to another part of the solid environment. The animal can thus, as we would say, "see where he is going." The act of turning or steering is, therefore, a visual as well as a muscular event. To turn in a certain direction is to shift the center of flow in that direction relative to the fixed structure of the optic array. The amount of turn is exactly correlated with the angular degree of shift. The behavior of aiming at a goal object can now be specified (although the properties of a figure in the field of view which arouse this behavior have not yet been described). To aim locomotion at an object is to keep the center of flow of the optic array as close as possible to the form which the object projects.

### (iii) Approaching without Collision

Approach to a solid surface is specified by a centrifugal flow of the texture of the optic array. Approach to an object is specified by a magnification of the closed contour in the array corresponding to the edges of the object. A *uniform* rate of approach is accompanied by an *accelerated* rate of magnification. At the theoretical point where the eye touches the object the latter will intercept a visual angle of 180°; the magnification reaches an explosive rate in the last moments before contact. This accelerated expansion in the field of view specifies imminent collision, and it is unquestionably an effective stimulus for behavior in animals with well-developed visual systems. In man, it produces eye blinking and aversive movements of the head, even when the stimulus is a harmless magnification of a shadow on a translucent screen. At lesser intensities this "looming motion," as it might be called, presumably yields lesser degrees of aversion, or a slowing down of approach. The fact is that animals need to make contact without collision with many solid objects of their environment: food objects, sex objects, and the landing surfaces on which insects and birds alight (not to mention helicopter pilots). Locomotor action must be a balance between approach and aversion. The governing stimulation must be a balance between flow and non-flow of the optic array. The formula is as follows: contact without collision is achieved by so moving as to cancel the centrifugal flow of the optic array at the moment when the contour of the object or the texture of the surface reaches that angular magnification at which contact is made.

## (iv) Steering among Obstacles

Fish, birds and arboreal animals live in a cluttered environment, that is, one whose open spaces are encroached upon by solid surfaces. Nevertheless, they swim, fly, or take a course among these obstacles with great precision. Many species do so only when the medium is illuminated, that is, they depend on vision. The obstacles are specified in the optic array by contours with internal texture; the open spaces are specified by the areas between such contours. The background areas may be untextured homogeneous color, like the sky, or densely textured surface color, like the earth. The question is, what governs the taking of a course during such locomotion? Symmetrical magnification of a textured contour specifies a collision course toward an obstacle, but a skewed magnification, where the center of flow is outside the textured contour, specifies a non-collision course. So long as an animal keeps the focus of centrifugal flow outside the textured contours and within a homogeneous or densely textured area, he will not collide with a solid object. This formula, it may be noted, is simply the reciprocal of that for aiming at a goal object. The properties of a textured contour by which is specified either an obstacle on the one hand or a goal object on the other have not yet been considered.

## (v) Pursuit and Flight

Predatory animals pursue and preyed-upon animals flee. These biologically complementary forms of behavior must both be controlled by transformations of optical pattern. Approach to a stationary goal object has been described. A fugitive goal object is specified when the optic array as a whole flows from a center, but when a textured contour within it does not expand. The object is then moving away and being pursued. Absolute angular magnification of the contour means catching up and minification of the contour means falling behind. Hence, the rule by which a big fish can catch a little fish is simple: maximize its optical size in the field of view. From the point of view of the prey, the expansion of a textured contour in the optic array means the approach of something. This in itself may touch off the reaction of flight if it comes within the field of view. Preyed-upon animals need eyes which can register this abstract optical event in the rearward as well as the frontward direction, and very generally they seem to have developed eyes with a panoramic binocular field (Walls, 1942). What exactly *is* flight? The formula is again simple. It is so moving as to minimize the optical size of the expanding contour. This will necessarily involve a centripetal flow of that hemisphere of the optic array which contains it and a centrifugal flow of the opposite hemisphere. If the optical size of the contour decreases, the animal is getting away; if it increases despite the contraction of the surrounding field, the animal is being overtaken. There is one other geometrical possibility of stimulation: contraction of a contour in an otherwise static array. This means something *going* away. Probably it does not touch off the reaction of flight as expansion of a contour does in preyed-upon animals. This hypothesis needs empirical testing.

### (vi) The Complexities of Terrestrial Locomotion

For simplicity, the formulae of the theory have referred, so far, to locomotion in a medium of water or air. They are sufficient to show the possibilities of a circular control or "feedback" type of stimulus-response analysis for understanding the locomotor behavior of fish and birds. There are, however, terrestrial animals. The surface of the earth is a substratum. Locomotion can occur, mechanically speaking, in two possible ways: by exerting force against the medium and avoiding contact with the substratum, or by exerting force against the substratum and keeping in more or less continuous contact with it. The latter type, terrestrial locomotion, seems to have developed later in evolution. Terrestrial animals utilize a great variety of mechanical procedures—crawling, gliding, hopping, walking, running, and the like, but they all push against the ground in one manner or another. For these animals, touch is available to play some part in controlling locomotion—actually *change* of contact stimulation, or tactual motion. There is also classical muscle-joint kinesthesis which, in these animals, is never discrepant with visual kinesthesis as it may be for the fish or the bird in a flowing medium. Since these modes of controlling stimulation run parallel in terrestrial man, it has been easy for the human psychologist to overlook the visual mode. Only since man began to fly aircraft has the visual component in the guidance of locomotion forced itself on the attention of psychologists. And yet it was always there to be observed. Consider the perception of "footing" in a man who is making his way over rough terrain. Or, better, consider the oculomotor coordinations of a cat, or of any animal which runs with "due regard" to the footing. The visual aspect of the performance is just as precise as the muscular aspect. The animal has only the information supplied by the optical array to a moving point (or a pair of them) and yet it adjusts its behavior to the convexities and concavities and other physical properties of the surface ahead of it. This consideration reminds one that animals respond to invariants as well as changes of stimulation—to the permanent properties of the environment as well as to their own motions in it. We should return to the problem of the exteroceptive function of vision and note whether the problem is reformulated after first considering its proprioceptive function. Animals are capable not only of locomotion in, but also of orientation to, their environment, that is, of object perception and even what psychologists have called "space" perception.

## IV. VISUAL ORIENTATION IN ANIMALS

Animals are not continually on the move; they sometimes remain at rest. Often the only movements that can then be observed are eye-movements. This means that the resting animal is exploring the optic array even if he is not exploring the environment. It is tempting to believe that the animal is still making some kind of implicit responses to the solid surfaces around him even if he is not explicitly poking his nose into things. He is certainly oriented to gravity and to the substratum when he maintains a constant posture. He is probably also oriented to the distant objects of his environment when he remains in the same place. In the fifth assumption, we may indeed find a basis for the latter kind of orientation. It seems to be possible for him to identify and react to the objects of his world by virtue of the optical properties of the light reflected from them to his eye. One might even wish to suggest that the animal, in his way, *perceives* the objects of his world.

Animals make different kinds of locomotor reactions to different objects. They approach food or shelter, they avoid obstacles, they pursue prey and they flee the predator. These are discriminative reactions and they require a different kind of stimulus-response theory than do the control reactions heretofore considered. We must now consider actions which are specific to those features of the optic array which do *not* change during locomotion rather than those which do. Such features of stimulation are not response produced and the responses are not circular. In such behavior the S-R linkage is between permanent entities of the environment and acts which are appropriate to them. The distinction between an S-R theory of *control* reactions and an S-R theory of *identifying* reactions is important for behavior theory.[6] It is true that an automaton can be designed which will aim at, approach, and pursue a pre-set target (as witness military missiles) and that no automaton has yet been designed which will recognize targets appropriate to its own needs (apart from its designer's) and act accordingly. But it would be wrong to categorize the first kind of reactions as *automatic* and the second kind as *voluntary*. This dichotomy is as pernicious as the one between sensory and perceptual processes. The true distinction is probably that between the properties of stimulation which vary over time and those which do not.

### (i) Object Perception

By the fifth assumption, material objects, substances in the solid state, are specified by the textures and contours of the optic array, and they stop locomotion. However, a solid object, by virtue of its chemistry and biochemistry, may constitute food for an animal. Or it may constitute a mate, or young, or shelter, or an obstacle, or an enemy. These higher-order properties of solids are specified

---

[6]Gibson (1966b, pp. 44–46) later abandoned the S-R theory employed here, replacing it with the distinction between exploratory perceiving and performatory acting. A modified version of this S-R approach can be found, however, in Gibson (1967c). (Eds.)

by higher-order properties of the light in the optic array. For example, there is internal pattern as well as texture in the light reflected from an object and there is shape as well as contour. There is a frequency distribution in such light which specifies in a complicated way what men call "color." Moreover, if the object is alive and moves there will be deformations of its contour and internal pattern which specify it as animate, and which may further specify it as one or another kind of animate thing. In so far as an animal can discriminate these variables of the optic array, he can discriminate the properties of objects which render them not only bump-into-able and walk-on-able but also mate-with-able, or get-underneath-able, or edible, or likely to cause pain. And to this extent, he can identify the significant classes of objects in his environment, that is, he can respond to them differently as the objects themselves differ in biophysical ways (Gibson & Gibson, 1955a). These are the so-called "goal-objects" of an animal's environment, the ones which are related to the animal's needs, which induce approach or avoidance, and which man describes as having valences or meanings in the perceptual field. The hypothesis is that the values of objects as well as their solidity are specified with some degree of reliability in the optic array. Mere physical solidity has a value for locomotion and collision. Chemical and biological properties of higher order have values for nutrition, reproduction, and survival. The animal's task is to detect these properties at a distance.[7]

Contemporary behavior theorists either take for granted that objects constitute stimuli ("stimulus objects") and thus beg the question of how objects are responded to, or else they assume vaguely that pattern stimuli are "cues" for behavior and thus slip around the problem of object perception. (The latter point is illustrated by comparing the use of "cue" by a student of behavior such as Miller—Miller & Dollard, 1941—who takes the concept very lightly, and a student of perception such as Brunswik, 1956, who takes the concept very seriously.) But this will not do. During locomotion, the patterns at the receptor surfaces of an animal are necessarily in flux, the objects being projected as changing patterns rather than constant patterns. If we wish to believe that an animal can respond to a constant object in the course of his behavior we should first resolve this apparent contradiction. There are two alternatives. We can assume that the animal somehow constructs a perceptually constant object from the kaleidoscopic field of sensations: this is the starting point for classical theories of perception. Or we can assume that the animal is sensitive to the mathematically invariant properties in the stimulus flux which correspond to the physically constant object: this is the alternative which seems more promising for the future.[8] During the locomotor transformations of the pattern of the optic array

---

[7]Gibson (1977b; cf. Ch. 4.9) developed these ideas concerning the functional properties of objects into his theory of affordances of objects for behavior. (Eds.)

[8]For more recent discussions of these alternatives, see Gibson & Gibson (1972), Johansson (1977) and Reed & Jones (1979). (Eds.)

the property of color remains, of course, invariant. During these perspective transformations many geometrical properties such as the kind of texture, or the angularity or curvature of the pattern also remain invariant. There are plenty of invariant variables in the flux of optical stimulation on the basis of which an animal can identify classes of permanent objects. The empirical question is whether animals are, or come to be, sensitive to them.

### (ii) Orientation to the Visible Environment

Animals seem not only to recognize constant objects, but to orient themselves to a constant environment, that is, to any permanent arrangement of solid surfaces. The homing behavior of many species suggests that the animal is able, on familiar ground, to find its way from any one place to any other significant place; territorial behavior also suggests that he can respond, in some sense, to the habitat as a whole; and exploratory behavior suggests a kind of striving to extend the boundaries of this whole. How can this complicated behavior be supposed to depend on vision? Consider the pattern of an optic array to a stationary position. For land animals the lower hemisphere, roughly, will be textured and patterned by the surfaces and objects of the earth. But not only solidity is specified in the array; the slants and slopes and the facings of this arrangement of surfaces are specified by *gradients* of the optical texture (Gibson, 1950a, Ch. 6). The edges are specified by *steps* of the texture variables, and convexities or concavities are specified by *changes* of gradient. In short, the lay of the land, the jumping-off places, the interspaces, barriers and obstacles, as well as the level stretches, are given by the geometry of the optic array. Depending on the locomotor capacities of the animal, this terrain provides definite possibilities or impossibilities for crawling, walking, climbing and the like. And if the animal can discriminate the textural variables it can discriminate among potential paths for locomotion. A potential path is a stretch of surface extending away from the animal which affords the kind of locomotion for which the animal is equipped. A barrier or obstacle is a surface which does not afford locomotion. There are transitional cases between path and barrier, to be sure, and a cliff or vertical edge is a special type of barrier, but the definitions will serve well enough for theoretical purposes. (The responses of rats to a "visual cliff" have recently been studied under laboratory conditions—Walk, Gibson & Tighe, 1957—and they show the kind of aversion predicted by this theory). A terrestrial animal is always encircled, then, by a radiating set of paths or barriers. Each angular sector of the optic array specifies the possibility of locomotion in that direction. A level path of unlimited distance is given by a gradual increase of textural density up the array to the horizon. A barrier is given by a region over which density remains constant, and its distance by the point at which the change in the density gradient begins. A falling-off place is given by an abrupt increase in density upward in the array. A margin between land and water (a barrier for a non-swimmer) is given by a change in the kind and rigidity of texture together with a change in color. Confinement consists of barriers in all directions; freedom consists of paths in all directions. To the extent that the animal can respond to these variables of the encircling optic array, we may now conclude, he has locomotor orientation to his environment. He perceives the possibilities of locomotion surrounding him. *And this is probably what should be meant by asserting that an animal has visual space perception.*

### (iii) Orientation to the Environment Outside the Range of Vision

The visible environment may be limited by enclosing surfaces such as those of a laboratory maze, and even in an open medium it is limited by the acuity of the eye, the clearness of the medium, and the level of the illumination. An animal, nevertheless, can learn in some degree to go to places and objects outside of these limits (Rabaud, 1928; Thorpe, 1956) just as a man can learn to find his way about a house, the streets of a city, or the highways of a state. How is this behavior to be accounted for, and in what sense is it visually determined? It is not explained by the unchanging pattern of an optic array to a single position. Consider, however, the transformations of pattern of an optic array to a moving position, as described in the seventh and eighth postulates. We have assumed that a family of continuous transformations is itself an optical stimulus, and that the properties which remain invariant under transformations also remain stimuli during such flux. The former specifies the particular path of locomotion taken; the latter specify the permanent arrangement of surfaces. An animal that explores its environment in the course of time moves from each of many places to each of many other places and, just as each place corresponds to a unique pattern, so each movement corresponds to a unique transformation. The visual flux of a locomotor animal, as it goes about its business, consists of a sequence of transformation families interspersed with periods of non-transformation. Since these families each begin where the preceding one ended, they are linked. The entire life of the animal is co-extensive, in fact, with a single grand family of optical transformations which specify the history of its travels and explorations. This fact should be taken into consideration in any theory of maze learning or, more generally, of how an animal learns its way about. The successive patterns of the optic array are not a series of discrete pictures like a series of nonsense syllables which have to be associated; they are parts of a continuous transformation with a temporal pattern of its own. The nature of this temporal pattern—the direction of the change of the momentary patterns—is probably something which an animal can sense and, if so, we do not have to postulate the conditioning of a series of responses to a series of discrete stimuli as Hull (1952) does in his theory of the goal-gradient and the habit-family. Hull chops a temporal pattern into ·a set of static patterns and is then faced with the problem of integration. The integration of behavior is partly explainable in terms of the pre-existing integrity of stimulation, and by the hypothesis that an animal learns to respond to it. If maze learning is to be explained in S-R terms we must recognize that the stimuli *to which responses are made* change as well as the responses themselves (Gibson & Gibson, 1955a). In the course of learning, a whole temporal pattern may become the effective stimulus for a single integrated act.[9]

The controversy over "response learning" and "place learning" has now reached major proportions in psychology (Woodworth & Schlosberg, 1954, Ch. 21; Thorpe, 1956, Ch. 5), but neither side has troubled to analyse the optical stimulation. Hull's theory of maze learning asserts that it is the acquiring of a sequence of movements. Tolman's theory asserts that it is the acquiring of a cognitive map of the maze (Tolman, 1948). If Hull's theory could profit by utilizing the notion of continuous transformation, Tolman's theory could profit by the notion of invariant variables of stimulation under transformation. The perceiving of the possibilities of locomotion surrounding an animal does not, as Tolman assumes, require a theory of sign learning or the interpretation of sensory cues. Space perception can be explained with greater parsimony by kinds of stimulation hitherto neglected in sensory physiology. Knowing the possibilities of locomotion *outside* the limits of momentary vision, that is to say the cognitive mapping of the extended environment, can be explained in part by the recurrent, constant, or invariant properties of such stimulation which are discovered during exploratory behavior.[10]

### (iv) The Learning of Visual Orientation by Exploration

Animals learn to get about the environment and they also learn *about* the environment. The first kind of learning is called behavioral and the second cognitive, but nothing prevents us from making both assertions. If an animal goes to where something is we can infer that he knows where it is. In either case the experimental evidence suggests that the learning depends on *exploratory* activity. Artificial environments such as mazes have provided much of the evidence, but the conclusion holds for natural environments as well, the evidence coming from work on homing and foraging (Thorpe, 1956). No other kind of stimulation is as informative about the environment as light when it is many-times reflected in a medium. The best means of exploring an environment is (a) to point the eyes in various directions, and (b) to plant them at various station points. It seems probable that eyes are sensitive to the transitions between visual patterns as well as the patterns themselves. Certainly locomotion is guided thus. A transformation may be more significant than a form, in fact, since it carries all the

---

[9]Gibson's later theory of occluding edges (Ch. 2.7) serves to make this argument more concrete. As Neisser (1978, pp. 98–99) notes, "Every occluding edge defines a region that could be brought into view by some movement, and thus marks the potential location of things presently unseen." (Eds.)

[10]Menzel (1978) reviews more recent work on cognitive maps. (Eds.)

information that a form does plus that carried by the kind of transition. There are families and superfamilies of such information in focusable light. The more of it an animal can react to the more efficiently and quickly he can go from place to place in his environment, and the more he can learn what the arrangement of his environment is. This kind of learning is by no means the only kind, to be sure, but it is an important one.

# 2.4

## The Uses of Proprioception and the Detection of Propriospecific Information*

The terms sensory and motor, when applied to the nervous system, are not precisely descriptive, for not all sensory impulses yield sensations and not all motor impulses yield movements. The physiologist speaks of afferent and efferent impulses instead, which are exact terms. The human engineer speaks of input and output, which are still more descriptive. Thus, when we want to talk about the input to the nervous system produced by its own output we can use the engineer's term *feedback,* or the physiologist's term *reafference* (Von Holst & Mittelstaedt, 1950). However, the available terms from psychology carry meanings that imply the theory of special conscious sensations and are weighted with history. The *muscle sense* dates from 1826 but the term is not very useful because it leaves out of account the return inputs from the joints.[1] *Kinesthesis* dates from 1880 but it implies sensitivity to movement whereas it ought also to imply information about the postures of the limbs and body.[2] The *vestibular sense* registers movements of the head, but only accelerations, and it also contributes to reflex postural equilibrium of the body, head, and eyes. *Somaesthesis* is a useful term, but too general. Boring (1942), of course, is the authority on all this.

---

*This paper was presented at an American Psychological Association symposium on the Role of Reafferent Stimulation in Perception, September 1964. It has not been published previously.

[1]The idea of a muscle sense comes from the work of Thomas Brown and Charles Bell. (See Bastian (1880, appendix) and Sherrington (1900).) (Eds.).

[2]The term ''kinesthesis'' was coined by Bastian (1880). Bastian (1887) includes a debate on the concept of kinesthesis with commentary by Hughlings Jackson, David Ferrier and others. For a recent review of work on kinesthesis, see McCloskey (1978). (Eds.).

From behavior theory there comes the old term *circular reflex,* which implies part of what we want to talk about. It was used, for example, by G. H. Mead and E. B. Holt in theories of the development of speech in the child and of social imitation. There is also Hull's term *response-produced stimulation* which is useful but implies acceptance of Hullian theory. Finally, there is available the term *proprioception.*

This word is practically synonymous with kinesthesis in modern usage. It is so used by the other contributors to this symposium. But, with apologies, I want to have it mean general self-sensitivity, that is, the fact that an animal stimulates itself in many different ways by nearly all of its activities, from the lowest to the highest, including the activities of looking, listening, touching, smelling, and tasting.

Sherrington, when he distinguished between proprioception and exteroception, in 1906, had a great insight. He suggested, and should have made us realize more fully, that an individual animal needs information about its own activities as well as information about the environment in order to function in the environment. It must have both to get along.[3] But Sherrington was so much influenced by the classical theory of mutually exclusive senses, each with its sensory nerve, that he could only ascribe proprioception to a class of proprioceptors and exteroception to a class of exteroceptors. In 1906 no one could doubt Johannes Müller's law of the special sensory qualities of the receptors and their nerves, nor that the resulting sensations were the sole basis for the getting of information. The notion that proprioception is a general function, not a special sense even now may sound strange after a half a century. But the modern concept of feedback or reafference is not that of a special sense. Return inputs to the nervous system, we now realize, may come through any of the sensory channels, not just through the receptors in the muscles, the joints, and the inner ear. The control of locomotion depends on the eyes; the control of manipulation on the eyes, joints, and skin; the control of speech on the ears, and so on. But this is proprioception in the exact meaning of the term.

A recurrent and unsolved puzzle now becomes obvious. How does an individual tell the difference between an input caused by its own activity and one caused by an external event if both come over the same nerve? If proprioception is not confined to a distinct anatomical class of proprioceptors separate from another class of exteroceptors, how is an input that is propriospecific distinguished from one that is exterospecific? For example, in the case of the eye, how is a shift of the retinal image over the retina when it is caused by a rotation of the eye any different from one that would be caused by a rotation of the world? This is the old problem of why we do not see the world move when the eyes move. There are many other examples, although they are less well known. The skin can be moved over a stationary object or an object can be moved over the stationary

---

[3]Thinès (1977, Ch. 3) reviews this aspect of Sherrington's work in considerable detail. (Eds.).

skin; the cutaneous stimulation may then be identical but the two cases are not confused in perception, and the question is why?

This puzzle, it seems to me, is even deeper and more far reaching than these examples suggest. In driving an automobile, in wielding a hammer, or in exploring the shape of an unfamiliar object in the dark, there is a complex concurrent *mixture* of response-produced stimulation and environment-produced stimulation. Consider the visual stimulation. One component of the visual flux is specific to the individual while another is constrained by the external arrangement of things or by external events. The same is true of the cutaneous flux of stimulation, for part of it is self-produced and another part is object-produced. It is even true of the flow of vestibular stimulation, for some of the forces on the little weighted hair-cells are initiated by the individual, some by external pushes, and some underlying component is due to the incessant pull of gravity. At cocktail parties, the sound of one's own voice is mixed with the sound of other voices. How can the individual sort out the mishmash of sensations and perceive their causes? If Müller was right about the specificity of sensations to receptors and only to receptors, and if Locke was right about sensations being the only ultimate source of perception, how does any person or animal distinguish between the feedback to the nervous system and the feed-in to it? What is the difference between the propriospecific information and the exterospecific information? In the terms of Von Holst (1954) what is the difference between reafferent and exafferent nervous impulses over the same nerve?

Von Holst's solution to the puzzle, as I understand him, is to imagine a central neural hookup that can distinguish the sensation following a motor command from the same sensation *not* following a motor command. To do this, the brain needs to keep a "copy" of each output, and determine whether or not an input matches it. If there is a match the input is given a proprioceptive quality; if not an exteroceptive quality. Von Holst's theory need not involve consciousness, but the explanation is in the same tradition as the hypothesis that a *feeling of innervation* always accompanies the arousal of a motor pathway—a hypothesis that carried the theory of sensations to its ultimate extreme.[4]

It seems to me that a more radical solution to the puzzle is called for. If proprioception is a general function of the overall perceptual system, cutting across the classical senses, then the subjective sensation-qualities have nothing to do with it. I make a sharp distinction between the input of information and the input of conscious sensation. The puzzle disappears if one simply postulates that the neural input is different when it is propriospecific than when it is exterospecific. The input that specifies its source, to be sure, comes in larger chunks than the one that specifies only its anatomical point of origin, but it is truly

---

[4]The controversy over innervation sensations was quite vigorous towards the end of the 19th century. James' (1890) chapter on the will is a good introduction to the debate. (Eds.).

informative and does not have to be corrected or supplemented as the bare sensory data would have to be.[5]

On this theory, proprioception utilizes whatever anatomical equipment is available for the pickup of information, just as exteroception does. The changing pattern of nervous input contains invariants that specify what is constant and variations that specify what is varying. We can now begin to study propriosensitivity and exterosensitivity as such. We can afford to recognize that the state of the body and the state of the world are interdependent, and that both must be detected in perception. We can take account of the phenomenal fact that our experience usually has both subjective reference and objective reference at the same time.

It is true that, for this approach a number of cherished assumptions have to be thrown overboard. We have to suppose that sensations as conscious contents are neither the causes of perception nor the components of perception, but are merely incidental. If perception is based on the pickup of information, it may or may not be accompanied by sense-data. We have to suppose that the classical senses, the conveyers of bare sense-data, are in large part mere artifacts of human analytic introspection. We shall have to define a new set of perceptual systems, recognizing that they are not mutually exclusive. We must suppose that organs of perception exist, incorporating the receptor-cells and receptive fields of single afferent neurons, but these organs have to be defined in functional not anatomical terms. The organ of sight, for example, consists of two eyes, not one. The organ of touch consists of the limbs and trunk, not just the skin. We can then suppose that the sensory qualities, intensities, extensities, and protensities celebrated by Titchener may reflect the receptors excited but not the organs at work. The great Cornell program of a complete inventory of the possible sensations becomes irrelevant for the study of perception. The study of the energy thresholds for sensation in measured amounts of intensity or frequency is relevant only to the receptors, not the perceptual organs. We must suppose that the psychophysics of intensity and frequency, however elegant a discipline, will not lead to a psychophysics based on the *information* in light, sound and mechanical energy, that is, information about the environment and the body of the observer.

The hypothesis being entertained is that there exists information for proprioception and that it can be registered. The sensations resulting from reafference are a matter of no consequence. This is a very disruptive hypothesis but it frees us to think in other ways. We have long wanted to acknowledge that the senses are active, exploratory, and search-oriented but the very term *sense* prevented this. We have failed to distinguish between active perceptual organs and passive

---

[5]The same idea seems to be behind Granit's (1973) theory that coactivation vitiates the need for reafference in muscle and articular proprioception (see Miles and Evarts, 1979, for discussion). (Eds.).

receptors. Consequently the study of the *orienting* capacities of the eyes, ears, nose, and hands has proceeded in a theoretical vacuum, and they had to be lumped together with behavior. The *adjusting* of perceptual organs, the overt acts of attention in looking, listening, smelling, tasting, and touching, can now be understood as an activity of extracting the invariants from potential stimulation, that is, the act of optimizing the pickup of external information. This suggests that the adjustments of the eyes, ears, nose, mouth, and hands are skills capable of development, but skills in their own right, not subordinate to motor performances.

The remarkable thing about this new concept of active exteroception, as contrasted with the old one of passive exteroception, is that we can no longer consider the stimulation of the retina (for example) apart from the ocular adjustments of accommodation, of intensity modulation, of stabilization, fixation, and exploration, that determine what the retinal image will be. The normal everyday retinal image is a truly *obtained* stimulus, not an *imposed* one as we have so long assumed.[6] The ocular adjustments are continually producing new retinal images so as to pick up the potential information in light. Note the implication. The ocular system has to be sensitive to the imperfections of a retinal image in order to make these adjustments. The system has to be propriosensitive in order to work. But the *sensations* incidental to focussing, fixating, exploring, and pursuing have nothing to do with their function, which is to achieve clear perception. When the eye shifts its fovea from one item of interest to another and the retina moves relative to the retinal image the input simply reflects and controls the shift of attention, and it is beginning at the wrong end to ask why the world does not seem to move. A pure transposition of total pattern, with gain of new detail on one side and loss of old detail on the other *specifies* an eye-movement, and this information is normally registered as such.

The feedback of the retina from ocular adjustment and ocular exploration is very much worth study, but we should not forget its perceptual purpose in considering what kind of sensation, if any, accompanies this feedback. Its modality or quality may be that of the retina if it is experimentally brought into consciousness but its meaning is that of an adjustment; it is information about the state of the ocular system. Reafference is part and parcel of the perceptual process inasmuch as it controls the activity of the perceptual organs in their search for external stimulus information. If there were time, I would try to show that this rule works just as well for the ear-head system in active auditory localization, for the hand-body system in active touching, and for the nasal-respiratory system in active smelling or sniffing, and in what we call "following our nose."[7] The perceptual systems all include what Pavlov termed orienting

---

[6]Gibson (1962a) applied this theory to touch and later (Gibson, 1966b) to all the perceptual systems. Cf. Wall's (1970) application of this idea to touch and kinesthesis. (Eds.).

[7]These are all discussed at greater length in Gibson (1966b). (Eds.).

responses, and they are all neatly hooked up with the basic system of postural orientation to gravity and the surrounding environment. That system is notoriously one which operates in a continuously circular fashion to achieve an equilibrium state. So do the higher perceptual systems.

Here is a role, then, for reafference or proprioceptions to play in perception. What about its role in overt behavior? We are fairly familiar with the latter from the rise of what is called cybernetics. And we may be tempted to assume that reafference is all one thing, working the same way in perception as it does in performance. But this, I think, would be a mistake. Performance modifies both the environment *and* the perception of the observer, whereas perception can modify only the stimulus information obtained from the environment. That is, by the education of attention the observer can isolate invariants, extract the critical features of things, and enhance his ability to detect small differences. I do not want to depreciate learning by doing; I only want to assert the possibility of learning by looking.

Motor learning cannot go to its limit unless it is accompanied by perceptual learning, but perceptual learning can proceed with very little muscular action except for the exploratory adjustments of the eyes, ears, and hands. The fallacy of the theory of *response-produced cues* as an explanation of perceptual learning lies in the assumption that the motor responses *as such* improve the discrimination of things. Hidden in the gross motor responses are more subtle activities of the perceptual organs that fix on and clarify the relevant stimuli. Along with this goes a ''tuning'' of the nervous centers that filters out irrelevancies. This is not an obvious kind of behavior. It is an activity but it deserves the name of perceptual activity and it cannot simply be thrown into the pot of motor responses.[8]

The perceptual systems include muscles, to be sure, but some of them like the eye muscles cannot do much to change the environment. They are exploratory, not performatory. The input is optimized, not the output. Eye and ear movements tend toward an equilibrium state of clarity, not of need-reduction. In exploratory activity the observer has to *move,* that is, move his eyes, his head, his hands, or even move to a new point of view. He has to do so in order to find out what is lawful, regular, recurrent in the world. He can only do this by isolating what remains invariant in a self-produced flow of changing stimulation. The permanent objects and their layout then emerge from the flow of perspectives. But the observer does not *necessarily* have to perform a task or achieve a purpose during this exploration.

If what I call proprioception is a general function instead of a special sense, and if it is normally a component of all the active exteroceptive systems, what sort of classification of the perceptual systems is possible and what sort of

---

[8]Most modern theories of reafference still hold that the motor output or feedback provides the information for discrimination, as opposed to Gibson's idea of action as adustment to perceptual information. (Eds.).

terminology do we use? This is a fair question. I am sorry to be a troublemaker but the only answer is a flexible terminology until a new consensus is reached. (Actually the classification of the special senses themselves, much as we might hope it to be clear, is a thorough muddle).

A new classification of the perceptual systems will have to start out with the information they register, and we now know that there is a great deal of redundancy in perception, that is, multiple cues for the same thing, or multiple equivalent information. The perceptual systems therefore have overlapping functions for getting external information although, of course, they do not overlap completely. Only the eyes can register the color of a surface, and only the skin can register its temperature, but the eye and the hand both can register its roughness or texture, its size, its inclination to gravity, and both systems can register its distance within about three feet. Beyond that, the eyes have to take over. Each perceptual system has some special virtue but none seems to neglect available information just because another system gets it too. Detection organs seem to relish redundancy, and a fire that is simultaneously seen, heard, felt, and smelled is experienced as one fire, not as four sensations. Consequently a classification of perceptual systems cannot be made as a mutually exclusive list in the way that it was hoped the senses could be listed.

Efforts to account for the "unity of the senses" in exteroception have not succeeded, and perhaps it is now clear why. As conveyers of sensation they cannot be unified, and their cooperation remains a puzzle. As detectors of information, however, their unity is just what they have in common and their diversity is what they do not.

If this is true the adaptation that occurs when the input of one perceptual system is put in conflict with the input of another is a problem in the resolution of information, and the question of the change in one sensation modality relative to the other is secondary. The ancient puzzle, going back to Bishop Berkeley, of whether we should *believe in vision* on the one hand or touch on the other, of which sense we should *trust,* is actually a problem of information pickup but it was thought to be a problem of sensory modalities because the modes of sensation were the only recognized channels of information.

The experimental evidence suggests to me that, in cases of discrepancy of information, the individual learns what is invariant. The learning is not, therefore, a matter of one sense modality altering another, or correcting it. No one is intrinsically more trustworthy than another. It is a matter of discovering what specifies the real layout of the world. And adaptation in this sense could occur in either the visual system or the haptic system independently or both together.[9]

Adaptation to prismatic distortion of the visual input, and to the resulting unstability of the phenomenal world when the head moves, seem to be facilitated by exploratory activity. But this does not mean that behavior determines perception; it only implies that perception, like behavior, is an activity of the individual.

---

[9]See Pick (1980) for a recent review of work on haptic perception. (Eds.).

# 2.5

# The Problem of Temporal Order in Stimulation and Perception*

## A. INTRODUCTION

Between 1950 and 1954 Lashley wrote three related papers entitled "The Problem of Serial Order in Behavior" (1951), "Dynamic Processes in Perception" (1954), and "In Search of the Engram" (1950). He was deeply concerned with the puzzle of time and memory, with the way in which temporal order enters into behavior, perception, and learning. He had been searching all his life for the physiological basis of memory—for the engram—but he had to conclude that he had discovered nothing as to its real nature and that no one else had either. The idea that the traces left by experience might be sensorimotor connections in the brain he liked no better than the older notion that traces were little images impressed on the neural tissue. Both of these ideas were inconsistent with the results of his experiments. "I sometimes feel," he said, "that the necessary conclusion is that learning just is not possible. It is difficult to conceive of a mechanism which can satisfy the conditions set for it" (1950, p. 477). "It seems certain that the theory of . . . paths from sense organs to association areas to the motor cortex is false . . . It is not possible to demonstrate the localization of a memory trace anywhere within the nervous system . . . and the so-called association areas are not storehouses for specific memories" (1950, p. 478).[1]

---

*Journal of Psychology, 1966, 62, 141–149. Copyright 1966 by The Journal Press, Inc. Reprinted by permission. This paper was the Psi Chi address delivered at the Eastern Psychological Association Meeting, April, 1965.

[1] See Masterton & Berkley (1974) for an overview of the difficulties encountered by the hypothesis of a sensory, motor, and association division of the cortex. Young's (1971) book is a useful history of the origin of many of these associationist ideas. (Eds.).

At the very end of the paper, however, Lashley sounded another note. He suggested that "the learning process must consist of the attunement of the elements of a complex system in such a way that a particular combination or pattern of cells responds more readily than before the experience" (1950, p. 479). No one knows how this might occur, and the suggestion is vague, but note that this idea is novel. If learning is a kind of *resonance* in the nervous system, a tuning of the system to certain inputs, then it is not any sort of storage of engrams or depositing of traces. Let us follow up this idea. It suggests to me an astonishing hypothesis, that learning does not necessarily depend on memory as it has always been conceived. Perhaps we should re-examine the problem of temporal order as Lashley started to do. Perhaps the mechanism of learning that proved so elusive can be found in the solution of that problem.

## B.    THE MUDDLE OF MEMORY

There is no satisfactory definition of memory that I can find, except the common sense one that appeals to introspection—the faculty of remembering. It cannot be defined as the rearousal of past experience, for surely not all memory is a matter of conscious experience. It cannot be defined as any lasting modification of neural function, for that would include growth. It cannot be defined as the general dependence of the present on the past, for that confuses memory with causation. Experimental psychologists usually do not even try to define memory except in terms of the experiments they perform. Memory is what the memory methods are concerned with. But the trouble with this is that a great many experiments requiring the reproduction of items presented, or the recognition of them, could be and often are called experiments on perception instead of memory. The act of drawing a visual pattern, or matching it to a sample, may be taken either as form-perception or as memory for form. The objective operations do not distinguish memory from perception. Only our subjective feeling about them separates the two kinds of activity. We have the feeling that perception is confined to the present, whereas memory refers to the past. But this distinction, be it noted, is wholly introspective. Moreover, as will be evident later, it cannot be made with any clarity.

There is another way, you might suppose, in which the activity of perception could be separated from the activity of memory—namely, by assuming that all sensitivity to simultaneous inputs constitutes perception and all sensitivity to successive inputs constitutes memory. The idea that form or space is perceived, whereas sequence or time is remembered, lurks vaguely at the back of our psychological thinking; but it is surely mistaken.[2] As I will try to show, the

---

[2]This is the theory Kant elaborated in the "Transcendental aesthetic" of the *Critique of Pure Reason* (1781/1929). (Eds.).

pattern and sequence of stimulation are too closely interwoven, space and time are too interdependent, for this formula to be true.

## C. THE POSSIBLE SOURCES OF CONFUSION

### 1. The Before-After Relation

One reason for the muddle of memory, I suspect, is our failure to consider the problem of temporal order *objectively*. We have habitually conceived time as consisting of past, present, and future, instead of a dimension defined by the relation of prior to subsequent. The stream of consciousness, as William James described it, exhibits the travelling moment of present time, the feeling of "now," and this divides the stream into a past extending in one direction and a future extending in the other. But the stream of stimulation has no such unique moment. Neither does the flow of external events. A man is aware of *now* but a clock is not. Consequently, a man is aware of his "past" but the clock is not. All the clock does is conform to the relation of before-after. Objective time, consisting of the sequential order of events, has no past and no memory.[3]

### 2. The Fallacy of Assigning Perception to the Present and Memory to the Past

We have been assuming, without ever examining the assumption, that memory applies to the past, perception is confined to the present, and the kind of activity we call expectation or prediction applies to the future. The separation of these activities, and of the physiological basis sought for each, has only an introspective criterion to justify it. The classification is questionable and I wonder if we can afford to keep them separate. Perception, memory, and expectation smell of faculties.

In the first place, an exact division between the present and the past by means of introspection has never been possible; and we, therefore, do not know when perception leaves off and memory begins. The travelling moment of present time is not a razor's edge, as James observed, for that would cease to exist; there is a "sensible" present, although no one has been able to measure its duration. I would add that we cannot be sure when perception stops and *expectation* begins, either, for a recent experiment at Cornell with an expanding silhouette in the field of view (Schiff, 1965), strongly suggests that the perception of approach and the expectation of collision are not separate.

Even more cogent is the evidence for the perception of motion. A change of visual pattern in time or a displacement of one part of the array relative to the rest of it is perceived, not remembered; and a visible motion may go on for a long

---

[3]Čapek (1961) has argued that modern physics can no longer utilize this conception of "objective time." Cf. Wiener's (1948) discussion of two concepts of time. (Eds.).

time, or may even be endless, like that of a whirlpool or a waterfall. Perception is an activity, not an instantaneous event shrunken to the razor's edge. The same is true of the perception of rhythm or any auditory sequence. The lower animals react to an optical motion as if it were a simple stimulus, where they would not react at all to a motionless pattern. Kinesthetic stimuli, like acoustic, must have duration to exist. Every possible sensation, in fact, by Titchener's criteria, must have the attribute of protensity.

### 3. The Fallacy of Assigning Pattern to Perception and Sequence to Memory

The perception of time has been recognized in psychology, or by some psychologists, but they have never faced up to the contradiction between this kind of time and memory-time, subjective time. We have accepted space-perception as a valid problem, but have been uncomfortable about time-perception. We have attempted to keep separate the problem of detecting patterns (objects) and that of detecting sequences (events). And hence the equivalence of pattern and sequence, of space and time, has seemed to be a puzzle which had better be swept under the rug than confronted.

For example, a series of items can be presented to a subject either in adjacent order (with an exposure device) or in successive order (with a memory drum); and the same groups are apprehended in the spatial distribution as in the temporal distribution. Is the first a span of perception and the second a span of memory? The apprehension is equivalent in both cases.

The eyes of primates and men work by scanning—that is, by pointing the foveas at the parts of the scene in succession. The eyes of rabbits and horses do not, for they see nearly all the way around at once and have retinas with little foveation. Does this mean that a horse can perceive his environment, whereas a man can apprehend it only with the aid of memory? I once thought so (1950a, p. 158 ff.) on the theory that successive retinal images must be integrated by memory, but this now seems to me wrong. It is truer to suppose that a visual system can substitute sequential vision for panoramic vision, time for space. Looking around is equivalent to seeing around, with the added advantage of being able to look closely. It is no harder for a brain to integrate a temporal arrangement than a spatial arrangement.

### D.  THE EXPERIMENTAL STUDY OF SEQUENTIAL PERCEPTION

My suspicions about the orthodox theory of memory are based on 15 years of research having to do with the perception of moving things or processes and with the control of locomotion. A good many of these experiments were unpublishable because they did not work out. But those that failed and those that worked both point to the general conclusion that the flow of stimulation, its transformation, reveals the activity of perception better than the unchanging form, the picture, that we generally use as a stimulus. A form, in fact, is nothing but a continuous nontransformation just as nonmotion is a special case of motion. Hence, the perception of space is incomprehensible unless we tackle it as the problem of space-time. Even the cues for depth, the unambiguous ones, are kinetic and not static. I mean by these the parallax information that comes from moving about in the world.

Parenthetically, let me say that the experiments began to be intelligible only when optical motion was clearly distinguished from material motion, the proximal stimulus from the distal source of stimulation, and only after it was realized how remarkably unlike the motion of an object the motion of light is. A perspective transformation is unlike a rotation and a magnification is unlike an approach, but each *corresponds* nevertheless to its objective event. I will not try to summarize these experiments here, but some of their implications are interesting.[4]

We found that continuous optical transformations can yield quite simple perceptions, but that they yield two kinds of perception at the same time, one of change and one of nonchange (Gibson & Gibson, 1957). The perspective transformation of a rectangle, for example, was always perceived as both something rotating and something rectangular. This suggests that the transformation as such ⟵ is one kind of stimulus information, for motion, and that the invariants under transformation are another kind of stimulus information, for the constant properties of the object. The constancy of the phenomenal object in such experiments, far from being destroyed by the variation of momentary sensation, may be enhanced by it (Gibson, 1963). This hypothesis of a persisting stimulus underlying a flux of changing stimuli, of invariant variables accompanying the variant variables, is a very powerful one. I am tempted to call it a fact, since it is a familiar idea in mathematics, and we should have thought of it long ago. There is almost always some permanence imbedded in any change. Note particularly that this continuing stimulus, if it is registered, explains the phenomenal constancy and identity of the object without any appeal whatever to a cumulative memory process.

The study of pattern vision in men and animals has been going on for a long time, and the theoretical problems are familiar ones. The study of what I will call (for the moment) change-of-pattern-vision is only beginning, and its theoretical problems are new. We may have to relinquish the old presuppositions in studying the new field. If, as is likely, transformations over time were the usual stimuli in the course of the evolution of visual systems, and nontransformations over time were rare and exceptional, then the primacy of form or pattern comes into question. There is no "form" left in a continuous transformation. It has vanished, and all that remains is the invariants.[5] Form discrimination as we test it by the presentation of two stationary pictures is irrelevant. There are individual

---

[4]Cf. Chs. 1.2 and 2.6. (Eds.).
[5]Cf. Ch. 3.5. (Eds.).

pictures in a strip of motion picture film but not in the visual system of an insect. It is no wonder, then, that a lower animal may have good motion discrimination with poor stationary pattern vision. Hints of this primitive sensitivity are still obtainable in our own pictorially educated vision. The afterimage from watching the expansion or contraction of the light from a rotating spiral is contraction or expansion respectively, and the direction of this apparent motion does not depend on the comparison of two different patterns at two different times. So far from motion being the comparison of two static pictures, it is the other way round—a static picture is only the null case of motion.

## E. NEW THEOREMS

Not only in vision but also in active touch and obviously in audition, the natural input to the perceptual organ is a changing array of stimulation—not a stationary one. The registering of the change is one task of the nervous system, and the detection of the underlying permanence is another. Perhaps, as Lashley suggested, the brain resonates to whatever is invariant under transformation and becomes increasingly attuned to it with recurrence over time. If so, perception and learning could be accounted for without any assumption of memory considered as an accumulation of traces. The brain would be a self-tuning resonator, not a storehouse.

A number of theorems are implied by this theory of apprehension, and I will try to make them explicit.

*1.* A succession can be perceived without having to convert all its elements into a simultaneous complex.

As Boring (1942, p. 576) points out, psychologists have generally accepted the proposition that a succession of items can be grasped only if the earlier ones are "held over" so as to be combined with the later ones in a single composite. Hence comes the theory of traces, requiring that every percept begins a trace, that they accumulate, and that every memory trace can theoretically reinstate its percept. The whole line of reasoning can be pushed into absurdity. The alternative is to deny the proposition on which it is based.[6]

*2.* Stimulation normally consists of *successivities* as well as *adjacencies*, and either will excite a receptive system.

This says that there are two kinds of order in stimulation, adjacent and successive (Gibson, 1950a, p. 63), the latter being on the same footing as the former. A visual margin between dark and light is a stimulus of the first sort, and a visual transient between dark and light is one of the second sort. The important fact in

---

[6]Loftus and Loftus (1980) present data from memory research which seem to argue against the trace theory. (Eds.).

either case is the direction of the intensity step. An upward margin is never confused with a downward margin, and an "on" is never confused with an "off." The retina in fact contains anatomical units that detect both kinds of transition, the spatial and the temporal. The sequential detectors do not have to make a comparison of intensity *now* with the memory of intensity *then* (an *off* receptor surely does not need a memory), and similarly the adjacent detectors do not have to compare intensity above the margin with intensity below it (or to the right and to the left of it).

Note that stimulation is asserted to be relational by definition and that sensations of absolute brightness are left out of account as being irrelevant.

*3.* The detection of *different-from-before* is simply an alternative to the detection of *same-as-before*, and both are primitive.

This says that the perception of a change or transformation is the reciprocal of a perception of nonchange or nontransformation. Neither requires an act of comparison. If the principle is extended over time, recognition can be explained as the detection of same-as-before without the requirement that the new percept be compared to the trace of the old one and be judged to match. Similarly the perception of novelty, the opposite of recognition, can be explained as the detection of different-from-before without having to assume that the memory is searched for traces of the past and no match is found.[7]

The problem of phenomenal identity in perception experiments using sequential stimulation (e.g., moving shadows) is not fundamentally different from the problem of recognition in memory experiments using sequential stimulation.

*4.* With increasing elaboration of the successive order of stimulation and the adjacent order of stimulation, limits are finally reached to the apprehension of both successive units and adjacent units.

This says that the temporal structure of stimulation and the spatial structure are both grouped into units, sometimes hierarchical and sometimes unrelated units, and that apprehension can span only a limited number of these units. In short, apprehension spans time—more exactly, events in time—but this does not have to be conceived as a span of memory, or as "primary," "immediate," or "short-term" memory. Apprehension also spans objects in space, and this does not have to be conceived as exclusively a span of perception. It is as if the brain could register only so many different successive events occurring in the same place and only so many different objects existing at the same time in different places.

As an example of what is meant by *successive units* in the above theorem, consider the following. The last paragraph may be said to consist of 571 letters, or 112 words, or 26 phrases, or four sentences, or one thought. Which unit do we choose for a description of the source of stimulation? (The same question arises if we consider the voice instead of the writing.) Clearly, all are legitimate. Each

---

[7]Shaw and Pittenger (1978) develop this idea further. (Eds.).

kind of unit is nested within a superordinate unit, and each kind is composed of subordinate units. There is no clear end in either direction, either of higher or lower order. And the same principle of forms within forms applies to the events of the natural world as to language. There is a *grammar* of events and a corresponding grammar of stimulation. Since there are normally no absolute units with which a psychologist can rest content, the choice of units is not a matter of psychological theory. It is only a matter of their being appropriate for the level of apprehension being considered.

5. In this theory, the function of perceiving is to maintain the contact of an organism with its environment.

Since, for an active organism in an eventful world, the stimulus energy is a continual flux, the main problem of perceiving is to detect the information that specifies the objects of the world—that is, to register the invariants under transformation. This is a solution to the puzzle of perceptual constancy. More than that, it resolves certain perplexities in the theory of memory, for it implies that what we call memory and recognition is often only a special case of invariant-detection. *Recollection* is then a sort of human luxury, an incidental ability to contemplate the past. Learning can occur without the intervention of remembering, just as thought can be imageless, and just as perception, in my view, can be sensationless.


## F.  CONCLUSION

The puzzle of the detection of both change and permanence in the world goes back nearly 2500 years. Heraclitus and his followers argued that all is flux and permanence is illusory. Parmenides argued that the world is immutable and change is illusory. His pupil, Zeno, even argued that motion is illusory. The controversy was a standoff until it was supposedly resolved by the doctrine that the atomic elements explain the permanencies while their separation and recombination explain the changes. But this resolution is not satisfactory to a psychologist, for it does not apply very well to the problem of what the *information* might be for apprehending both change and permanence.

The French have a neat saying, *Plus ça change, plus c'est la même chose*. It asserts, I think, the reality of permanence within change, of invariants underlying transformation. More than that, it suggests that the identify of a thing, its constancy, can emerge in perception only when it is observed under changing circumstances in various aspects. The static form of a thing, its image or picture, is not at all what is permanent about it. A form frozen in time is ambiguous information and is not a typical stimulus for our receptive surfaces. Only when the perspectives flow can we notice the distinctive features of the solid object. The invariants can be detected only if there is opportunity to distinguish them from the variations. This is surely not a matter of storing up all the cross-sections of past experience and of performing mental operations on the composite brought up to date. Let us not treat memory like a sacred cow, just because we are sometimes aware of remembering.

## G.  SUMMARY

The concept of memory in its relation to perception is a muddle. If we accept the fact of sequential perception, rejecting the fiction of momentary pattern-perception, matters become more intelligible. If perception involves the apprehension of a changing world, not a frozen one, the problem is that of detecting invariants under transformation. The permanence can be isolated just because the perspectives change. The latter do not have to be stored up and put together in a composite. The mechanism of perceptual learning is one in which the nervous system resonates to the invariants of the stimulus flow, as Lashley suspected, not one of storage and retrieval of engrams. The recalling of the past, the capacity (in some persons) to summon memory images into consciousness, may well be a quite incidental accompaniment of learning, not its basis.

# 2.6 What Gives Rise to the Perception of Motion?

## PART I: WHAT GIVES RISE TO THE PERCEPTION OF MOTION?*

Experimental studies of the perception of motion in the past, especially of visual motion, have failed to resolve the old puzzles or to yield any kind of general explanation. The root of the trouble may be a persistent misconception of what gives rise to the perception—an erroneous but plausible assumption about the stimulus.

What is the effective stimulus that always elicits a sensation or perception of motion? The physical motion of an object in the world, one might answer, but this is obviously not sufficient unless the object is illuminated or luminous, and unless it lies within the field of view of the observer. The motion must be specified somehow in the light to an organism and it must also enter an eye. When it is specified in the light and does enter the eye the animal almost always detects it, as the study of behavior shows. This is what is meant by saying that animals are very sensitive to "motion." But physical motion is not the same as optical motion.

A mobile object is not the only cause of motion detection. Because of motion parallax, the observer will also see a kind of motion when he himself moves or is moved in the environment, all objects being stationary. In this case, the human

*Psychological Review, 1968, 75, 335-346. Copyright 1968 by the American Psychological Association. Reprinted by permission. This was written as a summary of research carried out under Gibson's Office of Naval Research Contract. Two earlier summaries were published as Gibson (1954b) and Gibson (1957a, Ch. 1.2 herein). The final summary is available from the Navy as Gibson (1975c).

observer describes the motion of objects as only "apparent." Distinguishing between the "motion" of objects and the "movement" of the observer (Gibson, 1954b), it is clear that both cases will cause an optical motion of some sort in the light to the eye. This light, and only this light, contains the effective stimulus.

In the past, however, we have assumed that the retinal image was the proximal stimulus for vision. We have analyzed light-stimulation in terms of the retinal image, not in terms of the array of light to the eye (as we shall see, the two are not equivalent). For this reason, it has long been assumed as if it were self-evident that some *displacement of the retinal image over the retina* must be the effective stimulus for an impression of motion. I will call this the *retinal image displacement hypothesis*.

This hypothesis is clearly incorrect, for a retinal displacement does *not* elicit any sensation of motion during the saccadic *scanning* movements of the eyes between fixations, nor during the spontaneous correctional or tremor movements of the eyes during fixations. The first fact is an old puzzle (why does the world not seem to move when the eyes move?) and the second is a new puzzle arising from the discovery of an optical way to "stabilize" the retinal image on the retina during a fixation. In the absence of any other hypothesis to take its place, however, a number of ad hoc theories has arisen to explain the failures of the retinal image displacement hypothesis. One theory is that a retinal sensation *does* occur during an eye movement but that it is canceled out in the brain.

I shall argue that the hypothesis should be discarded, but let us first consider the reasons for its plausibility and persistence.

1. Some displacements of the retinal image relative to the retina *do* seem to yield sensations of motion. During pursuit fixation of a moving object in the environment, the image of the environment moves across the retina and the phenomenal world behind the object is often said to exhibit an "apparent" motion. (But at the same time, the object is also seen to move although its image is *not* displaced regularly over the retina, so there is a paradox here.) During after-nystagmus, the vertigo arising after cessation of prolonged artificial body-rotation, the phenomenal world has a disconcerting apparent motion—a motion said to result from the slow phase of the after-nystagmus but not from the fast phase. During a forced movement of the eyeball, as when it is pushed by a finger, there is an apparent motion of the environment, and much has been made of this observation during a century of theorizing, from Helmholtz to Von Holst.

2. It is true that an abrupt displacement of a spot of light in an otherwise homogeneous field of darkness will elicit a sensation of displacement (e.g., Hick, 1950). A rapidly moving spot of light yields the impression of a *streak*. But a slow motion of the spot cannot be observed, and a stationary spot may be seen in illusory motion after it has been fixated for some time in the dark—the so-called autokinetic phenomenon.

3. The hypothesis of retinal image displacement for the sensation of motion is analogous to other assumptions about the effective stimuli for other sensations.

The location of a luminous spot on the retina is supposed to yield a sensation of location. The intensity of a stimulus on the retina is supposed to yield a sensation of brightness, and the wavelength of the stimulus a sensation of color. The form of the stimulus is supposed to yield a sensation of form and the angular extent of the stimulus a sensation of extendedness. A brief pulse of stimulation on the retina is supposed to yield a brief flash of sensation. Accordingly, a motion of the stimulus over the retina should always yield a sensation of motion. It is assumed not only that these stimuli yield the corresponding sensations but also that the sensations depend upon the respective stimuli. All of these assumptions can be challenged (Gibson, 1966b) but they have seemed to support one another because they were mutually consistent. They are all part of the classical theory that a two-dimensional retinal image delivers two-dimensional visual sensations, to which depth must be somehow added.

4. The retinal image displacement hypothesis is taken to be consistent with the fact that the aftereffect of inspecting an environmental motion is localized on the retina—the negative afterimage of motion that results from looking at a slowly rotating disk, or a Plateau spiral, or a moving belt behind a window (or a waterfall). It is said to be analogous to the negative afterimage of hue or brightness in being a patch of disembodied motion in the visual field like the patch of filmy color constituting an afterimage. But this way of describing the aftersensation may be inadequate, as will be evident later; it may prove to be not so much a patch of motion as an aftereffect of the optical change that occurs at the *boundaries* of the disk, window, or waterfall.

5. The whole history of research on stroboscopic motion (Boring, 1942, Ch. 15), including Wertheimer's (1912) theory of the phenomenon, implies the hypothesis that displacement of a stimulus over the retina is the necessary condition for a perception of motion. Wertheimer was only concerned to explain why this displacement could be discontinuous instead of a dense sequence of momentary stimuli at a dense series of adjacent retinal points as commonsense and physics would suppose. He assumed a neural process of "short-circuiting" in the brain, never doubting that the retinal image was projected to the brain. It is possible, however, that stroboscopic motion can be subsumed under change of pattern in the image and does not have to be thought of as displacement of a stimulus.

6. The whole history of research on the just noticeable speed of motion and the discrimination of different speeds implies the assumption that a sensation must occur with a sufficient displacement of the stimulus over the retina and must increase with increasing displacement per unit of time. Many of these experiments in the psychophysical tradition have been reprinted or summarized by Spigel (1965) in his book of readings on the perception of motion. The present author's criticism of these experiments is also reprinted in this book (pp. 125–146). I objected that the supposed absolute threshold of the sensation of motion differs with different arrays of stimulation, and that the supposed differential

threshold depends on how far apart the standard and the variable motions are in the field of view. Angular speed of motion has thus not yielded to psychophysical measurement, for the experiments that attempt to isolate it are unsatisfactory.

In general, psychologists and physiologists have not been able to conceive any other possible visual stimulus for motion than "the successive stimulation of adjacent retinal loci," as Spigel phrases it (1965, p. 2). I too once asserted that since the retinal image is a two-dimensional projection of focused light on a sensitive anatomical surface, "when we say that it undergoes motion we must always mean motion with reference to that surface (Gibson, 1950a, p. 31)." This assertion now seems to me wrong. The effective proximal stimulus, more exactly the effective stimulus-information, can be conceived in a wholly different way. I shall argue that motion *of* the retinal image is a misconception and that motion *in* the retinal image, a change of pattern, is not displacement with reference to the retina.

## The Misconception Underlying the Retinal Image Displacement Hypothesis

For centuries we have thought of the retinal image as a picture projected and focused on a screen, the image being mobile and the screen fixed. The image is supposed to be freely transposable over the retina. But actually it is the other way round. The image is perfectly stationary, being anchored to the world, and the retina moves relative to the image. The retina is *continually* moving behind its image. Exploratory eye movements are necessary with highly foveated eyes like ours in order to bring the fovea successively to bear on details of the total image. Tremor of the eyes, moreover, is incessant and vision fades away when it is artificially canceled. In this cancellation experiment the term "stabilized retinal image" is a misnomer, for the normal image is always stable and the experiment only causes the image to vibrate in synchrony with the retina.

If the image is thought to be freely transposable over the retina we are faced with the puzzle of how it can be equivalent for vision when it excites a different set of receptors in the retina. But this is to state the question wrongly, for it is the retina that sweeps and vibrates in the course of its normal functioning. The puzzle is not one of a transposable image but of a mobile retina. In short, a retinal image from the natural environment *cannot* be displaced over the retina for it is the retina that is displaced over its image—the extended or potential image which the eye explores by sampling (Gibson, 1966b, Ch. 12).

The problem is not just one of which moves relative to the other—the retina or the image. In truth, to put the matter radically, the natural retinal image is not an image at all. We are accustomed to visualize it in terms of photography, as a frozen sample of the structure of the ambient light at one station point at one moment of time. This bears enough similarity to a flat photographic image on a plane surface to perpetuate the misconception. But actually each eye samples the field of view of the head, the head turns to sample the whole array of the ambient light, and the body moves from one vista to another in the environment. All higher animals do so, not just man. The retina sweeps over a potential image in time, revealing a new crescent of the array and abandoning an old one. It is not an image projected on a plane but on a sphere. The eye-head system can look around so as to produce a microcosm of the environment inside the eye "like a panoramic painting of the world shrunken to the interior of a 1-inch sphere (Gibson, 1966b, p. 259)." And, even further, this panorama is merely one of a continuous family of transformations corresponding to each of the possible paths of locomotion in the environment. If we are going to say that what a man sees as he gets about in the world depends on his retinal images we have got to stop thinking about them as flat snapshots projected and focused on a sensitive anatomical screen in a small spherical darkroom.

It should now be evident that the retinal image as we habitually conceive it is not equivalent to the array of light coming to the eye, and not even equivalent to the sector of the array *entering* the eye. For the problems of vision, image optics will not suffice and ecological optics will have to be formulated. The latter is at a higher level of analysis than the former.

## The Possible Causes of Motion Stimulation

If we discard the retinal image displacement hypothesis as a basis for motion detection what alternatives do we have? We may have to give up the theory that retinal sensations are the data for perception. What other information is available? There is good evidence to show that some visual perceptions of objective motion occur in the absence of visual sense data, perceptions that are "amodal" in that they do not have the defining attributes of the visual mode (Michotte, Thinès, & Crabbé, 1964). One can detect occluded motion if the information for occlusion is available (Reynolds, 1968).[1] As for the detection of subjective movement, psychologists have struggled in vain for a century with the puzzle of whether kinesthesis is one mode of sensation, or is multimodal, or perhaps amodal (Boring, 1942). The assumption that there is a fixed number of senses is probably untenable. So perhaps the time is ripe for a theory of perception and proprioception based on higher-order information instead of on sensory data.

To make a fresh start, consider the possible sources of optical motion in the light to an eye for a living animal in a natural environment. (The kinds of optical motion from an apparatus in a laboratory or a display intended to produce motion will be considered later.) What kinetic events have corresponding optical events that could induce an experience of motion or movement if the light entered an eye? There are two main types of such an event: motion of an object in the environment and movement of the observer. The latter may be subdivided into

---

[1]Cf. Ch. 2.7. (Eds.)

four categories, however, so that the list of sources comes to five: motion of an object, locomotion of a whole animal in the environment, movement of the animal's head on its body, movement of an eye in its head, and movement of an extremity of its body.

Other kinds of motion is described by astronomy and physics need not be considered. The motion of the environment in space does not concern us because it is not given in light except by obscure information. Motion of the environment relative to an animal is impossible, although a rotation of it can be simulated with a so-called optokinetic apparatus. The motion of a physical particle is only given in light when the array has been highly magnified. Let us examine the five types to determine what they entail in the way of optical information.

### Objective Motion

Any surface or object in the environment that reflects (or emits) light can move in a variety of ways relative to the permanent environment and can thus alter the perspectives of its texture and its edges in the ambient light. Rigid objects can move, in accordance with Newton's laws, in ways that are analyzable by three dimensions of translation and three axes of spin. Viscous or elastic surfaces can move in ways that are very difficult to analyze, the turbulent flow of liquid and the motions of the skin of an animal being examples.

What are the optical motions corresponding to the six parameters of rigid material motion? They are by no means copies or representations. They can be treated mathematically as families of perspective transformations by methods of projective geometry (Gibson, 1957a, but see also the modified and extended analysis of Hay, 1966).[2] This treatment, however, is limited to the consideration of the plane faces or facets of an object, the geometrical polygons, and their transformations in the optic array. What about a polyhedron, a many-faced solid object? When it turns, so that unprojected faces become projected, and vice versa, there is information for the back faces as well as the front faces. Another mathematical treatment than one confined to perspective transformations is required. There has to be an analysis of occlusion and disocclusion.

This approach, moreover, leaves out of account the background of a solid object, not only its back side. Objects are not ordinarily seen against the sky or in darkness. The hiding or screening of one surface by another and its opposite, the revealing or uncovering of it, are typical of object motions in a terrestrial environment. Motion of an object toward the observer involves not only more of its figure but less of its ground, and motion away from the observer involves the opposite. Even a frontal motion of an object does not yield simply a frontal displacement in the visual field, as we have assumed. There is a progressive

---

[2]In 1957, I assumed that there are six families of perspective transformations corresponding to the six Newtonian motions, but this is not correct. Transformations specify motions, as Hay has shown, but the correspondence is not this simple.

occlusion of the background at the leading edge and a progresive disocclusion at the trailing edge, apart from the "motion." Quite possibly this is the essential information for the perception of what we call its motion.

Evidently the occlusion transformation (if it may be called that) must be analyzed and experimentally isolated as well as the projective transformations and size transformations.

The optical motions corresponding to the types of viscous or elastic motion of a surface have been little studied. There is not even a classification of such motions. Fieandt and Gibson (1959) set up one such optical transformation, corresponding to "stretch," and Gibson and Pick (1963) considered one kind of transformation in the light coming from a human face, but the problem has scarcely been touched.[3]

In general, the optical information for environmental events other than simple displacements has been neglected (although the array from a motion picture screen carries an enormous amount of it). One reason for this neglect is probably our preoccupation with retinal displacements.

### Locomotion of the Observer

Whenever the station point of an eye in a head on the body of an individual is displaced relative to the iluminated environment, actively or passively, a transformation of the whole array of ambient light results, termed *motion perspective* (Gibson, Olum, & Rosenblatt, 1955). This is not to be confused with differential displacements of parts of the retinal image over the retina, the supposed cue of *motion parallax* (e.g., Gibson, Gibson, Smith, & Flock, 1959). An observer can explore this total transformation of the ambient array just as he can explore the total nontransformation of the frozen array that exists when the station point of the eye remains motionless. Motion perspective has been analyzed for the surface of the earth from horizon to horizon, as it applies in aviation, and gradients of velocity have been analyzed for the slant of a plane surface (Flock, 1964a). But the ordinary environment contains edges, and locomotion therefore involves occlusion-transformations at edges. These kinetic edge effects may well be more important than gradients of velocity as information for perception. The slightest shift in the station point of an eye makes them evident. When long continued, they constitute the transitions from one vista to another as the traveler moves through the world. But, as noted, they still await a precise mathematical description.

The point to be emphasized about motion perspective, including edge-effects, is that it does *not* elicit a perception of objective motion but a detection of

---

[3]Johansson (1973) introduced one technique for studying the perception of biological motions, and a number of further studies using his technique have since been made (cf. Johansson, von Hofsten & Jansson, 1980). (Eds.)

subjective movement. With an introspective attitude, to be sure, a human observer can report on *apparent* centrifugal flow of the visual field ahead when he drives a car but he is ordinarily simply aware of his locomotion in the rigid world. Is this awareness *visual* or is it *kinesthetic?* No answer can be given. I have called it *visual kinesthesis,* but a better statement is to say that it is nonmodal or sensationless, that is, that the classical sensations are irrelevant for it.

Motion perspective in any case provides information. It affords control or active locomotion. It also permits the registering of passive locomotion. Volition, together with classical muscle-joint proprioception, accompanies it in the first case but not in the second. But the global flow of motion perspective is information in its own right; it provides the *only* valid information for a bird in a headwind as to its motion or nonmotion with respect to the earth.

It is important to realize that motion perspective caused by locomotion entails change in the *whole* of the textured ambient array whereas the alteration of perspective caused by an objective motion entails only change in *part* of the ambient array, the remainder being frozen. If this part-whole difference can be picked up by a visual system, the difference between motion in the world and locomotion of the self would be specified by the input of the system, and an explanation in terms of a special brain process to correct the retinal sensation would not be required.

### Head Turning and Head Rotation Relative to the Body

In vertebrates, head turning is exactly linked with compensatory eye turning so as to keep the eyes in a fixed posture relative to the ambient array for as much of the time as possible (Gibson, 1966b, Chs. 4 & 9). Nevertheless, when the head turns or is turned its field of view sweeps across the ambient array and a new sample is available for the binocular system. In primates the head's field is approximately a hemisphere. The same thing happens when the head is rotated on an axis parallel with the shoulders, in looking up or down. The shift of the field of view relative to the whole sphere of available light can be noticed by introspection; there is a kind of uncovering and covering up of one's surroundings. But this shift or sweep is not seen as a visual motion except in postrotation vertigo; ordinarily one is imply aware of the head turning (or being turned) in a stationary world. The input from the neck (or from the semicircular canals, with passive turning) confirms this head turning with information from a different source. When the head is tilted to one side, however, or passively rotated on a saggital axis, a visual sensation of motion is easier to notice. This head movement does not yield a new sample of the ambient array; instead there is roughly the same sample with a rotation of each retina behind its retinal image. The subjective visual field tilts and it is *almost* as if the world were tilting. When the available array is reduced to a vertical luminous line in darkness the line *does* appear to tilt, the Aubert phenomenon, although not as much as the actual tilt of the retina relative to the image of the line. An illusory visual sensation seems to arise with tilts of the head but not with sweeps or shifts of the field of view, and it seems to be enhanced by impoverishing the optic array.[4]

Note that the information to specify head rotation is not contained in the optic array (unless the station-point of an eye is displaced relative to the environment). Head rotation is specified only by a shift or rotation of the *borders of the field of view*, borders corresponding to the nose and eyebrows. What moves is a sort of *window* opening on the optic array. The occlusion and disocclusion of the structure of the array can be noticed easily if one holds a tube in front of one eye and then looks about. The world does not move but the window does. If, however, a lens or an inverting lens-system is inserted in the tube so as to alter the occlusion transformation an illusory motion of the world results.

### Eye Movements Relative to the Head

The established types of eye rotation are the small saccades or tremor movements during fixation, the large saccadic eye movements, vergences, pursuit movements, compensatory nystagmus during head turning, and after-nystagmus. They all entail displacement or sweep of the retina behind the potential retinal image, but two of them are accompanied by illusory visual sensations and the rest are not. These two are the apparent motion of the background during pursuit and the apparent motion of the environment during vertigo, to which must be added the apparent motion of the environment during a *forced* movement of an eye. In line with the new conception of stimulus information, we need an explanation of why the apparent motions arise. We need no explanation of why they do *not* arise during the majority of eye movements, for motion of the retina is ordinarily registered as eye movement, that is, as sensationless proprioception.

In the theory of sensation-based perception there has to be a position sense of the eye, a feeling of the gaze-line relative to the skull (and thus relative to the skeleton and thus relative to the substratum). Only by means of such a position sense could input of retinal points be corrected so as to yield visual directions-from-here. But, despite all efforts, the position sense has not been demonstrated to exist. The eye has no joint, as the elbow has to register the position of the forearm, and the eye muscles seem to register strain rather than angular position, so that the perception of visual direction remains a puzzle. However, if the ambient optic array (or the potential retinal image) is recognized as a fact of optics to which the ocular system conforms, no special position sense of the eye need be assumed. The animal does not have to "feel" to "know" where his eye is pointing for he

---

[4]There is considerable experimental literature on the classical problem of the perceived uprightness of the phenomenal world despite the tilt of the retinal image, but this is not quite the same as the problem of its *stability*, which is here considered. For an introduction to the former controversy, see Gibson (1952b) and the references given.

can, as it were, "see" where it is pointing (although this need not be a reportable visual sensation). If eye movements can be registered relative to the array they do not have to be registered relative to the skull, skeleton, and ground (Gibson, 1966b, Ch. 12).

Returning to the illusory sensations of motion, the explanation may be that, under some conditions, the displacement of the retinal stimulus relative to the retina becomes *obtrusive*. A subjective or introspective attitude is one such condition, an abnormal oculomotor adjustment is another, and a reduction of the information in the ambient optic array is probably a third. Under such a condition the distinguishing of an objective motion from a subjective movement may become difficult. The input of the receptors, or the simpler receptive units, of the retina will become evident when the information sought by the exploratory visual system becomes obscure.

### Movement of an Extremity of the Body

Many of the higher animals have limbs that are visible, that is, enter the field of view of the head. Movements of the extremities relative to the main body constitute a large part of the animal's behavior. The classical sense of movement, kinesthesis, is supposed to register and provide for voluntary control of such movements. This afferent input comes principally from the joints of the skeleton (Gibson, 1966b, Ch. 6). But clearly an input will also occur from the eyes if the movement of the foot, paw, or hand is in the field of view. The skills of the primate come largely from looking at the hands. The visual feedback is covariant with the articular feedback. The information for positions and connected sets of positions (movements) is the same in both perceptual systems.

The visual motion of an extremity is somewhere between a subjective movement and an objective motion. It partakes of both proprioception and exteroception. The hand moves both with reference to the body and with reference to the world. Its projection is continuous with the body in the optic array and yet it is almost a figure on a ground like the projection of an object in the environment. The transformations arising from this quasi-object include all those that arise from a true object; occlusions of the environment, perspective transformations, and those corresponding to elastic motions. When the human infant watches his moving hand he is probably differentiating the set of those optical motions, thereby improving both his perceptual skill and his proprioceptive skill. Experimental studies of this phenomenon with infant monkeys have been carried out (Held & Bauer, 1967).

When an adult is performing manipulation his eyes move in all possible ways, fixating, scanning, pursuing, altering convergence, and compensating for movements of his head. The enormously complex motions of the retinal image relative to the retina are not registered at all in this situation. But the information in the optic array from the hands, the tools, and the stationary background of the environment, that is, the occlusions, the perspective and topological transformations, are registered with precision by the retino-neuro-muscular system. The optic array itself is the frame of reference with respect to which these informative optical motions occur.

## A Theory of the Optical Information for Perceiving Motion and Detecting Movement

A distinction has been drawn between perception and proprioception that cuts across the modes of sensation. There is information in ambient light for both objective motion and for two types of subjective movement, locomotion of the observer and movement of his limbs. Two other types of subjective movement, head turning and eye turning (the movements of the visual system itself), are not specified by transformations in the array or changes of its structure but by changes in the *sampling* of the array.

To be explicit, (a) when a figure in the array transforms with occlusion effects the motion of an object is specified. (b) When the total array transforms with occlusion effects the movement (locomotion) of the observer is specified. (c) When a certain familiar elastic protrusion enters the array the movement of a limb is specified.

These optical motions are registered by exploratory adjustments of the head-eye-retina system. (d) When the borders of the ocular orbits sweep across the array head turning is specified. (e) When the retina sweeps over the potential retinal image in one of the several ways possible for the oculomotor system an eye movement is specified. These five hypotheses together constitute a new theory that resolves puzzles of long standing.

According to this theory, reportable visual sensations of motion may or may not accompany the pickup of these types of information. They are merely symptomatic of information pickup in any case, not the basis of it. The important kinds of information that the retina seems to register are continuous *transformations* of form and texture and *disruptions* of texture (the occlusion transformation).

## Implications for Research

Most of the known experiments and demonstrations concerned with visual motion presuppose the retinal image displacement hypothesis and the general theory of sensations (e.g., Spigel, 1965). Experimenters have engaged in a misguided effort to scratch the retina with a focused pencil of light in much the same way that they would scratch the skin with a stylus. The new theory suggested calls for new experiments.

1. An obvious need is for clarification of what is meant by optical transformations. Even more important are the disruptions of optical texture, the kinds of discontinuity or rupturing that can occur in an array. Methods of displaying such

stimulus information are by optical shadow-projection, by animated film projected on a screen, and by computer-generated displays.

2. Points of light in otherwise homogeneous darkness do not serve to simplify the conditions for motion perception, as previously assumed, but only to reduce the information in an array. Textured and structured light is needed if the optical motions in the light are to be controlled and systematically varied.

3. The practice of requiring the subject to fixate a stationary point so as to keep the retina stationary in space during a presentation of motion does not achieve the intended purpose of isolating a displacement over the retina, for whatever moves relative to the fixation spot will constitute either change of pattern or will involve occlusion effects.

4. The ingenious optical procedure of "stabilizing" the human retinal image (actually of moving a beam of light so as to match the spontaneous movements of the eye during fixation) should be recognized as complicating, not simplifying, the normal activity of the retina. Similarly, the neurophysiological results of applying motions to the stationary retina of a paralyzed eye (e.g. Hubel & Wiesel, 1962) are highly suggestive but cannot be expected to reveal the neurophysiology of a mobile eye in an intact visual system.

5. The neurophysiological puzzle of how the form of a retinal image can be recognized when the form of the physiological image in the receptors of the retina is altered by an eye movement (the problem of Gestalt transposition) becomes an unnecessary difficulty in the new theory. Neither a form on the retina nor a displacement of it over the retina need be registered—only the *information* in the structure and transformation of an array. The conception of a physiological image, a picture transmitted to the brain, can be finally discarded. Experimenters can permit a moving eye and a changing array without having to worry about the eye-camera analogy.

6. New experiments are possible on the aftersensation of motion obtained in a patch of the visual field occupied by a moving belt, or a slowly rotating disk or an expansive or contractive motion coming to the eye from a Plateau spiral. The aftersensation has been described as an image filled with motion in the opposite direction, but it might just as well be an aftereffect at the contour of the patch arising from the disruption of optical texture at the contour. Rotation involves a *shearing* of the inner texture relative to the surrounding texture; expansion or contraction involves *destruction or creation,* respectively, of the inner texture at the boundary. The crucial factor might prove to be not the "motion" as such but the kinetic discontinuity.

7. The perception of the speed of motion of an object on a background might prove to depend on the rate of occlusion of the background at the edges of the object. For an object on the earth, this optical information is invariant with changes in the size and distance of the object. The constancy of perceived speed for such an object would thus be explained directly, whereas the kind of speed given by extent of retinal displacement per unit of judged time, speed as defined

in physics and conceived in empty space, runs into all the difficulties of the theory of how sensations are corrected by depth perception (Reynolds, 1968). The explanation of Brown's velocity transposition phenomenon, elaborating the suggestion of Smith and Sherlock (1957), might be attempted along the same lines, although this involves the complexities of window motion as distinguished from terrestrial object motion.

8. In general, new conceptions of motion perception go along with new conceptions of space perception, although evidence for the latter has not been considered in this review. The information in light for the perception of surfaces and surface layout, and the nature of this perception, has been considered elsewhere (Gibson, 1966b, Chs. 9–12).

9. The apparatus that can be used by a psychologist for systematically varying the information in a kinetic display is rapidly becoming more versatile. The technologies of film and television are adaptable to experiments. Moreover, the methods being tried in a new branch of art, kinetic art, are themselves experiments of a sort. The "abstractions" that arise from a changing optic array are much more interesting and more diverse than those from a painting. The perception psychologist can seize the opportunity to isolate information *about* events and episodes without having to make representations *of* events and episodes.

The kinetic "image" projected on a screen, opaque or transparent, is a method of controlling the light to the eye of an observer. It need not be thought of as a replica, copy, or representation of the environment, as an *image,* but as a *carrier of information*, in this case event-information. One can use an aperture or a window with a disk or a belt behind it instead of a projection screen; or cause a patch to move along a slot in a screen, as Michotte did in his many experiments; or put drawings on a phonograph turntable; or use a cathode-ray tube, or a television tube; whatever device is employed should be thought of as a way of experimenting with the information in light.

In summary, these nine suggestions for future experiments are based on a new conception of what gives rise to the perception of motion. It is not the motion of light over the retina, as we have been tempted to assume, but something that happens in ambient light. This is not easy to specify and measure, but it is surely a change in the structure of the array and it is open to investigation.

## PART II: MEMO ON MOTION*

The physical motions of bodies and particles have been described and specified with great success, in terms of displacement (and spin) with respect to a chosen "frame of reference," that is, a coordinate system with three axes using linear (and angular) coordinates. This is the basis of Newtonian mechanics.

*Unpublished manuscript, October, 1968.

Similarly the physical motion of light in space, considered as particles or waves, can also be described and specified by the same system, except that a considerable modification of it was introduced by the theory of relativity. Nevertheless a modified three-dimensional frame of reference is still the basis of physical optics.

But what frame of reference if any, is appropriate for describing the "motion of light" in quite another sense of the term—the "motion" *by means of which* the motions of bodies in an environment are seen (and the movements of an observer himself)? How are the transformations of pattern in the ambient optic array to be specified? In *ecological* optics (based on the steady state of multiply reflected illumination between opaque surfaces) what we have to describe is change in the perspective *projection* of objects, and change in the projection of the whole environment during locomotion. Moreover we have to describe the change from *projected* to *unprojected*, and *vice versa*, in the ambient light, that is, the effect of changing *occlusion* when the object (or the observer) moves. Is *any* coordinate system appropriate for these descriptions?

Gibson, Olum, and Rosenblatt (1955) analyzed what they called "motion perspective" for locomotion with respect to the surface of the earth, defining a pair of *angles* as the coordinates of each point in the array. They were thus able to describe the flow pattern of the array as something distinct from the *contrast pattern* of the array, but the analysis did not take account of occlusion, that is, of objects being concealed or revealed at an edge. In this case elements of the array disappear and appear (are *deleted* or *accreted*). Elements that do not exist *have* no coordinates. In this case a coordinate system is of no use.

The optical events that seem to constitute the information for the perception of material motions are not themselves motions. If so, they cannot be described by changing coordinates (pairs of numbers). Another kind of analysis is needed than the one which has been so powerful in physics.

# 2.7 The Change from Visible to Invisible: A Study of Optical Transitions*

Gibson suggested (1957a) that *physical* motions, the motions of material objects, should be distinguished sharply from the corresponding *optical* motions that make them perceptible to an O. Several kinds and variables of optical motions were described, all of which were loosely termed "optical transformations," and these were illustrated in a motion picture film (Gibson, 1955b).

We have recently been concerned, however, with another class of events, the perception of which needs to be understood. When an object *disappears from sight,* how is this event perceived and what is the optical basis for the perception? The question, far from having an obvious answer, is puzzling. The present study attempts to give an answer. It is illustrated by another motion picture film, a sequel to the first.

The term *disappearance* means a change from visible to invisible and the opposite term *appearance* means a change from invisible to visible. But this pair of terms is ambiguous, for there are two quite different kinds of events to which it may refer, that is, two ways in which an object may disappear and appear. It may *go out of sight* or *come into sight,* on the one hand, and it may *go out of existence* or *come into existence* on the other. The two cases are profoundly different, and human or animal Os clearly need to distinguish between the two cases if they are to cope with the permanent parts of their environment as contrasted with the impermanent parts—if they are to discriminate the persisting from the nonpersist-

*\*Perception & Psychophysics*, 1969, *5*, 113–116. Copyright 1969 by The Psychonomic Society. Reprinted by permission. Written in collaboration with G. Kaplan, H. Reynolds, & K. Wheeler. There is an accompanying film illustrating this paper (Gibson, 1968c).

ing things. A thing that disappears merely because it is no longer projected by light to the O's point of view is not to be confused with a thing that disappears because it is no longer projected by light at all. The former can still be seen from another point of view; the latter cannot be seen from any point of view.

Note that an illuminated environment is being taken for granted in this discussion. We are not here considering the disappearance and appearance of *light,* or the sensation of light. We are talking about the disappearance and appearance of a material *surface* in the *presence* of light, that is, a perception. The theoretical distinction between sensation and perception has been elaborated by Gibson (1966b). We are assuming that the disappearance of the whole environment with the absence of illumination and the reappearance of the whole environment with the presence of illumination is quite another problem than that of the disappearance and reappearance of a *part* of the environment, the whole of which is unaltered. The latter problem only is our present concern.

The question becomes, therefore, whether or not in the changing array of light to a point of observation there is a distinct kind of stimulus information for the perception of something that goes out of and comes into *sight* and another for the perception of something that goes out of and comes into *existence.* If the optical transitions are different in the two cases, and perhaps in their subtypes, a new perceptual theory is needed. We do not face the difficulties of the traditional explanations of how animals and children learn to *form concepts* of permanent things (e.g. Piaget, 1929), but we must explain how animals and children learn to *distinguish* between permanent and impermanent parts of the environment.

This new formulation of the problems that arise from the facts of visibility and invisibility owes much to the experimental work of Michotte (e.g., Michotte, Thinès, & Crabbé, 1964). But there is an essential difference inasmuch as we consider the possibility of available stimulus information for the types of object disappearance and Michotte did not.

*Going out of Sight and Coming into Sight.*    Consider the first case. A part of the environment, or a detachable object, may go out of sight because (a) it is hidden by another part of the environment, or (b) because it is hidden by another part of itself, or (c) because it becomes so distant from the point of observation that it "vanishes."[1] The last subcase implies a level terrain that is unobscured out to the horizon; the first two subcases imply the existence of an *edge.* The event of becoming hidden by an edge results from straight-line projection in the light that fills an iluminated space, that is, from the fact that, for a given station point, some illuminated surfaces of the total layout are projected to it and others are unprojected. Some of them "face" the station point and others do not. We have

---

[1]These ideas are further developed with respect to the perception of extent and objects at a distance in Gibson (1976a). (Eds.)

various words for becoming hidden like *covering* and *screening* but the best word for it is *occlusion*. Optical occlusion deserves much more study than it has ever received in perspective geometry. As for the third subcase, the object that vanishes because its distance becomes too great, it is also a consequence of the geometrical laws of perspective projection but it does not involve edge-occlusion; it involves the "vanishing point" of perspective and the "horizon" of the earth, or the principle of what will be called optical minification.

Occlusion, then, entails one thing in front of another, or one surface in front of another, with reference to a point of observation. It has been called interposition or "superposition" in the literature of pictorial depth-perception. But actually *change* of occlusion is what occurs in life as objects move and as Os move about in the world. Stationary occlusion as represented in a picture of frozen optic array has been studied by perceptionists but change of occlusion has not.

Vanishing into a point does not entail the relation in-front-of (or behind) but it has been studied and puzzled about for centuries. The kinetic fact that the projection of an object shrinks to a point as its distance increases, and the stationary fact that parallel lines on the earth are projected as lines that converge to a point on a horizon are at the very heart of our conception of abstract space.

It is important to note that, in all three subcases, going out of sight is reciprocal to coming into sight; one is simply the inverse of the other. The motion of an object that makes it disappear always has an opposite that makes it reappear; similarly, the locomotion of an O that makes anything disappear can always be reversed so as to make it reappear.[2]

*Going out of Existence and Coming into Existence.* Consider next the second case. When an object or part of the environment ceases to "exist," the fact is that its physical state has been changed by disintegration, solution, evaporation, sublimation, combustion, or dissipation. The surface that reflected light has ceased to exist. To be sure, the atomic matter has not; the latter has been *conserved,* as the physicists say, although its structure is altered. Nevertheless, even if matter cannot be annihilated, a light-reflecting surface can.

Conversely, an object can come into existence by crystallization or coagulation or condensation or sedimentation or, at a higher level of chemistry, by cell-growth. When it does, it begins to reflect light and becomes visible. But note that these processes by which an entity comes into visible existence are not simple reversals or opposites of the processes by which it goes out of visible existence, as are the motions and locomotions of the first case. The processes of dissolution and biological death are usually irreversible. This fact is connected with what the physicists call *entropy*.

---

[2]Thus these are reversible events, whereas events involving, e.g. the vanishing of a substance are non-reversible (cf. Ch. 2.8). The events described in (2a), (2b) and (2c) are illustrated in Gibson (1968c) and Gibson & Kaushall (1973). (Eds.)

# THE OPTICAL TRANSITIONS CORRESPONDING TO THESE TWO CASES

We are now prepared to study the optical transitions that arise from these different events. What are the changes in the optic array at a point of observation that can be distinguished by an O?

## (1a)  Progressive Covering and Uncovering

When the edge of one surface conceals or reveals another surface in the world, what happens in the structure of the optic array? What happens optically seems to be as follows. The adjacent units of optical texture on one side of a possible division in the optic array are preserved while adjacent units of optical texture on the other side of the division are progressively added to the array (uncovering) or are progressively subtracted from the array (covering). The *decrementing* of texture corresponds to a surface being concealed while the *incrementing* of texture corresponds to a surface being revealed. That side of the dividing line on which there is deletion or accretion always corresponds to the surface that is *behind;* that side on which there is neither, always corresponds to the surface that is *in front* (Kaplan, 1969). Gibson (1966b, p. 203) called this optical transition "wiping and unwiping" but these terms are metaphorical and are not mathematically precise. An effort to formalize the above rule is given in the appendix to this paper.

Note that this formula says nothing about the absolute *motion* (transposition) of objects in the world or of the O's position in the world, nor does it say anything about the absolute motion of the elements of optical texture in the array. Progressive deletion of texture can result from either a rightward motion of the covering surface or a leftward motion of the covered surface; progressive accretion can result from either a leftward motion of the covering surface or a rightward motion of the covered surface; in short, a thing can be *covered* by either of two physical motions. The special case of an object that moves behind a stationary occluding edge is only one case. It has attracted attention because of the paradoxical fact that the motion of the object continues to be "seen" after it is no longer projected in the optic array. Reynolds (1968) has verified this discovery of Michotte and has further investigated the experience of occluded motion.

When this optical transition of progressive accretion or deletion is experimentally produced by a motion picture display, an occluding edge is in fact perceived by an O, although the display consists only of a random texture divided into two parts. When the incrementing or decrementing of texture ceases, the edge is no longer perceived and a continuous textured surface is seen instead (Gibson, 1968c). These facts cannot be illustrated with a stationary picture; the reader should view the film if possible. The diagram given in the appendix, however, may be of help in visualizing the phenomena.

### (1b) The Conversion of a Surface into an Edge

A "movable" object in the environment is one that is detached from the permanent layout of the environment. Such an object, if opaque, occludes not only a part of the environment (the "ground" or "background") but also a part of itself, namely its "back" surface as distinguished from its "front" surface. Considering a polyhedron (an object with plane surfaces that face in different directions) we can assert that when it is rotated (or when an O moves around it) a *front* face is converted into a *back* face. As the slant angle of the front face increases the perspective projection of its form and texture is increasingly transformed; the transformation is loosely called "foreshortening" and its limit is a geometrical line. The optical figure and its components are compressed, as it were, along one dimension only. Meanwhile, or course, the slant angle of another face of the object *decreases,* its form and texture undergoing the reverse transformation.

A motion picture display of this optical transition does indeed yield the perception of a surface that is seen to turn until it passes through the position of "edge on." (A randomly textured cube was employed, but another polyhedron would have served.) The surface no longer *faces* the O but it persists phenomenally as a face of the object that has gone out of sight (Gibson, 1968c). When the sequence is reversed by running the film backward, a perfectly normal perception occurs of a surface that has *come into* sight.

### (1c) The Vanishing of a Surface into the Distance

When an object progressively becomes more distant from the point of observation its counterpart in the optic array shrinks, and the limit of this contraction is a geometrical point. If the object is in the sky or on level terrain it will not be occluded or hidden but it will nevertheless vanish by "minification." The figure corresponding to the front face of the object undergoes a size-transformation, all ratios or proportions in the figure being preserved until its visual angle becomes zero. The reverse transformation occurs when an object becomes progressively closer to the point of observation.

When this optical change is displayed on a motion picture screen the percept is of something that goes out of sight into the distance. This fact has been exploited in animated cartoon films. When Mickey Mouse is seen to zoom off at enormous speed he disappears without ceasing to exist. With magnification, similarly, a percept results of something coming out of the distance, that is, of approach. This can be simulated with a point-source shadow-projector (Gibson, 1957a) and the method has been used by Schiff (1965) to investigate the reactions of animals to the information for approach.

In conclusion, there do seem to be specific optical transitions corresponding to these three types of the events called *going out of sight* and *coming into sight.* Moreover, there is some evidence to show that animals and children distinguish the transitions and perceive the corresponding events. It should now be possible to carry out formal experiments with animals and children at various stages of development. Some research with human infants confronted with progressive occlusion and disocclusion of an object has been reported by Bower (1967) but the rationale of these experiments is not the same as that of our demonstrations.

We now turn to the events called *going out of existence* and *coming into existence*. The corresponding optical transitions are more complex and are not so easily described. An attempt will be made, however, to specify three examples that can be displayed on a motion picture screen.

### (2a) Evaporation and Sublimation

When a puddle of water evaporates or a chunk of solid carbon dioxide sublimates, the projected contour in the optic array shrinks and the optical texture within the contour changes, but in a way quite unlike the shrinkage and change that occur with optical contraction or minification. The figure shrinks irregularly, the texture does not become more dense, and ratios do not remain invariant. Phenomenally, the object is seen to disappear but it is *not* seen to vanish into the distance.

A motion picture display of a piece of "dry ice" disintegrating against a dark background yields the perception of something that ceases to exist. When the sequence is reversed in temporal order by running the film backward, the perception is "strange." There is then a suggestion of *growth* and of a substance that increases in size but this is not the same as the optical magnification that corresponds to the approach of an object out of the distance.

### (2b) Fading Away by Increasing Transparency

The mythical conception of ghosts or spirits, expressed in the Platonic conception of form without substance, has sometimes included the assumption that an opaque reflecting surface can become transparent, like one of water or glass, and can then become wholly nonreflecting, like air itself. This event does not actually occur but some men have believed that it could. It is inaccurately called "dematerialization" by believers in spirits, the opposite process being "materialization." A discussion of the optics of transparency is offered by Gibson (1966b, p. 216).[3]

The optical information for this hypothetical event can be produced by the method of double-exposing photographic film, and it is often used in the motion picture transition termed a "dissolve." Occasionally it has been used in cinematography to yield the illusion of an object or a man becoming a ghost.

A motion picture display can be made beginning with a textured rectangle on a differently textured background, progressing to a mixture of the texture of the background with that of the rectangle, and ending with the texture of the back-

---

[3]Cf. Gibson (1976a) (Eds.)

ground only. The O of this display perceives a rectangular object that goes out of existence. He does not report that it goes into the distance, or is hidden, or turned away. The opposite transition yields an experience of coming into existence, and it is even more anomalous.

### (2c) Being Consumed by Eating

Of all the kinds of substantial objects in the environment one of the most attractive is that of food objects. They are discriminated at an early stage of development and are further differentiated throughout life. They are peculiar, however, in being relatively impermanent; they disappear when they are eaten. One subclass of human food objects disappears from the optic array in successive "bites."

A motion picture sequence has been made beginning with a white disk on a black ground, with curved segments of the disk being successively deleted (cut out) from the periphery inward. This optical transition is different from the *continuous progressive* deletion of adjacent texture elements that corresponds to occlusion of an object. Os of this display are unanimous in perceiving a cookie or its equivalent that is being *eaten up*. The object is clearly seen to go out of existence. It is possible that even young children will perceive the same event with this display if they have come to notice that the successive deleting of curved parts of a figure corresponds to something being eaten. When the sequence is reversed in temporal order, another quite different event is perceived, but it is very "strange" for the adult Os and it would probably also prove to be so for the child.

The three transitions described above do not exhaust the possibilities. (We have not yet attempted to simulate the optics of melting or crumbling or breaking, although it could probably be done.) Nevertheless, a tentative conclusion would be that the two general ways in which an object can disappear are easily distinguished, and that they are distinguishable on the basis of optical stimulus information. Something that goes out of sight but continues to exist is not confused with something that disappears because it ceases to exist.

## DISCUSSION

It has long been taken for granted by developmental psychologists and philosophers of perception that the young child differs from the adult in the following respect: he cannot help believing that something which goes out of sight ceases to exist (Piaget, 1929). This follows from the theory of sensation-based perception, that is, from the assumption that when the sensation ceases the perception must cease, and the further assumption that imagination can take the place of sensation. But it now seems very doubtful that a young child has the belief that whatever goes out of sight ceases to exist. His perceptions are probably not based on his fleeting sensations but on the visual pickup of optical information. His perceptions are in Michotte's term "amodal" (Michotte, Thinès, & Crabbé, 1964). When the optical information is of one general sort the persistence of an object is specified; when it is of another general sort the nonpersistence of the object is specified. All the child has to do is distinguish the two general cases. Developmentally, he may have to learn to distinguish them but the development is one of perception, not of belief.

The optical transitions described in this paper, and displayed in the accompanying film, are of two general types. One is a *reversing* transition and the other is not. All of the reversing transitions looked equally natural whether the film was run forward or backward; the others did not look natural when the film was run backward. The reversing optical transitions are caused by motions of the object and by movements of the O from one place to another; the nonreversing optical transitions are caused by the destruction or creation of the reflecting surfaces that constitute an object. There are mathematical properties of the reversing transitions to specify the temporal existence of the object, both preexistence and postexistence; the properties of the nonreversing transitions specify either the going out of existence or the coming into existence of the object.

In his experimental studies of the "screening effect" and the "tunnel effect" with moving visual forms, Michotte confronted a paradox: the fact of the phenomenal persistence of an object after it had been occluded by an edge. On the traditional assumption that the sensation of an object, the color patch in the visual field, is entailed in its perception, a nonpersisting sensation *cannot* yield a persisting perception. An occluded object ought to be indistinguishable from a destroyed object, whereas it is in fact distinguishable. A radical resolution of the paradox is to assume that the sensation of an object is *not* entailed in its perception; all that is required for perception is the colorless and formless information to specify a persisting object on the one hand or a destroyed object on the other.

## APPENDIX

### The Hypothesis of Deletion/Accretion for Edge Perception

Consider the following string of symbols:

12345FGHIJ

They are intended to stand for adjacent elements of optical texture across an *optic array*. The nature of these "elements" is unspecified and the absolute locations are unspecified; they are simply adjacent. The numerals and the letters do not necessarily stand for two kinds of elements; they only imply that the array is divisible into two parts.

1. If the elements 12345 are preserved and the elements FGHIJ are progressively deleted from the array in the order FGH . . . , an occluding surface is specified by the numerals and an occluded surface by the letters: an edge is specified at Element 5, and depth is to the *right*.

2. If the elements FGHIJ are preserved and the elements 12345 are progressively deleted in the order 543 . . . , an occluding surface is specified by the letters and an occluded surface by the numerals; an edge is specified at Element F, and depth is to the *left*.

3. If the elements FGHIJ are preserved and the elements 12345 are progressively *accreted* in the order 678 . . . , an occluding surface is specified by the letters and an occluded surface by the numerals; an edge is specified at Element F, and depth is to the *left*.

4. If the elements 12345 are preserved and the elements FGHIJ are progressively *accreted* in the order EDC . . . , an occluding surface is specified by the numerals and an occluded surface by the letters; an edge is specified at Element 5, and depth is to the *right*.

Hence the part of the array that suffers deletion or accretion corresponds to a surface that is *behind* and is being concealed or revealed. The part of the array that is preserved corresponds to a surface that is *in front* and is concealing or revealing. The terminal element of the array that is preserved corresponds to the *edge*. A test of this hypothesis has been carried out by Kaplan (1969), along with another hypothesis dealing with the impression of mere depth-at-an-edge without the impression of one surface existing behind another.

# 2.8

## The Problem of Event Perception*

## INTRODUCTION

The first difficulty in formulating the problem of the perception of events is to decide what is to be meant by an *event*. After that we can go on to study the activity of an observer in perceiving one, and distinguishing it from others. For this, we have to analyze the stimulus information that is available to an observer, formulate hypotheses about the process of perception, and finally test them with experiments that provide stimulus information.

The defining of an event for purposes of studying perception involves several questions about which psychologists have not been clear. First, we are surely concerned with *physical* events in some sense of the term, not *mental* events. Only the former are relevant to perception. But are we concerned with *all* physical events including those on the cosmic and the atomic scales or only those on the terrestrial scale?[1] Next, we must surely include behavioral events, but where do we stop? Should we exclude events in the nervous system and the brain? The locomotor acts of animals are events for perception, very significant events, but then we must ask whether an act of locomotion by the observer himself is to be counted as an event for perception? It is obviously different from an act of locomotion by another animal. Finally, we must try to get clear about the relation of *motions* and events so as to decide whether or not events are composed of motions.[2]

---

*Unpublished manuscript, undated. (Written in 1971). This manuscript, unlike other unpublished papers of Gibson's, states that it is a "Preliminary draft, not yet for publication."

[1] This issue is discussed at far greater length in Gibson (1979a, part 1). (Eds.)

[2] Cf. Chs. 1.7, and 2.6. (Eds.)

## PHYSICAL EVENTS AND ECOLOGICAL EVENTS

We are concerned with the problem of perception, not with the much larger and more difficult problem of scientific knowledge. Human adults can know about astronomical events, chemical events, and even atomic events but what they perceive directly is terrestrial events. Animals do not have scientific knowledge and children have to be taught it. What we all share is the ability to detect objects of moderate size and events of moderate duration—those that occur in seconds, not microseconds or eons. Knowledge of ecological events by the child precedes knowledge of physical events in general by the adult. What happens in atomic lattices, test tubes, and the universe is, to say the very least, harder to see than what happens in the environment of animals.

To put the matter radically, physics cannot go from a universe of atoms to a world of surfaces without a conceptual leap that physicists avoid thinking about, but that biological scientists cannot afford to neglect. The consequences of this neglect will be evident later.

The evolution of perceptual systems sets limits to what animals can apprehend directly. These systems incorporate receptors that have to be stimulated. The perceiving of ecological events depends on stimulus information obtained through eyes, ears, and fingers that are directly affected by ambient light, sound, and contact, whereas the knowing of "physical" events depends on information at an entirely different level, obtained indirectly with instruments or by experiment, and still more indirectly by means of pictures and language.[3] We are concerned with ecological events.

## BEHAVIORAL EVENTS AND PHYSIOLOGICAL EVENTS

Animals and men perceive the behavior of other animals and other men, what we loosely call their "movements," but not the muscle-contractions, and certainly not the nerve-impulses, that underlie the behaviors. The movements of limbs, the deformations of the body, and the transients of vocalization are observable without the mediation of instruments. These have been called "molar" as against "molecular" behavior; they are activities of an organism at the ecological level of size and duration, measured in centimeters and seconds, not in microns or miles and not in microseconds or years. Animate movements include changes of posture, orienting responses, manipulations, "expressive" movements, and movements of the animal from place to place, that is, locomotions.

Is a behavioral act of the *observing* animal to be considered an event for perception, for example, his own locomotion? He is certainly aware of this kind

---

[3]The problem of mediated awareness is discussed in Chs. 3.2, 3.4, and 3.6, cf. Gibson (1979a, Ch. 14). (Eds.)

of molar behavior by virtue of all the kinds of sensitivity called proprioceptive, but is it an event for *perception?* This question has led to endless debate in psychology and philosophy over "private" perception, so called, *vs.* "public" perception.[4] Confusion can be avoided, I suggest, if we discard the orthodox idea that proprioception is one of the senses and acknowledge that it is an accompaniment of perception—of *all* perception (Gibson, 1966b, Ch. 2). I take the word to mean "awareness of self."

The fact is that movements of the observer himself have to be allowed for in order to understand his perception of the environment. At a minimum, even without gross responses, a perceiver has to orient his trunk, head, and eyes, making a series of adjustments and maintaining the posture of these body-parts, in order to see the world at all. Otherwise he is asleep. Hence one cannot be aware of the stream of events in the world without having at least some awareness of the stream of events in the body.

In the event of locomotion men and animals do see their own displacements in the environment as well as the displacements of objects and other animals, although it is surely a special kind of seeing. The two kinds of displacement are never confused—or almost never. The distinguishing of objective motion and subjective movement (Gibson, 1954b) is an old puzzle for the theory of perception but the solution may prove to be simpler than has been supposed.

## THE RELATION BETWEEN MOTIONS AND EVENTS

Since Newton discovered the laws of motion and laid the foundation for mechanics, physics has concentrated our attention on the motions of rigid bodies, translations and rotations along or around any of the axes of space. This analysis worked beautifully for falling bodies and machines with rigid parts and, what was most impressive, the science of mechanics could be extended up to the celestial and down to the atomic scale. The perceptionist, however, confines himself to mechanical events on the intermediate scale. But he cannot limit his concern to these only for he must also consider biological events, which are in general fluid or visco-elastic motions of surfaces. When a substance flows, stretches, contracts, bends, turns, twists, writhes, or in general *deforms* the ecological occurrence is usually significant and needs to be perceived.[5] But mechanics or kinetics does not work so well in this case.

Whenever it can, physics reduces non-rigid motions to the component rigid motions of particles because of the powerful mathematics that can be applied to the latter. When events can be reduced to motions and motions can be analyzed

---

[4]Cf. Ch. 4.5. (Eds.)

[5]See Johansson (1973) and Pittenger & Shaw (1977) for more on the perception of biological motion. (Eds.)

into quantities of space and time proofs are possible. We are told that ''anything that exists exists in some quantity,'' and the perceptionist is urged to quantify the stimuli he takes into the laboratory so as to fulfill the requirements of scientific method. Most psychologists have dutifully tried to do so, including the writer. But I am now convinced that this analytic reduction is hopelessly inadequate to define an ecological event. It does away with the features of an event that enable it to be perceived.

The necessary characteristic of an *event*, I propose, is that it has a beginning and an end. But this is not necessarily characteristic of a motion. The term *motion* is ambiguous; it can refer either to a displacement that starts and stops or to the amount of displacement per unit of time. The former is a fact, the latter an abstraction. One is the event but the other is only a velocity. Since uniform velocity does not occur in nature (uniform ''motion'' as Newton put it)[6] we postulate *instantaneous* velocity, ds/dt, for purposes of analysis, and then go on to postulate second and third derivatives, and so on. If we need to analyze the rotary motion or spin of a body we do the same thing using units of angle instead of units of displacement. The beginning and the end of the displacement (or turn) have vanished from the analysis. Calculus fails to describe the beginning and the end of the occurrence. In differential geometry the *structure* of the event disappears.

Perceptionists have tried to determine the threshold for perception of velocity, the barely noticeable speed of an object or a moving belt (Spigel, 1965; Gibson, 1968a). The efforts have failed. Observers can see a displacement or an occlusion but when they try to see a pure velocity an event or a series of events takes its place. There will be more of this later. If I am right there is no threshold for detection of velocity, or of any derivative of motion inasmuch as beginnings and ends, transients, events, have to exist for any perception to be possible.

The flow of liquid or viscous substances, as I understand it, is never perfectly uniform and continuous. Events arise like shearing, overtaking, deforming, and vortex formation.[7] The ideal but nonexistent river whose parts all move with the same velocity throughout all time is nevertheless the metaphor we use when we refer to the ''flow of time.''

## SPACE AND TIME; ENVIRONMENT AND EVENTS

It should have been clear long ago that there is no such thing as the perception of space but only the perception of environmental layout. Similarly there is no such thing as the perception of time but only of events.[8] Physics and mathematics begin with empty space, three reference axes, the dimension of time, and bodies

---

[6]In fact, almost all motion perception experiments have used uniform velocity (or a polar projection thereof). Runeson (1977) critically reviews much of this research. (Eds.)

[7]Cf. Stevens (1974, Ch. 2). (Eds.)

[8]Cf. Gibson (1975a). (Eds.)

that move. Biology and psychology, on the other hand, must begin with an environment, a medium, and surfaces (solid, viscous, liquid) that undergo change. We are tempted to think of the medium, air, as being space but this misleads us. Part of an environment is transparent and part of it is opaque whereas geometrical space is everywhere transparent; its lines and planes do not hide anything that lies *behind* them, as edges and surfaces do.

Physics *geometrizes* the world, for mathematical reasons that have been suggested. Biology and psychology, however, cannot do so without losing hold of their basic concept of the terrestrial environment. Mathematical physics goes so far as to geometrize the already pure dimension of time itself, in the interests of understanding the universe. But this would be a compounded mistake for biological science since it would leave us with nothing whatever to be perceived—neither environment nor changes of the environment. This tendency in physics has been deplored by Whitrow (1961) in a book called *The Natural Philosophy of Time*.[9]

The notion of environment implies some solid portion that is persistent, the "permanent" terrestrial layout, and some portion that is not, the changing layout. The medium, where animals can move about, is filled with illumination (to say nothing of sounds and odors). There are loci in the medium at which an animal could be positioned, and these loci are rather different from the points of geometrical space. They are potential points of observation, with a specific optic *array* at each point. The set of all these loci constitute the possible paths of locomotion for a single observer and also the positions that could be taken simultaneously by a host of observers (Gibson, 1966b, p. 192). This is why the concept of environment is neither "subjective" nor "objective"; it implies the surroundings of any single observer and those of all observers, without contradiction. The possibility of locomotion by observers must be assumed. This is the heart of ecological optics as distinguished from physical optics (Gibson, 1966b, Ch. 10) and this is the basis for an explanation of how an animal sees his own locomotion in a stable environment and distinguishes it from the displacements of objects and the locomotions of other animals.

An *environment* as thus defined is distinguished from a *chaos*, where there is no stable surface of support and where either clouds of matter continually deform, or bodies in space move in random fashion. Animals could not live in a chaos.

## A CLASSIFICATION OF ECOLOGICAL EVENTS

Having decided what is to be meant by an event, a tentative classification is possible. If an event is something with a beginning and an end it can be repeated; an occurrence can recur. A sequence of events then exists. A very familiar kind

---

[9]Čapek (1976) has a comprehensive review of this literature. (Eds.)

of sequence is of identical events, such as the swings of a pendulum, the revolutions of a crank, or the oscillations of a floating cork. A sequence has a frequency and a frequency, unlike a velocity, can be perceived. Moreover it can be perceived *directly;* the segregated events do not have to be counted by the observer. For this direct perception, the frequency cannot be too high or too low. The rate of occurrence of "steps" when a man strolls, walks, or runs is visible (also audible) and this, not his speed, is what we perceive. In order to perceive speed one would have to sense units of abstract time (like seconds) and units of abstract distance (like centimeters) and then compute it. One would have to perceive "space" and "time." But there *are* no natural units of space except the components of a surface and no natural units of time except events.

In the laboratory experiments on the perception of velocity mentioned above, using a moving belt behind a window (the "waterfall" apparatus) or an object rotating in front of a surface, what the observer detects, whether he knows it or not, is frequency—the frequency with which the parts of one surface hide and reveal the parts of the other surface. And when we judge the "speed" of an automobile we are probably detecting the frequency with which its edges occlude the trees or bushes of the background, or the squares of pavement (Gibson, Kaplan, Reynolds, & Wheeler, 1969). I am suggesting that the visual system contains nothing analogous to a speedometer but that it might have something like a tachometer without a scale.

The events of a sequence need not all be identical, of course, like oscillations or waves or cycles. At another extreme the events of a sequence may be all different, as when an experimenter presents an observer with a series of nonsense syllables to be "remembered," or a series of unrelated pictures. Metronome beats or light flashes are cases of pure repetition and nonsense items are cases of no repetition but neither is characteristic of natural sequences.[10] Environmental sequences commonly have cycles embedded in longer cycles, that is, *nested* events.

Consider the events in speech or music or pantomime or ballet (or in the sexual courting behavior of animals, for that matter). There are some different events and some similar events in the sequence. There will be shorter events that make up longer events and these making up still longer events. All are units of a sort, in the way that syllables, words, phrases, sentences, and discourses are units. Units are nested within other units. And the remarkable fact is that both the superordinate and the subordinate events can be perceived.

Note that in a structured sequence of this sort there is no fixed frequency, for beginnings and endings depend on the duration of the event we select for attention. The number of discrete events *cannot be counted.* Hence a numerical "span" of apprehension or memory is not to be expected.

---

[10]This contrast between natural and nonsense events is brought out by the research discussed in Jenkins, Wald & Pittenger (1978). (Eds.)

Can a continuing process like the flow of a river be treated as a sequence of events? A perfectly uniform stream does not exist, I argued, and even if it did it could not be perceived. A real river has different velocities in different parts with vortices that begin and end, and with ripples and bubbles that come and go. Deformations are perceived although velocities are not. A deformation is probably an event. (I am not sure of this, but I think that a deformation must have an end).

The behaviors of animals are visco-elastic events, as was suggested, with beginnings and ends, although they occur in nested sequences. An example of a unitary event is the "expressive movement" of the human face, as in smiling or frowning. The overall shape of this surface, or surface layout, is composed of subordinate shapes, called *features* (forehead, eyes, nose, mouth). There is a deformation of the overall shape and of the component features, consisting of a departure from the normal layout and a return to the resting state. The specific event of smiling or frowning has meaning by virtue of the fact that it is embedded in a particular sequence, a longer event that constitutes a course of action. As we have already argued, the psychologist cannot afford to reduce the facial expression to muscle-contractions.

In contrast to these biological events are the mechanical events of the environment. There are the rigid motions of levers, wheels, cranks, slides, rollers, rockers, pendulums, gears, pinions, escapements, screws, hinges, pistons (and sometimes the non-rigid motions of springs). Each of these so-called motions is an event. When the parts of a complex machine are assembled there will be a nested hierarchy of parts, with sub-assemblies, and when the machine is *running* there will be a nested hierarchy of *synchronous events*. (Note that this latter is quite different from the nested hierarchy of *sequential* events found in the behavior of animals, and in speech, music, and the theater. The machine does not exhibit sequential nesting; it does the same thing over and over in a repetitive way.) The combination of subordinate synchronous motions into a superordinate motion when a complex machine is running is the basis, I think, for what Johansson (1950) has called "configurations in event perception."

Finally, a class of events should be mentioned that might be called changes of state as contrasted with changes of shape, layout, or position. When a substance undergoes evaporation, sublimation, diffusion, vaporization, crumbling, or breaking, a surface is destroyed and when there is condensation, crystallization, or biological growth a surface comes into existence. At the particle level, to be sure, nothing is destroyed and nothing is created. But at the ecological level objects can and do go out of and come into existence (Gibson et al., 1969).

This kind of ecological event must be sharply distinguished from the kind when objects go out of sight and come into sight but have permanent existence. We tend to confuse them because we use the loose terms *appearance* and *disappearance* for both. But to use these terms is to confuse the objects of the world with the projection by light of the objects in the world. A fixed object that is concealed at one point of observation is revealed at another. An observer who moves so as to get the object in sight does not see a *new* object but only a newly *revealed* object. Locomotor occlusion and its inverse are thus a kind of optical event but not a physical or material event. I call it an optical transition. The transition involves self-reference as well as object reference, like the going out of sight of one wall of a room and coming into sight of another when an observer turns his head.[11] There can also be occlusion without locomotion or head-turning, of course, when one object goes behind another (Michotte, Thinés & Crabbé, 1964). The displacement of the object is then a true ecological event and the occlusion is an optical transition. In short ecological *events* must not be confused with the optical *transitions* in an ambient array. The events may be *specified by* the transitions but they are by no means the same kind of thing. We have long confused them because of a false analogy between physical "motions" and optical "motions," and paid for the mistake with wasted efforts.[12]

## THE OPTICAL INFORMATION FOR EVENT PERCEPTION

The next step is to ask what changes of the ambient optic array correspond to ecological events? These changes constitute the available information for perceiving events. It should be kept in mind that an optic array at a fixed point of observation consists of units like bits of optical texture, projected forms, and superordinate forms, in a nested hierarchy. All these components of an ambient array will be called "units" even though they may vary in angular size. They are the projections of the adjacent facets, faces, and surfaces of the environmental layout to a point of observation. (The void of empty space, the blue sky, does not provide *any* optic array.) It is taken for granted that a *changeless* optic array, one with a "frozen" structure, arises from and specifies a stationary point of observation in a world without events, a fixed observer in a fixed layout. When we speak of a *changing* optic array we must refer both to the persistence of its component units and to the possible lack of persistence of these units. (Astronomical motions thus do not provide a changing optic array.)

The general hypothesis is that ecological events are specified by *disturbances* in the optic array. A change, mathematically speaking, can be either of two kinds, that which preserves one-to-one mapping of elements and that which does

---

[11]This is the principle of "reversible occlusion" (Gibson, 1979a, pp. 191–195) cf. Ch. 2.7. (Eds.)

[12]It should be noted that Gibson's distinction between ecological events and optical transitions is not the distinction between distal and proximal stimuli; rather, it is a distinction between ecological events (among the surfaces of the environment) and ecological information for perception (within media of the environment), both of which are "distal." Ecological information is a structure in an environmental medium that specifies an environmental fact. See Chs. 4.3 and 4.4 for more on the proximal-distal distinction. (Eds.)

not; a disturbance here refers to the latter kind. It is a change that entails loss or gain of some of the adjacent units in an array, that is, a disturbance in the persistent units. This is to be distinguished from a disturbance in the *adjacent order* of *persisting* units, which will be discussed later.[13]

This hypothesis is quite different from previous hypotheses about change in the optic array. It does not refer to the *motion* of units (certainly not to the motions of stimulating light-points) nor even to the relative *displacements* of units in the array. It does not even appeal to the *transformations* of units considered as forms or point-sets, since all these changes imply one-to-one sequential correspondence of elements. It says that neither "optical motions and transformations" (Gibson, 1957a) nor "continuous transformations" of any sort (Gibson, 1968a) are adequate to describe the information for event perception. It is simply not the case that each unit of a stationary array goes into a corresponding unit of a subsequent array except in a special limiting case. Unhappily, then, neither the axioms and postulates of projective and perspective geometry nor the powerful mathematics of analytic geometry are sufficient for our purposes.

The general hypothesis of "disturbances" in the optic array has a number of underlying assumptions which I will try to make explicit.

1. It is assumed that the environment is not a *chaos* but has a relatively permanent layout in large part. The ambient array from a chaos would have *no* persistence of its component units or mapping of successive arrays. It would resemble what we call *scintillation*.

2. It is assumed that the surfaces of the layout are never wholly transparent, and that the layout is never wholly "open" but always more or less "cluttered." The ideal example of an open layout is a flat terrain with no occluding edges out to the horizon, and this is the limiting case analyzed by Gibson, Olum, and Rosenblatt (1955) in which continuous gradients or optical flow occur during locomotion. Another example of the limiting case is a closed bare room, without apertures or furniture. All faces and facets of the layout are then projected to all points of observation. But in actual cluttered layouts there exist what we call "objects," protuberances or detached bodies, that occlude some parts of the layout at some points of observation. The world in general is full of occluding edges. This means, parenthetically, that my attempt to explain the perception of surface layout in terms of continuous optical *gradients* (texture-density, flow, disparity) is incomplete (Gibson, 1950a). What needs explanation is the perception of cluttered as well as open layout.

3. It is assumed that all terrestrial displacements of objects, all visco-elastic events, all mechanical events, and all changes of existence, in fact all the events listed in the previous section including subjective movement and locomotion occur with reference to the permanent cluttered layout, especially the background surface, and therefore entail change of occlusion. When an object is displaced it

---

[13]Cf. Ch. 1.7. (Eds.)

occludes the background and when it turns it occludes its own back. When it goes behind a part of the layout its surface is occluded by the "frontground" and when it comes from behind this optical transition is reversed. The approach of an object progressively covers the wall behind it and its recession uncovers it. Animal behaviors and deformations of shape are not different in this respect from rigid displacements. The mechanical displacements of levers, wheels, pendulums, and crankshafts involve the displacements of occluding edges. The evaporation of a puddle, the dematerialization of a solid, and the fading of a smoke-ring reveal whatever was behind it previously. Even the hand-movements of the observer himself, and his locomotion over the ground by walking, driving, or flying involve progressive change of occlusion at a moving edge. Finally, turning the head, that closest of events to the self, uncovers one part of the ambient array while covering up another.

This third assumption is the one most likely to evoke disagreement. The objection might be made that it certainly does not hold for events in the cloudless sky, or in the night sky, or in complete darkness, where no textured background exists. The reply is that the empty sky and empty darkness constitute the limiting case of a *non-layout,* and the optically limiting case of a *non-array.* Only when a bird flying overhead occludes at least *part of itself* during flight do we perceive an event. Moving spots of light in utter darkness do not represent an event, in our sense, for the spots do not constitute an optic array. They constitute only optical atoms in an optical void, by analogy with material atoms in the void. Such optical transitions are not the prototype of optical information as we have assumed but only an impoverishment of it. The carryover from physics is inappropriate. The fallacy is to assume (as I once did) that "an optical motion is a projection in two dimensions of a physical motion in three dimensions" (Gibson, 1957a, p. 289; see also Johansson, 1964). The fact is that ecological events *cannot* be projected in one-to-one fashion.

## WHAT DO DISTURBANCES SPECIFY?

A disturbance in the optic array, i.e., a disturbance in the persistence of its units, may be either a progressive gain or loss of units on one side of a contour or a substitution of different units. The former specifies coming into sight or going out of sight at an occluding edge, change of occlusion, and is so perceived (Gibson et al., 1969). The latter probably specifies change of existence, although this has not yet been verified by experiment. At any rate, increments or decrements of optical texture are distinguishable from substitution of one texture for another; this corresponds to the fact that occlusion-change in the array means something radically different from existence-change in the world.

The new hypothesis for event perception does not affect the rule that a changeless ambient array specifies a wholly motionless observer in a world wholly without events. But animals are never motionless except when asleep (or when trying to avoid notice by a predator). It is still true that, for the limiting case of the "open" layout, continuous gradients of optical flow specify locomotion of the observer in a stable environment, the direction of this locomotion, the imminence of collision, and other useful matters. The centrifugal flow of the array dcreases to zero at the center of magnification (or minification) and also decreases to zero at the horizon of the earth (Gibson et al., 1955). The units of the array "vanish" at the horizon, along with the transforming of these units; they "open up" ahead and "close in" behind as we fly over the earth. Thus, even in this idealized layout, there is something analogous to gain and loss of the units of the optic array, and therefore a violation of pure mathematical correspondence.

Note that disturbances in the optic array of the gain-or-loss type are precisely the same in an otherwise frozen array as they are in an otherwise flowing array. Hence the detecting of occluding edges when an object is displaced, with deletion at the leading edge and accretion at the trailing edge, is as much possible for a moving observer as for a stationary observer. But the detecting of *fixed* occluding edges by a stationary observer is much more difficult than for a moving observer. This is why an observer standing still in a thick woods, cannot distinguish "what belongs to one tree and what to another . . . But the moment he begins to move forward, everything disentangles itself . . . as if he were looking at a good stereoscopic view of it" (Helmholtz, 1866/1962, vol. 3, p. 296). The information for occlusion in a frozen array is impoverished.[14] And the information in a flowing array is not due to "motion parallax," as Helmholtz thought, but to optical accretion/deletion.

## DISTURBANCE IN THE ADJACENT ORDER OF PERSISTING UNITS

So far we have considered only a disturbance in the *persistence* of the adjacent units of an optic array. We now consider a less common disturbance in the *adjacent order* of persisting units, of what is next to what, of arrangement. (Perhaps this is a problem in topology but I cannot find it treated; topology has not yet been applied to the optic array.) Each unit of a person's frozen array corresponds to itself in a subsequent frozen array but there has been a disruption of adjacency.

One kind of disruption occurs in the changing array from a *semi-transparent* surface or substance as distinguished from an *opaque* surface. Water or glass or swirling mist yield the perception of one thing behind another, but without opaque occlusion. E. J. Gibson, Gibson, Smith, and Flock (1959) displayed an array with two sets of interspersed units. When frozen, it provided the informa-

---

[14]In a frozen array occlusion is reduced to interposition. (Eds.)

tion for an opaque surface, but when one set of units was displaced relative to the other it seemed to specify one transparent surface in front of another—at least that is what was perceived. The adjacent order of units in the frozen texture had been destroyed; more exactly it had been partially permuted. To quote, "It was a peculiar sort of permutation, to be sure, for each of the two sets of elements retained an adjacent order, but the disruption of order as between these sets broke the original continuity. And this produced the perception of different surfaces with separation between" (p. 46). Presumably, if there had been a *complete* permutation of the original array nothing but a chaos would have been visible. The fact that one can drive a car on a rainy night, with an optic array coming from multiple moving reflections and changing blurs on the glass windshield, and nevertheless see the road instead of a chaos bears witness to the mathematical wisdom of the visual system.[15]

Another kind of optical disruption without gain or loss of optical units comes from one opaque surface sliding across an adjacent opaque surface at a crack, without any occluding edge. Adjacent order is preserved in both parts of the array except at the linear (or circular) rupture. I do not know how to describe this optical transition in mathematical terms. There need be no contrast contour in the array—only the break in adjacency. It is probably a limiting case since all but ideal cracks in a surface layout will entail some change of occlusion.

## THE PROCESS OF EVENT PERCEPTION

With some idea of what the *information* is for event perception we can begin to study the *process* of perception. If the foregoing analysis is right, or even partly right, the process is not at all what we have supposed it to be. We have assumed, first, that it is based on retinal sensations of motion; second, that it entails an organizing of the pattern of retinal motions, and, third, that there has to be a special process of cancelling out the "reafferent" sensory inputs caused by eye movements. Along with these we have also assumed, fourth, a picture transmitted to the brain at each moment of time, a sort of physiological image by analogy with the image of the photographic camera and a sequence of images in time by analogy with the motion picture camera. The latter assumption is actually not consistent with the former but efforts have been made to reconcile them.

I have already argued that whatever gives rise to the perception of motion it is not retinal motion (Gibson, 1968a). That is, it cannot be "the successive stimulation of adjacent retinal loci" (Spigel, 1965, p. 2). I have here argued that it cannot even be *optical* motion considered as displacement of optical units, and still further that the ecological source of optical change is not *physical* motion in the Newtonian sense.

---

[15]See Gibson (1976a) and Mace & Shaw (1974) for more on transparency and motion. (Eds.)

The second assumption fails equally when the structure of the ambient light is taken to be the basis of perception instead of the retinal image. There is no pattern of retinal displacements and not even a pattern of light-point displacements in the ecological optic array.

The third assumption is gratuitous if there is no necessity of cancelling out the sensory inputs caused by eye and head-movements—if they are taken to be simply the invariant accompaniments of sampling the ambient array, to be part of the flow of self-awareness coming from the exploratory visual system.[16] The retinal image displacement hypothesis arises from a misconception of the way the eye works (Gibson, 1968a, p. 338).

The fourth assumption, based on the motion picture analogy, is perhaps the most misleading of all. Despite a belief in irreducible sensations of motion we are tempted to believe in a sequence of discrete pictures each sensed or perceived for itself. We then try to reconcile them with such hypotheses as the "persistence of vision," or "apparent" motion due to neural short-circuiting, or "traces" of past stimuli that link them with the present stimulus. We are hopelessly confounded by the distinction between "present" experience and "past" experience although no one has ever been able to say what a "present" experience is. More generally, we contrast perception with memory and assert that perception depends on memory. But the explanation of storage and retrieval are becoming more and more elaborate.[17]

I have already argued that the perception of sequences does not depend upon memory in the sense of storage and retrieval of traces (Gibson, 1966a). Surely the perception of an *event* as described here does not depend on recall or recollection. A unitary event is a unit of experience. But what about a sequence of *nested* events of considerable duration? If they constitute a single event, it seems to me, it is perceived. Consider the two extreme cases of *pure* event-repetition and *no* event-repetition. I think that only in the latter case, exemplified by nonsense figures (or nonsense syllables) does storage-and-retrieval memory enter into consideration. Only then is there a "span" of short-term memory and a "transfer" to long-term memory. At the other extreme, the repetitive set of brief events, the whole episode surely does not involve memory. No one would claim that an immediate recurrence, end-to-beginning, requires recognition in the sense of comparing this percept with the trace of the past percept and noting the match. The sequence and its frequency are directly grasped.

All the above only goes to show that the process of event perception is not what we have supposed it to be. But it is prerequisite to a fresh start on the problem. We have to conceive of stimulus information for ecological events, not stimuli. We have to think of a kind of stimulus information that is unaltered by eye-movements or head-movements, or even locomotor movements—a kind that

---

[16]Cf. Chs. 2.4 and 4.4. (Eds.)

[17]Cf. Bransford, McCarrell, Franks & Nitsch (1977) and Turvey & Shaw (1979). (Eds.)

is invariant under these changes. We have to take into account the fact of occlusion and disocclusion as specified by the optical transitions in an array at a moving point of observation and at a stationary point of observation. It is helpful but not sufficient to think of mathematical transformations of the optic array. A promising hypothesis is that the information for events is to be found in *perturbations* of the structure of the array, and two kinds called disturbances and disruptions have been defined. These can occur in a sequential nesting of units for a changing array, and they can also occur in a synchronous nesting of units for the ambient array (things happen in sequence and they also happen at the same time). We cannot hope to establish a psycho*physics* for the perception of events, physics being of no help, but only a kind of psycho-*optics*, and this must be a novel kind of optics that considers the environment, not a branch of physics that considers only radiant energy.

# 2.9 Ecological Physics, Magic, and Reality*

## I. THE LAWS OF ECOLOGICAL PHYSICS

I have argued that the invariants of ecological physics are not the same as the invariants of physics. The former are *tacit*, not *explicit*. They are regularities known to common sense. They refer to the "medium-size dry goods" of the world, not the atomic or the cosmic. Children and animals learn these laws from observing everyday events, not by mastering a discipline in school.

When it is said that a magician or a conjuror "defies the laws of physics" it is these laws that are meant, not those in the textbooks. People take them for granted. I suggest that magic is only interesting and mysterious to a child *if these regularities are implicitly known*. I will try to make some of them explicit.

1. A substantial object tends to persist and the *more* substantial the *more* persistent. Rock lasts. Smoke does not.[1]
2. The major surfaces of the habitat are nearly permanent with respect to layout. But living or animate *objects* (objects are closed surfaces; see Gibson, 1979a, p. 307) change their shape when they grow or move, although they retain an underlying non-change.
3. Some objects, the bud and the pupa, transform. But no object is converted into an object that we would call entirely different, as frog into prince. The change is visible as such, and the changes produced by manipulations, by ecological transformations, and biological transformations are observed by children.

---

*Unpublished manuscript, August, 1979.
[1]Cf. Ch. 4.7. (Eds.)

4. A thing can go out of existence in various ways that can be observed, as breaking, pulverizing, dissolving, burning, evaporating (Gibson, 1979a, Ch. 6). These ways of being destroyed are not reversible, and this fact can also be observed. The whole habitat cannot go out of existence, only parts of it.[2]

5. Things can go out of *sight* in several regular ways that can also be observed. They can be hidden in the *dark,* in the *distance,* and by *occlusion* at an edge when things are displaced, or when the observer moves. It is a notable fact that these changes *are* reversible, and are seen to reverse.

6. A surface that has gone out of existence cannot be seen at all either with illumination or from any point of observation. A surface that has only gone out of sight can be seen from other points of observation if there is illumination. A surface that has gone out of sight continues to exist, and *is perceived to exist if the transition to being hidden was observed* (the "tunnel effect," Gibson, 1979a, p. 190ff).

7. A substantial object cannot come into existence except from another substance. It cannot be created from nothing, from the air. Nevertheless some human beliefs (based perhaps on the observation of clouds) assert the existence of spirits, ghosts, and demons that can "materialize" from the air and become visible or "melt into" the air and become invisible. This doctrine is a feature of many religions (e.g., that of the Magi, hence magicians). But the theory that children spontaneously "believe in magic" is contrary to the evidence. It is the other way around. They spontaneously believe in non-magic. Wishful imagination is best understood in the light of this fact.

8. A substantial detached object must come to rest on a horizontal *surface of support.* If an object rests on any other surface it is *attached.*

9. A detached object cannot rest at one place and then rest at another place without being *displaced.* Both rest and displacement are optically specified by the occluding edges of the object relative to the background, in the optic array.

10. A solid object cannot penetrate another solid surface without breaking it (crumbling or disintegrating of the surface). Nothing can penetrate a *liquid* surface suddenly without *splashing.*

11. When the integrity of an ordinary solid surface is broken, as when a rope is cut or a plate is broken, it cannot be restored except by special operations such as tying or mending. (Liquid surfaces, and living surfaces are broken and restored spontaneously, by other rules.)

12. The occluding edge of an opaque object or sheet *screens* (hides, conceals, or *puts out of sight*) part of the background, all of the far side of the

---

[2]The distinction between going out of existence and going out of sight, on which the present essay depends, is explained in great detail in Chs. 2.7 and 2.8 (Eds.)

object itself, and any other object that is temporarily positioned within the envelope of its visual solid angle. But occlusion is progressive and reversible. The occluding edge can be seen as such and hence to that extent, the hidden as well as the unhidden surfaces can be seen (Gibson, 1979a, Ch. 11). Certain conditions under which an occluding edge *cannot* be seen as such will be described in Part III below.

These 12 laws, rules, or regularities are surely not exhaustive. They are the ones I can put into words. The last, especially, is hard to formulate. It probably cannot be formulated at all in the usual terms of physical optics.

## II.  IMPOSSIBLE EVENTS THAT A MAGICIAN CAN MAKE US PERCEIVE

An event that would violate the laws of ecological physics if it occurred would be impossible. Nevertheless, someone who knows how to manipulate and control the information available to an observer for *perceiving* events can make him perceive such an impossibility. (Note that the observer can *perceive* a happening without necessarily *believing* that it happened: he may assume that it was a "trick." Seeing does *not* always entail believing). The magician does so by suppressing the optical information for what really happened or by preventing the observer from picking it up and, more rarely, by artifically producing information for the impossible happening. The literature of magic is full of practical wisdom about how things are seen, but it makes little reference to physics or optics. I refer to the magic of prestidigitation, not to the whole vast area of fairy-tale, fantasy, mystery-magic and "psychic" phenomena.

The kinds of impossible events that we can be made to perceive seem to be as follows:

1. A solid object is seen to "vanish" instead of merely to be hidden, covered, or concealed, that is, progressively occluded. More exactly it is inferred to go out of *existence* inasmuch as the optical information for its going-out-of-sight-and-continuing-to-exist has been eliminated. Sometimes a person is made to appear to "go up in smoke," as when a burst of smoke is produced in front of a trap-door on the floor of the stage through which the person drops. More often a small object is suddenly dropped into a hole under cover of a hand, or is "secretly" transferred to the *other* hand than the one that is "seen" to hold it, or is pulled up a sleeve by a rubber band. (The explanations of sleight-of-hand or legerdemain given by magicians suffer, not surprisingly, from not knowing the ecological optics of progressive occlusion. They emphasize "misdirecting the attention," which is insufficient).

2. A solid object is seen to "materialize" instead of being progressively uncovered or revealed, the information for the real event having been suppressed, or made so abrupt ("presto," the magician says) as to be undetectable.

Thus, for example, a bouquet of collapsible flowers comes out of its container too rapidly to be seen, or an invisible window-blind snaps up during an interval below the threshold of displacement-perception. Hence the object *is not perceived to have pre-existed* as it would be if it were disoccluded more slowly.

3. The integrity of the surface of a solid object that has been cut or broken is restored without mending (a ribbon, rope, or a sawed-in-two woman) in violation of Rule 12 above.

4. A solid object that has been destroyed is recreated (Rule 4). In both of these tricks the substitution (or whatever) is not perceived because the information for perceiving it has not been admitted into the optic array *at the observer's position*.

5. A substantial object is displaced from one location to another without having been transported from one to the other in violation of Rule 9. The displacement as motion is not seen, only the result of the displacement.

6. A solid object goes through a solid barrier without breaking its surface in violation of Rule 11. The actual penetration is not seen, only the result of it.

7. A solid substantial massive object (e.g., a lady in a flowing dress) floats in the air without being attached to any surface of the environment, in violation of Rule 8. This is called *levitation* by conjurors. The means of support is hidden.

8. A solid substantial object is changed into an "entirely different" object (in violation of Rule 3) by a conversion such as billiard ball into bouquet. Only the outcome of the supposed conversion is seen, not the process.

*Conclusion.*   It seems fair to conclude that a real event can go unperceived if the specifying optical motions in the array are eliminated and that another event that is ecologically impossible can be perceived if some optical information for it, however sketchy, is presented instead in the optic array. If the beginning and the end of a pseudo-event are displayed the observer perceives it, or tends to do so, by analogy with "stroboscopic motion."[3] The display of two images at separated places can yield the perception of one object being displaced. (For an attempt to deal with other forms of misperception cf. Gibson, 1966b, Ch. 14).

## III.  THE CONDITIONS UNDER WHICH UNHIDDEN SURFACES CAN EXIST UNSEEN IN THE FIELD OF VIEW

We take it for granted that a surface with its edges, the near side of an object, can be seen (Rule 12). We say that if it is illuminated it forms a retinal image, and that is the *stimulus* for seeing. If the surfaces of obstacles or enemies were often invisible we should be in a very bad way! But nevertheless there is an exceptional condition in which even the front of an object is unseen. It is when there is no

---

[3]For an ecological analysis of stroboscopic motion see Warren (1977) and Warren & Shaw (1978). (Eds.)

discontinuity in the optic array to separate the surface of the object from the surface of its background, that is, no contrast, border, or margins of any sort. The occluding edge of the object cannot be seen because the surface of the object and the surface of the ground behind it are indistinguishable. This condition can only be achieved with a delimited field of view, like that of a stage, and with strictly controlled artificial illumination. Magicians know this. The light must come from the edges of the proscenium arch and, according to Burlingame's *Magician's Handbook*[4] "with reflectors throwing the light in the face of the audience." The walls and floor of the stage are covered with black velvet, which has the lowest reflectance of any surface known. An object or person covered with black velvet against a background of black velvet cannot be seen, even if moving. It is perfectly real, unhidden, having a retinal image of sorts, but unperceived. A person dressed in white *can* be seen, and so can any object with a surface of higher reflectance. A woman with her head in a black bag is a headless woman. A black velvet screen dropped suddenly in front of anything visible will "vanish" it. But the gradual deletion of texture at the occluding edge must be suppressed.

You might suppose that the phenomena of so-called *camouflage* provide other examples of invisibility. The word is only a cover, however, for ill-understood facts, and the literature is a muddle.

A case similar to the black velvet stage-setting, I suspect, is that of so-called Arctic "whiteout" when a uniform snow-covered plain and a sunless sky of the same luminance, seen through the windshield of a vehicle, yields the perception of a complete void—an alarming experience. The circumstances under which a field of view will lack all optical texture or contrasts, all discontinuities, all *structure* are fortunately exceptional and there are no circumstances, I think, in which a whole ambient field will lack structure.

Psychologists have not studied these phenomena at the perceptual level. There is another condition where an unhidden surface can be unseen, however, that *has* been investigated. It is what I call the clean-sheet-of-glass experiment (Gibson, 1979a, Ch. 9). Plate glass cannot be distinguished from whatever is behind it in the absence of highlights and reflections. It is invisible or, as we say, transparent. A mirror yields phenomena that are similar in some respects (Fig. 10.16 in Gibson, 1966b, p. 218).

I am convinced that the surfaces of a box with an open front, together with their corners, could be made to vanish at a fixed point of observation even if their matte reflectances were gray or white instead of velvet black. It would be necessary to project exactly a beam of light on the back wall of reduced intensity such as to compensate for the reduced luminances coming to the eye from the slanted walls, floor, and ceiling. If the contrasts at the dihedral corners are eliminated the surfaces themselves cannot be seen. But this is not easy to achieve.

The control experiment for the "optical pseudotunnel" described in Gibson,

---

[4]Cf. Gibson, Purdy & Lawrence (1955). (Eds.)

(1979a, p. 153) is another case of unseen surfaces that nevertheless exist in the field of view.[5] One sees film or fog or sky instead of the surfaces. To my way of thinking all these cases of surface-perception or non-perception are expressions of the animal's ability to distinguish surface from air. The original experiment was Metzger's, the observer's eye being confronted with a homogeneous "Ganzfeld" as contrasted with a surface having "microstructure." (Gibson, 1979a, p. 150). My observers saw *nothing*.[6] (Metzger's observers said they saw "space" instead of a "plane"; I interpret the results ecologically instead of geometrically.) The ability to distinguish a surface from *nothing* (*no* substantial *thing*) is fundamentally the same as the ability to distinguish the surface of an object from the surface of its background.

## IV. THE CONDITIONS UNDER WHICH EXISTING SURFACES ARE SEEN TO EXIST

Let us go behind Koffka's admirable question *Why do things look as they do?* and ask *Why are things seen?* The naive answer is *Things are seen because they exist.* It is clearly wrong. A surface can exist and *not* be seen as my examples prove. The accepted scientific answer is *Things are seen because they exist within the present field of view and because each has a near surface reflecting the illumination and because a point-to-point image of each surface is formed on the retina and because these images are transmitted to the brain.* I maintain that this answer cannot be right either. We see surfaces that exist outside the present field of view (e.g., behind the head, the far sides of opaque objects, etc.) and we can fail to see a surface within the field of view. Separate images of discrete objects are a myth. The brain is not an organ that operates on "images" in any case.

The true answer is something like this. *A surface in a layout is seen because the optical invariants at a travelling point of observation specify its substance, texture, edges, dihedrals, and state of being at rest or in motion, these being the characteristics of an existing surface, and because the optical invariants are extracted by the eye-head-brain-body system of an observer.* I include under the term "layout" both enclosures and objects. I concede that things can be seen at a *fixed* point of observation, or in a *display* of information, but not with the multiple assurance of their existence that comes from a travelling point of observation, or from walking around an object.[7] Note that "seeing" is supposed to involve a system, not a channel for inputs to the brain.

These are the conditions, I suggest, for perceiving a particular object or place

---

[5]Cf. Gibson et al., 1955. (Eds.)

[6]Many of these issues are discussed in Ch. 1.6 (Eds.).

[7]For more on the limits of a single point of view see Ch. 3.4 and Gibson (1978b). (Eds.)

to exist (to be in existence). It is seen to persist when it is seen to go out of sight, and to have preexisted when it is seen to come into sight (Gibson, 1979a, p. 256ff.).

Can we perceive an object or place to be *nonexistent?* That sounds like an odd kind of perceiving. It is what we do, however, after we see the object or place destroyed (pulverized, burned etc.). To remember it is not the same as to "remember" a particular thing that is hidden.

Do we ever "see" a nonexistent object or place as if it existed? I do not mean the *virtual* object in a mirror, or a *mirage* in the desert air, or a *pictured* object behind the picture, but a *hallucinated* object, a thing for which no invariants are present in the ambient light even when the presumably drugged or diseased observer walks around it. If it is true that the absence of all structure in the light specifies air, i.e., "nothing" in the sense of *no thing,* the answer must be that we do not and cannot. If so, the doctrine that hallucinating is indistinguishable from seeing must be false (Gibson, 1979a, p. 257; also Gibson, 1970b). Finally, the perceiving of possible and impossible events discussed in Part I and II should not be confused with the perceiving or not perceiving of surfaces discussed in Part III and IV, although they are related. Events *occur* or do not. Surfaces *exist* or do not, but some come into and go out of existence, or undergo less drastic changes, or are displaced or *not* displaced, and all of them come into and go out of sight. The formula for perceiving the occurrences is actually somewhat simpler than the formula for perceiving the existents.

Major James J. Gibson shooting movie film (Balboa Island, California, 1945).

Meeting of a summer conference group.
Left to right: Wilson Wathall, Urie Bronfenbrenner, Richard Solomon, Karl Dallenbach, David Katz, Robert Blake, Robert MacLeod, James Gibson.
(Cornell University, Ithaca, New York, 1952).

The Gibson family.
Left to right: Eleanor (Jackie), Jean, Jerry, and Jimmy.
(Ithaca, New York, 1952).

International Conference on Perception.

Left to right: Wolfgang Metzger, Fritz Heider, George Klein, James Drever, Robert MacLeod, James Gibson, Hans Wallach, Egon Brunswik, Gunnar Johansson, Ivo Kohler, Julian Hochberg, T. Arthur Ryan.

(Cornell University, Ithaca, New York, 1954).

Eleanor and James Gibson with Ivo Kohler.
(Innsbruck, Austria, 1956).

James Gibson at the Workshop on Ecological Optics.
(Cornell University, Ithaca, New York, 1970).

James Gibson with Gunnar Johansson.
(Johansson's summer home on the Baltic Sea, Grässö, Sweden, 1976).

James Gibson receiving an honorary doctorate from Uppsala University.
(Uppsala, Sweden, 1976).

# 3

# THE PERCEPTION OF PICTURES

Edward Reed
and Rebecca Jones

## INTRODUCTION

How we perceive pictures was a problem Gibson puzzled about throughout his entire career. From his dissertation on the perception and reproduction of drawings (Gibson, 1929) to the chapters devoted to pictures in *The Ecological Approach to Visual Perception* (1979a, Chs. 15 & 16), Gibson sought to describe what pictures are and to explain how we perceive them. The study of pictures was important to Gibson's development as a theorist. His early experimental work on picture perception challenged theories based on physiological optics and provided one impetus for founding a more adequate, perceptually based optics. In his later work, pictures challenged Gibson's own theory that vision is based on formless invariants of optical structure revealed by transformations. Because the static optic array coming from a picture presents none of the optical transformations normally obtained by a moving observer, picture perception might seem to be based on the forms marked on the picture surface rather than on formless invariants. By extending the ecological approach to the perception of pictures, Gibson clarified both his concept of information and his distinction between direct and indirect perception

A question central to all the papers in this section is "how do pictures perform their representational function?"

Gibson's efforts to answer this question are evident in his repeated attempts to define a picture. These various definitions were testable hypotheses about what a picture is, such that it can provide information for an absent object or scene. Gibson carefully explored the implications of his definitions, and, when the definitions did not measure up to the facts of perceiving, he willingly modified them. The changes over the years in Gibson's definitions of a picture reveal his growing dissatisfaction with physiological optics and chart the development of ecological optics.

Gibson's concern with pictures as special objects of perception began with his Air Force research on methods of pilot selection and training. Some of this work is discussed in "Pictures as substitutes for visual realities" (Ch. 3.1), which is a chapter from Gibson's first book, *Motion Picture Testing and Research* (1947). At that time, Gibson's primary objective was to determine the scope of and limitations on the use of pictures in a practical setting. This applied emphasis is evident in the pragmatic definition of a picture offered (a flat, framed rectangle, filling only part of the field of view) and in the choice of research problems (such as the effectiveness of pictures for group viewing). However, the results of experimenting on these practical problems led to new and important theoretical issues.

In the first part of the chapter, Gibson reported experiments on the effects of viewing pictures from different angles and distances on the perception of shape and distance. Based on physiological optics, one would expect significant perceptual distortion for observers viewing a picture from either an oblique angle or the wrong distance. However, Gibson found no such distortions, indicating that these theoretical limitations on picture perception have no practical significance. In the second part of the chapter, Gibson discussed other characteristics of pictures that in fact do limit their usefulness as substitutes for visual realities and noted that many of them would not be predicted on the basis of physiological optics. These results suggested to Gibson that picture perception is not governed by the laws of physiological optics alone, and that we need an optics more relevant to perception to account for the facts of picture perception.

"A theory of pictorial perception" (Ch. 3.2) was Gibson's first comprehensive account of the perception of pictures. Again, with practical problems such as education and testing in mind, Gibson set out first to describe a general theory of "surrogates," and second to give a detailed account of the perception of those special surrogates, perspective pictures. The fundamental issue in this essay is *fidelity*, or how a surrogate can be faithful to its referent. Gibson argued that fidelity is a dimension with poles of conventionality and projection. Symbols lie on the conventional end, whereas pictures lie on the projective end.

In spite of the questions raised by his wartime research about the usefulness of physiological optics for describing picture perception, Gibson nevertheless used it in formulating his definition of a faithful picture. He hypothesized that a faithful picture is a surface that reflects a sheaf of light rays to a point that is the same as the sheaf of rays coming from the depicted scene. According to this view a picture performs its representational function by providing the eye with the same variations in light energy as would the depicted scene. Some of the implications of this point-projection theory are that viewing from the unique station point is important for undistorted perception, that line drawings and caricatures have less fidelity than photographs, and that with a high-fidelity surrogate mediated perception of a pictured object can become just like direct perception of the real object. Research into some of these implications by Gibson and his colleagues over the next decade (Gibson, 1956; Ryan & Schwartz, 1956; Smith & Gruber, 1958) contributed to the reformulation of this theory.

By the time Gibson revised his point-projection theory of picture perception in "Pictures, perspective, and perception" (Ch. 3.3), his thinking about vision had changed radically. In order to account for many puzzling and provocative facts about seeing, he had developed his theory that perception is based on *information* (Chs. 1.3, 4.3, 1979a, Part 2) and had founded th discipline of ecological optics as the study of optical information (Chs. 1.4, ι.6). This powerful new approach had important implications for his theory of picture perception and contributed to the solution of some contradictions inherent in the point-projection theory.

The first half of Chapter 3.3 is devoted to describing the information available for seeing the environment, and the second half contains an application of this theory to the displaying of information by pictures. Gibson argued that perception of the environment is based on ambient optical structure consisting of nested visual solid angles. By extrapolation, Gibson argued that pictorial information consists not in brightness variations in the sheaf of light rays at the eye, but in the structure of the optic array in terms of higher-order relational variables. Thus, a line drawing, which preserves relational information but not a point-by-point projection of light energies, may provide as accurate information as a photograph.

Although in this paper Gibson vigorously applied his new information-based theory of perception to pictures, the lure of fidelity and the persuasiveness of the illusion of reality from pictures caused him to retain one important component of the point-projection theory. This was the notion that fidelity can be defined in terms of the extent to which a picture sends the same sheaf of rays to a station point as would the scene it represents. Rather than abandoning this notion, Gibson added to it the concept of *functional* fidelity, which he defined as the degree to which a picture presents the same relational variables as would the depicted scene. This somewhat peculiar mix of ecological and physiological optics left a major problem that only a thorough application of ecological optics could solve: Caricatures are paradoxical in that they do not present either the same sheaf of rays or the same nested visual solid angles as the things they represent; yet, in a sense they are more faithful representations than photographs. At the heart of this problem was the appeal of the idea that a faithful picture, duplicating an optic array down to the level of color and brightness variations of the smallest elements, could transcend representation and function as a presentation of the depicted scene.

In "The information available in pictures" (Ch. 3.4), Gibson broke the shackles of physiological optics and provided a comprehensive account of how representational pictures of all sorts (caricatures as well as photographs) provide information. He repudiated the dimension he previously had proposed between projection and convention and showed how neither a projection theory nor a symbol or conventionalist theory could account for the facts of picture perception. In his new information-based theory of picture perception, Gibson argued that a picture performs its representational function by providing the same kind of information about an object as is found in the ambient arrays of the ordinary environment. This information consists of formless and timeless invariants of optical structure that specify the distinctive features of depicted objects. This theory is broad enough to cover all types of informative pictures, from photographs to line drawings to caricatures, and addresses some issues not even considered in Gibson's earlier papers (e.g., ambiguous drawings and pictures of nonexistent objects). Also, Gibson dismissed the possibility that the illusion of reality from pictures could ever be complete, because pictures always provide information for both the scene they represent and the surface they are. Mediated perception cannot become direct perception by stages; the two are very different.

"On the concept of 'formless invariants' in visual perception" (Ch. 3.5) provides a clarification of the theory that picture perception depends not on forms but on formless invariants. In Chapter 3.4, Gibson argued that pictures provide the same kind of information as is normally found in the ambient light of the ordinary environment, and that this information consists of optical invariants. However, a problem arises because the frozen optic array coming from a picture specifying a depicted object does not undergo the transformations that an optic array coming from a three-dimensional scene does. How can picture perception be based on formless invariants if there are no transformations?

In Chapter 3.5, Gibson presented several facts and arguments supporting the position that picture perception must be based on formless invariants rather than on forms or projections. For example, pictures specify entire solid objects, not just one view or a "ghostly shape." Optical invariants can specify hidden surfaces (Ch. 2.7), but forms or projections, the alternative bases for picture perception, are informative about only one aspect or view. Many other analogous arguments are presented, all supporting the view that invariants alone are adequate for explaining the facts of picture perception. Gibson admitted that we scarcely have begun to understand formless invariants but argued that future research should be devoted to their analysis (Ch. 1.7). Such research not only would enhance our understanding of picture perception but also would enrich the ecological approach to perception in general.

Pictures are unique objects in our world. Although they are themselves only flat surfaces with markings on them, they provide information for solid objects that are absent or even nonexistent. How pictures perform their representational function is an important problem for the ecological approach to vision, in that its solution requires the elaboration of some of the principles of ecological optics and the extension of the theory of information pickup. Pictures also provide a concrete way of approaching the issue of mediated awareness, and thus they constitute a link with an ecological approach to cognition. This was an avenue Gibson was beginning to explore, as can be seen from the notes included in Chapter 3.6 (cf. his work on hallucination and visualizing, 1970b; 1974b; 1979a, Ch. 14), and which ought to be pursued further in the elaboration of the ecological approach to psychology.

# 3.1 Pictures as Substitutes for Visual Realities*

In the tests devised by the Film Unit[1] and in most of the research on identification of aircraft, an underlying problem was repeatedly encountered, the problem of the appropriate use of *pictures*. The majority of these pictures were photographic—a category which includes both still pictures and motion pictures—but some were artificial in the sense that they consisted of nonsense shapes or highly schematic objects. These also could be either still or moving. Whether they were viewed on a projection screen or were seen in the form of photographic prints or drawings, they all had in common the characteristic of possessing a rectangular frame which filled only a small part of the observers' total visual field. They also were characterized by the fact that the screen or the paper on which the picture appeared was inevitably flat, and could be seen as such by the observers. These two characteristics may be taken as a preliminary definition of what is meant by a picture.[2]

Pictures in general afford one method of setting up a "miniature reality." For teaching, training, general communication and entertainment they rival language in importance. They are easier to apprehend than language and presumably are perceived more directly. But the apprehension of pictures has its own rules which

---

*Chapter 8 from James J. Gibson (Ed.) *Motion picture testing and research* (Washington, D.C.: U.S. Government, 1947).

[1]The Psychological Test Film Unit of the Perception Research Unit was established, with Gibson as its head, in October 1943 at Santa Ana Army Air Force Base. Its primary goal was the construction of aptitude tests for aircrew by means of research and development of motion picture displays. For more information see Gibson (1944). (Eds.)

[2]Gibson (1979a, pp. 270–271) provides a summary and critique of his various definitions of a picture. (Eds.)

are different from those which apply to the understanding of language. And likewise the perceiving of pictures is governed by a different set of psychological conditions than is the perceiving of the situations represented by them. The visual situation represented in a picture, whether still or moving, is not only shown "in miniature," i.e., ordinarily reduced in size, but is subject to other differences and limitations. These differences become important when pictures are employed for exact purposes in psychological tests or for controlled types of training.

As described in the foregoing chapters of this report, a variety of scenes have been represented by pictures in the course of test construction and research. The following examples may be listed: the scene of distant airplanes flying through the sky at different velocities; a schematic instrument panel; the shapes of aircraft against the sky, both moving and motionless; the scene showing locomotion of the observer during a landing; the scene showing flight over the ground during a series of changes of direction. In the chapters to follow, even more complex scenes are required to be represented, such as the distances of objects in the third dimension, and the task of sighting a hand-held machine gun on an attacking enemy pursuit plane. A number of principles were found to operate in the presenting of these pictures to observers for testing or training purposes, which may be brought together briefly in the present chapter. They fall under two main headings, the equivalence of a picture viewed at different angles and at different distances, and the limiting differences between a picture and the scene represented by the picture. With respect to viewing conditions, there appear to be fewer limitations on the use of pictures than optical principles would lead one to suppose. With respect to pictures as substitutes for natural vision, however, there are more limitations than are often recognized.

## THE EQUIVALENCE OF A PICTURE VIEWED AT DIFFERENT ANGLES AND AT DIFFERENT DISTANCES

The data presented in Chapter 4 [Not reprinted here. (Eds.)] demonstrated that within limits, the *performance* of an observer taking a motion picture test was independent of the angle at which he viewed the picture and the distance at which he viewed it. No direct evidence was available in these experiments with regard to the *appearance* of the picture. The most likely interpretation was that it had an equivalent appearance despite changes in the retinal image produced by different viewing angles and distances. The question of practical importance is this: does the *scene represented* in the picture become modified when the picture is viewed at an acute angle or at an "unnatural" distance?

*Constancy of Representation at Different Angles of View.* Ordinary experience in viewing photographs or pictures suggests that there is a considerable degree of latitude in the angle which the line of sight can make with the picture without distortion. It is known that the *shape* of an object seen in a straight-front position is perserved when the object is tilted or turned; this fact is given the name of "shape constancy." Presumably a picture, and the scene within the frame of the picture, are governed by an extension of the same fact of perception.[3]

In order to study this principle, a simple experiment was performed and repeated on various occasions with different observers, employing a projector, a screen, and slides showing several types of scenes. The setup is diagrammed in Figure 23. The normal arrangement of projector and screen is shown on the left. An observer viewing this screen picture at an angle reports that the *picture frame is rectangular,* and *the scene represented is not distorted,* although his retinal image is nonrectangular and foreshortened. The explanation of this fact must lie in the simultaneous perception of the screen as oblique. The theory suggested is that there exists an automatic compensation in visual perception for viewing at an oblique angle.[4]

As a partial test of this theory the arrangement shown on the right was tried out, the projector throwing an oblique image. In a head-on view, the picture projected on the screen now appears foreshortened and distorted (the retinal image being distorted in the same way as before). But it also looks distorted when the eye is moved over to the same oblique point of view taken by the projector, the retinal image in this position being completely rectangular. When both projector and eye are on the same line of projection, optical distortion disappears. The critical variable in these different situations is apparently the perception of the screen as an oblique surface. The oblique-view compensation seems to be able to preserve the "constancy" not only of a normal picture but also of a distorted picture. This interpretation is consistent with the observation that when one looks at the arrangement shown on the right with half-closed eyes, or tries to see the picture as an image dissociated from the screen, the distortion diminishes and its appearance comes close to being rectangular.

The implications of these results, although incomplete as a formal experiment, suggest that the viewing of pictures is governed not by the laws of optics taken by themselves but only as they are modified by principles of space perception. The principle of spatial constancy seems to be applicable.

*Constancy of Representation at Different Distances.*    The scene represented in a snapshot or picture appears to the ordinary observer to be relatively unaffected by the distance at which it is held or viewed. Likewise a photograph may be enlarged or reduced in size without any obvious change in its capacity to represent a scene. There are probably limits to both of these generalizations, but

---

[3]Rosinski & Farber (1980) review the literature on the effects of oblique viewing on picture perception. (Eds.)

[4]This is the central thesis of Pirenne's (1970) theory of picture perception. (Eds.)

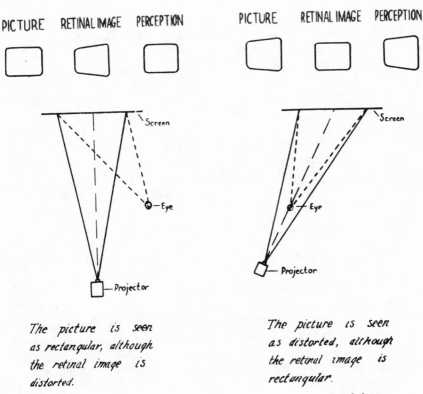

FIG. 23.    The effect of oblique-view compensation in viewing projected pictures: Perceptual shape-constancy.

the limits have apparently not been determined. People unquestionably have *preferences* in the viewing distances they select voluntarily for looking at photographs, museum pictures, and motion pictures. The Film Unit was unable to discover any empirical study of the basis of such preferences, or whether they are consistent. There is, however, an assumption which is accepted by photographers and is emphasized in the literature of photography that there exists only one proper distance at which a photographic picture should be viewed. This distance is *that at which the visual angle subtended by the picture at the eye of the observer is just equal to the visual angle subtended at the camera lens by the scene registered* (Henney & Dudley, 1939). In other words, the viewer must take such a distance that the proportion of the picture to his total field of view is the same as the proportion of the scene registered by the camera to the total field; the eye must be at a viewpoint equivalent to where the camera was. This requirement is said to be necessary if the distance and the relative positions and dimensions in the three-dimensional scene photographed are to be correctly represented and if they are to appear natural. It should be noted that, according to this rule, if a picture has been increased in size by photographic enlargement or by projection on a screen, the unique viewing distance must be increased in proportion to the degree of enlargement. This rule is not observed in practice, as indeed it could not be, in the viewing of motion pictures and in the showing of slides by projection to an audience. All members of the group cannot be seated at the "natural" viewing distance. The question is troublesome, and the problem arises as to whether the rule *ought to be* observed in the interests of correct representation.[5]

The evidence accumulated by the Psychological Test Film Unit on this question has already been presented in Chapter 4 and in the experiment on the apparent range of represented aircraft in Chapter 7. [Not reprinted here. (Eds.)] In the latter experiment there was a tendency for the apparent distance from the observer to the airplane pictured, indefinite as it was, to be the same whether the picture was viewed at 10 feet, 20 feet, or 40 feet. This result was in contradiction to the rule of the unique viewing distance. In these pictures, however, there were few cues to the perception of distance apart from the relationship of the object to the frame. Other pictures possessing perspective and representing three-dimensional scenes were subsequently observed under similar circumstances. The perspective, distance, and relative dimensions of these scenes did not appear to be distorted even though very considerable departures were made from the rule of the natural viewing distance.

The rule states that the observer of a picture must duplicate the visual angle of the camera that took the picture. Otherwise, it implies, his retinal image will not be a projected copy of the image which a spectator of the original scene would have had. But there is no proof that his retinal image needs to be such a copy. The visual surroundings of the picture-viewer consist of the room in which the picture is shown; the visual surroundings of the original spectator consist of the unrepresented parts of the total scene. These are quite different surroundings, and it is not legitimate to apply the optics of one situation to the optics of the other.

The evidence on the effect of viewing distance, together with other observations, suggested a perceptual rather than an optical theory of viewing pictures. In the case of photographs of three-dimensional scenes the *standpoint of the observer is itself represented in the scene*. The location of the observer in the space portrayed may not be exact, but it is never wholly indefinite. It depends, for one thing, on the amount of foreground visible (*cf.* Chapter 9). [Here, Ch. 1.1 & 2.2. (Eds.)] The location of the observer in this space is something entirely distinct from his location in the space in which the picture is shown—the classroom, theater, or photographic salon. The location of the observer in the represented space, so long as he "loses himself" in it (or more accurately, *sees himself* in it) seems to be little affected by his location in the room-space which contains the picture. The picture itself is perceived in a substantially equivalent way whether

---

[5]See Lumsden (1980) for a review of the literature on the effects of magnification and minification on picture perception. (Eds.)

its retinal image be relatively small or relatively large. This result may be explained on the basis of perceptual constancy. It is presumably for the above reason that the space represented in the picture is substantially equivalent whether its retinal image be relatively small or relatively large.

In all probability, too great a strain can be put upon this compensating ability of visual perception at extreme departures from the "natural" visual angle subtended by a picture. The appearance of photographs or motion pictures taken with telescopic lenses and the appearance of pictures taken with extremely wide-angle lenses indicate that distortions of representation in the third dimension do occur. The limits at which these distortions begin to assert themselves are not known; the conclusion for present purposes is simply that the tolerance in allowable viewing distances for pictures is considerable.[6]

## THE SCOPE AND LIMITS OF PHOTOGRAPHIC REPRESENTATION

The attempt to represent complex spatial scenes for purposes of testing or instruction encounters both opportunities and difficulties. Photography is undoubtedly the most powerful method of accomplishing such representation, especially if one includes motion picture photography and the animation of drawings. Many striking and realistic effects can be achieved. But the differences between photographic representations and the process of seeing directly are nevertheless considerable.[7] The visual and other mechanisms of man which yield his perception of a spatial world are, although subject to defects, superior to the mechanisms of representation by camera and picture at its best. In the course of the Film Unit's research, a tentative set of generalizations was gradually developed concerning the differences between the view yielded by the human visual mechanism and that yielded by photographic representation. In constructing tests for perceptual functions, it became evident that certain aspects of perception could, and others could not, be represented by pictures. Motion pictures added enormously to the possibilities but certain basic limitations were still present. A camera is capable of a good many kinds of "seeing," and a motion picture camera is capable of even more kinds. But no camera is capable of seeing as the eye sees. Inasmuch as some of the capacities of natural vision are not as obvious as universal possession of them might suggest, the differences and similarities are worth pointing out.

### Angle of View

The field of view of the eyes is very much wider than that of the usual type of camera. Photographic representation has a narrow field of view, seldom exceed-

---

[6]See Pirenne (1970) for research on this topic. (Eds.)

[7]Cf. Gibson (1979a, pp. 280–283) for discussion of this issue. (Eds.)

ing 45° to 50° laterally. It therefore lacks the feature of peripheral vision, and consequently a picture is necessarily seen with surroundings which are extraneous to it. The only exception to this rule is panoramic projection of images, which may be passed over. What the observer of a screen of a photograph sees "out of the corner of his eye" is not the scene of the picture but the room in which it is shown. This rule becomes significant when it is desired to represent, for example, the view of a flier over terrain in which he must locate landmarks. The narrow field of the camera is a handicap which has to be taken into account.

## The Effects of the Picture Margins

It follows from the above considerations that a picture must necessarily have margins. It cannot exist simply as a field of view; it is always an object within the field of view and therefore has a contour, which is conventionally a rectangular frame. The frame of a picture exercises a profound influence on the scene represented. Since the frame is always aligned with the vertical and horizontal directions of the room in which the picture is viewed, it becomes (or tends to become) the "frame of reference" with respect to which the orientation of the scene is judged. In the case of still pictures, if an object is not aligned with the frame, the object appears tilted, even though in actual fact it may have been the camera that was tilted. Even a scene showing terrain, horizon, or buildings tends to look like a tilted world in such circumstances, or like a hillside if that interpretation is possible, because of the strong tendency for the frame of the picture to determine the vertical and horizontal axes of the space represented. For this reason the camera in ordinary photographic work must be held in strict horizontal alignment and pointed horizontally forward. Under certain circumstances the camera may be successfully pointed up or down, as in aerial photographs, but only if there are cues in the scene to the unusual orientation of the viewer and his line of regard.

In the case of motion pictures *showing locomotion of the observer over the ground*, during flight for example, the frame of the picture may also, within limits, be shifted from the straight-front posture. It may be represented as applicable to the airplane and not to the ground. The experience of diving and turning can be shown with some success; the ground does not tilt up or rotate but instead the observer dives or turns. Banking is more difficult to represent; since the picture frame tends to be horizontal, the horizon itself tends to rotate and the observer then becomes disoriented. All efforts to *show the observer himself in space* by means of motion pictures must take account of the fact that the picture frame is an artificial frame of reference which comes between the observer and the spatial world depicted.[8]

---

[8]Warren (1976) discusses the uses of motion pictures for studying visual proprioception. (Eds.)

## The Weak Sense of Orientation in Pictures

If one contrasts the facts just described with the kind of viewing of which natural human vision is capable, the differences are striking. The eyes, unlike the camera, need not be aimed straight ahead and held upright. One can lean over, look up, or lie on one's side without the slightest tendency for the visual world to tilt or swing. The explanation presumably lies in the fact that our retinal images, unlike motion picture images, are accompanied by and compensated by a postural sense of the orientation of the head and the eyes.[9] The perceiver of a photograph or screen picture *is not necessarily made aware by it of the orientation of the camera that took the picture.* In ordinary vision the perceiver is automatically and immediately adjusted to the orientation of his eyes by the existence of another sense.

This is not to say that the camera, and especially the motion picture camera, cannot represent orientation at the point of view of the observer and the direction in which he is looking, but only that there are definite limitations on this capacity. The only cues available for it are those which are present in the visual scene itself, and they are frequently not wholly adequate. The amateur who attempts to photograph a skyscraper by pointing his camera up at it gets a picture which is an adequate reproduction of his own retinal image but which looks unnatural. The explanation is not that the perspective is exaggerated, as sometimes is suggested, but more probably that the sense of looking up is missing from the picture. The spatial frame of reference for the scene is not clearly indicated, and the building may seem to lean away from the vertical or otherwise look "queer."

## The Incapacity of Motion Pictures to "Look Around"

Early motion pictures were made with a motionless camera which registered a scene analogous to a theatrical stage or a still photograph. The motion was confined to the action shown and did not extend to the camera itself. "Pan" shots and "dolly" shots were a later development. Although modern motion picture technique employs a camera which moves with some freedom from one character to another and from one part of a scene to another, the shift in the "view" of the camera is usually slow and of no considerable degree. If it is desired to represent an object or event outside the field of view of the camera, a cut is normally employed rather than a moving camera.

This is not the state of affairs with natural vision. The eyes perceive a visual scene by a process of scanning it, i.e., they move from one fixation point to another, sometimes over a wide angle, by saccadic eye movements. A peculiar feature of these eye movements is that they are extremely rapid and that, for reasons only partially understood, the scene does not blur or even appear to move

---

[9]This hypothesis, developed in Gibson & Mowrer (1938) was later rejected by Gibson (1952b); cf. Ch. 2.4. (Eds.)

as the eyes sweep across it.[10] The changed orientation of the eyes is automatically sensed. If a motion picture camera is turned rapidly from one line of regard to another, the picture blurs. Its capacity to shift direction is therefore limited, and the process of scanning or looking around has no real counterpart on the screen.

When the motion picture camera is used to portray subjective experiences, as it is on rare occasions in commercial films and as it was employed to good effect in a few wartime training films, the limits on the kinds of "seeing" possible for it become a matter of importance. Conceivably they could be extended by novel techniques. The use of a "fast pan" instead of a cut under special circumstances to approximate the experience of scanning a scene might provide such an extension.[11]

## The Absence of a Focus of Attention in Pictures

The natural visual field has the characteristic of possessing a center at which vision is clearest. This center corresponds to the fovea of the eye—the part of the retina best equipped anatomically for exact perception. The periphery of the visual field becomes progressively less clear and vision fades or ceases at extreme angles. The margins of the visual field are not abrupt, as is the frame of a picture, and they are little noticed.

In contrast to this a picture lacks a central focus. The viewer may concentrate on any portion of it at will, and it is organized not by a gradient of clarity from center to periphery but by principles of what the artist calls composition. The camera cannot fixate on a scene in the strict meaning of the term; it cannot narrow the attention to a single object or a single portion of an object. The only means which the motion picture medium has of simulating the effect of concentrating attention is the conventional sequence of a long shot, followed by a medium shot, followed by a closeup. The part of a scene to be examined is, in effect, progressively enlarged until it fills most of the screen.

## Absence of Binocular Parallax in Pictures

A picture, although it represents a three-dimensional space and may do so very adequately, is always at the same time seen as a two-dimensional object. The flat appearance of a still picture may be minimized and perhaps even destroyed by methods such as viewing a photographic print or transparency through an enlarging lens. The effect is to enhance the apparent depth of the picture to a marked degree. But a single photographic picture, unlike natural vision, presents the same stimulus to both eyes and consequently lacks the type of depth perception attributable to stereoscopic vision. The significance of this fact will be discussed in greater detail in Chapter 9 [Here, Ch. 1.1 & 2.2 (Eds.)]. Stereoscopic pictures add

---

[10]See Ch. 2.6 for more on this phenomenon. (Eds.)

[11]For more on cinematographic technique see Gibson (1979a, Ch. 16). (Eds.)

the cue of binocular parallax to other depth stimuli already represented in the individual single photographs, but they still retain some of the characteristics of a picture by virtue of having only a limited field of view and possessing a rectangular marginal frame.

## The Point of View of the Camera and the Location of the Observer

Most pictures which show a terrain or which have perspective give some indication of the location of the observer in the space represented, and some give a definite indication. The position of "here" can always be made out, i.e., the point at which the observer is standing. This point is not actually in the picture, but it is in the space represented by the picture. It is usually, but not necessarily, at approximately the point where the camera was located. The focal length of the lens employed, however, has an effect on this apparent standpoint, the result of a telescopic lens being to move it forward into the scene and the result of a wide angle lens being to move it backward from the scene.

Change of location of the observer, or locomotion, is represented by motion pictures with a considerable degree of success. The visual stimuli which make this possible are discussed in detail in Chapter 9. [Here, Ch. 1.1 & 2.2 (Eds.)].

# 3.2 A Theory of Pictorial Perception*

A distinction is possible between what is commonly called experience at first hand and experience at second hand. In the former one becomes aware of something. In the latter one is *made aware* of something. The process by which an individual becomes aware of something is called perception, and psychological investigators have been concerned with it for generations. The process by which an individual is made aware of something, however, is a stage higher in complexity, and this has scarcely been touched upon by modern experimental psychology. It involves the action of another individual besides the perceiver. Although a precise terminology is lacking for this two-stage process, it is readily described in ordinary language: we speak of *being informed, being told, being taught, being shown, or being given to understand*. The principal vehicle for this kind of indirect perception is, of course, language. There is another vehicle for obtaining experience at second hand, however, and this is by way of pictures or models. Although much has been written about language, there is no coherent theory of pictures. The attempt to analyse how a picture conveys information is a necessary but highly ambitious undertaking. The following essay cannot claim to do anything but set up working hypotheses for an important field of investigation.[1]

---

*Audio-Visual Communication Review*, 1954, *1*, 3–23. Copyright 1954 by The Association for Educational Communications and Technology. Reprinted by permission.

[1]Gibson (1979a, Chs. 14 & 15) later refined this distinction between direct (first hand) and indirect (second hand) perceiving, and elaborated the theory that indirect perception forms a link between perception and cognitive or linguistic functions (cf. Ch. 3.6). See Hagen (1974; 1976) for another theoretical model of picture perception. (Eds.)

## I.  WORDS, PICTURES AND MODELS AS
## SUBSTITUTES FOR REALITIES

An obvious fact about perception is that it is different for different things, that is, our percepts are specific to the various features of the physical environment surrounding us. We discriminate among these features and we can identify objects, places, and events when we encounter them on another occasion. This discriminating and identifying of things is an important part of what goes on when we say that we *learn*. Learning requires not only that we make the appropriate reactions but also that we be sensitive to the appropriate stimuli. An important aspect of education, or of any kind of special training, military, industrial, or professional, is an increasing ability to discriminate and identify things.[2]

The training situation, however, is not always the same situation as that for which the individual is being trained. This fact holds for the child at home, the student at school, and the military trainee before he sees action. The learner must ordinarily be given an acquaintance with objects, places, and events which he has never physically encountered. The expedient is to train the individual in artificially constructed situations and expect that his learning will *transfer* to the novel situation, and this is essentially what any teacher does. The artificial construction of these situations is the crux of the matter. They must present adequate substitutes for the objects, places, and events later to be met with, if the latter are to be successfully discriminated and identified. The teacher can use oral and written words to induce this kind of secondhand experience, to "arouse an image," but he has always felt the need for other substitutes in addition. Pictures, films, drawings, models, and displays, along with diagrams, graphs, charts and maps are also, he is convinced, useful. Precisely why they are useful needs to be understood.

What kinds of substitute-stimuli are best for informing or teaching, or which kinds are better for what purposes? What are the advantages of pictures and motion pictures? What are the advantages of words? What are the limitations of both? Should pictures be realistic or schematic? Do pictures reproduce the perception of real three-dimensional space? These are all practical questions, but they involve difficult theoretical problems.

## II.  DEFINITION OF THE TERM "SURROGATE"

In order to understand how pictures convey information it will be necessary to have some general theory of how information is conveyed. Before attempting to specify the difference between pictures and words we should examine them to see how they are alike. The term *surrogate* is proposed to cover both, and a theory of surrogates will be formulated as a first step toward a theory of pictures.

The traditional or common sense explanation of how one man conveys infor-

---

[2]Cf. Ch. 4.2. (Eds.)

mation to another is simply that men have ideas, and that ideas are transmitted. The idea is said to be "expressed" in language, the words "carry" the idea, and the idea is then "grasped" or "taken in." An idea may be expressed by a picture as well as by words. It is hardly necessary to point out that this is no explanation at all. The "transmision of ideas" by words and pictures implies, when taken literally, that these vehicles carry their ghostly passengers unaltered from one mind to another. We shall therefore dispense with the term "idea" and state our definitions in terms of behavior.

A surrogate will be defined as a *stimulus produced by another individual which is relatively specific to some object, place, or event not at present affecting the sense organs of the perceiving individual*. The implications of this definition should be explored both for what it includes and what it does not include. It says, in the first place, that a surrogate is an artificial stimulus constituted or produced by the behavior of another organism. Consequently, a surrogate is *not* the same thing as a substitute stimulus or a preparatory stimulus or a conditioned stimulus, as these are ordinarily defined in psychology, for these include merely physical conjunctions of events. Clouds are not a surrogate for rain, nor is the smell of food a surrogate for food. These are *signs,* but not surrogates.

In the second place, the definition says nothing about what the stimulated individual will *do* in the presence of a surrogate. All it implies is that he may have a kind of mediated or indirect perception of what the surrogate is specific to. It is true, of course, that perception is a form of organic response, but this kind of response probably has the primary function of identifying or discriminating features of the environment; it is implicit rather than overt and it does not in any reliable way tell us what the individual will do.

Thirdly, the definition implies the action of one individual on another, a social influence, or an elementary form of communication, but the emphasis is on one aspect of communication only. The definition is concerned with the *mediating of a perception* rather than the *arousing of an action* in one's fellow man. Long ago, De Laguna (1927) pointed out that speech had two general functions, that of "proclamation" and that of "command." An act of speech might at one extreme merely proclaim the existence of a certain state of affairs, or at another extreme merely command a certain action. Usually it did both, but the two functions were said to be distinguishable. More recently, Skinner (1957) has distinguished between the "tact" and the "mand" in verbal behavior. Many social scientists have contrasted the transmitting of knowledge with the effort to control action, or "information" as against "propaganda." Surrogate-making as here considered, then, will apply only to the first kind of communication, not to the second. A general theory of communication including the function of persuasion would require many definitions and assumptions about human motivation and conduct, and is a greater undertaking than the writer here intends. The present theory is admittedly incomplete.

Fourthly, the definition says that a surrogate must be relatively specific to an absent object, place, or event. "Specific" here means a one-to-one relationship between different surrogates and different things; it does not mean that the things specified are necessarily concrete objects or particular places or never-to-be-repeated events. On the contrary, they may be abstract or universal things. Evidently the meaning of specificity is a crucial part of the definition. (Perhaps it is also the part of the theory to follow which most needs criticism and elaboration.)[3] The specificity of surrogates to their referents is analogous to what was called an obvious fact about direct perception—that it is different for different physical things. We assume that direct perceptions correspond to realities, or rather that they come more and more to do so as the perceiver learns. Accordingly we are primarily interested in how perceptions *mediated by surrogates* also come to correspond to realities. Clearly, this kind of apprehension can only be specific to a referent if the intervening surrogate was itself specific to a referent in the first place. The interesting fact about the specificity of a surrogate is that it depends on the psychological activity of its producer, that is, on the precision of *his* apprehension. Surrogate-making, whether it be naming, drawing, or modelling in clay, consists largely in what the writer has elsewhere called *identifying reactions* (Gibson, 1950a).

The above definition of surrogates may usefully be compared and contrasted with a recent explicit definition of *signs* by Charles Morris (1946). The present formula owes much to his rigorous discussion, but there are fundamental differences between them. Morris distinguishes between *iconic* signs and *non-iconic* signs. The former include images and pictures; the latter include words. Morris understands that no sharp line can be drawn between them. But he has very little to say about the former and his theory is applied not to them, but to language. In contrast, the present theory is directed toward pictorial communication and language is slighted. A surrogate as defined here is less inclusive than a sign as defined by Morris, in that the former is always something produced by an organism whereas the latter may be any feature of the stimulating situation. Moreover, surrogates exclude in large part the difficult category of "expressive" or "emotive" signs, that is, reactions which are specific to the state of the organism rather than to the features of his environment. The present emphasis, in short, is cognitive.

## III. THE PRODUCTION OF SURROGATES

Human organisms are chronic makers of surrogates. Some of their reactions yield only temporary stimuli (sounds, gestures, and so-called expressive movements) while others yield permanent stimulus-objects (picture-making, modelling, writing). It would be useful to classify and list, first, the fundamental motor acts which either constitute or produce surrogates and, second, the complex motor acts or technologies which man has learned for producing them. These sources of

---

[3]The concept of optical specificity is elaborated in Ch. 1.4. (Eds.)

stimulation are necessarily such as always to be either easily seen or easily heard by normal perceivers.

The fundamental motor acts are (a) the making of vocal sounds, such as cries or speech; (b) the making of movements of the face, hands, arms, or body, which includes gestures, postures, and mimicry; (c) the making of tracings on a surface of some kind, which includes drawing, painting and the special case of writing; (d) the shaping of a substance by moulding it, cutting it, or fitting pieces together, which includes sculptures, toys, and models of all kinds, and finally; (e) the making of mechanical sounds by manipulating an instrument or blowing into it, which includes sound-signalling and above all, music. If this list is exhaustive, it suggests that there are only a limited number of basic reactions appropriate for surrogate-making.

During recent history, to be sure, complex operations have been invented for making all these fundamental surrogates, which enable them to be conveniently reproduced, stored, and transmitted. Secondary surrogates are the result. The earliest technique of this sort, writing, is an instance of making a permanent surrogate to substitute for a simpler but temporary surrogate, i.e., tracings which are a substitute for speech. Writing probably evolved in the history of civilization from drawing, which is a primary surrogate (Hogben, 1949). The main techologies for secondary or tertiary surrogates seem to be (a) printing, which substitutes for writing; (b) sound-recording and reproducing, which substitutes for speech and music; (c) photography, which substitutes for drawing, painting, engraving, and other methods of altering a surface by hand, and which, together with photo-engraving, has flooded our environment with pictures; (d) cinematography, which enables a picture to represent time as well as space; (e) vacuum-tube images, both pictorial (television) and symbolic (radar), the end of which is not yet in sight, and finally; (f) various techniques for replicating things in three dimensions and thereby making models, displays, exhibits, panoramas, and simulators intended to produce all kinds of ''synthetic'' realities.

It should be noted that there is a characteristic of primary surrogates which the secondary or tertiary surrogates tend to lack, namely the personal style of the producer. Speech, gesture, handwriting, drawing and artistic style are notably ''expressive'' of the person who performs them (Allport & Vernon, 1933). His reaction is specific, in other words, to himself or to his mood in addition to being specific to an object. The more complex products tend to lack this personal character. A painter is usually identifiable from his pictures but a photographer seldom is.

## IV.   THE CONSEQUENCES OF SURROGATE-MAKING FOR THE PERCEIVER AND THE PRODUCER

The most obvious consequence of surrogate-making is that another person can apprehend objects, places, and events perceived only by the first person. This makes possible a sort of vicarious experience for other individuals; the writer of a book, for instance, can produce mediated perceptions in many other people, and they may be people who live in distant places or even will not be living until future times. He can make them see what he has seen and hear what he has heard. A similar power is commanded by the painter, the movie maker, the teacher, and the parent. One person can, as we say figuratively, transmit knowledge to others. What is equally important, however, is the fact that the first person can *exchange* surrogates with other persons. This makes possible a common body of perceptions among the group; it influences their direct perceptions and it may lead to a sort of consensus of experience, a common world in which mediated percepts and direct percepts are no longer separate.

The making of a surrogate, we must remember, necessarily involves self-stimulation whether or not it ever stimulates anyone else. Stimulation is fed back into an organism synchronously with its action. A speaker hears his own voice; an actor feels his own gestures; an artist sees his own pencil-movements. As a result, the perceptual process and the surrogate-making process tend each to lead into the other, and the two become inextricably mixed. As Morris (1946) and others before him have pointed out, this circular response in children, in conjunction with the facts of social stimulation, eventually converts a vocal sound into a symbol. The symbol-process then comes to occur in the absence of another person and even in the absence of the stimulating object to which the original perception was specific. At this stage of development the individual "thinks." Since the same circular operation occurs for other surrogates as well as for vocal ones, it is not unreasonable to suppose that a person can learn to think in terms of drawings or graphs or models (and of the manipulations which produce them) as well as in terms of words. It may even be possible to infer, later on in this essay, that in certain respects such thinking is more easily performed than is verbal thinking.

## V.  CONVENTIONAL AND NON-CONVENTIONAL SURROGATES

An attempt can now be made to formulate the difference between words and pictures. All surrogates are specific to their referents, but the correspondence between a word and its object is probably not the same as that between a picture and its object. Morris faced the same problem when he considered that a great many signs are, as he put it, "iconic" (1946, pp. 23, 191). His formula is very simple: a sign is iconic to the extent that it has itself the properties of what it denotes, or to the extent that it is similar to what it denotes. An image or a portrait of a man has many (but not all) of the properties of the man himself.

This statement is illuminating but it does not go very far, as Morris might be the first to admit. What *kinds* of properties can a surrogate share with the thing it stands for? In what respects is it similar? Can a surrogate be wholly unlike its object? And what if the object be abstract, so that there is little to be denoted?

Consider two extreme cases of what can be meant by the correspondence of one thing to another, first the correspondence of a license-plate to an automobile and second the correspondence of a shadow to the tree that casts it. The plate is specific to the car because of an arbitrary pairing of the two and because of a rule of social conduct that says plates may not be exchanged or duplicated. The shadow is specific to the tree because it is a geometrical projection of the tree on the surface of the ground by rays of light from the sun.

By analogy with the license-plate and the shadow, one may suggest that surrogates at one extreme are specific to objects, places, and events by *convention*, while surrogates at the other extreme are specific to the same things by *projection*. Language and algebraic symbols tend to fall toward the former pole and pictures or motion pictures toward the latter. Diagrams and graphs fall somewhere in the middle. Considering a language as a set of sounds produced by vocal reactions (or an equivalent set of tracings produced by manual reactions) the obvious fact to consider is that some groups of men have one set while other groups have different sets. A given object has different names in different languages. On the other hand the enormous number of photographic snapshots existing all over the world constitute a single set. A given object could be matched with its photograph by any human being without having to learn laboriously a special vocabulary of photographs. The object and its name have an extrinsic relation, whereas the object and its picture have an intrinsic relation.

Non-conventional, projective or replicative surrogates seem to be characterized by a very interesting possibility, which will require closer examination later. It is the theoretical possibility of the surrogate becoming more and more like the original until it is indistinguishable from it. For visual perception, and under certain viewing conditions, a model can be elaborated until the artificial scene is equivalent to the natural one. Under very special viewing conditions a motion picture can probably also be so elaborated that the perceiver is led to suppose that what he sees is an actual situation and an actual sequence of events. This possibility is *not* characteristic of a conventional surrogate.

Both conventional and non-conventional surrogates may, of course, be relatively unspecific to their referents, and to this extent the resulting perceptions will also be unspecific. Language may be vague or ambigous (Black, 1949, Ch. 2) and so also may pictures. *In the case of pictures the relation will be called one of greater or lesser fidelity; in the case of words the relation will be called one of greater or lesser univocality.* Maximum fidelity of a picture or model will be defined later, in terms of geometry and optics. Maximum univocality is very difficult to define; the task will be left to the students of semantics and of information-theory.

A number of propositions about words and pictures seem to follow from the foregoing assumptions, of which four will be stated.

1. In general, children have to learn the correspondence of a surrogate to its object in order to make use of it. *The more nearly a surrogate is projective or replicative, the less does associative learning need to occur. The more nearly a surrogate is conventional, the more does associative learning need to occur.*[4] Pictures and models are closer approximations to direct perception than words and symbols are.

2. Distinguishing between concrete objects, places, and events on the one hand, and abstract properties, qualities, or variables of them on the other, *the more nearly a surrogate is replicative or projective the less is it capable of referring to abstractions and the more must its referent be concrete.* Conventional surrogates, however, do not have this limitation. *The more arbitrary a surrogate, the more is it free to specify anything, abstract or concrete.* Verbal responses, for example, may be either names which identify objects or adjectives and adverbs which specify their properties. Picture-making can also identify objects and specify properties, but it cannot name an object and describe it *separately.* Verbal surrogates enable us to separate abstractions from concrete things and respond to them in a special way. With symbolic responses we can make propositions and hence perform logical and mathematical thinking. A realistic picture on the contrary, cannot state a logical proposition.

3. If purely conventional surrogates exist at one extreme and purely replicative surrogates at the other, there are "mixed" surrogates which are intermediate. These are specific to their referents partly by virtue of univocality and partly by virtue of fidelity. This applies particularly to pictures made by hand, which will be called "chirographic." The shift in human pre-history from picture-making (such as cave paintings) to picture-writing (such as Chinese characters) is apparently a development away from fidelity toward univocality. The development of Western painting up until the advent of photography is partly a matter of striving for fidelity, but artists at all times have also sought to specify general or abstract features of the world. Cartoonists, for instance, do so. *Mixed surrogates, especially chirographic pictures, specify both concrete objects, places, and events and general or typical objects, places, and events.* In other words, graphic conventions or graphic symbols may be incorporated in a picture as distortions of line, shape, proportion, or color. This reduces fidelity, but it may increase univocality. The latter effect, however, depends on the *establishment* of the convention.

4. A conclusion seems to follow from the foregoing paragraph, which may be controversial. *A chirographic picture cannot at the same time possess high fidelity for something concrete and high univocality for something abstract.* The introduction of graphic symbolization into a picture necessarily sacrifices its capacity to represent. The effort to gain abstractness entails a loss in concrete-

---

[4]See Ch. 4.2 and Gibson & Gibson (1972) for arguments against the theory of associative learning. (Eds.)

ness. The sacrificing of fidelity, that is to say distortion, should have the result of making the observer's perception vague and his behavior unspecific, *as a general rule*. Only when the distortion is such that artist and observer both accept it as a univocal symbol is the sacrifice worth while. The artist's intention may have been to make evident some typical or significant feature of the original, but if his distortion is not established as specifying it, the observer is only puzzled. If his distortion *does* specify it, the picture can evoke not only a mediated perception of something concrete, but also an apprehension of its general, abstract, or universal features.

## VI.  THE FIDELITY OF A MODEL

Certain types of surrogates, it was asserted, are characterized by fidelity (replicative or projective). Models and pictures are examples. Other types of surrogates are characterized by univocality, without fidelity. Words and symbols are examples. "Fidelity" must now be defined. It should be treated as a matter of degree, and the definition should be mathematical. The geometry of fidelity needs to come up for discussion. We will begin with models.

*A faithful model can be defined as a physical object whose various surfaces have the same dimensions as the corresponding surfaces of the original object, and hence are geometrically congruent with them, but which is made of a different substance than the original.* When the ratios of dimensions are the same, and the surfaces are geometrically similar instead of congruent, it is a *scale* model, and this is the commonest kind. Color can be reproduced as well as shape and structure. A model as thus defined will produce a retinal image identical with that of the original and, as an object, will be visually indistinguishable from the original. The *surroundings* of the original are not reproduced, however, and the ground on which the figure appears will then be different.

A model can be fabricated for a *place* as well as for an object in it, with the same definition as above. An example is a stage-setting, or the simulated cockpit of an airplane. A *working model* can be constructed in which movements and the course of events are replicated, although this begins to be difficult. Theoretically, this simulation of a total situation could be elaborated indefinitely, but if the purpose is a visual surrogate, it will soon become more economical to utilize a *picture* or a *motion picture* instead of a model if the observer's viewing position can be confined to one spot.

A model has several dimensions of fidelity: shape and proportion, motion, size, color, texture, and the like. Since a learner does not need to become familiar with *all* the properties of an absent situation in order to learn how to deal with it, there is theoretically no need to simulate all its properties in a model. The properties which are relevant or significant for his future behavior are the important ones.

The most obvious kind of non-fidelity of a model is any distortion of shape. Consider, for instance, a set of scale-models of different military aircraft used for the purpose of learning to identify and name the originals. As a general rule, distortion on the models would lead to confusion and poor aircraft recognition. There is evidence to suggest, however, that a distortion which exaggerates some *unique* or *characteristic* feature of an airplane relative to all the others may lead to *improved* identification of it (Gibson, 1947, Ch. 7). The phenomenon may be related to the caricaturing of faces by drawing, and it is consistent with the fourth proposition of Section V. This prediction can be tested experimentally.

## VII.  THE FIDELITY AND SCOPE OF A PICTURE

The fidelity of a picture, like that of a model, has to be defined geometrically, and only as an extreme case. *A faithful picture is a delimited physical surface processed in such a way that it reflects (or transmits) a sheaf of light-rays to a given point which is the same as would be the sheaf of rays from the original to that point.* This definition is intended to apply to paintings, drawings, color prints, photographic prints, transparencies, projected slides, movies, television pictures, and the like, when taken as cases of pure representation. The definition is equivalent to saying that a picture may be considered as a geometrical projection, and that the relation of a picture to its original is given by a polar projection of a three-dimensional solid on a plane. If the center of projection is taken as infinitely distant from the solid, the polar projection becomes a parallel projection, and the picture correspondingly becomes a map, or a plan view, such as is employed in engineering drawing. This unique point for every picture is what makes the viewing position for a picture important, as will be later evident.[5]

In the above definition a sheaf of rays is "the same as" another when the adjacent order of the points of color in the cross-section of one is the same as the adjacent order in the cross-section of the other. As the light-energy varies along any cross-sectional axis of one, so must it vary along the corresponding axis of the other. *To the extent that this condition is fulfilled, the picture will be said to have fidelity.*

All the above applies to a "still" picture, and the fidelity defined is momentary only. *If in addition to the same adjacent order of color points, there exists the same succesive order of color instants the picture will be said to have temporal fidelity.* If the temporal pattern in the picture is that of the original, complex qualities like the motion, sequence, change, growth, and pace of the original can be reproduced. The motion picture and the television image are techniques for approximating this state of affairs. It should be noted that the points and instants referred to above do not have to be the theoretical points and instants

---

[5]In standard accounts of perspective geometry this point is called the station point (Gill, 1974). (Eds.)

of mathematics, but may be finite units of area and finite intervals of time. The unit areas of the half-tone photograph exemplify the former, and the 1/24 second intervals of the standard motion picture exemplify the latter.

Along with fidelity, another important property of a picture is its scope. A picture was defined as a *delimited* surface, which is to say a picture has edges, commonly rectangular. If the surface is flat, the sheaf of rays projected by it to the "given point" is necessarily less than 180° in solid angle, and usually much less. Some pictures, such as murals, intercept a wide angle; other pictures, such as portraits, intercept a narrow angle. *The scope of a picture is the angular sector of the original environment intercepted by it.* One picture, in other words, may be a surrogate for a wide piece of the absent scene and another may be a surrogate for only a narrow piece of the absent scene, or perhaps only for a single object in it. When an environment needs to be represented, or when the background of or relations between objects, people, or events is important, a picture of wide scope is called for. When only a single object, person, or event needs to be represented, a picture of narrow scope may be sufficient. The scope of a photographic picture, for instance, is the angular amount of light intercepted by the lens of the camera. Scope should not be confused with degree of enlargement of a photograph. It is determined wholly by the lens used. A picture taken with a telephoto lens has a narrow scope and one taken with a wide-angle lens has a wide scope no matter what the size of the print in either case may be. The scope of a picture may be reduced by masking or cropping it, but it cannot be increased by photographically enlarging it. Neither can it be increased by holding the picture close to the eye or coming toward it for a close look. The retinal image of the observer is thereby magnified but the scope of the picture remains unaltered.

The fact that a picture is a surface with a boundary means that a picture can never, practically speaking, fill the entire field of view of its observer, which at any one moment occupies nearly a solid angular hemisphere. It is always surrounded by something else *not* the picture (the room for instance); it is a figure on a ground in psychological terminology. An effort to overcome this limitation can be made by increasing the scope of the picture and employing a *curved* instead of a flat surface. Panoramic still pictures have long existed, and semipanoramic motion pictures are now being exploited. The psychological effect of this increased scope is very striking. Even a completely circular panorama, however, cannot surround the observer below his feet as well as to his right and left, since there has to be a physical floor to stand on. Only a full-scale model of a situation can do that.

## VIII. SPACE IN PICTURES

A serious misunderstanding has existed for a long time about the physical fact that a picture is a two-dimensional surface. The misunderstanding takes the form of asserting that one cannot see three dimensions or depth in a picture. What one "sees" is a patchwork of flat surface-colors which serve as clues, and then one "infers" depth in the scene. This account of the matter is mixed up with a second more basic misunderstanding which assumes that the retinal image itself is a picture (this assumption being false) and then goes on to assert that we can only see flat sensations of color in the world around us and must infer its depth. There is at least a germ of truth in the first misunderstanding, for anyone who looks at a picture can see a flat surface, if he attends to it as such. (The second misunderstanding is less excusable, for very few people who look at the world can see a flat surface in front of their eyes.) If, however, the man who looks at a picture does *not* give special attention to the surface as such, he perceives a three-dimensional scene. How is it possible to assert that he can see a flat surface and can also see a three-dimensional scene?

The misunderstanding about pictures arises because it is only half of the fact to say that a picture is a two-dimensional surface. It is a surface *and it is also a peculiar sheaf of rays*. The sheaf of rays is an essential part of the total fact of a picture. The fact of physical optics (the sheaf) and the fact of physical chemistry (the processed surface) must be combined. The surface as such is flat, but the surface as the source of a sheaf of rays may be equivalent to that of the original scene, and the latter is not flat. The hypothesis to be proposed is that a picture can ordinarily be perceived in two different ways, as a surface and as a three-dimensional scene, and that this is so because the sheaf of rays ordinarily contains within it elements which are specific to a flat surface and also elements which are specific to a three-dimensional scene.

There can be no doubt whatever that a picture is capable of yielding a perception of depth and distance. It is, no doubt, the kind of depth and distance obtained when we close one eye, but this is not so different from the kind obtained with two eyes as the traditional theory asserts. The supplementary stimulation for depth-perception obtained from the second eye is not, on the one hand, negligible, but neither is it, on the other hand, basic or essential for depth-perception (Gibson, 1950b, Ch. 6; Gibson, 1947, Ch. 9).

When, under very special circumstances, a picture *cannot* be seen as a flat surface—when an observer who compares a photograph with the original scene cannot say which is which—it is because the elements in the sheaf of rays which are specific to a surface have been carefully eliminated. This involves (a) arranging for the picture to be viewed through an aperture, and for the original scene to be viewed through a similar aperture; (b) making the physical texture of the surface very fine; and (c) processing the surface so that the ray-bundle has high fidelity. A good deal of informal evidence for the success of this experiment exists, but it needs to be systematically performed.

It should be noted that our definition of a faithful picture implies not only a surface and a sheaf of light rays, but a unique viewing point. A picture is unlike a model in that theoretically it should be viewed with a single eye placed at its center of projection and kept motionless. Actually, and in practice, people do not satisfy these conditions very well when they look at a picture. They use two eyes, move about, and look from positions farther or nearer, above or below, and to the right or left of the center of projection (although they do, at least, always keep the picture nearly upright). These circumstances make the sheaf of rays *at the retina* (actually a pair of them at two retinas) rather different from the ideal sheaf of the theoretical picture, and plenty of stimulation is thus ordinarily provided for seeing the picture as a delimited flat surface.

Several propositions can now be formulated about space perception relative to picture-perception.

1.  Since two distinct systems of stimuli operate when a picture is viewed in the ordinary way, two kinds of perception ought simultaneously to occur: first, that of a three-dimensional scene (the situation represented) and, second, that of a delimited flat surface which is part of a different scene (the room, say, in which the picture is shown). There is evidence for this proposition, and more should be obtained.

2.  The mediated perception evoked by a picture is a space-perception, that is to say, it is three-dimensional. There is already evidence that the size of distant objects can be accurately judged in a photographic scene (Gibson, 1947, Ch. 9), or in other words, that size-constancy holds for this kind of perception. There is need for more evidence of this kind.[6] We need to know whether accuracy of spatial judgments is increased when the fidelity of the photograph approaches a maximum, and also what happens to the perception when the fidelity is much reduced.

3.  If two distinct spaces are capable of being seen when viewing a picture, two correspondingly different sets of spatial judgments should be obtainable from the observer. One set would consist of judgments of the distance from the eye to the picture. Another set would consist of judgments of the distance from the point of view of the picture to a specified object in the picture. Phenomenally, the first distance would be in the space of the room and the second would be in the space of the picture. These two spaces should prove to be incommensurable. A similar experiment might require judgments of the size of the picture in contrast with judgments of the size of an object represented in the picture.[7]

## IX.  THE UNIQUE VIEWING-POINT FOR A PICTURE

Insofar as any picture is a geometrical projection, it must have a unique center of projection. Although this point lies in the air on a theoretical perpendicular to the

---

[6]For research bearing on this question, see Hagen, Glick & Morse (1978) and Hagen & Jones (1981). (Eds.)

[7]See Ch. 3.4, p. 279ff and Gibson, 1979a, p. 282 for reports of such experiments. (Eds.)

plane of the picture, it is just as important for the picture as the deposits of pigment (or silver halide or dye) on its surface. In the case of a chirographic picture, constructed with some regard to the laws of perspective, it is the "station-point" for the "picture-plane" (Ware, 1900). In the case of a photographic picture it is at the perpendicular distance given by multiplying the focal length of the lens of the camera by the degree of enlargement of the picture (Henney & Dudley, 1939). This is the point at which an eye must be stationed if the eye is to be stimulated by the same sheaf of light rays which was included in the angular scope of the picture. In other words the visual solid angle of the picture at the eye should equal the scope of the picture, or, in still other words, the eye should be so stationed relative to the picture that it takes in the same light that the camera did when the picture was taken (or that the painter's eye did when he made the picture).

The point has already been made that this ideal viewing position is departed from rather widely in looking at paintings, snapshots, projected slides, movies, and especially television pictures. The question which naturally arises is *what happens to the phenomenal space of the picture when a departure is made from the unique viewing-point?*

Compare the sheaf of rays to the center of projection and the sheaf of rays to the eye, when these are not the same. The latter is *magnified* when the eye is nearer the picture. It is *diminished* when the eye is farther from the picture. (It is also *compressed horizontally* when the eye is to the right or left of the center of projection, and is *compressed vertically* when the eye is above or below the center of projection, but these deformations will not be considered at present.) We may now put this question: How is the three-dimensional object corresponding to a given sheaf of rays related to the three-dimensional object corresponding to a *magnified* (or diminished) but otherwise similar sheaf of rays? Would the latter object be simply *enlarged* (or reduced), or would it also be *deformed?* Geometrical analysis demonstrates that the object would have to be deformed as well as altered in size. The deformation consists in a relative shortening of its depth dimension in the case of magnification, and a relative elongation of its depth dimension in the case of diminishment. The implication is that depth in the space of a picture viewed from "too near" is shortened, whereas depth in the space of a picture viewed from "too far" is elongated. Whether this geometrical analysis will predict what happens to the *phenomenal* space of a picture is an empirical question which ought to be put to the test.[8]

There is good evidence, obtained with groups of aviation cadets during the last war, that various types of abstract perceptual discrimination *not involving any discriminations of depth,* when tested by the projecting of motion pictures in a classroom, are not affected by the distance of the eyes from the screen, that is, by the angular magnitude of the picture (Gibson, 1947, Ch. 4). This fact seems to suggest that the importance of the unique viewing-point for a picture depends on

---

[8]Cf. Rosinski & Farber (1980), Sedgwick (1980), and Lumsden (1980). (Eds.)

the kind of perception the picture is intended to produce. Perhaps the chief consideration is whether the perception needs to be correct with respect to depth or distance.

The issues involved in picture-viewing are highly complex, including as they do problems of spatial perception and perceptual constancy. The main puzzle for a general theory of perception can be put in this way: there is evidence to show that a retinal image which is magnified, diminished, or laterally compressed is in some respects equivalent to the unaltered image as a stimulus for perception. There is also evidence to show that a retinal image which undergoes such an elastic deformation is in other respects *not equivalent* as a stimulus for perception. What are the viewing-conditions under which the first statement holds and what are the conditions under which the second statement holds?

The perception of pictures viewed *obliquely,* i.e., at an angle to the surface, presents a similar set of problems regarding phenomenal distortion and phenomenal constancy. A method of investigating them has been described by the writer (Gibson, 1947, p. 170ff.).

## X. THE APPROXIMATION OF PICTORIAL PERCEPTION TO DIRECT PERCEPTION

References have already been made to the experiment of arranging that a picture and the original scene represented be viewed successively, under aperture conditions, and the possibility that the observer will be unable to distinguish one from the other. The picture most likely to yield success in this experiment is probably a large photographic color-transparency; if the original scene involved movement, it would have to be a motion picture. Indistinguishability from the original has long been attained with *models* of certain things, for example, wax flowers, and there seems to be no reason why it could not be realized in pictures.

The experiment is theoretically important since it constitutes a test of the validity of the definition of a picture with fidelity given in Section VII. It exemplifies the limiting case in which an object and the surrogate for it can have precisely the same effect on an organism, and in which the pictorial quality of a picture-perception vanishes. But its greatest importance, perhaps, is in demonstrating negatively the visual factors which, under ordinary viewing-conditions rather than aperture-conditions, make a picture seem what it is, namely, a surface, a substitute, or a mediating object (Gibson, 1951b). These factors constitute a second system of optical stimulation, we postulated, which makes possible two kinds of spatial impressions and two kinds of judgments for the observer.

It is possible to add "realism" to a still picture in various different ways besides the aperture-method described. The semipanoramic picture, and the circular panoramic picture constitute one way. The motion picture is another way. It is possible to combine these effects in semi-panoramic motion pictures, as Waller has done in the "Cinerama." The stereoscopic picture and the stereoscopic motion picture is still another way. Color, sound, "stereophonic sound," the "subjective camera" method of shooting motion pictures, and perhaps others, are all techniques for increasing realism. It is the writer's opinion, however, that there are basic discrepancies among these lines of effort, at least between the stereoscopic and the panoramic, which will make it impossible to use them simultaneously in one grand effort to achieve "complete realism."

The *graphic* method of constructing a surrogate for a situation is fundamentally different from the method of building a *model* for it, or a full-scale replica. The replica for a situation has a ground on which one can stand. Any graphic method (including photography, cinematography and stereophotography) presupposes the use of either a *room* or a *viewing-device*, and this limits the ultimate illusion of reality. A viewing-device eliminates the sight of one's nose, hands, body, and one's feet on the floor, which is an important component of direct visual perception.[9] A panoramic picture includes this component but necessarily introduces some kind of a junction between the room one stands in and the picture itself. The dilemma might be expressed by saying that it is intrinsically impossible to get the ego of the observer completely into the space of the picture. There will probably always be some tendency to experience *two* spaces, one incompatible and incommensurable with the other.

## XI.  THE FIDELITY OF CHIROGRAPHIC PICTURES

Little has been said so far about hand-made pictures as distinguished from lens-made pictures. Hand-made or chirographic pictures include paintings, drawings, cartoons, caricatures, animated drawings, and a host of others. Their fidelity, as defined, is generally lower than that of photographic pictures, although this is not true of necessity. As early as the 17th Century, some paintings of still-life achieved a level of fidelity barely reached by modern color photography. The reason for chirographic lack of fidelity, perhaps, is this. A picture, like a model, has many dimensions of fidelity to the object, rather than a single dimension. The object has many visual properties, but the most important ones (for most human purposes) are the form, shape, and proportion of its edges and surfaces. These can be rendered by *outlines*, which are very easy to trace on a surface by hand. If we assume that a perceiver does not need to be given *all* the properties of an absent object in order to know how to deal with it, but only those which are *relevant* or *significant*, it is a waste of effort to simulate them all. The photograph reproduces them all indifferently. The chirograph reproduces them selectively. It can be (and has been) argued by artists that such selective emphasis may clarify the observer's perception of the object in a way that no photograph can

---

[9]For more on visual proprioception, see Chs. 2.3 and 2.4. (Eds.)

do. The truth of this assertion is a problem in perception and cognition for which there is no present solution, but at least the assertion is not unreasonable.[10] The danger of low fidelity is vagueness or nonspecificity. When the artist either omits some dimensions of fidelity or departs from fidelity by distorting form, he takes the risk, but he may achieve a picture which clarifies and specifies instead.

## XII.  THE ADVANTAGES AND DISADVANTAGES OF REALISM IN PICTURES

Why, one might ask, do picture-makers strive for increased realism or, more exactly, why does a certain class of them do so? Why do children like realistic toys? Why the appeal of photography? of the movies? of television? of color-movies? of stereoscopic color movies? Only an intuitive kind of answer can be given until a workable theory of surrogates is more fully developed, but it might be of this sort: that human beings have a need for first-hand experience; that an increasing proportion of experience comes at second-hand in the modern world; and that they therefore need the closest thing they can get to first-hand experience.

A realistic picture, notably a movie, makes the observer "forget himself," or "lose himself in the scene," or "takes him out of himself." So also, of course, does the reading of history, or a novel, or a book on how to do carpentry, but the realistic picture does so with less effort on the part of the observer. And there are good reasons for the greater simplicity and directness of this kind of perception, as we have seen. Pictures and models are better than words and symbols for learning about concrete things, tools, mechanisms, or organisms, about particular places, scenes, and environments, and about existing events, processes, and sequences. If this is what needs to be learned, the surrogates for them should be "realistic."

On the other hand, proponents of the spoken and written word have argued that this kind of learning makes no demands on the "imagination" of the learner. No one knows what the imagination is, precisely, but it does seem likely that men need to apprehend abstract things and general rules, as well as to perceive concrete objects. Words and symbols (including graphic symbols and geometrical drawings) are essential for learning about properties, variables, groups, classes, and universals. Men can make propositions with symbols, and discover new ones by manipulating old ones. They can mutually exchange propositions, and formulate general laws. If this is what needs to be learned, the surrogates for them should be arbitrary and conventional. Both kinds of surrogates have their value.

---

[10]See E. J. Gibson (1969, Ch. 18) for an analysis of the importance of distinctive features in picture perception. (Eds.)

# 3.3 Pictures, Perspective, and Perception*

The writer of this essay is an experimental psychologist with a long-standing interest in the problem of how we see. As concerns vision, a perceptual psychologist like myself stands somewhere between the physicists and the physiologists on the one hand, and the critics and philosophers on the other.

It seems to me that a great deal of the current discussion about pictorial communication and pictorial art is confused. We often use the same word for different things. One of the worst sources of misunderstanding is the nature of perspective representation. Another is the nature of the perceptual process itself. If we could agree on what the facts of perspective are for ordinary vision, we should be better able to discuss its validity for painting. And if we could get rid of certain historical prejudices about the act of perception in everyday life, we could consider more clearly the special kind of perception aroused by a picture.

## PERSPECTIVE

The fundamental problems in pictorial communication, as I understand it, are first, the relation of the picture to the world, and second, the effect it will have on the perceiver.

The term ''perspective'' has several different meanings. It can refer to the various techniques of painting or drawing which give the illusion of a scene in depth. This is what it usually means to artists and architects. It can refer to the geometrical projection of a form on one plane to a form on another plane by a

*Daedalus, 1960, 89, 216-227. Copyright 1960 by Daedalus. Reprinted by permission.

bundle of lines intersecting at one point. This is what it means to a mathematician. Or it can refer to a certain way of seeing a natural scene as a patchwork of colors; that is, to "seeing in perspective." This is what it has meant to philosophers and psychologists who believed it important to analyze visual sensations. These various meanings often get mixed up in discussions of perspective.

There is, however, a single fact which underlies them all and makes them intelligible—the fact of the behavior of light in the world of animals and men.

*The Fact of Ambient Light.*    If we forget about abstract empty space and consider the concrete world, the important thing about light is that it fills the air and surrounds the individual on all sides. Light that has been reflected and scattered by surfaces is the light by which things are seen. Ambient light carries information, which can be observed simply by looking around. Illumination consists of a reverberating flux, echoing in straight lines throughout the open spaces of a terrestrial environment. During the day it is as much a part of the environment as are the reflecting surfaces themselves. It can be registered anywhere the individual may go. In fact the changes of light from moment to moment are the principal controls that govern his locomotion.

*The Optic Array at a Station Point.*    The rectilinear propagation of light means this: that the echoing light flux consists of interlocking bundles of rays. Each bundle consists of rays intersecting at a common point, and there is one such bundle for every point in the open air. Every such point is a potential station point for an eye—a place where an eye might be stationed. Rays are not only projected from a source; they are also introjected, as it were, to a point. We are concerned only with the converging bundles of rays. Each of these may be termed an optic array.[1]

We need not think of an optic array as composed of lines, however. At the station point, it consists of differences in the intensity and frequency of light in different directions.[2] The reason for this is that light is altered in energy and wave-length composition when it is reflected; and different surfaces, or parts of a surface, alter it in different amounts. A given pencil of light in an optic array will have imposed on it a certain relative intensity and a certain relative "color" with respect to other pencils of the array. An optic array, therefore, is a matter of transitions from one adjacent pencil to another—not of rays. The rays are useful fictions. The absolute intensity and the absolute color of a pencil do not matter to the eye; what matters is the structure and the relative composition of an optic array. These relational properties are constant under all conditions of illumination. In short, the mathematical structure of an optic array

---

[1]For a critique of this definition of an optic array, see Ch. 1.4, part 2. (Eds.)

[2]This use of the term station point is more general than standard usage (see note 5, Ch. 3.2). Gibson (1979a, p. 66) gives a clear distinction between a station point and a point of observation. (Eds.)

corresponds to the light-reflecting capacities of the surfaces surrounding the station point. It carries information about the world. For example, whereever the array is textured, there are surfaces in the world; wherever the array is homogeneous or untextured, there is only sky.

The structure of an optic array can be analyzed, for example, by angular coordinates. Or it can be treated topologically in terms of the contours between regions of different intensity.[3] A complete optic array can be projected only on a sphere. A part of an optic array—one sector of the total pie, as it were—can be projected on a plane. At best, this can represent less than half the array. If the plane is small, with rectangular edges, the projection begins to resemble that of a window or an ordinary picture. The familiar meanings of the term "perspective" begin to apply. But note that the principles which underlie all varieties of perspective, which make them intelligible and can reconcile the riddles they pose, are the fact of the optic array itself, and the further fact of different optic arrays at different station points.

An optic array is something external to and independent of an eye. It is quite different from a retinal image. The latter will be considered separately.

*A Generalized Geometry of Perspective.*   It is possible, therefore, to think of perspective as a more general science than the rules of representative drawing, or the description of visual sensations, or even the transformations of forms on one abstract plane to forms on another plane. It would be the geometry of the ways in which light specifies the world of surfaces from which the light is reflected.[4] Linear perspective of the classical sort would only be a small part of it, for that is merely the perspective of the edges of rectangular objects. There is also the perspective of the textures of inclined surfaces, the gradients of texture-density, the steps of density at the edges of objects, the ratios of densities in different directions, and still other variables of higher order.

Above all, there is the perspective of change of position, as distinguished from the perspective of position. When the station point moves, the whole structure of the optic array undergoes transformation. A new set of variables arises to confirm the information in static perspective. The parameters of transformation are specific to the motion of the station point; the invariants under transformation are specific to the permanent properties of the environment.[5] The optic array has a unique structure for every station point in the world. And the change in structure of the array is unique for every change of station point in the world. This is essentially what is meant by saying that ambient light carries information about the world.

---

[3]Cf. Ch. 1.7. (Eds.)

[4]Gibson conceived of ecological optics as originating from geometrical optics and perspective geometry. (Eds.)

[5]Cf. Chs. 1.2, 2.3, and Gibson, Olum & Rosenblatt (1955). (Eds.)

*Images.*   It will have been noted that nothing whatever, so far, has been said about images, retinal, photographic, or other. Environmental optics, unlike physical or physiological optics, is not concerned with images but with the fundamental conditions which make images possible. A differentiated optic array depends on two things: a source of light to illuminate the surfaces, and a medium free of dust or fog which would veil the contours; but it does not depend on the formation of an image. The structure of an optic array may or may not be registered by an animal with eyes; it exists, whether or not an animal occupies the station point.

The common belief that vision necessarily depends on a retinal image is incorrect, since the eye of a bee, for example, does not have a retinal image. What eyes do is to pick up all the useful information in light of which they are capable; retinal images are merely incidental in the process. The human eye explores an optic array by taking in cones of the array in sucession. The process could be compared to the way a searchlight beam is moved around a dark environment, with the difference that the light is being absorbed instead of being emitted.

*The Fallacy of Comparing a Retinal Image to a Picture.*   We can now clear up a misunderstanding which has persisted for centuries: the notion that a retinal image is like a picture. However a picture may be defined, everyone would agree that it is something to be looked at by an observer. A retinal image is not something to be looked at by an observer. It is therefore profoundly unlike a picture. There is a distribution of energy on a sensory mosaic, but it is not a replica, or a copy, or a model, or a record. It is a continous "input," as computer theorists say. It starts impulses in the optic nerve. The retinal image is easily visualized, but one should do so only at one's peril, for it encourages the fallacy of assuming a little man in the brain who looks at the retinal image. Whenever one is tempted to think in this way, one should remember the eye of the bee. A retinal image is no more like a picture in the eye than an auditory stimulus is like a phonograph record in the ear.

The designers of lenses and optical instruments are as badly mixed up about their so-called images as anyone else. What they do is to manipulate light in ways which enable us to get more information out of it than we ordinarily would. To magnify a cone of an optic array, as by a telescope or a microscope, is to alter the light entering an eye so that its fine structure becomes big and bright enough for the eye to pick up. Magnification can be accomplished either by producing a large picture on a screen to be looked at, or by applying an instrument directly to an eye and pointing it at the light coming from the real thing. In either case, it is the light to the eye that counts.

The human retinal image is only one stage in the human process of seeing. What the instrument makers, the photographers, the visual educators, and the artists in their own way are trying to do is to aid or enhance the process of seeing.

By "seeing" I mean understanding, not the special process of considering one's sensations or the special act of seeing in perspective.

## PERCEPTION

Perception is the having and achieving of knowledge about the world, and visual perception is the most exact kind of perception. The process depends on the stimulating of receptors, but receptors are combined into whole input systems with harmonious functions.[6] The ocular system of man is the most elaborate input system of all. It responds to the optic array of the moment and to the changes of the array over time. Such is its stimulus—or, more correctly, such is the flowing array of potential stimulation to which it responds.[7] The eyes react by exploring the array, fixing and converging on certain details, sharpening the contours by focusing the lens, and pursuing a moving bit of detail. The sequence of fleeting retinal images is scarcely detectable in perception; what emerges is a phenomenal scene together with its interesting features.

The essence of perception is selective attention to something important. The receptive system "tunes itself" by adjusting the apparatus for clear reception. The lens-retina-nerve-muscle system is not passive but active. It continually creates new stimuli for itself, searching out in an optic array the relations, ratios, grades, and invariants of pattern which specify facts of the world. The amount of potential information in the light reaching the eyes is unlimited.

As a consequence of the unlimited possibilities for informative stimulation, and of the exploring and selecting activity, two conclusions follow with regard to perception: first, it depends on stimulation; and second, it depends on the interests of the individual observer. These conclusions have appeared contradictory in the past, and the horns of a dilemma seemed inescapable: the perceiver can only mirror the world, or else he creates the world for himself. But this is a false issue.

The perceiver who has observed the world from many points of view, as we say, is literally one who has traveled about and used his eyes. That is, he has looked at the furniture of the earth from many station points. The more he has done so, the more likely it is that he has isolated the invariant properties of things—the permanent residue of the changing perspectives. Only because of the perspective transformations do the permanent properties emerge in perception. And only thus can he see the world as a whole, with every part connected to every other. The artist is a perceiver who pays special attention to the points of view from which the world can be seen, and one who catches and records for the rest of us the most revealing perspectives on things.

Perceiving, I have suggested, is the having or achieving of knowledge about

---

[6]These ideas were revised and clarified in Ch. 4.4 and Gibson (1966b). (Eds.)
[7]Cf. Ch. 4.3. (Eds.)

the world. But visual perceiving often enough does not feel like knowing; instead, it feels like an immediate acquaintance or a direct contact. To see a thing, a place, an event, an animal, or a person means to be in touch with it. What is to be said about this difference between immediate and mediated perception?

There are different degrees of mediation for different kinds of perception, all the way from the direct impression to the roundabout inference. One dimension varies between certainty and uncertainty; this depends, for example, on good illumination or poor illumination—that is, on the amount of potential information in the existing conditions of stimulus. Another dimension is between first-hand acquaintance at one extreme and hearsay at the other. This is a kind of mediation we should now consider—perception at second hand—that is, perception through the eyes of another person.

## THE NATURE OF PICTURES

The above discussion of perspective and the further discussion of the perceptual process are intended to make possible an explicit statement of what a picture is and what it does. Whether or not the formula I suggest is acceptable, it will have at least the virtue of being clear: in general, a picture is a human artifact which enables another person to perceive some aspect of the visible world in the same way that the artist, the maker of the artifact, has perceived it. This definition is intended to apply to any picture—any drawing, painting, photograph, motion picture, or television image, whether representational or not—so long as it is intended to be looked at.

Concretely, a picture is always a physical surface, whether of canvas, paper, glass, or some other substance, which either reflects light or transmits it. It is an object, in short, commonly a flat rectangular one, but what is unique about it is the light coming from it. The surface has been treated or processed or acted upon in such a way that the light causes a perception of something other than the surface itself. It delivers a sheaf of light rays to a station point in front of the surface, rays that contain information about quite another part of the world, perhaps a distant world, a past world, a future world, or a wished-for world; a delicious world or a horrifying world; but at any rate some part or aspect of a world which is not literally present at the station point. If an eye is actually stationed in front of the picture, and if its possessor can register the information contained in the sheaf of rays, then the picture has served its fundamental purpose. There has occurred a perception at second hand—a vicarious acquaintance with an absent scene.

*The Ways of Making Pictures.*   A picture is not only a surface but also, and more truly, an artificial optic array. The surface must have been treated or processed or acted upon in such a way as to determine the texture and structure and wave-length composition of the light to the station point. Many ways of doing this have been invented over the thousands of years of human history. But fundamentally they are of two types: a picture can be made by hand and eye, or it can be made by some adaptation of the photographic camera. The virtues of each method need to be considered objectively.

*The Fidelity of a Picture.* It is theoretically possible to construct a dense sheaf of light rays to a certain point in a gallery or a laboratory, one identical in all respects to another dense sheaf of light rays to a unique station point thousands of miles away on the surface of the earth. If each of the two pyramids of light were isolated from the surrounding optic array by an aperture or peephole, an eye could not detect any difference between them: the perceiver would be unable to say which was the artificial and which the natural scene. This follows from an elementary principle of psychology which says that, other things being equal, two identical instances of stimulation must arouse the same percept. Vision depends on the structure of the optic array, however this may have been caused.

The complete identity of two ray sheaves, point for point, with respect to intensity and wave-length composition, is in practice impossible. For one thing, the density of rays in a natural array is infinite; the texture of ordinary light is informative, no matter how finely it is analyzed microscopically, whereas the texture of an artificial array begins to show only the grain of the photograph or the pigment when it is analyzed. For another thing, the range of intensities in a natural array with good illumination exceeds the range of intensities coming from the best photographic transparency, and far exceeds that from the most meticulous painting. Still further, the wave-length composition of artificial dyes or pigments on a film or a canvas cannot be made to match exactly the spectral composition of the light from natural surfaces.

But this simple physical identity of the ray sheaves is not necessary for the success of the experiment described above. An eye responds primarily to the transitions and relations of an array—the relative variables instead of the absolute magnitudes of physical radiation. The texture of a pictorial array at a station point need be no finer than the acuity of the eye; the intensities are unimportant compared to the contours and gradients of intensity; and the "colors" of a pictorial array need be preserved only in relation to one another and to the prevailing ilumination in order to specify quite well the main classes of surface pigmentation. Consequently, two pyramids of light to a station point may be functionally identical as stimuli without being physically identical as energy inputs.

The experiment of constructing a picture indistinguishable from the original scene has been carried out, although it is not fashionable nowadays. In the centuries prior to photography, painters were often fascinated with the type of picture called "trompe l'oeil"—that is, a painting which could be illuminated and arranged so as to deceive the eye with a perception of a room, a relief, a doorway, or a still life in full three-dimensional reality. The experiment can be done within certain limits with a photographic transparency or a photomural, and it is successful even when the pictorial scene is arranged side by side with the original scene pictured.

The fidelity of a picture can be defined as the degree to which its surface sends the same sheaf of rays to its station point that is sent to a certain fixed station point at the scene represented. But a picture's *functional* fidelity to the scene represented is simply the degree to which the variables to which the eye is sensitive are the same in one array as the other. Complete fidelity of the latter sort is achievable.

An eye is particularly sensitive to contours—that is, to abrupt transitions of intensity in light. A line specifies a contour to an eye without replicating the different brightness on either side of the contour. This is why a line drawing can have a considerable fidelity to an original scene without any matching of brightness or color. An eye is also particularly sensitive to the straightness of contours and the alignment of details in light. Straight contours in a projection mean straight edges in the world. Hence it is, probably, that linear perspective in a picture is so compelling for most people. It is only one feature of the general geometry of perspective, as I argued above, but it is one to which the human eye is particularly sensitive. Man lives in an environment of buildings and pavements whose edges he has generally made rectilinear.

Fidelity of form and proportion in a static picture entails that the perspective be "correct." It is automatically so in a photograph taken with a camera having a well-designed lens system, where the print is viewed with a single eye at a perpendicular distance equal to the focal length of the lens. It is also correct for a representative painting made in accordance with the techniques discovered by the Renaissance painters when viewed from the station point. They come to the same thing, since both derive from the theory of rays intersecting a picture plane and from the fundamental experiment of the pinhole camera.

The faithful representing of solid objects with respect to form and proportion is not to be scorned, although it may be pedestrian work for an artist. It permits the vicarious experiencing of an absent thing or the mediated perception of a distant place. It is perception at second hand, to be sure, but the greater the fidelity of the picture, the more it resembles perception at first hand. It may be only a fixed window on the part of the world in question, a mere peephole on reality, but with all its limitations it is a kind of visual education. Anatomical drawings, scientific records, documentary pictures, and even travel snapshots of distant places are all ways of getting knowledge about the shapes of things, and this is important knowledge.

*The Illusion of Reality from Pictures.* The optical stimulus provided by an ordinary picture may be indistinguishable from that provided by the scene represented, when the latter is viewed with one eye through a window. The viewer is transported to the scene in question. But at best the perception aroused fails in three respects to be lifelike. First, the viewer cannot look around the scene. Second, he cannot move around in the scene nor can he observe anything moving in it. Third, he cannot obtain the binocular parallax resulting from the use of both eyes. The illusion of reality is incomplete, and no observer of an ordinary picture would ever suppose that he had literally been transported to the scene.

The makers of pictures, at least those with commercial ambitions, have generally wanted to remedy these defects in the lifelike quality of pictorial perception. They would like, if possible, to create a complete illusion of reality. In the effort to do so, they have tried to extend the scope of a pictorial array, to give it progression in time, and to make different arrays to each eye.

*1. The Scope of a Pictorial Array.* The scope of a picture may be defined as the angular size of its sheaf of rays at the proper station point. The field of view embraced by a picture determines to a considerable extent the illusion of being at the scene pictured. The easel painter and the photographer are limited in the size of the field they can represent. The flat canvas and the photographic print are of fixed dimensions, and the taking in of any larger field than about 45 degrees each way is extremely difficult.

The ordinary picture is a selection from the total scene—a choice of a certain angular sector which the viewer is permitted to observe. The situation is not like "life," in which every viewer can choose for himself what to observe. The alternative to an ordinary picture is a panoramic picture—that is, an array of increased scope.

Panoramas of battle scenes or historic events used to be very popular. Such a picture must be painted on a curved surface, cylindrical or spherical. It can be designed to fill the field of view of an observer who does not move his head, a hemispherical array—or it can be designed to fill the whole environment of an observer who turns around, a roughly spherical array. There are still a few circular buildings in various countries which house complete panoramas. The constructing of panoramic arrays by photographic projection methods is difficult. The semipanoramic motion picture, in the form of "Cinerama," is full of optical compromises, but most movie-goers agree that it nevertheless yields a strong illusion of reality. It is being employed, apparently, to satisfy the urge of people to see the world—that is, to witness strange events and popular spectacles.

*2. Progression in Time.* The greatest achievement in the pursuit of the illusion of reality was the invention of the motion picture. It is poorly named, for the picture does more than respresent motion or physical movement; it imitates time. The light surrounding a living person is a continuous flow of transformations and changes which specify the sequence of events in the neighborhood. This is what cinematography succeeds to some extent in representing.

The static picture can represent, it is true, a critical moment in time. The artist can choose the significant cross section in a continuous process or the high point of an event. But the pictorial array is itself unchanging, and the picture inevitably gives some suggestion of a dead and frozen world.

A camera which records a pictorial array over time, a cinematic or kinescopic camera, can "pan," or "dolly," or "cut," or "fade." This is to say, in effect, that it can look around after a fashion, can perform locomotion, can shift attention from one place to another, and can indicate the passage of time. It does all this in addition to recording simple motions. These are some of the perceptual capacities of the living observer, and hence the cinematic screen picture can imitate natural perception.

*3. Different Arrays to Each Eye.*    More than one hundred years ago it was proved by Wheatstone that the slight discrepancy between the inputs to the right and left eyes explains in part how we see the depth of a scene. This disparity of pattern, when artificially produced by a device called the stereoscope, yielded an illusion of depth.

With any such device, each eye must be located close to the proper station point of its corresponding picture. A stereoscopic panorama, therefore, is almost inconceivable. For the same reason, stereoscopic motion pictures are unsatisfactory to those viewers in a large group whose position relative to the screen is not optimal. The idea of combining all the inventions for improving the realism of a picture into one grand display—the panoramic, stereoscopic, colored motion picture—is probably impractical.

What can be said about these technical achievements as to the fidelity of pictorial representation and the lifelike quality of pictorial presentation? They help to satisfy men's curiosity about the world. They convey knowledge of a sort. They make perception effortless by approximating the natural kind of perception. They permit an almost direct acquaintance with things, events, places, and people. But they leave nothing to the imagination; perhaps they stultify it. They might be said to encourage in the observer passivity rather than activity. They do not impose the emphasis of the artist on the perception of the viewer.

## THE EDUCATION OF ATTENTION

A picture, I have suggested, conveys an aspect of the world as the maker of the picture has seen it. The "world" should be in some sense real, but it is not necessarily the literal existing world, and the "aspect" need not be a literal perspective from an existing station point.

If there is actually information in light, and if it is unlimited in amount, then each perceiver must select that part of the potential information he needs. When perceiving is mediated by a picture, some part of the selecting has already been done. Even a photograph is selective in its own way; but a painting is more selective, and in a different way. Each painter has his own habits and skills of selecting information from light. Each age of painting and each culture has its way of selecting what is important to see. If the artist emphasizes the information about the world that people need, he has done them a service. If they can register such information, he has made their vision more acute. Their eyes will become more sensitive, not at the level of anatomy or physiology, to be sure, but at the level of psychology. At this level, the subtleties and complexities of light are enormous. And hence the different ways of seeing the world are equally variable, though all may be valid.

Under this theory, selection and abstraction in painting are understandable. But what about "distortion" in nonrepresentative painting as the ordinary person thinks of it—that is, departures from fidelity to form and proportion? Why are people and places so often represented by modern painters as literally deformed, in the geometrical sense of the term? The answer, perhaps, is that only certain departures from literal representation are genuinely informative. Consider the representation of a human face. The caricaturist who has real insight into personality departs from an exact portrait in a single direction. The deformation is just that which shows the differences between this individual and all other individuals—the real differences, the traits of the person. In this case the deformation is not false but, in a paradoxical sense, true.

From what I know of the perceptual process, it does not seem reasonable to assert that the use of perspective in paintings is merely a convention, to be used or discarded by the painter as he chooses. Nor is it possible that new laws of geometrical perspective will be discovered, to overthrow the old ones.[8] It is true that the varieties of painting at different times in history, and among different peoples, prove the existence of different ways of seeing, in some sense of the term.[9] But there are no differences among people in the basic way of seeing— that is, by means of light, and by way of the rectilinear propagation of light. When the artist transcribes what he sees upon a two-dimensional surface, he uses perspective geometry, of necessity. Human visual perception is learned, but not in the same way that we learn a language. It can be acquired by education, but not by the kind of education that consists in memorizing a new set of symbols. What the artist can do is not to create a new kind of vision, but to educate our attention.

---

[8]This is Gibson's argument with Goodman. Cf. Ch. 3.4. (Eds.)
[9]Cf. Hagen (1979). (Eds.)

# 3.4

## The Information Available in Pictures*

Underlying all the discussions of representation there are currently two conflicting theories of what a picture is. The first theory assumes that it consists of a sheaf of light rays coming to a station point or perceiver, each corresponding to a spot of color on the picture surface. The second theory assumes that it consists of a set of symbols, more or less like words, and that a painting is comparable to a written text. On the first theory, a picture can represent a real object or scene insofar as the light rays from the picture are the same as the light rays from the original. On the second theory, a picture can stand for a real object or scene insofar as the language of pictures is understood. The second theory says that one has to learn to "read" a picture, much as the child has to read written speech, but the first theory denies this and asserts that as soon as a child can perceive an object directly he can perceive it in a picture.

One might suppose that these theories as stated are merely extremes, and that they can somehow be combined. But attempts to reconcile them have not been successful, or at least I find them unsuccessful and I have come to believe instead that both theories are wrong. We need a new theory of what a picture is. I will try to suggest later what it might be but first let us get clear about the two opposing positions, what the force of the argument is in each case and why in the last analysis they fail.

*Leonardo, 1971, 4, 27–35. Reprinted with permission from Leonardo, 4, 27 (1971). Copyright 1971 by Pergamon Press, Ltd.

## THE POINT-PROJECTION THEORY OF PICTORIAL INFORMATION

By the eighteenth century the technique of perspective representation, discovered by painters in the Renaissance, had matured along with the developing science of optics (cf. Fig. 24). An English mathematician could assert in 1715 that in order to produce a perfect painting of objects, "the Light ought to come from the Picture to the spectator's Eye in the very same manner as it would do from the Objects themselves" (Taylor, 1715). It would be as if the light came through a window, to be sure, corresponding to the frame of the picture but if each light ray from a spot of pigment on the canvas were the same in wavelength and intensity as each light ray from a spot on the front face of the object coming to the eye through the window, then the two bundles of light rays would correspond and the representation of the object would be complete. At the time of this assertion, Isaac Newton's treatise on *Opticks* had been published and it was widely read.

This theory of the perfect picture seemed to fit exactly with the theory of visual perception based on the retinal image that was developing at the same time. Newton asserted with confidence that:

> the Light which comes from the several points of the Object is so refracted as to . . . paint the Picture of the object upon that skin called the *Retina* . . . And these Pictures, propagated by motion along the Fibres of the Optick Nerves into the Brain, are the cause of Vision. For accordingly as these Pictures are perfect or imperfect, the Object is seen perfectly or imperfectly (Newton, 1730/1952, p. 52).

The theory of point-projection (along with the theory of the projected retinal image) has proved to be very powerful over the centuries. Light is, in fact, projective; one can project shadows or transparent pictures and the abstract notion of point-to-point correspondence is part of the branch of mathematics called projective geometry. Fifteen years ago I wrote an essay called "A Theory of Pictorial Perception" (1954c) in the effort to make it explicit for students of visual education. I defined the *fidelity* of a picture by analogy with the fidelity of a sound recording, assuming that it could go from a maximum to no fidelity at all. A faithful picture was *a delimited surface so processed that it yielded a sheaf of light-rays to a given point which is the same as would be the sheaf of rays from the original scene to a given point*, that is, *when the adjacent order of the points of color in the cross-section of one corresponded to the adjacent order in the cross-section of the other* (1954c). I should have added, *and when the forms in the one cross-section are congruent with the forms in the other*. This is essentially the same as the eighteenth-century definition quoted above. I did hedge it somewhat by suggesting that the *variations* in the adjacent light energy across one array might correspond with the *variations* across the other, thus introducing the notion of corresponding contrasts or relations instead of corresponding points of light. I was aware of the fact that the light intensities from a world range over

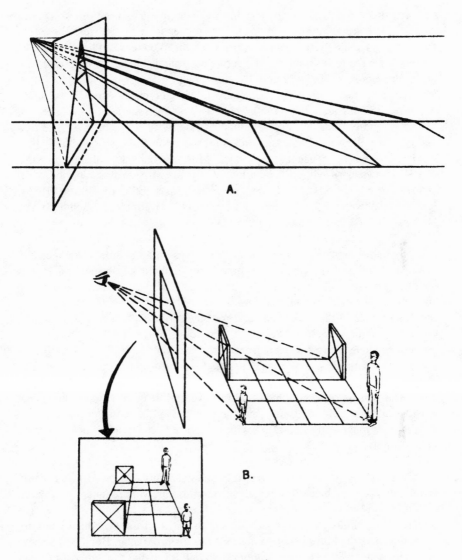

FIG. 24. The principles of pictorial representation.

The projection on a picture-plane of a regular pavement extending into the distance is shown in A. The main laws of linear perspective can be observed, especially the vanishing point at the horizon. The projection of a scene on a window of the picture-plane is shown in B. Note the angular size relations and the transformations of square-into-trapezoid. Straight edges are projected as straight lines in the picture (straightness is invariant). The perspective of surface texture is not shown, only what are called *outlines*. In both cases, note that it is the optic array that is the stimulus, not the image.

extremes that cannot possibly be matched by the light intensities from a picture. I did take some account of the paradox that if another station point were chosen for the light-rays than the uniquely proper one, the picture would no longer be faithful since the forms would no longer be congruent. In short, I had some idea of the limitations of the definition but not enough to reject it.

I amended this defnition considerably in a later paper entitled: *Pictures, Perspective, and Perception* (1960a) but I still retained the notion of a sheaf of light rays and did not discard the notion of fidelity in terms of rays. The new definition I will propose is based on ecological optics, not geometrical optics, and it transcends the concept of light rays.[1] Most of what was said about pictures in 1960, however, I will still stand by. A series of studies over a period of 15 years has been carried out at Cornell on pictorial perception by Gibson (1956), Ryan and Schwartz (1956), Smith and Gruber (1958), Smith and Smith (1961), Hochberg (1962), Hochberg and Brooks (1962) and most recently Kennedy (1970).

In the latter part of my 1954 essay, there was an admission which actually invalidated the point-by-point projection theory, although I did not realize it at the time. I said that a picture actually had many different dimensions of fidelity to an object, not just one, and that lines or outlines in a hand-made picture could faithfully represent the edges and corners of the surfaces of the world, although, of course, the lines could not represent their colors or textures. But this actually gives the whole thing away; the definition can only apply to a painting or photograph, not to a line drawing. There is *no* point-to-point correspondence of brightness or color between the optic array from a line drawing and the optic array from the object represented. There is some sort of correspondence but it must be of a very different kind than the one defined. In order to describe this relational or higher-order correspondence, we need a new optics not limited to rays of light.

Finally, there is still another objection to the point-projection theory, with its definition of fidelity in terms of light-rays and the forms they project on a plane. It does not apply to the caricature. The cartoonist's drawing of a man is not even a faithful projection of the shape of his features and his body. It does not represent his curves and contours. We say that it is distorted, which can only mean that the man represented is a *deformed* or *distorted* man. But this statement is somehow not right. The caricature may be faithful to those features of the man that distinguish him from all other men and thus may truly represent him in a higher sense of the term. It may correspond to him in the sense of being uniquely specific to him—more so than a projective drawing or a photographic portrait would be. And this is a compelling objection to the whole theory that pictorial information can be reduced to light rays.

One might try to salvage part of the theory by supposing that distortion in

---

[1]Cf. Chs. 1.4, Part 2, and 1.7. (Eds.)

caricatures is exceptional; it is not actually a kind of representation but a kind of graphic symbolism like the using of words. I was tempted by this compromise in 1954. I assumed that when an artist sacrificed projective fidelity the only justification was that he adopted graphic conventions, that is, codes which had to be agreed upon by all. I assumed that the only two possible kinds of specification were by *projection* or by *convention*. A caricature, therefore, was a mixture of the two. But this was only to combine incompatible notions. A caricature is *not* a mixture of optical projection and symbolic distortion but something different from either one. In the end, I will suggest that it is an effort at displaying relevant information.

Why, then, is the point-projection theory being considered so plausible? It is, first of all, consistent with physical optics and with the doctrine of visual sensations that seems to follow from it. This says that the pattern of light entering the eye consists of irreducible bits of color and brightness and that these are the *only* information the eye gets. These spots cannot specify the objects and surfaces from which the light comes; they can only specify sensations of color and brightness. All the rest of perception is a matter of interpretation. For example, the distance of an object, the third dimension of space, is either a matter of learning what the clues for distance are or else of having an unlearned intuition about them. But interpretation depends on sensations. Hence a picture that reconstitutes or represents the mosaic of color sensations from an external scene will arouse the same process of perception that the external scene would. This is the argument and it seems to be very convincing.

The force of the argument comes in part from the evidence said to show that a faithful picture can fool the observer into the feeling that he is looking at a reality instead of just a picture. Since two identical retinal images will yield the same perception, according to the theory, they should yield the same feeling of reality. This is the "illusion of reality" that has fascinated men over the ages. It is represented by the legend of Pygmalion, for whom the image and the reality were identical. It is the theme of a comprehensive and eloquent book by E. H. Gombrich (1961). Nearly everyone has been deceived, at one time or another, into taking a picture for the real thing. So we tend to accept the conclusion that a picture can be, as a limit, indistinguishable from the thing pictured. But this is a vague and slippery statement, as will be shown later. If it means that the perception of something pictured can gradually *become* the direct perception of that something, then it is not true.

## THE SYMBOL THEORY OF PICTORIAL INFORMATION

Artists themselves have never cared much for this point-projection theory of pictorial representation for it seemed to prescribe and constrain what they should do. Painters, critics and historians of art have rebelled against the whole concept of the perfect picture and the faithful image. But since the concept had the powerful support of optics and the physiology of the eye, the justification of the rebellion was not easy.

Twenty-five years ago, Kepes wrote a book called the *Language of Vision* (1944) and recently Goodman (1968) has written another book called *Languages of Art*. I think I understand what these two writers are saying. They are suggesting that a picture is composed of symbols, that the clearest examples of symbols are the letters and words of a language and that, therefore, one can learn to read a picture as the child learns to read English.

Kepes maintained that the components of a picture were not spots of sensation but something else:

> Just as the letters of the alphabet can be put together in innumerable ways to form words which convey meanings, so the optical measures and qualities can be brought together in innumerable ways, and each particular relationship generates a different sensation of space. The variations to be achieved are endless (1944, p. 23).

He gave illustrations of what he called this space-language in his book (cf. Figure 25). The light rays as such, he said "are only a haphazard chaotic panorama of mobile independent light-happenings" (p. 31). This point, that light rays are each independent of every other, had been made by the Gestalt theorists.

Similarly, if much more elaborately, Goodman stresses the analogy between

FIG. 25.    "Study of transparency" by Clifford Eitel, from G. Kepes, *Language of Vision*, Paul Theobald and Co., 1944. Reprinted with permission of the publisher.

pictorial representation and verbal description. "Representations, then, are pictures that function in somewhat the same way as descriptions. Just as objects are classified by means of, or under various verbal labels, so also are objects classified by or under various pictorial labels" (1968, p. 30). He accepts the theory that an act of perception is essentially an act of classification by the observer, assuming that classes have to be imposed on the data.

Now if painting is a language, then just as a new language can be invented (an artificial language like Esperanto, for instance) and can be learned by mastering its vocabulary and grammar, so a new mode of visual perception can be invented by painters and this can be learned by all of us if we succeed in mastering its elements. This revolutionary belief is, indeed, what motivates a good many modern painters. They intend not merely to educate our visual perception of the world but to give us a radically different kind of perception and make us discard the old kind. Arnheim, for example, in *Art and Visual Perception* (1954, p. 93) asserts boldly that only a kind of "shift of level" is needed "to make the Picassos, the Braques, or the Klees look exactly like the things they represent." These paintings do not now represent things for us, he seems to admit, but they will come to do so.

Is this theory correct? A crucial issue in the debate is whether or not the use of perspective in painting is a *convention*. The assertion that it is was made long ago by the art historian Irwin Panofsky (1924–1925) and it has been upheld by Kepes (1944), by Arnheim (1954) and by Goodman (1968). I once maintained in opposition, that:

> it does not seem reasonable to assert that the use of perspective in paintings is merely a convention to be used or discarded by the painter as he chooses . . . when the artist transcribes what he sees upon a two-dimensional surface, he uses perspective geometry, of necessity (1960a, p. 227).

But Goodman (1968, p. 12) disagrees:

> In diametric contradiction to what Gibson says, the artist who wants to produce a spatial representation that the present-day Western eye will accept as faithful must defy the "laws of geometry".

The main contribution of Goodman's book is not reflected in these quotations. When he is discussing pictures, especially paintings, he accepts the analogy with language but he also tries to work out the principles of what he calls *notation* and to apply them to all the various arts. This attempt does not seem to bear directly on the issue of what a picture is; he is clarifying a different problem, not here considered.

The controversy is interesting and important but it is plagued by confusion and misunderstanding. The disrespectors of geometry appeal to so-called inverse perspective in painting. Here is Kepes speaking, from the *Language of Vision:*

Chinese and Japanese painters assign to linear perspective a diametrically opposite role from that given it by Western painters. In their system parallel lines converge as they approach the spectator. They open up the space instead of closing it (1944, p. 86).

But let us be clear about this. It is certainly not true that parallel lines in the world (actually the edges of surfaces) converge as lines on a projection plane as the external edges approach the spectator; the lines must *diverge* as the edges become closer. No rule or canon of inverse perspective could possibly be *systematic,* that is, it could not be consistently applied in the practice of projecting a layout of surfaces on a picture-plane. I do not know why Oriental painters (and Medieval painters and sometimes children) often represent the edges of table-tops and floors as diverging upward on the picture surface instead of converging upwards but I know that they do not have a *system.* I suspect that this so-called inversion of linear perspective was quite unintentional and that the explanation is not simple.

What if anything, then *is* conventional in a representative picture, if perspective is not—what is arbitrary or prescribed? Only the rules for observing the picture surface, which are as follows: it should be seen with one eye, it should be upright and perpendicular to the line of sight instead of slanted and its distance must be just such that the visual solid angle from the picture is the same as would be the visual solid angle from the thing pictured. These rules, note, are highly restrictive and cannot be enforced on the spectator. But when they are not followed, there results a little-understood phenomenon vaguely called ''perspective distortion.'' There is also another prescription to enhance the illusion of reality that is *never* followed in practice: there should be an aperture in front of the eye hiding everything but the picture itself.[2]

The *system* of perspective projection, its optical geometry is a very pretty thing. But it has to be distinguished from the *practice* of perspective. Almost from the discovery of the system, the practice has proved to be less than satisfactory to painters. It was unsatisfactory for the very good reason that people cannot be made to look at a picture in the way prescribed. The system had to be compromised for the spectator's benefit in *ad hoc* ways, for example, to minimize perspective distortion. Painters and sympathetic critics put the blame on the system, not distinguishing it from the practice of perspective. Most of them did not understand or care about the abstract elegance of perspective geometry. For example, they confused the habit of putting a vanishing point in the center of the picture, which is a matter of composition, and, therefore, to be freely chosen, with the system of perspective projection as such.

And thus, if I am right, when artists stopped using perspective entirely as a

---

[2]An exception to this is the display of anamorphs and *trompe l'oeil* paintings, which typically includes a viewing aperture. Unlike ordinary pictures, these sorts of paintings are not appreciated unless they are so viewed. (Eds.)

guide to painting, they may have had good reason but the reason given should not have been that perspective is a convention. For they might be interpreted to mean that the science of optics is itself a convention. They might be saying that optics is not just ill-formulated for the purpose of understanding pictorial perception but it can never be formulated for that purpose. The first statement I believe. The second I deny, for I have some ideas about how to reformulate optics.

## A NEW THEORY OF PICTORIAL INFORMATION

If a picture is neither the source of a sheaf of different light rays each corresponding to a spot on the surface, on the one hand, nor a layout of graphic symbols like writing, on the other, what is it? I suggest that it is a display of optical information and that optical information does not consist of either spots of color or conventional figures with assigned meanings. It comes in an optic array, to be sure, but the array is composed of a hierarchy of nested units, not of rays. Information is contrasted with energy. There has to be enough stimulus energy in an optic array to excite the retinal receptors but the stimulus information is what counts for perception. And stimulus information is invariant under all sorts of changes in stimulus energy.

Here is a formal definition. *A picture is a surface so treated that a delimited optic array to a point of observation is made available that contains the same kind of information that is found in the ambient optic arrays of an ordinary environment.* This definition covers both the photograph and the caricature. It admits that a photographic color transparency can provide an eye with *almost* the same brightness and color contrasts that the cone of light intercepted by the camera provided. The *relations* of luminous intensity and spectral composition of the stimulus energies in the two arrays are in sufficient correspondence to make the low-order stimulus information very nearly the same. But the definition is broad enough also to admit the case of a caricature, where the contrasts of luminous energy are quite different and even the forms are different but where the high-order information to specify a particular person is common to both arrays. In short the optic array from a picture and the optic array from a world can provide the same information without providing the same stimulation. Hence, an artist can capture the *information* about something without replicating its *sensations*.

The above definition is based on a new theory of perception as well as a new formulation of optics. It assumes that two perceptions can be the same without their accompanying sensations being the same. It implies that visual sensations are not necessary for visual perception, strange as this may seem. Perception is based on the pickup of information, not on the arousal of sensation, and the two processes are distinct. Having sensations is at most only an accompaniment of perceiving, not a prerequisite of perceiving. Visual sensations are a sort of luxury incidental to the serious business of perceiving the world. I have argued all this, of course, in *The Senses Considered as Perceptual Systems* (1966b).[3]

The heart of the theory is the concept of optical information. Information consists of *invariants,* in the mathematical sense, of the structure of an optic array. Let us consider the information for the perception of an object in the environment. When one sees an object one does *not* ordinarily see its front surface, in perspective. One sees the whole of it, the back as well as the front. In a sense all of its aspects are present in the experience. It is an object in the phenomenal visual *world,* not a form in the phenomenal visual *field* (Gibson, 1950a). How can this be so? The basis of this direct perception is not the form sensations, or even the remembered sequence of these forms, but the *formless and timeless invariants that specify the distinctive features of the object.* These are the information for perception.

But what about the indirect perceiving of an object when one is presented with a picture of it? The picture, we have always understood, is only one of an infinite family of perspectives of the object, frozen in time. But we can now understand that an *informative* picture contains the same kind of timeless invariants that a sequence of perspectives contains. If it does not provide the eye with these invariants, it is not a good picture of the object (for example, if it is not depicted from a favorable point of view). The fact is that even when one sees a pictured object one ordinarily does not see its front surface only but the whole of it. This is an unsolved paradox for sensation-based theories of perception but it follows immediately from the present theory.

The timeless invariants become more obvious over time, it is true, in a motion picture as compared with a still picture but some of them at least are still present in the latter. When one walks around an object, or sees it rotating, its optic array undergoes perspective transformation and the whole family of perspectives is available to the eye, so that the invariants are easy to see and the single perspectives are not; in fact, it is then almost impossible to see a single perspective. This is the normal way of seeing an object. On the other hand, when one holds still it is easier to see the single perspective than when one moves around. But this is *not* the normal way of seeing an object.

## THE NAIVE ATTITUDE AND THE PERSPECTIVE ATTITUDE

There is evidence to suggest that animals and young children do not notice the aspects of an object or the perspectives of the environment. (An aspect or perspective is an *appearance* at a single stationary point of view.) The world does not appear as a frozen patchwork of flat colors confined by the boundaries of the temporary field of view (Gibson, 1950a, Ch. 3). What they notice is the set of invariant distinctive features of objects and the rigid layout of environmental

---

[3]Cf. Chs. 4.4 & 4.5. (Eds.)

surfaces. They see the non-change underlying the change. This is the naive attitude.

I also believe that our primitive ancestors, before the discovery of pictorial representation by the cave painters, had never noticed the aspects of objects and the perspectives of the environment. They could only take the naive attitude toward the world. Why should the Ice Age hunters have noticed that a mammoth had a different *appearance* from the front, the side, the rear and above? Why should they have observed that a thing *appears* to get smaller as it gets farther away? What use would there be to have paid any attention to linear perspective, and vanishing points and the optical horizon? But as our ancestors began increasingly to make pictures they began to notice these appearances. They began to see aspects, perspectives, in short *forms*. The man who painted the mammoth on the cave wall *had* to notice and remember one aspect (usually the side view) since the necessity of making tracings on a flat surface required it. And so it was, I think, that some men began sometimes to take the perspective attitude in viewing the environment. They began to be able to see the world as a picture (Gibson, 1966b, Ch. 11). But they had to learn to do so.

The modern child also has to learn it. He is surrounded by pictures and is encouraged by his parents to convert his scribblings into representations as soon as possible. But this is not easy, for contrary to orthodox theory, he does not experience his retinal image. And so, in learning to draw, he has to learn to pay attention to the projected forms as distinguished from the formless invariants. If the young child experienced his retinal image he should not *have* to learn to draw. The "innocent eye," far from registering points of color or even patches of color, picks up invariant relations (E. J. Gibson, 1969).

If I am right, then, the modern adult can adopt a naive attitude or a perspective attitude. He can attend to visible things or to visual sensations. And it is much the same when he looks at a picture as when he looks at the world. He can notice only the information for the perception of what is represented or he can pay attention to the picture as such, to the medium, the technique, the style, the composition, the surface and the way the surface has been treated. It is possible of course to shift from one attitude to the other and some pictures fairly compel us to go back and forth from the virtual object that is *in* the picture to the *real* object that *is* the picture. It is possible to combine these attitudes in various ways.

This duality, I suggest, is the essence of representation. Ordinarily one can perceive both the picture as a thing and the thing pictured. There is optical information to specify the surface as such and, in the same array, information to specify a quite different layout of surfaces. There are thus two concurrent levels of surface perception and two corresponding levels of depth or space perception. One is the space in which the picture lies and the other is the space in which the objects pictured lie. I have made experiments to verify this duality. If you place a photomural on the wall of a room representing (say) a road and trees, and if you then put an observer at the proper station point, you will find that he can "perceive" the distance of one of the trees and its height. He confidently estimates that it is a hundred paces away and twenty feet high, with about the same accuracy as when he is actually standing on the road that was photographed. But he can also, on request, perceive and estimate the distance and the height of the *picture*. This object is seen to be three paces away and four feet high. The distance and size of the tree and the picture are not commensurate, for they are not in the same space. The space of the road and the space of the room are not continuous with one another.

When you come to analyse the optic array from the room-and-picture, you find that it contains information for both the perception of the room-space and the perception of the picture-space. Neglecting binocular disparity and the focussing of the lens, the optical texture is present to specify both the surface of the road and the surface of the photograph, and the *gradients* of texture are present to specify both the distance of the tree and the distance of the wall.

## BUT WHAT ABOUT THE ILLUSION OF REALITY?

The point-projection theory of the perfect picture asserted that the objects represented would be seen "through the frame of the picture as if through a window" and, if this was true, it was implied that the pictured scene would be indistinguishable from the real scene. This analogy with a window opening on another world, a magic window, inspired painters for centuries and we owe a great debt to Gombrich (1961) for reminding us of it. But, like most analogies, it can be misleading. The margins of a picture, the frame, could never be mistaken for the occluding edges of a window, since the use of two eyes or the slightest movement of the head would betray the difference. That is, the existence of a world outside the window and extending behind the edges of the window, as contrasted with the non-existence of such a world, is specified by the kind of optical information called accretion-deletion of elements (Gibson, Kaplan, Reynolds & Wheeler, 1969). And so, despite all the stories of paintings that are said to deceive observers into trying to lift the curtain, or eat the grapes, or walk into the scene (Gombrich, 1961, p. 206), I am sceptical. There would be *information* for seeing these things, of course, but there would also necessarily be information for seeing a *painted* curtain, *painted* grapes and *painted* scene. The notion of an image that is literally and actually indistinguishable from the reality is a myth. Pygmalion's cold statue was not a girl and the image that Narcissus saw in the pool was insubstantial, as he could have discovered at any time.

The fallacy encouraged by an uncritical acceptance of the "illusion of reality" is the belief that the perception of something pictured can *pass over into* the perception of it. A mediated perception cannot become a direct perception by stages. No matter how faithful, how lifelike, how realistic a picture becomes, it does not become the object pictured. Perception at second hand will never be perception at first hand.

A related fallacy is the belief that a picture is *similar* to the object pictured (which is false to begin with) and the notion that when similarity reaches a maximum it becomes identity.

## WHAT ABOUT PICTURES OF NON-EXISTENT OBJECTS?

The new definition of a picture does not suggest, as did my old definition, that there must exist in the world, or have existed, an original scene for which it is an imitation, a substitute, a surrogate or a literal representation. There are pictures of mermaids, of angels, of buildings not yet constructed and of events that will never happen. The information provided by a picture is information for perceiving, in the widest sense of the term, not only for remembering something in the past but also for conceiving something in the future, in short for apprehending. The invariants of pictorial information are timeless. The experience obtained by a picture is *as if* one were confronted with a material layout of light-reflecting surfaces but *only* as if.

## WHAT ABOUT AMBIGUOUS DRAWINGS AND REVERSIBLE FIGURES?

Displays which are ambiguous or reversible with respect to what is seen have been interpreted as proving that perceiving depends more on the perceiver than it does on the external stimulus. In the illusion of reversible figure-ground and that of reversible perspective, it is as if there were two different things in the same place. The fact of two alternative percepts from the same drawing is very puzzling. The light to the eye has not changed when a pair of faces is seen instead of a goblet but the percept has (cf. Fig. 26).

If such drawings are analysed as sources of information instead of mere stimulation, however, the puzzle becomes intelligible. The information in the array is equivocal (Gibson, 1966b, p. 246). There are two incompatible kinds of pictorial information in the light to the eye and the percept changes when the beholder shifts from one kind to the other. The information for depth at an edge, for what hides what, has been carefully arranged to specify two different and opposite directions of depth. Equivocal representation in drawings of the edges and corners of surfaces in the world has recently been studied and is reported by Kennedy (1970).

## DISCUSSION

Two theories of pictorial perception have been described. Either we can *see* what is depicted in the same way we can see it when it is not depicted but confronts us

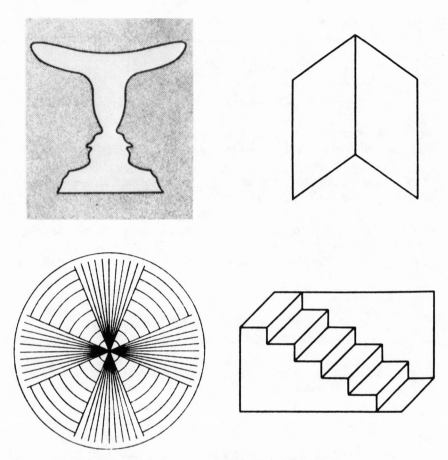

FIG. 26.   Reversible surface—or—air and reversible convexity—or—concavity. On the left are two examples of ambiguous figure and ground (the goblet-faces display and the alternate Maltese crosses). On the right are two examples of reversible "perspective" (the ambiguous book and the ambiguous staircase). Stare at the center of each drawing for a time; observe what happens.

or we can *understand* what is depicted in the same way we can understand it when it is described verbally. No other alternative has been considered in the debate.

   Neither theory is correct. It is true that perceiving what is represented is more like *seeing* it than like *understanding* it by reading or hearing about it. But it is not true that perceiving what is represented can ever be exactly like perceiving it in the world. Conversely, pictorial perception has more immediacy than the understanding of words. But all visual perception, indirect or direct, is based on the pickup of information, not on the having of sensations; it is based on the information in an optic array not on the rays of radiant energy.

To speak of the information in an optic array does not imply that it consists of conventional symbols or that pictures constitute a language, for some of the basic principles of optics still underlie the reformulated discipline that I call *ecological optics* (Gibson, 1966b, Chs. 9–11). Herein lies an alternative to both the analogy with classical optics and the analogy with language. The structure of a picture is allied to the structure of perspective geometry, not to the structure of language. Both pictures and language *have* structure, to be sure, and in this limited sense it is possible to say that both have a sort of *grammar*. But the informative structure of ambient light is richer and more inexhaustible than the informative structure of language. Animals and men could see things long before men began to describe them and we can still see many things that we cannot, as yet, describe.

It is surely true that picturing is a means of communication and a way of storing, accumulating and transmitting knowledge to successive generations of men. So is speaking-hearing a means of communication and writing-reading a way of accumulating and transmitting knowledge. But the difference is that picturing exploits some of the information in the structure of the light, the space-filling light that is everywhere available as long as a clear medium of water or air has existed on this planet. And this is what visual perceiving does.

Not only do we perceive in terms of visual information, we also can *think* in those terms (Arnheim, 1969). Making and looking at pictures helps us to fix these terms. We also can think in terms of verbal information, as is obvious, and words enable us to fix, classify and consolidate our ideas. But the difference is that visual thinking is freer and less stereotyped than verbal thinking; there is no vocabulary of picturing as there is of saying. As every artist knows, there are thoughts that can be visualized without being verbalized.

It is possible to suggest a new theory of pictorial perception only because a new theory of visual perception has been formulated. The latter is based on the radical assumption that light can convey information about the world and, hence, that the phenomenal world does not have to be constructed by the mind (or the brain) out of meaningless data. This assumption, in turn, depends on a new conception of light in terms of the array at a point of observation—light considered not merely as a stimulus but also as a structure. These ways of thinking about perception and light are unfamiliar but they clarify murky puzzles of long standing and they make the art of depicting very much more intelligible than it has been. It is now possible to distinguish between the pictorially *mediated* perception of the features of a world and the *direct* perception of the features of the surroundings, and yet to understand that there is common information for the features they have in common.[4]

---

[4]A useful book has just been published that clarifies the little understood pheonomenon of perspective distortion in pictures. It is *Optics, Painting & Photography* by M. H. Pirenne (Cambridge: Cambridge University Press, 1970). Professor Pirenne has misgivings, like me, about the theory that perspective is a symbolic convention. He defends, as I once did, the point-projection theory of pictorial information, although cautiously. But he accepts the eye-camera analogy, as I do not, and thus the new theory here proposed will seem very strange to him.

# 3.5 On the Concept of "Formless Invariants" in Visual Perception*

One of the many meanings of the term *form* is the *face* of a solid object (Gibson, 1951a). The face of a polyhedron is a flat surface, a polygon. One of the faces of a polyhedron is the *front* face, that is the surface facing the point of observation. When an observer moves (or when the object itself is moved) the *projected form* of this *surface-form* undergoes a continuous sequential perspective transformation (Gibson, 1957a) The *optical* form undergoes change but the *substantial* form does not. The mathematician can think of this change as a family of geometrical forms, each linked to every other by a specific transformation and this conception is implied by projective geometry, a conception of forms outside of time.

The perceptionist, however, thinks of it as a change in time. If he displays a continuous sequence of this sort, obtained by projecting a transforming shadow on a translucent screen, he finds that it will arouse the perception of a rigid surface in motion (Gibson & Gibson, 1957). It was first concluded from this experiment that such a sequence (or geometrical family) of optical forms was a "stimulus" for the perception of the face of an object. The term *stimulus* was being used in a very general sense, in a sense of the term that I have now abandoned, and I would now say instead that the sequence contained *information* for the perception.[1] Note that only one face of an object is being considered. How one goes from the perception of the face of an object to the perception of the *whole* object was not explained at that time. More of this question later.

---

*Leonardo*, 1973, 6, 43–45. Reprinted with permission from *Leonardo*, 6, 43 (1973). Copyright 1973 by Pergamon Press, Ltd.
[1]Cf. Ch. 4.3, part 2. (Eds.)

In these first experiments, the hypothesis of *invariants* in the sequence of perspective transformations was implicit. It gradually became more explicit, however, and by 1966 I could write as follows:

> Continuous optical transformations can yield two kinds of perception at the same time, one of change and one of non-change. The perspective transformation of a rectangle, for example, was always perceived as both something rotating and something rectangular. This suggests that the transformation, as such, is one kind of stimulus information, for motion, and that the invariants under transformation are another kind of stimulus information, for the constant properties of the object ... There is almost always some permanence imbedded in any change ... The primacy of form or pattern comes into question. There is no "form" left in a continuous transformation. It has vanished and all that remains is the invariants (1966a).

This is a very radical hypothesis. It suggests that the perception of an object does not depend on a series of percepts, each of one *image* of the object, that is, perceptions of its forms or perspectives, but depends instead on the invariant features of the forms or perspectives over time. Object-perception does not depend on form-perception but on invariant-detection. And these invariants are "formless," that is to say, they are not themselves forms. Form-perception is thus shorn of its importance. (This is too bad just at a time when form-perception is beginning to arouse a new level of interest among experimental psychologists! I am suggesting that the research on the discriminating of forms and patterns, however interesting, has no relevance to the perception of the *environment,* only to *pictures* of the environment.)

If this was a radical hypothesis in 1966, a still more radical extension of it was to follow. The formless invariants of the face of an object specify that particular face of the object. But what specifies the *back* face (or faces) of an object? The back of an object is the part that is *hidden* by the front of the object. What specifies the surface that goes out of sight at one edge of the turning object and comes into sight at the other edge? Perspective transformations in the array do not specify this; only an optical transition that is *not* a transformation will do so (Gibson, Kaplan, Reynolds & Wheeler, 1969). The information for the perception of going-out-of-sight is beginning to be understood, however, and there seem to be invariants that specify the occluding edge, that is to say, a surface layout where a front face adjoins a back face. Note that these invariants are even more "formless" than the invariants under changing slant, if that is possible. An occluding edge is not a form, although it is, to be sure, a feature of surface layout.

The hypothesis of invariants, even in its early and less radical form, has met with a certain incredulity from perceptionists and artists. It seems to contradict some of our deepest convictions about vision. Surely, they say, the perception of an object can be aroused by a *picture* of the object, a still picture, and, since it presents no transformation, it can display no invariants under transformation. The information for perception is in the *form*, not in any formless invariants, and, in this case (if not in all cases), object-perception *does* depend on form perception.

For some years, I was silenced by this argument, even if not convinced. But then I asked, is it conceivable that there *are* formless invariants in a picture, paradoxical as this may sound? Do we learn to detect invariants in a frozen array as well as in a changing array? Is it possible that the information in a picture does not consist of the forms in that picture?

By now there are a number of facts and lines of reasoning to support the hypothesis that invariants are information for perception, even in the special case of pictorially mediated perception.

1. It can be argued that primitive men did not "pay attention to the perspectives of things until they learned to draw and to perceive by means of drawing. Before that time they needed only to detect the specifying invariants of things that differentiated them—their distinctive features, not their momentary aspects or frozen projections. Young children are also, I think, not aware of aspects or forms as such ... The *invariants* in a pictorial array, the information *about* the dog, cat, man, house or car, are picked up very early but the embodiment of the ghostly shape of an object is not noticed" (Gibson, 1966b p. 236). This is to say, that in any picture of a cat, the young child sees *catness* and not the side view or front view of a cat, as the case may be. The front view and the side view specify the same cat and are seen as such.

2. In observing a caricature or a political cartoon one often does not notice the lines as such (the figure-on-ground, the tracings on the surface) but only the information they convey about the distinctive features of the person caricatured. The caricature may be a poor *projection* of his face but good *information* about it.[2] The "form" of the face is distorted but not the essential features of the face.

3. In the course of wearing spectacles that *distort* or *deform* the retinal image, for example prismatic glasses or even glasses with the upper half prismatic and the lower half not, it has been discovered that the perception of objects and of the environmental layout tends to become correct (Kohler, 1951/1964). This suggests that the information is not carried by the "form" of the retinal image and the perception is not based on it but on something else.

4. In observing line-drawings in general, when they represent solid objects we do not see silhouettes or cutouts like paper-dolls but modelled and rounded surfaces. A line is perceived as an occluding edge, that is, as the margin between the front surface and the back surface of an object (Kennedy, 1970).[3] The ancient doctrine that form-perception is primary and object-perception secondary is thus a mistake.

---

[2] See Perkins & Hagen (1980) for a discussion of caricature. (Eds.)
[3] Cf. Kennedy (1974). (Eds.)

5. In observing the so-called "vanishing point" of the railroad tracks at the horizon, I suggest that one does not in fact see the apex of an angle but *very great distance*. Even in a photograph or drawing of the tracks one does not perceive a triangle but the tracks "in the distance." In other words, the horizon in ecological optics is not so much a geometrical line as a mathematical invariant. An object goes out of sight by becoming too far away to see, not by vanishing into a point.

6. In reading, it seems quite clear that we do not notice or even see the alphabetic forms of the letters on the page but only the distinctive features of letters and their combinations (E. J. Gibson, 1969, Ch. 19).

7. Finally, there is a developing new hypothesis which says that a representative picture is best conceived not as a projection of the world on a picture plane by rays, as we have been taught, but as a source of graphic information about the world (Gibson, 1971a). The optic array from a picture can provide the same information as an optic array from the world without having to provide the same points of stimulation. The hypothesis is based on ecological optics instead of physical optics.

A good picture is not just one out of a vast family of perspectives. It contains graphic information, not forms, and this information is of the same kind as the mathematical invariants that become noticeable during a sequence of perspective transformations.

A good picture does not *have* to be in point-to-point correspondence with the facing surfaces of an actual concrete world (although a picture *can* be just such a projection and a photograph *is* one). It may specify a world that never was or, more exactly, the relevant features or affordances of an environment that is more interesting than any world that ever was.

In *The Perception of the Visual World* (1950a), I distinguished between what I called *retinal texture* and *surface texture*. Unhappily, however, the notion of projective correspondence between two kinds of texture is not adequate to the whole problem of perception. There is not just one kind of *texture* of a surface; there is, for example, a *pigment structure* and a *layout structure* (Gibson, 1966b, p. 208 ff). When bumps and hollows on a surface become deep enough, projective correspondence clearly fails. Here is a list of cases where elements of optical texture fail to correspond with elements of surfaces in the environment:

1. As given above, only *facing* surfaces are projected, *occluded* surfaces are not projected to the point of observation.
2. In the case of a transparent (but semi-textured) surface in front of another, there are *two* surfaces "projected" to the point of observation but in a sense of the term quite different from the above.
3. Cast shadows on a surface (as distinguished from the attached shadows arising from bumps and hollows) are independent of the texture of the surface (its layout structure and pigment structure) but yield an optical texture in the array.

4. Specular reflections of the source of light that bounce off a surface cause elements of optical texture that do not correspond to elements of the structure of the surface (e.g. multiple reflections or the scintillating reflections from water).

5. Luminous elements in a surface (radiating rather than reflecting light) will cause an optical texture that does not correspond to the texture of the surface.

Here, as in pictures, there are formless invariants.

Let me try to sum up. There is usually information in an optic array—either the stationary optic array from a picture to its proper station point or the changing optic array from an environment to a point of observation, usually a moving point. What does this information consist of? Does it consist of spots of light or darkness, or bits of color? Surely not; that is merely an array of sensations. Does it consist of contours or border-contrasts between patches of different intensity? No, although that is a little better. Does it consist of forms or *gestalten* on a background? Or perhaps of groups of forms? No, not even forms. None of these formulas is adequate. The information must consist of features of optical structure that we do not have adequate words to describe. But we can say that the units of structure are "nested"; there are subordinate and superordinate units.[4]

The information-bearing features are things like the following: alignment or straightness (being "in line" but not necessarily a line as such) as against bentness or curvature; perpendicularity or rectangularity; parallelity as against convergence; intersections; closures and symmetries. These features are present in an unchanging array but they are best revealed in a changing array, one kind of change being transformation. We have scarcely begun to understand them and neither mathematics nor the gestalt hypothesis has been adequate for the task. But it is along those lines that we should proceed.

---

[4]Cf. Ch. 1.7. (Eds.)

# 3.6

## Notes on Direct Perception and Indirect Apprehension

*Unpublished manuscript, May 1977.

### PART I: A NOTE ON DIRECT PERCEPTION, VARIOUS KINDS OF INDIRECT APPREHENSION, AND DEGREES OF INDIRECTNESS*

Direct perception, I suggest, is fundamental to all less direct kinds of apprehension or cognition.

*I. Direct Perception at First Hand of Ecological Things and Events.* This is perception at the level of substances, surfaces, and the medium, of ecology as distinguished from physics. It is based on stimulus information, i.e., invariants, picked up during exploration and locomotion. Direct perceiving includes one form of so-called remembering, that is, awareness of occluded surfaces as well as of surfaces seen-now-from-here. In general the affordances of things is what gets attended to, not the modalities, qualities, or intensities of the accompanying sensations, i.e., affordances for manipulation, locomotion, nutrition, and social interaction. Direct perception matures with age and improves with practice.

The perceiving of celestial objects, of events in the sky, and of the causes of optical phenomena such as rainbows is inadequate, however, to the extent that scrutiny is impossible and exploration cannot occur. The perceiving of microphysical objects and events is inadequate to the extent that the eye cannot be brought close enough and the visual solid angles are too small for good vision.

*II. More or Less Direct Perception of the Very Distant and the Very Small by Means of Simple Instruments.* Our species has invented various aids to perception, ways of improving, enchancing, or extending the pickup of information. The natural techniques of observation are supplemented by artificial techniques, using tools for perceiving by analogy with tools for performing.

The simplest optical instruments are correcting spectacles or hand-held magnifying glasses. An artificial lens can be either a substitute for, or a supplement to, the natural lens-system. The telescope enabled a man to see that the moon was not a luminous goddess in the heavens, but a land with mountains (Gibson, 1979a Ch. 9). The microscope enabled him to see unknown forms of life in a drop of water. These magnifying instruments do not significantly modify the invariants of structure in an array, and thus perception *does not require interpretation* to any great degree. But the radio telescope and the electron microscope convert or translate the optical information into a new form, and the display does require interpretation.

*III. Indirect Apprehension by Means of Information-Converting Instruments.* There are various devices that *convert* information, for example information to which the perceptual systems are not attuned into information which a perceptual system is adapted to pick up directly. Some examples are the photographic transparency made with X-rays, the "snooperscope," the spectroscope, the image-enhancing devices of photographic engineering, the sound spectrograph and, at a far extreme of indirectness, the cloud-chamber. Instruments have never been classified from the point of view of the optical information they provide but they could be. There are also non-optical devices for perceiving, like litmus paper. They all display *invariants,* I believe, but the apprehension of what is specified is not *direct* as in scrutinizing, listening, feeling and tasting. Perhaps the interpretation of these invariants becomes more nearly direct with practice, or does so in some cases, but an interpretation is nevertheless required.

*IV. Apprehension by Means of Measuring Instruments.* I suggested in (1979a, Ch. 8) that the *affordance*-dimensions of things and surfaces should not be confused with their *metric* dimensions. The former are seen and felt directly, relative to one's body, whereas the latter are apprehended indirectly by means of measuring sticks, and by the act of counting. The child who sees directly whether or not he can jump a ditch is aware of something more basic than is the child who has learned to say how wide it is in feet or meters.

The very small and the very large dimensions, the atomic and the galactic, are not directly perceived although, of course, they can be measured in metric units and treated mathematically. So also are very fast and very slow events. And so are very light and very massive objects, whose mass cannot be felt but can be measured in grams. The fundamental measuring instruments are the meter stick, clock, and balance, but their units combine to make higher units. We can get pointer-readings from all sorts of meters, photometers, volt meters, speedometers, accelerometers, and so on. One can learn to "read" the instrument, as we say, but this is radically different from perceiving directly the property measured.

There are no psychological scales on this theory, only affordance-dimensions, and the physical scales that we learn are intellectual constructions.

So far I have been describing apprehension at first hand in the sense that, even with an instrument, only one observer is involved. What about perception at second hand, when there is an information-giver between the perceiver and the world? I include perception mediated by man-made depictions and, of course, apprehension mediated by man-made descriptions, that is, by language, both spoken and written. But I shall contrast information that has been put into a picture with information that has been put into words and thus distinguish these two kinds of apprehension.

*V. Indirect Perception of Objects, Events, Places or Persons the Information for which has been Captured by a Picture-Maker.* I am suggesting that the optical information in a picture has been *captured* by its maker whereas the information in a description has been *converted*. The inv riants in the array from a picture have always been selected from what was avai abl: in the environment and have often been emphasized (especially in caricature) but they are of the same sort as the invariants in a natural array. The information does not require interpretation. In this respect looking at a picture is like looking through a telescope.

In any picture, chirographic or photographic, information to specify the surface on which it is made is unavoidable and can be noticed by an exploring observer. Hence pictorially mediated perception involves a dual awareness, a concurrent pickup of the information for what is pictured and the information for the picture as a surface.

The photographic camera is, of course, also a passive optical instrument. But when used by an information-giver it can be selective as much as a drawing or painting can be. The main difference is that a man can draw or paint something that is wholly imaginary, non-existent, or fictional, although he cannot photograph it.

A picture is not *similar* to what it depicts. Hence the term *representation* should not be used for it. And the term *image* is hopelessly vague. A picture is a source of information.

*VI. The Obtaining of Information that has been Put into Words.* Of all the uses of speech and language perhaps the most obvious is that of *conveying* or *transmitting* information from person to person and parents to children, and of *storing* information in written form so that it accumulates. Useful facts about the world can thus be obtained from your playmates, your mother, your teacher, and Aristotle himself.

Knowledge that has been put into words or, similarly, into numbers can be said to be *explicit*.[1] It is rather different from the knowledge got by direct

---

[1]For a thorough discussion of explicit versus tacit knowing, see Polanyi (1958). (Eds.).

perception, by the simpler instruments, and by pictures. Not all information about the world *can* be put into words and numbers. Sometimes there are no words for what can be seen and captured in a picture. Is this because no verbal description is possible, or only because it has not yet been formulated? I suspect that the information about the world that can be easily pictured is of a different *kind* than the information that is easily made explicit. How does the psychologist characterize them? To say that the former is "iconic" and the latter not is both useless and mystifying. To say that the former is "abstract" and the latter "concrete" is not adequate. To say that words are "coded" while pictures are "uncoded" is partly true but not good enough. To say that a picture specifies by projection (as against convention) is not correct. We need to make a fresh start.[2]

## PART II: VARIOUS KINDS OF COGNITION*

There are two quite different kinds of visual cognition, the direct perception of the surfaces around us together with their utilities, and the perception of man-made *markings* on surfaces together with the kinds of awareness that can be mediated by such marks. The meanings of surfaces and the meanings of marks are learned in quite different ways. Consider them separately.

1. I have suggested that the environment consists basically of substances, surfaces, places, objects, and events.[3] These perceivables have a special kind of meaning that I call affordances; animals and children learn to see what they afford *for them*. The learning is tacit, not explicit, i.e., most of it is not put into words. They are perceived by looking around and getting around (*ambient* and *ambulatory* vision, as described in *The Ecological Approach*, 1979a). They are learned out of school, by encountering the substances, surfaces, places, objects, and events of the terrestrial environment.

These parts of the world have not been recognized by psychologists and philosophers as what animals perceive. They are "nested"; they are not discrete entities or denumerable units, and they cannot be inventoried. Substances, surfaces, places, etc. do not differ from one another along single dimensions. They have meaningful combinations of dimensions, i.e., features, that constitute their affordances. They are not at all like the traditional "objects of perception." Hence we cannot study the development of our ability to discriminate them by isolating and controlling one variable at a time in the orthodox way. The theory of sets does not apply to them. They are not categorized except insofar as names are applied to them; they are simply perceived. And they are certainly not "stimuli."

---

[2]The details of the arguments against these dichotomies may be found in Ch. 3.4 (Eds.).

*Unpublished manuscript, July 1979.

[3]See Chs. 1.9, 2.3, 2.8, and 4.9. (Eds.).

2. The perception of the linguistic and numerical forms and symbols used to stand for the elements of speaking, writing, thinking, and computing is quite different. Their meanings are attached by association. The meaning of an alphanumeric character or a combination of them fades away with prolonged visual fixation, unlike the meaning of a substance, surface, place, etc. Letters and numbers are only about 5000 years old. They are conventional. There are only a few of them. They go into lists. They are discrete. They have to be memorized. They make items that are unconnected with the rest of the world. Letters can form nonsense syllables (but there is no such thing as a nonsense place or a nonsense event).

Marks on a surface are not parts of the ambient environment. They are scanned in a special way. They are often presented in an exposure-device, or they can be flashed in a tachistoscope so that scanning is eliminated and a single snapshot is supposedly transmitted to the brain. This makes each item a discrete "stimulus," a single retinal "image." Items are convenient for an experimenter, since they can be quantified. They lend themselves to the theory that cognition consists of the "processing" of inputs.

Consider the difference between the learning and forgetting of a list of items in the laboratory and the learning of the nested and connected places of one's habitat. They are not comparable. The same laws do not hold. Animals and children learn the habitat by locomotor exploration. They cut across property lines. They see where to go and how to go, and what places are good for what. They connect the hidden places with the place that is seen now from here. They can "orient" (turn to) relevant places. They see where they are relative to where they might be. Is this perceiving, or remembering, or knowing, or is it behaving? Or what? Maze learning does not capture it. It is surely not a sequence of responses to stimuli (as Hull believed) but it is just as surely not the constructing or consulting of an internal *map* as is now fashionable to suppose (and as Tolman once suggested for lack of a better formula). Neither conditioned responses nor expectancies are good enough to account for it. Place learning is a primitive kind of cognition, akin to perception, that involves visuo-motor activities, opaque geometry, reversible occlusion, the cluttered environment, and a whole new set of problems for psychology. Mainly it requires the hypothesis of unchanging invariant structure that underlies the changing perspective structure of the ambient light during locomotion.

3. and 4. There are still other kinds of cognition, of course, that are suggested in Chapter 14 of *The Ecological Approach* (1979a). There is knowledge of the very small and the very large, mediated by instruments such as the microscope and the telescope. And there is the awareness of the worlds of fiction and of imagination, both of one's own and of others. Cognitive psychology should push out beyond the cramping limits of laboratory stimuli.

# 4

# IMPLICATIONS OF ECOLOGICAL REALISM

Edward Reed
and Rebecca Jones

## INTRODUCTION

The essays included in this section are broader in scope than those in previous sections, in that they reveal some of the implications of Gibson's ecological approach for the whole of psychology. In the course of developing his theory of perception, Gibson performed critical analyses of a number of psychology's basic ideas such as the concepts of form, stimulus, and learning. These analyses, several of which are included here, illustrate Gibson's gift for concise description while documenting the development of the ecological approach and its widespread relevance.

The strategy taken by Gibson in analyzing problems was to select a fundamental problem, carefully articulate its components, and describe the important approaches to that problem. Next, the various approaches were compared and evaluated with respect to both conceptual rigor and empirical adequacy. Finally, novel ideas and approaches to the problem were suggested that avoided the difficulties discovered in the early approaches. Gibson's ecological realism is well-illustrated in this manner of analysis and in his choice of problems for discussion. Often he chose to discuss problems that had been avoided or overlooked by other researchers whose theories obscured the need for such efforts. The uniqueness of Gibson's method of ecological analysis is illustrated throughout these essays by the detailed attention given to the facts of the environment, and in his precise and systematic discussions of these facts.

Most importantly, Gibson's ecological realism enabled him to reject consistently both sides of classical debates in psychology and to propose better foundations for psychological theorizing. In these essays Gibson showed how both parties to the disputes between elementarists and holists, empiricists and nativists, and behaviorists and cognitivists have shared wrong assumptions about the relation between animals and their environment. Gibson's searching analyses of these issues exposed the weakness and imprecision of the assumptions on which these classical debates are founded, resulting in his rejection of the overarching dichotomy between mental (subjective, meaningful) and physical (objective, meaningless) properties, in favor of the concept of an ecological level of reality at which meanings and purposes are as real as bodies.

The first paper in this section, "What is a form?" (Ch. 4.1), consists of a detailed analysis of the central concept of Gestalt theory, the notion of form, pattern, or arrangement. Gibson's critical review of the numerous conceptions of form reveals many ambiguities and vagaries in the use of "form" that have given rise to confusions in theories of object and picture perception. One of the most pernicious problems is that of treating the stimulation at the retina as a kind of form, which leads to a confusion over whether form is the distal or the proximal stimulus, or a function of organization in the brain. Gibson argued that it is meaningless to investigate *how* we perceive form until we have established *what* it is that is perceived. As an attempt to solve this problem, Gibson formulated a classification of form that includes three major types, each of which requires special investigation and explanation. He claimed that, as those three areas were developed, the problem of "form perception" would disappear, along with the dichotomy between elementarism and holism, which is based on the issue of how we see form. This early analysis of what counts as a form provided a firm basis for Gibson's later research on what there is to be seen (Chs. 1.8, 2.8, 3.4, 4.9), on the structure of the optic array (Chs. 1.4, 1.6, 1.7, 2.6, 2.7), and on the perception of pictures (Section 3).

Gibson's rejection of the problem of form perception and the concomitant dichotomy of elementarism versus holism had important implications for his subsequent analyses of learning, the concept of the stimulus, and the nature of sensory activity. These implications are discussed in Chapters 4.2–4.4, beginning with an essay written in collaboration with E. J. Gibson, "Perceptual learning: Differentiation or enrichment?" Traditionally, the problem in perceptual learning has been the issue of how much of perception is learned. Sharing the assumption that we must go beyond the information given to the senses, nativists and empiricists have argued whether the enrichment we provide for the meager sensory inputs is primarily innate or acquired, and thus whether much or only a little of perception is learned. The Gibsons argued against both types of enrich-

ment theories, proposing a radically different specificity or differentiation theory
according to which the information available for perception is indefinitely rich
and detailed, rather than impoverished. Thus, perceptual learning is a process of
discriminating or differentiating variables of stimulation rather than of adding
meanings to impoverished stimulus input. Whereas associationists such as Postman (1955) described perceptual learning as a change in response to the same
stimulus, the Gibsons argued that perceptual learning involves a change in what
is responded to, namely, subtler details of structure in stimulation. This new
conception of perceptual learning opened up a variety of novel and fruitful areas
for investigation (E. J. Gibson, 1969; E. J. Gibson & Spelke, in press) and
provided the basis for some of Gibson's claims concerning his new reasons for
realism.

In "The concept of the stimulus in psychology" (Ch. 4.3), Gibson pursued
his strategy of revealing the strikingly different and even contradictory ways in
which psychologists use the same term. Although the $S$-$R$ approach has domi-
nated American psychology throughout the twentieth century, Gibson's essay is
the only systematic analysis of the crucial stimulus concept. The principle
sources of confusion in understanding the concept of the stimulus, according to
Gibson, lie in establishing the relations between stimuli and responses (do stimuli
trigger responses?; are they sufficient causes?; must they be defined independently of responses?), and in characterizing stimuli (do they exist only at the
receptor level?; what constitutes a single, separate stimulus?; what is the structure of stimuli, and how do they specify their environmental sources?). Gibson
spent much of his career answering these questions, and his alternative to classical approaches, which is merely hinted at in this essay, was that there are *no*
stimuli or inputs that cause behavior and perception. Instead, he argued that
perception and action are based on information and are the achievements of
purposeful creatures, rather than responses caused by circumstances. Gibson thus
relegated the $S$-$R$ concept to receptor-level physiology and began developing his
own psychophysiology of purposive systems.

"The useful dimensions of sensitivity" (Ch. 4.4) is an early version of Gibson's theory of the perceptual systems (Gibson, 1966b; Chs. 2.4, 2.5) and
reveals some of the consequences of rejecting the assumption that stimuli cause
perception. He argued that a rejection of the $S$-$R$ formulation entails denying the
classical doctrine that afferent impulses are the mechanism of perceptual sensitivity. In its place he offered his conception of perceptual sensitivity as an active
and purposeful process of attention that involves output as well as input. As
demonstrated by Gibson's (1962a) experiments on active touch, normal perceiving involves investigatory movements in conjunction with sensory processes.
Thus, the classical analysis of tactile, gustatory, chemical, auditory, and visual
inputs leading to sensations should be replaced with the analysis of the activities
of feeling, tasting, smelling, listening, and looking. The traditional theory that

holds that touch with a passive hand or vision with a fixed head are simple, basic cases of perceiving are wrong; afferent impulses are not the basis of sense perception, and sensations are not necessary for perception.

In "New reasons for realism" (Ch. 4.5), Gibson summarized the implications of his theory of information, arguing that it provides support for both a new theory of perception and for realism in epistemology. If the information for perceiving consists of invariants across transformations in the ambient energy fields that are specific to their source, then many of the classical problems in psychology and philosophy disappear. The problem of form perception dissolves into the problem of identifying the information available to specify the various types of form that are perceived. The important question in perceptual learning is not the origin of the supplementations, whether innate or acquired, for the meager sense data, but what information can be differentiated from the indefinitely rich available supply. Discrete stimuli (whether punctate or holistic) cannot cause perception; nor can passive sensory processes be the basis for perceiving; perceivers must actively look, listen, touch, and so forth, to use the information available that specifies the objects, organisms, places, and events around them.

Gibson also proposed profound alterations in the philosophy of knowing based on his concept of information. Prior to Gibson, knowledge had to be explained as the outcome of the subjective processing of objectively caused sense inputs. By founding his epistemology on ecological information, Gibson showed that it is possible to transcend the plethora of contradictions and puzzles that have arisen over the centuries as philosophers have argued whether knowledge can be considered objective in spite of its subjective components. Gibson's philosophical position, which has come to be called direct or ecological realism (Gibson, 1972; Michaels & Carello, 1981; Reed & Jones, 1979; Shaw, Turvey, & Mace, 1982), holds that our perception of the world is direct and our knowledge of it can be objective because information specifies its source. Gibson argued that objects and events in the environment are themselves real and meaningful, and that they are what animals perceive, desire, know, and act upon directly.

The papers included in Chapter 4.6, "The theory of proprioception and its relation to volition" and "Note for a tentative redefinition of behavior," extend the ecological approach to the questions of what is behavior and how is it controlled. Gibson rejected the still widely held theory (Gallistel, 1980; Norman, 1981) that behavior consists of responses or hierarchies of responses triggered either by stimuli or central (cognitive, motivational) states. Instead, he argued that behaviors consist of nested postures and movements, controlled by perception. Any functioning perceptual system may control behavior, organizing the postures and movements with respect to both the environment (exteroception) and the self (proprioception). Previous input theories of perception had led to output–input comparison theories of the relation between perception and behavior (Gallistel, 1980, Ch. 7; von Holst, 1954). According to these comparison theories, animals distinguish their own actions (proprioception) from externally determined events (exteroception) by using efference to evaluate afferent impulses: Actual input is compared to expected (on the basis of efferent impulses) input, and a correspondence means a successful action, whereas a mismatch signals an externally determined behavior or event. Against this theory, Gibson argued that any perceptual system can function both proprioceptively and exteroceptively, if the relevant information is available. The relation between behavior and perception is not through a comparison process but through the use of perceptual information to guide action. Gibson showed that unique deformations in the optic array specify the various postures and movements people make (e.g., locomotion, limb movements, exploration) and also the goals of behavior, such as the affordances of objects in the environment. Gibson's novel account of behavior and its control opens up the possibility of developing a realistic psychology of action, one that transcends the limitations of current cognitive *S-R* approaches.

Since at least the time of Parmenides and Heraclitus, philosophers have puzzled over the problem of how we come to have knowledge of a real, stable world given the blur of changing appearances (Hyland, 1973). In psychology the analogous problem is how we see solid and persisting objects on the basis of the fleeting, fluctuating, and fragmentary, flat retinal image. The answer has always been that sensations are interpreted through concepts that add meaning and depth, fill in the gaps, and provide stability. In "The new idea of persistence and change and the old ideas that it drives out" (Ch. 4.7), Gibson argued that both Parmenides and Heraclitus were wrong, and that the modern theory that knowledge is constructed on the basis of sensations is false. As an alternative Gibson offered his theory that both persistence and change, both variance and invariance, are necessary components of the information for perception, and change and nonchange in the world are perceived concurrently. The implications of this theory are that we can perceive things without having sensations caused by them, and that the distinction between the present and the past, which many theorists use to differentiate perception and memory, may be even more indistinct than William James suspected. Gibson's theory of the perception of the whole persisting and changing environment, by means of variances and invariances detected over time, requires a reformulation of many concepts central to psychology and philosophy, such as stasis and flux, perceiving and remembering, and knowledge and sensation.

Gibson's radical break with traditional psychology over the concepts of the stimulus, learning, sensory processes, and knowledge has confused many people who insist on interpreting his revolutionary ideas within the older framework. One of the most common misapprehensions of Gibson's theory is dealt with in "The myth of passive perception" (Ch. 4.8). If inputs from sense organs are the basis for perception, then a great deal of mental activity (the making of associations or information processing) must occur to transform the inputs into something useful and meaningful. Gibson has denied that such mental activity occurs, and as a result his critics accuse him of having a passive theory of perception. In this paper Gibson refuted that claim, showing that his theory of information pickup involves the active purposeful search for and detection of information by perceptual systems. Because information specifies its source and because the perceptual systems have evolved to detect that information, there is no need for mental processes that interpret, organize, or in some way transform information. Gibson's theory of active information pickup is clearly presented in both *The Senses Considered as Perceptual Systems* (1966b) and *The Ecological Approach to Visual Perception* (1979a, Ch. 14), although the type of activity he discusses is quite different from that incorporated into sensation-based theories of perception. The ecological approach to perception has important implications for the study of the process of perceiving, because if information is not processed in stages, each of which involves some transformation of the information, then the standard tools and experimental strategies of information-processing psychology are inappropriate for the study of perceptual activity.

Over the last 15 years of his career, Gibson united his various contributions to psychology into a single coherent framework or ecological approach. An idea fundamental to this approach is the concept of *affordance*. Affordances are those aspects of the environment that offer possibilities for behavior to an animal; they are what organisms perceive and act upon. In the "Notes on affordances" (Ch. 4.9) presented here, we have collected nine previously unpublished "purple perils" on affordances written after Gibson first introduced the concept (1966b, pp. 273-274, 285), but prior to his last statement of the theory (1979a, Ch. 9). These essays reveal the development of Gibson's thinking about affordances and deal with aspects of affordances not thoroughly discussed in his published works on the subject.

The first six essays included here all deal with classifying the visible properties and the affordances of the environment, and with refining the affordance concept. Gibson argued that what a thing is and what it means are not separate; nor is perceiving what a thing is independent of perceiving what it means. An analysis of the visible properties of the environment must therefore be done at the ecological (as opposed to a mathematical, physical, or phenomenal) level, and the classification of affordances must rest on what exists that can be perceived at that level.

In refining his theory of affordances, Gibson showed how it points the way to a unified psychology concerned with the behavior of purposeful creatures in a meaningful environment. The concept of affordances is so integrative and fundamental because it transcends the centuries-old doctrine of animal-environment dualism, the assumption that behaving animals and their environment can be studied separately. Previous theorists of purposive behavior such as Lewin (1936) and Tolman (1932) conceived of goals as mental objects found in or inferred from subjective experiences caused by physical objects. Thus, goal objects were thought to change with changes in the needs, knowledge, and experience of the organism, whereas meaningless physical objects remained unaffected by such organic changes. According to Gibson, affordances are specific to the potential relations between an organism and its environment but do not depend on organisms' psychological states for their existence. Thus, affordances are neither subjective nor objective and both; they go beyond that false dichotomy.

In the latter three essays included here, Gibson explored some of the possibilities for applying the ecological approach and the theory of affordances to social perception and behavior, architectural design, and ontology. Gibson argued that the basis of social existence is the ability of one organism not only to perceive the affordances of other creatures but also to perceive what objects, places, and events afford for other organisms (Gibson, 1979a, pp. 135, 141). This sharing of the environment is possible because there is information for perceiving that is independent of a single point of view. Because some observers can learn to perceive what other observers perceive, and because observers can record (in pictures or words) and display what they perceive, social behavior is possible.

The theory of affordances provides a unified conceptual structure with which to analyze the environment of animals and people at a meaningful, ecological level. Architects manipulating substantial surfaces of enclosures design their creations in terms of the affordances of those surface layouts: Walls, floors, doors, shelters, and paths are words we use to refer to what the human-built environment affords us. According to Gibson, these meaningful properties of the environment, although known tacitly, not explicitly, are primarily what is seen. The theory of affordances provides psychology with a detailed analysis of the different sorts of entities that animals may perceive, know, desire, and act upon. Objects are only one sort of environmentally meaningful entity, places and events are others; different still are the environmental facts of the self, its actions, ideas, intentions, and needs. All of these entities exist in the environment, and all can be perceived or known, either directly or indirectly. The great importance of the theory of affordances is in its constant reminder to us of the many kinds of things that are relevant to the behavior of animals, and therefore of the necessity of developing psychological theories that encompass these many different aspects of behavior and experience.

Perceiving the meaningful world and acting to change it are the fundamental psychological accomplishments of any creature. Gibson has shown us the rich information around us waiting to be used if only we will look, listen, and explore our surroundings. This ecological information supports meaningful activity because it specifies the affordances of things for our behavior. Information does not cause perception, nor do affordances cause action, but both are necessary for the achievements of perceiving and acting. Without information specifying the environment and specifying ourselves, we could not apprehend our environment or our place within it. Without an environment of objects and events that afford acting upon, we could do nothing. If we attend, we will perceive; and if we continue to attend, we will learn to perceive more acutely. If we act, there will be information for how to achieve our goals; and if we continue to act and to attend, we will learn how to accomplish our goals more effectively. Throughout his half-century-long career, Gibson's thoughtful and deep consideration of the perplexities of psychological theorizing and his careful attempts to resolve these problems greatly enriched psychology. Gibson's work not only offers profound insights into both animal and human behavior but also shows us what we must do and where we must look to learn even more about the ecological facts of animate behavior.

# 4.1 What is a Form?

## PART I: WHAT IS A FORM?*

The term *form* is used by different people to mean different things and by the same person to mean different things on different occasions. It can refer to the curved surfaces of a human female or the contours of a crankshaft, to a polyhedron or the style of a man's tennis game. *Shape, figure, structure, pattern, order, arrangement, configuration, plan, outline, contour* are similar terms without distinct meanings. This indefinite terminology is a source of confusion and obscurity for philosophers, artists, critics, and writers. It is an even more serious difficulty for scientists and psychologists. Ambiguity is excusable in the preliminary exploration and discussion of a problem, but it cannot be tolerated when a theory has reached the stage of experimental verification. A more rigorous terminology is very much needed. The psychological problem of how animals and men *perceive* form requires a definition of what it is that is perceived. Experiments in the field of form-perception and constancy of shape can only be decisive if one experimenter knows what the other is talking about.

When the environment of an individual is said to consist of objects, places, and events, a rough threefold classification of "formal" properties is suggested. One ordinarily applies the term *form* to an object, *arrangement* to a place, and *order* to an event. We might agree that the perception of a single object (one delimited by a surface), the perception of a set of objects (a region of space), and the perception of what happens to objects (movement and sequences in time) are

---

*Psychological Review*, 1951, 58, 403-413. Copyright 1951 by the American Psychological Association. Reprinted by permission.

three distinguishable problems each of which deserves a terminology of its own. The terminology with which this paper is concerned is the first.[1] The only kinds of visual form we shall undertake to deal with here are those associated with or derived from physical objects. Perhaps the simplest kind of shape is that embodied in an isolated object. If so, the effort at definition should begin with this kind.[2]

Even in this limited sense there seem to be at least three general meanings for the term form. There is first of all the substantial shape of an object in three dimensions. Second, there is the projection of such an object on a flat surface, either by light from the object or by the human act of drawing or the operation of geometrical construction. Images, pictures, drawings, and outlines are examples of form in this second sense. Third, there is the abstract geometrical form composed of imaginary lines, planes, or families of them. In this last sense of the term, form is said to be farthest removed from "substance." The reservation should be noted, however, that geometrical forms are presented to students as perfectly substantial black marks on white paper.

If one simply puts the question, How do we perceive form? without distinguishing between these three meanings of the term, a clear answer can hardly be given. Nevertheless, the problem of form-perception in psychology has usually been put in this way. What are the main solutions to the problem of form-perception? One kind of answer is to suppose that man simply has a form-sense. This is in effect no answer at all. It is still accepted, however, especially among ophthalmologists and physiologists. An alternative kind of answer is to assert that man somehow *learns* to perceive form. This answer is also widely accepted among some psychologists, although no one has been able to show just how this learning might occur. A third and more sophisticated answer is that of the Gestalt theorists who propose the general formula that the excitations on the retina are converted into forms by a process of organization in the brain, and who look to the general "laws of form" for an explanation of form-perception.[3] All these

---

[1]This terminology and analysis owes a great deal to the Gestalt static geometry of visual space, although it differs from that analysis in important respects (cf. Gibson, 1948; 1950a, Ch. 1). Gibson's later rejection of the hypothesis that space is perceived required a reconsideration of the definitions here put forward (see part 2 of this chapter). Gibson (1979a, Section 1) later developed an environmental physics of spatial layout using a different three-way distinction of surfaces, substances and media. Arrangement and form apply only to surfaces (cf. Chs. 1.8 and 3.4). (Eds.)

[2]There are, of course, many other formal properties of the environment even beyond those listed, such as the expression of a face, the composition of a painting, and the structure of a family. All these are unquestionably perceived, but they are so complex that the task of the psychologist is probably one of exploratory experiment rather than attempting to make exact definitions. Some psychologists in the tradition of phenomenology have tried to describe these higher-order varieties of form. The *overall* quality of a picture or a poem which makes it "good" would not be made any more intelligible, however, by imposing a terminology on critics of art and literature. The writer is only proposing that we be precise at a simple level where it may be profitable.

[3]The original laws of visual organization were formulated by Wertheimer (1923) on the basis of observations with spots, lines and outlines, and their implications were developed by Koffka (1935).

answers seem to take it for granted that a form is simply a form and that since everyone knows what the term means there is no need to specify it. Whether the form referred to is a physical thing or is an abstract property of a physical thing is not clear. Experimenters sometimes refer to *a form*, which implies that it is concrete, and at other times to the *form of a thing*, which implies that it is abstract. The only way to discover what they mean is to examine what they put in front of the observer's eyes during the experiments. In the vast majority of studies of form-perception it is artificial deposits of one or another sort on a paper surface. The theories of visual form, on the whole, have been based on evidence obtained with outline drawings.

It will be argued here that drawings are particularly inappropriate objects with which to begin a study of the perception of form. A drawing is a human production never found in a natural environment; it is complicated by being a thing with which men communicate with one another; it is not a simple presentation to sense-organs but a *representation* or a substitute-object. As a stimulus for perception it is convenient, but it is far from being the primary or fundamental stimulus which psychologists have usually taken it to be.

The reasons for supposing that the primary kind of form is a drawn form would make a long chapter in the history of scientific thought. A main reason, however, is the classical assumption that two-dimensional vision is immediate, primitive or sensory, while three-dimensional vision is secondary, derived, or perceptual. One must first see a plane form before one can see a solid form. This notion is connected with the argument that the three-dimensional properties of things can have no correlates in a two-dimensional retinal image, and that the three-dimensional properties must therefore be reconstructed by the mind or the brain. The writer has suggested elsewhere that this argument is a fallacy (Gibson, 1950a). So far from plane vision being primary and solid vision secondary, it is the other way around: There is overwhelming evidence to show that solid vision is primary and that plane vision is acquired only with training and by adopting a special attitude. The impression of a visual *world* may well prove to have a straightforward explanation; the impression of a visual *field*, however, is a very sophisticated kind of seeing and its explanation is far from being simple.[4]

It is possible to revise the traditional view that our visual sensations are two-dimensional and our perceptions are three-dimensional. When the doctrine is thus turned upside down it may appear strange on first insepction, but its intelligibility is much improved. The existing theories of form-perception aim first at two-dimensional form. If they fail to be convincing, the reason may be that three-dimensional impressions which have the property of shape are actually

---

The effort of Köhler (1940; Köhler & Wallach, 1944) to explain form-perception appears to be a search for laws of electrical current flow in the brain rather than laws of perceived form. Köhler believes, however, that these will ultimately prove to be the same, on the basis of his hypothesis of "isomorphism" between cortical process and phenomenal percept.

[4]See Boring (1952a,b) and Gibson (1952a) for discussions of the visual world and visual field concepts. (Eds.)

easier to account for than two-dimensional impressions which have the property of form. Perhaps the theories have been off on a false scent.

After a criticism as sweeping as the above, it is only fair to invite some return. A set of definitions and distinctions will therefore be proposed for the main types of visual form. If they are unacceptable, at least they will be clearly so. What are the various intelligible meanings that can be assigned to the term?

*1a. Solid Form.*   The closed physical surface enveloping a substance of some kind; the margin between two states of matter (usually between a solid and air). The surface may be curved or it may be composed of adjoining flat surfaces with edges; the former type can always be treated mathematically as a special case of the latter when the number of flat segments is very large. Organisms tend to have curved surfaces and to change their form with growth (Thompson, 1942); fabricated objects and a few natural objects like crystals tend to have adjoining flat faces and to resist transformation.

Objects have solid forms in the sense defined. When we perceive a detached object we also *see* a solid form—the depth, relief, or modelling of the surface. How we do so is a problem of long standing.

*1b. Surface Form.*   A flat physical surface with its edges; the face of an object (or one of the faces of a thin sheet of material such as paper). A surface-form always has an orientation which we shall term *slant*. Slant can be defined as the angle of inclination of the surface to the line of sight or, if preferred, to the axis of gravity (Gibson, 1950c).

Perceiving a surface-form involves perceiving both the slant of the surface and the form of its edges; an impression of form is never obtained without some accompanying impression of the angle at which the surface lies, either frontal or inclined. The problem of shape-constancy, so-called, is better formulated as the problem of seeing shape-at-a-slant.

If the modelling of a solid form is reducible to the varying slants of its faces, a solution for the problem of how we see slant ought to provide a solution for the problem of depth and relief. The slant of a surface is a physical variable which is simpler to define and easier to manipulate than is the modelling of an object.

*2a. Outline-Form.*   Physical tracings made with ink, pencil, or paint on a surface, which geometrically *represent* the edges of a surface-form or the margins of a solid form. These tracings have a finite thickness; they are drawn lines rather than the theoretical lines of geometry. They have two margins instead of the one margin exhibited by the edge of an object.

The perception normally aroused by an outline-form is quite unlike the outline itself. The paper surface is scarcely seen and a different surface seems to emerge within the outline. The paper surface appears to become "background" and to recede while the inclosed surface seems to take on "figural" qualities and to stand out (Koffka, 1935). This, however, is a sophisticated report. Most observers perceive an object and do not see tracings on a surface at all. When you press the question, however, they tell you that they do not literally see a physical object but a picture of it. Hence the perception is not like that of a solid form.[5]

*2b. Pictorial Form.*[6] Any representation of a physical object on a surface by drawing, rendering, painting, photography or other means. This would include outlines, silhouettes, plan-views, engineering drawings, and perspective drawings; it extends to transparencies, images projected on a screen, motion pictures and in short, to the vast variety of things we call pictures. One feature is generally to be found—a frame, usually rectangular, edging the surface on which the representation appears. A pictorial form is normally presented to the eyes with the surface perpendicular to the line of sight, that is, at a zero slant.

Some pictures represent other physical properties of an object in addition to the margins and surfaces of the object, such as color, texture, shading, and motion. A color photograph or a 16th century Dutch still-life are examples. If a sufficient numbers of variables has been incorporated in the deposits of pigment or dye on the surface, an instructive result may be achieved by an ingenious experimenter. He may fool an observer into believing he sees a real object instead of a picture. When it is carefully arranged that the picture is seen through an aperture so that the frame is invisible, the head is motionless, and only one eye is used, *the resulting perception may lose its representational character.* This may be termed a "peephole situation." In these circumstances, a pictorial form is equivalent to a solid form or, as we say, the observer has the illusion of reality.[7] It may be noted that his retinal image closely resembles the one he would have in an actual peephole situation with a solid form.[8] What this demonstration brings out is the fact, often forgotten, that a pictorial form *as ordinarily viewed* induces a quite different type of visual perception from that of a solid form.

Any pictorial form, including the special case of a simple outline form, has been defined as a representation of an object. We therefore need a definition of a representation. How is one made? The fundamental types are (a) the plan and (b) the perspective of a surface-form.

---

[5]A corollary of this definition is that the figure-ground phenomenon has been derived from the perception of outline-forms, not from a study of all forms or of all perception. The universality of the phenomenon as ordinarily described is therefore questionable. It is one of the most convincing tenets of Gestalt theory in its battle with elementarism but whether it will serve as the fundamental basis for a complete theory of perception is not so certain.

[6]The papers in Section 3 discuss various aspects of pictorial form and picture perception. (Eds.)

[7]This assumes that the viewing conditions for the solid form are exactly the same as those for the pictorial form. Such a situation can be set up experimentally, but is otherwise an unlikely occurrence (Hagen, Jones & Reed, 1978). For a critique of this image based account of pictorial perception, see Ch. 3.4. (Eds.)

[8]Other techniques of pictorial viewing which aim at the complete illusion of reality, notably stereoscopic movies, are impressive but fail to achieve this end. As long as the frame is visible, a picture will look like a picture.

*2c. Plan-Form.*   Outlines indicating the plan-projection or "plan-view" of the edges of a surface form. A plan-view is exemplified by an engineering drawing. It does not involve a transformation. The terms projection and transformation will be defined later.

*2d. Perspective-Form.*   Outlines indicating a perspective-projection or "perspective view" of the edges of a surface form. This always involves a transformation (relative compression or foreshortening). We say that such a drawing shows the object *in perspective.*

It is true that, after training, adults can visualize the perspective-form of an object they see without having a drawing or picture in front of them. This training is what enables artists to *make* perspective drawings without using special optical or geometrical tehniques. Children, in general, cannot do so. This ability to visualize a thing on a picture-plane is probably what lends plausibility to the unfortunate doctrine that we have sensations of form mediated by a "form-sense." The assumption is that the retinal image of a three-dimensional object is a perspective picture in two dimensions and that hence the resulting sensation must be a perspective-form in two dimensions. The doctrine is then faced with the knotty problem of how the sensation can be converted into a three-dimensional perception.

*2e. Nonsense-Form.*   Tracings on a surface (a pictorial form) which do not specifically represent (are not a projection of) a recognizable object. A drawing may be meaningless because (a) the projection is crude or inaccurate or (b) the tracings are accidental, like a child's scribble or the contours of an ink-blot, or (c) the tracings have a plan or system not *designed* to be a projection of a recognizable object. These latter are what modern artists often construct and call *abstract forms,* but they should be distinguished from the abstract geometrical forms to be defined later. They are also called non-objective forms or non-representational forms, and these terms are better. It should be noted that a drawing may also be meaningless for a quite different reason, because, although it is an accurate projection of an object, the object is not recognizable to the observer. Biological drawings and mathematical construction are often of such a nature.

The fact is that nonsense-forms are never nonsensical; they are never actually meaningless to an observer, but are simply unspecific or ambiguous. The perceiver discovers a succession of objects in the picture or, if not objects, then surfaces, edges, and fanciful constructions which are often aesthetically interesting.[9]

We come next to the genuinely abstract forms of geometry. They are certainly not substantial surfaces and edges although they are just as certainly connected with these things. They are also not tracings on paper, although they are represented or symbolized by such. They are in a class by themselves.

---

[9]Gibson (1951c, 1956) developed this point with reference to projective tests. (Eds.)

*3a. Plane Geometrical Form.*   An imaginary closed line on an imaginary plane. A geometrical line has no width and a geometrical plane has no thickness. A geometrical line is indicated or suggested by a substantial tracing on a substantial surface, but the two should not be confused. Geometrical lines and planes can be specified by the equations of analytic geometry more accurately than they can be drawn on paper. For the practised mathematician equations are often preferable to drawings. Geometrical forms are infinitely variable and only a very few special cases of them have names. Words like *triangle, rectangle, square, circle* stand for only the most familiar geometrical forms.

*3b. "Solid" Geometrical Form.*   An imaginary closed surface in an imaginary space of three dimensions. The forms of solid geometry are, of course, no more solid than the blue sky. They are the prototype of all ghosts. They are, in fact, the ghosts of objects just as planes are the ghosts of surfaces, lines the ghosts of edges, and points the ghosts of particles. We can conceive a geometrical form but we cannot see it in the same sense that we see an object, for the form is an abstract property of many objects.

*3c. Projection. Projected Form.*   A geometrical form on one plane which is in an exact correspondence with a form on another plane, the correspondence being defined as point-to-point or one-to-one. The relation between a form and its projection is physically exemplified by an object and its shadow (silhouette) or an object and its pinhole-image, that is to say by optics. If the planes of the two forms are parallel, the forms are geometrically similar or congruent, like scale-drawings or plan-views; if the planes are not parallel, one form is a perspective-transformation of the other.

Conceived thus, a given plane geometrical form is only one of an infinite set of perspective-transformations. The physically analogous fact is that when an objective surface-form is projected on another surface by light, the differing orientation of the form to the surface yields a set of different perspective-forms. The *psychologically* analogous fact, one might suppose, would be that when a surface-form is viewed at different angles of regard, the perceiver obtains a set of different perspective-impressions. The difficulty for psychology is that under ordinary circumstances he does not; instead he obtains a constant percept of the surface-form with a varying impression of slant.

## The Problem of Form-Perception

The above definitions provide a terminology which can now be applied. Returning to the original question of how we perceive form, the obvious reply must be, what *kind* of form? The question must be divided into three or more questions. Solid or surface forms, pictorial forms, and geometrical forms—these at least must be treated separately.

*Perceiving Surface-Forms.*    If the psychologist can explain how we see a given face of a solid object having a certain form at a certain slant, the explanation of how we see the whole object in three dimensions can be derived. This is the problem of shape-constancy. It has usually been assumed, in thinking about shape-constancy, that seeing a form without slant was simpler than seeing a form with slant. Since the retinal image is flat, there is supposed to be a retinal form, a two-dimensional form, or a "pattern-stimulus," which initiates the process of perception. But what could this retinal form possibly be? It is clearly neither a substantial form nor an abstract geometrical form. Perhaps it is a pictorial form—the "retinal picture" of commonsense psychology. Nothing, however, could be more mistaken. A picture is something to be looked at. The retinal image could only be a picture if there existed a perceiver behind the eye to look at it. The retinal image is none of the kinds of form defined; *it is in fact not a form at all*. It is a complex of variables of light-energy, definable in terms of steps and gradients but not in terms of physical edges, geometrical lines, or graphic outline (Gibson, 1950a). Ordinarily there is a dual complex of energy (a pair of images) on a bifurcated receptor-surface (a pair of retinas). We do not see our retinal images; we see an object, and the process is mediated by the images. The images as such may prove to be definable in terms of *order* (perhaps the kind of order exemplified by the number-series) but not *form*. The writer believes that the retinal images should be conceived as a kind of "ordinal stimulation" (Gibson, 1950a, Ch. 5).[10]

In order to understand the perceiving of a surface-form, therefore, the problem is to specify the variables of stimulation which elicit the perceived properties of the object—the slant of the surface together with the form of its edges. Both the surface and its edges are specifically given in retinal stimulation but they are not represented there. The pair of images is a correlate but not a copy of the object. The nearly constant appearance of these edges at differing slants in the case of ordinary naive perception will probably prove to be simply a by-product of the specifying of this stimulation. The dependence of phenomenal slant-shape upon the impression of slant may then be clarified.

*Perceiving Objects Mediated by Pictures.*    The question of what and how we see when we look at a picture of some kind is quite different from the question formulated above. The process of object-perception is surely simpler than the process of picture-perception. Despite the fact that men have been making drawings for thousands of years and during the past century have invented a variety of displays which our ancestors never dreamed of, we know very little

---

[10]In connection with the analysis of visual images in terms of variables, it is interesting to note that closed geometrical forms are variables when one considers their perspective transformations, and that different kinds of geometrical forms (*e.g.*, triangle, square, circle) can probably be specified in terms of variables, although little mathematical effort has been expended in this direction. (Eds: This is the origin of the ideas developed in Ch. 1.2).

about what happens within us when we see a picture. This much is certain, however. Pictures are *on* a surface whereas substantial objects *are* a surface. Moreover pictures *stand for* substantial objects in addition to *being* substantial objects. An outline-form, a painting, a photograph, or a radar screen-picture are each a sign of something else. What the observer ordinarily perceives is the object, place, or event represented, and this fact poses a special problem of perception.

Take for example an outline-form, *i.e.,* a line drawing on paper. It is almost impossible to avoid seeing the properties of a surface-form having edges which stand out from the background. This "piece of surface" may have a form and a slant quite different from the form of the tracings and the slant of the paper. This last fact is so important that an experimental demonstration of it is worth reporting.

The outline-forms illustrated, (Fig. 27) drawn on cards, were shown in succession to an observer with the instructions, "Tell me what you see *on the card.* Keep looking at it, and if what you see changes describe it also." For each card the verbal descriptions were recorded and later classified. Every 0 reported two or more perceptions within 60 seconds and some had as many as seven. Ten 0s were used.

At no time did any 0 describe anything like black deposits or marks or traces on a white surface. All the terms and phrases used fell into three other classes: *lines and angles, geometrical figures,* and *solid objects with physical surfaces.* The first two kinds were very infrequent; the great majority of terms referred to objects. Evidently what every 0 saw "on the card" was seen with what might be called the pictorial attitude. The physical objects reported were highly variable,

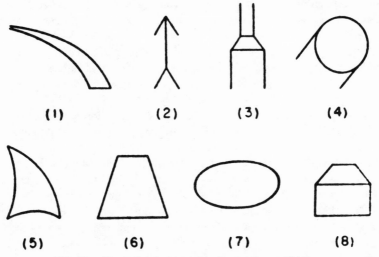

FIG. 27.   The outline forms used in the experiment. (Eds.)

differing from one 0 to another and successively for the same 0. They could be divided into two sub-classes: (1) objects for which the outline-form was a plan-view, and (2) objects for which it was a perspective-view. With only one or two exceptions, *every observer saw every outline-form in each of these two ways.* The first drawing could be a horn or a road curving up a hill, the second an arrow or a tent-roof, the fourth a pulley with rope or a cannon-muzzle, the sixth a truncated pyramid or a carpet on the floor, and so on. It is obvious that a single outline-form may elicit perceptions of two quite different solid forms. The form of a surface with its edges (*e.g.,* the carpet) may be very different from the outlines representing the edges of such a surface (*e.g.,* the trapezoid).

It should now be clear why outline drawings are not appropriate stimulus-objects with which to begin the study of form-perception. They are habitually taken to stand for something other than what they are and, more important, what they stand for is often equivocal. An outline, representing as it does only the edges of a surface, may stand for any *object which projects that particular outline,* including some very queerly shaped surfaces. For instance, a given trapezoid, or a trapezoidal pencil of light-rays, may stand for a square at a given slant but it may also stand for any of an infinite set of different trapezoids at other different slants. Conceiving the matter in this way, it is only to be expected that the perceiving of outline-forms is fluid, changeable, and seems to have a spontaneous character. The perceptions they arouse are unstable because they are equivocal representations. It is not necessary to infer that the stimulus-distribution is unstable, nor to suppose that it moves in the direction of equilibrium or "good form." Nearly all the research on form-perception has utilized outline-drawings as stimuli. If it be granted that these are actually *pictures of forms,* the research is irrelevant to the problem. A genuine psychophysics of form-perception will have to deal with "shape-slant," *i.e.,* with transformations of form which co-vary with degrees of slant. In contrast with an outline drawing, a pair of retinal images of the usual sort contains stimulus-variables for the perception of slant (Gibson, 1950c). Only in "peephole situations" are these stimulus-variables so impoverished that the perception of slant becomes ambiguous.

*Visualizing Geometrical Forms.*    To the question of how we perceive form in the third general meaning of the term, the answer is probably that geometrical forms are not perceived at all. Geometrical forms have no stimuli or, more exactly, are not in psychophysical correspondence with stimuli. They are not seen directly like substantial forms, or indirectly like represented substantial forms, but instead are conceived or abstracted from innumerable past seeings of both. Not much is known about the process of abstraction or concept-formation, but it is fairly certain that a child can identify a simple object at a very early age, a represented object at a later age, and a concept at only a much later age. The geometrical forms we are talking about are conceptual or general. It must be remembered that the geometrical triangle referred to in a theorem is a triangle in general, not just the particular form in the geometry textbook.

What kind of forms *are* the drawings in the textbooks then? One might be tempted to say they are pictorial forms, but this would not be strictly correct. Outline-forms do not represent geometrical forms in the way that they represent the edges of surface-forms, or objects. A geometrical drawing may be said to signify a whole set of projective transformations. A set of transformations is even more ghostly than a single geometrical form. An outline taken in this sense is more nearly a symbol than it is a picture. The relationship of *standing for* is more dependent on an arbitrary convention, and therefore on learning, than it is in the case of a picture. Consequently an outline-form presented to an observer without any other indications of the object represented is even more ambiguous than it was made out to be in the last section. In addition to being equivocal as a picture, it is a symbol for a bevy of geometrical ghosts. To assume that it constitutes a simple "stimulus" for perception is completely misleading.

*Patterns and Textures as Distinguished from Forms.* The term pattern has so far neither been used nor defined. In psychological usage it seems to refer to (1) a group or arrangement of single objects, or (2) a group of artificial traces on a surface, such as the patterns used to exemplify Wertheimer's laws of visual organization, or (3) a group of natural inhomogeneities on a surface. In the latter meaning, a pattern passes over into being a *texture*. The latter term, in the writer's opinion, should mean an arrangement of visible particles not *on* but *in* a surface—the visible structure of a surface itself. This is important because of the possibility that the optically corresponding texture of the retinal image of the surface is the adequate stimulus-condition (or one of the stimulus-conditions) for the impression of the surface (Gibson, 1950c). The writer has suggested that the impression of a surface is essential for the perception of determinate visual space (Gibson, 1950a). The interrelationships between visual acuity, visual texture, surface-perception, and space-perception remain to be defined.

The first and second meanings of the term pattern—a grouping or arrangement—need definition and analysis as much as any of the others, but the task is beyond the scope of this paper. So also do "structure," "sequence" and the higher order varieties of *Gestalten*. The feeling of mystery that attaches to all such words ought to be dispelled, because they will be even more interesting when comprehended.

*Conclusions.* A number of explicit definitions of visual forms have been proposed out of a conviction that psychologists should come down to earth and say exactly what they mean when they talk about form. The suggestion was made that the kind of forms heretofore studied—pen or pencil tracings—is artificial, and as a type of stimulus for perception is equivocal. Such forms are either projections of disembodied edges or symbols for ghostly abstractions. The forms we need to investigate first are embodied in chunks of physical surface. The kind of form for which there exists an unequivocal stimulus is a form imbedded in a surface—that is to say, a shape-at-a-slant. When a form is not imbedded in a surface (and when, as a result, contour-stimulation is not accompanied by surface-stimulation) the resulting percept is ambiguous. Since the slant of the presumed surface is equivocal, the form is also equivocal, and what the observer sees is open to the influence of assumed probabilities, clues, unconscious inferences, the standards of past experience, or the social norms of group life. Since nearly all the experimental research on form-perception has been performed with outline-stimulation alone, we are tempted to conclude that *all* form-perception depends on probabilities, inferences, and norms—in other words, on subjective factors. This conclusion is unwarranted. Important as these factors no doubt are, the primary problem for psychologists is to isolate the invariant properties in visual stimulation which are in psychophysical correspondence with constant phenomenal objects. According to the proposed definitions *solid* forms and *surface*-forms are realities. *Outline*-forms and also *pictorial-, plan-, perspective-,* and *nonsense*-forms are representations which the perceiver takes to stand for realities. For these a special theory of picture-perception is required. *Geometrical* forms, both *plane* and *solid,* are abstractions which cannot even be represented, strictly speaking, but can only be specified by symbols. If the definitions are accepted, there is no such thing as form-in-general with the universal characteristics ascribed to it by Gestalt theorists. None of the above forms is a whole which is different from its parts. None is organized in any special sense. None is in the least dynamic. It is possible to understand, however, why these characteristics have been ascribed to visual *Gestalten.* The reason is probably that we have studied only the disembodied varieties of form—*i.e.* ghost shapes—which are ambiguous representations or equivocal symbols, and which consequently yield fluid, variable, or inconsistent percepts.

If such be the case, the effort to determine what happens in the brain when one perceives form-in-general will prove to be fruitless. Theories such as those of Köhler (1940, Köhler & Wallach, 1944) and, more recently, Hebb (1949) seem to be efforts of this sort. At least three separate levels of theory will be required: first, a theory of how we perceive the surfaces of objects—a theory of slant-shape or, in older words, of shape-constancy; second, a theory of how we perceive representations, pictures, displays, and diagrams; and third, a theory of how we apprehend symbols. There is no reason to suppose that the physiological concomitants of all these experiences will be the same; in fact, since pictures and symbols presuppose objects, their physiological explanations will probably have to be found at increasing levels of complexity. When these three levels of theory have been developed, the category of "form-perception" in psychology will have evaporated.

## PART II: TOWARD A NOMENCLATURE OF FORM, PATTERN AND SHAPE*

This note is a revision of a proposed set of earlier definitions (Gibson, 1951a) aimed to improve communication. It is based on the discussion of the term *image* in Ch. 11 of *The Senses Considered as Perceptual Systems*, 1966b. Ten definitions are offered for various types of *form*, of *pattern*, and of *shape*. At least this number of distinct meanings seems required.

### Form

1. *Pictorial* form (including *drawn* form, *outline* form, *painted* form). This consists of tracings or deposits on a relatively smooth surface. Such a form can be registered by vision but not by touch; it is a graphic display. It may or may not be a representation (cf. Gombrich, 1961).
2. *Surface* form. This is the flat face of a substantial object (polyhedron) as determined by its edges (dihedral angles). It is a source of optical stimulation when the face is illuminated and of mechanical stimulation (touch) whether or not it is illuminated. We say that the form can either be seen or touched (felt).
3. *Perspective* form. This is an abstraction from perspective geometry and the theory of representation. It is not a source of stimulation at all; it is not perceptible by either vision or touch; it exists only in an *optic array*. But it has been taken to imply a "retinal" form which arouses a "sensation" of form. A special case among perspective forms is the *frontal* form (when the face of an object is perpendicular to the line of sight).[11]
4. *Geometrical* form. This is an even further mathematical abstraction, the ghostly shape exemplified by the triangle, square, circle, etc. It must be depicted by tracings on a surface if any stimulation is to occur. Nevertheless, human children are trained to visualize and name such forms in the absence of depiction, and the resulting tendency to reify them is a cause of confusion.

### Pattern

5. *Texture* pattern. This should be understood to mean the arrangement of the small parts of a material surface, or the "composition" of the surface. The pigment composition of a *smooth* surface is given only in light to an eye; the structural composition of a *rough* surface is given both to the eye and to the exploring hand.
6. *Optical* pattern (or optical *texture*). This is the relatively fine structure of the optic array. Optical texture is not to be confused with material composition,

---

*Unpublished manuscript, October, 1967.
[11]See Chs. 3.2 and 3.3 for more on perspective. (Eds.)

although it contains a great deal of *information about* the surface and its composition. Optical texture is generally not experienced as such in the way that optical form (perspective) is said to be experienced as a sensation.

7. *Spot* pattern. This is an ambiguous term. It can mean either an array of *luminous* spots (as from the night sky) resulting in patterned visual sensations but an indefinite perception, or it can mean an array of *surface* spots which yields a direct perception of the surface and also the pattern of spots. When the arrangement of spots as such is attended to, a variety of semi-perceptual experiences will arise, e.g. the phenomena of grouping or clustering as studied by *Gestalt* theorists. With a graphic array of spots and strokes a variety of *coded* patterns can be established for associative learning (e.g. letters and symbols). The resulting percepts are properly called *mediated* as distinguished from *direct*.[12]

## Shape

The term *shape* can be used as synonymous with *form,* but it will not be so used here. It is here understood as three-dimensional.

8. *Solid* shape. This is the arrangement of the enveloping surfaces of an object. If the outer skin consists of *flat* surfaces, the object can be analyzed as a polyhedron with adjacent faces (surface forms). If the skin consists of *curved* surfaces, it can be analyzed in terms of concavities, convexities, and saddles. Such a shape can be perceived visually only over time (the object being *turned* around or the the observer having to *move* around) and the information for this perception is presumably the optical invariants under perspective transformations.[13] It can be haptically perceived all at once insofar as it can be *grasped* otherwise it must be perceived over time by exploratory feeling, presumably by *mechanical* invariants of haptic touch. Note that a polyhedral object as defined here is not to be confused with a ghostly geometrical polyhedron, nor is a curved object to be confused with the ideal surfaces of *conics*.

9. *Transparent* solid shape. A special case in which all edges (dihedral angles) of both front and back faces are projected in the optic array. Whenever there is binocular disparity or optical motion (or both) the solid shape is detectable; otherwise it is ambiguous (as in wire figures or line drawings representing wire figures).

10. *Empty* solid shape. The arrangement (layout) of the *interspace* (medium) between reflecting surfaces; an *enclosure* (e.g. a room). When large, this constitutes the visible and tangible *environment* of an observer.[14]

---

[12] Cf. Ch. 3.6 and Gibson (1979a, pp. 258–263). (Eds.)
[13] Cf. Ch. 1.2. (Eds.)
[14] Cf. Ch. 4.9, Part 8. (Eds.)

# 4.2 Perceptual Learning: Differentiation or Enrichment?

## PART I: PERCEPTUAL LEARNING: DIFFERENTIATION OR ENRICHMENT?*

The term "perceptual learning" means different things to different psychologists. To some it implies that human perception is, in large part, learned—that we learn to see depth, for instance, or form, or meaningful objects. In that case the theoretical issue involved is *how much* of perception is learned, and the corresponding controversy is that of nativism or empiricism. To others the term implies that human learning is in whole or part a matter of perception—that learning depends on comprehension, expectation, or insight, and that the learning process is to be found in a central process of cognition rather than in a motor process of performance. In this second case, the theoretical issue involved is whether or not one has to study a man's perceptions before one can understand his behavior, and the controversy is one of long standing which began with old-fashioned behaviorism.

These two sets of implications are by no means the same, and the two problems should be separated. The problem of the role of learning in perception has to do with perception and the effect of past experience or practice on it. The problem of the role of perception in learning has to do with behavior and the question of whether we can learn to do something by perceiving, or whether we can only learn by doing it. The questions, then, are these: (*a*) In what sense do we learn to perceive? (*b*) In what sense can we learn by perceiving? Both questions are important for the practical problems of education and training, but this paper will be concerned with the former.

---

*Psychological Review, 1955, 62,* 32–41. Copyright 1955 by the American Psychological Association. Reprinted by permission. This paper was written with Eleanor J. Gibson.

## IN WHAT SENSE DO WE LEARN TO PERCEIVE?

This question has roots in philosophy and was debated long before experimental psychology came of age. Does all knowledge (information is the contemporary term) come through the sense organs or is some knowledge contributed by the mind itself? Inasmuch as sensory psychology has been unable to explain how as much information about the world as we manifestly do obtain is transmitted by the receptors, some theory is required for this unexplained surplus. There has been a variety of such theories ever since the days of John Locke. An early notion was that the surplus is contributed by the rational faculty (rationalism). Another was that it comes from innate ideas (nativism). In modern times there have been few adherents to these positions. The most popular theory over the years has been that this supplement to the sensations is the result of learning, and that it comes from past experience. A contemporary formula for this explanation is that the brain stores information—possibly in the form of traces or memory images but conceivably as attitudes, or mental sets, or general ideas, or concepts. This approach has been called empiricism. It preserves the dictum that all knowledge comes from experience by assuming that past experience somehow gets *mixed with* present experience. It assumes, in other words, that experience *accumulates,* that traces of the past somehow exist in our perception of the present. One of its high-water marks was Helmholtz's theory of unconscious inference, which supposes that we learn to see depth by interpreting the clues furnished by the depthless sensations of color. Another was Titchener's context theory of meaning, which asserts that we learn to perceive objects when a core of sensations acquires by association a context of memory images.

Over a generation ago this whole line of thought was challenged by what seemed to be a different explanation for the discrepancy between the sensory input and the finished percept—the theory of sensory organization. The gestalt theorists made destructive criticisms of the notion of *acquired* linkages among sensory elements and their traces. Instead they asserted that the linkages were *intrinsic,* or that they arose *spontaneously,* taking visual forms as their best example. Perception and knowledge, they said, were or came to be *structured.*

The theory of sensory organization or cognitive structure, although it generated a quantity of experimentation along new lines, has not after 30 years overthrown the theory of association. In this country the old line of empiricist thinking has begun to recover from the critical attack, and there are signs of a revival. Brunswik (1952, pp. 23 ff.) has followed from the start the line laid down by Helmholtz. Ames and Cantril and their followers have announced what might be called a neoempiricist revelation (Cantril, Ames, Hastorf, & Ittelson, 1949; Ittelson, 1951; Kilpatrick, 1952). Other psychologists are striving for a theoretical synthesis which will include the lessons of gestalt theory but retain the notion that perception is learned. Tolman, Bartlett, and Woodworth began the trend.

Leeper (1935) took a hand in it at an early date. The effort to reconcile the principle of sensory organization with the principle of determination by past experience has recently been strenuously pursued by Bruner (1951) and by Postman (1951). Hilgard (1951) seems to accept both a process of organization governed by relational structure and a process of association governed by the classical laws. Hebb (1949) has recently made a systematic full-scale attempt to combine the best of gestalt theory and of learning theory at the physiological level. What all these theorists seem to us to be saying is that the organization process and the learning process are not inconsistent after all, that both explanations are valid in their way, and that there is no value in continuing the old argument over whether learning is really organization or organization is really learning. The experiments on this issue (beginning with the Gottschaldt experiment)[1] were inconclusive, and the controversy itself was inconclusive. Hence, they argue, the best solution is to agree with both sides.

It seems to us that all extant theories of the perceptual process, including those based on association, those based on organization, and those based on a mixture of the two (including attitudes, habits, assumptions, hypotheses, expectation, images, contexts, or inferences) have at least this feature in common: they take for granted a discrepancy between the sensory input and the finished percept and they aim to explain the difference. They assume that somehow we get more information about the environment than can be transmitted through the receptor system. In other words, they accept the distinction between sensation and perception. The development of perception must then necessarily be one of supplementing or interpreting or organizing.

Let us consider the possibility of rejecting this assumption altogether. Let us assume tentatively that the stimulus input contains within it everything that the percept has. What if the flux of stimulation at receptors *does* yield all the information anyone needs about the environment?[2] Perhaps all knowledge comes through the senses in an even simpler way than John Locke was able to conceive—by way of variations, shadings, and subtleties of energy which are properly to be called stimuli.

---

[1]Gottschaldt (1929) contrasted the effects of past experience (in the form of repetition) with the role of organization (e.g., good form for figures) on the perception of form. In some cases, observers' expectations for seeing hidden parts of a figure did not show any systematic relation to frequency of presentation, but were instead influenced by organizational factors. As Gibson (1941a, pp. 790–791) pointed out, these results argue against the importance of past experience in current perception only on the assumption that set (here, expectation) itself is not the product of past experience. This is why the controversy was inconclusive: neither proponents nor opponents of empiricism were able to specify what should count as an experiential factor in perception. (Eds.)

[2]In Chs. 1.5 and 1.6 it is explained why this formulation is incorrect; stimulation of receptors is not the same thing as information for a perceptual system (cf. Ch. 4.4; Gibson, 1966b, pp. 1–7, 31–44). (Eds.)

## THE ENRICHMENT THEORY VERSUS THE SPECIFICITY THEORY[3]

The entertaining of this hypothesis faces us with two theories of perceptual learning which are clear rather than vague alternatives. It cuts across the schools and theories, and presents us with an issue. Is perception a creative process or is it a discriminative process? Is learning a matter of enriching previously meager sensations or is it a matter of differentiating previously vague impressions? On the first alternative we might learn to perceive in this sense: that percepts change over time by acquiring progressively more memory images, and that a context of memories accrues by association to a sensory core. The theorist can substitute attitudes or inferences or assumptions for images in the above Titchenerian proposition, but perhaps all this does is to make the theory less neat while making the terminology more fashionable. In any case perception is progressively in *decreasing correspondence with stimulation*. The latter point is notable. Perceptual learning, thus conceived, necessarily consists of experience becoming more imaginary, more assumptive, or more inferential. The dependence of perception on learning seems to be contradictory to the principle of the dependence of perception on stimulation.

On the second alternative we learn to perceive in this sense: that percepts change over time by progressive elaboration of qualities, features, and dimensions of variation; that perceptual experience even at the outset consists of a world, not of sensation, and that the world gets more and more properties as the objects in it get more distinctive; finally, that the phenomenal properties and the phenomenal objects correspond to physical properties and physical objects in the environment *whenever learning is successful*. In this theory perception gets richer in differential responses, not in images. It is progressively in *greater* correspondence with stimulation, not in less. Instead of becoming more imaginary it becomes more discriminating. Perceptual learning, then, consists of responding to variables of physical stimulation not previously responded to. The notable point about this theory is that learning is always supposed to be a matter of improvement—of getting in closer touch with the environment. It consequently does not account for hallucination or delusions or, in fact, for any kind of maladjustment.[4]

The latter kind of theory is certainly worth exploring. It is not novel, of course, to suggest that perceptual development is a matter of differentiation. As phenomenal description this was asserted by some of the gestalt psychologists, notably Koffka and Lewin. (Just how differentiation was related to organization,

---

[3]This contrast between enrichment and specificity (differentiation) theories of perceptual learning is strikingly paralleled by Popper's (1963) later, but independently developed, distinction between the "bucket" and the "searchlight" theories of the sources of knowledge. (Eds.)

[4]For these cases, see Gibson (1966b, Ch. 14; 1970b; 1979a, pp. 243-245). (Eds.)

however, was not clear.) What *is* novel is to suggest that perceptual development is always a matter of the correspondence between stimulation and perception—that it is strictly governed by the relationships of the perceiver to his environment. The rule would be that, as the number of distinct percepts a man can have increases, so also the number of different physical objects to which they are specific increases. An example may clarify this rule. One man, let us say, can identify sherry, champagne, white wine, and red wine. He has four percepts in response to the total possible range of stimulation. Another man can identify a dozen types of sherry, each with many varieties, and numerous blends, and so on for the others. He has four thousand percepts in response to the range of stimulation. The crucial question to ask about this example of differentiated perception is its relation to stimulation.

Stimulus is a slippery term in psychology.[5] Properly speaking stimulation is always energy at receptors, that is, proximal stimulation. An individual is surrounded by an array of energy and immersed in a flow of it. This sea of stimulation consists of variation and invariants, patterns and transformations, some of which we know how to isolate and control and others of which we do not. An experimenter chooses or constructs a sample of this energy when he performs a psychological experiment. But it is easy for him to forget this fact and to assume that a glass of wine is a stimulus when actually it is a complex of radiant and chemical energies which is the stimulus. When the psychologist refers to stimuli as cues, or clues, or carriers of information he is skipping lightly over the problem of how stimuli come to *function* as cues. Energies do not have cue properties unless and until the differences in energy have correspondingly different effects in perception. The total range of physical stimulation is very rich in complex variables and these are theoretically capable of becoming cues and constituting information. This is just where learning comes in.[6]

All responses to stimulation, including perceptual responses, manifest some degree of specificity, and, inversely, some degree of nonspecificity. The gentleman who is discriminating about his wine shows a high specificity of perception, whereas the crude fellow who is not shows a low specificity. A whole class of chemically different fluids is equivalent for the latter individual; he can't tell the difference between claret, burgundy, and chianti; his perceptions are relatively undifferentiated. What has the first man learned that the second man has not? Associations? Memories? Attitudes? Inferences? Has he learned to have perceptions instead of merely sensations? Perhaps, but a simpler statement might be made. The statement is that he has learned to taste and smell more of the qualities of wine, that is, he discriminates more of the variables of chemical stimulation. If he is a genuine connoisseur and not a fake, one combination of such variables can

---

[5]Cf. Ch. 4.3. (Eds.)

[6]For a clarification of the difference between energy as stimulation and energy as stimulus information, see Chs. 1.3, 1.4, 4.3, 4.4 and also Gibson (1979a, pp. 55–58). (Eds.)

evoke a specific response of naming or identifying and another combination can evoke a different specific response. He can consistently apply nouns to the different fluids of a class and he can apply adjectives to the differences between the fluids.

The classical theory of perceptual learning, with its emphasis on subjective determination of perception in contrast to stimulus determination, gets its plausibility from experiments on errors in form perception, from the study of illusions and systematic distortions, and from the fact of individual differences in and social influences on perception.[7] The learning process is assumed to have occurred in the past life of the experimental subject; it is seldom controlled by the experimenter. These are *not* learning experiments insofar as they do not control practice or take measures before and after training. True perceptual learning experiments are limited to those concerned with discrimination.

One source of evidence about discriminative learning comes from the study of the cues for verbal learning. The analysis of these cues made by one of the authors in terms of stimulus generalization and differentiation (E. Gibson, 1940) suggests the present line of thought. It has also led to a series of experiments concerned with what we call *identifying responses*. Motor reactions, verbal reactions, or percepts, we assume, are identifying responses if they are in specific correspondence with a set of objects or events. Code learning (Keller, 1943), aircraft recognition (Gibson, 1947), and learning to name the faces of one's friends are all examples of an increasingly specific correspondence between the items of stimulation presented and the items of response recorded. As a given response gains univocality, the percept is reported to gain in the feeling of familiarity or recognition and to acquire meaning.

## AN ILLUSTRATIVE EXPERIMENT[8]

In order to provide a clear example of such learning, we studied the development of a single identifying response. The S was presented with a visual item consisting of a nonsense "scribble"; his recognition of it was tested when it was interspersed in a series of similar scribbles, and then the single showing and the multiple presentation were repeated until the item could be identified. We devised a set of 17 scribbles intended to be indistinguishable from the critical item on the first trial, and another set of 12 items intended to be distinguishable from the critical item on the first trial.

---

[7]Gibson (1951b) discusses this literature at greater length. (Eds.)

[8]This experiment was first reported at the meeting of the American Psychological Association in September 1950 in a paper read by Eleanor J. Gibson, and an abstract has been published (Gibson & Gibson, 1950). (Eds.: Experiments that further developed these ideas may be found in Gibson, Gibson, Pick & Osser, 1962 and Pick, 1965).

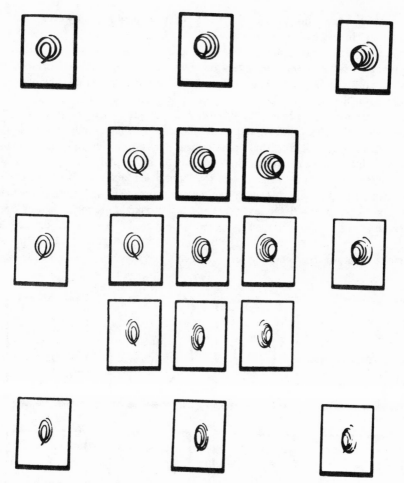

FIG. 28.   Nonsense items differing in three dimensions of variation.

The items which had to be differentiated are shown in Figure 28. The critical item, a four-coil scribble, is in the center and 16 other items are arranged outward from it. The eighteenth item (a reversal of the critical item) is not shown. It may be noted that there are three dimensions of variation from the critical item: (a) number of coils—three, four, or five, (b) horizontal compression or stretching, and (c) orientation or right-left reversal. The latter two kinds of variation were produced by photographic transformation. There are three degrees of coil frequency, three degrees of compression, and two types of orientation, which yields 18 items. Since one of these is the critical item, 17 remain for use in the experiment. The reader may observe that when these differences are verbally specified and the figures are displayed for immediate comparison, as in Figure

28, they are clearly distinguishable. The Ss of the experiment, however, saw the items only in succession.

The 12 additional items presented on each recognition trial are shown in Figure 29. Each differs from every other and from all of the set of 18. The differences from the scribbles were intended to be sufficient to make them appear different at the outset to Ss with a normal amount of experience with drawn forms. The 30 items (12 plus 18) were printed photographically on stiff 2 in. × 4 in. cards with black borders, and made into a pack. The material available for any one learning trial consisted of the critical item plus a shuffled pack of cards among which were interspersed four replicas of the critical item.

The S was shown the critical item for about 5 sec. and told that some of the items in the pack would be exactly like the one shown. The series of 34 was then presented each with a 3-sec. exposure and S was asked to report which of them were the same figure. The identifying response recorded was any report such as "that's it" or "this is the one I saw before." The S was never told whether an identification was correct or incorrect. A record was kept not only of the identify-

FIG. 29.  Nonsense items differing in many dimensions of variation.

ing responses, but also of any spontaneous *descriptions* offered by S, which were later classified as *naming* responses and *qualifying* responses.

At the end of the first trial the critical figure was presented a second time and another shuffled pack was run through. The procedure of examining a figure and then trying to identify it when mixed with a series including figures of both great and little similarity was continued until S made only the four correct identifications in one trial. Three groups took part in the experiment: 12 adults, 10 older children (8½ to 11 years), and 10 younger children (6 to 8 years).

*Results.* In this experiment, learning is taken to be an increase in the specificity of an identifying response or, in other words, a decrease in the size of the class of items that will elicit the response. The data therefore consist of the number of items (out of a probable maximum of 17) reacted to as if they were the critical figure. As will be evident, this class of undifferentiated items was reduced as a result of repetition. The three groups of Ss, however, began to learn at very different levels and learned at very different rates. The results are given in Table 1. For adults, the class of undifferentiated items at the outset was small (Mean=3.0), and only a few trials were needed before this class was reduced to the critical item alone (Mean=3.1). Two of these adults were able to make no other than correct identifying responses on the first trial. Both were psychologists who could have had previous acquaintance with nonsense figures. The learning task was so easy for this group that not much information about the learning process could be obtained. At the other extreme, however, the younger children "recognized" nearly all of the scribbles on the first trial (Mean=13.4), which is to say the class of undifferentiated items was large. The number of trials needed

TABLE 1
Increase in Specificity of an Identifying Response for Three Age Groups

| Variable | Adults (N = 12) | Older Children (N = 10) | Younger Children (N = 10) |
|---|---|---|---|
| Mean number of undifferentiated items on first trial | 3.0 | 7.9 | 13.4 |
| Mean number of trials required for completely specific response | 3.1 | 4.7 | 6.7* |
| Percentage of erroneous recognitions for items differing in *one* quality | 17 | 27 | 53 |
| Percentage of erroneous recognitions for items differing in *two* qualities | 2 | 7 | 35 |
| Percentage of erroneous recognitions for items differing in *three* qualities | 0.7 | 2 | 28 |

*Only two of the younger children achieved a completely specific identification. The mean number of undifferentiated items on the last trial was still 3.9.

to reduce this class to the correct item was so great that most of the Ss could not be required to complete the experiment. Two out of 10 reached the criterion, but for the remainder the trials had to be stopped for reasons of fatigue. After an average of 6.7 trials the mean number of undifferentiated items was still 3.9. One child had so much difficulty with the task that E finally gave differential reinforcement by saying "right" or "wrong" after each presentation of a card. Although this procedure helped, wholly specific identifications were never achieved. The failures of the younger children to discriminate did not seem to be due merely to "inattention"; they understood that they were to select only the figures which were *exactly* the same as the critical figure.

For the older children (between 8½ and 11 years of age) the results were intermediate between these extremes. For them the particular task and the particular items were neither too hard nor too easy. The average number of undifferentiated items on the first trial was 7.9, and all children succeeded in reducing this to a single item after a mean of 4.7 trials.

Table 1 also indicates for each group an important fact about the unspecific responses: they tend to occur more often as the differences between the test item and the critical item become fewer. As Figure 28 shows, a given scribble may differ in *one* quality or dimension (thickness, coil frequency, or orientation), or in *two* of these qualities, or in all *three* of them. Five of the scribbles differ in one feature, eight differ in two features, and four differ in three features. It will be recalled that the 12 additional forms shown in Figure 29 differed from the critical item with respect to *more* than three features. Amount of difference can be usefully stated as number of differing qualities or, conversely, amount of sameness as the fewness of differing qualities.[9] The lower half of Table 1 gives the percentage of occurrence of false recognitions in the case of scribbles with one quality different, with two qualities different, and with three qualities different. These percentages are based on the number of times the items in question were presented during the whole series of trials. The "dissimilar" figures, which had many qualities different, yielded a zero percentage of false recognitions except for a few scattered instances among the younger children.

*Discussion.*    The results show clearly that the kind of perceptual learning hypothesized has occurred in this experiment. A stimulus item starts out by being indistinguishable from a whole class of items in the stimulus universe tested, and ends by being distinguishable from all of them. The evidence for this assertion is that the specificity of S's identifying response has increased. What has happened to produce this result?

The Ss were encouraged to describe all the items of each series as they were

---

[9]Experiments on primary stimulus generalization have usually varied the magnitude of a *single* difference, not the number of differences, between the critical stimulus and the undifferentiated stimulus. However, our method of quantifying "amount of difference" has much to recommend it.

presented, and a special effort was made to obtain and record these spontaneous verbal responses for seven of the older children. In general they tended to fall into two types, either naming responses or qualifying responses. Considering only the responses to the 17 scribbles, the record showed that the frequency of the latter type increased during the progress of learning. Examples of the former are nouns like *figure 6, curl, spiral, scroll*. Examples of the latter are adjectival phrases like *too thin, rounder, reversed*. It is notable that the latter are responses not to the item as such but to the relation between it and the critical item. They are analogous to differential judgments in a psychophysical experiment. An adjective, in general, is a response which is specific not to an object but to a property of two or more objects. It is likely, then, that the development of a specific response to an item is correlated with the development of specific responses to the qualities, dimensions, or variables that relate it to other items. The implication is that, for a child to identify an object, he must be able to identify the differences between it and other objects, or at least that *when* he can identify an object he *also* can identify its properties.

The verbal reactions of the children to the 17 scribbles, both naming and qualifying, could be categorized by E as specific or nonspecific to the item in question. These judgments were necessarily subjective, but they were carried out with the usual precautions. Although a single adjective cannot be specific to a single item, a combination of adjectives can be. An example of a nonspecific reaction is "another curlicue," and of a specific reaction is "this one is thinner and rounder." The latter sort may be considered a spontaneously developing identifying reaction, not of the "that's it" type, it is true, but nevertheless fulfilling our definition. The mean number of such verbal reactions on the first trial was 7.7 out of 17, or 45 per cent. The mean number of such reactions on the last trial was 16.5, or 97 per cent. This suggests that, as a single identifying response becomes increasingly specific to one member of a group of similar items, verbal identifying responses also tend to become specific to the other members of the group. As the class of indistinguishable items which will elicit one response is diminished, the number of responses which can be made to the class increases.

## OTHER EVIDENCE

Another source of experimental evidence about perceptual learning comes from psychophysics. Contrary to what might be expected, psychophysical experimenters over the years have shown a lively interest in perceptual learning, or at least in the bettering of perceptual judgments with practice. One of the authors has recently surveyed this neglected literature insofar as it concerns improvement of perception or increase in perceptual skills (E. J. Gibson, 1953). There is a great quantity of evidence about progressive change in acuity, variability, and accuracy of perception, including both relative judgments and absolute judgments. It proves beyond a shadow of doubt that the notion of fixed thresholds for a certain set of innate sensory dimensions is oversimplified. Discrimination gets better with practice, both with and without knowledge of results. An example may be taken from the two-point threshold on the skin.

As long ago as 1858 it was discovered that there is a certain distance at which two points are felt double by a blind-folded subject that is characteristic of the area of the skin tested. At the same time, it was found that only a few hours of practice in this discrimination had the effect of reducing the distance to half of what it had been (Volkmann, 1858). Later experiments showed that the lowering of the threshold continued slowly for thousands of trials; for instance, it might go from 30 mm. to 5 mm. during four weeks of training. Moreover, the improved discrimination transferred to other untrained areas of the skin, transfer being nearly complete for the bilaterally symmetrical area. It was found that blind subjects had very much lower thresholds than seeing subjects even at the beginning of testing (Jastrow, 1894; Whipple, 1924). The experimental improvement was largely lost after a period of disuse. It seemed to depend on confirmation or correction of the judgment, or, in the absence of that, on the development of a sort of scale from "close together" to "far apart" (E. J. Gibson, 1953). It is clear that any theory of supposedly distinct sensations of oneness and twoness never had any support from these data. As one writer put it, the observer adopts different and finer *criteria* of doubleness. What might these criteria be? We suggest that the stimulation is complex, not simple, and that the observer continues to discover higher-order variables of stimulation in it. The percept becomes differentiated.

## CONCLUSION

There is no evidence in all of this literature on perceptual learning, nor is there evidence in the experiment reported in the last section, to *require* the theory that an accurate percept is one which is enriched by past experience, whereas a less accurate percept is one *not* enriched by past experience. Repetition or practice is necessary for the development of the improved percept, but there is no proof that it incorporates memories. The notion that learned perception is less and less determined by external stimulation as learning progresses finds no support in these experiments. The observer sees and hears more, but this may be not because he imagines more, or infers more, or assumes more, but because he discriminates more. He is more sensitive to the variables of the stimulus array. Perhaps the ability to summon up memories is merely incidental to perceptual learning and the ability to differentiate stimuli is basic. Perhaps the dependence of perception on learning and the dependence of perception on stimulation are not contradictory principles after all.

This theoretical approach to perceptual learning, it must be admitted, has points of weakness as well as points of strength. It accounts for veridical perception, but it does not account for misperception. It says nothing about imagination or fantasy, or wishful thinking. It is not an obviously useful approach for the study of abnormal behavior or personality, if one is convinced that a man's perceptions are the clues to his motives. But if one is concerned instead with the practical question of whether training can affect favorably a man's perception of the world around him, a very productive field for theory and experiment is opened up.

## PART II: WHAT IS LEARNED IN PERCEPTUAL LEARNING? A REPLY TO PROFESSOR POSTMAN*

Contemporary association theory, says Professor Postman (1955), formulates the problem of perceptual learning in terms of associations between stimuli and responses instead of associations between sensations and memory images. He seems to admit the theoretical difficulties in the way of an enrichment theory when the associations refer to phenomenal experience, but he implies that they are avoided when the associations refer to S-R connections. Here lies our main disagreement, for we do not believe that the difficulties can be so easily avoided. By reformulating the problem, can the associationist escape a reformulated difficulty? Professor Postman may not have to face the issue of whether perceptual learning is the enriching or the differentiating of experience, but he has to face another issue—whether such learning is a change in the attachment of responses to stimuli or an increase in the specificity of responses to stimuli.

Our critic should not suggest that the differentiation hypothesis we proposed is limited to conscious perception, or that it cannot be given a stimulus-response formulation. We believe it can be stated either in the language of phenomenology or in the language of behavior theory. The useful portions of both are inter-translatable. In the fable of the two winebibbers (perhaps from California and New York, respectively) we were at some pains to put the abstruse contrast between a tutored and an untutored palate in strict stimulus-response terms. And in the sample experiment we offered, concerning the development of an isolated identifying response, the procedure and the outcome were stated in these terms—namely, that there resulted an increased specificity of response to stimulation accompanied by an increase in the ability to respond differentially to the dimensional variables of the stimuli. An interesting thing about this outcome, however, was that it is also formulable in terms of what the subjects were aware of.

---

*Psychological Review, 1955, 62, 447–450. Copyright 1955 by the American Psychological Association. Reprinted by permission. This paper was written with Eleanor J. Gibson, as a reply to Postman (1955).

Professor Postman objects to the differentiation hypothesis for perceptual learning, presumably even in S-R terms, because no mechanism is proposed to account for the progressive change. It "begs the question" of learning; it does not explain *how* learning occurs (pp. 443–444). He must imply that the association hypothesis can account for the change and does explain how. But he himself, when discussing the difference between psychological and physiological associationism betrays a certain lack of confidence in the explanatory power of the concept. It is true that the history of psychology is full of "laws of association" having empirical validity, and that there are as yet no accepted "laws of differentiation" or "laws of stimulus-response specificity." But the age and respectability of the term "association" should not give it more explanatory power than it has. Our alternative hypothesis is not a theory but only the promise of a theory, and its explanatory value remains to be seen. It points to facts the explanation of which must be sought. It is concerned with the question of what is learned in perceptual learning, not how it occurs, or at least not as yet. "What is learned?" is the first question to ask, we think; the question of the mechanism is secondary.

Even learning theorists who limit their research to animal behavior have been arguing the fundamental question of what learning is instead of how it occurs. Considering the performance of an animal before, during, and after practice, what *kind* of change in performance exists? Only if this is understood does the psychologist know what to try to explain. The "what is learned?" debate has so far been concerned with the response side of the stimulus-response formula. If a psychology of perceptual learning is to develop along with a psychology of motor learning the question must be faced on the stimulus side. This was the question explicitly formulated in our original paper. In what sense do we learn to perceive?

Professor Postman has his own idea of what perceptual learning is. He believes that it is "a change in the nature of responses evoked by . . . stimuli" (p. 440). It is also described on the same page as "changes in stimulus-response relationships under controlled conditions of practice" or, a little later, as "the attachment of new responses, or a change in the frequency of responses, to particular configurations or sequences of stimuli." The emphasis is wholly on the change in the responses. We argue that where perceptual learning is concerned, it ought to be on the change in what the organism responds *to*. We suggested that perceptual learning consists of responding to variables of stimulation not previously responded to. We believe that the emphasis on change in the effective stimuli for responses will greatly increase the explanatory power of S-R theory. The stimulus can no longer be thought of as a bit of energy at a single receptor, true, but it never should have been so conceived in the first place. The organism is surrounded by energies of every sort and description. How they function as cues—that is, how certain variables and variations of this energy come to be specifically responded to—is the basic problem for perceptual learning. Just here is where psychophysics can help. Classical psychophysics has always been concerned with the correspondence between variables of energy and variables of response, although it was a serious mistake to suppose that the correspondence was innate or immutable.

The above quoted descriptions of perceptual learning, if taken as definitions, are not consistent with one another. It is said to be a *change,* either in the nature or responses, or in the frequency of responses, or in the stimulus-response relationships. But it is also said to be an *attachment* of responses to stimuli. This term reveals the strain of associationist thinking which we criticized and called the enrichment hypothesis. The changes in S-R relationships are not adequately described by speaking of the attaching, or connecting, or the forming of bonds between stimuli and responses. The inadequacy is evident if we inquire what is *new* in learning—new responses or new stimuli? Or is it merely the connections that are new? The change in S-R relationships that occurs with learning, we suggest, is one of progressive specification and abstraction. The organism discriminates and conceptualizes at the same time that he elaborates his repertory of responses. If both stimuli and responses are to be conceived as "molar" rather than "molecular," as Postman should be willing to admit, the change cannot be conceived as one of attachment between entities.

The main difficulty in the way of the traditional enrichment theory is its implication that learning involves a decreasing psychophysical correspondence between perception and stimulation. But the associationism of stimulus and response, Postman says, avoids this difficulty. Does it? We suggest that it only refuses to face the difficulty. Postman himself pleads that he does not wish to prejudge the question of increasing or decreasing correspondence between perception and stimulation. He suggests that we let the facts decide whether practice does or does not result in improved discrimination. He will assert that perceptual learning has taken place when the *relative frequencies* of judgments of *same* or *different, larger* or *smaller, higher* or *lower* have changed (p. 440). He seems not to care whether the judgments are correct or incorrect. The student of perception, however, has to face the problem of verdical judgments. He has to count or compute *errors.* The experimental methods for studying discrimination require it. Let us try to push Postman to the wall. Does he really wish to assert that a progressive decrease in discriminative accuracy (increase in variable error or constant error) should be considered learning?

We come finally to the problem of signs and symbols, and the perception of meaning. Our specificity hypothesis cannot account for such facts, it is said, and yet this is required of a theory of perceptual learning. ". . . sign-perception would appear to be, almost by definition, an associative phenomenon: an object can be perceived as a sign only by virtue of the fact that the organism has associated the sign object with the object specified" (p. 445). This sounds very convincing. It is true that the theory of association comes into its own when treating signs, signals, symbols, indicators, cues, clues, surrogates, or substitute stimuli. The relation between a word and its referent has fascinated thinkers for centuries. Perhaps this is why the theory of association has lasted for centuries. It should be noted, however, that in the quotation above Postman falls back on the kind of association he has rejected—that between objects of experience. To have made the same point in terms of association between stimulus and response would have been much more difficult. The plausibility lent to classical association theory by its success with signs and symbols is not inherited intact by an S-R association theory.

The relation between a word and its referent is the best example of an association. It is arbitrary; it seems wholly unlike the relation between a pitch and a tone, or a wave length and a hue. Is it then the relation which should be postulated to exist between a stimulus and a response, as Postman does? In the case of perceptual responses, this seems to violate some of the facts.

A stimulus-response theory with emphasis not on association but on specificity of responses and discriminative behavior could be extended to explain meaning, signs, and symbols even though it has not yet been formally attempted. We do not agree that the specificity hypothesis breaks down when it comes to the problem of human reactions to man-made sources of stimulation. Just because they are man-made, the problem of perception is one stage more complicated with such objects than it is with objects of the natural environment, and the problem of perceptual learning is equally more complicated. Nevertheless the basic tenet of the specificity approach still holds: men learn to perceive symbols by a process which involves an increase in the specificity of their responses to physically different symbols.[10] Symbols, like natural objects, must be differentiated or identified in order to be carriers of meaning. They come in sets, not singly. And it is quite possible that the meaning of a symbol, in the mathematico-logical sense, is given by its univocality within the set. This seems to be the assumption which has proved so fruitful in information theory. The meaning of a symbol in the psychological sense may be given by the univocality of the response to the stimulus. Note the difference between this formula and Postman's. He says the organism has perceived the meaning of a stimulus "when it has learned to make the appropriate response" (p. 445). We would say *when it has learned to identify the stimulus relative to all possible stimuli.*

A theory of perceptual learning which takes the line suggested would unquestionably throw a great burden on the stimulus. The specificity hypothesis for perceptual learning depends on the validity of a psychophysical approach to perception itself. The organism must be ultimately capable of response to extremely high-order variables of stimulation, including those of temporal succession, if meaning is to be explained in this way. Professor Postman has pointed out what seem to be implausible complexities of such stimulation. Others could be cited which seem equally absurd on first consideration. The only possible answer to this argument is to ask for time to test the absurdities experimentally. Meanwhile the possibility of a new empiricism based on discrimination at least should be considered along with the old empiricism based on association.

---

[10]Gibson & Gibson (1972) show how a specificity and differentiation theory might be applied to the learning of speech and reading. For more on reading, see Gibson & Levin (1975). (Eds.)

# 4.3

## The Concept of the Stimulus in Psychology

### PART I: THE CONCEPT OF THE STIMULUS IN PSYCHOLOGY*

It seems to me that there is a weak link in the chain of reasoning by which we explain experience and behavior, namely, our concept of the stimulus. The aim of this paper is to find out what psychologists mean by the term stimulus, with the hope of deciding what they *ought* to mean by it. After a short look at the history of the term, I will try to uncover the sources of confusion in modern usage. In the end, perhaps, the concept will be clarified. If not, certain contradictions will have been brought to light.

The experimental study of the stimulus began in the eighteenth century, so far as I can tell, with an investigation of the curious things that could be done to make a frog's leg twitch. The experimenters discovered what is now called the nerve-muscle preparation. Galvani and later Volta gave their names to electricity as well as to physiology by their experiments. In the early nineteenth century Johannes Müller applied these discoveries to the philosophers' problem of the human senses, the gates of knowledge. The nerves of sense, he pointed out, can be excited by a variety of unnatural agencies such as electrical current. Since the mind is acquainted only with the qualities specific to the sensory nerves, not with the stimuli, how it gets knowledge of the material world became more puzzling than ever. Later in the century, Sherrington was to emphasize the extent to which receptors are naturally protected against such irrelevant stimuli by the structural specialization of sense organs. But meanwhile it had been discovered that the

*American Psychologist, 1960, 15, 694–703. Copyright 1960 by the American Psychological Association. Reprinted by permission. This paper was presented as a Presidential Address to the Eastern Psychological Association, New York, N.Y., 1960.

skin would yield sensations only at certain discrete points. Here was a fresh puzzle. The separate receptor cells of all the sense organs came to be seen under the microscope, and the punctate character of the sensory process seemed to be established.

During all this time, the physical scientists were discovering the laws of energy and triumphantly measuring it in its various forms, electricity, momentum, light, heat, sound, and the results of chemical reaction. It became possible to measure certain variables of energy at sense organs, at least the simple ones like frequency and amount. Thresholds of reportable sensation were established. Fechner, following Weber, conceived the grand scheme of a measurement formula for consciousness, relating its judged intensity to a simple variable of the stimulus. Psychophysics was born.

Whatever could be controlled by an experimenter and applied to an observer could be thought of as a stimulus. In the growing science of human psychology, it became evident that this was the independent variable of an experiment, to be isolated and systematically varied. Much more complex things than physical energies could be presented to the sense organs—words for instance. These were also called stimuli, although the stimulus conditions manipulated, recency, frequency, meaningfulness, were vastly different from the variables of the psychophysical experiment.

In the latter part of the nineteenth century the concept of the reflex arc was applied to the adaptive behavior of animals. It had been thought to explain the strictly mechanical actions of the body ever since Descartes.[1] Reflexes had stimuli. The situations of animals could be systematically altered and the reactions observed. Organisms obviously responded to such stimuli, and the experimenter could apply them more freely than he could venture to do with human beings. To shorten a long story, such experiments came to be merged with human experiments and the outcome was a general stimulus-response psychology. This was a great success, especially in America. But stimuli for animal psychologists were not the same as stimuli for sensory physiologists and stimuli were still different for the students of perception and learning.

Enough has been said to show that in the twentieth century we have inherited a mixed batch of ideas about the stimulus. We constantly use the word but seldom define it. We take it for granted. We have behavior theory in full bloom, and perception theory in ripened complexity, but who ever heard of stimulus theory? As a preliminary effort in this direction, I have made a survey of what modern writers seem to mean by the term. Some writers define it, but not many. My method was to collect quotations from books. I then put them into opposition to one another. The ways of conceiving the stimulus are often in flat contradiction. Occasionally one book can be quoted against itself. The issues interlock, of course, but I have separated them into eight areas of disagreement and will treat

---

[1]An excellent history of the reflex concept is provided by Fearing (1929/1971). (Eds.)

them separately. In what follows, I will quote without comment, for the most part, keeping my own opinions to the end.

*I*. For Freud, the only use of the term stimulus that is discoverable in the *Collected Papers* (1949) is to refer to a motivating force. This, after all, is the dictionary meaning of the word—something that arouses or impels to action. In ordinary speech we refer to the stimulus of hunger or fear, which may compel extreme forms of behavior. Freud does not often use the term, but when he does, a stimulus is something to be satisfied or warded off.

Psychologists and physiologists, however, have generally used the term for the arousing of a sense organ instead of a whole individual. But they do not wholly agree about this. Some accept both meanings. Neal Miller asserts that "any stimulus has some drive value" (Miller & Dollard, 1941, p. 59). However, Skinner believes that "a drive is not a stimulus," and that although "the term has the unfortunate connotation of a goal; or spur to action," we must not be misled by this popular meaning of the word (1938, p. 375). Here, then, is the first area of disagreement in our way of conceiving the stimulus: *does a stimulus motivate the individual or does it merely trigger a response?*

*II*. Pavlov said that "a stimulus appears to be connected with a given response as cause with effect" (1927, p. 10). This is a forthright assertion. Similarly Watson took as the whole aim of psychology the predicting of the response, given the stimulus, and the specifying of the stimulus, given the response (1924, p. 10). But contrast this with the caution of Hilgard and Marquis. "We refer to a stimulus as an instigator (and no more is intended than that the stimulus is in some sense the occasion for the response" (1940, p. 73). Evidently what Pavlov and Watson meant by a stimulus is not what Hilgard and Marquis meant. Nearly all psychologists now follow the second line. It is allowed that a stimulus may cause a reflex, but not an act.[2] Woodworth was one of the first to emphasize that the stimulus does not in itself determine the response; factors in the organism intervene to help determine it. The discussion of intervening variables or mediating processes has by now filled volumes.

The same rule is taken to hold for experience. It is allowed that a stimulus may cause a sensation, but not a perception. M. D. Vernon, for example, states that "the nature of the percept is not . . . determined by the physical qualities of the stimulus, but is largely a function of constructive tendencies in the individual" (1952, p. 47).[3] But I have been arguing the opposite for some time, that the percept is in very good correspondence with the physical variables of the

---

[2]This theory of "occasionalism" dates back to Malebranche in the 17th Century (see Radner, 1978). (Eds.)

[3]Vernon's constructivism was inspired by the work of Bartlett (1932), whose ideas have again become influential (Neisser, 1976). (Eds.)

stimulus. *Can a stimulus be taken as the sufficient cause of a response, or can it not?* This is a second area of confusion in our concept of the stimulus.

*III.* Skinner has recently noted that "we frequently define the stimulus by the very doubtful property of its ability to elicit the response in question, rather than by any independent property of the stimulus itself" (1959, p. 355). He suggests no remedy, however, for this doubtful scientific behavior, and he seems to be confessing a sin without pointing the way to salvation. In truth many psychologists do give a circular definition of the stimulus. Skinner himself believed in his first book that "neither term (stimulus or response) can be defined as to its essential properties without the other" (1938, p. 9). Neal Miller has said "a response is any activity by or within the individual which can become functionally connected with an antecedent event through learning; a stimulus is any event to which a response can become so connected" (Miller & Dollard, 1941, p. 59). Miller, in fact, has argued that this circular definition of the stimulus is not only necessary but is theoretically desirable (Koch, 1959, p. 239). He seems to have abandoned completely the specifying of a stimulus by variables of physical energy. But listen to Estes. "By, *stimulus,* I refer to environmental conditions, describable in physical terms without reference to the behavior of an organism" (Koch, 1959, p. 455), and Hayek says, "the distinction between different stimuli must be independent of the different effects they have on the organism" (1952, p. 9).

Here is a disagreement. The student of psychophysics will argue that we must define our stimulus by certain operations of physical science, not by the judgments of our subject. Otherwise how are we ever to discover what stimuli can be discriminated and what cannot? When the stimulus is difficult to specify in objective physical terms, however, investigators tend to avoid the difficulty and describe it as that which is responded to, or that which is perceived. A few go further and, by arguing that an experimenter cannot define the stimulus anyway except in terms of *his* perception, reach a philosophical position of subjectivism.[4] There is an ancient puzzle to which students of philosophy are treated—whether there exists any sound when a tree crashes in the forest with no living being there to hear it. It is a question of how to conceive the auditory stimulus. It seems to remain a puzzle for a good many psychologists.

I think the central question is the following. Is a stimulus that which *does* activate a sense organ or that which *can* activate a sense organ? Some writers imply that a stimulus not currently exciting receptors is not a stimulus at all. Others imply that a stimulus need not excite receptors to be called such. They allow of *potential* stimuli. Witness Guthrie's assertion that stimuli are "potential occasions" for the initiation of sensory activity, and that "the physical stimuli, though present, may not be effective" (Koch, 1959, p. 178). The former concep-

---

[4]James (1890, I, p. 196) called this the "psychologist's fallacy". (Eds.)

tion allows physical energy to be called a stimulus only when some response can be observed; the latter allows the possibility that stimulus energy may be present without necessarily being responded to. The latter seems the better concept. With the former meaning, one could never speak of a subthreshold stimulus, and this is a useful term. An effective stimulus on one occasion may be ineffective on another. And there are various response criteria by which a threshold can be measured.

The distinction between effective and potential stimuli is made by a few theorists, but its implications have not been traced, and the idea remains undeveloped. The concept of a permanent environment of *objects* is widely accepted, but not the concept of a permanent environment of *potential stimuli*.[5]

The third area of disagreement is this: *must a stimulus be defined independently of the response it produces—in physical terms rather than terms of behavior or sensory process?*

*IV.* For Pavlov a stimulus could be anything in the terrestrial world. Any event he could think of to use in an experiment he would call a stimulus, and he employed tones, bells, the sound of bubbling water, lights, rotating objects, pictures on a screen, acid in the mouth, food, a scratch on the back, or electric shock. This common sense usage of the term persists among a good many behaviorists. Spence has said that the term stimulus means to him, "the physical or world situation, with its different aspects or features" (1956, p. 39). For Neal Miller anything that is discriminable is a stimulus or, as he calls it, a cue, these terms having the same meaning. For Skinner, a stimulus is simply "a part, or modification of a part, of the environment" (1938, p. 235). To be sure, he says, it must "refer to a class of events the members of which possess some property in common" (p. 34). Because stimuli have this "generic nature," the practice of calling a bell an auditory stimulus and a book a visual stimulus, is as he puts it, "frequently successful" (p. 235). All these writers persist in believing that somehow the things of the environment can *stimulate* us, and they refuse to be worried by the paradox that only receptors at the skin of an individual can actually be stimulated.

This definition of the stimulus is considered naive by perception psychologists. Stimuli are energies, not objects. In Troland's words, "the stimulus may be defined as the specific physical force, energy, or agency which brings about the stimulation of a given receptor system" (1930, p. 9). This conception has the authority of a century's research on the senses. In 1834, Johannes Müller argued that a stimulus was whatever excited one of the "nerves of sense." To the modern neurophysiologist, a stimulus is energy that depolarizes a living cell—especially, but not exclusively, a nerve cell. For Jennings in 1906, studying the ameba, a stimu-

---

[5]J. S. Mill spoke of the "permanent possibilities of sensation" (cf. Gibson, 1966b, p. 223). (Eds.)

lus was a type of change in the immediate environment that produced a change in behavior (1906, p. 19) and there existed precisely five types: chemical, mechanical, thermal, photic, or electrical. Woodworth says that "a stimulus is any form of energy acting upon a sense organ and arousing some activity of the organism" (1929, p. 223). Koffka wishes to call stimuli "the causes of the excitations of our sense organs" (1935, p. 79), but he, more than any other theorist, faced up to the contradictory meanings of the term and proposed a formal distinction between the "proximal" stimulus and the "distal" or "distant" stimulus. He made us consider the paradox that although perception and behavior seem to be determined by the distal object, they can in fact only be aroused by the proximal stimulus.[6]

Not all psychologists are willing to grapple with this paradox and, in truth, it is baffling. If the proximal stimulus for a given object is altered with every change of the observer's position in space, if it is different on different occasions, we are faced with an absurdity. We must suppose that a countless family of different stimuli can all arouse the same percept. Most behaviorists speak of the stimulus-object as if, by hyphenating two words with different meanings, the absurdity were removed. As men of common sense they see the need of reducing to one the countless number of stimuli that can arouse a single percept, and in this surely they have a point. But perceptionists, being unable to take the easy way out, struggle to construct theories of how different stimuli might arouse the same percept, the theories of perceptual constancy. So far, no theory has been agreed upon. Is it possible that common sense is right without knowing it, and that every family of proximal stimuli arising from one object is, in a sense, one stimulus?

Here is a fourth disagreement: *do stimuli exist in the environment or only at receptors?* There is a suggestion that both usages of the term are somehow correct, but it has not been explained.

*V.* Osgood says that "a stimulus may be defined as that form of physical energy that activates a receptor" (1953, p. 12). But he does not tell us whether he means by a receptor a single cell or a mosaic of receptor cells, that is, a sense organ. Others besides Osgood are undecided about this question, or have not thought about it. Hull knew what he thought. For him, the retinal image was a pattern of stimuli (1943, p. 37) and a single light ray was a stimulus (p. 33). "A stimulus element is a stimulus energy which activates a single receptor-organ" (p. 349). This is straightforward. Woodworth says that "of course the light entering the eye and striking many rods and cones is a collection of stimuli rather than a single stimulus," but in the next paragraph he suggests that "the sudden cessation of a light" is a stimulus (1929, p. 28). Köhler was fairly explicit on the question, saying that an organism responds to "an objective constellation of

---

[6]Brunswik (1956), Heider (1959), and Holt (1915) discuss the distinction between distal and proximal stimuli at great length (cf. Ch. 1.6). (Eds.)

millions of stimuli'' (1929, p. 179) and Koffka also assumed that stimuli on the retina or the skin were local events (1935). But Nissen, on the other hand, asserts that ''a stimulus involves a pattern of stimulation, spatial or temporal'' (Stevens, 1951, p. 374). Many other writers define stimuli as the occasions for activation of a sense organ, not of a receptor cell, and speak as if a pattern were a stimulus. There is a vast difference between a pattern of stimuli and a stimulus pattern, but we have not sufficiently thought about it. Is a ''pattern'' a single stimulus or is it a number of separate stimuli?

The notion that a stimulus is what excites a cell, and is therefore *punctate*, seems to many theorists the only rigorous definition. On this account Hull had to introduce the postulate of afferent neural interaction to explain molar behavior as distinguished from molecular responses. The gestalt psychologists had to develop the theory of sensory organization in order to explain perception. But Lashley once said that

> the stimulus to any reaction above the level of a spinal reflex involves not the excitation of certain definite sensory cells but the excitation of any cells of a system in certain ratios, and the response may be given to the ratio even though the particular cells involved have not previously been excited in the same way (Murchison, 1934, p. 476).

This passage suggests the idea that higher levels of reaction require us to define higher orders of stimulation. Lashley seems to be saying that a ratio may be itself a stimulus, not just a relation between two stimuli. But note that the gestalt theorists, by conceiving all stimuli as local events, did not come to think in this way.

A controversy has long been going on over the question of how an individual could respond to a relation. It began with Köhler's evidence that a chick will select the brighter of two gray papers instead of the absolute brightness of a particular paper. Köhler thought it demonstrated a relational process in the brain; Spence has gone to great lengths to show that it could be explained in terms of absolute responses to each piece of paper, subject to the so-called principle of stimulus generalization. But the simplest explanation would be that the effective stimulus in the experiment was the direction of the difference in brightness in the field of view. In line with this solution to the problem, students of vision conceive that a margin is a visual stimulus, perhaps *the* visual stimulus, and a margin in the array of light to an eye is strictly a ratio, that is, a relation between measured intensities.

Here is the fifth source of confusion: *when is a pattern or relation to be considered a single stimulus and when a number of separate stimuli?*

*VI.* The notion that a stimulus can only be something punctate is related to the notion that a stimulus can only be something *momentary*. The gestalt psychologists pointed out that a melody is perceived, but they never suggested that a melody was a stimulus. The notes of the melody were taken to be the stimuli. But what about the transitions between notes, or the "transients" of acoustical engineering? Are they stimuli? The investigators of speech sounds seem to think so, but the auditory literature of sensation is vague on this question. And if a short transition is a stimulus, why not a long transition or temporal pattern?

In vision, experimenters have not been able to make up their minds as to whether an optical motion was a stimulus or a series of stimuli. The retina and also the skin are very sensitive to motion. It ought to be simple, but the facts of the stroboscope and the phi-phenomenon have been interpreted to imply that it is complex. Motion is taken to be change of location, as it is in classical physics, and it is then reasoned that the impression of location must be fundamental to any perception of a change of location.

On the other hand the generalization is frequently met with that a stimulus is *always* a change. This is very confusing, in fact it is one confusion piled on another. I think that writers who make this assertion have in mind the experiments showing that an unchanging stimulus soon ceases to be effective for perception. They are thinking of sensory adaptation. What changes in that case is not the stimulus but the process of excitation. For the retina, the skin, and the olfactory organ, sensory adaptation does occur. For example, the steady application of an image to a human retina, by the method of artificially stabilizing the image, eventuates in a wholly ineffective stimulus. But note that the steady application of focusable light to a human eye does not. This stimulus never becomes wholly ineffective, even with the best voluntary fixation, because of slight movements of the eye itself. This means that retinal stimulation is by no means the same thing as optical stimulation. They are different stages in the chain of events that leads to vision. A "change in stimulation" means something quite different when it is produced by some adjustment of the sense organ itself than when it is produced by an external event.

Is optical motion, then, meaning a change in the pattern of focusable light to the eye, to be considered a stimulus? Experiments based on this assumption are beginning to appear. In the recent Cornell research with optical transformation (Gibson & Gibson, 1957) we not only think of this as a stimulus, we have come to think of nonchange of pattern as simply a special case. Stability, after all, is only definable as absence of motion. Similarly, a form is definable as a non-transformation. In this conception, sequence is a dimension of stimulation whether or not change occurs.

The great virtue of this conception of sequence is that it suggests a simple solution to the puzzle of perceptual constancy. Two types of nonchange are distinguishable, first, nonmotion of a pattern and, second, invariance of a pattern during motion. The invariant contained in a family of the perspectives arising from a single object is a single stimulus. Hence there is only one stimulus for a single object, and the common sense opinion is right after all.

The sixth conceptual issue is this: *when does a sequence constitute a single and when a number of separate stimuli; also, can a single enduring stimulus exist throughout a changing sequence?*

*VII*. Users of the Rorschach test assume that a stimulus field can be either structured, or, as they put it, *unstructured*. I could find no explicit definition of unstructured stimulation in the literature but only examples of the material to which the term is applied—inkblots and other items used in the so-called project-ive tests.[7] The idea of structured stimulation comes from gestalt theory but only from a vague, tentative, and undeveloped hypothesis of gestalt theory—the ex-ternal forces of organization as distinguished from the internal forces of organiza-tion. Koffka, for example, was so preoccupied with the ways in which the individual *structured* his stimulus field that he scarcely considered the ways in which it might already *have* structure (1935). In fact, he wrote sometimes as if it had none, as if all structure had to be imposed on it, because the stimuli them-selves were meaningless points.

This uncertainty about the existence of structure in the stimulus for perceived form still persists. But since Koffka's time, and partly inspired by him, some experimenters are beginning simply to assume it, and to apply mathematics to the structure of a stimulus. They would not agree that an inkblot is in any sense an unstructured stimulus. A picture has one structure, an inkblot has another, but it does not lack structure. That can be said only of a film-color or the cloudless blue sky. The structure of an array may have ambiguous or equivocal components, as Koffka showed, but that is not the same thing. The capacity of light to carry structure to an eye may be impoverished or reduced experimentally but it re-mains. The structure of light may not specify anything familiar to the subject, or to any observer, but it is a geometrical fact. The subject may be unable to register the structure because it is nonsense to him, or he overlooks it, or he was not told to look for it, or his eyes are defective, or he is too young, or for a dozen other reasons, but it is still in the light. So, at least, some experimenters would argue.

What can be meant by an unstructured stimulus field is thus a matter of disagreement. The seventh question is: *how do we specify the structure of a stimulus?*

*VIII*. The conception of stimuli as physical energies seems to imply that, in themselves, they have no significance or meaning. Especially if they are consid-ered to be only spots of energy at brief moments of time it is clear that they specify little or nothing about the environment. Light, heat, mechanical, acousti-cal, chemical, and electrical energy are far from being objects, places, events, people, words, and symbols, but nevertheless they are the only stimuli that can

---

[7]Cf. Gibson (1956). (Eds.)

affect receptors. This theory of the meaningless stimulus has been an accepted doctrine for a long, long time in the study of the senses. It leads to the notion of the sense datum—the bare sensation, or raw sensory impression, and thence to the persistent problem of how animals and men can be supposed to perceive objects, places, events, and one another.

Students of behavior, however, without questioning the doctrine of the empty stimulus, often act as if they did not believe it. Beach speaks for comparative psychologists when he says, in describing how birds feed their offspring, "young birds exhibit a gaping response which *stimulates* the parent to place food in the nestling's mouth" (Stevens, 1951, p. 415). He takes it for granted that light rays can specify the event called gaping and refuses to worry about it further. Students of perception do worry about this question, but they are not consistent. On the one hand, they firmly assert that nothing gets into the eye but light of variable wave length and intensity, not objects, or events, or facts of the environment. On the other hand, they often say that light "carries" information about the environment, or that stimuli "provide" information to the perceiver. If this is so, the stimuli must specify something beyond themselves, and they cannot be empty of meaning.

A sort of compromise between the informative stimulus and the empty stimulus is provided by the use of the term *cue*. According to Woodworth, "a cue, as used in psychology, is a stimulus which serves as a sign or signal of something else, the connection having previously been learned." (1958, p. 60.) Stimuli are conceived by analogy with messages, or communication in code. Brunswik thought of stimuli as *indicators* of environmental facts, by analogy with pointer readings, emphasizing, however, that they had only a probable connection with the fact in question (1956). Boring has suggested that stimuli may be taken as *clues,* and this term points to Helmholtz's theory of unconscious rational inference from the sense data (Harper & Boring, 1948).

Merely to call the stimulus a cue, sign, signal, message, indicator, or clue does not tell us what we need to know. The question is to what extent does the stimulus specify its source, and how does it do so? Is it possible that the use of these verbal metaphors only prevents us from facing the problem? Or consider the use by modern information theorists of a neutral term like *input*. When they compare the organism to a communication system or to a black box, the internal working of which has to be discovered, are they avoiding the obligation to consider the environment of an organism and the relation of stimuli to the environment?

The problem of the connection between stimuli and their natural sources has not been taken seriously by psychologists. Stimuli have not even been classified from this point of view, but only with respect to the sense organs and the types of energy which carry stimuli. It is a problem of ecology, as Brunswik realized when he wrote about the "ecological validity" of cues (1956). I think the problem has been obscured, and our recognition of it delayed, by our failure to separate it into parts. The connection between natural stimuli and their sources is not the same as the connection between *social* stimuli and their sources, for example, the connection between words and their referents. This latter problem, surely, is distinct. Semantics is one thing, ecology is another; and a science of environmental stimuli may not prove to be as difficult as a science of symbols, once we put our minds to it.

I have maintained that optical stimuli, for example, gradients of texture in the light to an eye, specify environmental objects by the relation of *projection*. To me this is not at all the same as the relation by which words specify objects, which I would call one of *coding*. But however this may be, we face another unanswered question, the eighth: *do stimuli carry information about their sources in the world, and how do they specify them?*

## SOME POSITIVE HYPOTHESES

Can anything useful be salvaged from these various contradictory usages and definitions? No one could be blamed for being pessimistic about it. S. S. Stevens, who has thought hard and long about stimuli, concluded that it is futile even to attempt a general definition of the stimulus in psychology. Psychology as a whole, he says, can be equated with the problem of defining the stimulus, that is, giving a complete definition of the stimulus for a given response. To be able to do so would require that we specify "all the transformations of the environment, both external and internal, that leave the response invariant." And "for no response have we yet given a complete definition of the stimulus" in this sense (Stevens, 1951, p. 31ff.) If I understand him, what Stevens chiefly had in mind is the puzzle of constancy. He was saying that we do not know how to specify, in the chaos of literal proximal-energy stimulation, the actual cause of a given response. This is a discouraging truth.

But, unlike Stevens, I have hopes, and even some positive hypotheses to suggest. Once the contradictory assumptions about stimulation are made explicit, we can try to resolve them. For one thing we might search for an invariant component in the bewildering variety of functionally equivalent stimuli. Perhaps there is an invariant stimulus for the invariant response, after all. Many sorts of higher order variables of energy may exist, only awaiting mathematical description. They will have to be described in appropriate terms, of course, not as simple functions of frequency and amount. We must not confuse a stimulus with the elements used for its analysis. We must learn to conceive an array not as a mosaic of stimuli but as a hierarchy of forms within forms, and a flux not as a chain of stimuli but as a hierarchy of sequences within longer sequences.

*Molar Stimuli.*   Ever since Tolman, behavior theorists have been agreeing that psychology is concerned with molar responses, not molecular ones. Accordingly, we try to observe and measure what an organism is doing, not how all its muscles are contracting. With this kind of observation on the response side there should be a corresponding kind of observation on the stimulus side. We should try to discover what an organism is responding *to,* not what excites all the little receptors.[8] Of course all the muscles may be contracting and all the receptors may be excited, but observation at that level is the job of the physiologists.

The same recommendation can be made for the study of perception. The gestalt theorists have demonstrated the fact of molar experience, but they did not look for molar stimuli. These may very well exist outside the laboratory and, with ingenuity, can perhaps be isolated in the laboratory. If so, we shall have a new and powerful kind of psychophysics.

This conception of molar stimuli is not wholly new. Forty-five years ago, E. B. Holt was convinced that cognition, along with behavior, was a constant function of stimulation. In this he agreed with Pavlov and Watson. But Holt emphasized that the stimulus *of which* cognitive behavior was a function was more abstract and more comprehensive than the stimulus of classical psychophysics. As one passes from reflexes to behavior, the effective stimulus "recedes," as Holt put it (1915, *passism*). By the *recession* of the stimulus he meant that it seems to be located far out in the environment rather than close by in the receptors. And he also meant that as cognition develops, the stimulus of which it is a function recedes more and more. Following this suggestion, one might conclude that a change in response implies a change in the stimulus to which the response is made. Learning would then involve not only alteration of behavior but also an alteration in the effective stimulus.[9] Presumably its molar character has gone up a stage in the hierarchy.

*Potential Stimuli.* Evidently the hypothesis of potential stimulation, accepted casually by some theorists, has quite radical but unrecognized implications. We have long acknowledged the almost unlimited possibilities for new responses in learning theory; why not equally vast possibilities of new stimuli? The environment, so considered, would consist of a sort of reservoir of possible stimuli for both perception and action. Light, heat, sound, odor, gravity, and potential contacts with objects surround the individual. But this sea of energy has variables of pattern and sequence which can be registered by sense organs. They can be explored, either at one station-point or by moving around in the environment. The fields of radiating sound and odor, together with the flux of light rays reflected from surfaces, make it possible to respond to things at a distance. The changes of pattern in time serve as controlling stimuli for locomotion and manipulation. The variables and covariables and invariables of this stimulus environment are inexhaustible.

---

[8]Brentano (1874/1973) called this responding to or directedness the intentionality of psychological acts (see Aquila (1977) for a review of work on this concept). (Eds.)

[9]Cf. Ch. 4.2. (Eds.)

Surprisingly little has been written about stimuli. The sensory physiologists, of course, have read their physics and chemistry. But physical science portrays a sterile world. The variables of physics make uninteresting stimuli. Why is this true? I think it is because psychologists take for stimuli only the variables of physics as they stand in the textbooks. We have simply picked the wrong variables. It is our own fault. After all, physicists are not primarily concerned with stimuli. They have enough to do to study physical energies without worrying about stimulus energies. I think that we will have to develop the needed discipline on a do-it-yourself principle. It might be called ecological physics, with branches in optics, acoustics, dynamics, and biochemistry. We cannot wait for the physical scientists to describe and classify potential stimuli. The variables would seem to them inelegant, the mathematics would have to be improvised, and the job is not to their taste. But it is necessary. And if successful, it will provide a basis for a stimulus-response psychology, which otherwise seems to be sinking in a swamp of intervening variables.[10]

Consider, for example, the physics (that is to say the acoustics) of speech sounds. As recently as 1951, in the *Handbook of Experimental Psychology* (Stevens, p. 869), the fact that a word is perceptually the same when whispered as it is when shouted was taken to prove that the physical characteristics of sound waves, frequency, intensity, and so on, cannot tell us about speech. Speech perception would require a psychological theory, not physical measurement. But the invention of the sound spectrograph seems to have shown that certain higher order variables of acoustic energy are the critical constituents of speech and the stimuli for hearing it. These newly discovered invariant patterns of sound are completely physical, even if they had not previously been studied in physics. What was needed to understand the psychophysics of hearing words was not more psychology but more physics.[11]

For another example consider the optics of an array of light. The physical variables applying to the point source and the image point do not explain the seeing of a surface. But my own work shows that the variables of an optical *texture* do account for the seeing of a surface, and that by manipulating textures an experimenter can produce synthetic perceptions of objects (Gibson, Purdy, & Lawrence, 1955). Gradients, patterns, and other invariants are not part of existing geometrical optics, but they are physical facts. What was needed for a psychophysics of visual perception was not more theorizing about cues but more attention to geometrical optics.

*Effective Stimuli.*    An effective stimulus can now be defined. It is one which arouses receptor activity, or recorded neural impulses, or sense organ ad-

---

[10]Gibson (1966b, pp. 1–7; 1979a, pp. 1–3, 149) later argued against S-R psychology, theories using intervening variables, and other input processing theories (cf. Chs. 4.6 and 4.8). (Eds.)

[11]Shankweiler, Strange, & Verbrugge (1977) review problems associated with describing the speech signal. (Eds.)

justments, or overt responses, or verbal judgments—whichever criterion one chooses. Note that the idea of fixed innate thresholds of sensation is rejected. It was always a myth, for every psychophysical experimenter knows that the threshold obtained depends on the method used and the response criterion chosen.

In short, whether or not a potential stimulus becomes effective depends on the individual. It depends on the species to which he belongs, on the the anatomy of the sense organs, the stage of maturation, the capacities for sense organ adjustment, the habits of attention, the activity in progress, and the possibilities of educating the attention of the individual. Such facts make up the field of perceptual development and perceptual learning. At the lower levels they are called facts of sensory physiology; at the higher levels, facts of attention or exploration, but they are all one problem. Animals seem to be driven to make potential stimuli effective. They use their receptor equipment, probably, in as great a variety of ways as they use their motor equipment. From this point of view, it seems to me, the senses begin to make sense.

*Stages of Specificity.*    Johannes Müller began the study of the way in which the modes of experience are specific to the excitations of nerve fibers. Sherrington and others showed how the excitations of fibers were generally specific to the patterns of the stimulus. Ecological physics will tell us the extent to which the proximal stimuli are specific to their sources in the world.[12] If experience is specific to excitation, and excitation to stimulation, and stimulation to the external environment, then experience will be specific to the environment, within the limits of this chain of specificities. The first two stages have long been under investigation. The last is ripe for study. There has been a controversy over whether or not visual stimuli can specify their objects (for example, Cantril, 1950), but it can be settled, for the facts are discoverable, and arguments should await evidence.

*The Informative Capacity of Molar Stimuli.*    If the structure and sequence of stimulus energy can be analyzed, potential stimuli can be described and arranged in a hierarchy. There will be subordinate stimuli and superordinate stimuli, of lower order and higher order. So conceived it is reasonable to assume that stimuli *carry information* about the terrestrial environment. That is, they specify things about objects, places, events, animals, people, and the actions of people. The rules by which they do so are to be determined, but there is at least enough evidence to warrant discarding the opposite assumption under which we have been operating for centuries—that stimuli are necessarily and intrinsically meaningless.

---

[12]See Gibson (1966b, pp. 1–7) for arguments against the proximal-distal distinction, and Chs. 2.8, 2.9 and Gibson (1979a, part 1) for more on ecological physics. (Eds.)

*Natural Stimuli, Pictorial Stimuli, and Coded Stimuli.* I have suggested that, instead of continuing to employ the careless analogies of our present loose terminology for stimuli—cues, clues, signals, signs, indicators, messages, inputs, and the like—we make a systematic study of the laws by which stimuli specify their sources. We need to know the laws of stimulus information. Almost certainly these will not be the laws which govern the transmission of information in human systems of communication. The natural world does not literally *communicate* with the sense organs. The potential physical stimuli arising from an event are not to be compared to the physical stimulus arising from the *word* for that event. We cannot hope to understand natural stimuli by analogy and with socially coded stimuli, for that would be like putting the cart before the horse. Just this, however, is what we tend to do when we speak of the "signs" for depth perception and the "messages" of the senses. We cannot afford to speak of coded information for the sense organs when we mean stimuli, for some of these are coded and some are not.

A systematic study of the specifying power of stimuli will put the problem of meaning in perception on a new footing. It will take several forms, depending on the kinds of relations discovered. My guess is that there will be at least three, corresponding to the stimuli from things, from pictures, and from words. It is true that men, besides learning to perceive objects, also learn to apprehend things by way of perceiving pictures and words. These mediated perceptions get mixed with direct perceptions in the adult. But we shall have to disentangle them before we can have a complete theory of human perception.

## CONCLUSION

The foregoing distinctions and assumptions seem promising to me. But I would agree that a stimulus theory cannot be established by merely asserting it. The scientific question is whether all these new kinds of stimuli exist. I suggest that we look for them in the environment and then try to bring them into the laboratory.

It is still true that the stimulus is the prime independent variable of a psychological experiment. I quote from Underwood (1957):

> One may vary more than one stimulus condition in a given experiment . . . but to draw a conclusion about the influence of any given variable, that variable must have been systematically manipulated alone somewhere in the design. Nothing in analysis of variance, covariance, Latin squares, Greco-Latin squares, or Greco-Arabic-Latin squares has abrogated this basic principle (p. 35).

If Underwood is right, the secret of a good experiment is to discover the relevant stimulus before doing the experiment. The moral of my argument is that a systematic search for relevant stimuli, molar stimuli, potential stimuli, invariant stimuli, specifying stimuli, and informative stimuli will yield experiments with positive results. Perhaps the reservoir of stimuli that I have pictured is full of elegant independent variables, their simplicity obscured by physical complexity, only waiting to be discovered.

## PART II: NOTE ON THE DISTINCTION BETWEEN STIMULATION AND STIMULUS INFORMATION*

For an information-based theory of perception that purports to replace sensation-based theories of perception the distinction between *stimulation* and *information* is crucial. Can it be made explicit?

It has long been known that the stimulation of receptors is not *sufficient* for perception. Receptors are *touched off* or *fired* by stimuli for which they are more or less specialized, that is, mechanical, chemical, radiant or photic energy, but the stimuli do not specify the sources in the environment from which they come. As Johannes Müller asserted long ago, sensations are specific to receptors, not to objects in the world. And this is the age-old puzzle of sensation-based theories of perception. Sensations must be supplemented. But how?

Strictly speaking, then, a stimulus is any event that excites a receptor and initiates afferent neural impulses. A group of receptors can only be excited by a group of stimuli; a mosaic of receptors must be excited by a mosaic of stimuli; even overlapping receptive *fields* in a mosaic must be excited each by its own stimulus. This is the one-stimulus-to-one-receptor hypothesis. It cannot be avoided. The realization that when stimuli are so conceived they are *independent* of one another was one of the puzzles that led to Gestalt theory.[13] The assumption that receptors are excited independently of one another led the Gestalt psychologists to their theories of the "grouping" of sensations and the supposed laws of sensory "organization." For it follows that the relations among a group of stimuli are only observable as the relations among a group of sensations. Even a simple difference between two adjacent stimuli would have to be registered either by some kind of comparison of two adjacent sensations (a "comparator") or by some neurological equivalent (a "field"). Intensity of visual stimulation has to be converted into frequency of nerve impulses ("brightness") for each anatomical receptive unit before the process of visual perception can even begin. And when the *mobility* of the retina (and the skin) is taken into account these difficulties become still more formidable for any theory that aims to explain perception in terms of receptor inputs.[14]

---

*Unpublished manuscript, March, 1972.

[13]Köhler (1913/1971) called this puzzle of the independence of stimuli from one another the constancy hypothesis for sensations (not to be confused with perceptual constancy). (Eds.)

[14]See Ch. 2.6 for more on sensation-based approaches to vision during eye movements. (Eds.)

Red, Niz, Poredail

The conception of a structured *array* of ambient light (or an array of contacts, vibrations, or substances), is entirely different from the notion of stimuli that impinge on receptors. Information about the environment consists of the invariants of structure in a continuous flow. Stimuli, together with *groups* of stimuli, *patterns* of stimuli, *relations* among stimuli, and *series* of stimuli become irrelevant except insofar as one wishes to study the neurophysiology of receptors and the firing of peripheral and central neurons. The array *consists* of contrasts and transitions, not of stimuli, and not of groups, patterns, or series of stimuli.[15] As psychologists we can now afford to admit the strict hypothesis of one-stimulus-to-one-receptor. We can agree that points and flashes of light do elicit sensations without having to derive perceptions therefrom. We can allow that prods do arouse reflex responses without trying to build behavior out of such supposed units.

It is perfectly legitimate to apply physical stimulation to an animal or an observer to see what he does or says, but one should not expect to learn about perception or behavior in this way. For the latter purpose the experimenter must provide or display information. The fact that he must *stimulate* the retina (or the skin or the cochlea) in order to do so is incidental. The haphazard applying of ''stimuli'' to subjects without concern for environmental meaning has led to a vast literature describing anomalous perceptions and puzzling behaviors. In such an experiment the subject does his best to discover an invariant, but it is often one that the experimenter had not planned and does not understand.

The concept of a *stimulus* in psychology and in common speech is broad, loose, and vague, unlike the strict meaning the term has been given here, that is, the energy that triggers a receptor. Formerly I, too, used the word loosely. In *The Perception of the Visual World* I referred to a contrast in the retinal image, or a line, or a gradient of texture-density as a ''stimulus.'' I even asserted that a relation could be a stimulus, and agreed that the retinal image was the stimulus for an eye. There were stimuli for perceptions, I thought, as well as stimuli for sensations; stimuli of ''higher order'' as well as those of ''lower order.'' But this was a mistake. The concept applies to a passive receptor, not to an active perceptual system; it belongs to physiology at the neural level not at the level of homeostasis.

Information that specifies the source in the environment from which it comes does not consist of separate stimuli. Hence the patterns or forms of stimuli do not need to be perceived. They do not have to be organized. Ambient light, sound, and the pressures that the world can exert on the skin are structured and unified and segregated at all levels of size and duration before the light, vibration, or pressure ever get to the receptors in the form of stimuli.

---

[15]See Chs. 1.4 and 1.7 for more on the structure of the optic array. (Eds.)

# 4.4 The Useful Dimensions of Sensitivity

PART I: THE USEFUL DIMENSIONS OF SENSITIVITY*

What I am going to talk about is the relation of sensing to perceiving. We have all believed that we understood the process of sensation fairly well and that only the process of perception gave us difficulties. But I am going to suggest on the contrary that a straightforward theory of perception is possible and that it is our understanding of sensation which is confused.

First let us make sure that there is really a problem in how to treat sensing and perceiving. Some psychologists now maintain that there is no difference between them in fact. The distinction has broken down; they say it has no validity and we should forget it. I think that what they mean is this. An individual can make discriminations in many ways. We can say either that he is *sensitive to* many variables of stimulation or that he can *experience* many kinds of differences between things but what has importance, the argument goes, are only the facts of discrimination, not whether they are called sensory or perceptual. There is something valid in this argument. I would call it the experimentalist's position—stick to the facts and cut the cackle! It is enough to determine just what differences an animal, a child, or a man can respond to and what others he cannot. This limited aim of psychology might be called simple psychophysics (not metric psychophysics) and it is good experimental science. But it provides no explanation of how the individual keeps in touch with with the environment around him.

---

*American Psychologist*, 1963, *18*, 1-15. Copyright 1963 by the American Psychological Association. Reprinted by permission.

The problem of perception, then, the problem of contact with the environment, still remains.[1]

The variables of sensory discrimination are radically different from the variables of perceptual discrimination. The former are said to be dimensions like quality, intensity, extensity, and duration, dimensions of hue, brightness, and saturation, of pitch, loudness, and timbre, of pressure, warm, cold, and pain. The latter are dimensions of the environment, the variables of events and those of surfaces, places, objects, of other animals, and even of symbols. Perception involves meaning; sensation does not. To see a patch of color is not to see an object. To see the extensity of a color is not to see the *size* of an object, nor is seeing the form of a color the same as seeing the *shape* of an object. To see a darker patch is not to see a shadow on a surface. To see the magnification of a form in the field is not to see an approaching object, and to see the expansion of the whole field is not to observe one's own forward locomotion. To have a salty taste is not to taste salt, and to have a certain olfactory impression is not to smell, say, a mint julep. To feel an impression on the skin is not to feel an object, nor is having sensations of strain and pressure to feel the weight of an object. To feel a local pain is not to feel the pricking of a needle. To feel warmth on one's skin, is not to feel the sun on one's skin, and to feel cold is not to feel the coldness of the weather. To hear sound is not the same thing as to hear an event, nor is to hear an increasing loudness to hear the approach of a sounding object. Finally, let us note that having a difference of sound sensation in the two ears is by no means the same as to hear the direction of a sound. The last case is instructive, for we do not in fact have such binaural differences in sensory experience but we do localize sounds.

Having sensations is not perceiving, and this fact cannot be glossed over. Nevertheless, perceiving unquestionably depends on sensing *in some meaning of that term*. That is, it depends on sensitivity or the use of the sense organs. To observe, one must sense. The question I wish to raise is whether or not it is true that to observe one must have sensations.

I realize that any inquiry into the relation of sensing to perceiving raises the ghosts of formidable men. It is disconcerting to feel that Locke, Berkeley, and Hume are looking over one's shoulder, or that Kant and two generations of Mills are raising their eyebrows. A perceptual theorist can get into staggering muddles, and he does well to be cautious. Nevertheless, I have a set of hypotheses to propose and you may judge it both for internal contradictions and for conformity with the facts. My first suggestion, the general thesis, is that the useful dimensions of sensitivity are those that specify the environment and the observer's relation to the environment. There are other dimensions of sensitivity which do

---

[1]These statements can be read as criticisms of Gibson's earlier theories of perception (Gibson, 1950a, 1959a; Chs. 1.1, 2.2, 3.1). For further criticisms see Gibson (1966b, *passim*) and Gibson (1979a, p. 149, Ch. 14). (Eds.)

not specify such facts and relations, but they are not useful in this way, being only incidental to the activity of perception.

A whole set of correlative hypotheses go along with this radical thesis. They need to be understood before it begins to have plausibility, and the theory should be considered as a whole. The facts of sensory psychology and sense physiology are so varied and voluminous that it is not easy to stand back and take a fresh look at the evidence. Moreover, each of us is apt to have his own private opinion about the data of his senses. But if you will suspend belief in the standard doctrine of sensation and question your favorite introspections, I hope to convince you that the explanation of sense perception is not as difficult and roundabout as it has always appeared to be.

Consider first the puzzle of perceptual constancy. I will not attempt to review the experiments measuring the tendency toward constancy which are limited to vision and which, in any case, are indecisive. Instead I will point to the general evidence for an invariance of perception with varying sensations. This invariance appears not only in vision but also in other senses, notably those excited by mechanical energy, hearing, and touch. The paradox of constancy—the "distal focusing of perception" as Egon Brunswik (1956) put it, is more than a matter of color, size, and shape constancy; it is the heart of the problem of useful sensitivity.[2]

Figure 30 is a picture of a patchwork of visual sensations. Note that it is a cross section of a wide-angle cone of light rays which might enter a human eye, the left eye in this case. Figure 31 is a longitudinal section of such a wide-range cone. It is stationary and momentary as represented in the picture, but whenever the eye moves to a new fixation point it will take in a new cone of rays. At that station point in the room there exists a complete optic array of available stimulation, the array being sampled and explored by new fixations. Figure 32 shows that if the *man* moves instead of his eye moving, the pattern of the entering array is *transformed,* that is, every patch of color in the array changes form, and the patch work as a whole is altered.

All this is simply the outcome of the laws of ambient light, or what might be called optical perspective (Gibson, 1961a). The laws of *pictorial* perspective with which we are more familiar are a special case involving the sheaf of rays at a picture plane (Gibson, 1960a). Figure 33 is an illustration of so-called linear perspective on a picture.

The sensations of the visual field shift with every movement of the eye, and transform with every movement of the head. But, the perception of the room remains constant throughout. There is invariance of perception with varying sensations.

There are two kinds of seeing, I argue, one resulting in the experience of a visual field and the other in the experience of a visual world (Gibson, 1950a).

---

[2]Gibson (1965a) discusses constancy at greater length. (Eds.)

FIG. 30. Momentary cross-section of the light entering a human eye.

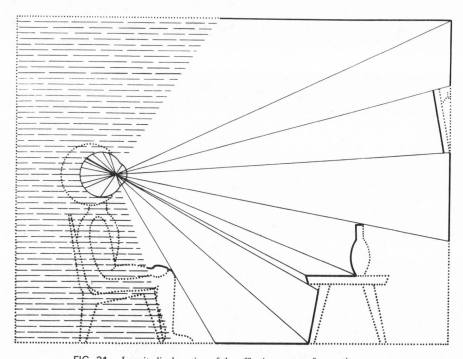

FIG. 31. Longitudinal section of the effective sector of an optic array.

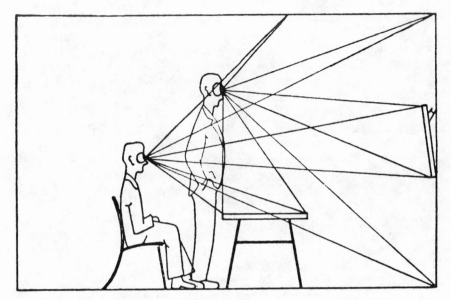

FIG. 32. Perspective transformation of the patchwork of an optic array due to change of viewpoint.

The field is bounded; the world is unbounded. The field is unstable; the world is stable. The field is composed of adjacent areas, or figures; the world is composed of surfaces, edges, and depths, or solid objects and interspaces. The field is fluid in size and shape; the world is rigid in size and shape. As pure cases, they are distinct, although in many experimental situations the observer gets a compromise experience between the two extremes. However, these experimental situations are seldom ones in which the observer is free to explore a complete

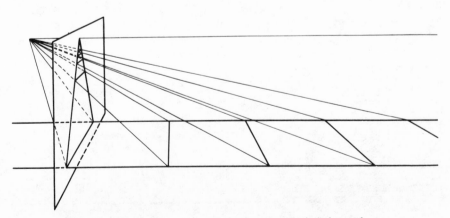

FIG. 33. The special case of a ray sheaf at a hypothetical picture plane.

optic array with his eyes, and are never ones in which he is allowed to move about so as to obtain a series or family of perspectives.

The visual *field* ahead of the observer during locomotion expands in a sort of centrifugal flow goverened by the laws of motion perspective. The visual *world* during locomotion is phenomenally quite rigid. Sensation varies but perception is invariant. To be sure, the observer sees his locomotion. The expansion of the field ahead *specifies* locomotion. This suggests a strange and radical hypothesis—that the visual sensation in this case is a symptom of kinesthesis, having reference to the self instead of the world, and that it has nothing to do with the visual perception of the world (Gibson, 1958b).

Another case is that of the perception aroused by the perspective transformation of a silhouette in an otherwise empty field of view. As an experiment, this does not require a panoramic motion picture screen, and it can be carried out in a laboratory. There results a perception named stereokinesis, or the kinetic depth effect, or simply rigid motion in depth (Gibson & G son, 1957). Behind the translucent screen in such experiments, at an indefinite dis ance, there appears a virtual object moving in space. The form of the silhouette changes; the form of the phenomenal object remains invariant. The observer can see a change of form if he attends to the flat screen, but what he spontaneously reports is a rigid object. Ordinarily the transformation is seen as motion of the object, not as a sensation.

Another example is the familiar one that the color of the surfaces of the environment, including the white to black series, do not change as the illumination goes from brilliant to dim. The corresponding sensations, however, the film colors obtained by seeing a surface through an aperture, vary widely with illumination. The perception of whiteness is quite a different matter from the sensation of brightness. With the available stimulus of a complete optic array, the ambient light reflected from a whole layout of surfaces, one can detect the actual physical reflectance of each surface. The absolute luminous intensity of a color patch determines the sensation of brightness, but only if it is taken in isolation.

Finally, I remind you of the difference between the binocular sensations of objects in depth and the binocular perception of the depth of objects. When one attends to his visual sensations one can notice the doubling or diplopia of images in the field of view; crossed diplopia from here to the fixated object, and uncrossed diplopia beyond that point.[3] This doubling changes with every change in convergence, especially as we look to or away from what our hands are doing. We ought to see nothing as single except what lies on the momentary horopter. But of course we see everything as single, that is, we perceive it so. There is a phenomenal unity of each object despite an ever-varying doubleness of its sensation.

Auditory perception, we say, is based on a different mode or department of sense from visual perception. But the paradox of invariant perception with vary-

---

[3]For further details, see Gibson (1950a, p. 100ff.) (Eds.)

ing sensations holds nevertheless. Consider those very peculiar and special sounds, the phonemes of speech. They are acoustically analysable, it is true, in terms of intensity, frequency, and the frequency spectrum, but their distinctive nature consists of higher-order variables which are now beginning to be specified. Phonemes are the same at quite different levels of pitch and loudness, and hence are phenomenally constant for the voices of men, or women, or children. Speech cannot only be voiced; it can also be murmured, shouted, whispered, or sung. It can be emitted in falsetto, or even by a sort of whistling, without completely destroying the distinctive features which define the phonemic units of speech. They are invariant with changes of auditory sensation.

Consider also the hypothetical sensations that a hearer would get during auditory localization—the different sense impressions or sense data from the two ears. The main stimulus differences are ones of intensity and time of onset. As we know from the experiments of Wallach (1940) and others, the hearer turns and tilts his head from side to side, as if exploring, when he hears an unseen event. For a repeating sound, this means that the relative loudnesses and onsets of sensation are continually changing during the head turning. But the perception is that of a fixed or constant direction of the sound in space. As a matter of fact there is no evidence to show that any man or animal ever heard the changes of binaural sensations when turning his head. There is no awareness of such a flux. Binaural disparity never becomes conscious as binocular disparity can (Rosenzweig, 1961). I prefer to believe that the binaural mechanism is an active system which responds to disparity and tends to react by nullifying it, that is, by pointing the head toward the source of sound. The system responds to the sound field in the air, and we are misled when we consider only the wave train entering each ear separately.

So much for hearing. It is the sense of touch, so-called, that provides the clearest examples of the invariance of perception with varying sensations. In the last two or three years I have been running a series of experiments to test the limits of what an observer can do by touching or feeling without vision, that is, to discover what he can detect or discriminate about surfaces, edges, interspaces, objects, and motions in the neighborhood of his body. In these experiments we can compare the classical results obtained with passive punctate stimulation of the skin (intensity, locus, duality, and motion of a cutaneous impression or a pattern of such impressions) and the results obtained with the self-produced stimulation of touching. In general, an observer can perceive the properties of an object by active touch with quite surprising success. So also, of course, can a blind person. The following results come from a long series of observations (Gibson, 1962a).[4]

---

[4]Katz (1925) and Revesz (1950) founded the study of active touch (haptic perception); see Pick (1980) for a recent review. (Eds.)

*Rigidity.*    For example, when pressing on a rigid object with a finger, or squeezing it with the hand, there is an increase of sensation and then a decrease, or usually a flow of changing intensities. The perception, however, is of a constant rigidity of the surface. One simply feels the object. The impression on the skin as such is hard to detect. When one is touched *by* the same object instead of touching it, however, the variation of intensity is easy to detect. An observer can distinguish correctly between two protuberant surfaces, one rigid and the other yielding, when he presses them, but not when they are pressed on his passive skin.

*Unity.*    When feeling one object between two fingers, only one object is felt, although two separated cutaneous sensations occur. This is a surprising fact when you consider it. The different local signs of these impressions have seemingly dropped out of the experience. The result is the same whether the object is held with two, three, four, or five fingers; the multiplicity of impressions on the skin has no effect on the perception of spatial unity of the object. It can be held by two hands and still be one object. It can be felt by many combinations of all 10 fingers, in rapidly changing combinations, and the perception of the object is all the better for it.

*Stability.*    Active touch is exploratory and the observer tends to slide his finger over a corner or protuberance of a hidden object. The impression is then displaced over the skin and a feeling of tactile motion would be expected to occur. But the object is perceived to be stationary in space, and the tactile motion is not noticed. The perception is stable although the sensation is moving.

*Weight.*    When one holds or lifts an object, the judgment of its weight is easier than when it is allowed simply to press downward against the skin of the supported resting hand. In active lifting, a whole set of additional inputs is involved. Besides the end organs of the skin and the deeper tissue, the receptors of the finger joints, wrist joints, and arm joints are excited, and the whole neuromuscular feedback system of the arm is activated. The flux and array of pressure sensations and articular sensations from a dozen or so joints ought to be of bewildering complexity. It probably would be if introspection could detect all that goes on in hefting a weight. But what the observer perceives is the mass of the object, unchanging despite the changing sensations. A weight comes to be as well or better perceived, in fact, when the object is shifted back and forth from one hand to the other. Something invariant emerges from this seeming mishmash of excitation. The perception is equivalent to that which accompanies the controlled and isolated sensory impressions of the standardized weight-lifting experiment.

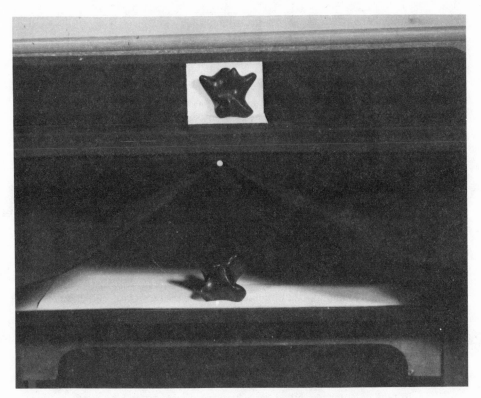

FIG. 34.   The visible object and the tangible object.

*Shape.*   A method of investigating the perception of unfamiliar shape by active touch is illustrated. Figure 34 shows an object behind a curtain with another identical (or different) object visible on a turntable. Figure 35 shows an observer feeling the object with both hands and judging whether the visible one is the same or different. Alternatively he might be required to match it with one of 10 visible objects, as shown in Figure 36. The degree to which these sculptured free forms differ among themselves is illustrated in Figure 37, where two are identical and the third different, and also in Figure 38, a view from the side. All these objects have six protuberances in front, and a rounded back. The ordinary observer, after very little practice, can distinguish among the tangible objects and match them to their visible replicas with little error (Caviness & Gibson, 1962).

The haptic system of the exploring hand is sensitive to the variables of solid geometry, not those of plane geometry. It gets nothing of a flat picture, but it gets a great deal of the shape of a solid object. The hand can detect all of the following properties: the slant of a surface, the convexity or concavity of a surface, the edge or corner at the junction of two or more surfaces, and the separation of

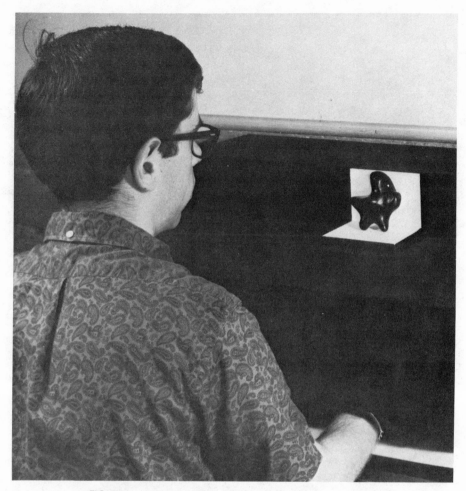

FIG. 35.    An observer looking at one object and feeling another.

two edges, as our experiments demonstrate.[5] Now it has always been assumed that the skin must be analogous to the retina—that it is a sensory mosaic which registers the form or pattern of the receptors excited. The skin and the retina can, in fact, do so when they are passively stimulated, and this has been taken to be their basic or sensory function.

If the cutaneous form sense is the basis for the feeling of objective shape, however, an impossible paradox arises. The series of cutaneous pressure patterns with a pair of exploring hands is something like that of a kaleidoscope; it

---

[5]Cf. Gibson & Backlund (1963). (Eds.)

FIG. 36. The ten sculptured objects used.

seemingly has no rationale, and no single pattern is ever like the shape of the object. Nevertheless, from the inputs of the skin and the joints together, from the sensory system if not from the sensations, a remarkably clear perception of shape arises. The phenomenal shape of the object is invariant although the phenomenal patterns of sense data fluctuate and vary from moment to moment.

*Conclusion.* From all these facts of vision, hearing, and touch we ought to conclude that sensations are not the the cause of perceptions. This is a strange statement. But I am willing to draw this conclusion. Conscious sensory impressions and sense data in general are incidental to perception, not essential to it. They are occasionally symptomatic of perception. But they are not even neces-

FIG. 37. Close-up of two identical and one different object.

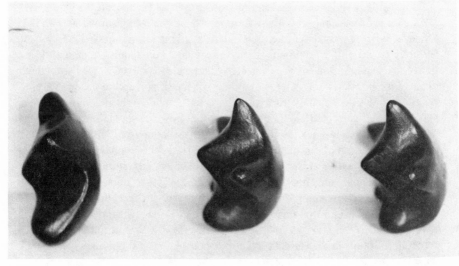

FIG. 38.    Side view of three objects.

sary symptoms inasmuch as perception may be ''sensationless'' (as for example in auditory localization). Having a perception does not entail the having of sensations.

The difficulty in accepting this conclusion is how to explain sense perception *unless* by way of sensations. But there is a way out of this difficulty, and that is to distinguish two meanings of the word ''sense''. Sensitivity is one thing, sensation is quite another.

The first meaning refers to the effects of stimulation in general. The second refers to conscious impressions induced by certain selected variables of stimulation. We can now assert that in the first meaning sensory *inputs* are prerequisite to perception, but that in the second meaning sensory *impressions* are *not* prerequisite to perception. In other words the *senses* are necessary for perception but *sensations* are not. In order to avoid confusion it might be better to call the senses by a new term such as *esthesic system*.[6] We can then distinguish between sensory perception and sensory experience, between perception as a result of stimulation and sensation as a result of stimulation. The variables of stimulation that cause the first must be different from those that cause the second. Likewise the dimensions of sensitivity to informative stimuli must be different from those to uninformative stimuli.

---

[6]This is the only place in which Gibson used this term. He later spoke of *perceptual* systems (Gibson, 1966b) and made a distinction between imposed stimulation (passive reception) and obtained stimulation (active detection). Under normal circumstances stimulation is obtained, not imposed. (Eds.)

How is the invariance of perception with varying sensations to be explained? By higher-order variables of stimulation which are themselves invariant, and by the sensitivity of esthesic systems to such invariant information. This kind of sensitivity is useful to animals. It may be innate, or acquired, or a little of both—that is a question for experiment. We can study it directly. We do not have to solve the puzzle of how there can be invariance of perception despite varying sensations. We do not have to inquire how sensations might be converted into perceptions, or corrected, or compensated for, or how one set of sensations might reciprocally interact with another set. If the sensations are disposed of, the paradox of perceptual constancy evaporates. Clearly the hypothesis of stimulus invariants is crucial for this explanation, and I will have to return to it later. Note that with this approach, a seemingly useful tool of experimenters, the index of constancy loses its meaning. It ceases to be a measure of perceptual achievement. The supposed baseline of this ratio, the "retinal" size, shape, or brightness, cannot be used in a computation of the achievement if it is not the basis of the perception. It falls in a different realm of discourse, and it simply is not commensurable with perceptual size, shape, or brightness.

*What are sensations?*    We might well pause at this stage to consider what is being discarded. Just what are these experiences that the perceptual theorist should no longer appeal to? I suggested at the beginning that our understanding of sensations has always been obscure. The reason for this, I think, is that the term sensation has been applied to quite different things. Let us examine the various meanings of the word to be found in philosophy, psychology, and physiology.

1. The theoretical concept. Theories of perception, as already noted, have always assumed that sensations were the necessary occasions of perception; that they were entailed in perceiving. This is precisely the assumption that is being challenged by my distinction between sensation and sensitivity. Its plausibility comes only from the evidence that *stimuli* are the necessary occasions of perception. I shall argue that none of the kinds of experience which have been called sensory *requires* this theoretical assumption.

2. The experimentalist's concept. In psychophysical experiments the variables of sensation have been taken to be correlates of the variables of physical energy which the experimenter could apply to his observer. In the past, the latter have tended to be those which were fundamental for physics proper, and which were controllable by borrowing the instruments of optics, acoustics, and mechanics. The favorite physical variables were intensity and frequency for wave energy, along with simple location or extension, and time or duration. But these dimensions of stimulation have little to do with the environment. They are fundamental for physics but not necessarily so for sense organs. The dimensions of available stimulation in a natural physical environment are of higher order than these, being variables of pattern and change. We are beginning to be able to control these natural stimulus variables. Note also that the stimuli of classical

psychophysics are *applied* to a passive observer by an experimenter whereas the stimuli in perceptual psychophysics are *obtained* by an active observer (although the opportunities for obtainable stimulation are provided by the experimenter). The experiences resulting from these two situations are apt to be different, as the experiments on active touch demonstrate.

3. The physiological concept. The early physiologists discovered the receptor elements of the sense organs and assumed that these cells (rods, cones, hair cells, etc.) were the units of a receptor mosaic. Hence a sensation was taken to be a correlate of a single receptor, that is, the end organ of the nerve fiber. But we are now fairly sure, after recording from single fibers with microelectrodes, that the functional units of a sense organ are not the anatomical cells, but groupings of cells. It was also assumed, after Johannes Müller, that a specific mode or quality of sensation corresponded to any given nerve or fiber. But this generalization too, can no longer be supported since, for one thing, the same fiber can participate in different groupings and have thereby different receptive functions.[7] When Müller insisted that the mind had no direct contact with the environment but only with the "qualities of the sensory nerves," he was confusing sensitivity with sensation. He assumed that the function of the senses was to provide sensations. He was right, surely, to maintain that perception depends on stimulation but wrong to maintain that it depends on the conscious qualities of sense. A sense *organ* has to be defined as a hierarchy of functional groupings of cells, and they are not always adjacent anatomically.

4. The analytic concept. The attempt to reduce consciousness to its lowest terms by introspection culminated in Tichener. A sensation was taken to be an irreducible experience not analysable into components—a simple datum. It is fair to say that the attempt failed. Sensations as combining elements are no longer advocated, although the elegance and force of the structuralist program was such that traces of it are still influential in psychology. Conscious perceptions *cannot* always be reduced to conscious sensations, as the Gestalt theorists have shown. It is clear that sensation in this meaning of the term is not prerequisite to perception.

5. The empiricist's concept. According to Locke and all the thinkers influenced by him, sense impressions are the original beginnings of perceptual experience prior to learning. They are innate, and pure sensations are had only by the new-born infant. They are without meaning and probably without reference to external objects. They are data for thought (or inference, or interpretation, or association, or other kinds of learning, either automatic or rational). What they are like has been the subject of endless inquiry, and this explains our strong curiosity about the first visual experiences of the congenitally blind after the operation for cataract. The theory that original experience was composed of sensations has always appealed to psychologists because the available alterna-

---

[7]Uttal (1973) comprehensively reviews these issues for each sensory modality. (Eds.)

tives, nativism and rationalism, implied either a faculty of perception or a faculty of reason. But we can reject sensation as the original beginning of perception and accept useful sensitivity as something present from the start of life without being driven into the arms of faculty psychology. We can also avoid the nagging difficulty that infants and young animals (and the cataract patients, in my opinion) do not, on the evidence, seem to have the bare and meaningless sensations that classical empiricism says they should have.

6. The concept of an experience with subjective reference. There is still another possible meaning of the term sensation. It is the meaning used in saying that a stomach-ache is sensory rather than perceptual. The same could be said of an after-image as compared with an object, for it seems to refer more to the observer than it does to the outer world. In cases of passve tactual experience, the observer can feel either the impression on the skin as such or the object as such, depending on how he directs his attention. It is as if the phenomenal experience had both a subjective pole and an objective pole. Pain is ordinarily subjective (although there may be some objective reference, e.g., a pin) and vision is ordinarily objective (although there can be a subjective aspect, e.g., dazzle), but all senses, in this view of the matter, carry both subjective and objective information. The observer's body, as well as his environment, can always be noted, together with the relation between them. The body and the world are different sources of stimulation; there is propriosensitivity as well as exterosensitivity. Sherrington was wrong only in supposing that there are separate proprioceptors and exteroceptors. All organs of sensitivity, I suggest, have this dual function.

Note that sensation considered as the subjective pole of experience is quite different from the other meanings of sensation. This is not the provider of data for perception or of messages or elements, nor is it the innate beginning of perception. This is a legitimate and useful meaning, but not the classical one— the basis of the experience of the external world.

*Conclusion.* Having examined the various kinds of experience that have been called sensory, I conclude that no one of them is required as the necessary occasion of perception. Several of them do undoubtedly occur in a man who introspects, or who serves as subject in an experiment, but the explanation of perception can dispense with all of them.

## RECONSTRUCTION OF A THEORY OF SENSITIVITY

If sensitivity is distinguished from sensation, and if perception depends on the former but not the latter, we will have to make a fresh start on the explanation of perception. We will have to discard many cherished doctrines and formulas (like separate and distinct modalities of sense), to clarify and find words for new things (like stimulus patterns and transformations), and to devise new experimental methods (such as how to control stimulus information instead of traditional stimuli). What are the requirements of a theory of perception not mediated by sense data?

Obviously it will have to show that sensitivity, with or without accompanying sensations, is adequate for all the manifold properties of perception (Gibson, 1959a). It will have to show that the afferent inputs to the nervous system of a child or man are rich enough to explain the degree to which he is aware of the world (but the inputs are taken to be those of active systems, not passive receptors or even sense organs). It will have to show that there is information in available stimulation (but the potential stimuli are taken to be limitless in variables of higher order). It will have to show that there are constants in the flow of available stimulation in order to explain constancy. It will have to show that these invariants in ambient light, sound, and mechanical contact, do in fact specify the objects which are their sources—that something in the proximal stimulus is specific to the distal stimulus (Gibson 1960c).[8] It will have to suggest how these invariants can be discovered by the activity of selective attention (but there are hints of such a mechanism in what we already know about sense-organ adjustments, so-called, and about the selective filtering of higher nerve centers). It will have to explain propriosensitivity (self-perception) along with exterosensitivity (object perception), but without appealing to the oversimplified doctrine of a special sense of kinesthesis.

Moreover, the theory will have to explain all the observations and experiments of past generations which seem to make it perfectly evident that the observer *contributes* meaning to his experience, that he *supplements* the data, and that significance *accrues* to sensation. I have assumed limitless information in available stimulation from the natural environment. Therefore, the explanation must be that the *experimenter* has limited the available information in all such experiments, or else that, in a natural situation, the available stimulus information is impoverished, as by darkness or a disadvantageous point of view. Psychologists are accustomed to use stimulus situations with impoverished, ambiguous, or conflicting information. These have been devised in the hope of revealing the constructive process taken to characterize *all* perception. In these special situations there must indeed occur a special process. It could appropriately be called *guessing*. But I would distinguish perceiving from guessing, and suggest that we investigate the first and try to understand the second by means of corollaries about deficient information.

The theory will have to provide an explanation of illusions, not only the optical ones but those of all other channels of sensitivity. The postulates of stimulus information and stimulus ecology, however, suggest ways in which the various illusions can be, for the first time, classified into types and subtypes of misperception, with the reasons therefore. A proper description of the informa-

---

[8]Gibson's subsequent emphasis on perceptual systems actively obtaining stimulation forced him to abandon the sensori-motor dichotomy and, therefore, the proximal-distal distinction (cf. Gibson, 1966b, p. 4). (Eds.)

tion in an optic array will necessarily include a description of the information in a picture, and the ambiguous, conflicting, equivocal, or misleading information that can be incorporated in a picture. Note that illusions will be treated as special cases of perception, not as phenomena which might reveal the laws of the subjective process of perception.

Finally, the theory will have to be consistent with the known facts about social perception and all the information that has accumulated about the perception and learning of symbols and words. Here, you may think, a sensitivity theory of perception must surely fail. Even allowing that physiognomic and expressive character may have some basis in complex stimulation, words can have no meaning except that supplied by the perceiver. But this objection, cogent as it may sound, entirely misses the point. Once it is granted that stimuli may carry information, or have meaning, the whole theory of meaning is revolutionized, and we have to make a new start on it. Once it is granted that a child or a man can develop sensitivity to the invariants of the ecological stimulus environment it is no great step to admit that he can also learn to respond to the invariants of the social and the symbolic environments. The laws by which stimuli specify events and objects are not, of course, the rules or conventions by which chosen events or objects stand for others, but both are lawful. If animals and children can register perceptual meanings it is not surprising that children and adults can go on to register verbal meanings. However, just as the child does not first have a repertory of sensations and then attach meanings, so also he does not first hear a vocabulary of words and then attach meanings.

## Role of Attention in Perception

An entirely different picture of the senses has emerged. For this to happen, we had to suppose that their sole function was not to yield sensations. Instead of mere receptors, that is receivers and transducers of energy, they appear to be systems for exploring, searching, and selecting ambient energy. The sense organs are all capable of motor adjustment. Figure 39 is a diagram which supplements and alters the usual stimulus-response diagram. It shows on the left the modification of stimulation by reactions of the exteroceptive system, and on the right the modification of reactions by stimulation of the proprioceptive system. The latter is familiar nowadays under the the name of feedback, that is, the neural loops essential for the control of behavior. But the loops on the left are just as essential as those on the right. The organism has two kinds of feedback, not one. There are two kinds of action, in fact, one being *exploratory* action and the other *performatory* action. Muscles can enhance perception as well as do work and some, like the eye muscles, have this function exclusively. The hands, mouth and nose, ears, and eyes are all in their own way active systems, as the body is. The primary reaction to pressure on the skin is exploration with the fingers. Chemicals at the nose and mouth first elicit sniffing and savoring. Sound at the ears causes head turning. Light at the eyes brings about focusing, fixating, converging, and exploring of the light. Note that the outcome of all these ad-

the modification of stimulation by reactions of the exteroceptive sense organs

the modification of reactions by stimulation of the proprioceptive system

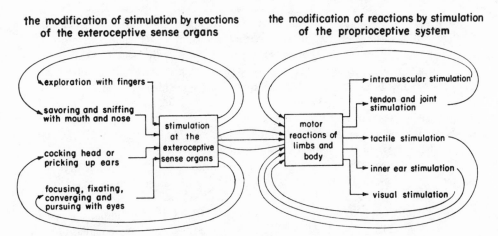

FIG. 39.   The feedback loops for exploring stimulation and those for controlling behavior. (The angular lines represent physical action; the curved lines represent neural action.)

justments is to obtain stimulation or, rather, to obtain the maximum information from the available stimulation.

This new picture of the senses includes attention as part of sensitivity, not as an act of the mind upon the deliverances of the senses. Every esthesic system is an attentional system. Attention is not an intervening process, therefore, but one that starts at the periphery. It also continues to select and filter the already selected inputs at nerve centers, as we know both from introspection and from the evidence obtained by microelectrode recording.

## Pattern and Change of Stimulation

Consider the sense organs in the old way, each as a population of receptive units. We have thought of the retina, the skin, the tongue, and perhaps the olfactory epithelium as examples of a sensory surface, a mosaic. Even the Organ of Corti and the lining of the statocysts may be conceived in this way. But note, parenthetically, that the flat surface analogy does not hold at all for the articular sense, that is, the set of receptors for all the joints of the skeleton. The point is that any population of receptive units is capable of delivering a *simultaneous array of neural inputs* (although it is gratuitous or false to call this a two-dimensional pattern or picture, as we do for the retina and are tempted to do for the skin). Apart from this muddle, every sense, then, is a pattern sense. Equally, they are all capable of delivering *a sequence or stream of neural inputs or changes in the simultaneous pattern*. Every sense is therefore a transformation sense as well as a pattern sense.

Consider next the stimulation for these senses, the *proximal* stimulation. In every case it also is a simultaneous array and a successive flux. There are two kinds of order in stimulation, as I once put it, adjacent order and sequential order

(Gibson, 1950a). Pattern and change are characteristic of stimulation in general, unless it has been sterilized by an experimenter, and here is where the information lies. For example, pattern and change occur at the retina and the skin—even more at the dual retina and the two-handed skin, as the experiments reported have shown. They occur at the basilar membrane of the cochlea as, respectively, the momentary sound spectrum and the transients of sound; moreover the binaural disparity patterns change with head movement. The simultaneous pattern of input from all joints of the skeleton taken together is a highly intricate and interlocked configuration, yet its slightest transformation seems to be registered when the individual moves. Pattern and change occur at the gustatory and olfactory surfaces, and even for the statocysts and the semicircular canals. Pattern and change are universal.

Now, sensory physiologists have always recognized the importance of patterns of stimulation and tried to relate them to the sensory projection areas of the brain. What they have not understood is transformations of pattern. They have tried to imagine a cortical correlate of form, which is difficult enough (as witness Hebb's recent attempt to explain visual form perception, 1949), but not the changes of form which I have described. A tabulation may help to clarify the problem (Table 2).

The motionless frozen observer with his eyes fixed on a motionless frozen world gets a pattern of stimulation from each of his senses (Type I stimulation) but the situation is hardly typical. The array at the eyes is comparable to a panoramic still picture. If he moves, or if something moves, the arrays change (at the eyes, the skin, and the joints, for instance) in specific ways or dimensions (Type II stimulation). I have worked out the dimensions of transformation for the eyes, and it ought to be possible to do this for the other systems. Subjective movement and objective motion (A and B) normally yield different stimuli even at the eyes. The observer can see himself moving, as one does in automobile driving, and even see his own eye movements, as in observing the shifting of an afterimage, but these are perceptions with subjective reference. They are "proprioceptive." We might say that the stimuli are propriospecific, since they carry information about the self.

TABLE 2
A Classification of Stimulus Variables for Perception

---

I. The unchanging stimulus array. *Unvarying variables.* Dimensions of pattern, form, and structure as such

II. The changing stimulus array. *Varying variables*
   A. Self-produced transformation—specifies *motion of self*
      1. With a sense-organ exploration—control of *attention* (e.g., eye movement)
      2. With gross motor reactions—control of *performance* (e.g., locomotion)
   B. Other-produced transformation—specifies *motion of object*

III. The *invariants* in a changing stimulus array. *Invariant variables*
   *Unchanging* dimensions under transformation—specify *rigid surfaces and objects.*

---

The third type of stimulus variable is crucial since it is taken to explain the invariance of object perception. Change of an array usually involves nonchange. Some order is preserved in every transformation. Neither at the eye nor the skin nor at any other organ does the energy scintillate, as it were, like the random flashing of the fireflies in a field. There are always invariant variables alongside the varying variables. They are specific to (but not copies of) the permanent properties of external things. It is not a paradox that perception should correspond to the distal object, although it depends on the proximal stimulus if the object is in fact specified in the stimulus. The Ames demonstrations purporting to show that optical stimulation can *never* specify objects depend on a frozen array from which the invariants cannot emerge.

Consider the difference between *unvarying* and *invariant* variables of stimulation (Type I and Type III). In the former case the stimuli that would be invariant do not get separated off from the those that would vary if the array underwent transformation. The frozen array, the case of continuous nontransformation, carries less information. The case is one that never occurs in life. A prolonged freezing of the pattern of stimulation on the retina or the skin, in fact, yields an input which soon fades away to nothing.

The normal world is sufficiently full of motions and events to make a stream of stimulation. But even without external motions a flow is produced. The normal activity of perception is to explore the world. We thus alter its perspectives, if events do not alter them for us. What exploration does is to isolate the invariants. The sensory system can separate the permanence from the change only if there is change.

In vision, we strive to get new perspectives on an object in order to perceive it properly. I believe that something analogous to this is what happens in the active exploratory touching of an object. The momentary visual perspectives, of course, are pictures or forms in the geometrical sense of that term whereas the momentary tactual perspectives are not. Nevertheless they are similar since, for an object of a given solid shape, any change of cutaneous pattern like any change of retinal pattern is *reversible*. The impression of the object on the skin, like its impression on the retina, can recur by a reversal of the act that transformed it. The successive patterns thus fall into a family of patterns which is specific to the object. I submit to Hebb the suggestion that the first problem in perceptual physiology is not how the brain responds to form as such, unvarying form, but instead how it responds to the invariant variables of changing form. I think we should attempt a direct physiological theory of object perception without waiting for a successful theory of picture perception.

## Invariant Properties of a Changing Stimulus Array

The crux of the theory of stimulation here proposed is the existence of certain types of permanence underlying change. These invariants are not, I think, produced by the acquiring of invariant responses to varying stimuli—they are *in* the stimuli at least potentially. They are facts of stimulus ecology, independent of the observer although dependent upon his exploratory isolation of them. This kind of order in stimulation is not created by the observer, either out of his past experience or by innate preknowledge. Just as the invariant properties of the physical world of objects are not constructed by the perceiver, so the invariant properties in available stimulation are not constructed by him. They are discoverable by the attentive adjustments of his sense organs and by the education of his attention.

Some of these stimulus invariants are extremely subtle. The ultimate subtleties of the information in stimulation may well be unlimited. But other invariants are quite simple and easily detected. The optical texture that specifies a physical surface (in contrast with the textureless patch that specifies an empty space) is invariant with illumination and under all transformations of perspective. Introspectively we say that one yields a surface color and the other a film color, but the spatial meaning is what counts, not the introspection. The textures of earth, air, and water are different, and the differences are constant. So are the differences that specify to the young of any species the fur, feathers, or face of the mother. The intensity and wave length of the light are irrelevant. The infant seems to be sensitive from the beginning, more or less, to such external stimuli as these. The tablet of his consciousness may be nearly blank at birth, as Locke believed, but the impressions that do appear are vague perceptions, not bare sensations. The earliest dimensions of sensitivity are useful ones.

Classical sense impressions, I think, are something of which only a human adult is aware. They tend to arise when he introspects, or when he tries to describe the content of experience, or the punctate momentary elements of perception, or when simple variables of physical energy are experimentally isolated for him by a psychologist, or when stimuli are applied to his receptors instead of his being allowed to obtain them for himself. Far from being original experiences, they are sophisticated ones; they depend on having had a great deal of past experience.

This is not to deny that perception alters with learning or depends upon learning. Instead it points to a different kind of learning from that we have previously conceived. Unquestionably the infant has to learn to perceive. That is why he explores with eyes, hands, mouth, and all of his organs, extending and refining his dimensions of sensitivity. He has to separate what comes from the world and what comes from himself. But he does not, I think, have to learn to convert sensations into perceptions.

## PART II: A NOTE ON CURRENT THEORIES OF PERCEPTION*

What underlies the current theories of perception, all of them, from which the "ecological approach" departs? I seem to detect the following set of assumptions:

---

*Unpublished manuscript, July, 1974.

1. Information about the world comes only through the organs of sense.

2. Information about the world that *has* come through the organs of sense in the past is stored in memory and is added to what is *now* coming through the senses.

These are the two basic assumptions of empiricism. The second is necessary because "sensations" by themselves are insufficient for perception. There are still theorists, however, who disagree with them and make a different assumption:

3. Information about the world exists in the *mind*. What comes through the organs of sense has to be *interpreted* by the mind. This seems to be the basic assumption of rationalism. And insofar as the information in the mind is supposed to be innate (to exist at birth) it is also the basic assumption of nativism. Rationalism and nativism, although allied theories, are not quite the same.

The conflict between these theories has persisted for centuries. Empiricism is generally preferred but nativism and even rationalism have adherents. No theory has won. We need to go deeper. What are the presuppositions that underlie all three of these assumptions? What do they *agree* on? I think I discern the following:

4. What comes through the sense-organs must be mere *signals* from the world, since it seems impossible for a complete *picture* of the world to get through, or even a series of pictures. "Signals" are a *metaphorical description* of sensations. Strictly speaking, sensations are specific to receptors and not to the world (J. Müller).[9]

5. Perception is some kind of *internal operation* of the brain (the seat of the mind) on the signals from the world, e.g., interpretation, addition, supplementation, or organization, but in any case a "processing" of the input.[10]

6. What exists in the brain or the mind when perception has been achieved is a sort of *representation* of the world that more or less *corresponds* to it.

7. We can understand the perception of the world separately from the awareness of the body of the perceiver *in* the world (the self or ego) since different sense organs are involved, the exteroceptors in the first case and the proprioceptors in the second case (along with the interoceptors).

I propose to reject these four presuppositions in favor of others. This is also to reject the classical theories of perception, nativism, rationalism, and even empiricism.

---

[9] Modern sensory physiologists might hold that sensations are specific to receptive units and not to receptors; cf. Ch. 4.3, part two. (Eds.)

[10] Cf. Ch. 4.8. (Eds.)

Instead of (4) I suggest that nothing "comes through" the sense organs, neither signals nor pictures, since these organs are components of perceptual systems that extract invariants from the flux of stimulus energy surrounding the observer. Invariants are specific to the world but *not* to the receptors stimulated.

Instead of (5) I suggest that perception is a circular process in which outputs to the perceptual organs from the brain are as important as inputs from the organs to the brain. The claim that impulses in the sensory nerves are *signals* is rejected. The nerves should not be compared with channels for communication. The brain is *not* the seat of the mind.

Instead of (6) I suggest that the act of perceiving is one of becoming aware of the environment, or picking up information about the environment, but that nothing like a *representation* of the environment exists in the brain or the mind which could be in greater or lesser correspondence with it—no "phenomenal" world which reflects or parallels the "physical" world.[11]

Instead of (7) I suggest that the perception of the environment is necessarily accompanied by "co-perception" of the self in the environment since each entails the other. All the perceptual systems obtain information about the self along with information about the world. This must be so if they register their own adjustments as well as the results of these adjustments.

What about the first three assumptions that distinguish between empiricism, rationalism, and nativism?

We can now reformulate (1) to assert that information about the world is only obtained by the activity of the perceptual systems. Information does not simply "come through," or impress itself on a mind that is blank at birth however, as sensations caused by stimuli are supposed to do. The mistake of the empiricists was to think that information about the world could only be got by way of these imposed sensations.

We can also reformulate (2). Information about the world that has been obtained will continue to be obtained, and the information-pickup will improve with practice. This is perceptual learning. But this does not imply that information is stored in memory. The information continues to be available outside the skin, i.e., the invariants that specify the world. Perception is a skill, not a constructing of the mental world out of psychic components. The observer has no *need* to store information. The fact that he can recall, recollect, imagine, and think about parts of the environment "not present to the senses" is a different matter entirely. This fact does *not* prove that memories are combined with sensations so as to yield perceptions.

Assumption (3) seems to me simply wrong and is to be rejected, not reformulated. Information about the world does not exist in the mind. The rational mind of rationalism, as contrasted with the emotional body, is a myth. The inborn

---

[11] See Ch. 4.9 for more discussion of the distinction between the phenomenal and the real world. (Eds.)

mind of nativism, as contrasted with the mortal body, is a fallacy. The empiricists opposed these doctrines and held that information is got by a natural process, not a mystical one. They were right, even if they never understood the natural process. But actually they never completely freed their theories of mentalism.

What we need in psychology is a theory which avoids the plague of mentalism, even in the diluted form accepted by empiricism, without falling into the opposite error of stimulus-response mechanism. The new assumptions above are an effort in this direction. Whereas all the classical theories are based on neural *inputs* and constructive operations on these inputs (sensations) the new theory is based on neural *loops* and their hypothetical capacity to resonate to invariants over time (information).[12] Moreover the new theory aims to explain not only the perception of the environment but also the co-perception of the self.

The behaviorist movement tried to rid psychology of mentalism, and had some success, but it never had any success with the genuine problems of perception and cognition. We are now witnessing a great revival of interest in perception and cognition, but unhappily a regression to mentalism seems to go along with it. The good features of behaviorism are being lost in the retreat of psychologists into the old concern with sensations and images. The S-R formula has failed but the emphasis on action and adjustment is still valid. The explanation of perception, accordingly, should be functional. The acceptance of inputs and images actually goes hand in hand with the belief in discrete stimuli and countable responses. Both are out of date.

The modern theory of automata based on computers also has the virtue of rejecting mentalism but it is still preoccupied with the brain instead of the whole observer in his environment. Its approach is not ecological. The metaphor of inputs, storage, and the consulting of memory still lingers on. No computer has yet been designed which could learn about the *affordances* of its surroundings. Computer-theorizing still clings to the tradition of rationalism.[13] The ecological approach to perception cannot depend on it.

---

[12]Cf. Ch. 2.5. (Eds.)

[13]See Searle (1980) for a discussion of the rationalistic tradition behind the computer metaphors used in modern psychology. (Eds.)

# 4.5 New Reasons for Realism

## PART I: NEW REASONS FOR REALISM*

If *invariants* of the energy flux at the receptors of an organism exist, and if these invariants correspond to the permanent properties of the environment, and if they are the basis of the organism's perception of the environment instead of the sensory data on which we have thought it based, then I think there is new support for realism in epistemology as well as for a new theory of perception in psychology. I may be wrong, but one way to find out is to submit this thesis to criticism.

In this paper the theory of perception will first be outlined and then, insofar as they are separable, the reasons for realism will be presented. Only a bare skeleton of the theory need be stated since it has recently been published in book form.[1] It will be convenient to limit the discussion to the central problem of the perception of terrestrial objects and events. Under "objects" I will include the earth and its fixtures, the comparatively unchanging properties of solid things, in contrast to the sky, where such determinate objects do not exist. Under "events" I will include moving objects. The problems arising when human gestures, speech, or writing are the sources of perception will be largely excluded, although some reference must be made to pictures.

---

*Synthese, 1967, *17*, 162–172. Copyright 1967 by D. Reidel, Publishers. Reprinted by permission.

[1]Gibson (1966b) represents the present form of the theory. A less developed stage (part of which I would no longer defend) can be found in Gibson (1959a). A still more immature theory can be found in Gibson (1950a). The germ of it is in Gibson (1948).

## I. THE THEORY OF INFORMATION-BASED PERCEPTION

Existing theories of perception begin with the unquestioned assumption that it is based on sensations (sense impressions, or sense data), and then go on to postulate some kind of operation that must occur to convert them into percepts. It is taken for granted that sensation is entailed in perception. The theory of information-based perception begins with the assumption that sensory impressions are occasional and incidental symptoms of perception, that they are not entailed in perception. It is therefore not obliged to postulate any kind of operation on the data of sense, neither a mental operation on units of consciousness nor a central nervous operation on the signals in nerves. Perception is taken to be a process of information pickup.

The channels for sense impressions in animals and men are distinguished from what are called perceptual systems. The former consist of bundles of nerve fibers connecting passive receptors with corresponding points in the brain, and they are supposed to be mutually exclusive. The latter consist of both incoming fibers from organs containing receptors and outgoing fibers back to these organs and they are not supposed to be mutually exclusive but to overlap one another. The sensory nerves are supposed to deliver distinct signals to the brain that elicit correspondingly distinct qualities of experience in this theater of consciousness. The perceptual systems are assumed to make orienting and exploratory adjustments of the perceptual organs and to resonate in a particular way when a distinct kind of information is picked up. The senses yield an awareness of the receptors that have been stimulated by small amounts of energy, radiant, mechanical, thermal, or chemical. The perceptual systems yield an awareness of objects—one that sometimes does not include any awareness of the receptors stimulated. It is admitted that the qualities of sight, sound, touch, taste, and smell are interesting and that they reflect important facts of neurology. They are not to be confused, however, with the acts of looking, listening, touching, tasting, and sniffing which have a quite different neurological basis.

The sensitivity of the retina, the cochlea, the skin, the tongue, and the nasal membrane can be studied by the methods of sensory physiology and classical psychophysics but the shifting patterns of nervous input obtained when the eyes move, the head turns, the hand gropes, and the mouth works are only half of an input-output circle, and this circular act of attention has an entirely different order of sensitivity. It focusses not on stimulation but on stimulus information.

### 1. The Existence of Stimulus Information

The first assumption of this theory of perception is that certain properties of the energy flux at the skin of an active animal do not change, whereas other properties do. The former are invariant, the latter variant. It is further assumed, and can be demonstrated, that the invariants of stimulation correspond to invariant properties of the environment. Hence they are said to be ''information about'' the environment. The stimulus energy impinging on a perceiver must have pattern or structure in order to convey information in this meaning of the term. The ambient light, sound and odor in the surrounding medium, along with the mechanical and chemical contacts that arise from the substratum and its fixtures, are forms of stimulus energy that contain stimulus information.

Consider light, for example. Physical optics has been interpreted to imply that light carried information only about atoms, not about objects.[2] But when the student of vision believes this he makes the mistake of adopting the physicist's assumptions about radiant light from energy sources. He needs to make assumptions instead about *ambient* light from the surfaces of the terrestrial world. The latter is subject to laws of perspective geometry, not laws of photon tracks. The student of useful vision should be concerned with ecological optics, not physical optics; with the kind of light by which things are seen, not with the kind of light that is seen. The structure of an array of ambient light from the earth is the same from noon to sunset. Certain properties of this structure are invariant under perspective transformations as the observer moves from place to place. And these invariants are specific to the substances of which objects are composed, to the edges of objects, and to the layout of their surfaces. The intensity of light in any patch of the ambient array varies with the time of day and with the position of the observer, so that it carries *no* information about objects.

The primary receptors in the retina of the eye, the photo-sensitive rods and cones, are stimulated by radiant energy within certain limits of intensity and frequency. At this level the physiology of the eye and the physics of stimulus energy are cognate. It can be shown that the excitation of photo-receptors brings about corresponding sensations of brightness and color under certain special laboratory conditions. But when a retinal image is formed, even one with only a few margins or contrasts, it begins to have structure, and we must shift from physical optics to ecological optics. The retina itself has a structure of interconnecting nerve fibers, and we must shift from the level of a photo-receptive mosaic to a still-to-be-understood level of higher-order units in the nervous system. The simple correspondence of brightness to intensity and of color to frequency no longer holds. In short, we must think about the stimulus information for the system, not the stimulus energy for the receptors.

## 2. The Fact of Invariance over Time

It is assumed that the pattern of the ambient light, the ambient sound pressures, and the ambient mechanical pressures on any living animal is continually chang-

---

[2]This implication, and the further one that we can only *know* about particles, not objects, seemed overwhelming to me and to many other scientists 37 years ago. I read it in A. S. Eddington, *The Nature of the Physical World*, New York 1929. It took me years to get over it. I now realize that Eddington's physical world was that of the sky, not the earth.

ing. No stimulus array is ever frozen for any length of time except in the case of a sleeping or otherwise unconscious observer. There is the special case of a laboratory observer who tries to keep still and hold his eyes fixed but even then his eyes, head, and limbs manifest some tremor. Consequently the notion of an unchanging stimulus pattern is an unrealized abstraction, and the even more abstract notion of a fixed constellation of punctate stimuli is a myth. The realities of stimulation involve change in time. Stimulus information about objects resides, therefore, in invariant properties of the transforming array over time. This applies both to vision and to touch.

Taking vision as our example, consider a picture. We have supposed that it is the prototype of visual stimulation instead of the flowing picture that results from locomotion. The information about objects is much reduced in peephole vision, that is, in the optic array from a frozen picture, and ambiguities of size, distance, edges, and layout arise in viewing a picture. Such pictorial contradictions have been studied for centuries by painters and psychologists alike. All such ambiguities are removed when the experimenter substitutes the object for its picture so that the observer can walk around the object and see it in different perspectives.

If this is true, the function of a visual system is not to register the perspectives of things, their forms or color patches in the visual field, but to register the invariants that underlie the changing perspectives. Form-perception is an incidental symptom of this capacity, not its basis; the so-called sensations of form that we notice in a picture, or when we consider things as silhouettes, are not entailed in the perceiving of objects. Perception in the newborn does not begin with a flat patchwork of innate visual sensations to which depth must be added by some operation such as learning; perception begins at birth with whatever capacity the infant has to pick up the invariants in the stimulus flux that are significant for him.

## 3. The Process of Extracting Invariants over Time

The invariant properties of a changing stimulus array correspond to the invariant properties of the environment. What about the *variant* properties? The child must learn to separate the invariants from the variants more and more precisely as he grows up, and to focus his attention on them if he is to learn more and more about the world. He typically does so by exploration, that is, by changing the stimulus patterns on his eyes and skin so as to isolate what remains unchanged. During exploration of a stationary world, all such changes or transformations specify nothing more than his own movements. They have subjective reference to his own body. Since each transformation is obtained as a "feedback" from a movement, he can reverse the transformation by reversing his movement. The child can thus *control* the variants but not the invariants of stimulation. This fact probably has something to do with the way in which he can extract the latter from the mixture.

Let us note that the detecting of those variants of stimulation that can be controlled is not a channel of sense or a mode of sensation. The classical sense of kinesthesis does not cover it. Nor is this kind of detection a kind of perception. It is best described as a component of all the perceptual systems, the *propriospecific* component.

We can now take a further step. We note that not all transformations are caused by movements of the observer. Some are produced by motions of objects in the world, such as falling bodies, rolling stones, and moving animals. How can the child separate the variants caused by external events from the variants caused by his bodily movements? How can he know that the whole world has not moved, for example, whenever he moves his eyes? This is an old and controversial question in psychology.[3] A possible answer is, by extracting a still higher order of invariant. The uncontrollable variation, the one that cannot be reversed by reversing an exploratory movement, is information for an external event just as the invariant that remains after a controllable variation is information for an external object. If the *extracting of invariants over time* is the key process in perception, it can be assumed to occur at higher levels, including those called "intellectual."

## 4. The Continuity of Perception with Memory and Thought

All theories of sensation-based perception imply a categorical distinction between perception and memory, the former depending on *present* stimulation and the latter on a retrieval of the traces of *past* stimulation. A difficulty for these theories is that no sharp division between perceiving and remembering can be discovered in experience. The present merges with the past indistinguishably, and no good criterion has been found to separate them. The theory of information-based perception, on the other hand, implies that perception and memory are not sharply separated, either logically or phenomenally, since the dimension of time has been incorporated in the very definition of stimulus information.

Present stimulation is supposed to appear directly in consciousness as sensation. Past stimulation is supposed to have left traces that can appear in consciousness as memory images. Percepts are often supposed to be mixtures of sensations and memory images. Concepts and thoughts are supposed to be pure memory images without any admixture of sensations. The trouble with this theory is that perceivers are seldom able to distinguish by introspection between the sensations and the memories, and thinkers, although sometimes aware of images, often report that their thoughts are "imageless."

---

[3]Cf. Ch. 2.6. (Eds.)

The theory of information-based perception avoids these difficulties by assuming that neither sensations nor images are entailed in having knowledge of the world. The resonating of a cognitive system to invariants over time implies attention to objective facts, present, past, or future. The symptoms of stimulation may or may not appear as sensations in perception. The symptoms of casting one's attention over the whole world or over a great span of time may or may not appear as images in thought. It makes no difference, for they are incidental to knowledge, not essential for it.

In this theory, the old problem of how single memory images of an object might be fused into a concept is no longer a problem. The problem of how a concept might be imposed on a new percept disappears. The puzzle of the invariance of perception despite varying sensations, the "constancy" of the phenomenal size, shape, and color of objects, is no longer a puzzle. And the really staggering problem of the phenomenal persistence of objects when they are no longer "present to the senses" because they have been hidden by other objects is quite capable of solution when we realize that the awareness of an object does not depend on an awareness of its patch of color in the visual field.

## 5. Summary

Four hypotheses have been outlined above: (1) the existence of stimulus information, (2) the fact of invariance over time, (3) the process of extracting invariants over time, and (4) the continuity of perception with memory and thought. Whether or not they are verifiable (and this is not the place for a marshalling of evidence) they go together and provide a theory of perception. Granting it some plausibility, what does it imply about the old philosophical puzzles of our knowledge of the external world and our confidence in it?

## II.  IMPLICATIONS FOR EPISTEMOLOGY

It seems to me that these hypotheses make reasonable the commonsense position that has been called by philosophers direct or naive realism. I should like to think that there is sophisticated support for the naive belief in the world of objects and events, and for the simple-minded conviction that our senses give knowledge of it. But this support is hard to find when the senses are considered as channels of sensations; it becomes easy when they are considered as perceptual systems.

Highly ingenious philosophical arguments have been advanced in this century that give roundabout support for the common man's position. It is my impression (although I could be wrong) that all these forms of realism presuppose what I have called the theory of sensation-based perception, and that this is why the arguments have to be roundabout. What happens if we entertain the theory of information-based perception?

## 1. Immediate or Direct Experience

The doctrine that all we ever experience directly is the flow of our sense data implies that our experience of objects and events is indirect. Perception is mediated by sensation. This doctrine leads straight to the sense-datum controversy, since it is just plain false to assert that sense data are all we ever experience "directly."

For this doctrine we now have a substitute. There can be direct or immediate awareness of objects and events when the perceptual systems resonate so as to pick up information *and* there can be a kind of direct or immediate awareness of the physiological states of our sense organs when the sensory nerves as such are excited. But these two kinds of experience should not be confused, for they are at opposite poles, objective and subjective. Only the former should be called perceptual experience. There can be an awareness of other bodily organs than the sense organs, as in hunger or pain, and these are also properly called sensation. The concentrating of inner attention on the states of the receptors, however, as occurs when we are aware of after-images, double images, and "ringing in the ears," is unnatural. Psychologists, philosophers, and schizophrenics who make a habit of it are called "introspective" or "introverted" by the common man.

What about *indirect* awareness? This term should now be reserved primarily for the apprehension of things and events by means of surrogates or human artifacts, including pictures, words, sound-reproducing devices, and microscopes. I suspect that the experience is called indirect in such cases to the extent that there is a concurrent *direct* perception of the surface of the picture, the sounds or letters of the words, the scratching of the record, and the sight of the turntable, in short, of the mediator as such. Whether or not the terms *indirect* and *mediated* should be applied to cases of apprehension by judgment and inference I am uncertain.[4] But I am quite certain that there is no such thing as a phonograph record in the ear and no such thing as a picture in the eye—no reproduction of an external event or object that the organ transmits to the brain.

## 2. The Detection of Colors and Sounds

The man-in-the-street has always supposed that the colors of objects are one thing, whereas the colors of a rainbow or a sunset or an oil-slick are a different matter. He sees the color of a surface *in* the surface, although he may see other colors that appear to be in the light. But this simple fellow has been told he is wrong ever since Newton's discovery of spectral wavelengths, for colors are only in the light, not in objects. Even more, he is told by physical optics and physiological optics that colors are only in *him* since light consists of waves (or photons—both are true, sorry!). The poor man is bewildered but he goes on seeing colors in surfaces. More exactly, he sees very much the same color in the

---

[4]Cf. Gibson (1979a, Ch. 14). (Eds.).

same surface despite change in the amount, kind, and direction of the illumination falling on it. The light is variant, the color is invariant, so of course he sees the color in the surface, not in the light.

Ecological optics, I think, gives promise of assuring him that he is right after all. It postulates stimulus information in the ambient light from a layout of reflecting surfaces, as noted. The various reflectances of these surfaces, their types of natural pigmentation, help to determine the structure of the ambient light. The invariants of structure that specify classes of natural pigments (as in ripe *vs.* unripe fruit, for example) are highly complicated and remain to be worked out, but some progress is being made in doing so.

Physical acoustics tells the man-in-the-street that sensations of loudness, pitch, and pitch mixture are in his head, and only arise because they correspond to the variables of sound waves in the air. He could not possibly *hear* a mechanical event; he can only infer it from the data. But nevertheless he goes on hearing natural events like rubbing, scraping, rolling, and brushing, or vocal events like growling, barking, singing and croaking, or carpenter's events like sawing, pounding, filing, and chopping. Ecological acoustics would tell him that the vibratory event, the source of the waves, is specified in certain invariant properties of the wave train. These properties (the transients for example) are the same over the whole field of sound waves centered on the mechanical disturbance and extending outward in the medium. Information about the event is physically present in the air surrounding the event. If the man is within earshot, he hears the event.

In short, there is a proper meaning of the word ''color'' that refers to a distinctive feature of a solid substance. There is a proper meaning of the word ''sound'' that refers to a distinctive feature of a mechanical disturbance. The doctrine of secondary qualities comes from a misunderstanding.

## 3. Public Experience and Private Experiences

The ecology of stimulus information, as distinguished from the physics of stimulus energy, describes fields of available stimulation. In any given air space there exist fields of three types: (1) overlapping fields of airborne compression waves from mechanical events (''sounds''), (2) interpenetrating fields of perspective projections from reflecting surfaces (''sights'') and, (3) fields of diffusing volatile substances from plants and animals (''odors'').[5] They rise and fall in intensity, but they have been generally available to the ears, eyes, and noses of terrestrial animals for millions of years. They have controlled the locomotion of animals toward or away from the sources of these fields. They

---

[5]The volatile parts of plants and animals are sometimes called ''essences'' by odor-chemists. This suggests the fact that the vapors.of many things specify them, that is distinguish them from other things, and this is what I mean by information about things.

constitute what might be called public information for the perception of events, objects, and organisms.

The ambient stimulation for an individual perceiver at any one location in such an air space is not the same as at any other location, but the information is the same and, since he moves about, he can have the same perceptions that another perceiver could have. A whole crowd of perceivers, in fact, could all hear, see, and smell the same things. They could also hear, see, and perhaps smell each other. Each one, finally, could hear his own voice and footsteps and see his own body.

Now I suggest that this state of affairs can define what might be called levels of increasing "privacy" of perception. All observers can obtain exactly the same information about a tree if they all walk around it and get the same perspectives. Each observer gets a somewhat different set of perspectives of his own hands than any other observer gets, although there is much in common. But the perspective of one's own nose is absolutely unique and no one else can ever see it from that particular point of view. It is a completely private experience. It is always there whenever one's eyes are open—or rather it is always "here."[6]

The tree, the hand, the nose, are increasingly *private*. The negative afterimage is still more private, and in a special way. It is a pure *sensation*, we say.

What about sensations? If it is right to say that these curious experiences are a sort of detection of the physiological states of the sense organs then they are the most private of all forms of awareness. No one else can have my sense data. No one else can experience my headaches or my hunger or my heartbeat for that matter. But if we agree that knowledge of the world is not in principle reducible to sense data, as I urge, there is no reason to be puzzled by the contradiction between the private nature of sensations and the public nature of perception. If sensations are the basis of perception there is every reason for attempts to show that they are not as private as they seem, no matter what intellectual acrobatics are required. But if they are not the basis of perception we can relax and allow them their place at the subjective pole of experience without danger of falling into the ridiculous pit of solipsism.

## 4. Summary

Both the psychology of perception and the philosophy of perception seem to show a new face when the process is considered at its own level, distinct from that of sensation. Unfamiliar conceptions in physics, anatomy, physiology, psychology, and phenomenology are required to clarify the separation and make it plausible. But there have been so many dead ends in the effort to solve the theoretical problems of perception that radical proposals may now be acceptable.

---

[6]What happens when a man sees his nose in a mirror, a *virtual* nose, is interesting but it has too many ramifications to be followed up here.

Scientists are often more conservative than philosophers of science. I end, therefore, as I began, with a plea for help.

## PART II:   ARE THERE SENSORY QUALITIES OF OBJECTS?*

As a scientist who believes that philosophical debate is a good thing for theory-making, I am grateful to J. W. Yolton (1968–1969) for his appreciative criticism. I will confine my reply to one of his points only, his assertion that my theory of perception underplays the role of the "sensory qualities of objects" in the pickup of information.

Yolton says that the information acquired in perception is "frequently (perhaps in an extended sense always) sensory." What does he mean by "sensory?" If he means that all such information depends on sensitivity, I agree, but if he means that it depends on the having of subjective sensory impressions, I do not. The difficulty arises with such qualities of an object as *hot, red, hard,* and *large.* These, he says, are sensory qualities. But I argue that these only differ from other qualities of objects (edible-inedible, ripe-unripe, smooth-textured, friend or enemy) in this respect: that the subjective sense-impressions are more noticeable, more available to introspection, more *obtrusive.* I want to suggest that there are no special qualities of objects that have to be designated as *sensory.*[7]

In the course of detecting the temperature of a surface by the hand it may be almost inescapable that we should have a sensation like *hot.* When we perceive the differential reflectances of things it is easy to have the sensation of *red.* When testing for the composition of an object the feeling of *hard,* the unyielding resistance to my grasp, may be noticeable. And in observing the size of an object one may well be impressed by how *large* it looms in the field of view. But these impressions do not require us to believe that the temperature, reflectance, composition, and size of an object are qualities with a special status.

To be explicit, I argue that there are no such entities as the *sensory* qualities of objects; if there are none they can have no role to play in the pickup of information about the environment. It seems to me that a quality of an object belongs to the object and that the quality of a sensation does not.

I take the word "sensation" to mean a subjective experience. Such experience, of course, *does* have qualities (and also intensities and durations). An enormous variety of such experiences is surely possible. The accepted classification of them seems to me quite inadequate. Some sensations, I suspect, are the

---

*Synthese*, 1968–1969, *19*, 408–409. Copyright 1969 by D. Reidel, Publishers. Reprinted by permission. This paper was written in reply to Yolton (1968–1969).

[7]See Gibson (1979a, p. 31) for a fuller account of the qualities of objects. (Eds.)

result of paying attention to the eyes, the ears, or the skin; they arise when one asks how it feels to perceive the world. Others are specific to postures and movements of the body; still others to the internal organs and physiological states of the body like hunger. We have only vague terms like "somaesthesis" and the so-called "body image" to denote them. Perhaps whatever specifies the organism as existing in its environment is to be called sensation. The temporary array of perspective appearances of the world is called the field of visual sensations, or the visual field, and this, I think, is the best index an observer has of himself as *here*. So I have to admit that the study of sensations is important for an understanding of one's awareness of the self even when I deny that it is basic to an understanding of one's awareness of the world.[8]

---

[8]See Ch. 4.6 for an information-based account of self-perception, as opposed to this sensation-based theory. (Eds.)

# 4.6 Notes on Action

Notes on Action

## PART I: THE THEORY OF PROPRIOCEPTION AND ITS RELATION TO VOLITION: AN ATTEMPT AT CLARIFICATION*[1]

It sounds reasonable to assume that there is a close connection between proprioception and the voluntary control of movement. An individual needs to know what he has done in order to decide what to do next. Something like this reasoning seems to underlie the enthusiasm for Von Holst's theory of "reafference" and the "efference copy."[2] But it seems to me misguided. Proprioception, especially visual proprioception, will have to be understood in its own right before we can even begin to wrestle with the formidable problem of volition.

Followers of Von Holst assume that all movements except for "reflexes" are caused by motor *commands* initiated in the brain. An *efferent copy* of the command is stored and compared with the afferent input. If the input cancels the copy, it is interpreted as proprioception; if not, it is interpreted as exteroception.[3] This is thought to explain (for example) why the world does not seem to move when the eyes move.

I have a different theory of proprioception based on perceptual systems in-

---

*Unpublished manuscript, June, 1974.

[1]Gibson (1941a, pp. 801–810) discussed the dichotomy between voluntary and involuntary behavior and questioned the existence of a single dimension between involuntary and voluntary activity (cf. E. J. Gibson, 1939; J. J. Gibson, 1936a). (Eds.)

[2]Von Holst & Mittelstaedt (1950). See Gallistel (1980) for a review of theorizing concerning "efference copies" and "corollary discharges" as supplements to sensations in perception. (Eds.)

[3]Gibson's critique here also applies to more recent versions of this theory in which the motor copy is not hypothesized to cancel out afferent input, but rather as an information signal in a system set to evaluate afference (see McKay, 1973 for details). (Eds.)

385

stead of sensory channels. For the visual system, I assume that a disturbance in the structure of the optic array is *exterospecific* if it specifies a motion or event in the environment. It is *propriospecific* if it specifies a movement of the observer himself relative to the stable environment, a locomotion, *or* if it specifies a movement of a *part of the observer's body* relative to the body as a whole. Note that a movement of the observer or of a part of his body may be passive as well as active, i.e., may be imposed instead of initiated (as in passive locomotion in a vehicle, or passive turning of the head in a rotating chair, or passive movement of a limb). Hence a "motor command" *is not necessarily entailed in a bodily movement*. The first question is what distinguishes an optical motion or disturbance that is exterospecific from one that is propriospecific? Is there a difference between the optical consequences of an external event and those of a bodily movement?

There seem to be three types of bodily movement, either active or passive: first, locomotion, or displacement of the point of observation (the head) relative to the environment; second, limb-movement relative to the body (e.g., manipulation); and third, exploratory movement of the head-eye visual system itself, i.e., head-turning and eye-turning. Consider them in order.

*Displacement of the point of observation.* Locomotion has the inevitable consequence of what I have called *motion perspective* in the ambient optic array.[4] This kind of optical change specifies locomotion and nothing else, just as an unchanging optic array specifies a motionless observer. That is to say, there is no possible event in the normal environment that could bring about this unique optical change, given the facts of ecological optics—no motion in the environment that could cause this motion in light. The fact that a man who faces a "Cinerama" screen can be given a temporary *illusion* of locomotion only reinforces this assertion. Motion perspective involves the complete ambient array. It is strictly propriospecific.[5]

*Limb movement relative to the body.* An *occupied* point of observation involves not only an ambient optic array but also a *field of view*, i.e., a sample of the ambient array that is specific to the observer himself (Gibson, 1979a: Ch. 13—Eds.). The limbs and body of the animal normally *protrude* into the field of view, and the hands of a primate are important "semi-objects" in the field of view. A primate usually sees the movements of his hands. These optical deformations are also strictly propriospecific. No possible event in the environment could cause these particular optical changes.

*Head-turning and eye-turning.* When the head is rotated on either a vertical or a horizontal axis the edges of the field of view "sweep" across the ambient

---

[4]Cf. Ch. 2.2 and Lee (1974). (Eds.)

[5]A number of experiments corroborate this claim (Lee & Lishman, 1977a, 1977b; Lishman & Lee, 1973; Warren, 1976). (Eds.)

optic array, revealing its structure at the leading edge and concealing it at the trailing edge. This occurs whether the head rotation is active or passive, obtained or imposed. It is uniquely propriospecific; it specifies head-turning relative to the persisting array projected form the persisting environment. Note that the environment cannot possibly rotate around the animal. When this impossibility is artificially simulated with an "optokinetic drum" the observer "feels" himself being turned (or "sees" himself turning—it makes no difference which).[6] Animals in this experiment generally compensate by turning so as to maintain the same field of view, this being one way of maintaining a posture.

There are, of course, rotations of the *eyes* in the head that are compensatory for head-turning, and these are perhaps the most fundamental of all eye-movements. This adaptive nystagmus underlies all the more complex ocular adjustments, including those that accompany the foveated eyes of some animals, and it serves the same function, of stabilizing the eyes relative to the environment except for saccades.

The sweeping of the edge of the field of view across the ambient array, the visual sensation, can scarcely be noticed by the human observer. It is ordinarily simply registered for what it is, a specific of head-turning relative to the environment. And the rapid shift of the *occular* field of view that accompanies a saccadic eye rotation cannot be noticed at all. I suggest that it too is normally registered for what it specifies, a saccade. There is a history of theorizing about the puzzle of why no retinal sensation of "motion" is obtained when the eyes jerk, during the century from Helmholtz to Von Holst, but I think it is a false puzzle.[7] The shift of the retina behind the potential retinal image, the extended image, is normally propriospecific. I suspect that all the experimental results with eye-movements and points of light in a dark room can be reconciled with this hypothesis but this is only a suspicion. The rapid displacement of a point in the dark may prove to be indistinguishable from an equivalent rapid rotation of the eye in that situation. If so, it is one of the very rare cases in which visual exteroception need be confused with visual proprioception.

The foregoing theory of visual proprioception says nothing about volition. It applies as well to passive movements as to active movements. Proprioception is taken to be the awareness of the self that accompanies the perception of the environment.

What about intended movements, then? And what about the "intentionality" of perception, the active, striving nature of perception when an observer is seeking information instead of simply having it presented to him? This seems to me a question at an entirely different level. And it is not answered by supposing that the brain issues commands to the muscles, for that is the worst sort of

---

[6]This feeling of head-turning has long been claimed to be the result of afference from or efference to the eyes during the nystagmic eye movements that occur in this situation (Dichgans & Brandt, 1978). However, a recent experiment has shown that visual proprioception of head rotation is independent of eye movements (Brandt, Dichgans & Koenig, 1973). (Eds.)

[7]McKay (1973), L. Matin (1972), and E. Matin (1974) review this literature. (Eds.)

mentalism. Between so-called involuntary reflexes and so-called voluntary movements there are surely many intermediate kinds of action. They will never be worked out unless the voluntary-involuntary dichotomy is abandoned. Reflexes are not machine-like on the one hand and purposive acts are not soul-like on the other.[8] It is fruitless to assume that behavior develops by an increasing voluntary control of primitive involuntary reflexes. What sounds to me promising is to begin with the assumption that active perception is controlled by a search for the affordances of the environment and that active behavior is controlled by the perceiving of these affordances.

## PART II: NOTE FOR A TENTATIVE REDEFINITION OF BEHAVIOR*

If behavior does not consist of responses what does it consist of? The failure of the stimulus-response formula in psychology is being recognized more and more widely but what do we have to take its place?[9] An interest in studying behavior should not be confused with the assumptions of behaviorism. The most stultifying of these was the formula of responses or reactions, originally supposed to be triggered by stimuli but later extended to include those "emitted" by an organism in the absence of stimuli. All kinds of responses and response-combinations have been postulated including "inner" responses, "mediating" responses, and "molar" responses; but the formula cannot be made to work in psychology, and it should be abandoned.

A substitute formula might be that behavior consists of *postures* and *movements*. Can this be developed? Note that postures and movements are *controlled* rather than being either triggered or emitted, as responses are. They are controlled by information, both external and proper, but not by stimuli. That is, there is always a flow of both exterospecific and propriospecific information available. A flow of information is not composed of "signals." Note also that the classical division of responses into types called involuntary (reflexes) and voluntary does not apply to postures and movements. They are *all* controlled and to say that some control is voluntary is to say nothing. The theory of motor "commands" is self-defeating. Can we now formulate a sort of taxonomy of behavior that makes sense?

---

[8]Recent research on reflex components of stepping (Forssberg, Grillner, & Rossignol, 1977), standing (Nashner, 1976), and looking (Gonshor & Melvill-Jones, 1976; Miles & Eighmy, 1980) have shown that reflexes are not responses mechanically coupled to stimuli, but are somewhat adaptive and functional. Conversely, research on simple voluntary movements (Nashner & Cordo, 1981) has revealed automatic and mechanical components of volition. (Eds.)

*Unpublished manuscript, June, 1975.

[9]Even the most anti-behavioristic of cognitive psychologists have not replaced the S-R formula so much as supplemented it (Dennett, 1975). (Eds.)

## Postures

Behavior depends on posture and is inseparable from it. This is true in two ways. First, a fixed posture of the body and its members never persists for long; it gives way to a movement, which is a change from one posture to another.[10] Even an equilibrium posture like the upright stance consists of small corrective movements. A stance is an orientation to the surface of support, to gravity, and to the sky-earth contrast. A posture is an *orientation to the environment*. A posture involves both a whole and its parts, that is, a body and its members. A "member" is a moveable unit of the body.

Second, any movement entails the altering of a special posture while maintaining a general posture. Thus, walking involves keeping an upright posture; and pointing with the arm involves a stance of the body. There is always some non-change underlying the change of posture.

## Movements

Animate movements have very little to do with Newtonian motions, and mechanics alone is a poor guide to their study. How can animate movements be classified? An obvious distinction is between movement of the whole body and movement of a body-member.

1. Movement of the body-unit relative to the environment layout. There are two abstract pure cases here (a) the displacement of a body relative to the rigid environment i.e., locomotion from place to place, and (b) the "turning" of the body from one orientation to another i.e., the rotation of the body. In walking they are usually combined. There are additional sub-cases of body-rotation ("pitch" and "roll") which, in the case of terrestrial locomotion but not aquatic or aerial, involve "falling," that is, a failure of the upright stance.

Note that all these cases are mechanically complex involving a positive and a negative acceleration, although they are biologically simple. The movement of the head generally "leads" the movement of the rest of the body in these locomotions and turns.

2. Movement of a body member relative to the body-unit.

*a. Head-movement.* The head is the principal member of the body. It can *turn* relative to the trunk, or *nod* or *tilt* (and the eyes in the head then undergo a compensatory movement which keeps them anchored to the optic array and the fixed environment). Note that a head-movement can occur during a locomotion movement of the body relative to the environment.

---

[10]Recent work on the mechanisms underlying reaching (Bizzi, 1980) and standing (Nashner & Woolacott, 1979) have shown that postures can change into movements and back (or to a new posture) with great speed. Work on stepping and standing shows that vision plays an important role in controlling the postures and movements underlying balance and locomotion (Berthoz, Lacour, Soechting, & Vidal, 1979). (Eds.)

*b. Eye-movement.* The eyes can move relative to the head, that is, can rotate. Actually they can do so on any of three axes. The types of eye-movement have been listed and measured. The eyes, head, trunk, and legs make a sort of hierarchy of body members. The eyes and head are oriented to the source of environmental information currently being picked up.

*c. Arm and hand movement.* The arms move relative to the trunk and the hands relative to the arms. This is the kind of primate behavior called *manipulation.* If the stance of the body is maintained the hands can thus move relative to the layout of the environment, that is, reach, grasp, push, pull, and also point, throw, catch, and strike (see later).

*d. Leg movement.* For bipeds, when the legs move relative to the trunk they also move relative to the surface of support and thus *propel* the animal. This is terrestrial locomotion. Primates are also capable of "arboreal" locomotion, or climbing, etc.

The classes of movement so far listed would fall under the kinds of behavior called locomotion, perceptual exploration, and manipulation. (For "acrobatic" movements, see later.) But there are also kinds of behavior loosely called "performatory" and "sexual" and "social."[11]

*e. Movements that change the environment.* There are movements of the hands, feet, and jaws that change the layout of the environment or the composition of its substances, or even their existence. Detached objects can be displaced (transported, thrown, kicked) or shaped, or destroyed. Doors can be opened, liquids can be splashed or poured, and food-objects can be eaten. Traces can be made on surfaces. That is to say, events of the environment can be brought about. When tools are used the movements of the hands cause motions of the tool that in turn cause motions or other changes of the layout.

*f. Movements for sexual and familial interaction.* The sequence of preliminary and consummatory behaviors connected with reproduction is complex and well known. The movements are oriented to another animal of the complementary sex and the control of these movements depends not only on proprioception but also on exteroceptive perception of the movements of the other individual. The type of behavior called *nurturant* follows the same rule.

*g. Movements for social interaction.* These include predator and prey behaviors, fighting and competition, cooperation, and also various kinds of social play, especially in children.

---

[11]Cf. Gibson (1966b, pp. 56–57) for a functional taxonomy of movement systems. (Eds.)

*h. Movements for social communication.*[12] Postures and gestures of the body, limbs, and hands serve for communication from one animal to another as for example in the act of pointing. But the gestures of the face that we call "expressions" are important for man in the conveying of information about intentions. And, above all, the complex gestures of the vocal tract that produce sounds are a superior means of communication, unaffected by darkness or by occluding edges. In my terminology the face and the vocal mechanism are "members" of the body as much as the head and limbs. They adopt postures and move from one posture to another just as the body does, and the hand. They have a repertory of positions and transitions between positions which are clearly not responses to stimuli.

*i. Movement for its own sake.* Finally, a type of movement should be listed which is less controlled by exteroception than the others, that is, by objects and events at a distance from the observer. The movements of the dance are of this sort, at least in dancing alone. They obviously go from one posture or "pose" to another. The movements of children in "play" are also often self-controlled, as in tumbling, jumping, whirling around, etc. This kind of play does not need a "plaything," or a "playmate," only a surface of support.

The heart of the foregoing classification, however incomplete, is the substitution of postures and movements-between-postures for responses to stimuli. The postures and movements are felt and seen *relative to the environment.*

## Behavior and Perception

What is the relation of perception to behavior thus reformulated? It is more intimate than the relation of sensation-based perception to response-based behavior ever could be. Perception of the environment is always accompanied by co-perception of the self (*proprioception* in my new meaning of that term). We pay attention mainly to the affordances for behavior of the environmental layout—its *behavioral* geometry you might say, as distinguished from its *abstract* geometry. Thus exteroception is seldom divorced from proprioception.[13] The orienting of a perceptual system and the orienting of behavior go together. (But the orienting movements of sense organs and of body members are not reflex responses as Pavlov thought.) The dichotomy of "sensory" and "motor" disappears. It was convenient only for a simplistic level of neurophysiology in any case.

It is still true that the extracting of information for the perception of the world

---

[12]Cf. Smith (1977). (Eds.)

[13]Lee (1978) suggests that the term "exproprioception" should be used to denote the mutuality of extero- and proprio-ception. (Eds.)

and the extracting of information for the bodily control of performances are different processes, even if complementary. The perception of a goal, its affordance, controls locomotion in one way whereas the visual proprioception of the optical outflow controls locomotion in an entirely different way. The bee who lands on a flower needs to both perceive the flower and control his flight. He has to see an invariant environment in order to identify the flower, and to see himself moving through the environment in order to guide his locomotion. The perceiving and the behaving go together but they are not the same process.

The theories of control so far advanced have been based on the stimulus-response formula; all they add is feedback or response-produced stimuli. A more adequate theory of the steering, guiding, or controlling of behavior can be based on the notion of perceptual systems with built-in proprioceptive functions, and the notion of a general orienting system.

# 4.7

## On the New Idea of Persistence and Change and the Old Ideas that it Drives Out*

We perceive that the environment changes in some respects and persists in others. We see that it is different from time to time, even moment to moment, and yet that it is the same environment over time. We perceive *both* the change and the underlying non-change. My explanation is that the perceptual systems work by detecting invariants in the flux of stimulation but are also sensitive to the flux itself.

The classical theories of perception assume that the flux of stimulation causes a flux of sensation, the basis of perception, and that the perception of permanent objects must somehow be constructed from this flux. One common explanation is that we have *concepts* which enable us to interpret the sensory flux. (The concepts may be acquired or innate; that is controversial.) For example, Piaget supposed that the child has to develop the concept of *object permanence* before he can perceive a persisting environment (cf. *Child's Conception of the World*). This explanation is in line with the old notion of the "operations of the mind" upon the "data of sense." Note that the flux of stimulation has often been taken to mean a sequence of *stimuli,* with a corresponding sequence of *sensations.* This assumption is convenient for experimenters.

The idea of permanence despite change, or permanence during change, can be applied to many phenomena. I believe that the so-called perceptual constancies of the psychology laboratory are special cases of it, that is, the constancy of the size, the shape, and the color of an object in experience.[1] But the constancies are

---

*Unpublished manuscript, November, 1975.

[1]See Koffka (1935, ch. 6) and Epstein (1977) for reviews of the literature on perceptual constancies. (Eds.)

far from being *representative* cases of it. (And since size and shape constancy refer only to the perception of an object they could not be applied to the perception of the ground *behind* the object in any case.) The deep question is *not* how a transforming color-patch in the visual field can lead to the perception of a constant near side of an object in the world but how the systematic coming and going of perspectives can lead to the perception of a solid object with a far side.[2]

Consider the causes of changing visual stimulation. What are the facts? Over and above the causes of changing illumination (which are complex) there are four sources of change in an optic array (Gibson, 1979a, Chs. 5-7—Eds.). First, the locomotion of an observer from one vista to another in a cluttered environment causes motion perspective in the ambient array.[3] Second, the motion of a persisting object or animal in the environment causes a local disturbance in the ambient array, a change in the perspective of the object.[4] Third, the head-turning of an observer as in looking around causes a change in the *sample* of the ambient optic array obtained by the eyes.[5] Fourth, the physical destruction of a surface in the environment like a cloud (an impermanent object) causes its projection to vanish from the optic array.[6] Note that, although the first and second kinds of optical change involve transformations of the sort studied in projective geometry, a change in projection at a point of observation, *all* of them involve the more radical change from projected to unprojected or the reverse. In the fourth case the surface ceases to reflect light and has no projection at *any* point of observation. In the first three the surface goes *out of sight* whereas in the fourth it goes out of *existence*. (See Table 3.)

All theories based on visual sensations admit that sensations fluctuate in the sense that patches of color in the visual field of the observer appear and disappear, i.e., come and go, as the observer moves about, as objects move, as the observer looks around, and lastly when substantial objects that *cause* patches of color in the field cease to exist. All that sensations can do is begin and end when the stimuli that cause them begin and end, i.e., go on and off. Sensations are thus of necessity temporary, fleeting, and impermanent. On the basis of color patches alone it would be impossible to distinguish between the moving observer, the moving object, looking around, and the genuine non-persisting object. Something more is needed than forms and colors in the visual field and hence the appeal to conceptual knowledge of objects and, in particular, the concept of object-permanence.

The theory that men and animals perceive change and non-change concurrently is quite different. We see that a displaced object is the same object but in a different location. We see a turning object as the same but showing a different

---

[2]Cf. Ch. 1.2. (Eds.)
[3]Cf. Chs. 2.2 and 2.3 (Eds.)
[4]Cf. Ch. 1.2. (Eds.)
[5]Cf. Ch. 2.6 and Hay (1966). (Eds.)
[6]Cf. Ch. 2.7. (Eds.)

TABLE 3
Four Kinds of Persistence/Change Pairings

| Ecological Event | Change in Optic Array | Visual Event |
|---|---|---|
| (1) Locomotion | Motion perspective; wiping of structure by faster elements | Visual proprioception of self movement; objects going out of sight to the rear |
| (2) Object motion | Local disturbance(s); wiping of structure by faster elements | Displacing object(s) going in/out of sight |
| (3) Head movement | Successive different samples; wiping of structure by faster elements | Progressive occlusion/ disocclusion at trailing/ leading edges of field of view |
| (4) Destruction of surface(s) | Vanishing of structure | Object going out of existence |

side. We see the same world with *me* in a different location.[7] We see that an animal is the same animal but in a different posture if it behaves. We perceive that a surface has the same color and texture but that its illumination is different when the sun comes out. We perceive that the water flows over the rocks but that it is the same stream. Above all, we perceive that the general layout of the opaque surfaces of the environemnt persists even when some of them are concealed by others although of course we "see" that the latter are concealed. We perceive the world behind the head, which is only to say that we are aware of the head. Note that some of these cases involve the detection of occluding edges. The most cogent examples of the phenomenal persistence of objects and surfaces despite the non-persistence of their sensations are of this sort. The retinal images come and go but the surfaces do not.

Next consider what is implied by the phenomenal "persistence" of surfaces that go out of sight, keeping in mind that going out of sight and coming into sight are reciprocal. It means the perceiving of surfaces as continuing to exist in the future and having existed in the past as well as existing in the present. But if we do in fact experience that persisting environment in this way, note that this is not *perception* in the traditional meaning of that term which refers only to experience of "the present" and relegates to *memory* all experiences of "the past" and to *expectancy* all experience of "the future." The meaning of the term perceiving will have to be extended to include remembering and expecting.[8]

---

[7] See Lasky, Romano & Wenter (1980) for experiments on the development of this perceptual ability. (Eds.)

[8] Michotte's (1962) experiments on phenomenal persistence without sensory input or sensations and Merleau-Ponty's (1962) phenomenology of the hidden anticipated Gibson's views here in several respects. However, neither these writers, nor later investigators of such phenomena (e.g., Kanizsa, 1979) thought the reality of hidden-but-seen was more than a *phenomenal* reality. (Eds.)

An occluding edge, as Kaplan's (1969) experiment showed, is not well specified with a frozen optic array. There has to be a progressive, ongoing change of the array concurrent with a non-change. In that experiment the change was described as either a progressive gain of structure (accretion) or loss (deletion) on one side of a contour, with non-change on the other side. Accretion yielded the perception of surface-being-revealed and deletion the perception of surface-being-concealed, i.e., going-behind and coming-from-behind. I suggest now that when a surface is being-revealed there is an *expectancy* of the hidden portion and when a surface is being-concealed there is a *memory* of the hidden portion, so you might say, but that actually it is a simple case of the perceiving of the surface. To me it is more like seeing than it is like imagining or recalling. We sometimes speak of "foresight" and "hindsight" instead of expecting and remembering, and these terms carry the suggestion that I am making.

William James was bothered by the puzzle of the *junction* of past and future in his description of the stream of consciousness.[9] He never doubted that they were separate but what would "the present" be? The borderline was not sharp; he could only suggest that the present goes a little way *into* the past, and perhaps the future. But this is simply a muddle. It will not do. Perhaps it is a false puzzle and the two are united in the fact of occluding edges. For at an occluding edge the present *hides* the past and also hides the future. During locomotion what is being concealed "goes into the past" and what is being revealed "comes from the future." But actually of course one simply apprehends the whole environment.

---

[9]Cf. Ch. 2.5. (Eds.)

# 4.8 The Myth of Passive Perception: A Reply to Richards*

J. L. Austin once remarked (in *Sense and Sensibilia,* 1962) that there was nothing so plain boring as the constant repetition of assertions that are not true. He was tired of hearing that all we can ever perceive is our private sense data, or at least that they are all we can ever directly perceive. I agree with Austin. This is why I have tried to formulate a theory of the direct perceiving of the environment without the necessity of sensations to mediate the process. Perceiving is information-based, not sensation-based. But now I keep hearing that I have a passive theory; that it does not recognize the *activity* of perceiving, and I am tired of that assertion for it is also not true.[1] The kind of activity I postulate is different, to be sure, and perhaps this is the source of the misapprehension.

The only kind of perceptual activity that my critics are willing to admit is *mental activity,* that is, the operations of the mind upon the deliverances of the senses. (You can substitute the operations of the brain upon the inputs of the sensory nerves if you like, but that will come to the same thing.) Different hypothetical operations have been proposed by different theorists of perception and every new generation sees new operations proposed, mostly new names for old operations. The kind of activity, however, that seems to me important is the looking, listening, touching, tasting, and sniffing that goes on when the percep-

*Philosophy and Phenomenological Research,* 1976, *37,* 234–238. Copyright 1976 by the University of Buffalo. Reprinted by permission. This paper was written as a reply to Richards (1976).

[1]This criticism of Gibson goes back at least to Epstein & Park (1964) and Freeman (1965). Versions of it may be found in Gregory (1972), Gyr (1972), Hamlyn (1977) and Ullman (1980). Replies to this criticism are found in Gibson & Gibson (1972), Gibson (1973b), Flock (1965), Mace & Pittenger (1975), Reed & Jones (1978, 1981), Jones & Pick (1980) and Reed (1980). (Eds.)

tual systems are at work. These acts involve adjustments of organs, not mere stimulation of receptors. They are not mental. Neither are they physical, for that matter, but functional. My notion of the pickup of information by the extracting of invariants over time involves the optimizing activity of a system and I believe it escapes the fallacies of mentalism on the one hand and those of stimulus-response behaviorism on the other.

The classical theories of sensation-based perception can only begin to talk about activity after sensations have been aroused by stimuli.[2] They postulate activities to supplement the sensations or to correct them, or to interpret them, or to organize them, or make inferences from them, or attach meanings to them, or fuse them with memories, or combine them with concepts, or impose logic on them, or construct a model of the world from them (the list could go on and on). But the theory of information-based perception can begin to talk about activity before sensations have been aroused by stimuli, an activity that orients the organs of perception, explores the ambient array, and seeks an equilibrium. For example, the adjustments of stabilizing the eyes, fixating them, turning them, converging them, accommodating the lens, and modulating the pupil are surely activities (but not reflexes) which are quite independent of visual sensations. And the mental compensation for sensations of motion resulting from eye movements is no longer a puzzle if the sensations are irrelevant.

Richards (1976) asserts that I have a theory of passive perception and implies that such a theory has been held by others as well. But I ask who are they? Has any theorist ever believed that perception was passive? I cannot think of one. No one has ever proposed that sensations were enough to explain perception, not since Thomas Reid distinguished them.[3] There have been psychologists and physiologists who were simply not interested in the problems of perception but that does not make them adherents to a passive theory. Richards accuses me of believing that ''the senses are merely conduits conveying unsullied information to mind about the real properties of the world.'' But I emphatically do not believe that and no experimental psychologist could possibly believe it. I reject the notion of conduits, the assumption of incoming messages, and I go so far as to question whether there are nerves that should properly be called ''sensory'' (Gibson, 1966b, p. 42). I suggest that the nervous system operates in circular loops and that information is never conveyed but extracted by the picking up of invariants over time. Information about the world is available in the light, sound, chemicals, and mechanical contacts that constitute the ''flowing sea of stimulus energy.'' So, to Richards' claim that my theory neglects the activity of perceiving I submit the counterclaim that it emphasizes an activity that is central to perceiving, a genuine activity. If it has been neglected this is only because of all

---

[2]One supposed alternative to sensation-based theories of perception is a motor theory. However, motor theories of perception are in fact complementary to sensation-based theories because they hold that perception arises only when motor responses (tacit or actual) organize the sensory data. See, e.g. Liberman, Cooper, Shankweiler & Studdert-Kennedy (1967). (Eds.)

[3]Reid (1785). (Eds.)

the loose talk about processes of the mind or of the brain which is the seat of the mind. If physiologists would forget their precious reflexes and sensations for a while and do a little thinking about perception and the adjustments of the organs of perception, they would begin to find out about this activity.[4]

It is quite true that I reject the doctrine of specific nerve energies as Richards points out. Especially I reject the implication of this doctrine for perception, the inference that if we cannot know anything but the "qualities of our nerves" the properties of the environment are forever beyond our ken. It may be a fact that electrical stimulation of the eye causes a sensation reported as "light" instead of "electricity" but one cannot make the inference about knowledge that Johannes Müller made, not if sensations of light are irrelevant for visual perception. Only if one assumes that sensations of light are the *necessary basis* of visual perception is one faced with the great mystery of how we see the surfaces of things.

It is true that my hypothesis of an inexhaustible reservoir of information about the environment outside the observer was not entirely clear in my essay entitled *Perception as a Function of Stimulation* (Gibson, 1959a) but it became clear by the time I published *The Senses Considered as Perceptual Systems* (Gibson, 1966b). I now make a sharp distinction between stimulus energy and stimulus information.[5] I would no longer suggest that an act of perception had a stimulus or could be touched off by stimulus energy (although a sensation, of course, has a stimulus and is touched off by it). This change in my theory has confused Richards, along with other readers, and I am sorry for the lack of clarity. The concept of the stimulus has had a baneful influence on psychology (Gibson, 1960c) and I myself have had trouble in getting free of it. I would now deny that there is ever a one-to-one correspondence between stimulation and perception. What I should have said was that perception is wholly constrained by stimulus information.

My theory of the available information in ambient light is radically different from the modern theory of information considered as signals, the mathematical theory founded by Shannon.[6] But my critics have not understood this fact, and here is another source of confusion. I argue that the perceptual systems are not to be compared to the media for human communication, that the inputs of a sensory nerve have nothing to do with messages, and the outputs of a motor nerve have nothing to do with commands. The world does not telegraph the brain and the brain does not telegraph the muscles; only a whole man sends telegrams. The brain is not a receiver nor a sender; not a homunculus but only an organ. Richards is quite wrong to say that I have appealed to *information theory* in order to buttress the concept of *information* that underlies my theory of perception.

My notion is that information consists of invariants underlying change. It does not consist of stimuli, nor of patterns of stimuli, nor of sequences of stimuli. A

---

[4]Wall (1970) attempts to do just this. (Eds.)
[5]Cf. Chs. 1.4, 1.6, 4.3 and 4.4 (Eds.)
[6]See Shannon (1948). (Eds.)

perceptual system does not respond to stimuli (although a receptor does) but extracts invariants. This notion is radical and unfamiliar but why should it be so difficult to comprehend? Gradients, transients, derivatives, ratios, and rates in a flowing array of energy are actually much more plausible than patterns of stimuli that go on and off at a mosaic of receptors.

Richards seems to take it for granted, however, that psychology cannot get along without the assumption of these discrete stimuli. He says "all that we have in immediate sensory stimulation is one receptor or a group of receptors firing in a certain sequence. . . . Relations, at least those to which Gibson here refers, are not real features of the physical world. . . . What is a border of light? In the natural world . . . there are only discrete photon units. . . . Borders are relations which exist only for cognating perceivers." But I deny just these assertions, all of them. Richards accepts the doctrines of physical optics, whereas I propose a new level of ecological optics.[7] He believes the orthodox physiologists whereas I believe they are out of date. There are some physiologists who reject the doctrine of specific nerve energies as strongly as I do.

Richards assumes that the retina, the optic tract, the lateral geniculate body, and the striate cortex "together constitute the organ of visual perception." He even leaves out the eye! I assert that the whole eye-head-retino-neuro-muscular system with all the precise adjustments involved in looking constitute the visual system.

Richards assumes that a "cognitive reworking" of the input of the sensory nerves is necessary for perception. He has to assume something of that sort since the sensory input is obviously insufficient, for example in the case of the optic nerve where the third dimension has been lost in the retinal image. So has every other theorist had to assume something like a reworking of the input, but they have not been able to agree on what it is. Anyone who believes the senses to be channels of sensation *has* to be a mentalist when it comes to sense perception. I, on the other hand, assume that cycles of input and output that reach an optimal state are necessary for perception. The brain is not the place where it occurs but only the central part of the perceptual system. I do not have to say anything whatever about inputs alone, or sensations, or the "processing" of inputs, or the traces they might leave. I am tired of hearing about cognitive reworking and organizational processing and intellectual machinery. It is time for a fresh start on this ancient problem.

I repeat what I said in reply to Gyr (1972) who is another critic of my theory. "A whole set of current experiments and controversies will go by the board if the modalities of sense are recognized as being unimportant for the activity of perception, for the theory of direct perception implies an equally direct awareness of the body of the observer and the adjustments of its perceptual organs. New experiments will have to be designed to test this theory" (Gibson, 1973b, p. 397).

---

[7]Cf. Ch. 1.4. (Eds.)

# 4.9 Notes on Affordances

## PART I: WHAT IS PERCEIVED? NOTES FOR A RECLASSIFICATION OF THE VISIBLE PROPERTIES OF THE ENVIRONMENT*

The abstract analysis of the world by mathematics and physics rests on the concepts of *space* and *time*. The study of sense perception by psychologists has conformed to this analysis. *Mass* is exemplified by what we call "objects," and *energy* by what we call "light." So it is assumed that we perceive space, time, and objects, and that we sense light (or color). This way of thinking about perception has a long history. The perceptible qualities of objects were classified in accordance with it. John Locke's list consisted of the primary qualities of *position, shape, size, duration, motion,* and *solidity,* to which was added the secondary quality of *color* and other non-visual secondary qualities (sound, taste, smell, and warmness or coldness).[1] Psychology is still trying to explain the perception of the *position* of an object in space, along with its *shape, size,* and so on, and to understand the sensations of *color.* The explanations are tortured and success is not in sight.

But a direct explanation of the perception of the properties of the visible environment may be possible if these properties are taken from concepts of ecology instead of from mathematics and physics. (Perhaps they are ultimately "reducible" to the latter, but the psychologist cannot wait for such a reduction.) What might such a list be? Here is a preliminary classification.

---

*Unpublished manuscript, August 1967.

[1] Locke's list varied from place to place in his *Essay.* It was Descartes who first determined to integrate physics and psychology by means of the doctrine of primary and secondary qualities (cf. Maull, 1978). (Eds.)

## Spatial Properties

(We do not visually perceive "space," but we do perceive the following persisting, i.e., relatively invariant, properties of the world.)[2]

1. *Surface layout.* This includes surface slant, corners (dihedral angles), curvature, and the edges of surfaces which occlude other surfaces. It includes the recession of the ground (distance from "here"). Finally, it includes objects, with the position of each object in the layout, the dimensions of the object (size) and the proportions of its faces (shape). The persistence or permanence of hidden objects is discussed below.
2. *Substance or composition.* This includes the solidity, liquidity, or viscosity of the substance, the color of the surface (reflectance and differential reflectance), and the texture of the surface (its small-scale layout).
3. *Lighting or illumination.* This includes cast shadows, attached shadows ("shading"), and direction of illuminations on a surface.

## Spatio-Temporal Properties

(We do not perceive "time" as such, but we do perceive changes or varying properties of the world, which are spatio-temporal.)

1. *Motions of rigid objects.* This includes displacements and rotations relative to the ground.
2. *Deformations of elastic objects.* This includes the flow of viscous or fluid surfaces.
3. *Progressive occlusion and disocclusion,* that is, the optical covering and uncovering of surfaces (objects) by edges. An object that is thus covered is specified as persisting. An object may also recede "into the distance" and persist.
4. *The ending and beginning of the solid state,* that is, the melting, decomposition, dissolution, etc., of an object or (occasionally) the opposite.
5. *The onset and cessation of illumination.* This includes many kinds of transients, both naturally and artificially produced (e.g., "flashes" of light).
6. *Animate motions and deformations.* This includes the whole realm of events in the animate and social environment, e.g., expressive movements and social signals.
7. *Events in general.*[3] For events with sufficiently abrupt onset and cessation is is possible to measure duration ("time"). For multiple events of this sort

---

[2]See Gibson (1979a, Part 1) and also Ch. 1.9 for more details on these properties of the environment. (Eds.)
[3]Cf. Ch. 2.8. (Eds.)

it is possible to measure frequency ("rate"). But, in general, the centimeter-gram-second system of physics can only be applied at present to uninteresting events in the visible environment.

Perceptual research needs a program newer than the one formulated in Newton's *Principles* and Locke's *Essay Concerning Human Understanding*.

### The Visual Detection of the Self [4]

Proprioception accompanies perception; we proprioceive visually as well as perceive visually, and this kind of detection is also spatio-temporal. We can detect the following characteristics or variables of the self as the center of the environment. (The information is multiple but we are considering only visual information.)

1. *The temporary posture of the body*. The upright or inclined posture of the head is "visible."
2. *The locomotion of the body*. The direction and speed of locomotion through the environment is "visible" (by means of motion perspective and the changing occlusion of surfaces at edges). This extends to locomotion in vehicles.
3. *The movements of the limbs*. Gross movements and fine manipulations are "visible." Both movements of the hands and of the tools grasped are thus registered (pointing, reaching and grasping, but also raking, pounding and trace-making).

Note that the term *perception* is reserved for the environment, and *detection* or *registration* is applied to the self. Note also that the visual registration of body movement may be either obtained or imposed, i.e., from an active or a passive movement (Gibson, 1966b, Ch. 2). Hence not all movements are self-produced, and not all inputs should be considered as "feedback" or "reafferent," as seems to be widely assumed. The problem of the registering of information is distinct from the problem of the purposive control of movement.

### PART II: A PRELIMINARY DESCRIPTION AND CLASSIFICATION OF AFFORDANCES*

The hypothesis that things have *affordances*, and that we perceive or learn to perceive them, is very promising, radical, but not yet elaborated (Gibson, 1966b, p. 285). Roughly, the affordances of things are what they furnish, for good or ill, that is, what they *afford* the observer. A list of examples and a classification is

---

[4]Cf. Chs. 2.4 and 4.6. (Eds.)

*Unpublished manuscript, February 1971.

needed; the reader is invited to make his own list, or to supplement the tentative list given below.

Not only objects but also substances, places, events, other animals, and artifiact have affordances. We might begin with the easy-to-perceive components of the environment consisting of surfaces and surface layouts. And we should assume a human animal as observer, to start with, since the list of affordances will be somewhat different for different animals.

I assume that affordances are not simply phenomenal qualities of subjective experience (tertiary qualities, dynamic and physiognomic properties, etc.). I also assume that they are not simply the physical properties of things as now conceived by physical science. Instead, they are *ecological,* in the sense that they are properties of the environment *relative to* an animal. These assumptions are novel, and need to be discussed.

In a theory of information-based perception, learning to perceive affordances is only one kind of perceptual learning or perceptual development. (For other kinds, see Gibson, 1966b, Ch. 13, esp. p. 283 ff, and E. J. Gibson, 1969, Ch. 5.)

The examples that follow are intended to be only suggestive.

  *I. Surfaces and surface-layouts related to posture and locomotion*
  —a stand-on-able surface or surface of support; a place that affords rest.
  —a walk-on-able surface, one that affords "footing" (For terrestrial locomotion the substratum must be nearly level and rigid; a water surface is excluded.)
  —a vertical rigid surface, an obstacle, affording collisions and barring locomotion.
  —an interspace or opening between obstacles, affording locomotion.
  —a falling-off place, the brink of a cliff, affording injury by collision with the ground.
  —a gap between two cliff-edges which (depending on its width) may afford jumping.
  —a stepping-down (or stepping-up) place, affording descent (or ascent).
  —a sit-on-able surface (affording sitting).
  —a stand-on-able object, stool, affording a high reach.
  —a climbable layout (tree, ladder, stairway).
  —a get-underneath-able surface, affording shelter (roof).
  *II. Surfaces that reveal or conceal; transparent or opaque*
  —an occluding surface, with its occluding edges (screen, wall, lid, clothing). An *opaque* surface.
  —a revealing surface (glass).
  —a place affording concealment of oneself from others (hiding place, "private" place).
  —a place or layout affording concealment of an object from others.
  (Note that children are deeply interested in the possibilities of occlusion, as in peek-a-boo and hide-and-go-seek and other games of concealment.)

*III. Objects affording manipulation and related activities* (We distinguish *portable* from *immovable* solid objects, and *graspable* from *non-graspable* solid objects.)

—a handle (a graspable object attached to a portable object).

—a hand-hold (a graspable object attached to an immovable layout).

—a stick (or rake). An elongated rigid object affording a long reach (or a long grasp).

—a tree branch (affording arboreal support to a primate).

—a throwable object, missile (rigid, graspable, movable, of moderate weight).

—an object that affords *hitting;* a club, hammer.

—an object that affords cutting; a knife, axe (having an edge with an acute dihedral angle).

—an object that affords *piercing;* needle, spear.

—an object that affords knotting, binding, lashing; string, thong, rope, thread.

—an object that affords *plugging;* a convexity that fits into and fills a concavity.

—a surface that affords support for useful objects; a bench, shelf, table.

—an object that affords *rolling* (sphere or cylinder) as distinguished from one that has a flat *base* and affords *sliding.*

*IV. Substances with affordances*

—a substance that affords pouring, dripping, dabbling. A *liquid.*

—a substance that affords smearing, painting, trace-making. A *viscous* substance.

—a substance that affords being shaped by manipulation. A plastic or malleable substance.

—a substance that resists change of shape. A solid with persisting shape and size. An object. (Note that the properties of a substance are not the same as the properties of an *object;* this fact is recognized in speech, if not in physics, by the use of a "mass noun" instead of a "count noun.")

—a substance or object affording nutrition. Food.

—a substance or object affording illness. Poison. (But note that both food-objects and poisonous objects afford *ingestion* and that they are sometimes hard to distinguish by optical information. Occasionally, if rarely, they are not even distinguishable by taste and smell, i.e., by the chemical value system.)

*V. The affordance of injury or benefit*

We now come to a consideration of the positive or negative "valences" of things. Phenomenologists maintain that they are facts of "immediate experience" but have not analyzed the biophysical basis of this perception. Nevertheless the perception *at a distance* of what something affords *if* encountered is said to be the great virtue of vision (cf. Berkeley's *New Theory of Vision,* 1709, on "the damage or benefit which is like to ensue.") A mechanical encounter or other energy-exchange may cause tissue damage. But the object, place, substance, event, or animal that affords injury need not be encountered; it can be *avoided, escaped,* or *averted,* if perceived.

> —the edge of a cliff affords falling.
> —a wall affords collision (but may afford climbing).
> —an approaching missile ("looming") affords injury.
> —a knife-edge affords being cut (but also affords cutting).
> —a fire affords being burned, but also affords warmth.
> —a snake affords being bitten.
> —a surface of deep water affords drowning, but a surface of shallow water affords bathing.

These places, events, or animate objects are all specified in an ambient optic array. In each case the affordance can be *seen,* I suggest, and this is not the same thing as saying that the injury can be *foreseen.* The argument is reinforced by the evidence to show that the *imminence* of collision is optically given, as in Schiff's experiment. But there are other places, substances, and events in an environment that are either *not specified* in an optic array, or not obviously, or whose affordances are *not visible,* or not without special training.

> —a potential rock-fall or avalanche is hard to see.
> —a lightning-bolt is not seen until it occurs.
> —the danger of sunburn or gamma rays is not visible.
> —the imminence of an "accidental" explosion is not indicated.

*VI. The detecting of affordances by young animals*

The human young must learn to perceive these affordances, in some degree at least, but the young of some animals do not have time to learn the ones that are crucial for survival.[5] Ethologists therefore are interested in what they call "sign-stimuli" and "releasers." If the foregoing is correct, however, the behavior in question should be reconsidered in terms of stimulus information, not of stimuli. A listing of releasers in these terms would be interesting.

## PART III: MORE ON AFFORDANCES*

At one extreme stands the fact that educated adults have a *conception of space,* i.e., mathematical or geometrical space, Euclidean, Cartesian, non-Euclidean, and so forth.

---

[5]For more on the development of the perception of affordances, see E. J. Gibson (1982) and E. J. Gibson and Spelke (in press). (Eds.)

*Unpublished manuscript, March 1971.

Then there is what psychologists have called the *perception* of space. Although it is a complete muddle, and full of contradictions, depth-perception implies distance-from *here,* and such perception recognizes at least the fact of a potential observer and a *surrounding* space.

Next there is what I call the perception of *layout*—the actual layouts of environmental surfaces, chiefly opaque solid surfaces, and the geometrical *components* of layout. Such perception depends on optical information for environmental places and objects at the set of all possible points of observation in the medium, and this takes into account both hidden (unprojected) and unhidden (projected) surfaces at a fixed point of observation.

Finally, at the other extreme, there is the perception of the *affordances* of environmental surface layouts (which includes objects and places and even *animate* objects). The activity of an observer that is afforded depends on the layout, that is, on the solid geometry of the arrangement. The same layout will have different affordances for different animals, of course, insofar as each animal has a different repertory of acts. Different animals will perceive different sets of affordances therefore. The perception is of *practical* layout, not *theoretical* layout, but it is nonetheless geometrical for all that.

Animals, and children until they learn theoretical geometry, pay attention to the affordances of layout rather than the mathematics of layout. Hence, although logically one advances from space to affordance, developmentally the progress is in the opposite direction, from affordance to space. The *formless invariants* in the light which the eyes of the very young pick up, instead of the forms of the visual field, are just those that specify affordances.

## PART IV: STILL MORE ON AFFORDANCES*

There has been a great gulf in psychological thought between the perception of *space and objects* on the one hand and the perception of *meaning* on the other. But when space and objects are defined in terms of the opaque solid geometry of surface layout, and when meaning is defined in terms of the affordances of places, substances, surfaces, and objects (hereafter termed "things"), these problems are seen to be linked. For example, what anything affords an organism depends in some degree on its shape or the features of its shape (solid shape, of course, not pictorial form). Hence it is that the shape of something is especially meaningful.

The meaning or value of a thing consists of what it affords. Note the implications of this proposed definition. What a thing affords a particular observer (or species of observer) points to the organism, the *subject.* The shape and size and composition and rigidity of a thing, however, point to its physical existence, the

---

*Unpublished manuscript, March 1971.

*object*. But these determine what it affords the observer. The affordance points both ways. What a thing *is* and what it *means* are not separate, the former being physical and the latter mental, as we are accustomed to believe.

The perception of what a thing is and the perception of what it means are not separate, either. To perceive that a surface is level and solid is also to perceive that it is walk-on-able. Thus we no longer have to assume that, first, there is a sensation-based perception of a thing and that, second, there is the accrual of meaning to the primary percept (the "enrichment" theory of perception, based on innate sensations and acquired images).[6] The available information for the perception of a certain surface layout is the same information as for the perception of what it affords.

The controversies over whether the values of things are "relative" or "absolute," and whether value is a subjective phenomenon or an objective fact, should be reinterpreted in the above terms.

## PART V: THE AFFORDANCES OF THE ENVIRONMENT*

The environment of animals can be described at different levels. At the level of fundamental physics it can be said to consist of matter and energy, of particles and their interactions. At a more familiar level, but still one described by physics and solid geometry, it can be said to consist of *substances*, a *medium*, and the *surfaces* between them.[7] With emphasis on the surfaces and their layout, the environment can be described in terms of substratum, enclosures, detached objects, edges, corners, convexities, and concavities; these are the *features* of surface-layout. Note that these features of the environment are geometrical, or mathematically abstract in some degree, but that they begin to be *meaningful*. Edges and corners and surfaces, for example, *combine* to make objects of use and enclosures for shelter. (They are best described by *synthetic* geometry, not by *analytic* geometry.) Then, next, the environment can be described as the *surroundings* of animals who live and get about in the medium. Finally, at the highest level, the environment can be described in terms of *what it affords the animals that live in it*. So considered it consists of objects, substances, places, events, and other animals, all of which have meaning. Note that what these things afford depends on the substances they are made of, the layout of their surfaces, and the ways in which the layout changes.

For example, certain substances afford nutrition but others do not, and a certain surface-layout affords locomotion whereas another does not. The behavior of the animal has to be controlled by the affordance (for him) of the

---

[6]Cf. Ch. 4.2. (Eds.)

*Unpublished manuscript, January 1972.

[7]See Gibson (1979a, Part 1) for more details on this distinction. (Eds.)

substance, object, or place. And this affordance has to be perceived by the animal if his behavior is to be controlled. True, the affordances of substances and surfaces differ for different animals. The ant, the bird, and the primate live in different "niches" as the ecologist puts it, but the reciprocity of the animal and its environment is the same for all.

The notion of affordances implies a new theory of meaning and a new way of bridging the gap between mind and matter. To say that an affordance is meaningful is not to say that it is "mental." To say that it is "physical" is not to imply that it is meaningless. The dualism of mental *vs.* physical ceases to be compulsory. One does not have to believe in a separate realm of mind in order to speak of meaning, and one does not have to embrace materialism in order to recognize the necessity of physical stimuli for perception.

The history of the concept of *affordance* may be illuminating. The term is reminiscent of a word coined by Kurt Lewin, *Aufforderungscharakter*. The term was first translated into English as *invitation-character* (by J. F. Brown in 1929) and later as *valence* (by D. K. Adams in 1931). The latter is more generally used (cf. Marrow's 1969 biography of Lewin). Koffka invented a new term, *demand-character,* when he wrote the *Principles of Gestalt Psychology* (1935). He maintained that the postbox "invites" the mailing of a letter; the handle "wants to be grasped"; the chocolate "wants" to be eaten; things in experience "tell us what to do with them" (p. 353). But the crux of this theory is that the demand character, like the valence, was assumed to be in the *phenomenal* object but not in the physical object. It was in the "field" for Lewin or, for Koffka, in what he called the "behavioral" environment but not in the "geographical" environment. In short, the value of something did not have any "physical" reality. The valence of an object was bestowed upon it by a need of the observer, and a corresponding tension in his field. Koffka agreed, arguing that the postbox has a demand-character only when the observer needs to mail a letter, for only then is he *attracted* to it. Thus the value of something was assumed to change as the need of the observer changed.

In contrast, the *affordance* of something is assumed *not* to change as the need of the observer changes. The edibility of a substance for an animal does not depend on the hunger of the animal. The walk-on-ability of a surface exists whether or not the animal walks on it (although it is linked to the locomotor capacities of that species of animal, its action system). The positive affordance of an object can be perceived whether or not the observer needs to take advantage of it. It offers what it does because it is what it is. The uses of things are directly perceived, as Lewin and Koffka sometimes realized, but this is *not* because of a force between the object and the ego in the phenomenal field, as they believed; it is only because the substance and the layout of the object are visible and these determine its use.

Similarly, the capacity of an object, place, or animal to injure the observer, its negative affordance, does not depend on his being afraid of it, or being repelled by it, or on his avoiding it. When a falling-off place (for example) is perceived, his locomotor behavior can be therewith controlled, but that does not imply that the mountain goat or the mountaineer automatically retreats from the cliff-edge.[8] It affords walking-along as well as falling-off. There are paths, obstacles, slopes, barriers, and openings in the terrestrial layout, as well as brinks, and they all either afford or do not afford locomotion.

The *affordances* of the environment are permanent, although they do refer to animals and are species-specific. The positive and negative *valences* of things that change when the internal state of the observer changes are temporary. The perception of what something affords should not be confused with the "coloring" of experience by needs and motives. Tastes and preferences fluctuate. Something that looks good today may look bad tomorrow but what it actually *offers* the observer will be the same.[9]

The notion of affordance, therefore, is not the same as the notion of *valence, invitation character,* or *demand character* although it is in the same line of theoretical development. The Gestalt theorists were not clear about it, for they could not resolve the subjective-objective dichotomy. They sometimes talked as if a valence were a fact of the environment but at other times as if it were only a fact of experience. The physical world for them was the world of physics as this was described by physicists like Eddington, without meanings or values, and thus they were forced to suppose in the last analysis that meanings and values were mental.[10] Now, forty years later, we should know better, for the environment is no longer quite so physical and experience is no longer quite so mental as it was then.

The meaning or value of anything consists of what it affords an observer, or species of observer. But what it affords the observer is determined by its material substance and its shape, size, rigidity, motion, etc. What it means and what it is are not separate, as we have been led to believe. And the observer who perceives the substance and the surfaces of anything has thereby perceived what it affords.

## PART VI: AFFORDANCES AND BEHAVIOR*

Affordances are invariant combinations of properties of things (properties at the ecological level) *taken with reference to* a species or an individual. I now add: with reference to its *needs* (biological and social) as well as to its action-systems and its anatomy. The affordances for behavior and the behaving animal are *complementary*.

Affordances are perceived, i.e., attended to.

---

[8]Cf. Ch. 1.3. (Eds.)
[9]Cf. Ch. 4.7. (Eds.)
[10]See the discussion of Eddington in Ch. 4.5. (Eds.)
*Unpublished manuscript, April, 1975.

Affordances do not *cause* behavior but constrain or control it.

Needs control the perception of affordances (selective attention) and also initiate acts.

Acts are *not* responses to stimuli, and percepts are not responses to stimuli. An observer is not "bombarded" by stimuli. He extracts invariants from a flux of stimulation.

Affordances, and the stimulus information to specify affordances, are neither subjective nor objective but transcend this dichotomy.

The actor/perceiver and the environment are *complementary*.

An affordance is not the outcome of a perceptual process, as a "meaning" is supposed to be.

## PART VII: NOTE ON PERCEIVING IN A POPULATED ENVIRONMENT*

A populated environment is not just a terrestrial environment with a special set of animated social objects in it. People *are* animated objects, to be sure, with complex affordances for behavior; but they are more than that. People are not only *parts* of the environment but also *perceivers* of the environment. Hence a given observer perceives other perceivers. And he also perceives *what* others perceive.[11] In this way each observer is aware of a shared environment, one that is common to all observers, not just *his* environment.

There are two interconnected reasons for having a shared environment, first, that every observer gets about and thus can take the point of view of another observer and, second, that an observer can be told about things he has never seen or shown pictures of these things. In the latter case he perceives what others perceive by way of the information they give him, that is, by perception at second hand, or vicarious perception. In the former case he perceives what others perceive without the mediation of words or pictures. In other words, speaking subjectively, I have the ability to see objects and places from your present standpoint; and I have the ability to learn about objects and places that you describe or portray. The two abilities go together. To know what *you* know, I must realize the partial identity of you and me, that is, I must in some sense be able to "identify" with you.

I must first of all come to understand that you and I can look at the same object and can *see* the same object even though your perspective view of it is not the same as mine, since you see it from *there* and I see it from *here*. Your perception and mine can be identical even though your "sensation" and mine can never be identical *at the same time*. The same invariants over time are available to both of

*Unpublished manuscript, August 1974.
[11]Cf. Gibson & Pick (1963). (Eds.)

us. I cannot occupy your point of observation *now* but I can in the future, and I could in the past. This, I suggest, is what is meant by the metaphorical assertion that I can "put myself in your place." (It means I can put myself in your position. But it does *not* mean that I can put myself in your body. I am a body myself, not a disembodied spirit, and two bodies cannot exist in the same position.)

If you see a head-on view of a bounding tiger and I see a side view, you are in greater danger than I am; but we both see the same tiger. We also see the same event: You see him approaching you and I see him approaching you.

Now consider perception at second hand, or vicarious perception. This is perception at a different level; perception mediated by communication and dependent on the "medium" of communication, like speech sound, painting, writing, or sculpture. The perception is indirect since the information has been presented by the speaker, painter, writer, or sculptor, and it has to have been *selected* by him from the unlimited realm of available information.[12] This kind of apprehension is complicated by the fact that direct perception of sounds or surfaces occurs along with the indirect perception. The sign is often noticed along with what is signified. Nevertheless, however complicated, the outcome is that one man can metaphorically see through the eyes of another in the case of the painter, and apprehend through the eyes and words of another in the case of the writer. The apprehensions of the traveller, the explorer, and the investigator become available to all men.

It is often believed that perceiving is a private affair, unique to the individual, whereas knowing is shared with others because of the common language. But this assumption of private perception and public knowledge is quite mistaken.[13] Even the direct perception of objects and surfaces is shared over time because of common points of observation and the ability to see from other points than the one now occupied. The mediated perception of part of the environment obtained by looking at a picture is shared, since it is a sort of window on another scene that anyone can look through. And the even more mediated perception (knowledge) obtained by a verbal description or a symbolic description of the sort found in mathematics is obviously shared with all others who have learned the language or the symbols.

The awareness of a common world, the sharing of our perceptions, is not entirely due to our verbal agreements with one another, as so many philosophers are tempted to believe. It is also due to *the independence of our perception from a fixed point of observation, the ability to pick up invariants over time*.[14] This *underlies* the ability to get knowledge by means of pictures and words. The social psychology of knowledge has a basis in ecological optics.

---

[12]For further discussion of mediated perception see Chs. 3.2, 3.4, 3.6, and Gibson (1979a, Chs. 14 & 15). (Eds.)

[13]Cf. Ch. 4.5 for a critique of the private-public dichotomy. (Eds.)

[14]Cf. Gibson (1974b). (Eds.)

## PART VIII: THE THEORY OF AFFORDANCES AND THE DESIGN OF THE ENVIRONMENT*

Architecture and design do not have a satisfactory theoretical basis. Can an ecological approach to the psychology of perception and behavior provide it?

Assume that the environment consists of *substances* and their *surfaces,* a surface being the interface between the substance and the medium, air. Assume also that surfaces have a more or less persisting "layout."

*Substances.* There exist natural substances like earth, clay, rock, water, and plant tissue. They can be modified by man, as when bricks are made of clay, mortar is mixed, wood is fabricated, and ore is smelted. Substances can be artificial, like glass, metal, or plastic. These are the "materials" of the designer, architect, and builder.

*Surfaces.* Similarly, the surfaces of substances and the "layout" of these surfaces can be natural, modified, or artificial. The horizontal surface of a pond or stream is a natural layout. The horizontal ground, or a hillside, or a cliff are kinds of natural terrestrial layout. But men have modified the shape of the terrain by levelling it, or making earthworks, ramps, ditches, and hedgerows. And men have formed quite artificial layouts by fabricating and constructing objects, enclosures, panels, walls, bridges, and tools.

Substances and their surfaces afford benefit or injury when they are encountered by a mobile animal. Different kinds of surface layout will afford different kinds of posture, different kinds of locomotor behavior, and different kinds of manipulation. Here are some examples of what the environment, natural or artificial, affords.

1. A solid horizontal surface affords *support*. A water surface does not.
   —A surface of support affords *resting* (coming to rest).
2. An extended surface of support affords *locomotion,* for a terrestrial animal.
3. A *vertical* solid surface stops locomotion and affords *mechanical contact*. It is a *barrier*.
   —A rigid barrier surface affords injury by abrupt contacts, i.e., collision. It is an *obstacle*. Deceleration is necessary to achieve contact without collision.
   —A *non-rigid* barrier surface can avert injury by collision.
4. A vertical *double surface,* that is, a wall or screen, affords *hiding behind,* that is, being out of sight of observers on the other side. This is true if the double surface is *opaque*.

---

*Paper presented at the Symposium on Perception in Architecture, American Society for Esthetics, Toronto, October 1976. Expanded on delivery. Previously unpublished.

5. A double surface at sufficient height above the ground affords *getting under*. It is a *roof*.

6. Any layout of surfaces that encloses an appropriate volume of air affords *shelter* (from the wind, cold, rain, snow). A cave, burrow, or hut.

    —An enclosure affords being out of sight of observers in all directions ("privacy") and thus it affords protection from predators. (All animals sometimes need to *hide*.)

7. An aperture or gap in an enclosure affords *entry* and *exit*.

    —It also affords *vision* within the enclosure by admitting illumination (sunlight).

    —It also affords *looking through* (both looking *out* and looking *in*).

    —It also affords long-term *respiration* (breathing fresh air).

    —Note that all the complexities of doors, windows, shutters, grilles, and panes of glass, etc., get their utilities from these basic affordances. (E.g., the misperception of a glass door is a real danger in modern buildings.)

8. A horizontal surface at about knee-height above the surface of support affords sitting, a *seat*.

9. A horizontal surface at about *waist-height* above the ground affords support for objects and facilitates manipulation of objects, e.g., tools, and materials for writing and reading, a workbench, desk, table.

10. A large drop-off in the surface of support affords injury by falling-off, a "brink." But a railing affords protection from falling off (like a fence, which is a barrier to locomotion).

    —A *small* drop-off in the surface of support affords stepping down without injury.

    —A series of "steps" in a *stairway* affords ascent or descent of a cliff by a pedestrian.

    —A *ladder* affords ascent or descent.

    —A *ramp* affords a different mode of ascent or descent.

Note that the separations, sizes, and shapes of the surfaces described are relative to the size and shape of the animal being considered, man. We design on what we call the "human scale." Small and large are relative. Now consider again the affordance of *locomotion* (#2).

11. An extended horizontal surface of support that is "uncluttered" affords *footing*, i.e., bipedal locomotion. If cluttered, however, it may not afford locomotion by planting the feet.

    —An aperture in the surface of support, a hole, or a foot-sized obstacle, affords *stumbling*. Either a concavity or a convexity does so. A small gap affords *stepping over;* a wider gap affords *jumping over;* a still wider gap affords *falling into* (consider the experiment on rats with a "jumping stand''). A small obstacle affords *stepping over;* a larger obstacle affords only *jumping over,* or *climbing over.*

12. A large gap in a barrier affords *walking* through. A smaller gap only affords *squeezing* through, or *ducking* under, or *creeping* under.
13. Any acute dihedral angle between two rigid surfaces, a ''sharp'' edge, affords *injury* on contact. But a junction of non-rigid surfaces does not. The latter explains the advantage of soft or padded surfaces in the artificial environment. Automobile interiors are now padded; why not domestic interiors?

We are now prepared to consider the visual perception of these surface layouts in advance of behavioral contact with them, that is, the perception of *what they afford.* For what we perceive first of all is not abstract color and space, as psychology has taught, but surfaces and their layout. Ecological optics provides a new explanation of how we see surfaces and their layout. They are specified by gradients, discontinuities, and other invariants in the *array* of light, not by the light as such.

We need to perceive the slant of the ground. We need to see the holes in it and the protuberances on it. We need to distinguish the solidity, rigidity and opaqueness of surfaces from their opposites. For *if* we can detect the gaps, separations, sizes, and shapes relative to our bodies, we will perceive directly and immediately their affordances for us. The meanings will be tacit, of course, not explicit, and whatever words we may apply to them will be inadequate, but that does not matter. Things will look as they do because they afford what they do.

Herein lies the possibility for a new theory of design. We modify the substances and surfaces of our environment for the sake of what they will afford, not for the sake of creating good forms as such, abstract forms, mathematically elegant forms, esthetically pleasing forms. The forms of Euclid and his geometry, abstracted by Plato to the immaterial level, have to be rooted in the substances and surfaces and layouts that constrain our locomotion and permit or prevent our actions. Surfaces have to be illuminated if they are to be seen. You cannot see them in darkness. But there is no use trying to illuminate a triangle.

Illuminated surfaces at a place in the environment are projected to a point of observation in the medium. The projections constitute what I call an ambient optic array. The surfaces constitute what I call a vista.[15] What one sees as he looks around is not a patchwork of forms but the possibilities of support, of falling, of resting, of sitting, of walking, of bumping into, of climbing; of taking shelter, of hiding, of grasping, of moving movable things, of tool using, and so on and on. There are also of course the possibilities of eating and drinking and those of social and sexual encounters, but I will leave them out of account. They

---

[15]Cf. Gibson (1979a, pp. 198–200). (Eds.)

are all in the surfaces of the vista. What I now want to emphasize is the fact that one also sees the possibility of *entering the next vista*, of going around the corner, or through the door, or over the hill. More exactly, one sees the occluding edges of the presently projected surfaces. A living observer is never frozen in the vista of the moment. Perceiving is sequential.

To see a vertical occluding edge is to see that it affords walking around, or peering around, or reaching around. This is a fact of ecological optics, not of physical optics. Of all the affordances I have mentioned this one is the most radical. For it implies that an observer perceives in some sense the surface that is occluded, that he detects the next vista. One sees around corners because one can go around corners in the course of time. The concept of the arrested image has misled us. The static picture is not the basic element of visual perception.

Architects need to pay attention to the affordances of locomotion and action in the layouts they design. To be oriented in a building (or a city, or a maze, for that matter) is to know where to go to get what you want. You have to open up a sequence of vistas until the final vista contains the surfaces of your goal. The perceiving of this affordance is made unnecessarily difficult in modern buildings.

The course in "basic design" with which architects now begin their training is at fault, I believe. It teaches *graphics,* on the assumption that an understanding of "form" is as necessary for architects as it is presumably for painters. But no one is ever going to understand "form," in my opinion. The use of the term only promotes confusion.[16] What architects are concerned with is the layout of surfaces.

## PART IX: A NOTE ON WHAT EXISTS AT THE ECOLOGICAL LEVEL OF REALITY*

I have been assuming that ecological reality (as distinguished from physical reality) consists of substances, the medium, the surfaces that separate them, and the varieties of surface layout. To these must be added the changes that occur in all of them, since they change in some respects and persist in others, the changes being no less real than the persistences. All such changes I call *events* (Gibson, 1979a, Ch. 6).[17]

The medium, the surface of support, and some substances are very persistent. Many local substances and layouts are very changeable, and their surfaces may even go out of or come into existence.

Substances, media, surfaces, layouts, and events are what there is to perceive, that is, know directly. Perceiving is extracting the information in ambient

---

[16]For a complete discussion of these issues, see Ch. 4.1. (Eds.)

*Unpublished manuscript, November 1978.

[17]Cf. Chs. 2.8 and 2.9. (Eds.)

light, sound, odor, and mechanical contact. The invariant combinations of features that constitute the *affordances* of these realities are what the animals pay attention to.

By this formula *objects* are by no means the only realities; an object is merely a substance with a topologically closed surface (a detached object) or a nearly closed surface (an attached object). An object is one form of layout and there are many other forms of layout such as enclosures, hollow objects, places, convexities, concavities, edges, corners, etc. It is an important form of layout, to be sure (animals are detached objects), but objects do not constitute reality and objects in space emphatically do not make up the world. There is an enormous variety of objects with affordances for human animals, and the imposing on them of *categories* using words (subordinate and superordinate) is what makes knowledge explicit instead of tacit, but the perceiving and naming of objects does not comprise the whole problem of perception as is often assumed.

On this formula *abstract* objects do not exist. There are, to be sure, realities that cannot be perceived directly but only known indirectly by means of instruments, measuring operations, pictures, and language, but it seems to me mistaken to call such realities "abstract" as against "concrete." Indirect knowledge based on communication (chirographic pictures and words) is uncertain and ill-understood by psychology.

The course of development of the perception of these different kinds of reality, by growth and by learning, is surely different. Consider learning to perceive detached *objects* and learning to perceive *places* (as in learning one's habitat). Moveable objects can be displaced, permuted in arrangement, put side by side for comparison, can be counted, and fall into a hierarchy of classes. Places, however, are nested within larger places, do not have sharp boundaries, cannot be displaced or permuted, are classified in a quite different way, and are learned in the course of locomotion (by the opening up of vistas). The ways in which children develop concepts of objects, therefore, cannot be the same as the ways in which they develop knowledge of places.

The ways in which children learn to perceive events are still different. Events at the ecological level are ill-understood; investigators are not even sure what an event *is*, being preoccupied with the "motions" of "objects." But the evidence suggests that very young children begin to distinguish happenings, transitions, deformations, displacements, and other changes in the environment before they distinguish objects.[18] Progressive and non-reversible events are distinguished from repeating or cyclic events by very young infants. The movements, sounds, and touches made by a person are especially worthy of attention since they specify what the person affords.[19]

---

[18]Cf. E. J. Gibson, Owsley, & Johnston (1978) and E. J. Gibson, Owsley, Walker, & Megaw-Nyce (1979). (Eds.)

[19]Cf. Spelke & Cortelyou (1980) and Walker (1980). (Eds.)

Events, like places, are nested, episodes being contained within longer episodes. For perception this nesting is what counts, not the metric dimension of empty time with its arbitrary instants and durations. Time as such, like space, is not perceived.

What about so-called "subjective" reality? Awareness of the persisting and changing environment (perception) is concurrent with the complementary awareness of the persisting and changing self (proprioception in my extended use of the term). This includes the body and its parts, and all its activities, from locomotion to thought, without any distinction between activities called "mental" and those called "physical." Oneself and one's body exist along with the environment. They are co-perceived. They are inescapable *in* the environment at the place called "here." They exist, but in a radically different fashion from the ecological realities. The two kinds of existence should not be confused. One's nose, hands, feet, heart, and stomach are co-perceived; and so are one's pains and itches and the aftereffects of stimulation (after images and feelings of vertigo); and so are one's ideas, insights, fantasies, dreams, and memories of childhood. But they should not be thought of as constituting a different realm of existence or a different kind of reality than the ecological, nor are they "mental" as against "physical."

# References

Allport, G., & Vernon, P. *Studies in expressive movement*. New York: MacMillan, 1933.

Aquila, R. *Intentionality: A study of mental acts*. University Park, PA: Pennsylvania State University Press, 1977.

Arnheim, R. *Art and visual perception*. Berkeley: University of California Press, 1954.

Arnheim, R. *Visual thinking*. Berkeley: University of California Press, 1969.

Austin, J. L. A. *Sense and sensibilia*. Oxford, England: Oxford University Press, 1962.

Avant, L. L. Vision in the Ganzfeld. *Psychological Bulletin*, 1965, *64*, 246-258.

Bartlett, F. H. *Remembering*. Cambridge, England: Cambridge University Press, 1932.

Bastian, H. C. *The brain as an organ of mind*. London: Kegan Paul, 1880.

Bastian, H. C. The "muscular sense": Its nature and cortical localization. *Brain*, 1887, *10*, 1-137.

Beck, J. *Surface color perception*. Ithaca, NY: Cornell University Press, 1972.

Benedikt, M. To take hold of space: Isovists and isovist fields. *Environment and Planning B*, 1979, *6*, 47-65.

Berkson, W. *Fields of force: The development of a world view from Faraday to Einstein*. London: Routledge & Kegan Paul, 1974.

Berthoz, A., Lacour, M., Soechting, J., & Vidal, P. The role of vision in the control of posture during linear motion. *Progress in Brain Research*, 1979, *50*, 197-209.

Bizzi, E. Central and peripheral mechanisms in motor control. In G. Stelmach & J. Requin (Eds.), *Tutorials in motor behavior*. Amsterdam: North Holland Press, 1980.

Black, M. *Language and philosophy*. Ithaca, NY: Cornell University Press, 1949.

Boring, E. G. *The physical dimensions of consciousness*. New York: Century, 1933.

Boring, E. G. *Sensation and perception in the history of experimental psychology*. New York: Appleton-Century-Crofts, 1942.

Boring, E. G. Visual perception as invariance. *Psychological Review*, 1952, *59*, 141-148. (a)

Boring, E. G. The Gibsonian visual field. *Psychological Review*, 1952, *59*, 246-247. (b)

Bower, T. G. R. The development of object-permanence: Some studies of existence constancy. *Perception & Psychophysics*, 1967, *2*, 411-418.

Boynton, R. The visual system: Environmental information. In E. C. Carterrette & M. P. Friedman (Eds.), *Handbook of Perception* (Vol. 1). New York: Academic, 1974.

Braddick, O., Campbell, F. W., & Atkinson, J. Channels in vision. In *Handbook of Sensory Physiology* (Vol. VIII). Berlin: Springer-Verlag, 1978.

**419**

Brandt, T., Dichgans, J., & Koenig, E. Differential effects of central versus peripheral vision on egocentric and exocentric motion perception. *Experimental Brain Research,* 1973, *16,* 476–491.

Bransford, J., McCarrell, N., Franks, J. J., & Nitsch, K. Towards unexplaining memory. In R. Shaw & J. Bransford (Eds.), *Perceiving, acting and knowing: Towards an ecological psychology.* Hillsdale, NJ: Erlbaum, 1977.

Braunstein, M. L. *Depth perception through motion.* New York: Academic Press, 1976.

Brentano, F. [*Psychology from an empirical standpoint.*] London: Routledge & Kegan Paul, 1973. (Originally published, 1874.)

Brodatz, P. *Textures; a photographic album for artists and designers.* New York: Dover, 1966.

Bruner, J. S. Personality dynamics and the process of perceiving. In R. R. Blake & G. V. Ramsey (Eds.), *Perception: An approach to personality.* New York: Ronald, 1951.

Brunswik, E. Thing constancy as measured by correlation coefficients. *Psychological Review,* 1940, *47,* 69–78.

Brunswik, E. Distal focussing of perception: Size constancy in a representative sample of situations. *Psychological Monographs,* 1944, *56* (254).

Brunswik, E. *The conceptual framework of psychology.* Chicago: University of Chicago Press, 1952.

Brunswik, E. *Perception and the representative design of psychological experiments.* Berkeley: University of California Press, 1956.

Burlingame, H. J. *The magician's handbook.* Chicago: Wilcox & Follett Co., 1942.

Cantril, H. *The "why" of man's experience.* New York: Macmillan, 1950.

Cantril, H., Ames, A., Hastorf, A., & Ittelson, W. H. Psychology and scientific research. *Science,* 1949, *110,* 461–464, 491–497, 517–522.

Čapek, M. *The philosophical impact of contemporary physics.* New York: Van Nostrand, 1961.

Čapek, M. (Ed.). *The concepts of space and time.* Boston: D. Reidel, 1976.

Caviness, J. A., & Gibson, J. J. The equivalence of visual and tactual stimulation for the perception of solid forms. Paper presented at the Eastern Psychological Association, Atlantic City, April 1962.

Cohen, W. Spatial and textural characteristics of the Ganzfeld. *American Journal of Psychology,* 1957, *70,* 403–410.

Costall, A. On how so much information controls so much behavior: James Gibson's theory of direct perception. In G. Butterworth (Ed.), *Infancy and epistemology.* Brighton, England: Harvester Press, 1981.

DeLaguna, G.A. *Speech: Its function and development.* New Haven: Yale University Press, 1927.

Dennett, D. Why the law of effect will not go away. *Journal for the Theory of Social Behaviour,* 1975, *5,* 169–187.

DeSilva, H. R. *Research on the scientific investigation of driving skill.* Massachusetts State College, Amherst (Now University of Massachusetts) F. E. R. A. Project #XS-F2-U-25. Boston: Reproduction Section Project #428, 1935.

Dichgans, J., & Brandt, T. Visual-vestibular interaction: Effects on self movement perception and postural control. In *Handbook of Sensory Physiology* (Vol. VIII). Berlin: Springer-Verlag, 1978.

Duncker, K. Über induzierte Bewegung. *Psychologische Forschung,* 1929, *12,* 180–259.

Eddington, A. S. *The nature of the physical world.* New York: MacMillan, 1929.

Eimas, P., & Miller, J. Effects of selective adaptation on the perception of speech and visual patterns: Evidence for feature detectors. In R. Walk & H. Pick (Eds.), *Perception and experience.* New York: Plenum Press, 1978.

Epstein, W. (Ed.) *Stability and constancy in perception.* New York: Wiley, 1977.

Epstein, W., & Park, J. An examination of Gibson's psychophysical hypothesis. *Psychological Bulletin,* 1964, *62,* 180–196.

Fearing, F. *Reflex action.* Cambridge, MA: M.I.T. Press, 1971. (Originally published in 1929.)

Fisichelli, V. R. Effect of rotational axis and dimensional variations on the reversals of apparent movement of Lissajous figures. *American Journal of Psychology*, 1946, *59*, 669-675.

Flock, H. R. Some conditions sufficient for accurate monocular perceptions of moving slant. *Journal of Experimental Psychology*, 1964, *67*, 560-572. (a)

Flock, H. R. A possible optical basis for monocular slant perception. *Psychological Review*, 1964, *71*, 380-391. (b)

Flock, H. R. Optical texture and linear perspective as stimuli for slant perception. *Psychological Review*, 1965, *72*, 505-514.

Forssberg, H., Grillner, S., & Rossingnol, S. Phasic gain control of reflexes from the dorsum of the paw during spinal locomotion. *Brain Research*, 1977, *132*, 121-139.

Fraenkel, G. S., & Gunn, D. L. *The orientation of animals*. London: Oxford University Press, 1940.

Freeman, R. B. Ecological optics and visual slant. *Psychological Review*, 1965, *72*, 501-504.

Freud, S. *Collected papers*. London: Hogarth Press, 1949.

Gallistel, C. R. *The organization of action*. Hillsdale, NJ: Erlbaum, 1980.

Gibson, E. J. Sensory generalization with voluntary reactions. *Journal of Experimental Psychology*, 1939, *24*, 237-253.

Gibson, E. J. A systematic application of the concepts of generalization and differentation to verbal learning. *Psychological Review*, 1940, *47*, 169-229.

Gibson, E. J. Improvement in perceptual judgments as a function of controlled practice or training. *Psychological Bulletin*, 1953, *50*, 401-431.

Gibson, E. J. *Principles of perceptual learning and development*. New York: Appleton-Century-Crofts, 1969.

Gibson, E. J. The concept of affordances in development: The renascence of functionalism. In W. A. Collins (Ed.), *Minnesota symposia on child psychology, Vol. 15: The concept of development*. Hillsdale, NJ: Erlbaum, in press.

Gibson, E. J. & Levin, H. *The psychology of reading*. Cambridge, MA: M.I.T. Press, 1975.

Gibson, E. J., Owsley, C. J., & Johnston, J. Perception of invariants by 5-month-old infants: Differentiation of two types of motion. *Developmental Psychology*, 1978, *14*, 407-415.

Gibson, E. J., Owsley, C. J., Walker, A., & Megaw-Nyce, J. Development of the perception of invariants: Substance and shape. *Perception*, 1979, *8*, 609-619.

Gibson, E. J., & Spelke, E. The development of perception. In J. Flavell & E. Markman (Eds.), *Cognitive development. Volume 3 of Handbook of Child Psychology*. New York: Wiley, in press.

Gibson, E. J., & Walk, R. D. The "visual cliff." *Scientific American*, 1960, *202*, 64-71.

Gill, R. W. *Basic perspective*. London: Thames & Hudson, 1974.

Gombrich, E. *Art and illusion: A study in the psychology of pictorial representation*. Princeton, NJ: Princeton University Press, 1961.

Gonshor, A., & Melvill-Jones, G. Extreme vestibulo-ocular adaptation induced by prolonged optical reversal of vision. *Journal of Physiology* (*London*), 1976, *256*, 381-414.

Goodman, N. *The languages of art*. Indianapolis: Bobbs-Merrill, 1968.

Gottschaldt, K. Über den Einfluss der Ehrfahrung auf die Wahrnehmung von Figuren II. Vergleichende Untersuchungen über die Wirkung figuraler Einprägung und die Einfluss spezifischer Geschehensverlaufe auf die Auffassung optischer Komplexe. *Psychologische Forschung*, 1929, *12*, 1-87.

Gottsdanker, R. M. The ability of human operators to detect acceleration of target motion. *Psychological Bulletin*, 1956, *53*, 477-487.

Graham, C. H. Visual perception. In S. S. Stevens (Ed.), *Handbook of Experimental Psychology*. New York: Wiley, 1951.

Granit, R. Linkage of alpha and gamma motoneurones in voluntary movement. *Nature* (*New Biology*), 1973, *243*, 52-53.

Gregory, R. Seeing as thinking. *Times Literary Supplement*, June 23, 1972, 707-708.

Gyr, J. Is a theory of direct visual perception adequate? *Psychological Bulletin*, 1972, *77*, 246–261.

Hagen, M. A. Picture perception: Toward a theoretical model. *Psychological Bulletin*, 1974, *81*, 471–497.

Hagen, M. A. Problems with picture perception: A reply to Rosinski. *Psychological Bulletin*, 1976, *83*, 1176–1178.

Hagen, M. A. A new theory of the psychology of representational art. In C. Nodine & D. Fisher (Eds.), *Perception and pictorial representation*. New York: Praeger, 1979.

Hagen, M. A., Glick, R., & Morse, B. Role of two-dimensional surface characteristics in pictorial depth perception. *Perceptual and Motor Skills*, 1978, *46*, 875–881.

Hagen, M. A., & Jones, R. K. Plane surface information as a determinant of pictorial perception. In J. Long & A. Baddeley (Eds.), *Attention and performance IX*. Hillsdale, NJ: Erlbaum, 1981.

Hagen, M. A., Jones, R. K., & Reed, E. S. On a neglected variable in theories of pictorial perception: Truncation of the visual field. *Perception & Psychophysics*, 1978, *23*, 326–330.

Hamlyn, D. W. The concept of information in Gibson's theory of perception. *Journal for the Theory of Social Behaviour*, 1977, *7*, 5–14.

Harper, R. S., & Boring, E. G. Cues. *American Journal of Psychology*, 1948, *61*, 343–351.

Hay, J. C. Optical motions and space perception: An extension of Gibson's analysis. *Psychological Review*, 1966, *73*, 550–565.

Hayek, F. A. *The sensory order*. Chicago: University of Chicago Press, 1952.

Hebb, D. O. *The organization of behavior*. New York: Wiley, 1949.

Heft, H. An examination of contructivist and Gibsonian approaches to environmental psychology. *Population and Environment: Behavioral and Social Issues*, 1981, *4*, 227–245.

Heider, F. Ding und medium. *Symposium*, 1926, *1*, 109–157. Excerpted as "Thing and medium" in Heider (1959).

Heider, F. *On perception, event structure, and psychological environment*. New York: International Universities Press, 1959. (Psychological Issues Monographs, Vol. 1, No. 3).

Held, R., & Bauer, J. Visually guided reaching in infant monkeys after restricted rearing. *Science*, 1967, *155*, 718–720.

Helmholtz, H. von [*Handbuch der Physiologischen Optik.*] Translated as *Physiological Optics*, New York: Dover, 1962. (1st German Ed: 1866/3rd German Ed.: 1909–1911).

Henney, K., & Dudley, B. *Handbook of photography*. New York: Whittlesey House, 1939.

Hick, W. E. Threshold for sudden change in the velocity of a seen object. *Quarterly Journal of Experimental Psychology*, 1950, *2*, 33–41.

Hilgard, E. R. The role of learning in perception. In R. R. Blake & G. V. Ramsey (Eds.), *Perception: An approach to personality*. New York: Ronald, 1951.

Hilgard, E. R., & Marquis, P. G. *Conditioning and learning*. New York: Appleton-Century-Crofts, 1940.

Hochberg, J. E. The psychophysics of pictorial perception. *Audio-Visual Communication Review*, 1962, *10*, 22–54.

Hochberg, J. E., & Brooks, V. Pictorial recognition as an unlearned ability. *American Journal of Psychology*, 1962, *75*, 624–628.

Hochberg, J. E., Triebel, W., & Seaman, G. Color adaptation under conditions of homogeneous visual stimulation (Ganzfeld). *Journal of Experimental Psychology*, 1951, 41, 153–159.

Hogben, L. *From cave painting to comic strip*. New York: Chanticleer, 1949.

von Holst, E. Relations between the central nervous system and the peripheral organs. *British Journal of Animal Behaviour*, 1954, *2*, 89–94.

von Holst, E., & Mittelstaedt, S. M. Das reafferenzprinzip. *Naturwissenschaften*, 1950, *20*, 464–476. Translated in von Holst, E. *The behavioral physiology of animals and man* (Vol. 1). London: Methuen, 1973.

Holt, E. B. *The Freudian wish*. New York: Holt, 1915.

Hubel, D. H., & Wiesel, T. N. Receptive fields, binocular interaction, and functional architecture in the cat's visual cortex. *Journal of Physiology*, 1962, *160*, 106–154.

Hughes, A. The topography of vision in mammals. In *Handbook of Sensory Physiology* (Vol. VII/5). Berlin: Springer-Verlag, 1977.

Hull, C. L. The goal-gradient hypothesis applied to some "fieldforce" problems in the behavior of young children. *Psychological Review*, 1938, *45*, 271–299.

Hull, C. L. *The principles of behavior*. New York: Appleton-Century-Crofts, 1943.

Hull, C. L. *A behavior system*. New Haven: Yale University Press, 1952.

Hurvich, L., & Jameson, D. *The perception of lightness and brightness*. Boston: Allyn & Bacon, 1966.

Hyland, D. *The origins of philosophy*. New York: Putnams, 1973.

Ittelson, W. H. The constancies in perceptual theory. *Psychological Review*, 1951, *58*, 285–294.

James, W. *The principles of psychology*. New York: Holt, 1890. (Dover reprint edition).

Jansson, G., & Börjesson, E. Perceived direction of rotary motion. *Perception & Psychophysics*, 1969, *6*, 19–26.

Jansson, G., & Runeson, S. Measurement of perceived oscillation. *Perception & Psychophysics*, 1969, *6*, 27–32.

Jastrow, J. Psychological notes on Helen Keller. *Psychological Review*, 1894, *1*, 356–362.

Jenkins, J. J., Wald, J., & Pittenger, J. Apprehending pictorial events: An instance of psychological cohesion. In C. W. Savage (Ed.), *Perception and cognition: Issues in the foundations of psychology*. Minneapolis, MN: University of Minnesota Press, 1978.

Jennings, H. S. *Behavior of the lower organisms*. New York: Columbia University Press, 1906.

Johansson, G. *Configurations in event perception*. Uppsala, Sweden: Almqvist & Wiksell, 1950.

Johansson, G. Rigidity, stability and motion in perceptual space. *Acta Psychologica*, 1958, *13*, 359.-370.

Johansson, G. Perception of motion and changing form. *Scandinavian Journal of Psychology*, 1964, *5*, 181–208.

Johansson, G. On theories for visual space perception: A letter to Gibson. *Scandinavian Journal of Psychology*, 1970, *11*, 67–74.

Johansson, G. Visual perception of biological motion and a model for its analysis. *Perception & Psychophysics*, 1973, *14*, 201–211.

Johansson, G. Spatial constancy and motion in visual perception. In W. Epstein (Ed.), *Stability and constancy in visual perception: Mechanisms and processes*. New York: Wiley, 1977.

Johansson, G., von Hofsten, C., & Jansson, G. Event perception. *Annual Review of Psychology*, 1980, *31*, 27–63.

Johansson, G., & Jansson, G. Perceived rotary motion from changes in a straight line. *Perception & Psychophysics*, 1968, *4*, 165–170.

Jones, R. K., & Lee, D. N. Why two eyes are better than one: The two views of binocular vision. *Journal of Experimental Psychology: Human Perception and Performance*, 1981, *7*, 30–40.

Jones, R. K., & Pick, A. D. On the nature of information in behalf of direct perception. *The Behavioral and Brain Sciences*, 1980, *3*, 388–389.

Julesz, B. *Foundations of cyclopean vision*. Chicago: University of Chicago Press, 1971.

Kanizsa, G. *Organization in perception*. New York: Praeger, 1979.

Kant, I. [*The critique of pure reason.*] (N. K. Smith, trans.). London: St. Martins, 1929. (Originally published as *Kritik der reinen Vernunft*, 1781 (1st) and 1787 (2d).)

Kaplan, G. Kinetic disruption of optical texture: The perception of depth at an edge. *Perception & Psychophysics*, 1969, *6*, 193–198.

Katz, D. *Der Aufbau der Tastwelt*. Leipzig: Barth, 1925.

Katz, D. [*The world of color.*] London: Kegan Paul, 1935. (Originally published as *Der Aufbau der Farbwelt*, 1930.)

Keller, F. S. Studies in International Morse Code I. A new method of teaching code reception. *Journal of Applied Psychology*, 1943, *27*, 407–415.

Kennedy, J. M. Line representation and pictorial perception. Unpublished PhD., Cornell University, 1970.

Kennedy, J. M. *A psychology of picture perception*. San Francisco: Jossey Bass, 1974.

Kepes, G. *Language of vision*. Chicago: Theobald, 1944.

Kilpatrick, F. P. *Human behavior from the transactional point of view*. Hanover, NH: Institute for Advanced Research, 1952.

Koch, S. (Ed.). *Psychology: A study of a science* (Vol. 2). New York: McGraw-Hill, 1959.

Koffka, K. *The principles of Gestalt psychology*. New York: Harcourt-Brace, 1935.

Kohler, I. [*Über Aufbau und Wandlungen der Wahrnehmungswelt*. Vienna: R. Mohrer, 1951] Translated as, The formation and transformation of the perceptual world. *Psychological Issues*, 1964, *3*(4).

Köhler, W. [On unnoticed sensations and errors of judgment] *Zeitschrift fur Psychologie*, 1913, *66*, 51-80. Reprinted in M. Henle (Ed.), *The selected papers of Wolgang Köhler*. New York: Liveright, 1971.

Köhler, W. *Gestalt psychology*. New York: Liveright, 1929.

Köhler, W. *Dynamics in psychology*. New York: Liveright, 1940.

Köhler, W., & Wallach, H. Figural after-effects: An investigation of visual processes. *Proceedings of the American Philosophical Society*, 1944, *88*, 269-357.

Langewiesche, W. *Stick and rudder*. New York: McGraw-Hill, 1944.

Lappin, J., Doner, J., & Kottas, B. Minimal conditions for the visual detection of structure and motion in three dimensions. *Science*, 1980, *209*, 717-719.

Lashley, K. In search of the engram. In *Symposium of the Society of Experimental Biology, Vol. 4: Physiological mechanisms in animal behavior*. New York: Academic Press, 1950.

Lashley, K. The problem of serial order in behavior. In L. A. Jeffress (Ed.), *Cerebral mechanisms in behavior*. New York: Wiley, 1951.

Lashley, K. Dynamic processes in perception. In J. F. Delafresnaye (Ed.). *Brain mechanisms and consciousness*. Oxford, England: Blackwell, 1954.

Lasky, R., Romano, N., & Wenters, J. Spatial localization in children after changes in position. *Journal of Experimental Child Psychology*, 1980, *29*, 225-248.

Lee, D. N. Theory of the stereoscopic shadow-caster: An instrument for the study of binocular kinetic space perception. *Vision Research*, 1969, *9*, 145-156.

Lee, D. N. Binocular stereopsis without spatial disparity. *Perception & Psychophysics*, 1971, *6*, 216-218.

Lee, D. N. Visual information during locomotion. In R. MacLeod & H. Pick (Eds.), *Perception: Essays in honor of James J. Gibson*. Ithaca, NY: Cornell University Press, 1974.

Lee, D. N. A theory of visual control of braking based on information about time-to-collision. *Perception*, 1976, *5*, 437-459.

Lee, D. N. The functions of vision. In H. Pick & E. Saltzman (Eds.), *Modes of perceiving and processing information*. Hillsdale, NJ: Erlbaum, 1978.

Lee, D. N. The optic flow field: The foundation of vision. *Philosophical Transactions of the Royal Society, London*, (B), 1980, *290*, 169-178. (a)

Lee, D. N. Visuo-motor coordination in space-time. In G. Stelmach & J. Requin (Eds.), *Tutorials in motor control*. Amsterdam: North Holland Press, 1980. (b)

Lee, D. N., & Lishman, J. R. Visual control of locomotion. *Scandinavian Journal of Psychology*, 1977, *18*, 224-230. (a)

Lee, D. N., & Lishman, J. R. Vision: The most efficient source of proprioceptive information for balance control. *Aggressologie*, 1977, *18*(A), 83-94. (b)

Leeper, R. A study of a neglected portion of the field of learning: The development of sensory organization. *Journal of Genetic Psychology*, 1935, *46*, 41-75.

LeGros Clark, W. E., & Medawar, P. B. (Eds.). *Essays on growth and form presented to D'Arcy Thompson*. New York: Oxford University Press, 1945.

Lewin, K.  Environmental forces. In C. Murchison (Ed.), *A handbook of child psychology*. Worcester, MA: Clark University Press, 1933.

Lewin, K.  *A dynamic theory of personality*. New York: McGraw-Hill, 1935.

Lewin, K.  *Principles of topological psychology*. New York: McGraw-Hill, 1936.

Liberman, A., Cooper, F., Shankweiler, D., & Studdert-Kennedy, M. Perception of the speech code. *Psychological Review*, 1967, *74*, 431-461.

Lishman, J. R., & Lee, D. N. The autonomy of visual kinesthesis. *Perception*, 1973, *2*, 287-294.

Lishman, J. R., & Lee, D. N. Visual proprioceptive control of stance. *Journal of Human Movement Studies*, 1975, *1*, 87-95.

Loftus, E., & Loftus, G. On the permanence of stored information in the human brain. *American Psychologist*, 1980, *35*, 409-420.

Lombardo, T. J. J. Gibson's ecological approach to visual perception: Its historical context and development. Doctoral dissertation, University of Minnesota, 1973. Dissertation Abstracts International, 1973-1974, *34*, 3534-3535B (University Microfilms No. 74-721).

Lumsden, E. Problems of magnification and minification: An explanation of the distortions of distance, slant, shape, and velocity. In M. A. Hagen (Ed.), *The perception of pictures* (Vol. 1). New York: Academic Press, 1980.

Mace, W. M. Ecologically stimulating cognitive psychology. In W. Weimer & D. Palermo (Eds.), *Cognition and the symbolic process*. Hillsdale, NJ: Erlbaum, 1974.

Mace, W. M. J. J. Gibson's strategy for perceiving: Ask not what's inside your head, but what your head's inside of. In R. Shaw & J. Bransford (Eds.), *Perceiving, acting and knowing: Towards an ecological psychology*. Hillsdale, NJ: Erlbaum, 1977.

Mace, W. M., & Pittenger, J. Directly perceiving Gibson. *Psychological Bulletin*, 1975, *82*, 137-139.

Mace, W. M., & Shaw, R. E. Simple kinetic information for transparent depth. *Perception & Psychophysics*, 1974, *15*, 201-209.

Mach, E. *Grundlinien der Lehre von den Bewegungsempfindungen*. Leipzig: Verlag von Wilhelm Engelmann, 1875.

MacLeod, R. An experimental investigation of brightness constancy. *Archives of Psychology*, 1932,(135).

Marmolin, H., & Ulfberg, S. Rörelse-perception och formförändring. [Perception of motion and change of form]. Unpublished report, Psychological Laboratories, University of Uppsala, Uppsala, Sweden, 1967.

Marrow, A. J. *The practical theorist: The life and work of Kurt Lewin*. New York: Basic Books, 1969.

Masterton, R. B., & Berkley, M. A. Brain function: Changing ideas on the role of sensory, motor and association cortex in behavior. *Annual Review of Psychology*, 1974, *25*, 277-312.

Matin, E. Saccadic suppression: A review and an analysis. *Psychological Bulletin*, 1974, *81*, 899-917.

Matin, L. Eye movements and perceived visual direction. *Handbook of Sensory Physiology* (Vol. VII/4). Berlin: Springer-Verlag, 1972.

Maull, N. Cartesian optics and the geometrization of nature. *Review of Metaphysics*, 1978, *32*, 253-273.

McCloskey, D. Kinesthetic sensibility. *Physiological Review*, 1978, *58*, 763-820.

McIntyre, C., Hardwick, C., & Pick, H. L. The content and manipulation of cognitive maps in children and adults. *Monographs of the Society for Research in Child Development*, 1976, *41*(166).

McKay, D. M. Visual stability and voluntary eye movements. *Handbook of Sensory Physiology* (Vol. VII/3/A). Berlin: Springer-Verlag, 1973.

Menzel, E. W. Cognitive mapping in chimpanzees. In S. H. Hulse, H. Fowler, & W. K. Honig (Eds.). *Cognitive processes in animal behavior*. Hillsdale, NJ: Erlbaum, 1978.

Merleau-Ponty, M. [*The phenomenology of perception.*] London: Routledge & Kegan Paul, 1962. (French ed. 1946).

Metelli, F. Achromatic color conditions in the perception of transparency. In R. MacLeod & H. Pick (Eds.), *Perception: Essays in honor of James J. Gibson.* Ithaca, NY: Cornell University Press, 1974.

Metzger, W. Optische untersuchungen am Ganzfeld, II. Zür Phänomenologie des homogenen Ganzfelds. *Psychologische Forschung,* 1930, *13,* 6-29.

Metzger, W. Beobachtungen über phänomenale Identität. *Psychologische Forschung,* 1934, *19,* 1-60.

Metzger, W. *Gesetze des Sehens.* Frankfurt: W. Kramer, 1953 (A much revised edition appeared in 1975).

Michaels, C., & Carello, C. *Direct perception.* New York: Prentice Hall, 1981.

Michotte, A. *Causalité, permanence et realité phénomenales.* Louvain: Publications Universitaires, 1962.

Michotte, A. [*The perception of causality.*] New York: Basic Books, 1963. (Originally published as *La perception de la causalité,* 2nd ed. 1954).

Michotte, A., Thinès, G., & Crabbé, G. Les complements amodaux des structures perceptives. *Studia Psychologica,* Louvain: Publication de l'Université de Louvain, 1964.

Miles, F. A., & Eighmy, B. Long-term adaptive changes in primate vestibulocular reflex I. Behavioral observations. *Journal of Neurophysiology,* 1980, *43,* 1407-1425.

Miles, F. A., & Evarts, E. V. Concepts of motor organization. *Annual Review of Psychology,* 1979, *30,* 327-362.

Miller, N. E. (Ed.). *Psychological research on pilot training.* AAF Aviation Psychology Reports No. 8. Washington: U.S. Government Printing Office, 1947.

Miller, N. E., & Dollard, J. *Social learning and imitation.* New Haven: Yale University Press, 1941.

Mollon, J. D. Neurons and neural codes. In K. von Fieandt & I. Moustgaard (Eds.), *The perceptual world.* New York: Academic Press, 1977. (a)

Mollon, J. D. Neural analysis. In K. von Fieandt & I. Moustgaard (Eds.), *The perceptual world.* New York: Academic Press, 1977. (b)

Morris, C. *Signs, language, and behavior.* New York: Prentice-Hall, 1946.

Müller, J. [*Elements of Physiology* (Vol. 2).] (W. Baly trans.). London: Murray, 1838. (German Original, 1834.)

Murchison, C. *Handbook of General Experimental Psychology.* Worcester, MA: Clark University Press, 1934.

Musatti, C. L. Sui fenomeni stereocinetici. *Archivio Italiano di Psychologia,* 1924, *3,* 105-120.

Nashner, L. Adapting reflexes controlling the human posture. *Experimental Brain Research,* 1976, *26,* 59-72.

Nashner, L., & Cordo, P. Relation of automatic postural responses and reaction-time voluntary movements of human leg muscles. *Experimental Brain Research,* 1981, *43,* 395-405.

Nashner, L., & Woolacott, M. The organization of rapid postural adjustments of standing humans. In R. E. Talbott & D. R. Humphreys (Eds.), *Posture and movement.* New York: Raven Press, 1979.

Neisser, U. *Cognition and reality.* San Francisco: W. H. Freeman, 1976.

Neisser, U. Gibson's ecological optics: Consequences of a different stimulus description. *Journal for the Theory of Social Behaviour,* 1977, *7,* 17-28.

Neisser, U. Perceiving, anticipating and imagining. In C. W. Savage (Ed.), *Perception and cognition: Issues in the foundations of psychology.* Minneapolis, MN: University of Minnesota, 1978.

Newton, I. *Opticks.* New York: Dover, 1952. (Reprint of 1730 ed.)

Nicod, J. *Foundations of geometry and induction.* London: Kegan Paul, 1930.

Norman, D. Categorization of action slips. *Psychological Review,* 1981, *88,* 1-15.

Osgood, C. E. *Method and theory in experimental psychology.* New York: Oxford University Press, 1953.

Panofsky, E. Die Perspektive als 'Symbolische Form', *Vorträge der Bibliothek Warburg, 1924–1925;* 258–331, Leipzig, 1927.

Pavlov, I. P. *Conditioned reflexes.* (Transl. by G. V. Anrep) London: Oxford University Press, 1927.

Perkins, D., & Hagen, M. A. Convention, context, and caricature. In M. A. Hagen (Ed.), *The perception of pictures* (Vol. 1). New York: Academic Press, 1981.

Piaget, J. *The child's conception of the world.* New York: Harcourt Brace, 1929.

Pick, A. D. Improvement of visual and tactual form discrimination. *Journal of Experimental Psychology,* 1965, *69,* 331–339.

Pick, H. Tactual and haptic perception. In R. Welsh & B. Blasch (Eds.), *Foundations of orientation and mobility.* New York: American Foundation for the Blind, 1980.

Pirenne, M. H. *Optics, painting & photography.* Cambridge, England: Cambridge University Press, 1970.

Pittenger, J., & Shaw, R. Perceiving the face of change in changing faces. In R. Shaw & J. Bransford (Eds.), *Perceiving, acting and knowing: Towards an ecological psychology.* Hillsdale, NJ: Erlbaum, 1977.

Polanyi, M. *Personal knowledge.* Chicago: University of Chicago Press, 1958.

Popper, K. *Conjectures and refutations.* New York: Harper & Row, 1963.

Postman, L. Toward a general theory of cognition. In J. H. Rohrer & M. Sherif (Eds.), *Social psychology at the crossroads.* New York: Harper, 1951.

Postman, L. Association theory and perceptual learning. *Psychological Review,* 1955, *62,* 438–446.

Purdy, J., & Gibson, E. J. Distance judgment by the method of fractionation. *Journal of Experimental Psychology,* 1955, *50,* 374–380.

Purdy, W. C. The hypothesis of psychophysical correspondence in space perception (Unpublished doctoral dissertation, Cornell University). Ann Arbor: University Microfilms, 1958, No. 58–5594.

Rabaud, E. [*How animals find their way about.*] (Translation of French original). New York: Harcourt, Brace & Co., 1928.

Radner, D. *The philosophy of Malebranche.* Amsterdam: Gorcum Publishers, 1978.

Reed, E. S. Information pickup is the activity of perceiving. *The Behavioral and Brain Sciences,* 1980, *3,* 397–398.

Reed, E. S., & Jones, R. K. Gibson's theory of perception: A case of hasty epistemologizing? *Philosophy of Science,* 1978, *45,* 519–530.

Reed, E.S., & Jones, R. K. J. J. Gibson's ecological revolution in psychology. *Philosophy of the Social Sciences,* 1979, *9,* 189–204.

Reed, E. S., & Jones, R. K. Is perception blind? A reply to Heil. *Journal for the Theory of Social Behaviour,* 1981, *11,* 87–91.

Reid, T. *Essays on the intellectual powers of man.* Cambridge, MA: M.I.T. Press, 1969. (Originally published, 1785.)

Restle, F. Coding theory of the perception of motion configurations. *Psychological Review,* 1979, *86,* 1–24.

Revesz, G. *Psychology and the art of the blind.* London: Longmans & Green, 1950.

Reynolds, H. N. Temporal estimation in the perception of occluded motion. *Perceptual and Motor Skills,* 1968, *26,* 407–416.

Richards, R. J. Gibson's passive theory of perception: A criticism of Müller's specific energies hypothesis. *Philosophy and Phenomenological Research,* 1976, *37,* 221–234.

Rogers, B., & Graham, M. Motion parallax as an independent cue for depth perception. *Perception,* 1979, *8,* 125–134.

Rosenbaum, D. Perception and extrapolation of velocity and acceleration. *Jouranl of Experimental Psychology: Human Perception and Performance,* 1975, *1,* 395–403.

Rosenzweig, M. R. Development of research on the physiological mechanisms of auditory localization. *Psychological Bulletin,* 1961, *58,* 376–389.

Rosinski, R., & Farber, J. Compensation for viewing point in the perception of pictured space. In M. A. Hagen (Ed.), *The perception of pictures* (Vol. 1). New York: Academic Press, 1980.

Runeson, S. On visual perception of dynamic events. Unpublished PhD Dissertation, Uppsala University, Uppsala Sweden, 1977.

Ryan, T. A., & Schwartz, C. Speed of perception as a function of mode of representation. *American Journal of Psychology,* 1956, *69,* 60–69.

Schiff, W. Perception of impending collision: A study of visually directed avoidant behavior. *Psychological Monographs,* 1965, *79*(604).

Schlosberg, H. Stereoscopic depth from single pictures. *American Journal of Psychology,* 1941, *54,* 601–605.

Searle, J. Minds, brains, and programs. *The Behavioral and Brain Sciences,* 1980, *3,* 417–457.

Sedgwick, H. The geometry of spatial layout in pictorial representation. In M. A. Hagen (Ed.), *The perception of pictures* (Vol. 1). New York: Academic, 1980.

Shankweiler, D., Strange, W., & Verbrugge, R. Speech and the problem of perceptual constancy. In R. Shaw & J. Bransford (Eds.), *Perceiving, acting and knowing: Towards an ecological psychology.* Hillsdale, NJ: Erlbaum, 1977.

Shannon, C. A mathematical theory of communication. *Bell System Technical Journal,* 1948, *27,* 379–423, 623–656.

Shaw, R., & Pittenger, J. On perceiving change. In H. Pick & E. Saltzman (Eds.), *Modes of perceiving and processing information.* Hillsdale, NJ: Erlbaum, 1978.

Shaw, R., Turvey, M. T., & Mace, W. M. Ecological psychology: The consequences of a commitment to realism. In W. Weimer & D. Palermo (Eds.), *Cognition and the symbolic process* (Vol. 2). Hillsdale, NJ: Erlbaum, 1982.

Sherrington, C. S. The muscular sense. In E. A. Schafer (Ed.), *Textbook of physiology.* Edinburgh: Pentland, 1900.

Sherrington, C. S. On the proprioceptive system especially in its reflex aspect. *Brain,* 1906, *29,* 467–482.

Skavenski, A., Hansen, R., Steinman, R., & Winterson, B. Quality of retinal image stabilization during small natural and artificial body rotations in man. *Vision Research,* 1979, *19,* 675–683.

Skinner, B. F. *The behavior of organisms.* New York: Appleton-Century-Crofts, 1938.

Skinner, B. F. *Verbal behavior.* New York: Appleton-Century-Crofts, 1957.

Skinner, B. F. *Cumulative record.* New York: Appleton-Century-Crofts, 1959.

Smith, O. W., & Gruber, H. Perception of depth in photographs. *Perceptual and Motor Skills,* 1958, *8,* 307–313.

Smith, O. W., & Sherlock, L. A new explanation of the velocity transposition phenomenon. *American Journal of Psychology,* 1957, *70,* 102–105.

Smith, P. C., & Smith, O. W. Ball-throwing responses to photographically portrayed targets. *Journal of Experimental Psychology,* 1961, *62,* 223–233.

Smith, W. J. *The behavior of communicating.* Cambridge, MA: Harvard University Press, 1977.

Spelke, E., & Cortelyou, A. Perceptual aspects of social knowing: Looking and listening in infancy. In M. Lamb & L. Sherrod (Eds.), *Infant social cognition: Empirical and theoretical considerations.* Hillsdale, NJ: Erlbaum, 1980.

Spence, K. W. *Behavior theory and conditioning.* New Haven: Yale University Press, 1956.

Spigel, I. M. (Ed.). *Readings in the study of visually perceived movement.* New York: Harper & Row, 1965.

Steinman, R., & Winterson, B. J. Binocular retinal image motion during active head rotation. *Vision Research,* 1980, *20,* 415–430.

Stevens, P. S. *Patterns in nature.* Boston, MA: Atlantic-Little Brown, 1974.

Stevens, S. S. (Ed.). *Handbook of Experimental Psychology.* New York: Wiley, 1951.

Stoeckel, R. B., May, M. A., & Kirby, R. S. *Sense and safety on the road.* New York: D. Appleton-Century, 1936.

Stratton, G. M. Some preliminary experiments on vision without inversion of the retinal image. *Psychological Review,* 1896, *3,* 611–617.

Stratton, G. M. Vision without inversion of the retinal image. *Psychological Review,* 1897, *4,* 341–360, 463–481.

Taylor, B. Linear perspective. London, 1715.

Thinès, G. *Phenomenology and the science of behavior.* London: Allen & Unwin, 1977.

Thompson, D'Arcy W. *On growth and form.* New York: Macmillan, 1942.

Thorpe, W. H. *Learning and instinct in animals.* London: Methuen, 1956.

Tinbergen, N. *The study of instinct.* London: Oxford University Press, 1951.

Todd, J., Mark, L., Shaw, R., & Pittenger, J. The perception of human growth. *Scientific American,* 1980, *242,* 106–114.

Tolman, E. C. *Purposive behavior in animals and men.* New York: Appleton-Century-Crofts, 1932.

Tolman, E. C. Cognitive maps in rats and men. *Psychological Review,* 1948, *55,* 189–208.

Troland, L. T. *Psychophysiology* (Vol. 2). New York: Van Nostrand, 1930.

Tschernak-Seysenegg, H. Über parallaktoscopie. *Archiv fur die geschichte der Physiologie,* 1939, *241,* 454–469.

Turvey, M. T., & Shaw, R. The primacy of perceiving: An ecological reformulation of perception for understanding memory. In L-G Nilsson (Ed.), *Perspectives on memory research.* Hillsdale, NJ: Erlbaum, 1979.

Ullman, S. Against direct perception. *The Behavioral and Brain Sciences,* 1980, *3,* 373–415.

Underwood, B. J. *Psychological research.* New York: Appleton-Century-Crofts, 1957.

Uttal, W. *The psychobiology of sensory coding.* New York: Harper & Row, 1973.

Vernon, M. D. *A further study of visual perception.* Cambridge, England: Cambridge University Press, 1952.

Volkmann, A. Über den Einfluss der übung auf das Erkennen raumlicher Distanzen. *Ber. d. Sachs. Ges. d. wiss., math. phys. Abth.,* 1858, *10,* 38–69.

Walk, R., & Gibson, E. J. A comparative and analytical study of depth perception. *Psychological Monographs,* 1961, *75,* No. 519.

Walk, R., Gibson, E. J., & Tighe, T. The behavior of light- and dark-reared rats on a visual cliff. *Science,* 1957, *126,* 80–81.

Walker, A. The perception of facial and vocal expressions by human infants. Unpublished PhD thesis, Cornell University, 1980.

Wall, P. D. The sensory and motor role of impulses travelling in the dorsal columns towards cerebral cortex. *Brain,* 1970, *93,* 505–524.

Wallach, H. The role of head movements and vestibular and visual cues in sound localization. *Journal of Experimental Psychology,* 1940, *27,* 339–368.

Wallach, H. *On perception.* New York: Quadrangle, 1976.

Wallach, H., & O'Connell, D. N. The kinetic depth effect. *Journal of Experimental Psychology,* 1953, *45,* 205–217.

Walls, G. L. *The vertebrate eye.* Bloomfield Hills, MI: Cranbrook Institute of Science, 1942.

Ware, W. R. *Modern perspective.* New York: MacMillan, 1900.

Warren, R. The perception ego motion. *Journal of Experimental Psychology: Human Perception and Performance,* 1976, *2,* 448–456.

Warren, W. Visual information for object identity in apparent movement. *Perception & Psychophysics,* 1977, *21,* 264–268.

Warren, W., & Shaw, R. The visual specification of events: A reply to Ullman. *Perception & Psychophysics,* 1978, *24,* 387–389.

Watson, J. B. *Psychology from the standpoint of a behaviorist.* Philadelphia: Lippincott, 1924.

Wertheimer, M. Experimentelle studien über das Sehen von Bewegung. *Zeitschrift fur Psychologie,* 1912, *61,* 161–265.

Wertheimer, M. Untersuchungen zur Lehre von der Gestalt, II. *Psychologische Forschung,* 1923, *4,* 301–350.

Whipple, G. M. *Manual of mental and physical tests, Part 1: Simpler processes.* Baltimore: Warwick & York, 1924.

Whitrow, J. G. *The natural philosophy of time.* London: T. Nelson & Sons, 1961.

Wiener, N. *Cybernetics.* Cambridge, MA: M.I.T. Press, 1948.

Woodworth, R. S. *Psychology.* New York: Holt, 1929.

Woodworth, R. S. *Dynamics of behavior.* New York: Holt, 1958.

Woodworth, R. S., & Schlosberg, H. *Experimental psychology.* London: Methuen, 1954.

Yolton, J. On Gibson's realism. *Synthese,* 1968–1969, *19,* 400–406.

Young, R. M. *Mind, brain and adaptation in the nineteenth century.* London: Oxford University Press, 1971.

# Complete Bibliography of James J. Gibson

Gibson, J. J. The reproduction of visually perceived forms. *Journal of Experimental Psychology*, 1929, *12*, 1–39.

Gibson, J. J., Jack, E. G., & Raffel, G. Bilateral transfer of the conditioned response in the human subject. *Journal of Experimental Psychology*, 1932, *15*, 416–421.

Gibson, J. J. Adaptation, after-effect and contrast in the perception of curved lines. *Journal of Experimental Psychology*, 1933, *16*, 1–31.

Gibson, J. J. Retroaction and the method of recognition. *Journal of General Psychology*, 1934, *10*, 234–236. (a)

Gibson, J. J. Vertical and horizontal orientation in visual perception. *Psychological Bulletin*, 1934, *31*, 739. (Abstract) (b)

Gibson, J. J., & Gibson, E. J. Retention and the interpolated task. *American Journal of Psychology*, 1934, *46*, 603–610.

Gibson, J. J. (Ed.) Studies in psychology from Smith College. *Psychological Monographs*, 1935, *46* (6, Whole No. 210).

Gibson, J. J., & Hudson, L. Bilateral transfer of the conditioned knee-jerk. *Journal of Experimental Psychology*, 1935, *18*, 774–783.

Gibson, J. J., & Robinson, D. Orientation in visual perception: The recognition of familiar plane forms in differing orientations. *Psychological Monographs*, 1935, *46* (6, Whole No. 210, 39–47).

Radner, M., & Gibson, J. J. Orientation in visual perception: The perception of tip-character in forms. *Psychological Monographs*, 1935, *46* (6, Whole No. 210, 48–65).

Gibson, J. J. A note on the conditioning of voluntary reactions. *Journal of Experimental Psychology*, 1936, *19*, 397–399. (a)

Gibson, J. J. Review of E. Freeman, *Social Psychology. Psychological Bulletin*, 1936, *33*, 664–666. (b)

Gibson, J. J., & Raffel, G. A technique for investigating retroactive and other inhibitory effects in immediate memory. *Journal of General Psychology*, 1936, *15*, 107–116.

Gibson, J. J. Adaptation, after-effect, and contrast in the perception of tilted lines: II. Simultaneous contrast and the areal restriction of the after-effect. *Journal of Experimental Psychology*, 1937, *20*, 553–569. (a)

Gibson, J. J. Adaptation with negative after-effect. *Psychological Review*, 1937, *44*, 222–244. (b)

Gibson, J. J., & Radner, M. Adaptation, after-effect and contrast in the perception of tilted lines: I. Quantitative studies. *Journal of Experimental Psychology*, 1937, *20*, 453–467.

Gibson, J. J., & Crooks, L. E. A theoretical field analysis of automobile-driving. *American Journal of Psychology*, 1938, *51*, 453–471.

Gibson, J. J., & Mowrer, O. H. Determinants of the perceived vertical and horizontal. *Psychological Review*, 1938, *45*, 300–323.

Gibson, J. J. The Aryan myth. *Journal of Educational Sociology*, 1939, *13*, 164–171. (a)

Gibson, J. J. Why a union for teachers? *Focus*, 1939, *2*, 3–7. (b)

Gibson, J. J. A critical review of the concept of set in contemporary experimental psychology. *Psychological Bulletin*, 1941, *38*, 781–817. (a)

Gibson, J. J. Review of S. H. Britt, *Social psychology of modern life*. *Psychological Bulletin*, 1941, *38*, 895–897. (b)

Gibson, J. J. Visual organization in relation to camouflage. In S. W. Fernberger (Ed.), *Perception*. *Psychological Bulletin*, 1941, *38*, 432–468. (c)

Gibson, J. J. History, organization, and research activities of the Psychological Test Film Unit, Army Air Forces. *Psychological Bulletin*, 1944, *41*, 457–468.

Gibson, J. J. Motion picture testing and research. Aviation Psychology Research Reports, No. 7. Washington: U.S. Government Printing Office, 1947. Pages 181–195 reprinted in D. Beardslee & M. Wertheimer (Eds.), *Readings in perception*. Princeton, N.J.: D. van Nostrand, 1958.

Gibson, J. J. Studying perceptual phenomena. In T. G. Andrews (Ed.), *Methods of psychology*. New York: Wiley, 1948.

Gibson, E. J., & Gibson, J. J. The identifying response: A study of a neglected form of learning. *American Psychologist*, 1950, *7*, 276. (Abstract)

Gibson, J. J. *The perception of the visual world*. Boston: Houghton Mifflin, 1950. (a)

Gibson, J. J. The implications of learning theory for social psychology. In J. G. Miller (Ed.), *Experiments in social process: A symposium on social psychology*. New York: McGraw-Hill, 1950. (b)

Gibson, J. J. The perception of visual surfaces. *American Journal of Psychology*, 1950, *63*, 367–384. (c)

Gibson, J. J. What is a form? *Psychological Review*, 1951, *58*, 403–412. (a)

Gibson, J. J. Theories of perception. In W. Dennis (Ed.), *Current trends in psychological theory*. Pittsburgh: University of Pittsburgh Press, 1951. (b)

Gibson, J. J. The visual field and the visual world: A reply to Professor Boring. *Psychological Review*, 1952, *59*, 149–151. (a)

Gibson, J. J. The relation between visual and postural determinants of the phenomenal vertical. *Psychological Review*, 1952, *59*, 370–375. (b)

Gibson, J. J., & Carel, W. Does motion perspective independently produce the impression of a receding surface? *Journal of Experimental Psychology*, 1952, *44*, 16–18.

Gibson, J. J., & Cornsweet, J. The perceived slant of visual surfaces—optical and geographical. *Journal of Experimental Psychology*, 1952, *44*, 11–15.

Gibson, J. J., & Dibble, F. N. Exploratory experiments on the stimulus conditions for the perception of a visual surface. *Journal of Experimental Psychology*, 1952, *43*, 414–419.

Gibson, J. J., & Waddell, D. Homogeneous retinal stimulation and visual perception. *American Journal of Psychology*, 1952, *65*, 263–370.

Gibson, J. J. Social perception and the psychology of perceptual learning. In M. Sherif & M. O. Wilson (Eds.), *Group relations at the crossroads*. New York: Harper & Brothers, 1953. (a)

Gibson, J. J. Review of E. F. Tait, *Textbook of refraction*. *American Journal of Psychology*, 1953, *66*, 678. (b)

Gibson, J. J. Ordinal stimulation and the possibility of a global psychophysics. *Proceedings of the 14th International Congress of Psychology*. Amsterdam: North-Holland, 1954. (a)

Gibson, J. J. The visual perception of objective motion and subjective movement. *Psychological Review*, 1954, *61*, 304–314. (b)

Gibson, J. J. A theory of pictorial perception. *Audio-Visual Communication Review*, 1954, *1*, 3–23. (c)

Gibson, J. J. Review of M. D. Vernon, *A further study of visual perception. Psychological Bulletin*, 1954, *51*, 96–97. (d)

Beck, J., & Gibson, J. J. The relation of apparent shape to apparent slant in the perception of objects. *Journal of Experimental Psychology*, 1955, *50*, 125–133.

Gibson, J. J. The optical expansion pattern in aerial locomotion. *American Journal of Psychology*, 1955, *68*, 480–484. (a)

Gibson, J. J. *Optical motions and transformations as stimuli for visual perception* (motion picture). State College, PA.: Psychological Cinema Register, 1955. (b)

Gibson, J. J., & Gibson, E. J. Perceptual learning: Differentiation or enrichment? *Psychological Review*, 1955, *62*, 32–41. (a)

Gibson, J. J., & Gibson, E. J. What is learned in perceptual learning? A reply to Professor Postman. *Psychological Review*, 1955, *62*, 447–450. (b)

Gibson, J. J., Olum, P., & Rosenblatt, F. Parallax and perspective during aircraft landings. *American Journal of Psychology*, 1955, *68*, 372–385.

Gibson, J. J., Purdy, J., & Lawrence, L. A method of controlling stimulation for the study of space perception: The optical tunnel. *Journal of Experimental Psychology*, 1955, *50*, 1–14.

Gibson, J. J., & Smith, O. W. The perception of motion in space. In *Symposium on Physiological Psychology* (ONR Symposium Report ACR-1). Washington, D.C.: Office of Naval Research, 1955.

Gibson, J. J. The non-projective aspects of the Rorschach experiment: IV. The Rorschach blots considered as pictures. *Journal of Social Psychology*, 1956, *44*, 203–206.

Gibson, J. J. Optical motions and transformations as stimuli for visual perception. *Psychological Review*, 1957, *64*, 288–295. (a)

Gibson, J. J. Technical and scientific communication: A reply to Calvert. *American Journal of Psychology*, 1957, *70*, 129–131. (b)

Gibson, J. J. Survival in a world of probable objects. Review of E. Brunswik, *Perception and the representative design of psychological experiments. Contemporary Psychology*, 1957, *2*, 33–35. (c)

Gibson, J. J., & Gibson, E. J. Continuous perspective transformations and the perception of rigid motion. *Journal of Experimental Psychology*, 1957, *54*, 129–138.

Gibson, J. J., & Smith, O. W. Apparatus for the study of visual translatory motion. *American Journal of Psychology*, 1957, *70*, 291–294.

Gibson, J. J., Smith, O. W., Steinschneider, A., & Johnson, C. W. The relative accuracy of visual perception of motion during fixation and pursuit. *American Journal of Psychology*, 1957, *70*, 64–68.

Gibson, J. J. The registering of objective facts: An interpretation of Woodworth's theory of perceiving. In G. Seward & J. Seward (Eds.), *Current psychological issues: Essays in honor of Robert S. Woodworth*. New York: Holt, 1958. (a)

Gibson, J. J. Visually controlled locomotion and visual orientation in animals. *British Journal of Psychology*, 1958, *49*, 182–194. (b)

Gibson, J. J. Research on the visual perception of motion and change. In *Second Symposium on Physiological Psychology* (ONR Symposium Report ACR-30). Washington, D.C.: Office of Naval Research, 1958. (c) Reprinted in I. Spigel (Ed.), *Readings in the study of visually perceived movement*. New York: Harper & Row, 1965.

Gibson, J. J. *Further experiments on optical motion and visual depth* (motion picture). State College, PA.: Psychological Cinema Register, 1958. (d)

Bergman, R., & Gibson, J. J. The negative after-effect of the perception of a surface slanted in the third dimension. *American Journal of Psychology*, 1959, *72*, 364–374.

Gibson, E. J., Gibson, J. J., Smith, O. W., & Flock, H. Motion parallax as a determinant of perceived depth. *Journal of Experimental Psychology*, 1959, *58*, 40–51.

Gibson, J. J. Perception as a function of stimulation. In S. Koch (Ed.), *Psychology: A study of a science* (Vol. 1). New York: McGraw-Hill, 1959. (a)

Gibson, J. J. After-effects: Figural and negative. Review of P. McEwen, *Figural after-effects. Contemporary Psychology*, 1959, *3*, 294–295. (b)

von Fieandt, K., & Gibson, J. J. The sensitivity of the eye to two kinds of continuous transformation of a shadow-pattern. *Journal of Experimental Psychology*, 1959, *57*, 344–347.

Gibson, J. J. Pictures, perspective, and perception. *Daedalus*, 1960, 216–227. (a)

Gibson, J. J. The information contained in light. *Acta Psychologica*, 1960, *17*, 23–30. (b)

Gibson, J. J. The concept of the stimulus in psychology. *American Psychologist*, 1960, *16*, 694–703. (c)

Gibson, J. J. Review of E. H. Gombrich, *Art and illusion. American Journal of Psychology*, 1960, *73*, 653–654. (d)

Gibson, J. J. Perception. In *Encyclopedia of Science and Technology*. New York: McGraw-Hill, 1960/1977.

Gibson, J. J. Ecological optics. *Vision Research*, 1961, *1*, 253–262. (a)

Gibson, J. J. The contribution of experimental psychology to the formulation of the problem of safety: A brief for basic research. In *Behavioral approaches to accident research*. New York: Association for the Aid of Crippled Children, 1961. (b)

Gibson, E. J., & Gibson, J. J., Pick, A. D., & Osser, H. A developmental study of the discrimination of letter-like forms. *Journal of Comparative and Physiological Psychology*, 1962, *55*, 897–906.

Gibson, J. J. Observations on active touch. *Psychological Review*, 1962, *69*, 477–491. (a)

Gibson, J. J. Introduction to I. Kohler, *The formation and transformation of the perceptual world*. New York: International Universities Press, 1962. (b)

Gibson, J. J. The survival value of sensory systems. *Biological prototypes and synthetic systems* (Vol. 1). New York: Plenum, 1962 (c)

Gibson, J. J., & Flock, H. The apparent distance of mountains. *American Journal of Psychology*, 1962, *75*, 501–503.

Gibson, J. J., Schiff, W., & Caviness, J. Persistent fear responses in rhesus monkeys to the optical stimulus of "looming." *Science*, 1962, *136*, 982–983.

✗ Gibson, J. J. The useful dimensions of sensitivity. *American Psychologist*, 1963, *18*, 1–15.

Gibson, J. J., & Backlund, F. An after-effect in haptic space perception. *Quarterly Journal of Experimental Psychology*, 1963, *15*, 145–154.

Gibson, J. J., & Pick, A. D. Perception of another person's looking behavior. *American Journal of Psychology*, 1963, *76*, 386–394.

Gibson, J. J. Constancy and invariance in perception. In G. Kepes (Ed.), *The nature and art of motion*. New York: Brazilier, 1965. (a)

Gibson, J. J. Review of R. J. Hirst (Ed.), *Perception and the external world. American Journal of Psychology*, 1965, *78*, 700. (b)

Gibson, J. J. The problem of temporal order in stimulation and perception. *Journal of Psychology*, 1966, *62*, 141–149. (a)

Gibson, J. J. *The senses considered as perceptual systems*. Boston: Houghton Mifflin, 1966. (b)

Gibson, J. J. James J. Gibson. In E. G. Boring & G. Lindzey (Eds.), *A history of psychology in autobiography* (Vol. 5). New York: Appleton-Century-Crofts, 1967. (a)

Gibson, J. J. On the proper meaning of the term "stimulus." *Psychological Review*, 1967, *74*, 533–534. (b)

Gibson, J. J. Invariant properties of changing stimulation as information for perception. In F. Klix (Ed.), *The organization of human information processing: Symposium von XVII Internationalen Kongress für Psychologie*. Berlin: Akademie-Verlag, 1967. (c)

Gibson, J. J. New reasons for realism. *Synthese*, 1967, *17*, 162–172. (d)

Gibson, J. J. What gives rise to the perception of motion? *Psychological Review*, 1968, *75*, 335–346. (a)

Gibson, J. J. Depth perception. In *International Encyclopedia of the Social Sciences*. New York: Macmillan, 1968. (b)

Gibson, J. J. *The change from visible to invisible: A study of optical transitions* (motion picture). State College, PA.: Psychological Cinema Register, 1968. (c)

Gibson, J. J. *The senses considered as perceptual systems*. London: G. Allen & Unwin, 1968. (d)

Gibson, J. J. Are there sensory qualities of objects? *Synthese*, 1968-1969, *19*, 408-409.

Gibson, J. J. Further thoughts on the perception of rigid motion. In J. Järvinen (Ed.), *Contemporary research in psychology of perception: In honorem Kai von Fieandt Sexagenarii*. Porvoo, Finland: Werner Söderstrom Osakeyhtiö, 1969. (a)

Gibson, J. J. *Vara sinnen som perceptuella system*. Stockholm: J. Beckmans Bockforlag, 1969. (b) (Translation of Gibson, 1966 b, by L. Eriksson.)

Gibson, J. J., Kaplan, G., Reynolds, H., & Wheeler, K. The change from visible to invisible: A study of optical transitions. *Perception & Psychophysics*, 1969, *5*, 113-116.

Gibson, J. J. On theories for visual space perception: A reply to Johansson. *Scandinavian Journal of Psychology*, 1970, *11*, 75-79. (a)

Gibson, J. J. On the relation between hallucination and perception. *Leonardo*, 1970, *3*, 425-427. (b)

Gibson, J. J. The information available in pictures. *Leonardo*, 1971, *4*, 27-35. (a)

Gibson, J. J. The legacies of Koffka's *Principles*. *Journal for the History of the Behavioral Sciences*, 1971, *7*, 3-9. (b)

Gibson, E. J., & Gibson, J. J. The senses as information-seeking systems. *The London Times Literary Supplement*, June 23, 1972, 711-712.

Gibson, J. J. A theory of direct visual perception. In J. Royce & W. Rozeboom (Eds.), *Psychology of knowing*. New York: Gordon & Breach, 1972.

Gibson, J. J. On the concept of "formless invariants" in visual perception. *Leonardo*, 1973, *6*, 43-45. (a)

Gibson, J. J. Direct visual perception: A reply to Gyr. *Psychological Bulletin*, 1973, *79*, 396-397. (b)

Gibson, J. J. *Die Wahrnehmung der Visuellen Welt*. Weinheim and Basel: Beltz Verlag, 1973. (c) (Translation of Gibson, 1950a, by V. Schumann.)

Gibson, J. J. *Die Sinne und der Prozess der Wahrnehmung*, mit einem geleitwort zur Deutschsprachigen Ausgabe bei J. J. Gibson. Bern, Stuttgart, and Wien: Verlag Hans Huber, 1973. (d) (Translation of Gibson, 1966b, by I. Kohler, E. Kohler, & M. Groner.)

Gibson, J. J., & Kaushall, P. *Reversible and irreversible events* (motion picture). State College, PA.: Psychological Cinema Register, 1973.

Gibson, J. J. A note on ecological optics. In E. Carterette & M. Friedman (Eds.), *Handbook of perception* (Vol. 1). New York: Academic Press, 1974. (a)

Gibson, J. J. Visualizing conceived as visual apprehending without any particular point of observation. *Leonardo*, 1974, *7*, 41-42. (b)

Gibson, J. J. *La percepción del mundo visual*. Buenos Aires: Edicianes Infinito, 1974. (c) (Translation of Gibson, 1950a, by E. Revol.)

Gibson, J. J. Events are perceivable but time is not. In J. T. Fraser & N. Lawrence (Eds.), *The study of time, II*. New York: Springer-Verlag, 1975. (a)

Gibson, J. J. Pickford and the failure of experimental esthetics. *Leonardo*, 1975, *8*, 319-321. (b)

Gibson, J. J. The implications of experiments on the perception of space and motion. Office of Naval Research Final Report (Contract No. N000 14-67A-0077-0005). Arlington, VA.: Office of Naval Research (Environmental Physiology), 1975. (c)

Gibson, J. J. Three kinds of distance that can be seen, or how Bishop Berkeley went wrong. In G. B. Flores D'Arcais (Ed.), *Studies in perception: Festschrift for Fabio Metelli*. Milano-Firenze: Giunte Editore, 1976. (a)

Gibson, J. J. The myth of passive perception: A reply to Richards. *Philosophy and Phenomenological Research*, 1976, *37*, 234-238. (b)

Gibson, J. J. Commentary and a further note on ''The relation between audition and vision in the human newborn'' by M. J. Mendelson and M. M. Haith. *Monographs of the Society for Research in Child Development*, 1976, *41* (4, Whole No. 167). (c)

Gibson, J. J. On the analysis of change in the optic array. *Scandinavian Journal of Psychology*, 1977, *18*, 161–163. (a)

Gibson, J. J. The theory of affordances. In R. Shaw & J. Bransford (Eds.), *Perceiving, acting and knowing: Towards an ecological psychology*. Hillsdale, N.J.: Erlbaum, 1977. (b)

Gibson, J. J. The perceiving of hidden surfaces. In P. Machamer & R. Turnbull (Eds.), *Studies in perception*. Columbus: Ohio State University, 1978. (a)

Gibson, J. J. The ecological approach to the visual perception of pictures. *Leonardo*, 1978, *11*, 227–235. (b)

Gibson, J. J. *The ecological approach to visual perception*. Boston: Houghton-Mifflin, 1979. (a)

Gibson, J. J. A note on E. J. G. by J. J. G. In A. D. Pick (Ed.), *Perception and its development: A tribute to Eleanor J. Gibson*. Hillsdale, N.J.: Erlbaum, 1979. (b)

Gibson, J. J. Foreward. A prefatory essay on the perception of surfaces versus the perception of markings on a surface. In M. A. Hagen (Ed.), *The perception of pictures* (Vol. 1). New York: Academic Press, 1980.

Gibson, J. J. [The ecological approach to visual perception.] Munich: Urban N. Schwartzenberg, 1981 (German edition of Gibson, 1979a).

Gibson, J. J. [The ecological approach to visual perception.] Tokyo: Saiensu-Sha Co., Ltd., 1982 (Japanese edition of Gibson, 1971a).

# Author Index

*Italics* denotes pages with bibliographic information.

# Subject Index